DARBYSHIRE
ON
THE ENGLISH
LEGAL SYSTEM

AUSTRALIA
Law Book Co.—Sydney

CANADA and **USA**
Carswell–Toronto

HONG KONG
Sweet & Maxwell Asia

NEW ZEALAND
Brookers—Wellington

SINGAPORE and **MALAYSIA**
Sweet & Maxwell Asia
Singapore and Kuala Lumpur

DARBYSHIRE
ON
THE ENGLISH
LEGAL SYSTEM

By

PENNY DARBYSHIRE PhD, MA
Reader in Law,
Kingston Law School,
Kingston University

EIGHTH EDITION

LONDON
SWEET & MAXWELL
2005

First Edition 1971
Second Edition 1977
Third Edition 1982
Fourth Edition 1987
Reprinted 1990
Fifth Edition 1992
Sixth Edition 1996
Seventh Edition 2001
Reprinted 2003
Eighth Edition 2005

Published in 2005 by
Sweet & Maxwell Limited of
100 Avenue Road, London, NW3 3PF
Typeset by Servis Filmsetting Ltd, Manchester
Printed in Great Britain by TJ International, Padstow, Cornwall

No natural forests were destroyed to make this product,
only farmed timber was used and replanted

A CIP catalogue record for this book is available from the British
Library

ISBN 0421 901 500

Foreword

On the publication of this eighth edition, the necessary change of title, from *Eddey & Darbyshire on the English Legal System*, is an appropriate moment for the original author to take stock.

My first obligation is to thank Penny Darbyshire for so ably editing the fifth, sixth and seventh editions. The rewriting involved more than justifies this new edition bearing her sole name.

My second obligation is to Sweet & Maxwell, who originally invited me to write the book in 1970. Over the ensuing thirty-five years I have worked with a number of editors and without exception, I have valued their help, enthusiasm and professionalism.

My third obligation is to Margaret Eddey, my wife. Apart from interest, advice and encouragement she typed the original manuscript, all later editions for which I was responsible for, not to mention five other student texts and various law articles. I am immensely grateful.

In the original Preface I wrote that "Lawyers will be well aware that there is never an opportune time to publish a book on the English Legal System". Every consequent edition has confirmed the accuracy of this statement. Change in the system appears to be both constant and inevitable.

One has only to compare the first edition with this eighth edition to acknowledge the immensity of changes, which have taken, and are taking place. The ever-developing importance of European Community law and the prospect of the European Constitution. The application of the European Constitution on Human Rights. The immense importance of the Internet and the need for lawyers and judges to have computer expertise. Current arguments concern the need to adapt the system to counter terrorism: arguments that question the appropriateness of Trial by Jury, and press the case for Identity Cards. In the day-to-day operation of the system changes of great importance have taken place in Civil and Criminal Procedure and in the Legal Aid system.

For the student it remains the case that a basic knowledge of the English Legal System is the prerequisite of any successful approach to legal studies. Whatever the student's particular field of interest any attempt to study that branch of the law in isolation is inevitably defective.

I am glad that the original text and the later editions have proved so successful in meeting the needs of students. As to the future, I have no doubt that we can look forward to many more editions of *Darbyshire on the English Legal System*.

Keith Eddey, 2005

Online Updates

A free online updating service is available in conjunction with this text. It can be found at *http://www.sweetandmaxwell.co.uk/academic/ updates/darbyshire/index.html*.

The site can also be accessed by going to the Sweet & Maxwell website (*www.sweetandmaxwell.co.uk*); clicking on "Academic"; clicking on "Students"; clicking on "Online Updates"; and clicking on "Darbyshire on the English Legal System".

The service will provide periodic updates, from 2006. It also contains additional material, such as an illustrated walking tour of legal London, a summary of the *Review of the Criminal Courts of England and Wales* (the Auld Review) and an essay on discrimination in the legal profession.

Contents

PART I: Sources

1. Understanding the English Legal System

2. Sources of English Law

3. Community Law: Its Impact on English Law and the English Courts

ix

CONTENTS

Table of Cases

Table of Statutes

Table of Statutory Instruments

Table of International and European Conventions and Legislation

Note on Neutral Citation of Cases

Where a case has been given a neutral citation number, this has been used in the text. Where none is available, the case has been cited by reference to the court and date only—this applies to cases pre-dating 2001 and the judgments of the European Court of Justice and the European Court of Human Rights.

Part I: Sources

1. Understanding the English Legal System

1. What is Law?

Societies and their subcultures govern themselves by countless 1–001 sets of rules of different types, written or unwritten. Without these codes of acceptable behaviour, there would be no society, no order, only chaos and anarchy. We conduct our lives according to all manner of learned or agreed rules of conduct. These include our own internalised moral code, unconsciously followed rules of etiquette and civilised behaviour. We may adhere to the tenets of a religion and a particular church. We may belong to a private organisation, such as a political party or a sports club with its own constitution and membership rules but none of the codes so far mentioned, however complex, carries the force of law. For instance, the constitution of the California Parent Teachers' Association is lengthier and much more complex than the English Courts and Legal Services Act 1990 but it is not law. It cannot be interpreted or enforced by a court.

What then is special about legal rules? To commit a gross generalisation and without getting involved in heavy jurisprudence (the philosophy of law), a rudimentary definition of law, within the English legal system, is a rule that is backed by a sanction for its breach, ultimately enforceable by a court, a tribunal or arbitration. There is considerable overlap between non-legal rules and the law. For instance, the basic rules of most major religions are astonishingly similar. Most of them condemn murder and so do all legal systems, although what constitutes murder and the punishment imposed differs from one legal system to another. In another overlap, dropping litter in the street would be condemned by most English people as anti-social behaviour but it is also illegal and subject to a fine enforceable in a criminal court. Nevertheless, many forms of anti-social behaviour,

3

such as spitting in a crowded street, would shock most people as a breach of the rules of civilised behaviour but are not illegal. Again, we must distinguish between the immoral and the illegal. Adultery is not illegal, though it is a breach of many people's religions or moral codes. Some MPs and peers think adulterous behaviour should have legal ramifications. They attempted but failed to amend the Family Law Bill 1996, to allow the judge to take account of such "faults" on the part of divorcing couples.

Sanctions for breach of the law take many forms, apart from the obvious example of sentences passed for breaches of the criminal law. When part of the Merchant Shipping Act 1988 was found by the European Court of Justice (ECJ), in the *Factortame* cases, to be in breach of the Treaty of Rome, the operation of the offending sections of the Act had to be suspended and the UK government had to compensate Spanish fishermen who had been prevented from plying their trade in British coastal waters. If I breach my contract with you, you can ask a civil court to impose a sanction on me by awarding damages against me or enforcing my obligations under the contract. If a minister makes a new set of regulations, they can be quashed by the High Court if she failed to follow procedure prescribed in the enabling Act of Parliament which gave her the power to make the regulations, such as consulting affected parties.

2. Distinguishing Between Different Types of Law

Substantive and Procedural

1–002   While the former prescribes, proscribes and regulates areas of human activity, the latter sets down rules for the manner of enforcing the law in relation to that activity. The Theft Acts and many leading cases define what conduct and mental elements constitute the offence of theft but the procedures for arresting the suspect, questioning, charging, and trying him are contained in several quite different statutes (Acts of Parliament), cases and sets of procedural rules.

Private and Public

1–003   The former governs relations between private citizens or bodies, the latter applies to public bodies which are publicly regulated and usually publicly funded, such as the departments of local and central government and public services, such as the Highways Agency. Dicey, one of the UK's most famous constitutional lawyers, boasted in 1885 that our law did not recognise this distinction, since all public bodies were equally bound by the ordinary law of the land, enforceable in the ordinary courts. While it is true to say that the English legal system does not provide a separate court structure for adjudicating on disputes arising with public bodies, as does the French legal system, the last century, especially the period since 1981, saw the massive growth in a body of law regulating the conduct of public bodies which all English lawyers would now acknowledge as public law. The study of public law is a requirement for entry to the legal profession and it covers such topics as regulating police behaviour and the judicial review (a check by the High Court) of the legality of decisions taken and rules made by public bodies.

Domestic and International

Our domestic law is applicable in and enforceable by the courts of England and Wales and, sometimes, throughout the UK. Public international law is contained in conventions and treaties devised and agreed to by groups of countries concerned to regulate activities in which they have a common interest or which take place across national boundaries, covering everything from air traffic to drug trafficking. Its interpretation and enforcement may be the task of an international court recognised in or established by such a treaty. Frequently, more detailed laws giving practical effect to treaty requirements are enacted into domestic law. Our Misuse of Drugs Act 1971 provides domestic law in accordance with the requirements of the international conventions on narcotics.

1–004

It is important to understand that Community law, often referred to as EU law, and the law of the European Convention on Human Rights are not foreign law, they have been incorporated into UK law but in different ways, as I explain in Chapters 3 and 4, below.

Civil Law and Criminal Law

Private civil law regulates relations between private persons or bodies and civil law is usually invoked only by those parties seeking to protect their private rights or interests. For instance, if I commit a tort against you, say, negligently backing my muck spreader over your gatepost, the State, as such, has no interest in taking me to court to sue for damages on your behalf but you may sue me in a civil court. Similarly, if I unfairly dismiss you, you may take me to an employment tribunal to ask for compensation but if you choose not to enforce your legal right to protection by the civil law, that is your prerogative. The State is not going to step in if you do not act. Having said that, elements of the State, such as government agencies, have a vast range of statutory and common law powers to invoke the civil law against private individuals and, of

1–005

course, a private party may take a civil court action against an element of the State, such as suing the police over a death in custody but all of these activities between citizen and State are subject to the rules of public law as well.

By contrast, a criminal offence is a wrong against the State and punishable as such, in the criminal courts. Criminal law is a type of public law. Whereas the State has no interest in pursuing your civil claim, if you are a victim of a crime, such as theft, the State may prosecute the offender, whether or not you wish to take action against him. The aim of taking a criminal case to court is to punish the wrongdoer, rather than to compensate, although our judges and magistrates may attach a compensation order to any sentence they pass. Just to confuse you, in English law, victims of crime retain the right of private prosecution so may prosecute the offender in the criminal courts, if the State chooses not to prosecute.

I know that my explanation may have confused the distinction, rather than clarified it but, in studying law, you will soon be able to recognise the difference. Suffice it to say that virtually all the foundation subjects studied in a law degree, such as tort, contract, land law, equity, most of public law and Community law are elements of civil law. Most of the criminal law we study is taught under the heading of criminal law. A true story may help to distinguish.

A story from the student world: my bike

1–006 When I was a law student, I was biking to college to sit the last of my finals when a car driver knocked me off my bike. The police arrived on the scene and took details of the accident and interviewed her and the witnesses. She was prosecuted in criminal proceedings in Kingston magistrates' court, pleaded guilty to the offence of careless driving and was fined. My solicitor, acting on my behalf, threatened to sue her in civil proceedings in Kingston County Court for damages for the losses I had suffered, as a result of her negligent driving. I needed the cost of a new bike and damages for the pain and shock of my injuries. Luckily, the driver's motor insurance company, acting on her behalf, agreed to settle out of court for the sum claimed by my solicitor. This was typical. As we shall see, the vast majority of civil disputes are settled out of court by the parties or their representatives. What is also typical was my solicitor's tactic of waiting for the outcome of the criminal case before threatening a civil action against her. A civil case is much easier to prove than a criminal one. The *quantum* (standard) of proof is lower so my solicitor knew that the driver's criminal conviction would make the civil case easy to prove. To help matters, the police had given him their file of statements, taken as criminal evidence, to use as civil evidence. (Incidentally, I still had to sit my private international law exam, in shock, with my right arm dislocated and my gashed knee bandaged. What cruel lecturers I had.)

Civil and criminal cases: getting the language right

Here is a list of the correct terminology used in most civil and criminal cases. Try to get it right.   **1–007**

CIVIL	CRIMINAL
The claimant	The prosecutor
sues	prosecutes
the defendant	the defendant
in the county court or High Court.	in the magistrates' court or Crown Court.
Most cases are settled without a trial, as no defence is entered.	Most cases are heard without a trial as the defendant pleads guilty.
If a defence is entered, the case goes to trial and it is heard before a single judge, who decides on fact and law. In exceptional cases, a jury decides.	If the defendant pleads not guilty, the case goes to trial and is heard by a district judge (magistrates' court) or lay magistrates, who decide on fact and law. In the Crown Court, the jury decides issues of fact (the verdict) and the judge rules on points of law.
If the judge finds the case proven, he enters judgment for the claimant.	If the magistrates or jury find the case proven, they bring in a verdict of guilty and convict the defendant.
He may make an order, *e.g.* an award of damages, against the defendant.	The magistrates or judge may pass sentence on the defendant, *e.g.* a fine or a term of imprisonment.
If the judge does not find the case proven, he enters judgment for the defendant.	If the magistrates or jury find the case is not proven, they acquit the defendant.

7

In either case, if the losing party appeals, she becomes "the appellant" and the other side "the respondent." If she seeks judicial review, she becomes the applicant.

3. What is the English Legal System?

1–008   The study of the English legal system applies to the powers, procedures and activities of the group of courts and statutory tribunals in England and Wales and the people who work in them and/or whose job it is to resolve legal problems. The legal systems of Scotland and Northern Ireland are quite separate. They have distinct court structures, different procedures and sometimes apply different rules of substantive law.

We speak of the English legal *system* as if it were a coherent structure with the constituent parts working in a smooth, interrelated fashion but it is very important to bear in mind that no-one has custom-designed it. Think of it more as a heap of *Lego* bricks, some of which are joined together, than a sophisticated construction of *Lego Technic*. It has been given to us in little boxes, over the last ten centuries and parts have been deconstructed and reconstructed from time to time. We fiddle with it. For instance, in the 1990s, Lord Woolf was concerned with how to improve access to civil justice and, in 1991–1993, the Royal Commission on Criminal Justice contemplated how the criminal process could be improved but no-one ever examines the workings of the whole structure. We take it for granted that we need two levels of first instance court (trial court). We take it for granted that we need both a Court of Appeal and the House of Lords or Supreme Court because it has been that way beyond living memory. Only students in tutorials and essays are tortured with such questions. The general issues paper of the Civil Justice Review, published in 1986, raised the radical question of whether we really need both the county courts and the High Court dealing with civil trials and the Master of the Rolls is asking the question again, in 2005. Lord Justice Auld in his 2001 *Review of the Criminal Courts of England and Wales* suggested a unified criminal court but such radical thinking is rare.

It is true to say, however, that, considering nothing much had happened in the English legal system since the 1870s, we have scrutinised and reconfigured an enormous number of bricks in our *Lego* pile since 1985, largely thanks to the Conservative Lord Chancellor, Lord Mackay, his Labour successor, Lord Irvine and the newest Lord Chancellor, Lord Falconer. Examining the English legal system with the eyes of an outsider, as he is a member of the Scottish Bar, no block of our system was sacrosanct to Lord Mackay. He was prepared to leave virtually no brick unturned, no question unasked. He made many enemies by his radical approach, daring to ask whether it was in the public interest that lawyers' monopolies should be protected and whether we should really assume that the litigant is better off being represented by a lawyer in an adversarial process. Another Scot, Lord Chancellor Irvine continued with the same approach.

Hallmarks of the English Legal System

The common law

The English legal system is a "common law" legal system. This means that many of our primary legal principles have been made and developed by judges from case to case in what is called a system of precedent, where the lower courts are bound to follow principles established by the higher courts in previous cases. The term "common law" historically distinguished the law made by judges in the royal courts in Westminster and commonly applicable in the whole of the kingdom, from the canon law (ecclesiastical law) or the local systems of customary law which predominated until 1066 and existed beyond.   **1–009**

Judge-made law is at least as important to us as the law made by Parliament. For instance, there is no statute telling us that murder is a crime and defining it for us. It is a common law crime. The required guilty act, of causing death and the necessary degree of guilt, malice aforethought, have been prescribed and defined, over the centuries, by judges. Similarly, the law of negligence was the invention of a judge who wanted to find a remedy for a woman who had suffered gastro-enteritis when she drank from an opaque bottle of ginger beer, wherein lurked the decomposing remains of a stray snail. She was given the ginger beer and thus had no contract with the retailer or manufacturer and we can assume Mr Slimey Snail was not a pet, endowed with his own third party liability insurance, so the judge, Lord Atkin, decided that, as a matter of principle, she should have a right to damages against the manufacturer, as they owed her a duty of care. Thus, he invented what became the law of negligence.

Adversarial procedure

Another of the hallmarks of the English legal system and all common law systems is that basic trial procedure is essentially adversarial. This means that the two parties to the case are left to their own devices to prepare and present their cases unaided by the court. Crass comparisons are made between this typical common law procedure and the type of "inquisitorial" procedure, with officials of the court involved in the fact finding process, which is said to be a hallmark of   **1–010** continental European legal systems. As we shall see, however, our trial system has not always been adversarial and inquisitorial elements are appearing at many points in the system. Also, it is wrong to label European procedural systems as inquisitorial.

Jury trial and orality

1–011   Historically, certainly since 1215, jury trial was central to the English legal system in both criminal and civil cases, although its use in civil cases is now rare and it is confined to the most serious cases in the criminal courts. The need to argue cases before a jury has certainly shaped our rules of evidence, procedure and our substantive law and has meant, historically, that most of each argument was presented to the court orally, through argument by the parties and oral examination and cross-examination of witnesses. Again, the emphasis on orality is rapidly disappearing, with the admission of more and more written statements and documentary evidence in hard copy and electronically retrievable form. Since 1995, in civil cases, lawyers now have to present the court with a skeleton argument so the advocate's art of oral story-telling is being replaced by a scene in a typical High Court room where all bewigged heads are face-down in "the bundle" of pre-served documents, flicking through to make cross-references, incomprehensible to the casual observer. It has taken some fun out of court watching, because it is difficult to follow the story.

Lay magistrates

1–012   The bulk of criminal cases are heard in magistrates' courts, mostly by lay justices. There are over 28,000 of them and no other legal system makes such heavy use of laypeople as decision-makers. In exporting the common law, we exported the concept of magistrates but they tended to be professionals. When you add to them the use of lay arbitrators, tribunal panel members and jurors, you start to realise how many important decisions are taken by laypersons in the English legal system.

4. The Mother of All Common Law Systems

1–013   Just as the UK Parliament has been called "the mother of parliaments," so I would call the English legal system the mother of all common law legal systems, worldwide. We exported the common law and our legal system, along with the English language, into our old colonies and the Commonwealth. The common law daughters of the English legal system include the US, Canada, Australia and New Zealand but we maintain our direct link with the living common law of some Commonwealth countries, both dependent and independent, through the Judicial Committee of the Privy Council. This court sits in London and is the highest court of appeal for those jurisdictions. Since it is mainly composed of Law Lords you can see that this provides for harmonious development of principle throughout all of these common law jurisdictions. Decisions of the Judicial Committee are persuasive and not binding precedents on the English courts but they are heavily influential, since everyone realises that when those senior judges metamorphose back into Law Lords they are hardly likely to contradict legal principles which they carefully established when doing their job as privy councillors.

This common law cross-fertilisation is by no means confined to Commonwealth countries, however. Certain areas of the common law, such as tort and criminal law, have developed globally, with judges in the courts of one country regularly persuaded by the reasoning of their brethren in another jurisdiction. You only have to flick through the pages of an English text on criminal law to see how other countries tackle some of the interpretive problems facing our criminal courts. Where no precedent exists, English judges may well be persuaded by a precedent from America, Australia or Canada. At the same time, English common law is still alive throughout the US, even in forms which have been replaced in England. For instance, the actions constituting an attempted crime in California are determined by old English case law, replaced in England by the Criminal Attempts Act 1981. Throughout the US, crimes are divided into felonies and misdemeanors, a distinction which we disposed of in 1967. They also chose to retain the harsh felony murder rule. Californian property law uses concepts straight out of medieval English property law, abolished by the English in the Law of Property Act 1925. If you buy property in the US, you may be astonished by quaint concepts and ancient English terminology.

Apart from judicial borrowing of precedents, there is a ceaseless interchange between academics in the common law world, in terms of writing, thinking, teaching and research. If you want to read the best of English legal history, you have to turn to American journals and books. American legal history is English legal history.

The Comparison with Other European Systems

Since, in our popular rhetoric and our legal analysis, we are always comparing ourselves with continental legal systems, notably the French and since we, along with all other EU Member States, now have to absorb Community law into our domestic legal systems, we students of the English legal system need to understand something more about another major "family" of laws, the "Romano-Germanic" family, as David and Brierley describe it, in   1–014

11

Major Legal Systems in the World Today. Apart from Ireland, a common law country, the legal systems of all our EU partners are, historically, members of that other major family.

Different Roots

1–015   The Romano-Germanic family was developed by scholars in the European universities from the Renaissance of the twelfth and thirteenth centuries. There was a need for an autonomous law, independent of canon (Church) law, to replace inadequate and bitty customary law. Scholars latched onto Roman law as a neat pre-existing body of rules and set about refining it. Law was seen as a fairly abstract body of principles of justice, and its teaching was linked to the teaching of philosophy, theology and religion. It emerged from France and Italy but was taught in this way in Spain, Portugal, Scandinavia, even Oxford and Cambridge. The teaching of national law was not taken up until the seventeenth and eighteenth centuries. The flexibility and abstract nature of this civil law refined and taught in Europe can be contrasted with the rigidity of the common law rules developing in the Westminster courts. Eventually, Roman law was translated into the basis of national laws for practical application. This could not be done in England because the rules of common law, devised and applied by the courts, were already too entrenched. From the thirteenth to the sixteenth centuries, the law as taught in the universities had considerable influence. Jurists, not governments, developed the law so the countries of the Romano-Germanic family had jurists and legal practitioners who took their concept of law, approach and reasoning from Roman law.

The study and refinement of Roman law naturally progressed to its codification. Codes were developed independently but the most influential of these was the Napoleonic Code of 1804. The French code was received in Belgium, the Netherlands, the Rhenish provinces, Luxembourg, Poland and Italy. Thanks to colonisation by the Spanish, Portuguese, French and Dutch, elements of Romano-Germanic law spread throughout South America, parts of North America (Louisiana, Quebec) and Africa. The French influence extends to Turkey, Egypt, Iran, Syria, Iraq, Japan, Taiwan, Vietnam and Cambodia. The Romano-Germanic family can, then be seen alongside the common law family, as populating a large part of the world. Certain countries have a mixture of the two. Examples are Scotland, Israel, South Africa, Zimbabwe and Botswana.

Because the French Napoleonic Code was absorbed into so many legal systems, this made France an even more fecund mother of legal systems than the English. Notice that Germany did not adopt the French code but devised one of its own so some comparativists talk of a French family and a German family.

And Different Branches

The same divisions of law can be found throughout the Romano- **1–016**
Germanic legal systems and some of them, such as "the law of obligations," are alien and incomprehensible to the common lawyer.

Written constitutions

The UK is one of only three countries in the developed world **1–017**
without a written constitution. As a consequence, we lacked any
notion of fundamental rights until very recently. There is almost no
awareness amongst the public at large of what the UK constitution
amounts to. There is no talk of fundamental constitutional rights, as
is common in Germany and France and as is drummed into each
small child's memory in the US, because we do not think we have
any. Indeed, we have only spoken in terms of human rights in the
last few years, since the Human Rights Act 1998 came into force, in
October 2000. In all our European partner states, along with all of
England's common law daughters, the legality of the law of the land
can be tested against a written constitution in a special constitutional
court and struck down if it offends against some constitutional
requirement. In the UK, on the other hand, we are used to the idea
that the law of our land is untouchable. Parliament is supreme and,
prior to 1973, only Parliament could undo what a previous parliament had done. Maybe it is this inability to conceptualise any law
superior to that made by Parliament which partly explains why we
reacted so badly to the effrontery of the rulings of the ECJ in the
Factortame cases, which resulted in the suspension of that part of the
Merchant Shipping Act 1988 that flew in the face of the Treaty of
Rome. Similarly, the Blair government reacted coolly in December
2004, when the law lords condemned the Anti-Terrorism, Crime and
Security Act 2001 as contravening the European Convention on
Human Rights (see Chapter 4, below).

Public law and private law

Romano-Germanic legal systems all recognise the distinction **1–018**
between public and private law which, historically, English
common law did not acknowledge. The French, for instance, have a
separate set of courts, headed by the Conseil d'Etat, administering
a separate body of public law developed by those courts to a sophisticated level by the first half of the twentieth century. French law
has, in this respect, been highly influential over Belgian and Dutch
law. Those countries also have courts which are modelled on the
Conseil d'Etat. In the English legal system, however, the development of public law was stifled, until the enactment of the Crown
Proceedings Act 1947, by the rule that the Crown could not be sued
and until 1981 by the difficulties in applying for judicial review. It is

only since the 1960s that we have acknowledged the separate existence of a body of public law, worthy of being taught as an independent subject. We still do not have a separate set of public law courts, along French lines but at least we now list all applications for judicial review to be heard in the administrative court by specialist judges, with a simplified procedure, which has allowed the rapid development of a coherent body of public law.

The concept of law

1–019   The very way in which law is conceived of in the legal systems of the Roman-Germanic family is radically different from the way we approach it and it has developed in the common law countries and this goes a very long way towards explaining why Community law and the judgments of the ECJ were so much easier, in the early days, for our European partners to assimilate than for us. This is how David and Brierley, in their classic analysis, explain la différence:

"In countries of the Romano-Germanic family, the legal rule is formulated, characterised and analysed in the same way. In this family, in which doctrinal writing is held in high esteem, the legal rule is not considered as merely a rule appropriate to the solution of a concrete case. It is fashionable to view with a certain disdain, and as casuistic, the opposite view which places the rule of law at the level of concrete cases only. Digests of decided cases, form books and legal dictionaries are certainly useful working instruments for practitioners, and they provide much of the raw material for jurists in their work. But these compilations do not enjoy the high prestige associated with legal scholarship. The function of the jurist is to draw from this disorganised mass first the rules and then the principles which will clarify and purge the subject of impure elements, and thus provide both the practice and the courts with a guide for the solution of particular cases in the future." (p.94)

In common law countries, just about the opposite is going on. The initial approach is one of pragmatism in individual cases, rather than abstract principle. The common law is developed, whether the judges are dealing with a judge-made law or interpreting a statute, on a case by case basis. The concern of the judge is to find the solution to the instant case. When a sufficient body of case law has developed, through the application and extension of judicial reasoning in the system of precedent, then it may be possible to elevate these judicial rulings to the level of principle. Examples of this abound. In public law, the principles of natural justice have developed in this way. The judges have, on a case by case basis, extended the right to a fair hearing in an unbiased tribunal from hearings in the inferior courts to all manner of decisions by administrative bodies.

Because judicial reasoning is such an important source of law, we are heavily dependent on law reports. Academics certainly comment on judicial reasoning but they cannot be said, for the most part, to be the source of legal doctrine themselves. Indeed, there was a convention that judges did not cite living authors. The exception is that, where there is no precedent, the courts will resort to examining what are known as "books of authority" by the early writers in the common law, from the seventeenth and eighteenth century and it is now quite common, for judges to refer to modern textbooks or articles.

Sources of law and the judicial approach

The primary source of law in the Romano-Germanic legal systems is undoubtedly codified law, the drafting and interpretation of which is influenced by or the task of academic jurists. In common law countries, we depend on a mixture of judge-made law (common law) and statute, as interpreted by judges, whose reasoned opinions we must read in the law reports. If we take the French legal system as a contrasting example, we can see that the judge is not considered to be a source of law. Indeed, following the revolution, judges' powers were curtailed and they were prohibited from creating binding rules of precedent, as Article 5 of the Code Civil now stipulates. Of course, this is constitutional theory but in reality, French judges have had to make law, to a certain extent, and some critics say that the notion that they do not make law is an academic myth. While even the judgments of the Cour de Cassation are not meant to form binding precedents, they are followed by the lower courts in most cases. Certainly French public law is almost entirely judge-made since it was developed after the Napoleonic era of codification. The French ambivalence is illustrated by the way law is taught. Textbooks emphasise codified law, legislation, with cases relegated to footnote illustrations, yet tutorials concentrate on case commentaries.

The nature of a judgment in French law could not be further from its English counterpart. Whereas some of our leading House of Lords decisions contain the reasoned opinions of five Law Lords, distinguishing and applying a long list of precedents and stretching through over 100 pages in the law reports, French judgments, even emanating from the Cour de Cassation, rarely amount to two pages. They are in the form of a syllogism: they set out the facts, the legal issue in context and the conclusion, without, usually, citing any previous case authority. Because judgments are so short, they are normally published accompanied by academic commentary. All this is explained by Dadamo and Farran, in *The French Legal System*.

1–020

Procedural differences

1–021   We most commonly see the English legal system contrasted with European systems in terms of procedure, notably criminal procedure. Broadly speaking, European systems were characterised as inquisitorial, with the examining magistrate, then the court, taking a significant part in fact-finding and examining witnesses. This caricature was contrasted with the adversarial or accusatorial system, which the common law population likes to emphasise is so much fairer, with the judge acting as an unbiased umpire, permitting both sides to prepare and present their cases and examine witnesses, independent of court interference. Both the English and continental legal systems have recently departed from the purity of their respective models, however, especially with the procedural changes of the 1980s and 1990s. One significant difference, which should be mentioned at this point, however, is that, whereas English barristers have been used to arguing most of their case orally in civil proceedings, until the requirement for written skeleton arguments in civil cases, from the 1990s, European advocates are much better trained in reducing their arguments into writing.

Bad Europeans

1–022   I have endeavoured to explain at some length the contrast between the English legal system and the Romano-Germanic systems of our EU partners for two reasons. First, we need to see where the English legal system sits, in worldwide terms and secondly, we need to understand why Community law seems a bit more difficult for us to get used to than for our European counterparts. Community procedural law and its concept of law are derived directly from the French legal system, the mother or sister of all the other EU legal systems, apart from Ireland and Germany. The Europhobe might say that, just as the Union seems to be in the political grip of the Franco-German alliance, so the French and Germans had sewn up Community law before we even got into the Common Market because, just as Community procedure is French, so substantive Community law is based on German (and American) competition law.

The French influence can be seen in these aspects of Community procedure. French is the working language of the court. Lawyers' oral submissions are strictly limited to 30 minutes' argument. Common lawyers, trained in the tradition of oral advocacy, have to be helped by the Court's staff to reduce their arguments into writing. The roles of the advocate-general and judge-rapporteur are modelled on the French. They have no common law equivalent. The system of references for preliminary rulings under Art.234 EC bears a direct similarity to references of questions of law from the French inferior courts to the Cour de Cassation. Again, there is no common law equivalent. The early judgments of the ECJ looked just like French judgments, with very little reasoning and no precedents cited. This was one of the most difficult aspects of Community law for the common lawyer to comprehend but the ECJ has now changed. For the sake of consistency, it takes serious account of its own precedents and cites them in its judgments and reported decisions contain much more reasoning than they formerly did, thus looking much more like common law judgments. The ECJ certainly accepts and applies broad principle in the same way that a court in a Roman-Germanic legal system would.

As I explained above, all other Member States have written constitutions which spell out the relationship of domestic law and Community law and citizens of all other Member States are used to having their statutes measured against a higher form of law, the constitution. We are not and, in the way in which British politicians reacted to some ECJ judgments, we showed that we simply did not appreciate that our enacting of the European Communities Act 1972 was a very significant derogation from the supremacy of the UK Parliament.

5. Keeping up-to-date with the English Legal System

The English legal system is by far the fastest changing area of **1–023** English law. Like all law books, this one, finished in 2005, will be out of date by the time you read it. If you are a law student, here are some tactics for keeping up-to-date in all your legal studies.

* Never buy out-of-date law books. They are as dangerous as last week's cream cakes. A search on *Amazon* or the publisher's website will indicate which is the latest edition.
* Show tutors/examiners that you have kept up to date by reading a quality daily newspaper, such as *The Times*, *The Financial Times*, *The Guardian* or *The Independent*. *The Times* has the greatest legal content, with a law supplement on Tuesdays. It also contains brief reports of recent cases, to help you keep up with your other legal studies. They are produced much more quickly than any other hard copy set of law reports. *The Guardian* contains useful analysis of social issues in the legal system, as does *The Independent*. If you cannot buy a paper, you can read them online. You can also search through old newspaper articles in various news

databases, such as *LexisNexis*, if your library has it. By getting into the habit of reading the newspapers, you can also make the law more interesting for yourself by understanding how law is about real people, in the real world. Law is not just in books.

* Take yourself off to court. The courts are a free source of daily entertainment, Mondays to Fridays. Justice in England and Wales is meant to be open to the public. Courts and tribunals are everywhere. Go and see how law operates in the real world, in sorting out people's disputes and responding to their offences. In this way you will learn a lot about procedure, the court structure, lawyers, magistrates and judges.

* Regularly browse the legal news journals, such as *The New Law Journal*, *Legal Action*, the Law Society's *Gazette* or *The Lawyer*.

* Visit relevant websites and check on What's New? The most useful for the English legal system is the Department for Constitutional Affairs (DCA), in charge of the courts, legal services and judges and magistrates. The Home Office is in charge of the police and the criminal justice system so visit its site periodically. The criminal justice system and Youth Justice Board have their own sites and the DCA site is user-friendly and has useful links. A quick, efficient and accurate way of keeping up with legal news is to browse through the press releases from these departments and then you can choose which topics to pursue on the site in more detail.

* Read my online updates to this book: *http://www.sweetand-maxwell.co.uk/academic/updates/darbyshire/index.html*.

WEBSITES RELEVANT TO THE ENGLISH LEGAL SYSTEM (CHECKED IN MAY 2005)

024

Association of Women Barristers: *www.womenbarristers.org.uk*
Association of Women Solicitors: *www.womensolicitors.org.uk*
Bar Council: *www.barcouncil.org.uk*
British and Irish Legal Information Institute: *www.bailii.org*
Butterworths, including NLJ index and *LexisNexis* and Butterworths Direct, which you can set up to give you a daily update: *www. butterworths.com*
Central Office of Information, including all press releases: *http://www.coi.gov.uk/*
Centre for Effective Dispute Resolution (ADR): *http://www.cedr.co.uk/*
Citizens Advice: *www.citizensadvice.org.uk*
Civil Justice Council: *http://www.civiljusticecouncil.gov.uk/*
Community Legal Service: *www.clsdirect.org.uk*

Council on Tribunals: *http://www.council-on-tribunals.gov.uk/*
Criminal Cases Review Commission: *www.ccrc.gov.uk*
Criminal Courts Review: *www.criminal-courts-review.org.uk*
CJSonline: *http://www.cjsonline.org*
Crown Prosecution Service: *www.cps.gov.uk*
Department for Constitutional Affairs, formerly the Lord Chancellor's Department: *http://www.dca.gov.uk*
European Court of Human Rights: *www.echr.coe.int*
EU institutions and documents, including European Commission and European Court of Justice: *www.europa.eu.int*
European Commission Representation in the UK, for EU news, publications, info and free email newsletter: *http://www.cec.org.uk/info/index.htm*
Google, search engine: *www.google.co.uk*
Government information: *http://www.direct.gov.uk/Homepage/fs/en*
Her Majesty's Courts Service: *www.hmcourts-service.gov.uk*
Home Office: *www.homeoffice.gov.uk*
Human Rights Unit info and links: *http://www.dca.gov.uk/hrucl/hramenu.htm*
International Courts of Justice are best accessed via the UN website: *www.un.org*
Judicial Studies Board: *http://www.jsboard.co.uk/*
JUSTICE: *www.justice.org.uk*
Justices' Clerks' Society: *www.jc-society.co.uk*
Law Commission, including reports: *www.lawcom.gov.uk*
Lawlinks, run by the University of Kent at Canterbury: *http://library.ukc.ac.uk/library/lawlinks*
Law Society, including the *Gazette*: *www.lawsociety.org.uk*
Law Society's Gazette: *www.lawgazette.co.uk*
LAWTEL (this is a subscription only database): *www.lawtel.co.uk*
Legal Abbreviations, contains 12,500 abbreviations: *www.legalabbrevs. cardiff.ac.uk*
Legal Action Group, including items from *Legal Action*: *www.lag.org.uk*
LexisNexis is a very comprehensive subscriber database: *http://web.lexis-nexis.com/xchange-international/*
Legal Services Commission: *www.legalservices.gov.uk*
Legal Services Research Centre (of the Legal Services Commission): *www.lsrc.org.uk*
Liberty: *www.liberty-human-rights.org.uk*
Office of Public Sector Informations, incuding Acts of Parliament and statutory instruments: *www.opsi.gov.uk*
Parliament, an excellent, very informative website, including many information leaflets on the Lords and Commons and legislative procedures, plus House of Lords judgments, *Hansard* and all Bills: *www.parliament.uk*

Privy Council: *www.privy-council.org.uk*

Review of Tribunals: *www.tribunals-review.org.uk*

Scottish Parliament: *www.scottish.parliament.uk*

Secretariat to the Law Officers' Department (Attorney-General): *www. lslo.gov.uk*

Social Science Information Gateway: *www.sosig.ac.uk/law*

Statistics: *www.statistics.gov.uk*

Sweet and Maxwell, law publishers, including free textbook updates: *www.sweetandmaxwell.co.uk*

US Supreme Court: *www.supremecourtus.gov*

Welsh Assembly: *http://www.wales.gov.uk/index.htm*

Westlaw, another very comprehensive subscriber database: *www.westlaw.co.uk*

BIBLIOGRAPHY

1–025   C. Dadamo and S. Farran, *The French Legal System* (1996).

R. David and J.E.C. Brierley, *Major Legal Systems in the World Today* (1985).

H.P. Glenn, *Legal Traditions of the World* (2000).

T. Honoré, *About Law: An Introduction* (1996).

FURTHER READING

1–026   If you want to read a really entertaining and wide ranging book, giving you a general introduction to English law, you cannot do better than, G. Rivlin, *Understanding the Law* (2004).

2. Sources of English Law

The sources of English and Welsh law are statute law (Acts of Parliament and Statutory Instruments), other delegated legislation, common law (case law made by superior judges), Community law, the European Convention on Human Rights, international treaties, the residuary royal prerogative and, less obvious nowadays, books of authority and custom. The UK Parliament delegated considerable law making power to the National Assembly for Wales, under the Government of Wales Act 1998.

2–001

The major problems with this multitude of sources today are lack of accessibility and the tremendous bulk of law being produced and the consequent confusion, even among lawyers and judges. The common law presumption that everyone knows the law is demonstrably false.

This chapter is a mere outline. For those who wish to know more about any of these sources of law, I strongly recommend that you read Manchester, Salter and Moodie's *Exploring the Law* and Zander's *The Law Making Process*. The latter provides a great explanation of how law is made and the former provides excellent examples of how English law develops from these sources.

1. Legislation

The most obvious source of codified law is an Act of Parliament, the UK Parliament. In the British constitution, a fundamental doctrine is that of parliamentary sovereignty which recognises that supreme power is vested in Parliament and that there is no limit in law to the law-making capacity of that institution. This is now massively tempered by membership of the Common Market, now European Union, since 1973 and the importation of the European Convention on Human Rights by the Human Rights Act 1998, in 2000. Nevertheless, unless it conflicts with Community law or the

2–002

Convention, what Parliament passes in the form of an Act will be put into effect by the courts. Where statute law provides a remedy, the citizen is expected to resort to that, not to a common law remedy: *Marcic v Thames Water Utlities* [2003] UKHL 66. A person whose property was flooded by overflowing sewers had an adequate statutory complaints procedure, without resorting to the tort of nuisance.

This acceptance by the courts of parliamentary supremacy is entirely a matter of history derived directly from the seventeenth century conflict between the Stuart Kings and Parliament. In that conflict, the courts took the side of Parliament and one result of their joint success was that, thereafter, the courts have been prepared to acknowledge the supremacy of Parliament within its own sphere, whilst Parliament has readily allowed the independence of the judiciary to become an acknowledged factor in the constitution. The contrast with countries with a written constitution (most countries) is, however, very marked in that their Supreme Courts have the power to overrule legislation as being "unconstitutional." No such power exists in the English legal system. In *British Railways Board v Pickin* (1974) an unsuccessful attempt was made to persuade the courts to intervene, on the grounds that the Board had obtained powers in a private Act of Parliament by misleading Parliament. The only role of the courts is to "interpret" the statutory provisions to the circumstances of any given case. If there is an element of human rights in issue, they must, where possible, interpret Acts so as to give effect to Convention rights and they are obliged to recognise Community law as supreme, if it conflicts with English law.

Another unsuccessful attempt to overturn an Act was made in 2005, in *R. (Jackson) v Attorney-General* [2005] EWCA Civ 126. In this case, pro-hunt supporters challenged the validity of the Hunting Act 2004, arguing that it was invalid because it was passed under a procedure laid down by the Parliament Act 1949 which was in itself invalid. The 2004 Act, banning foxhunting, had been hotly controversial. The Government had used their powers under the 1949 Act to pass the Bill through the House of Commons only, without the consent of the House of Lords, who had rejected a previous version. The 1949 Act had amended the Parliament Act 1911, which permitted a Bill to be passed by the Commons alone, in certain circumstances, provided a two year period had elapsed. The 1949 Act reduced that period to one year. Lord Woolf C.J. in the Court of Appeal (CA) remarked that it was very rare for the courts to entertain a challenge to an Act of Parliament but the Administrative Court, below, had been correct to admit the challenge. The 1911 Act was very unusual. The House of Lords, House of Commons and the King had used the machinery of legislation to make a fundamental change to the constitution. It was "perfectly appropriate" for the courts to consider the issue since they were helping Parliament and the public by clarifying the legal position when such clarification was obviously necessary. The Court held that the constitution could be amended by the legislature and it was clear that such an amendment was intended by the 1911 Act but that did not mean it was intended that the 1911 Act could not be amended by the 1949 Act.

The Queen in Parliament

The UK Parliament is made up of three constituent elements: the **2–003** monarch; the House of Lords; and the House of Commons. An Act of Parliament normally has approval of all three elements. Under certain conditions, it can be passed without the approval of the Lords, using the Parliament Acts 1911 and 1949. This has only been done a few times and occurred in 2004 with the Hunting Act.

The monarch's place in Parliament is a formality. She attends the opening of a new session of Parliament, as she does each autumn and after each General Election when a new government is elected, such as in 2005. She reads the speech from the throne, which is the Government's statement of its legislative proposals for the coming session of Parliament. The speech is written by the Prime Minister and does not in any way reflect her personal views. All legislation must receive the Royal Assent before it becomes law. It has not been refused since the reign of Queen Anne in 1707 and will never be refused; such is the strength of the constitutional convention that the monarchy does not interfere in politics.

Procedure

An Act of Parliament starts off as a Bill. Most Bills are **2–004** Government Bills. Their clauses will have been agreed by the "sponsoring" department which has instructed parliamentary counsel to draft the Bill.

Before the Bill becomes an Act of Parliament, and the clauses become sections, it must undergo five stages in each House. It may start off in the Commons or Lords. Once the Bill with any amendments has been approved both by the House of Commons and, normally, the House of Lords, it needs only the Royal Assent to become an Act of Parliament. It comes into immediate effect unless it contains its own starting date, or it has a provision which allows different parts of the Act to be brought into force at different times, by a minister making a statutory instrument to that effect. For instance, different parts of the Criminal Justice Act 2003 are now being brought into force, in 2005, the time of writing. The Human Rights Act 1998 came into force in 2000, to give the courts, public bodies and the public time to prepare. If you want to know more about parliamentary procedure and how Bills progress, read the excellent "Factsheets" on the UK Parliament website. For example, one especially useful sheet describes the parliamentary stages of a Government Bill. There is much information, easily understood, on the website. Even better, go and watch proceedings yourself, free. If you want to watch the Committee rooms, where Government policy is scrutinised and legislation is examined in detail, you can skip the queue.

The Form of an Act of Parliament (Statute)

Language

2–005   Statutory language must be precise. Every Act must relate to existing legislation on the subject so clauses often amend old Acts or cross-refer to others. Further, although the modern aim is to draft the law in plain English, the endeavour to close loopholes also makes Acts complex. In 1995, I watched an argument between a parliamentary draftsman and a tax lawyer, at a conference on legislation. The tax lawyer accused the draftsman of making the Finance Acts too complicated for ordinary people to understand. The draftsman retorted that if clients stopped paying tax lawyers like him large amounts of money to find loopholes, he could draft them in simpler language. Controversial or big Bills suffer many amendments, especially by the Government who introduced them. It is said that there is a tendency to introduce Bills in outline and fill in the details as they pass through Parliament. These factors combine to make statutes complicated and notoriously difficult for the lay person to understand. Although the earliest statutes had long titles and preambles, since the Short Titles Act 1896, Acts of Parliament have been given a short title and preambles have become the exception.

Citation

2–006   From 1963 every Act is given a Chapter number for the year in which it receives the Royal Assent. This abolishes the centuries-old system by which Acts were given a Chapter number for the session of the parliament in question designated by the regnal year of the monarch. This system could produce difficulties. For instance, 1937 under the former system was cited as "1 Edw. 8 and 1 Geo. 6." The present system is to refer to an Act by its short title and Chapter number for the year in question: for example, The Gender Recognition Act 2004 (c.7).

Acts are published by the Office of Public Sector Informtion (OPSI). It operates as part of the Cabinet Office. In practice, OPSI makes new legislation available for sale to the public as soon as it has been given the Royal Assent. It is available free online from the OPSI, with all public Acts from 1988.

Public Bills and Private Bills

A Public Bill is legislation which affects the public at large, and applies throughout England and Wales. Most Bills are Public and sponsored by the Government. A Private Bill is legislation which affects a limited section of the population, either by reference to locality or by reference to a particular family or group of individuals. These are known respectively as Local and Personal Bills. A Private Member's Bill is a Public Bill introduced by a back-bench Member of Parliament, who has been successful in the ballot. A Hybrid Bill may cover work of national importance but in a local area. Examples are the Channel Tunnel Bills of the 1970s and 1980s.

2–007

Consolidation, codification and statute law revision

Consolidation is the process by which provisions in a number of Acts of Parliament are brought together and re-enacted in one Act. It is not a method for changing the law but it does make the law easier to find. In order to ease the passage of such measures, they go through Parliament in a special procedure. In 2000 for example, the legislation concerning sentencing was consolidated in the Powers of the Criminal Courts (Sentencing) Act 2000.

2–008

Codification is the term used for an Act of Parliament which brings together all the existing legislation and case law and forms a complete restatement of the law. It can involve changes in the law and is thus one method of law reform. Recently, Lord Chief Justice Bingham, as he then was, added his weight to the academics' increasingly impatient demand for a codification of the criminal law and Professor Spencer added a persuasive and reasoned argument for codifying criminal procedure and the Government included plans for a code in its legislative proposals announced in its 2001 white paper, *Criminal Justice: The Way Ahead*. See more discussion on codification in Chapter 5, below.

The Law Commission, which was set up under the Law Commissions Act 1965, has, as one of its responsibilities, to keep under review all the law with a view to its systematic development and reform including, in particular, the codification of the law. It is consequently working at the present time on possible legislation which will, at some future time, codify particular branches of the law. The Law Commission also has overall responsibility for advising the repeal of obsolete and unnecessary enactments.

Since 1993/1994, a Special Public Bill Committee "fast-track" procedure has been used for legislation proposed by the Law

2–009

Commission and other non-contentious Bills. This "Jellicoe procedure" employs a committee of specialists (*e.g.* judges and lawyers on The Arbitration Bill 1996) instead of a committee of the whole House. Lord Chancellor Mackay's ill-fated Domestic Violence Bill 1995 was supposed to be one such Bill. Unfortunately, it proved to be very controversial and was lost. We come back to the Law Commission in Chapter 5, below.

Delegated Legislation

2–010   This is the name given to law made in documentary form by subordinate authorities acting under law-making powers delegated by Parliament or the sovereign, acting under her prerogative. Parliament does not have time or expertise to fill in the details or technicalities of the law so most big Bills are mere frameworks. The big difference between Acts of Parliament (primary legislation) and subordinate or delegated legislation is that the courts can quash the latter if it is outside the remit of delegated power (substantively *ultra vires*) or has not been made in a procedurally correct way (procedurally *ultra vires*). The CA confirmed that it was entitled to review subordinate legislation on the grounds of illegality, procedural impropriety or *Wednesbury* unreasonableness, even where it had been debated and approved by affirmative resolution of both Houses of Parliament. The Court was entitled to assess for itself the facts presented to Parliament as supporting the legality of the subordinate legislation. The extent to which a statutory power was open to judicial review on the ground of irrationality depended critically on the nature and purpose of the enabling legislation: *R. (Javed) v SS for Home Department* and joined cases [2001] EWCA Civ 789.

Such legislation can take the following forms.

Orders in Council

2–011   Parliament sometimes permits the Government through Her Majesty in Council to make law by way of an Order in Council. This is particularly true where an emergency is imminent. Orders in Council are sometimes issued under a prerogative power, as was the Order in Council concerned in the case of *CCSU v Minister for the Civil Service* (1984), otherwise known as "the GCHQ case", which Margaret Thatcher used to issue a ban on trade union membership in GCHQ. An Order in Council requires the formality of a meeting of the Privy Council in the presence of the Queen. Practically, the decision to use prerogative power in this way is made by the Cabinet, or a small section thereof.

Statutory Instruments

A more common form of delegated legislation is the power fre-   2–012
quently given to ministers to make law for a specified purpose. The
document containing this law is called a statutory instrument and
thousands are issued every year. As each one is published it is given
a number for the year, for example, the Greenhouse Gas Emissions
Trading Scheme (Amendment) Regulations (SI 2004/3390).
Statutory instruments have become of major importance as a source
of law. Much more law is contained in them than in Acts. Almost all
Community law comes into English law via statutory instruments,
like the one just mentioned.

Byelaws

Parliament delegates to local authorities and other public bodies the   2–013
power to make local laws or laws limited to their particular functions.
Thus local authorities can make town laws, or byelaws, for their areas.
For instance, there are often rules governing behaviour in parks or
leisure centres. Even so the authority has to obtain confirmation of the
byelaws from the named central government minister before the
byelaws take effect. The power to make byelaws also belongs to public
bodies such as the British Airports Authority. Byelaws can be quashed
on judicial review by the Divisional Court of the Queen's Bench
Division if they are *ultra vires*, or their illegality can be used as a
defence where someone is prosecuted for infringing them. This happened to Lindis Percy, a protester against US defence forces in this
country. She appealed to the Crown Court against her conviction for
breach of byelaws by repeatedly entering a secure defence installation
and the Crown Court upheld her appeal, holding the byelaws to be
ultra vires the Military Lands Act 1892, the enabling Act (facts in *SS for
Defence v Percy* (1999, HC)). Another example is *Boddington v British
Transport Police* (1998, HL), where B sought to defend himself from a
charge of illegally smoking on a railway carriage on the ground that
the posting of no smoking notices by Network South Central was *ultra
vires*. He was convicted and the House of Lords dismissed his last
appeal.

Welsh law

Wales gained considerable autonomy in making delegated legis-   2–014
lation for Wales, from 1999. Under the Government of Wales Act
1998 and subsequent legislation, this includes substantial areas of
government, such as agriculture, planning and the environment,
health and social services, education and industry, housing and
local government, sport and leisure and the Welsh language. In
turn, the Assembly has delegated many of its powers to its First

Minister, who leads the Welsh Assembly Government. For more detail, see the Assembly's website, below.

Comment on delegated legislation

2–015   Since the mid-point of the twentieth century, there has been increasing concern that Acts are mere frameworks, giving substantial powers to Ministers to fill in the details through delegated powers, usually using statutory instruments. For instance, the Access to Justice Act 1999 provides a new framework for the provision of legal services but leaves it up to the Lord Chancellor to devise a funding code to say what types of litigation will be publicly funded and leaves it up to regional bodies to allocate priorities in spending their budget. Concern has repeatedly been expressed that too much legislative power is being given to the executive. The Lords raised this concern in a debate in 1991, citing the Child Support Act, which gave over 100 regulation-making powers to the Minister and others, most of which were subjected to the negative procedure, by which a statutory instrument automatically becomes law unless concerns about it are positively raised in Parliament.

In recent years there has been concern over the frequent use of "Henry VIII" sections in Acts which permit a Minister to amend primary legislation, an Act, through a statutory instrument. In *Thorburn v Sunderland City Council* [2002] EWHC 195 imperial heroes challenged the validity of delegated legislation to amend the Weights and Measures Act 1985. It implemented an EC Metrication Directive and made it illegal to sell loose goods by the pound. The statute contained a "Henry VIII clause", allowing itself to be amended by subordinate legislation. The High Court dismissed the argument that Henry VIII clauses should only be used to make minor amendments to Acts. They also dismissed the argument founded on the doctrine of implied repeal, that the 1985 Act had impliedly repealed s.2(2) of the European Communities Act 1972.

A power for a Minister to "fast-track" an amendment to a piece of legislation which has been declared by the courts to be incompatible with the European Convention on Human Rights, is contained in the Human Rights Act 1998. This caused concern in the passage of the Bill through the Lords.

2. Statutory Interpretation

"Rules" for Statutory Interpretation

2–016   Inevitably, disputes arise as to the meaning or application of legislation and the task of the judges in this context is, therefore, described as that of statutory interpretation. Judges are not the only people who need to interpret statutes. Law lecturers and students and lawyers advising their clients need to do so. Judges of the lower courts need to interpret statutes for their own sake and sometimes for juries. Magistrates' clerks (legal advisers) need to know how to advise their bench. Civil servants and local government officers need to know how to apply the law to us. Most importantly, as ordinary citizens, all of us are presumed to know the law so we need to understand the way our business and social lives are regulated and what are our rights (*e.g.* as employee) and duties (*e.g.* to pay tax). Before I describe the "rules" for this I should explain that two experts on statutory interpretation, Cross and Bennion, insist that there are no such "rules". Bennion said Cross wrote his book to prove there were no such rules. In Bennion's own first edition, 1984, he said there are no such rules. "Instead there are a thousand and one interpretive criteria." (see Bennion's 1997 letter) Nevertheless, judges have developed a set of common law principles to help them interpret statutes that are known as the rules of statutory interpretation. It is important to understand that judges do not articulate the application of these "rules" but they do tend to apply them sequentially. The labels of these "rules" are now simply a construct for academic analysis. Cross and other commentators argue that judges now take a "contextual approach". (See Bell and Engle, *Cross on Statutory Interpretation*). In doing this, judges claim to be searching for "the will of Parliament" and sometimes they articulate this. For instance, in *R. v Chief Constable of the RUC Ex p. Begley* (1997), Lord Browne Wilkinson explained this limit on the House's role in developing the common law, as he saw it:

> "It is true that the House has power to develop the law. But it is a limited power. And it can be exercised only in the gaps left by Parliament. It is impermissible for the House to develop the law in a direction which is contrary to the expressed will of Parliament."

The first tactic judges use is to look for definitions of contentious words. The Interpretation Act is generally useful. One of its better-known sections provides that "unless the contrary intention appears (a) words importing the masculine gender include the feminine (and vice versa) (b) words in the singular include the plural, and words in the plural include the singular". Most statutes contain definitions of the words they use, especially if they are novel, so the Crime and Disorder Act 1998, s.85 defines "action plan order" and "drug treatment and testing order", for example. Sometimes words are left undefined and it is for the courts to determine their application. The Protection from Harassment Act 1997 does not define harassment but the High Court decided it did not include the activities of Microsoft, intimidating a software counterfeiter by provoking police raids, conducting oppressive litigation and telephoning the claimants at night: *Tuppen v Microsoft* (2000).

The first principle in interpretation is that the judge should apply the words according to their "ordinary, plain and natural meaning". In *Clarke v Kato* (1998) the House of Lords held that as a matter of ordinary language, a car park did not qualify as a road for the purposes of the Road Traffic Act 1988 so as to be an area in respect of which a motor insurance policy had to provide cover. The courts will always construe penal legislation restrictively, applying limited meaning to statutory language, as can be seen from *R. v Johnson, R. v Hind* [2005] EWCA Crim 971, cited in Chapter 10, below.

2–017 Unfortunately, the courts sometimes find themselves bound by the literal words of an Act into an interpretation which they consider leads to a daft result. In *Horsman* (1997) Waller L.J. said

> "the powers of the Court of Appeal flow only from statute, and however anomalous, if the words of the section are clear, there is no room for construing them in any other way . . . the question whether there should not be some amendment should be looked at with some haste".

R. v Smith [2002] EWCA Crim 2907 was another case where the CA reluctantly felt itself bound by a literal interpretation of statute. Section 14(5) of the Criminal Appeal Act 1995 seemed to say that once the Criminal Cases Review Commission (CCRC), on whatever grounds, had made a reference to the court, the appellant might add any further grounds, including those expressly rejected by the CCRC. Their Lordships were "very surprised indeed" at this and respectfully suggested an amendment.

Sometimes judges are frustrated that a legislative oversight can produce a harsh result in unforeseen circumstances. A poignant example was *R. v Human Fertilisation and Embryology Authority Ex p. Blood* (1996/1997). Diane Blood and her husband had decided to have a baby. Before she got a chance to conceive, her husband died of meningitis. While he was still in a coma, a sample of sperm was removed and frozen and his widow, Mrs Blood wanted to use it to conceive. The Human Fertilisation and Embryology Act required a man's written consent for the storage or use of his sperm in the UK. Much as the judge and the public had "universal sympathy" (Stephen Brown J.) for the weeping Mrs Blood's "double bereavement", he could not surmount the clear requirement of the Act. Baroness Warnock, whose committee's finding led to the Act, blamed herself for not foreseeing such a case and Lord Winston, the famous fertility specialist, called the result "cruel and unnatural". The CA too felt "all the courts . . . can do is give effect to the clear language of the

Act" (*per* Woolf M.R.). Happily, they allowed her appeal on a point of Community law. They ruled that she had the right to take the sperm for insemination elsewhere in the EU. She conceived in 1998.

Sometimes a case can be spared a bad outcome which would **2–018** result from a literal interpretation, because a second principle, which has become known as the golden rule, is that the literal application need not be applied, if to do so would lead to absurdity or to inconsistency within the statute itself. An outstanding example of the golden rule occurred in *Re Sigsworth* (1935), where a man was found to have murdered his mother. In the statute dealing with the distribution of the mother's estate it was laid down that the estate was to be distributed amongst "the issue". The son was her only child. The judge held that the common law rule that a murderer cannot take any benefit from the estate of a person he had murdered prevailed over the apparently clear words of the statute.

A third principle is that if the so-called literal or golden rules fail to assist, the judge is entitled to consider the "mischief" rule. This rule, which was first settled in *Heydon's Case* in 1584, allows the judge to consider: (1) what was the common law; (2) what was the defect or mischief in the common law; and (3) what remedy Parliament in the legislation has provided for the defect. Here, a judge is entitled to examine existing legislation and case law before coming to a decision, with the intention that the ruling will "suppress the mischief and advance the remedy." In *Bournewood Community and Health NHS Trust Ex p. L* (1998), the House of Lords held that the statutory predecessor to s.131(1) of the Mental Health Act 1983 was designed to cure the mischief caused by the assumption that compulsory powers had to be used unless the patient could express a positive desire for treatment, and to replace that by the offer of care, without deprivation of liberty, to all who needed it and were not unwilling to receive it.

The court is not easily persuaded to reject the plain words of the statute. Lord Scarman in *Stock v Frank Jones (Tipton) Ltd* (1978) explained that:

"if the words used by Parliament are plain there is no room for the anomalies test, unless the consequences are so absurd that without going outside the statute, one can see that Parliament must have made a drafting mistake . . . but mere manifest absurdity is not enough; it must be an error (of commission or omission) which in its context defeats the intention of the Act".

Nevertheless, in *Inco Europe v First Choice Distribution* (2000) the **2–019** House of Lords said the courts must be able to correct obvious drafting errors. In suitable cases, the court can add, omit or substitute words. Before doing so, they must be abundantly sure of three matters:

1. the intended purpose of the statute or provision in question;
2. that by inadvertence, the draftsman and Parliament had failed to give effect to that purpose in the provision in question; and
3. the substance of the provision that Parliament would have made, although not necessarily the precise words that it would have used, had the error in the Bill been noticed.

Drafting errors and omissions may occur because of the number of amendments made as a big Bill passes through Parliament. A famous example of this is s.16 of the Theft Act 1968, which became known as "a judicial nightmare" and remained uncorrected until the Theft Act 1978. Lord Goff closely examined *Hansard* and recounted its messy legislative history in *Preddy* (1996, HL) and commented:

"hurried amendments to carefully structured comprehensive Bills are an accident-prone form of proceeding; and the new s.16 . . . proved to be so incomprehensible as to be unworkable in practice".

Sometimes legislation proves to be completely unworkable and this has repeatedly occurred in the area of criminal procedure and sentencing, which has been the subject of far too much legislation. For instance, the Criminal Justice and Public Order Act 1994 purported to do away with committals from magistrates' courts to the Crown Court and to replace them with transfer proceedings. When Epsom Magistrates' Court tried to use the new transfer scheme in September 1995, the bench and clerk found it did not work. Eventually, the section was abandoned and a new scheme created in 1998. Academics and the Law Commission get very frustrated when they have warned that there are gaps in a Bill or defects and Ministers just ignore or even ridicule them. This frustration is expressed by Ashworth in an editorial of the March 1996 *Criminal Law Review* and has frequently been complained of by the late Professor Sir John Smith, especially when things go wrong, in the nature of "I told you so" comments in the *Criminal Law Review*.

Other "Rules" (Aids to Interpretation)

2–020   Where specific words are followed by general words, the general words must be given effect in the light of the foregoing specific words. This is called the *ejusdem generis* rule. An example is *Hobbs v CG Robertson Ltd* (1970) where the CA had to construe the following phrase concerning the provision of goggles in the Construction (General Provision) Regulations 1961 "breaking, cutting, dressing or carving of stone, concrete, slag or similar materials" to circumstances where a workman injured an eye, through the splintering of brickwork from a chimney breast which he was required to remove. The Court applied the *ejusdem generis* rule in holding that brick was not "a similar material" to stone, concrete or slag; the provision of goggles was, therefore, not compulsory and the workman's claim failed. A connected rule is that where, in a statute, there is a list of specified matters, which is not followed by general words, then only the matters actually mentioned are caught by this provision of the Act. The Latin phrase for this is *expressio unius est exclusio alterius*. In *R. v Inhabitants of Sedgley* (1831) a statutory provision for rating occupiers of "lands, houses, tithes and coal mines" was held not to apply to any other kind of mine and in *B v DPP* (1998), the CA applied the rule (not saying they were doing so) in interpreting the Sexual Offences Act 1956. The inclusion of a specific statutory defence in two sections demonstrated conclusively that Parliament did not intend that the defence should be available for other offences where a defence was not mentioned. The rule *noscitur a sociis* means that where two or more words follow each other in a statute, they must be taken as related for the purpose of interpretation. For example, in *Inland Revenue Commissioners v Frere* (1965) the House of Lords held that in the relevant phrase of the statute "interest, annuities or other annual payments" the word "interest" meant annual interest.

It is accepted practice that a statute must be taken as a whole. Consequently it follows that a judge must relate a word or phrase in a statute to its place in the context of the whole measure.

Other presumptions are as follows

(i)   There is no change in the existing law beyond that expressly stated in the legislation.

(ii)   The Crown is not bound unless the Act specifically makes it so. The Windsors can only be prosecuted for speeding because the Road Traffic Act binds the Crown.

(iii)   Legislation is not intended to apply retrospectively, unless this is expressly stated to be the case.

(iv)   Any change in the law affecting the liberties of the subject must be expressly and specifically stated.

(v)   Any liability for a criminal offence must be on the basis of fault, unless the words of the statute clearly intend otherwise.

(vi)   The legislation applies throughout the UK unless an exemption for Scotland or Northern Ireland is stated. Because Scotland, in particular, has its own legal and local government system, it is common for Parliament to legislate for

Scotland separately and now much of this legislative power has been passed to the Scottish Parliament.

(vii) If the provisions of two Acts appear to be in conflict, the court will endeavour to reconcile them, since there is no presumption of implied repeal. If reconciliation is not possible, logic demands that the later provision be given effect. For instance, *Padmore v Inland Revenue Commissioners (No.2)* (2001, HC), the Court had to resolve a conflict between two inconsistent tax provisions. The Chancery Division held that where the Act being construed is a consolidating Act, it is only permissible to take into account the earlier legislation if the later language is ambiguous, obscure or would lead to an absurdity. Where there is a conflict between two sections in the same statute, the court must do its best to reconcile them and may read words into the statute, to give effect to plain legislative intent.

(viii) Legislation must be construed so as not to conflict with Community law (see Chapter 3, below).

(ix) Legislation must be construed so as to give effect to the European Convention on Human Rights where possible (see Chapter 4, below).

(x) Parliament intends to give effect to international treaties to which the UK is a contracting party.

Extrinsic Aids

2–021   Judges decided that they would refrain from consulting *Hansard*, the report of debates on a Bill through Parliament and would only permit reference to preparatory documents to determine the mischief the Act sought to remedy. They set out guidelines in *Black-Clawson v Papierwerke* (1975, HL). The reason for this rule is that people should be entitled to know the law by taking an Act at face value. Furthermore the intentions of, say, the Lord Chancellor, in introducing the Courts and Legal Services Bill may have differed from the "intention of Parliament", in passing the Act, after it had been debated and amended. Because of this rule the judge was unable, theoretically, to make use of Parliamentary debates, reports of committees or commissions or what the government ministers involved had said about the measure as evidence of Parliamentary intent. This rule, that no extrinsic aids would be used, ensured that Parliament had a complete obligation to express itself precisely when making new law.

Serious inroads into this rule, significantly altering the judicial role in statutory interpretation, were made by the House of Lords in *Pepper v Hart* (1993). In this case, the question arose whether, under the Finance Act 1976, Parliament had intended school teachers at private schools to be taxed on the full value of the benefit in kind of the private education offered to their own children. The House of Lords ruled, erroneously, that this had been Parliament's intention. Their Lordships' attention was later drawn to the statement of the sponsoring minister. From this, it became clear that the true intention was that the teachers should only be taxed on the cost to their employers, which was minimal, so an Appellate Committee of seven Law Lords was reconvened and the case reargued, with reference to *Hansard*.

Their Lordships held that Parliamentary materials should only be referred to where:

"(a) legislation is ambiguous or obscure or leads to an absurdity;
(b) the material relied on consists of one or more statements by a minister or other promoter of the Bill together if necessary with such other Parliamentary material as is necessary to understand such statements and their effect;
(c) the statements relied on are clear" (*per* Lord Browne-Wilkinson).

Despite their Lordships' warnings that this new activity was to be the exception, judges and counsel in cases since 1993 have made frequent use of the *Pepper v Hart* principle, even where there is little ambiguity in a statute and case law has extended the rule to allow reference to preparatory material, such as green papers and white papers, and reports of the Law Commission and Royal Commissions. Even back in the 1970s, the Master of the Rolls, Lord Denning, and the Lord Chancellor, Lord Hailsham, said they always consulted *Hansard*. Drawing attention to the dangers of all this, the editors of *Cross on Statutory Interpretation* (1995 ed.) say it creates more work for lawyers, in advising clients and preparing litigation. Resorting to all these extrinsic aids, they comment, is no substitute for the clearest possible drafting of the text of the statute. Dame Mary Arden, when chairman of the Law Commission, warned of the dangers of *Pepper v Hart*. Ministers might prefer to have Bills drafted in general terms and make good the deficiency with a speech in Parliament. The executive might try to take short cuts by failing to get legislation accurate and relying on departmental notes on clauses. This would strengthen the power of the executive over Parliament. She said these dangers had been recognised. Departmental legal advisers scrutinised ministerial speeches in *Hansard* and if they were inaccurate, the Minister could correct a mistake at an appropriate point during further consideration of a Bill. In *R. v Secretary of State for the Environment, Transport and the Regions Ex p. Spath Holme Ltd* (2001), the Law Lords deprecated the frequent citation of *Hansard* and said that the conditions laid down in

2–022

Pepper v Hart should be strictly insisted upon. They were concerned with the cost of fruitless *Hansard* searches.

An example of the application of *Pepper v Hart* appears in *Mullen* (1999, CA), where Auld L.J. resorted to parliamentary debates to interpret the Criminal Appeal Act 1995. The case appears in Chapter 10 on criminal procedure, below. Looking at *Hansard*, he decided that the meaning of "unsafe" conviction in the amended form of the Criminal Appeal Act 1968 was meant to be the same as before the 1995 amendment. In other words, to restate the practice of the CA, over the years, in deciding what constituted sufficient grounds for quashing.

A very important example of the CA and the House of Lords referring to *Hansard* to help them in statutory interpretation was the case challenging the validity of the Hunting Bill, *R. (Jackson and others) v Attorney-General* (see above). Lord Woolf C.J., in the CA said the 1911 Parliament Act, which allowed legislation to be passed through the House of Commons only, in certain circumstances, was passed to resolve a constitutional crisis. An examination of *Hansard* disclosed beyond doubt that both the House of Commons and the House of Lords understood the extent of the constitutional change to which they were agreeing.

2–023   The courts are now much more ready to use extrinsic aids to interpretation than they used to be. For example, as can be seen from *R. v G & R* below, the House of Lords examined relevant Law Commission papers.

In *Westminster City Council v National Asylum Support Service* [2002] UKHL 38, the House held that explanatory notes could be used in interpretation, even if there were no ambiguity,

> "insofar as (they) cast light on the objective setting or contextual scene of the statute, and the mischief at which it is aimed . . . Used for this purpose Explanatory Notes will sometimes be more informative and valuable than reports of the Law Commission or advisory committees, Government green or white papers, and the like. After all, the connection of Explanatory Notes with the shape of the proposed legislation is closer than pre-parliamentary aids which in principle are already treated as admissible" (*per* Lord Steyn).

He meant they were more useful than those other materials because they are updated as a Bill passes through Parliament and changes its wording and meaning.

Different considerations apply in the case of a statute which incorporates an international convention. Here, exceptionally, the court must have regard to the full background so reference may be made to relevant material which explains the provisions in the convention. For a discussion of the approach of the English courts in interpreting international law in recent cases, including the *Pinochet* cases, see the very useful article by Qureshi.

Intrinsic Aids

The judge is, however, entitled to find assistance from the intrin-   2–024
sic aids contained in the statute itself; these include the long title, marginal notes, headings, which may be prefixed to a part of the Act, and Schedules, which are part of the Act although they do not affect words used in the body of the Act unless these are ambiguous. In *R. v Montila* [2004] UKHL 50, the House of Lords ruled that headings and side notes could be used in interpretation but less weight should be attached to them than to parts of the Act that are open to debate in Parliament. Preambles may also be used in statutory interpretation, although they are rarely used in modern statutes. Community legislation makes regular use of preambles. The famous "Eurobananas" Regulation of 1994, regulating standards of bananas, contains a preamble longer than the text. The European Court of Justice examines these preambles as a matter of course, in interpreting Community legislation.

Punctuation is referred to in interpreting the meaning of a sentence in the same way as we use it as an essential guide to the sense of normal everyday English.

Criticism

It can be gathered from the strictness of the approach articulated   2–025
by some judges that if the words of a statute fail to deal with a particular situation, there is no power in a court to fill the gap, despite the fact that Lord Denning M.R. often claimed "We fill in the gaps." This absence of provision is known as *casus omissus*, and in general the principle requires Parliament to pass a new statute to make good the deficiency. Lord Simonds in *Magor and St. Mellons RDC v Newport Corporation* (1952) said on this point "the power and duty of the court to travel outside them (the words of a statute) on a voyage of discovery are strictly limited . . .. If a gap is disclosed, the remedy lies in an amending Act."

This view is unrealistic. Generally Parliament, save in taxation cases, is very slow to amend faulty legislation. In recent years, however, the House of Lords seems to have grasped the nettle and become much more willing to give a purposive construction to legislation. In *Fothergill v Monarch Airlines Ltd* (1981, HL) Lord Diplock was explicitly critical of Lord Simonds' approach and lays the blame for unsatisfactory rules of statutory interpretation on the judges' "narrowly semantic approach to statutory construction, until the last decade or so".

Criticism used to be made fairly often and somewhat more infrequently now of the inflexible attitude of some judges in the task of statutory interpretation. In view of the difficulty of using language with an exactness which covers every conceivable situation, including the future, critics claim that the task of construction would be better done if judges took off their blinkers and considered all the circumstances which are relevant to the interpretation of the legislation in the particular case. Judging from the wide application given to *Pepper v Hart*, many modern judges agree with this criticism. Taking a broad, purposive approach, they apparently relish the opportunity to consult extrinsic aids. On the other hand, they may decline to do so in the face of clear language. An example is the *Kato* case above. Here Lord Clyde, speaking for the Law Lords, rejected an invitation to include car parks in the definition of "road" to give a purposive construction, because it would strain the word "road" beyond what it meant in ordinary usage.

2–026   Recently, some commentators have made sweeping statements that judges now favour a broad purposive approach. This simply is not true in most cases, as the above cases demonstrate and as can be seen from any trawl through recent *Times* law reports. The reason is that judges cannot use the purposive approach to avoid clear words. Lord Steyn said in *IRC v McGuckian* (1997, HL):

> "During the last 30 years there has been a shift away from the literalist approach to purposive methods of construction. When there is no obvious meaning of a statutory provision the modern emphasis is on a contextual approach designed to identify the purpose of a statute and to give effect to it".

(See his application of the purposive approach in *R. v A* [2001] UKHL 25 which I analyse in depth in Chapter 4 on human rights, below.) But Dame Mary Arden, quoting him, added that the courts can only apply a purposive approach where the purpose is sufficiently clear.

Nevertheless, one can identify some cases where judges clearly articulate that they are taking a purposive approach and they explain why. In one such case, judges were anxious to enforce safety on the railways and rejected the literal interpretation sought by Railtrack to excuse itself. Indeed, they even thought it regrettable that Railtrack had appealed the case, remarking that the sight of Railtrack engaged in litigation with its inspectorate was not likely to enhance public confidence: *Railtrack Plc v Smallwood* [2001] EWHC Admin 78. Another excellent and explicit example of a purposive interpretation is *Callery v Gray (No.1)* [2001] EWCA Civ 1117 where the CA had to make sense of the Access to Justice Act's provisions as to costs in conditional fee agreement cases (see Chapter 17 on legal services, below).

In interpreting the Parliament Act 1949 and assessing its validity, Lord Woolf C.J., in the 2005 case on the Hunting Act 2004 had regard to the fact that the 1949 Act had been generally accepted as a proper exercise of sovereign power by the Queen, the Lords, the Commons and the populace. A number of Acts had been passed according to the procedure it had set down.

Both the European Court of Human Rights and the European Court of Justice take a broad purposive approach to interpretation, described as "teleological". English and Welsh judges are well aware of this and use it themselves in relevant cases but some of them have adopted the habit in their interpretive tasks, even where the case has nothing to do with Community law or the Convention.   **2–027**

Another, in some ways more serious, criticism is that there is a lack of consistency in the application of the rules. It is suggested that judges may use whichever rule leads to the result which they wish to achieve; on one occasion they will rely on the literal rule, whereas on another they will reject it.

In a 1992 critique, *Making The Law*, the Hansard Commission recommended that for every Act of Parliament, the relevant government department and Parliamentary Counsel should prepare "notes on sections", an updated version of the "notes on clauses" prepared for a minister during the passage of a Bill. These should be published with the Act and used by the courts in interpreting it. See the research and critique by Sacks. She did research to try and ascertain whether judges are given sufficient guidelines to help them perform their task. She found that problematic wording in statutes did not always arise from careless drafting or because Parliament did not foresee a particular situation, as was commonly assumed. It was sometimes because "the Government either lacked clear objectives or, had deliberately intended to obfuscate in order to avoid controversy". References to *Hansard* did not help. "Time and again Members of Parliament pleaded for enlightenment." Worse, many difficult clauses received no debating time. She said this reflected badly on the parliamentary scrutiny process itself and called for the adoption of a method used by the French. She warned of the dangers of selective reading from *Hansard* and the inconsistent use of background reports. She repeated the recommendation of the Renton Committee and others that a statement of intent be included in every Act. This was done in the Courts and Legal Services Act 1990 but not in some of the other major statutes cited in this book. A Bill, she recommended, ought to be accompanied by a very detailed explanatory memorandum as it proceeds through Parliament. This was done in other parliaments.

At last, New Labour promised to make legislation more accessible and is attempting to fulfil that promise. Since the beginning of the 1998–1999 parliamentary session, Bills are being presented with fairly full "explanatory notes", written in clear and simple English. The note appears next to the Bill on the Parliament website and explanatory   **2–028** notes to Acts are available on the OPSI website. This is explained, and some of the difficulties of the drafter, by Christopher Jenkins, the First Parliamentary Counsel in an article which is well worth reading.

The attempt to make legislation more comprehensible has a long and somewhat fruitless history. The Statute Law Society was formed in 1968. Its main object was to procure technical improvements in the form and manner in which legislation is expressed and published so as to make it more intelligible. Its first report, in 1970, said procedures must be governed by the needs of the user. This was approved in 1975 by the Renton Committee. The Rippon Commission followed almost 20 years later and listed the following principles:

- Laws are made for the benefit of citizens.
- All citizens should be involved as fully and openly as possible in the way statute law is prepared.
- Statute law should be as certain and intelligible as possible for the benefit of citizens.
- Statute law should be rooted in the authority of Parliament and thoroughly exposed to democratic scrutiny.
- Ignorance of the law being no excuse, statute law had to be as accessible as possible.
- Although governments need to be able to secure the passage of their legislation, to get the law right and intelligible is as important as getting it passed quickly.

In the meantime, tax lawyers, among others, were still frustrated by the complexity of Finance Acts. In 1996, the Inland Revenue admitted tax law could be simplified and a rewrite project was launched. The Capital Allowances Bill 2001 was subjected to a four-stage consultative process involving users of tax legislation. Also in 2001, the Lords and Commons set up a Joint Committee on Tax Simplification Bills.

Tax lawyers and taxpayers are not the only people who get frustrated by confusing legislation. The group which undoubtedly has the biggest struggle and suffers from the greatest volume of legislation, as well as some of the most ill-drafted, complex and often unworkable legislation, are magistrates' clerks (legal advisers). The Justices' Clerks' Society tries to answer interpretive questions and frequently identifies lacunae in the law. They have formulated the policy that where there is a lack of clarity, any doubt should be resolved in the defendant's favour.

3. Case Law

2-029   Remembering that the English legal system is a common law system, indeed the mother of all common law systems, the significance of case law, *i.e.* common law, in creating and, presently, refining our laws cannot be underestimated. The law produced by the courts can be just as important as the law produced by Parliament. For instance, in 1991, the House of Lords abolished the rule protecting a husband from criminal responsibility for raping his wife. By case law, I mean the decisions of judges laying down legal principles derived from the circumstances of the particular disputes coming before them.

The Meaning of Precedent

The reason why such importance is attached to case decisions is explained by this doctrine of judicial precedent, which is also known as *"stare decisis"* (to stand by decisions). This doctrine, in its simplest form, means that when a judge comes to try a case, she must always look back to see how previous judges have dealt with previous cases (precedents) which have involved similar facts in that branch of the law. In looking back in this way the judge will expect to discover those principles of law which are relevant to the case under consideration. The decision which she makes will thus seek to be consistent with the existing principles in that branch of the law, and may, in its turn, develop those principles a stage further.

2–030

Because the branches of English law have been gradually built up over the centuries, there are now hundreds of thousands of reported case decisions available in hard copy, CD-Rom or online, with many more not included in the official Law Reports, on databases such as *Westlaw* and *Lexis* so that the task of discovering relevant precedents and achieving consistency is by no means simple. The standing of a precedent is governed by the status of the court which decided the case. Decisions of the House of Lords are obviously to be treated with the greatest respect, whereas a decision of a county court judge has normally limited effect. This quite common sense approach has developed into a rigid system under which precedents of the superior courts, if found to be relevant to the facts of a particular case, are treated as "binding" on the lower courts, so that the judge in the lower court must follow the reasoning and apply it to the case in hand. The judge is thus obliged to decide the case in accordance with binding judicial precedent.

The Doctrine of Precedent in Operation

The system operates as a hierarchy.

2–031

The European Court of Justice and the European Court of Human Rights

Decisions of the former are binding on all English and Welsh courts. Decisions of the latter must be taken account of.

2–032

The House of Lords/Supreme Court

2–033 Decisions of the House of Lords are binding on all the courts lower in the hierarchy. This is so not only where the facts of the later case are identical, which will be very rare, but also where the facts of the case call for the application of the same legal principle as in the House of Lords case. Until 1966, by reason of the binding nature of judicial precedent, a decision of the House of Lords, once made, remained binding on itself, as well as on all the courts lower in the structure. In 1966, by a formal Practice Statement, the House of Lords judges announced that in future they would not regard themselves as necessarily bound by their own previous decisions. The Practice Statement is worth quoting at length, as it gives us a neat summary of the arguments for and against a rigid system of binding precedent.

"Their Lordships regard the use of precedent as an indispensable foundation upon which to decide what is the law and its application to individual cases. It provides at least some degree of certainty upon which individuals can rely in the conduct of their affairs, as well as a basis for orderly development of legal rules. Their Lordships nevertheless recognise that too rigid adherence to precedent may lead to injustice in a particular case and also unduly restrict the proper development of the law. They propose, therefore, to modify their present practice and, while treating former decisions of this House as normally binding, to depart from a previous decision when it appears right to do so. In this connection they will bear in mind the danger of disturbing retrospectively the basis on which contracts, settlements of property and fiscal arrangements have been entered into and also the especial need for certainty as to the criminal law. This announcement is not intended to affect the use of precedent elsewhere than in this House."

There have not been many instances since the 1966 Practice Statement of the House of Lords departing from a previous decision. In *Herrington v British Railways Board* (1972) the Court revised a long-standing legal principle concerned with the duty of care owed to a child trespasser. In *R. v Shivpuri* (1986) the House of Lords departed from a decision given only one year earlier when reconsidering the law relating to criminal attempts. A recent and very significant instance of the Law Lords overruling their predecessors was *R. v G & R* [2003] UKHL 50 which reversed the effect of *R. v Caldwell* (1981), which had redefined and broadened the meaning of "recklessness" in the Criminal Damage Act 1971 (and consequently criminal law in general) to include offenders who had not foreseen a risk. The House noted that *Caldwell* had been subject to forceful academic, judicial and practitioner criticism, as producing unfair results. They examined the Law Commission's Draft Criminal Code Bill and its working paper prior to the 1971 Act and decided Parliament had never intended to broaden the ambit of the criminal law in this way. In this case, the House clearly saw themselves as justified in departing from precedent in correcting its unfair effects. By way of contrast, in *Jindal Iron and Steel Co Ltd v Islamic Solidarity Shipping Co Jordan Inc* [2004] UKHL 49, the House declined to overturn a 1957 precedent, because it had stood for 50 years, had worked satisfactorily, had not produced unfair results and an enormous number of transactions had taken place assuming that it was the law.

The Court of Appeal

The Civil Division of the Court of Appeal by its decisions binds all   **2–034** the courts in the structure except the House of Lords. The CA does bind itself for the future, according to the decision in *Young v Bristol Aeroplane Co* (1944) although it may escape if: (i) a later decision of the House of Lords applies; (ii) there are previous conflicting decisions of the CA; or (iii) where the previous decision was made *"per incuriam"*, *i.e.* in error, because some relevant precedent or statutory provision was not considered by the Court. A great example of such a decision, which the Divisional Court of the Queen's Bench Division held was decided *per incuriam* and thus not even binding on a magistrate, was *Thai Trading* (1998, CA), on the legality of a contingency fee agreement entered into by a solicitor. The House of Lords authority of *Swain v Law Society* (1983) had not been cited. It was obviously binding on the Court of Appeal and they decided wrongly, in ignorance of it, so *Thai Trading* is a *per incuriam* decision and not binding on any court. Note that the respondents in the case were unrepresented. With an increasing number of litigants in person, this problem is bound to occur, which is why judicial assistants were invented, in the 1990s, to do background research for judges in cases like this.

Lord Denning, when Master of the Rolls, tried to avoid this rule. The Criminal Division of the Court of Appeal does not consider itself always bound by its own decisions. Where the liberty of the subject is concerned, the court feels itself free to overrule a previous decision if it appears that in that decision the law was misunderstood or misapplied "and if a departure from authority is necessary in the interests of justice to an appellant": *R. v Spencer* (1985). An example of this occurred in *R. v Shoult* (1996, CA). A court led by Lord Taylor C.J., declined to follow *R. v Cook* (1995, CA), in considering an appeal against a prison sentence for a drink-driving conviction. This has especially applied since October 2000, where the court has chosen to modify the law in accordance with the European

Convention on Human Rights and can clearly be seen in the case law on the Criminal Appeal Act discussed in Chapter 10 on criminal procedure, below.

The High Court

2–035   Decisions of a single judge in the three divisions of the High Court are binding on the lower courts but not on other High Court judges. If a High Court judge is presented with a precedent from a previous High Court case he will treat the precedent as "persuasive", and not as "binding". Decisions by a Divisional Court are binding on judges of the same division sitting alone but not necessarily on future Divisional Courts: see *R. v Greater Manchester Coroner Ex p. Tal* (1985).

The County Court, the Crown Court and magistrates' courts

2–036   The decisions of these courts are seldom reported and not binding.

Binding and persuasive

2–037   It has already been explained that depending on the status of the court a precedent may be binding or it may be persuasive. Precedents which come from the Judicial Committee of the Privy Council or from countries within the common law jurisdiction, like Canada and Australia, are persuasive and the adoption of concepts from those foreign jurisdictions has led to developments in English common law, for instance, in criminal law and the tort of negligence. Sometimes, the House of Lords considers developments in other common law jurisdictions but decides not to adopt them into English law. This occurred in *Transco plc v Stockport MBC* [2003] UKHL 61. The House restated the rule in *Rylands v Fletcher*, rejecting a submission that it had been absorbed into the law of negligence, as held in the Australian High Court.

Terminology

2–038   Where a judge finds that a precedent to which he is referred is not strictly relevant to the facts of the case concerned, he is said to "distinguish" that case. As such, the case is not binding upon him. If, on the other hand, the judge holds that a precedent is relevant, and applies it, he is said to "follow" the reasoning of the judge in the earlier case.

When an appeal court is considering a precedent, it may "approve" the principle of law established in the case, or it may "disapprove" the precedent. It can "overrule" the principle of law established in a precedent if the case was decided by a court junior in status to it. A decision is said to be "reversed" when a higher court, on appeal, comes to the opposite conclusion to the court whose order is the subject of the appeal.

Ratio decidendi **and** *obiter dicta*

The most important and binding element of a judgment is the legal   2–039
principle which is the reason for the decision or *ratio decidendi* as it is
known; and then the remainder of the judgment, statements which
deal by way of explanation with cases cited and legal principles
argued before the court, are called *"obiter dicta"* or things said by the
way. The whole of a dissenting (disagreeing minority) judgment is
"obiter".

It is the *"ratio"* of a decision which constitutes the binding precedent; or *rationes* if there is more than one reason. So that when a
judge is referred to a precedent, the first task of the court is to decide
what was the *ratio* of that case, and to what extent it is relevant to
the principle to be applied in the present case. Whilst an *obiter
dictum* is not binding, it can, if it comes from a highly respected
judge, be very helpful in establishing the legal principles in the case
under consideration.

So important is it that a judgment should be accurately recorded
that, before publication in the "official" law reports, judges are asked
to check for accuracy the court reporter's version of the judgment.

Advantages and Disadvantages of a System of Binding Precedent

The main advantages of the doctrine are that it leads to consistency   2–040
in the application and development of the principles in each branch
of the law, and by virtue of this characteristic it enables lawyers to
forecast with reasonable certainty what the attitude of the courts is
likely to be to a given set of facts. The system is flexible in that it can
find an answer to any legal problem, and it is essentially practical in
that the courts are perpetually dealing with actual circumstances. It
must also be said that one result of the recording of cases over the
centuries is that the tremendous wealth of detail leads to considerable precision in the principles established in each field of law.

Critics argue that restriction on judicial discretion can be undesirable, and can lead to a judge, who wishes to escape from a precedent,
drawing illogical distinctions. Added to this is the difficulty, which
can occur in some Appeal Court decisions, of discovering exactly
what the *ratio decidendi* of a previous case is. This has been known to
be the case when the House of Lords decides an appeal by a majority
vote of three to two, and the three judges in the majority appear to
arrive at their decision for different reasons. An example of this difficulty is *Harper v National Coal Board* (1974) where the CA was, for this
reason, unable to discover the *ratio decidendi* of the House of Lords'
decision in *Smith v Central Asbestos Co Ltd* (Dodd's case) (1973). A
final factor, which is a practical problem, is that there are so many
cases being dealt with each year that inevitably there is increasing

complexity in each branch of the law. The sheer bulk of cases on commercial or criminal law is almost overwhelming and causes textbooks to become increasingly specialised and substantial. Even so, it can well happen that a case of importance is not reported, other than on *Lexis*, and so may go unnoticed for some considerable time. Such a case remains a precedent.

Law Reports

2–041   A system of binding precedent is dependent on the publication of reported cases. Law reporting dates back to the thirteenth century. The earliest case summaries were collected in manuscript form in what became known as the Year Books. These seem to have been prepared by students or practitioners and circulated among the judges and leading barristers. With the invention of printing, the production of law reports for sale to the legal profession, between the sixteenth and nineteenth centuries became common practice. They are published under the reporters' names. These reporters varied widely in their accuracy and reliability, but their law reports remain available, and have now been republished in a series called *The English Reports*, covering 1220–1865.

Since 1865, law reporting has been placed on a different basis, although it remains a matter for private enterprise. In 1870, the Incorporated Council of Law Reporting was established. It consists of representatives of the Law Society and the Inns of Court and publishes what have come to be treated as the Official Law Reports. (See Reeves on "Law Reporting from the 13th to the 21st Century"). The reports are published some considerable time after the judgment has been given, but are regarded as authentic. Approved judgments handed down in the High Court or CA can be copied immediately. Unapproved judgments are only given to the parties involved. High Court and CA decisions are available online, via the Her Majesty's Courts Service website and House of Lords decisions are available on the Lords' section of the Parliament website. The *Weekly Law Reports* (W.L.R.) and *All England Law Reports* (All E.R.), are published commercially by firms of law publishers. They are on hard copy and CD-Rom. All decisions of the Crown Court, High Court and above, whether or not reported elsewhere, are stored on *Westlaw* and *Lexis*. As well as these full reports, a number of law magazines carry summaries of recent case decisions, as do *The Times* and *The Independent*. Case summaries appear on another commercial database, *Lawtel*. Law reporting is done by barristers who attend the court hearing.

Citation of Judgments

2–042   In order to control the multiple citation of precedents of different value in reports of varying accuracy, the Lord Chief Justice issued three Practice Directions. Approved reserved judgments of the CA and High Court (the Supreme Court) can be cited as soon as handed down. If a case is reported in the official *Law Reports*, that one should be used. If not but it appears in the *Weekly Law Reports* or *All England Law Reports*, then they can be cited. If not reported in any of these, specialist private reports may be cited. Unreported cases may not be cited without permission. In civil courts, county court judgments and those on applications may not normally be cited.

Advocates are now required to state, in their skeleton argument, the proposition of law demonstrated by each authority they wish to cite and must justify citation of more than one authority for each proposition. If advocates wish to cite foreign authorities they must justify doing so and certify that there was no English authority on the point.

Advocates have a common law duty to the court to achieve and maintain appropriate levels of competence and care: *Harley v McDonald* [2001] UKPC 18. They still have a duty to draw to the attention of the court authorities which support their opponent's case. Doubtless this attempt by the judges to limit citations stems from the uncontrolled growth in the number of precedents lawyers will incorporate in their arguments, as demonstrated by a small piece of statistical research by Zander. In 2000, Zander showed that the number of authorities referred to in judgments had almost doubled since Diamond's research in 1965, from an average of 8.9 to 15.6. The percentage of those authorities cited which were unreported had almost quadrupled and the percentage of overseas authorities cited had increased from 3.7 per cent to 7.5 per cent. From 2001, all High Court and CA judgments are numbered and have numbered paragraphs, not pages. This neutral citation of judgments caters for those cited from electronic sources.

Do and Should Judges Make the Law?

Of course judges make law. That is the nature of the common law. 2–043
To pretend otherwise is silly. They created the law of tort. They invented the basic rules of contract. Murder is a common law crime. When a statute protecting people from harassment did not define harassment, obviously, the Government who introduced the Bill and Parliament who passed it as an Act were expecting the judges to define it and thus make the law. When judges reinterpret English law in accordance with the Treaty of Rome or other EU treaties or the European Convention, they are making the law. When judges find themselves dealing with an entirely novel set of circumstances, such as whether silent phone calls constitute an assault (*Ireland* (1997, HL)) or when the House of Lords overrules outdated and undesirable common law "rules" such as the marital exemption in

rape, they are making law (*R. v R* (1991, HL) and see especially CA judgments).

Nevertheless, the extent to which it is desirable to take this activity of rule creation has been the subject of endless debate. Many judges and academics have written on this subject but it is an argument of constitutional law and there is no space for it in this book confined to the ELS. A good starting point for the reader would be Zander's *The Law Making Process*, Chapter 7. The approach of those who would prefer to leave as much rule creation as possible to Parliament is typified by Bennion's 1999 article.

4. Prerogative Power

2–044   The residue of the monarch's power is exercised by the Prime Minister or another Government minister. The prerogative includes the power to conduct foreign relations, enter treaties, declare war and peace, confer honours, issue pardons, secretly vet jurors and a list of more uncertain activities. To help clarify them for us, a House of Commons Committee published a list of them in 2003. Where a statute deals with an activity previously exercised by way of prerogative power, the courts will presume that the statute has eclipsed and replaced it. In 2004, Professor Jeffrey Jowell suggested that they should be codified.

5. Custom

2–045   The common law was derived from the different laws of the existing Anglo-Saxon tribal groups in, for example, Kent and Wessex. The term "common law" emphasises the point. As England became one nation, with one king and one government, so the laws of the Anglo-Saxon regions had to be adapted into a national law common to the whole country. Since the difference between the regions stemmed from their different customary laws it is no exaggeration to say that custom was the principal original source of the common law and in this historical sense, custom, as the basis of common law, continued to play a part over the medieval period.

Customs were thus absorbed into the legal system, sometimes in the form of legislation and sometimes, particularly in the earliest period, by the judges giving decisions which were based on custom. The gradual result was that custom virtually disappeared as a creative source of law. An exception exists at the present day on a limited scale for cases where the courts can be convinced that a particular local custom applies. Usually in such cases, custom is pleaded as a defence as permitting the conduct in question. It is unusual, nowadays, for an argument to be based on custom and the rules for its acceptance are strict. Recognised custom does, however, play a very important part in the interpretation of international law. See below.

6. Books of Authority

A distinction is drawn between books of antiquity and those of   **2–046**
recent origin. Both categories are of importance and have a part to play in the system, but only the books of antiquity can strictly be regarded as a source of law.

In the first category fall certain ancient textbooks, any one of which by long-standing judicial tradition can be accepted as an original source of law.

The following works, most of which were written by judges, are accepted as books of authority —

Glanvill, *De Legibus et Consuetudinibus Angliae* (c.1189): authoritative on the land law and the criminal law of the twelfth century.

Bracton, *De Legibus et Consuetudinibus Angliae* (c.1250): mainly commentaries on the forms of action with case illustrations. A major study of the common law.

Littleton, *Of Tenures* (c.1480): a comprehensive study of land law.

Fitzherbert, *Nature Brevium* (c.1534): a commentary on the register of writs.

Coke, *Institutes of the Laws of England* (1628): an attempted exposition in four parts of the whole of English law.

Hale, *History of the Pleas of the Crown* (1736) (60 years after Hale's death): the first history of the criminal law.

Hawkins, *Pleas of the Crown* (1716): a survey of the criminal law and criminal procedure.

Foster, *Crown Cases* (1762): authoritative within its scope, which is concerned with the criminal law.

Blackstone, *Commentaries on the Laws of England* (1765): a survey of the principles of English law in the mid-eighteenth century intended for students. From the time of Blackstone on, writers of legal textbooks have fallen into the second category, that is, those of recent origin.

Modern textbooks are not treated as works of authority although   **2–047**
they are frequently referred to in the courts. Advocates are permitted

to adopt a textbook writer's view as part of their argument in a case. Judges will often quote from a modern textbook in the course of giving judgment; for example, *Re Ellenborough Park* (1956) the CA adopted the definition of an easement as defined in *Cheshire's Modern Real Property*. In *R. v Shivpuri* (1986) the House of Lords paid tribute to an article in the *Cambridge Law Journal* by Professor Glanville Williams. This article had a considerable influence on the court in persuading it to reverse its previous ruling. Sometimes the judge will decide that a statement in a textbook on a particular point is incorrect.

In *R. v Moloney* (1985) the House of Lords held that the definition of "intent" in *Archbold*, the virtual bible of criminal court practice, was "unsatisfactory and potentially misleading". The reason why no textbooks, since *Blackstone's Commentaries* were published in 1765, have been accepted as works of authority seems to be that: (i) case reports have become fuller and much more easily accessible; and (ii) by that time the principles of the common law were fully established, so that there was no question of a later textbook being itself a source of law.

7. International Law as a Source of English Law

2–048   There are two types, private and public international law. The former deals with such things as family law—what happens when there is a divorce between nationals of two different jurisdictions, who has care and control of the children and what happens if one kidnaps the children and takes them abroad. It also determines, for instance, what law should govern a dispute arising out of a car accident between nationals of two different states which takes place in a third. Private disputes between individuals or commercial organisations, such as those arbitrated in London, discussed in Chapter 12 on alternatives to the civil courts, may also be governed by elements of international law. Public international law (PIL) governs relations between states and the entities of states and creations of states such as the United Nations and the World Bank. Over the decades of the twentieth century and even before, we have created a number of fora to resolve international disputes. In the news at the moment is the War Crimes Tribunal for the former Yugoslavia. As I write, in 2005, the former President Milosovic is being tried before it, in the Hague, Netherlands. If you want to keep up-to-date with the Milosovic case or other indicted war criminals, or the progress of the War Crimes Tribunal dealing with Rwanda, then go to the UN website, have a look round it then click on the links to those two. PIL regulates such matters as the carriage of goods by air and sea, use of illegal drugs and war crimes. As individuals become more mobile in their domestic, social and working lives and with globalisation of the market place, so UK governments sign up to more and more treaties obliging us to enact domestic legislation (such as the Misuse of Drugs Act 1971) governing the lives of the citizenry and so we see more international litigation in the English courts. Qureshi's very useful article examines the attitude of the English courts to PIL issues, as manifested in recent case law, most famously, the *Pinochet* cases. One fascinating aspect of PIL this article explains is the recognition of custom in PIL. We bind ourselves to the explicit obligations of treaties but are also bound by the tacit rules of custom. Customary international law (CIL) is law which is a product of consensus amongst the community of nations. States regard it as binding in their dealing with other states. He quotes Lord Lloyd in the first *Pinochet* case (2000, HL) on the effect of CIL in English law:

"The application of international law as part of the law of the land means that, subject to the overriding effect of statute law, rights and duties flowing from the rules of (customary international law) will be recognised and given effect by the English courts without the need for any specific act adopting those rules into English law."

In applying and interpreting international conventions, the courts will apply a purposive construction, as the House of Lords did in *Sidhu v British Airways Plc* (1997). This case also determined that domestic common law cannot override a convention to which the UK is a contracting party. In this case, the parties sought to sue for damages at common law but the Lords held that their remedies were limited to those available for international carriage by air according to the Warsaw Convention. It provided a comprehensive code with a uniform international interpretation which could be applied in the courts of contracting parties, exclusive of any reference to domestic law.

Do not forget that the European Convention on Human Rights and the treaties of the EU have a massive effect on English law as well as generating rights and liabilities in public and private international law. They are such a significant source of English law that they merit separate chapters of this book.

BIBLIOGRAPHY

Dame Mary Arden, "Modernising Legislation" [1998] P.L. 65.   **2–049**
C. Banner and T. Boutle, "Challenging the Commons" (2004) 154 N.L.J 1466.

J. Bell and G. Engle, *Cross on Statutory Interpretation* (1995).

F. A. R. Bennion, letter, (1997) 147 N.L.J. 684.

F. A. R. Bennion, "A Naked Usurpation" (1999) 149 N.L.J. 421.

F. A. R. Bennion, *Statutory Interpretation* (2002) and (1st ed., 1984). *www.francisbennion.com*

The Right Honourable Lord Bingham of Cornhill, L.C.J., "A Criminal Code: Must We Wait Forever?" [1998] Crim. L.R. 694.

C. Jenkins, "Helping the Reader of Bills and Acts" (1999) 149 N.L.J. 798.

Professor Jowell was appearing on BBC Radio 4 in the *Unreliable Evidence* series.

C. Manchester, Salter and P. Moodie, *Exploring the Law* (2nd ed., 2000).

K. M. Qureshi, "International Law and the English Courts" (2001) 151 N.L.J. 787.

P. Reeves, "Law Reporting from the 13th to the 21st Century" (2000) 164 *Justice of the Peace* 1023.

V. Sacks, "Towards Discovering Parliamentary Intent" (1982) 3 *Statute Law Review* 143.

J. R. Spencer, "The Case for a Code of Criminal Procedure" [2000] Crim. L.R. 519.

United Nations: *www.un.org*

M. Zander, "What precedents and other source materials do the courts use?" (2000) 150 N.L.J. 1790.

M. Zander, *The Law Making Process* (6th ed., 2004).

Articles on the Diane Blood case in *The Times*, October 18, 1996.

FURTHER READING AND SOURCES FOR UPDATING THIS CHAPTER

2–050

Online updates to this book: *http://www.sweetandmaxwell.co.uk/academic/updates/darbyshire/index.html*

Parliament: *www.parliament.uk*

Welsh Assembly: *www.assembly.wales.gov.uk*

Scottish Parliament: *www.scottish.parliament.uk*

Office of Public Sector Informations: *www.opsi.gov.uk*

The Statute Law Review.

3. Community Law: Its Impact on English Law and the English Courts

"DETERMINED to lay the foundations of an ever closer union among the peoples of Europe". (The first aim of the preamble of the Treaty of Rome 1957.)

"The Treaty is like an incoming tide. It flows into the estuaries and up the rivers. It cannot be held back". (Lord Denning M.R. in *HP Bulmer v J Bollinger SA* (1974, CA).)

"The rise of the City firms of solicitors (and parallel firms in other cities) has made Britain the legal capital of Europe". (Robert Stevens, 1994.)

1. Community Law is Part of UK Law

Membership of the European Community has dramatically cur-   **3–001**
tailed the sovereignty of Parliament in the British constitution, in
certain contexts. It is simply unrealistic to consider the English legal
system or English sources of law in isolation from the EU, as the
ambit of Community power and now Union power is extended, so
the bulk of substantive law accelerates in growth, and it is no longer
appropriate to consider Community law as a single subject. Apart
from the Treaties and Regulations, which are directly applicable in
all Member States without further ado (and made binding in UK
law by the European Communities Act 1972, s.2), most statute law
comes into the UK "by the back door", through the medium of delegated legislation but it is scrutinised in Parliament by committees
in both Houses. For detail of parliamentary scrutiny of Community
law, see the free factsheets available from the Lords and Commons'
information offices and available on the UK Parliament website.

The interpretive and other judgments of the European Court of Justice (ECJ) are also a source of Community law and they and the EU Treaties and secondary legislation have to be interpreted by the English and Welsh courts. All our magistrates, judges and other adjudicators must treat questions as to the meaning or effect of the Treaties and Community instruments as questions of law to be determined in accordance with principles laid down by the ECJ. On any such question, they must take judicial notice of the Treaties, the *Official Journal of the Communities* and decisions or opinions of the ECJ or Court of First Instance (CFI). This is laid down in the European Communities Act 1972, s.3, as amended. This means that all ECJ rulings are binding precedents to be applied in the English and Welsh courts.

Here, I provide a simple and very basic guide to the institutions of the EU and the sources of Community law. It is essential, however, for every student of English and Welsh law to understand that they cannot ignore Community law. Regrettably, English lawyers, until the late 1990s suffered an appalling ignorance of Community law, which reflects the insularity of the wider British community. This chapter is the most basic of introductions. For a simple, well written and accurate account of Community law, I strongly recommend Steiner and Woods, *EC Law*, to which I am indebted for much of the content of this chapter. Foster's *Blackstone's EC Legislation* is updated annually and an indispensable accompaniment to any EU/ Community law, textbook. We are lucky to have a collection of brilliant textbooks written in the English language. My favourite is Weatherill and Beaumont, *EU Law* and Craig and De Burca's *Text, Cases and Materials* for a comprehensive materials collection.

3–002

> London is one of the major legal centres in the world. Historically a centre for international trade, insurance, litigation and arbitration, it now hosts massive American law firms, established here as a springboard into Europe. Indeed, firms from 40 different countries have offices in London. UK lawyers are the most mobile in Europe, the most likely to establish practice in the other Member States, a right established under an EC Directive. The sooner the English law student grasps just how important Community law is and the sooner she understands that it is a part of English law, not some foreign law imposed on us by Brussels, the better.

2. The Treaties

3–003

The Common Market was created by the signing of the Treaty of Rome in 1957. The primary aims of its first six members were

54

economic, to set up a common market in Europe but as the Treaty states, its signatories were "determined to lay the foundations of an ever closer union among the peoples of Europe . . . by . . . pooling their resources to preserve and strengthen peace and liberty". The Treaty remains an essential source of Community law, as well as the Community's constitution, at least until the new constitution is ratified, if ever. Incorporation of the Treaty of Rome and the other EU Treaties into English law was effected by the European Communities Act 1972. The other major instruments with which we must concern ourselves are the Single European Act of 1986, which created the single European market, effective by the end of 1992; the Treaty on EU (TEU, Maastricht Treaty), ratified in 1993, which extended the scope of Community competence and provided for economic and monetary union and Union citizenship; the Treaty of Amsterdam, signed in 1997 and in force in 1999 and the Treaty of Nice, in force in 2003, which expanded the Union from 15 Member States to 25. At the time of writing, 2005, it is proposed that the constitution of the EU will be reduced into writing but establishing it will be a slow process, as all 25 member states must ratify it and some will be holding referenda at home so their citizens can vote on whether to ratify.

The Union consists of three pillars: the European Community, which is the central law making and law enforcing unit and the two outside pillars, Justice and Home Affairs (JHA) and Foreign and Social Policy. If the proposed constitution is ratified, then this tripartite structure will dissolve. Decision-making in the outside pillars is largely a matter for the Council. It gives much more freedom to the Member States and involves fairly slow policy negotiations. Following the Treaty of Amsterdam, some policy areas were shifted from Justice and Home Affairs pillar to the central pillar, the EC, such as immigration and asylum and border checks (passport control). New elements have been added to the EC Treaty, such as the Protocol on Social Policy. The Amsterdam Treaty thus added a further dimension to the EC, based on fundamental rights. Very importantly, the ECJ's jurisdiction was extended beyond the EC into the JHA pillar but in a very restricted manner. (The UK pressure group JUSTICE considered co-operation in this third pillar to be ineffectual. They considered the lack of democratic and judicial control over the third pillar had "profound implications for human rights".) The Amsterdam Treaty also introduced closer co-operation between States.

The Nice Treaty resulted from the Inter Governmental Conference of 2000 and came into force in 2003. It provided for enlargement, alterations to the Council and Commission, increasing the Assembly and for some Art.234 references to be heard by the CFI.

In October 1991, the European Economic Area was created, **3–004** including States subjected to Community law on the internal market and competition but not represented in the institutions. Ten of those States joined the Union after the Treaty of Nice came into effect and Bulgaria and Romania may join by 2007.

3–005

> The six founder members of the Common Market in 1957 were France, Germany, Italy, Belgium, Luxembourg and The Netherlands. The UK joined in 1973. By 2002, the Union consisted of 15 counties after the accession of Denmark, Greece, Spain, Ireland, Austria, Portugal, Finland and Sweden. In 2004, the EU was joined by 10 more states: Estonia, Lithuania, Latvia, Poland, Hungary, the Czech Republic, Slovakia, Slovenia, Malta and Cyprus.

3. Institutions

3–006   The basic four EC institutions are the Parliament, the Council, the Commission and the Court of Justice. The other institution which necessitates a brief mention is the CFI. Notice that the Treaty of Amsterdam altered the Treaty Article numbers so the old ones appear bracketed.

Parliament (Article 190(137))

3–007   Members of this large assembly are directly elected by their Member States. It is essential to grasp that, unlike conventional Parliaments on the Westminster model, this is not the legislature of the Community, although its powers have been massively enhanced by the 1986 Single European Act and by the Treaty on European Union 1992, as explained below. This has gone some way to remedy the institutional imbalance in the Community and to remedy the "democratic deficit", complained of by critics, that the unelected Council is the primary legislature. The Treaties of Amsterdam and Nice extended its powers of co-decision. Parliament now has a legislative role on several levels, advisory and consultative, a right to participate in conciliation and co-operation procedures and a right of co-decision in certain defined areas. The Parliament has no real powers over the two outer pillars of the Union. It has a supervisory role over the Commission, which must report to it and answer questions. Parliament's dissatisfaction with the Commission led to all the Commissioners resigning in 1999. Some were reappointed. The Parliament has been influential over the other institutions in recognising and adopting the European Convention on Human Rights. (See Steiner and Woods, Chapter 2 or any other EC/EU law textbook for explanation.)

The Council (the Council of the European Union) (Articles 202–210(145–154))

This body is really the legislature of the Union. It is composed of   3–008
one representative minister from each Member State. These delegates change according to the nature of the subject under discussion.
For instance, on agricultural policy, states will send their agriculture
ministers. On economic issues, finance ministers will attend. When
the Council is composed of heads of state or government it is known,
confusingly, as the European Council. They meet at least twice a
year, with the Commission President, assisted by foreign ministers
and a Commissioner (Single European Act 1986, Art.2).

The Council's job is to ensure the Treaty objectives are attained. It
has the final say on most Community secondary legislation but, in
most cases, can only act on a proposal from the Commission. If the
EU can be said to have a legislature for its secondary legislation, this
is it. Following the implementation of the TEU, it shares decision-
making with the Parliament in some respects. Not only is the
Council criticised for being unelected (the democratic deficit) but it
lacks transparency. It is the only legislature other than North Korea
that sits behind closed doors.

Since it is not a permanent body, much of the Council's day to day
work, initially sifting and scrutinising Commission proposals, is delegated to COREPER, the committee of permanent representatives of
the Member States. It, in turn, delegates its workload to working
groups. Again, COREPER lacks accountability and transparency.

The Commission (Articles 211–219(155–163))

There is one Commissioner from each of the 25 Member States but   3–009
each must act independently of state control. They are appointed for
five years, renewable. Each Commissioner has a portfolio for a particular Union activity and heads a Directorate-General. For example,
the UK Commissioner, Peter Mandelson, has the portfolio for trade,
which is obviously very important. The present 2004–9 Commission
is headed by its President, José Manuel Barroso, the Portuguese
Commissioner. There was a delay in confirming this Commission, as
the original candidate for Commissioner for Justice, Rocco
Bottiglione, was exposed as believing that homosexuality was a sin
and holding very conservative views on women. It became clear that
if he stayed, the Parliament would veto the appointment of the
whole Commission so this illustrates the power of the Parliament.

The Commission's functions are as follows:

The motor

It takes the initiative on making new law and policy, because the   3–010
Council can only take important decisions following proposals of

the Commission but the Council may request the Commission to undertake studies and submit appropriate proposals. Nevertheless, this power of initiative makes it very powerful in setting the agenda of the Council and Parliament.

The watchdog

3–011   The Commission enforces the Member States' Treaty obligations and may take an errant Member State to the ECJ, under Art.226(169), should persuasion fail. An example is the ECJ decision against Italy in 2002 that it was in breach of the Treaty and Directive 89/48 in failing to provide foreign lawyers with the infrastructure and freedom to provide their services in Italy: *Commission v Italy* (2002, ECJ). Another example was the 2003 ECJ ruling that Italy was in breach of its treaty obligations in insisting that British chocolate should be called "chocolate substitute" because it contained vegetable fat other than cocoa butter: *Commission v Italy* (2003, ECJ).

The Commission can also impose fines and penalties on those in breach of EC competition law, or those who ignore decisions taken against them. Accordingly, the Commission has extensive investigatory powers. For instance, because Germany failed to comply with rulings on water purity and protection of birds, it imposed a daily fine of £350,000 while the infringement continued.

The executive

3–012   The Commission is, effectively, the Community executive. Policies formed by the Council need detailed implementation by the Commission. Much of this is done by legislation, which requires a final decision by the Council. The Commission has its own decision-making powers and enforces competition policy.

Negotiator

3–013   In relation to the EU's external policies, the Commission acts as a negotiator, leaving agreements to be concluded by the Council, after consulting the Parliament, where this is required by the Treaty.

3–014   What does the European Union do? In the EC it makes law and policy on: trade, customs, consumer affairs, economic and monetary union, agriculture, fisheries, competition, freedom of movement of workers, freedom to establish business, education and training, energy, the environment, food safety, employment and social affairs, sex equality, public health, regional policy, transport, tax. In the outer pillars of the EU, it makes policy and encourages co-operation on justice and home affairs, including human rights, foreign policy and security, external trade and humanitarian aid.

The Court of Justice (Articles 220–245(164–188))

> Do not confuse the ECJ with the European Court of Human Rights (ECtHR), described in Chapter 4, below. The ECJ sits in Luxembourg and interprets Community law for the 25 Member States of the EU. The ECtHR is **not** an institution of the EU, It interprets and enforces the European Convention on Human Rights for the 46 countries that have ratified the Convention. It sits in Strasbourg.

3–015

Composition

The Court consists of 25 judges: one for each Member State. They are assisted by eight Advocates General (A.G.s). It is the A.G.'s task to assist the Court, individually, by making a detailed analysis of all the relevant issues of fact and law in a case before the Court and submitting a report of this, together with recommendations, to the Court. Thus, they can express their personal opinions, which the judges cannot, and they can examine any related question, not brought forward by the parties. Article 223(167) of the Treaty stipulates that both judges and A.G.s "shall be chosen from persons whose independence is beyond doubt and who possess the qualifications required for appointment to the highest judicial offices in their respective countries or who are jurisconsults of recognised competence" (*e.g.* academic lawyers). Each judge and A.G. is appointed for a renewable term of six years. The British Advocate General, A.G. Jacobs has been in office since 1988.

3–016

Procedure

The Court's workload has increased massively since 1970. Then, 79 cases were brought before it and now hundreds of cases per year are lodged, with hundreds more being set down before the CFI. The latter was created to deal with this increased workload but, still, it has proved necessary to devise another coping mechanism. This has been the tendency to hear cases before a chamber of three or five judges, reserving the Grand Chamber of 13 judges for the more important cases. The full court (quorum 15) will only sit in exceptional cases.

The case for each party is submitted in written pleadings, oral argument being strictly limited to about half an hour per party. The common lawyers appearing before the Court, from Ireland and the UK find more difficulty in adjusting to this procedure than do lawyers from continental Europe. The President allocates one of the judges to act as a judge-rapporteur to each case. She prepares a public report after the written procedure, ready for the oral

3–017

hearing. It contains a summary of the facts and legal argument. She prepares a private report to the judges, containing her view of whether the case should be assigned to a chamber.

Meanwhile, an A.G. will also have been assigned to the case. They are not assigned to cases brought by or against their native Member State. The A.G. prepares an opinion which is delivered orally, at the end of the oral hearing. It contains a full analysis of relevant Community law, which may give a more complete and accurate account than that produced in argument by the parties, since the lawyers appearing in the case may appear before the ECJ only once in their legal careers.

3–018   The A.G. also gives his opinion as to how the Court should decide the case. It is true that the Court follows this opinion in most cases and it is thus a good indicator as to how the Court is likely to decide, as well as providing an essential explanation of the reasoning behind the Court's decision, after the event but this opinion should never be referred to as a "ruling", as is frequently misreported by the British news media.

After this, the A.G. drops out of the picture and the judges deliberate in secret, without interpreters, in French, the working language of the Court. (Since Finland and Sweden joined the EC in 1995, it has been argued that the Court should adopt English as a second official language, since this is the second language of Scandinavians but the cost of double translation would be prohibitive.) After deliberations, the judge-rapporteur will draft and refine the decision.

Function

3–019   Under Art.220(164), the task of the Court is prescribed as to "ensure that in the interpretation and application of this Treaty the law is observed". It is the supreme authority on all matters of Community law. In its practices and procedure, it draws on continental models, notably French procedure but in substantive law, it borrows principles from all Member States.

The EC Treaty is a framework, generally speaking, with few of its provisions spelled out in detail. This gives the Court massive latitude as a court of interpretation, in effect creating Community law and jurisprudence. Its boldness has been a matter of controversy but since we are watching the emergence of a whole new legal system and body of law, it is hardly surprising that the Court's decisions contain sweeping statements of principle, especially given that the EC Treaty is silent, even on such fundamentals as the relationship between Community law and national law (see *Costa v ENEL* (1964), below).

When developing new legal principles, the Court's first reference point is the objectives of the Community and the Articles of the

Treaty. Over the years, it has built up a massive body of reported decisions. Like our House of Lords, the Court is not bound by its own previous decisions but usually follows them. The judgment is a single one but without much indication of the reasoning behind it (especially in the older cases). This is where the submission of the A.G. comes in useful, as an explanation.

Jurisdiction

The Court's work consists mainly of the following list. **3–020**

1. Determining whether or not a Member State has failed to fulfil a Treaty obligation. Actions may be brought by the Commission or another Member State (Arts 226(169), 227(170)).
2. Exercising unlimited jurisdiction in reviewing penalties (*e.g.* fines imposed by the Commission). Actions may be brought by natural and legal persons (Art.229(172)).
3. Reviewing the legality of an act, or failure to act, of the Council or Commission or Parliament. A request for review may be made by a Member State, the Council, the Commission, or Parliament or, where it concerns them, by the Court of Auditors or European Central Bank. Any natural or legal person may challenge regulations or decisions which are addressed to them or concern them (Art.230(173)).
4. Deciding over compensation for damage caused by the institutions. Actions can be brought against the Community by Member States and natural or legal persons (Arts 235 (178), 288(215)).
5. Acting as a court of appeal on points of law from the CFI (Art.225(168)).
6. Giving preliminary rulings at the request of a national court or tribunal (Art.234(177)).

This last point is most important for our purposes, as this is the mechanism through which Community law is developed and interpreted in its domestic context, in English case law. Any case may be referred to the Court from any English or Welsh court or tribunal, under Art.234, where there is an item of Community law to be interpreted. The ECJ gives its interpretation and then remits the case to the domestic court, leaving them to apply that interpretation and then decide the case accordingly.

Note that the Treaty of Amsterdam provided for a very important extension of the Court's jurisdiction. Hitherto, it had only had power over Community law, emanating from the Community, the central pillar. It now has power to rule on decisions made in the Justice and Home Affairs pillar, subject to agreement by the

Member States. In these policy areas, however, only courts of last instance may refer from the Member States. See the latest edition of Foster for the wording of the Articles and the explanation of how the Court's powers were amended or added to by the Treaty of Nice. They are all in plain English and easy to understand.

Court of First Instance (Article 225(168a))

3–021   The Single European Act (1986) provided for the establishment of a Court of First Instance and it began its work in 1989. Like the ECJ, its task is to ensure that Community law is enforced in interpreting and applying the treaties (Art.220). Its 25 judges usually hear cases in chambers of three or five, any of whom, apart from the President, may be called upon (unusually) to act as Advocate General. Its jurisdiction was limited to disputes between the Community and its servants, cases involving Community competition law and applications for judicial review and damages in certain matters under the European Coal and Steel Community. In 1992, however, the TEU amended Art.168a to provide that the Council, acting on a request from the European Court, could transfer any area of the Court's jurisdiction to the CFI, except for Art.234(177) preliminary rulings. Accordingly, a lot of work was transferred down in 1993, to relieve pressure on the ECJ. By 1996, the CFI was hearing as many cases as the Court of Justice. There is a right of appeal from this Court, on matters of law, to the ECJ. From 2005, cases involving the EU's staff will be moved into the EU Civil Service Tribunal, created by the Treaty of Nice. The Nice Treaty also enabled certain Art.234 references to be transferred to the CFI.

3–022   ### Article 234(177) Preliminary Rulings

Article 234 enables any court or tribunal in any Member State to refer a point of Community law in a pending case to the ECJ for their interpretation. The Court's ruling on the point is then sent back to the national court to be applied in the case, which will have been suspended in the meantime. All national courts have a duty to apply and enforce Community law but this ability to refer when they are uncertain is designed to prevent divergent interpretation. These references are a significant volume of the Court's workload and they have proved to be the essential vehicle for the Court to develop its principles and precedent. Article 234, provides:

"The Court of Justice shall have jurisdiction to give preliminary rulings concerning:

(a) the interpretation of this Treaty;

(b) the validity and interpretation of acts of the institutions of the Community and of the ECB;

(c) the interpretation of the statutes of bodies established by an act of the Council; where those statutes so provide.

Where such a question is raised before any court or tribunal of a Member State, that court or tribunal may, if it considers that a decision on the question is necessary to enable it to give judgment, request the Court of Justice to give a ruling thereon.

Where any such question is raised in a case pending before a court or tribunal of a Member State against whose decision there is no judicial remedy under national law, that court or tribunal shall bring the matter before the Court of Justice."

Paragraph (b) includes all Art.249(189) legislative acts, described below and the Court has ruled that it also includes non-binding recommendations and opinions. The Court cannot rule on questions of national law so cannot rule that a national provision is incompatible with Community law but has said it will provide the national court with all necessary criteria to enable it to answer such a question. It will not rule on how law is to be applied by the domestic court but will offer guidance. It has interpreted international treaties entered into by the Community.

Although the reference procedure has been the major case law tool by which the ECJ has developed its general principles and coloured in the sketches of EC instruments by interpreting them, all references are bogged down in a frustrating backlog. The ECJ decided 665 cases in the year to 2004 but it had 840 pending and a further 531 new cases were lodged. The CFI is equally overloaded, hence the removal of staff cases from its workload, into the new tribunal, from 2005. According to the 2004 report, Art.234 referrals had taken an average of 23.5 months between referral and the decision taken by the ECJ. This is even worse than 2000, when they took 21.6 months. The UK has long complained that this delay is unacceptable, as the case in our courts, or another Member State's court is put into suspended animation for around two years while a decision is awaited from the ECJ.

National Courts or Tribunals that Can Refer

If parties have contracted to arbitrate, the arbitrator is not a court   **3–023** or tribunal within Art.234(177) but where the law imposes an arbitrator to resolve disputes, then a question can be referred to the ECJ. Even a body exercising functions preliminary to its judicial function may refer. In *Pretore di Salo v Persons Unknown* (1987, ECJ), an Italian public prosecutor, who would later act as examining magistrate, was allowed to refer. In *El-Yassini v Secretary of State for the Home Dept* (1996), the Court permitted a reference from an Immigration Adjudicator, because "the body" was a permanent officer, appointed by statute, hearing and determining disputes according to statutory powers. An independent arbitrator to whom parties had voluntarily submitted their dispute was not allowed to refer, however, in *Nordsee Deutsche Hochseefischerei GmbH* (1981).

The Discretion to Refer

3–024   The ECJ originally took a strict view that it was for the national courts and not for them to decide when a reference was necessary for the decision but it has emphasised that it will not answer hypothetical questions or act on references from non-genuine disputes which have been contrived simply to test Community law by means of an Art.234(177) reference.

The Court has specified that, for it to assume jurisdiction, it is essential for the national court to explain why it considers a preliminary ruling to be necessary and the national court must define the factual and legislative context of the question it is asking.

The question of the timing of a reference is left to the national court but the Court has requested that facts and points of national law be established in advance. A national court or tribunal cannot be prevented from making a reference by a national law that it is bound to follow the decision of a higher court on the same question of Community law. In other words, our Court of Appeal (CA) could still make a reference, if they considered it necessary, despite the existence of a House of Lords precedent on the same question of Community law. The Court emphasised in the *Rheinmuhlen-Dusseldorf* case (1973) that, as the object of Art.234 is to ensure that the law is the same in all Member States, domestic law cannot limit the lower court's power to make a reference if it considers the superior court's ruling could lead it to give judgment contrary to Community law.

"Necessary"

3–025   Note the use of the word "necessary" in the discretionary power to refer. The Court must consider a reference necessary. The ECJ defined this in *CILFIT v Italian Ministry of Health* (1981). There is no need to refer if:

(a) the question of EC law is irrelevant; or
(b) the provision has already been interpreted by the ECJ, even though the questions at issue are not strictly identical; or
(c) the correct application is so obvious as to leave no scope for reasonable doubt. This matter must be assessed in the light of the specific characteristics of Community law, the particular

difficulties to which its interpretation gives rise and the risk of divergences of judicial decisions within the Community.

The approach of the UK courts to the discretion to refer

In *Bulmer v Bollinger* (1974, CA) Lord Denning M.R. set out guide-   3–026
lines for English courts, other than the House of Lords, for deciding when it was necessary to make an Art.177(234) reference. They were influential in a number of cases but did not meet with uncritical approval. Bingham J. warned that the European court was in a better position to determine questions of Community law because, for instance, of their expertise, their unique grasp of all the authentic language texts of that law and their familiarity with a purposive construction of Community law. Once he became Master of the Rolls, he set out this important dictum in *R. v International Stock Exchange Ex p. Else* (1993, CA):

"if the facts have been found and the Community law issue is critical to the court's final decision, the appropriate course is ordinarily to refer the issue to the Court of Justice unless the national court can with complete confidence resolve the issue itself. In considering whether it can with complete confidence resolve the issue itself the national court must be fully mindful of the differences between national and Community legislation, of the pitfalls which face a national court venturing into what may be an unfamiliar field, of the need for uniform interpretation throughout the Community and of the great advantages enjoyed by the Court of Justice in construing Community instruments. If the national court has any real doubt, it should ordinarily refer."

Commenting on this case, Weatherill and Beaumont, in *EU Law*, praise Lord Bingham for doing a great service in creating a presumption that national courts and tribunals should make a reference if they are not completely confident as to how the issues can be resolved.

"This is a *communautaire* approach consistent with the spirit of judicial co-operation that is needed if the Article 234 system is to do its job of ensuring uniform interpretation of Community law throughout the Community."

It is, nevertheless, a rebuttable presumption so the English law reports have many examples of the courts declining to refer. An example is *R. v Ministry of Agriculture, Fisheries and Food Ex p. Portman Agrochemicals Ltd* (1994). Brooke J., in declining to refer, took account of the guidelines in previous case law but was influenced by the fact that neither of the parties wished for the case to be referred and that, given the usual 18-month delay to be expected in receiving the Court's interpretation, the answer would be redundant by the time they would receive it.

Some judges have warned that English courts should exercise great caution in relying on the doctrine of *"acte clair"* in declining to make a reference. The Court accepts that national courts will apply this doctrine, borrowed from French law, when the interpretation of a provision is clear and free from doubt (see below).

3–027   It is possible, in the English legal system, for an appeal to be made against a lower court's decision to refer. Such an appeal was successfully made in *Ex p. Else* (above), the CA holding that it was not necessary to refer.

The Obligation on National Courts of Last Resort to Refer

3–028   Two questions arise here. Firstly, when is a court "a court of last resort"? There are two theories, abstract and concrete. Under the former, only the House of Lords would be obliged to refer. Under the more practical concrete theory, any court from whom there is no appeal or from which appeal has been refused should be obliged to refer. The rulings of the ECJ seem to support the latter: *Costa v ENEL* (*obiter*). This seems to be fairer to the parties, especially where they have been refused permission to appeal and it seems more likely to achieve the harmonisation of law Art.234 is aiming at. The matter has been resolved by the ECJ itself in *Lyckeskog* (2002, ECJ). The ECJ held that courts which could be challenged did not fall into the category of court under an obligation to refer. Steiner and Woods comment that this decision is worrying in terms of access to justice because it presupposes the parties have the time and money to litigate right through to the last possible court before being able to obtain a reference. The second question relates to the circumstances in which the obligation to refer arises.

Although the wording of this paragraph looks mandatory, as if courts like the House of Lords must refer every point of EC law to the ECJ, the Court has ruled, in the *Costa v ENEL* case (see below) that this is not necessary where the question raised is materially identical to a question which has already been the subject of a preliminary ruling in an earlier case. In *CILFIT* (above) the Court spelled out what they considered to be the discretion available to courts of last resort, as above, despite the wording of Art.234. They said that courts of last resort have the same discretion as others, to decide whether a reference is necessary and that there is no obligation to refer if the criteria laid down are satisfied.

Satisfying the conditions for the application of the third *CILFIT* criterion will not, however, be easy, as the Court laid down the condition that the national court must be convinced that the matter is equally obvious to the courts of the other Member States and to the ECJ and they reminded courts that, in satisfying themselves of this criterion, they should bear in mind the plurilingual nature of that law and the Court's use of purposive and contextual construction. While many English judges would not shy away from a purposive and contextual approach, I am at a loss to see how the House of Lords has the facilities to delve into the domestic law reports of the other 24 Member States to see how a point has been variously interpreted by other national courts, in their many national languages.

There are modern examples of the House of Lords refusing to refer a case to the ECJ, mainly relying on the first *CILFIT* exception, that the Community law point was irrelevant, including a case in which they refused to follow the *Von Colson* principle: *Finnegan v Clowney Youth Training Programme Ltd* (1990, HL). In the very important 2000 case of *Three Rivers DC v Bank of England*, the House of Lords declined to refer. Nevertheless, in recent years, the House seems to have been generally more prepared to refer to the ECJ and seems more ready to apply European Court case law where it does not refer, such as in *Webb v EMO Air Cargo (No.2)* (1995, HL). The case is illustrative of the fact that, had the House not made a reference, it would have come to the opposite conclusion from that reached by the ECJ and would have refused an appeal which it was ultimately persuaded to allow. Of course the danger of not referring lies in the risk that different Member States will resolve the same issue in different ways.

There is now a practice direction, issued by the ECJ in 1999, stating when it is appropriate to make a reference but it really states the existing principles, as set out by ECJ case law. It was repeated in England and Wales as a Supreme Court Practice Direction for our CA and HL, for the guidance of all domestic courts and tribunals.

3–029

4. *Sources of Community Law*

The sources of EC law are as follows, in addition to the general principles and decisions of the ECJ:

3–030

1. The EC Treaty and Protocols, as amended by further treaties, such as the Single European Act 1986 and Treaty on European Union 1992.
2. EC secondary legislation (Regulations, Directives and Decisions).

3. International agreements entered into by Community institutions on the Community's behalf, using their powers under the Treaty.
4. Decisions of the ECJ and CFI. This includes the vast body of law and principle established by the ECJ.

Article 10(5) of the Treaty obliges all Member States to "take all appropriate measures, whether general or particular, to ensure fulfilment" of all these obligations.

Secondary Legislation (Legislative Acts)

3–031   The law-making powers of the Community institutions are laid down in Art.249(189) of the Treaty (as amended by the TEU). They are set out very clearly and students of English law need to know and understand this Article:

"In order to carry out their tasks and in accordance with the provisions of this Treaty, the European Parliament acting jointly with the Council, the Council and the Commission shall make regulations, issue directives, take decisions, make recommendations or deliver opinions.
    A regulation shall have general application. It shall be binding in its entirety and directly applicable in all Member States.
    A directive shall be binding, as to the result to be achieved, upon each Member State to which it is addressed, but shall leave to the national authorities the choice of form and methods.
    A decision shall be binding in its entirety upon those to whom it is addressed.
    Recommendations and opinions shall have no binding force."

These are all called "acts". Distinguish between binding and non-binding acts. Only the first three are binding.

- *Regulations* are generally applicable and designed to apply to all situations in the abstract. Since they are binding in their entirety and directly applicable in all Member States, they may give rise to rights and obligations for states and individuals without further enactment.
- *Directives* are binding as to the result to be achieved, upon each Member State to which they are addressed. The State thus fills in the details by enacting domestic law in accordance with the principles it is directed to effect.
- *Decisions* are individual acts, addressed to a specified person or persons or States. They have the force of law and, therefore, have effect without further expansion.

Acts which do not conform with procedural safeguards may be annulled. Recommendations and opinions have no binding force in law, although they are of persuasive authority.

5. Direct Applicability and Direct Effect

To understand the application of Community law, it is necessary to   3–032
have a basic grasp of the distinction between the principles of direct applicability and direct effect. It is also necessary to draw attention to the distinction between horizontal and vertical direct effect, that is, between provisions directly effective between individuals, giving rise to rights or obligations enforceable between individuals and provisions giving rise to rights of individuals against the Member States. When the European Communities Act 1972 took the UK into the EU, or Common Market, as it then was, EC law became directly applicable, in international law terms, as if it were domestic English law. The terminology becomes confusing, however, because provisions of international law which are found to be capable of application by national courts at the suit of individuals are also termed directly applicable. To spare confusion, therefore, all British writers on EC law have adopted the term "directly effective" to express this second meaning, that is, to denote provisions of EC law which give rise to rights or obligations which individuals may enforce before the national courts.

Whether a particular provision of EC law gives rise to directly effective, individually enforceable rights or obligations is a matter of construction, depending on its language and purpose. Since principles of construction vary from State to State, the same provision may not be construed as directly effective everywhere. For lawyers in the English legal system, whether a provision is directly effective is crucially important because, thanks to the concept of primacy of EC law, a directly effective provision must be given priority over any conflicting principle of domestic law. The EC Treaty specifies, in Art.249, that regulations are directly applicable but it has been left to the ECJ to set out, in a group of leading cases, which and when other EC provisions can have direct effect.

Treaty Articles

The issues of whether and when a Treaty Article could have direct   3–033
effect was first considered in the *Van Gend en Loos* case of 1962. The question arose as to whether Art.12 of the Treaty, which prohibited States introducing new import duties, could confer enforceable rights on nationals of Member States. The ECJ held that it could because the text of the Article set out a clear and unconditional duty

not to act. The prohibition was, thus, perfectly suited by its nature to produce direct effects in the legal relations between Member States and their citizens. The ECJ clearly thought it desirable that individuals should be allowed to protect their rights in this way, without having to rely on the European Commission or another Member State to take action against an offending Member State.

This case involved a flouted prohibition but ECJ case law soon extended direct effect to positive Treaty obligations, holding that an Article imposing upon a Member State a duty to act would become directly effective once a time-limit for compliance had expired. The ECJ has found a large number of Treaty provisions to be directly effective, in relation to free movement of goods and persons, competition law and discrimination on the grounds of gender or nationality.

The ECJ applies the following criteria to test whether a provision is amenable to direct effect. It must be:

- clear and precise, especially with regard to scope and application;
- unconditional; and
- leave no room for the exercise of implementation by Member States or community institutions.

The ECJ has, however, applied these conditions fairly liberally, with results as generous as possible to the individual seeking to rely on the Article.

3–034   Although the *Van Gend* case involved vertical direct effect, that is, a citizen enforcing rights against a State, later case law, notably *Defrenne v Sabena* (1975, ECJ) demonstrated that Treaty Articles could also have horizontal direct effect, that is, could be relied on between individuals, such as private employer and employee. A good example of the invocation of *vertically* directly effective Treaty Articles is the *Factortame* case, discussed below.

Regulations
3–035   Regulations are, as stated above, designed to be directly applicable and, thus, directly effective. It is important to understand that this means both vertically and horizontally.

Directives
3–036   Directives are an instruction to Member States to enact laws to achieve a certain end result, so it was originally assumed they could not be directly effective. Nevertheless, in *Grad v Finanzamt Traunstein* (1970, ECJ) the ECJ held that no such limitation applied. Here, a German haulier was allowed to rely on a Directive and decision on VAT which the German government had ignored. The direct

effect of Directives was confirmed in *Van Duyn v Home Office* (1974, ECJ). The ECJ held that Mrs Van Duyn, a Scientologist, was allowed to rely on a Directive to challenge the UK's refusal to allow her to enter the UK.

The conditions for effectiveness are the same as those applied to test Treaty provisions: clarity, precision, being unconditional, leaving no room for discretion in implementation. Once a time-limit for implementation has expired, the obligation to implement it becomes absolute but a directive cannot be directly effective before that time-limit has expired: *Ratti* (1978, ECJ). Where a State has implemented a directive inadequately, it is still possible for it to be declared directly effective, to make up for that inadequacy (*UNO* (1976, ECJ)). If they can be interpreted as directly effective, directives of course then have to be interpreted and applied by our courts and tribunals and the citizens and their lawyers affected by them, as if they were, say, a UK statute. Unlike statutes, however, we are given lengthy preambles to help us interpret them. If you take a look at any EC directive, you will see what I mean.

Horizontal or vertical direct effect?

One of the most significant but difficult issues before the ECJ in recent years has been the issue of whether directives can be declared effective horizontally, that is, to enforce private rights and obligations between private parties. All the case law referred to above relates to the enforcement of private rights against a State, giving vertical direct effect to a directive. The ECJ has no problem in declaring vertical direct effect since this is merely enforcing rights and obligations against a State which that State has omitted to effect in its own domestic legislation. It is not so keen, however, to hold private parties bound by a directive which a State has neglected to implement, when the default is clearly the State's.

3–037

The leading case on this issue is *Marshall v Southampton & South West Hampshire Area Health Authority (Teaching)* (1984, ECJ) but, as we shall see, subsequent case law, in particular the *Marleasing* case and *Foster v British Gas*, leave the law in a position which is far from clear. The decision in the *Marshall* case is clear enough.

Mrs Marshall was an employee of the Area Health Authority and she challenged their compulsory retirement age of 65 for men and 60 for women as discriminatory and in breach of the EC Equal Treatment Directive 76/207. Different retirement ages were permissible in domestic English law, under the Sex Discrimination Act 1975. On a reference from the Court of Appeal, the ECJ held that the different retirement ages did indeed breach the Directive and that Mrs Marshall could, in the circumstances, rely on the Directive against the State (here represented by the Area Health Authority) regardless of whether they were acting in their capacity as a public authority or her employer. The issue of horizontal and vertical effect of directives had been fully argued before the ECJ and they determined that:

".... a Directive may not of itself impose obligations on an individual and that a provision of a Directive may not be relied upon as such against such an individual."

This looks like a very straightforward refusal to permit directives to have direct effect but problems remain.

1. Here, Mrs Marshall could rely on the Directive against her employers because they were a part of the State so how is "State" to be defined? The wider the definition, the more individuals will be allowed to rely on directives as directly effective.
2. Is the time now ripe for directives to be given horizontal direct effect?
3. Has the ECJ permitted individuals to avoid the harshness of this ruling against horizontal effect by requiring domestic courts to apply directives indirectly, as a matter of interpretation (the *Von Colson* principle)?

What is the State?

3–038   In the *Marshall* case, then, an Area Health Authority was regarded as an arm of the State, as was the Royal Ulster Constabulary in *Johnson v RUC* (1984, ECJ), but what of other publicly funded organisations such as universities or publicly run corporations? The House of Lords sought a preliminary ruling from the ECJ on the status of the British Gas Corporation and in their response, in *Foster v British Gas* (1989, ECJ), the ECJ took the opportunity to provide a definition, although it is not, I am afraid, definitive. The Court ruled that a directive may be relied on as having direct effect against:

"a body, whatever its legal form, which has been made responsible, pursuant to a measure adopted by the State, for providing a public service under the control of the State and has for that purpose special powers beyond those which result from the normal rules applicable in relation between individuals."

The ECJ ruled that:

1. It was up to them to rule which categories of body might be held bound by a directly effective directive.

2. It was up to the domestic court to decide whether a particular body fell within that category.

On the first of these points, it is still unclear which bodies will be classed as part of the State. On the second point, the refinement of the concept of State is laid open to differences of interpretation by Member States' domestic courts.

The UK's definition of a state body was addressed in the 1992 case of *Doughty v Rolls Royce* (1992, CA). Here, the CA ruled that Rolls Royce did not qualify as part of the State, within the Foster definition because they did not provide a public service, nor possess any special powers, despite being wholly owned by the State. The issue as to what is an emanation of the State was addressed again by the ECJ in *Kampelmann v Landscaftsverband Westfalen-Lippe* (1997) and seems to have been expanded. The Court defined it by repeating the exact words they had used in Marshall but then added "or other bodies which irrespective of their legal form, have been given responsibility, by the public authorities and under their supervision, for providing a public service". See comment by Tayleur.

Should Horizontal Direct Effect now be Extended to Directives?

In three cases in 1993 and 1994, A.G.s separately argued that the   3–039
Court should reverse its decision in *Marshall* and give horizontal direct effect to directives. In the *Faccini Dori v Recreb Srl* case of 1994, an Italian student sought to rely on a 1985 Directive, unimplemented by Italy, to cancel a contract she had entered into with a private company and now regretted. A number of reasons had been put forward by the A.G.s in these cases and by academic commentators for an extension of the concept. For instance, the Court is prepared to give horizontal direct effect to Treaty Articles, despite the fact that, like directives, they are addressed to Member States. Secondly, the emergence of the single market in 1993 necessitated enforcing equality of the conditions of competition and the prohibition on discrimination. Thirdly, the TEU had amended the EC Treaty to require publication of directives in the *Official Journal* (so private persons had less excuse not to know their responsibilities under a directive). A full ECJ of 13 judges nevertheless declined to adopt this reasoning and extend the concept of horizontal direct effect. They reiterated that the distinguishing basis of vertical direct effect was that the State should be barred from taking advantage of its own failure to comply with Community law. In the 2004 judgement of *Pfeiffer*, the ECJ confirmed there is no horizontal effect of unimplemented directives.

Decisions

3–040   The *Grad* case, discussed above, confirmed that decisions could be directly effective, provided they meet all the required criteria. This does not pose any of the moral problems of horizontal direct effect of directives, since decisions are, in any event, only binding on the addressee.

International Agreements to which the EU is Party

3–041   The ECJ has shown an inconsistent approach to the question of which international agreements to which the EU is a party can be directly effective. The full picture can only be painted by the ECJ on a piecemeal basis, from case to case.

6. The Von Colson Principle and Marleasing: Indirect Effect

3–042   Where individuals seeking to rely on a directive cannot show that their opponent is a branch of the State, all may not be lost, because of a principle developed in *Von Colson and Kamann* (1983, ECJ). Miss Von Colson was claiming that the German prison service had rejected her job application in breach of the Equal Treatment Directive and German law provided inadequate compensation. At the same time, another claimant. Miss Hartz, was making the same claim against a private company. Thus, the issue of horizontal/vertical direct effect and the public/private distinction was openly raised in a reference under Art.177(234) before the ECJ. The ECJ avoided opening up these distinctions by ingenious reliance on Art.5(10) of the EC Treaty. Article 10 requires States to "take all appropriate measures" to ensure fulfilment of their community obligations. This obligation falls on all parts of a State, said the Court, including its courts. Thus, the courts in a Member State must interpret national law in a manner which achieves the results referred to in Art.189(249), *i.e.* the objectives of a directive. The German courts were obliged, then, to interpret German law in such a way as to enforce the Equal Treatment Directive. The ECJ added, however, an important qualification to this obligation: "it is for the national court to interpret and apply the legislation adopted for the implementation of the Directive in conformity with the requirements of Community Law, in so far as it is given discretion to do so under national law." These qualifying words were, however, moderated in *Marleasing* (below) to "as far as possible".

The significance of this case is that it provides horizontal effect in an indirect way. Even though EC law is not applied directly, it may still be applied indirectly through the medium of domestic interpretation. As one might expect, the application of the *Von Colson* principle very much depends on the interpretation of the domestic courts.

The principle was extended in a very significant way by the case of *Marleasing SA v La Comercial Internacional de Alimentacion SA* (1990, ECJ). The Court held that a national court was required to interpret its domestic legislation, whether it is legislation adopted prior to or subsequent to the Directive, as far as possible within the light of the wording and purpose of a directive, in order to achieve the result envisaged by it. To extend the principle even to legislation adopted prior to a directive is a large extension and, some would argue, may perhaps have an unfortunate effect in holding parties bound by a directive which was different in scope from the domestic legislation with which they were dutifully complying. Some argue this case is a large step towards accepting the horizontal direct effect of directives. The end result of such interpretation certainly appears to be the same, as far as the individual litigants are concerned. This principle has been applied many times over. One example was *Oceano Grupo Editorial v Rocio Murciano Quintero* (1998). Oceano sought to rely on Spanish law to bring an action in a Barcelona court. Part of the Unfair Contract Terms Directive, which only became enforceable in Spanish law after their claim arose, would have deprived the Barcelona court of jurisdiction. The ECJ reaffirmed that a national court is obliged, when it applies national law provisions, predating or postdating a directive, to interpret those provisions, so far as possible, in the light of the wording of the Directive, even if this meant ruling that it did not have jurisdiction to entertain the claim.

Further comments on this principle are necessary at this point: **3–043** first, the Court declined to apply the principle to extend criminal liability (*Pretore di Salo v Persons Unknown* (1986, ECJ) and many later cases). Secondly, it is unclear to what extent national courts are required to depart from national law in order to achieve the result sought by the Directive. To achieve such a result may involve the national court departing significantly from the wording of national law. For instance, in the *Von Colson* case, the national law clearly limited the compensation payable to the two women to a nominal amount, whereas the ECJ held that the Directive required the amount to be effective. It does seem, however, that the national court is not required to override the clear wording and intent of national law in order to make it comply with the Directive which cannot be construed as directly effective. This was confirmed in several cases, one being *Arcaro* (1995). Having said that, in *Centrosteel v Adipol*, the ECJ affirmed the requirement for interpretation of national law in the light of the wording and purpose of Community law even when this will impose an obligation on private parties. Thirdly, the ECJ has no jurisdiction to construe national law itself. It can only interpret the Directive and must leave it to the national court to construe national law in conformity with that interpretation.

7. Damages from a Tardy State: The Francovich *Principle*

3–044   Yet another remedy is available for a citizen who has suffered as a result of the non-implementation of a directive but where the conditions for direct effect are not satisfied. In another case giving a bold interpretation to Art.5(10), the ECJ held that, in certain conditions, the aggrieved citizen may have a remedy against the State in damages.

In *Francovich v Italy* (1991), the applicants were employees of businesses which became insolvent, leaving substantial arrears of unpaid salary. They brought proceedings in the Italian courts against Italy, for the recovery of compensation provided by Directive 80/987, which Italy had not implemented. The Directive guaranteed payment of unpaid remuneration in the case of insolvency by the employer. The applicants could not rely on the concept of direct effect, however, because the Directive's terms were insufficiently precise. The ECJ, nevertheless, held that the applicants were entitled to compensation from the State. Inherent in the Treaty, they said, was the principle that a Member State should be liable for damage to individuals caused by infringements of Community law for which it was responsible. Their interpretation rested, in particular, on Art.5(10), which places a duty on Member States to take all appropriate measures to ensure the fulfilment of Treaty obligations. The ECJ argued that to disallow damages against the State in these circumstances would weaken the protection of individual rights. The Court laid down three conditions for an individual claiming damages against a Member State for failing to implement or incorrectly implementing a directive:

1. The result laid down by the Directive involves the attribution of rights attached to individuals.
2. The content of those rights must be capable of being identified from the provisions of the Directive.
3. There must be a causal link between the failure by the Member State to fulfil its obligations and the damage suffered by the individuals.

The ECJ has left it up to each Member State to determine the competent courts and appropriate procedures for legal actions intended to enable individuals to obtain damages from the State. The procedures must be not less favourable than those relating to similar claims under domestic law and must not make it difficult or practically impossible to obtain damages from the State. In *Becker v Finanzamt Munster-Innestadt* (1981, ECJ), in clarifying the above conditions, the ECJ held that provisions of Directives can be invoked by individuals insofar as they define rights which individuals are able to assert against the State. Only a person with a direct interest could invoke a Directive but this might include a third party: in *Verholen* (1991, ECJ), a husband could bring a claim where his wife was discriminated against in a social security benefit, as it disadvantaged him.

Damages from a State whose Legislature Flouts Community Law

In *Factortame (No.4)*, properly known as the joined cases   3–045
Brasserie du Pecheur SA v Federal Republic of Germany and R. v Secretary of State for Transport Ex p. Factortame Ltd and others (No.4) (1996, ECJ), the Court extended the principle it had developed in *Francovich* to permit a claim of damages against a State, to instances where its national legislature had passed a law which was in serious breach of EC law. In the first case, French beer manufacturers were claiming damages against Germany for passing beer purity laws that effectively excluded the import of their beer. In the second case, the UK Parliament had passed the Merchant Shipping Act 1988, which effectively excluded foreign fishing vessels, notably Spanish, from their right to fish in British coastal waters, by laying down registration conditions of residence, nationality and domicile of vessel owners. Spanish fishermen complained that the Act offended against Art.52(43), which guarantees freedom of establishment. In prior cases, the Court had already ruled the domestic legislation to be in breach of EC law. What was now at issue was whether the aggrieved parties could claim damages against the respective states in the national courts. The *Factortame* case had been referred by the Queen's Bench Divisional Court for an Art.177(234) preliminary ruling. The ECJ decided the following (paraphrased):

1. The *Francovich* principle, making states liable for loss or damage suffered by individuals and caused by the State's breach of EC law, applied to all state authorities, including the legislature.

2. The conditions of a claim of damages in this context were:

    a. that the rule of Community law breached was intended to confer rights on the individuals who had suffered loss or injury;

    b. that the breach was sufficiently serious: the Member State had manifestly and gravely disregarded the limits on its discretion;

    c. that there was a direct causal link between the breach and the damage sustained by the individuals.

The State must make good the consequences of the damage, in accordance with its national law on liability but the conditions laid down must not be less favourable than for a domestic claim and must not make it excessively difficult or impossible to make a claim. (Comment: in the context of English law, it was virtually impossible for the Spanish fishing vessel owners to claim damages in the English courts, because we had no substantive or procedural law enabling a claim for damages against Parliament.)

3. Such a claim could not be made conditional on establishing a degree of fault going beyond that of a sufficiently serious breach of Community law.

4. Reparation must be commensurate with the damage sustained and this might include exemplary damages, where a public authority had acted oppressively, arbitrarily or unconstitutionally. It was left to the domestic legal system of each Member State to set the criteria for determining the extent of reparation.

5. Damages could not be limited to those sustained after a judgment finding such an infringement of Community law.

The upshot of these cases was, in 1996, that the onus was on the UK to find some procedure, in the English courts, for making a claim against the State for a breach of Community law by Parliament. Not only had we to find a procedure but were obliged to devise some substantive cause of action in damages. Neither the ground nor the procedure had to be too difficult to allow the Spanish claim. In 1997, the Spanish brought their claim through the Queen's Bench Divisional Court and were awarded damages. This was upheld by the CA then the House of Lords so the Secretary of State for Transport lost in all three courts. The House found that the Government, in introducing this legislation had acted carefully and deliberately to discriminate on grounds of nationality in the face of a clear and fundamental provision of the Treaty, former Art.7. This was done in good faith and to protect British fishing communities rather than to harm the Spanish but inevitably it took away or seriously affected their rights to fish. There was a fundamental breach of Treaty obligations. It was a sufficiently serious breach to entitle Factortame and 96 others to compensation in damages: *R. v SS for Transport Ex p. Factortame Ltd and others (No.5)* (1999, HL).

Notice that *Factortame (No.4)* was swiftly followed by a case which clarified how bad the breach of Community law had to be before damages could be claimed. In *R. v HM Treasury Ex p. British Telecommunications plc* (ECJ, 1996), the Court ruled that damages could be claimed by individuals who had suffered loss as a consequence of a State's enacting a Directive incorrectly (this much was not new). The important point about this case, however, was that they ruled that the breach of Community law was not sufficiently serious to merit damages. The UK had acted in good faith and simply made a mistake in its enactment into UK law of the relevant Directive. The wording of the Directive was ambiguous and several other Member States had also misinterpreted it so there was no manifest and grave breach of Community law, as required by *Factortame (No.4)*.

In 2003, the same cause of action was extended to a supreme   **3–046** court, in *Köbler v Republik Osterreich*. The ECJ held, however, that there could only be liability where there had been a manifest infringement of the applicable law.

Steiner and Woods point out quite rightly, however, that in the cases after this, the ECJ's application of the *Factortame-Brasserie du Pecheur* principles is inconsistent, despite their clarity. For instance, the result in *R. v Ministry of Agriculture, Fisheries and Food Ex p. Hedley Lomas Ireland Ltd*, two months after the *BT* case, was "surprising", because it found that a State's "mere infringement" of Community law might be sufficient to warrant an action for damages, where the State was not "called upon to make any legislative choices or has a considerably reduced choice, or none". In this case and *Dillenkofer*, the Court did not list and apply the principles listed in *Factortame-Brasserie du Pecheur* but did revert to its approach in the BT case, in *Denkavit* and other cases, then applied the stricter *Hedley Lomas* principles in another case against the UK MAFF. Examining more recent cases of the late 1990s, Steiner and Woods comment that the approach of the ECJ to "sufficiently serious" remains unclear (*EC Law*, Chapter 5).

8. General Principles of Law

Over its relatively short lifetime, the ECJ has built up and inter-   **3–047** preted a body of general principles. They must be applied in interpreting EC law, including EC elements of domestic law. They can be invoked by States and individuals to challenge community action or inaction, to claim damages and they can be used to challenge a Member State. These general principles, developed by the ECJ as the English courts have developed the common law, should be distinguished from the fundamental principles of the EC Treaty (*e.g.* free movement of goods and persons; non-discrimination). In part, the general principles are derived from fundamental rights in individual Member States. The ECJ could not be seen to be taking these away, nor could it leave EC law in a state conflicting with constitutional rights in any Member State so in *Internationale Handelsgesellschaft mbH v Einfuhr* (1970), the ECJ, while asserting the primacy of EC law, pointed out that respect for fundamental rights was part of EC law. The Court looks for principles common to Member States' constitutions and is guided by international treaties to which Member States are signatories, the most obvious and important being the European Convention on Human Rights. The rights include, for example:

- proportionality: administrative authorities must not use means more than appropriate and necessary to achieve their ends;
- legal certainty: includes the principle of legitimate expectation (same as English law) and the principle of non-retroactivity;
- natural justice: the right to a fair hearing (same as English law), the duty to give reasons, due process;
- the right to protection against self- incrimination;
- equality;
- subsidiarity (in the EC Treaty, now Art.5): the Community can only act if its objectives cannot be achieved by the Member States.

9. The EU and the European Convention on Human Rights

3–048   All the Member States are signatories of the Convention so one would think the obvious way for the ECJ to guarantee rights would be for the EU to be a signatory of the Convention. An attempt to do this was, however, declared invalid by the ECJ. The 1996 Intergovernmental Conference failed to have accession incorporated into the Treaty of Amsterdam. The ECJ will continue to apply the Convention rights within its jurisdiction. What happens in the Union, outside the EC and the relationship between Union law and the Convention is much more complex and was explored in the

Matthews case (1999, ECtHR). In this case, Ms Matthews, a British resident of Gibraltar, applied in 1994 to register as a voter in the European Parliamentary elections. Her application was denied. She then brought an action on the basis of the Convention, Art.3, Protocol 1 which provides that that the State will provide for elections by secret ballot to ensure free expression of the people in the choice of legislature. The ECtHR (note—not the ECJ) upheld her claim. The ECtHR drew a distinction between acts of the EU, which could not be challenged before it, as the EU is not a State party to the Convention, and acts of Member States of the EU Contracting States of the Convention. They remain responsible for ensuring that Convention rights are guaranteed and their obligation could not be set aside by subsequent Treaties entered into by the States. The ECtHR noted the ECJ's jurisprudence in which it recognised and protected Convention rights. Legislation emanating from the EU institutions had the potential to affect the citizens of Gibraltar to the same extent as Gibraltar's domestic legislation and the UK would thus be obliged to secure for the citizens of Gibraltar the rights guaranteed by Art.3, Protocol 1 of the Convention, irrespective of whether the elections involved were to the domestic or European Parliament. Further, Gibraltar was affected by the supremacy of EC law, as much as any other EC territory.

10. Direct Effect of Community Law in the UK

The European Communities Act 1972 gave legal effect to EC law in the UK. Pay close attention to the wording of s.2(1):   3–049

"All such rights, powers, liabilities, obligations and restrictions from time to time created or arising by or under the Treaties, and all such remedies and procedures from time to time provided for by or under the Treaties, as in accordance with the Treaties are without further enactment to be given legal effect or used in the United Kingdom shall be recognised and available in law, and be enforced, allowed and followed accordingly; and the expression 'enforceable Community right' and similar expressions shall be read as referring to one to which this subsection applies."

In the *Factortame (No.1)* case of 1990, the House of Lords interpreted "enforceable Community right" to mean directly effective legal right. This section gives effect to all directly effective Community law, whether made prior to or after the passing of the Act.

Section 3 binds all our courts to interpret matters of EC law in accordance with the rulings of the ECJ and requires our courts to take judicial notice of EC legislation and the opinions of the ECJ. Our courts have had no problem in applying directly effective provisions. They seem to have been reluctant in some cases, however, to apply the *Von Colson* principle. In *Duke v Reliance Systems Ltd*, Duke complained that she had been forced to retire at 60, despite her male colleagues' being permitted to work until 65. Equal Treatment Directive 76/207 was not enacted into domestic law until the Sex Discrimination Act 1986. Duke could not rely on the Directive as directly effective because her employer was a private company. She argued that the English courts should construe the unamended Sex Discrimination Act 1975 in a manner consistent with the Equal Treatment Directive, treating her enforced retirement as unlawful dismissal. The House of Lords considered the case of *Von Colson* but opined that it did not provide a power to interfere with the method or result of the interpretation of national legislation by national courts. They noted that the Equal Treatment Directive post-dated the Sex Discrimination Act 1975 and thought it would be unfair on Reliance to "distort" the construction of the Act to accommodate it. The House of Lords later applied the same objections in relation to the Northern Ireland legislation, despite the fact that it was passed after the Directive (*Finnegan*, 1990, HL).

3–050   Nevertheless, the House is prepared to make a distinction when construing national legislation that has been passed in order to implement a directive. In *Pickstone v Freemans Plc* (1989, HL) the House adopted a purposive construction in interpreting an amendment to the Equal Pay Act 1970, in order to make it consistent with the UK's obligations under the Equal Pay Directive. The same purposive approach was taken in *Litster v Forth Dry Dock & Engineering Co Ltd* (1989, HL). In this case, Lord Templeman said he thought the *Von Colson* principle imposed a duty on the UK courts to give a purposive construction to UK legislation which had been passed to give effect to Directives. In *Webb v EMO Air Cargo (UK) Ltd* (1992, HL), Lord Keith, giving the opinion of the House, said it was the duty of the UK court to construe domestic legislation in accordance with the ECJ's interpretation of a relevant Community Directive "if that can be done without distorting the meaning of the domestic legislation". He noted that, according to the ECJ, this obligation on the domestic courts only arises where domestic law is open to an interpretation consistent with a Directive. In this case the House agreed with the Court of Appeal, the Employment Appeal Tribunal and an industrial tribunal that the applicant had not suffered discrimination under English law. They nevertheless asked the ECJ to construe the relevant directive and the application of the principle of equal treatment to the circumstances of the case. The ECJ sent back its interpretation, flatly disagreeing with the House and ruling that the facts of the case disclosed discrimination. The House applied the ECJ's ruling in October 1995. The report provides an interesting example of how the House had to construe an English statute in accordance with EC law in a way which seemed to run contrary to the instincts of domestic courts at all levels, at that time.

11. Supremacy of Community Law in the UK

Curiously, the founding Treaty of the European Community, the   3–051
Treaty of Rome 1957, did not prescribe the supremacy of Community law over national law. It was left to the embryonic ECJ in developing its limbs, to describe the conception of its supremacy in *Costa v ENEL* (1964, ECJ). This quotation is as oft-cited and as jurisprudentially significant as Lord Atkin's famous neighbour principle, which did so much more than just resolve the problems caused when a snail was left to decompose in a bottle of ginger beer. In addition, the words below are so constitutionally significant, they should be learned and absorbed by every UK citizen, let alone every student of English law:

"By creating a Community of unlimited duration, having its own institutions, its own personality, its own legal capacity and capacity of representation on the international plane and, more particularly, real powers stemming from a limitation of sovereignty or a transfer of powers from the States to the Community, the Member States have limited their sovereignty rights, albeit within limited fields, and have thus created a body of law which binds both their nationals and themselves.
The integration into the laws of each Member State of provisions which derive from the Community, and more generally the terms and the spirit of the Treaty, make it impossible for the States, as a corollary, to accord precedence to a unilateral and subsequent measure over a legal system accepted by them on a basis of reciprocity."

By 1970, the Court had asserted the supremacy of EC law, even over Member States' constitutions (the *Internationale Handelsgesellschaft* case, 1970, ECJ). By 1977, in *Simmenthal*, the Court had explained that this meant that every court, however lowly, was under a duty to disapply national law in favour of Community law, where there was a clear conflict. Furthermore, in the *Factortame-Brasserie du Pecheur* case of 1990, the Court added that national courts must be capable of protecting claimed Community law rights in the face of clear contrary provisions in national law, pending the ECJ's final ruling on the precise nature of those rights.

The Effects of EC Sovereignty within the UK

3–052   In the European Communities Act 1972, the UK Parliament effectively gave away its legislative sovereignty in matters within the EC's sphere of activity, recognising the principle of supremacy of directly effective EC law over domestic legislation. The crucial words of s.2(4) are both retrospective and prospective:

"... any enactment passed or to be passed ... shall be construed and have effect subject to the foregoing provisions of this section".

This means that, where domestic law conflicts with directly effective EC law, the latter must be applied and the only way of altering this position is to repeal this subsection. The House of Lords recognised that this was the effect of this subsection in Factortame (1990) when they disapplied part of the Merchant Shipping Act 1988, the clear words of which flew in the face of established Community law rights, including freedom of establishment and non-discrimination.

In this case, as explained above, Spanish owners of fishing vessels sought to register as British so that they would have access to the British Fishing quota under the common fisheries policy. The 1988 Act attempted to limit registration to British managed vessels. Factortame and others sought a judicial review in the High Court of the legality of the Act. The High Court referred the question of Community law to the ECJ but, meanwhile, the procedural question of how to grant interim relief found its way up to the House of Lords. The House declined to grant an interim injunction against the Crown as an injunction could not, in English law, bind the Crown. Furthermore, they objected, the applicants' Community law rights were "necessarily uncertain" until determined by the ECJ and appeared to run directly contrary to Parliament's sovereign will. They sought a preliminary ruling from the ECJ. The Court answered by saying that where the sole obstacle preventing a national court from granting interim relief based on Community law is a rule of national law, that rule of national law must be set aside. Not surprisingly, when the ECJ ruled on the substantive question, they upheld Factortame's complaint that part of the Merchant Shipping Act ran contrary to Community law.

In *Equal Opportunities Commission v Secretary of State for Employment* (1994, HL), the House of Lords confirmed that the *Factortame* case had established that a declaration could be obtained in judicial review proceedings that an Act of Parliament is incompatible with Community law. In this case the House accepted the EOC's complaint that part of the Employment Protection (Consolidation) Act 1978 was in breach of Community law. The Act was subsequently amended by Parliament.

A Comment on *Factortame (No.4)*

The UK media reacted especially badly to the *Factorame (No.4)* 3–053
ruling, affronted at the thought of having to pay retrospective
damages to the Spanish for stopping them coming and raiding "our"
fish stocks. What is so ridiculous is that we reacted as if the ruling
were a surprise. When we passed this piece of protectionist legislation
in 1988, we were warned formally by the Commission, in 1989, acting
under their former Art.169 powers, that we were in breach of the
Treaty so we might have guessed that the ultimate punchline would
be that we would have to pay damages to the Spanish. We reacted
with the same indignant horror to *Factortame (No.1)*, in 1990, which
effectively ruled that a part of the Merchant Shipping Act would have
to be suspended, as if we were shocked at this assault on the legislative sovereignty of Parliament. Apparently many of us had not
noticed, or worked out that we had given this away, on joining the
common market, as it then was, in January 1973. As if to rub salt into
the wound made by *Factortame (No.4)*, in March 1996, the beef crisis
broke out within days of the judgment. We entered the hypocritical
position of arguing that the Court's powers should be curbed, by the
1996 Intergovernmental Conference (the renegotiation of Maastricht),
yet at the same time lodging a claim before the Court against the
Commission for losses caused by the export ban on British beef.

12. The Charter of Fundamental Rights (2000)

This was signed at the end of 2000. It is declaratory only and 3–054
therefore its legal status seems to be "soft law" but it has already
been referred to, in 2001, by the ECJ. There has been no judgment,
to date, which is based on the Charter of Fundamental Rights
(EUCFR).

It is addressed to the Community institutions and Member States
when implementing EC law. It put social and economic rights on the
same footing as civil and political rights. Examples of the rights are
listed below.

1. Dignity (*e.g.* right to life, prohibition on torture).
2. Freedoms (*e.g.* liberty and security, respect for private and
   family life, right to marry, freedom of thought, religion,
   expression; right to education).
3. Equality (*e.g.* non-discrimination, cultural, linguistic and religious diversity; rights for children, the disabled and the
   elderly).
4. Solidarity (*e.g.* workers' rights to information and consultation; social security, health care, environmental and consumer protection).

5. Citizenship rights (*e.g.* voting, good administration, access to documents, the Parliament and the Ombudsman and diplomatic and consular protection).
6. Justice (*e.g.* effective remedy and fair trial, presumption of innocence and fair trial).

The full text can be seen at *http://www.europarl.eu.int/charter/default_en.htm*.

As can be seen, there is an overlap with the European Convention on Human Rights, described in the next chapter, which is NOT a treaty of the EU. Articles 52 and 53 of the EUCFR specify that those rights that correspond to Convention rights must be given the same scope and meaning and while Community law can provide more generous protection, it must not fall below the protection guaranteed by the Convention.

In 2005, the European Commission is consulting on a Fundamental Rights Agency to advance the effect of the Charter. The UK Government argues that the Charter puts a brake not an accelerator on the powers of the EU.

13. The Corpus Juris *Project and the Creation of a European Area of Freedom, Security and Justice*

3–055   The Commission is pressing for a greater measure of control over criminal investigation and prosecution within Member States. It is thought this is needed to combat organised crime. The aim is to protect the financial interest of the EU (protecting the budget; tax evasion). It is directed at eight crimes: fraud, market rigging, abuse of office, misappropriation of funds, disclosure of secrets derived from office-holding, money laundering and receiving and conspiracy. Consequences may include a Community police force, customs service and courts and ultimately a legal service. In 2002, the Council decided to establish Eurojust to improve coordination between Member States in these matters. A European arrest warrant has already come into effect, as a result of a decision in 2002. It replaces extradition proceedings between member states with a system of surrender between judicial authorities. In 2004, the Commission adopted a proposal for a Council framework decision on certain procedural rights in criminal proceedings throughout the EU. All of these developments rest on the principle of mutual recognition where criminal justice systems operate differently, as they all do because, in practice, the interpretation of what constitutes a fair trial differs fairly radically throughout Europe. There have been examples from 2002–3 of English courts refusing extradition to France on the ground that the suspect would not get a fair trial and a similar refusal by a French court to extradite to Spain, on the ground that the suspect might be tortured. The problem with some of these proposed new rights, as Susan Alegre points out, is their vagueness so a right to legal advice does not even extend to a right to have a lawyer present during questioning. The jurisdiction of the ECJ to rule on matters of justice and home affairs, activities in the third pillar such as this, varies between the Member States. In the UK, the ECJ has no jurisdiction in this context. The proposed fair trial rights include:

1. access to legal advice before and at trial;
2. access to interpretation and translation;
3. protection for those who cannot understand proceedings, such as the mentally ill;
4. communication and consular assistance;
5. receiving a letter of rights.

For further discussion see Alegre and for detail, see the Commission website. If a Fundamental Rights Agency were established, as described in the previous section, it could monitor whether these rights were applied in practice. Stephen Jakobi, who has for many years run Fair Trials Abroad, a group of lawyers who endeavour to help those detained and tried abroad, is all too familiar with the shortcomings of other legal systems. He warned, in "Tattered Justice" (2002), that efficiently administered justice systems would be forced to recognize decisions made by under-funded and ill managed courts.

In 2005, Europol, the EU police coordinating agency claimed there were 4,000 criminal gangs operating in Europe. According to the International Monetary Fund, the profits of organized crime account for 2.5 per cent of the world's gross domestic product.	3–056

14. The Proposed Constitution

The aim is to integrate the Charter of Fundamental Rights, provide a clear acknowledgement of the Union's values and objectives and rename the laws as laws. The main changes are as listed.   3–057

1. The three pillars of the EU will be integrated.
2. The EU will have legal personality so will be able to ratify treaties (such as the European Convention on Human Rights).

3. It will incorporate the Charter of Fundamental Rights.
4. It spells out the (existing) supremacy of EU law.
5. It reduces the legislative procedures to six, and legislative acts, such as directives and regulations are renamed.
6. It provides a right for a citizens' initiative, permitting a petition of a million signatures to be sent to the Commission, inviting it to take a legislative initiative.
7. It gives a greater role for national parliaments to be consulted and kept informed of new policy and legislative initiatives.
8. It gives more power to the Parliament
9. It creates a Foreign Affairs Council, chaired by an EU Minister of Foreign Affairs.
10. The ECJ's competence will be extended to include foreign policy and certain areas of freedom, security and justice.

The Treaty establishing a constitution is the first item in Foster's *Blackstone's EC Legislation*. The Press section of the Commission website provides a press pack, including a summary, which is much more digestible than the overly large and detailed document.

BIBLIOGRAPHY

3–058   S. Alegre, "EU fair trial rights—added value or no value?" (2004) 154 N.L.J. 758.
M. Fletcher, "Fresh row brews over European rights Bill", *The Times*, October 2, 2000.
S. Jakobi, "Tattered Justice", *Counsel*, April 2002, p.18.
JUSTICE, "Justice in Europe", 1997.
S. Nash and M. Furse, "Human Rights Law Update" (1999) 149 N.L.J. 891.
R. Smith, "Fundamentally right" (on the EUCFR) (2005) 155 N.L.J. 229.
R. Stevens, "On being nicer to James and the children" (1994) 144 N.L.J. 1620.
T. Tayleur, "Emanations of the State" (2000) 150 N.L.J. 1292.

FURTHER READING AND SOURCES FOR UPDATING THIS CHAPTER

3–059   Online updates to this book: *http://www.sweetandmaxwell.co.uk/academic/updates/darbyshire/index.html*
Official portal to the EU: *http://europa.eu.int/* (click on your preferred language).
European Commission: *http://europa.eu.int/comm/index_en.htm*
European Commission in the UK: *http://www.cec.org.uk/* (you can read the weekly newsletter on the website or have it emailed to you free, by registering here).

ECJ, description: *http://europa.eu.int/institutions/court/index_en.htm* (then click on the link to the ECJ).

Portal to European Union Law, Eur-Lex: *http://europa.eu.int/eur-lex/ en/index.html*

The European Constitution has its own website but the full document is almost indigestible. Instead, try the Press Pack, which contains a summary, at *http://europa.eu.int/comm/press_room/ presspacks/constit/ index_en.htm*

The UK Parliament for excellent factsheets on EC institutions and law and details of how EC law and EU policy are scrutinised in both Houses: *www.parliament.uk*

J. Steiner and L. Woods, *EC Law*. Naturally it is essential to use the latest edition, as listed on *www.amazon.co.uk*

N. Foster, *Blackstone's EC Legislation* (new edition annually).

S. Weatherill and P. Beaumont, *EU Law* (use the latest edition).

P. Craig and G. De Burca, *EU Law, Text Cases and Materials* (use the latest edition).

4. The European Convention on Human Rights and English Law

"He regarded the European Convention as 'a gift from victory' in the Second World War, a product of victory over the principles and governance of wicked men, led by Adolph Hitler" (Attorney-General Lord Goldsmith QC, obituary for Lord Scarman, Law Lord 1977–1986, *Counsel*, February 2005.)

1. Incorporation into UK Law

The European Convention on Human Rights (the Convention) was drafted over 50 years ago by British lawyers. It grew out of disgust with fascism and an anxiety to protect basic freedoms. It is a Treaty of the Council of Europe. The UK, led by a Labour government, was the first signatory (1951). From 1966, the Government allowed individuals to bring claims against the UK. By 1998, 99 cases had been taken against the UK, more than any country except Italy, and the UK had been found to be in violation of the Convention 52 times. The UK was a frequent defendant before the European Court of Human Rights (ECtHR), partly because we lack a written constitution.

Prior to 2000, however, the individual could not assert their Convention rights through the domestic courts. Judges of the UK were powerless to apply it. The courts, in any event, took a fairly conservative approach, despite "ingenious and persistent invitations by counsel" to depart from domestic law (Lord Chief Justice Bingham in his maiden speech in the Lords, 1996). The Lord Chief Justice made a speech urging incorporation of the Convention and in the Court of Appeal (CA) he and his fellow judges expressed dissatisfaction with their powerlessness to allow appeals in a case which raised Convention issues: *R. v Morrisey* (1997). In the meantime, the

4–001

Conservative governments of the early 1990s had set their face against the incorporation of the Convention. They had grown hostile to the ECtHR, especially because of decisions such as that against Home Secretary Michael Howard in relation to sentencing juveniles and against the UK and in favour of the families of IRA members assassinated by the UK Government in the Death on the Rock case. Minister Michael Heseltine called this decision "ludicrous" and called for an alteration to the powers of the ECtHR. They sought a new fact-finding procedure and vetting of potential judges. They were dilatory in enforcing the judgments of the ECtHR which they did not like (see Bindman).

In 1996, the Labour opposition issued a consultation paper on their plans to incorporate Convention rights, should they be elected. The Lords had a two-day debate on the Constitution, in which, despite Lord Bingham's entreaties, the Conservative Lord Chancellor Mackay expressed the view that UK citizens were adequately protected by the common law. Enacting a Bill of Rights would, he feared, give the courts wide discretion over matters which were properly the preserve of Parliament. The generalised wording of the Convention would leave too much scope for judicial interpretation and litigation. Lord Irvine, then Shadow Lord Chancellor, opened the case for the Opposition, pointing out that the UK was virtually alone amongst the major nations of Western Europe in failing to give its citizens the means to assert Convention rights in the courts (see Hudson). Once in Government, in 1997, New Labour swiftly published a white paper, *Rights Brought Home*. In the Tom Sergeant Memorial Lecture in 1997, the newly appointed Lord Chancellor Irvine said:

> "The Human Rights Bill . . . will be a constitutional change of major significance, protecting the individual citizen against erosion of liberties, either deliberate or gradual. It will promote a culture where positive rights and liberties become the focus and concern of legislators, administrators and judges alike".

The Human Rights Bill would, he said, require judges to produce a decision on the morality of conduct, not simply its compliance with the bare letter of the law. He thought the traditional common law approach to the protection of liberties, described as a negative right (the right to do anything not prohibited by law), offered little protection against creeping erosion of individual liberties by a legislature. The Human Rights Act 1998 (HRA 1998) incorporated the Convention into English law on October 2, 2000. This means that the Convention rights became part of UK law and thus English law and could now be enforced by English and Welsh courts and tribunals.

Once the Act was about to come into force, the point was made 4–002
that our judiciary would become the guardians of individuals'
rights, as the Lord Chancellor called them in the Paul Sieghart
Memorial Lecture, 1999. The newspapers carried a number of articles expressing concern about the judicial appointment system,
manifesting a distrust of the Oxbridge white, male judiciary it produced, to enforce Convention rights. Liberals like Lord Lester had
campaigned for over 30 years for incorporation but the
Conservative Lord Kingsland reiterated traditional fears about the
Act, like those expressed above. (Their views were quoted in the
special *Times* supplement.)

The Human Rights Act 1998, in Force October 2, 2000
A straightforward explanation of the Convention's incorporation 4–003
into the English legal system is by Robin White in his excellent 1999
book, *The English Legal System in Action*. The Department responsible
for the enforcement of human rights in the UK is the Department for
Constitutional Affairs. On its website, under "People's Rights" you
will find the pages of its Human Rights Unit. These are very informative and contain the simplest explanations of our human rights, as
well as news on their development and application within our legal
system The pages contain links to the Convention, the UK's Human
Rights Act 1998, the European Court of Human Rights, news, minis
terial speeches, statistics, case outcomes, Parliamentary debates, other
official publications and links to other useful Human Rights sites.
    Section 1 and Sch.1 of the HRA 1998 restate Conventions and
Protocols as part of UK law with the exception of Art.13. Article 13
would have given a remedy for violation in any court or tribunal.
The Government did not want to give them sweeping, new, inappropriate powers. People have to seek remedies in the higher
courts, on appeal or in judicial review proceedings.
    Section 2 provides that when a court or tribunal is determining a
question in connection with a Convention right it "must take into
account" judgments, decisions or declarations of the ECtHR, and
opinions or decisions of the Commission or the Committee of
Ministers. Notice, as the white paper explained, that this does not
mean that the Court's decisions are binding. This is in distinct contrast with the binding decisions of the European Court of Justice
(ECJ), as provided by the European Communities Act 1972. Section
3 of the HRA 1998 says "(s)o far as possible, primary legislation and
subordinate legislation must be read and given effect in a way which
is compatible with the Convention rights". Notice that this applies
to all of us in interpreting legislation, not just the courts but the obligation is qualified. This is important. Section 6 makes it unlawful for
any public authority, including any court or tribunal, to act in a way

incompatible with a Convention right. Notice the meaning of "public authority" has been criticised by academics and others as too vague. (I discuss the point about "public" below). Any party to any legal proceedings can rely on a Convention right. This means, for example, that it can be used to apply for a stay (stop) of proceedings, or as a defence, or a ground of appeal or to found an application for judicial review. If a court or tribunal is satisfied of a violation, they may award anything appropriate within their jurisdiction. Damages or compensation may only be awarded by those courts or tribunals empowered to do so (s.8).

4–004   Where courts cannot interpret a piece of legislation as compatible, then certain courts may make a declaration of incompatibility, under s.4(2) but in the English legal system, only these courts have this power: High Court, Court of Appeal, House of Lords, Privy Council and the Courts Martial-Appeal Court. A lesser court or tribunal must apply the incompatible law and the case will have to be taken on appeal until one of these higher courts is reached. This may take two levels of appeal. For instance, the Employment Appeal Tribunal and Social Security Commissioners do not have this power. The declaration of incompatibility does not affect validity and is not binding on the parties (s.4). In any case where a court is considering making a declaration of incompatibility, the Crown (meaning the Government) is entitled to notice and to be joined as a party to the proceedings (s.5).

Section 11 provides for a fast track legislative procedure designed to remove the incompatibility, as described in Chapter 2 of this book on sources, above, so a minister can use a statutory instrument to amend offending primary legislation and, as explained in that Chapter, this "Henry VIII" section of the Act is controversial.

People can still apply to the ECtHR in Strasbourg but they will have to show that they have exhausted all domestic remedies.

4–005   When a new Bill is published, s.19 obliges the sponsoring minister to make a written statement that it is compatible or decline to make a statement but indicate that the Government wishes to proceed. A Joint Parliamentary Committee on Human Rights has been created.

The Act necessitated the biggest project in training judges and magistrates ever managed by the Judicial Studies Board. Like the ECJ, the ECtHR takes a highly purposive approach to legislative interpretation and, examining relevant case authorities since the Act came into force in 2000, we can see that our own judges have, to an extent, taken this approach themselves. It was obvious in 1998 that there would be an impact on precedent and existing judicial interpretations of statute and this has proven to be the case. In order to enforce a Convention right, the CA may consider itself not to be bound by previous binding precedents which are incompatible with Convention rights. This was explained in the 1997 White Paper *Rights Brought Home.* This can be seen in relation to criminal procedure and criminal appeals, as explained in Chapter 10 of this book, below. The Privy Council has held that provisions of constitutional human rights legislation "call for a generous interpretation, avoiding what has been called 'the austerity of tabulated legalism', suitable to give individuals the full measure of the fundamental rights and freedoms referred to": *Ministry of Home Affairs v Fisher* (1980).

A number of extra judges were created to deal with what the Government predicted would be a heavy workload generated by the HRA 1998. The statistical bulletin on the Department of Constitutional Affairs (DCA) website analysing court business in the year after the implementation of the Act discloses that its impact was not as significant as predicted during that period. During that year, there was an insignificant increase in civil court business and, indeed, by 2005, there has been a significant reduction in civil business. Many far-fetched claims have failed. In *R. (on the application of M and Leon La Rose) v Commissioner of Police of the Metropolis* [2001] EWHC Admin 553, the High Court warned lawyers that the Convention should not be invoked when the deprivation of rights was merely theoretical or illusory.

The Justices' Clerks' Society welcomed the Bill but warned that it   **4–006** provided scope for considerable time to be spent in argument at the magistrates' court which will not affect the result of the case at that stage. The justices are obliged to take account of Convention rights but are powerless to make a declaration of incompatibility. This, they feared, could lead to cumulative delay in contested hearings, although, by 2005, there are no statistics to test the validity of this prediction.

2. The Convention Rights

These are appended to the HRA 1998 as Sch.1, where they are   **4–007** spelled out in full. Briefly, they are, by Article:

  2. Right to life.
  3. Prohibition of torture.
  4. Prohibition of slavery and forced labour.
  5. Right to liberty and security.
  6. Right to a fair trial.
  7. No punishment without law.
  8. Right to respect for private and family life.
  9. Freedom of thought, conscience and religion.
10. Freedom of expression.

11. Freedom of assembly and association.
12. Right to marry.
13. Not incorporated into English law (see above).
14. Prohibition of discrimination.
16. Restrictions on political activity of aliens.
17. Prohibition of abuse of rights.
18. Limitation on use of restrictions on rights.

Some rights are absolute, such as 3. Some admit exceptions, such as 2 and most are subject to restrictions to ensure respect for other rights and freedoms.

3. The European Court of Human Rights

4–008 | Do not confuse the ECtHR with the ECJ, described in Chapter 3, above. The ECJ sits in Luxembourg and interprets Community law for the 25 Member States of the EU. The ECtHR is **not** an institution of the EU. It interprets and enforces the ECHR for the 46 countries that have ratified the Convention. It sits in Strasbourg.

4–009   The fulltime Court was opened, in 1998, replacing the two stage Commission and part-time Court. I describe its composition in Chapter 6 on the civil courts, below. Procedure is as follows. Each application is assigned to a section and a rapporteur. Three judges filter applications, with most decision-making done on the papers, and those cases deemed admissible go to panels of seven judges. The President of a chamber may invite other interested parties and other member states to join in the proceedings and the contracting state whose citizen is an applicant has a right to intervene. Initially, or at any time in proceedings, a case may be referred to a Grand Chamber of 17 judges "where a case raises a serious question of interpretation of the Convention or where there is a risk of departing from existing case-law", explains the Court's website. Chambers decide by a majority vote. Any judge who has taken part in the consideration of the case is entitled to append to the judgment a separate opinion, either concurring or dissenting, or a bare statement of dissent.

    Within three months of delivery of the judgment of a chamber, any party may request that the case be referred to the Grand Chamber if it raises a serious question of interpretation or application or a serious issue of general importance. An example of this occurred in the case of *Hatton v UK* (2001, ECtHR) on aircraft noise at Heathrow where the UK requested that a chamber's decision against it be referred to a Grand Chamber.

Following a finding of a breach of the Convention, the State is legally obliged to make reparation for the consequences of the violation. Where the domestic law affords only partial reparation, Art.41 provides that the Court can award an applicant "just satisfaction" for pecuniary and non-pecuniary damage. More details of the Court's procedure can be found on its website.

One practical drawback in the Court's functioning is its backlog,   4–010
as with the ECJ. Speaking at the Court's annual press conference 2003 in Strasbourg, the President told journalists:

"2004 will be a critical year for the ECtHR in terms of the next reform of the ECHR. As we have been saying for some time, the Court is struggling to cope with the ever-growing volume of cases pending before it—currently some 65,800 applications . . . Under the current arrangements the Court is required both to filter out manifestly inadmissible cases and adjudicate on the important cases raising new or serious issues under the Convention. It is increasingly difficult to carry out both these functions effectively. The new protocol must tackle this problem."

In the five years following the restyling of the Court (1999–2003), the Court delivered 3,308 judgments, compared with 389 in the five preceding years. Despite this increase in productivity, the backlog of cases has continued to grow. There were 38,000 new applications in 2003, more than twice as many as the number of cases terminated over the year (17,950).

In 2005, the Court's president urged all 46 member states to ratify the new Protocol 14, designed to remedy this backlog. It will change court procedure to try to streamline the process for cutting out unmeritorious cases. A single judge will be able to declare an application inadmissible if the applicant has not suffered any significant disadvantage.

The Court normally confines itself to declaring whether there has   4–011
been a violation of the Convention but in 2004 it took the unusual step of complaining of a Polish "systemic failure" to provide compensation for loss of property following repatriation after World War II. It called on Poland to remedy the legal defect, as it would affect 80,000 people, 167 of whom were in the queue of applications before the Court. If there are more such complaints of "systemic failure" and if they are resolved by the offending states then this should dissipate some of the backlog.

The Committee of Ministers

This is the decision-making organ of the Council of Europe and is   4–012
composed of the foreign Ministers of the 46 contracting States. It

supervises the execution of the Court's judgments and can check that a State has taken steps to amend offending legislation. The Court may, at the request of the Committee of Ministers, give advisory opinions on legal questions concerning the interpretation of the Convention and Protocols.

4. The Approach of the European Court of Human Rights

4–013   A.T.H. Smith explained the principles upon which the ECtHR has acted:

1. A generous approach is taken when determining what comes within the scope of the rights.
2. There are four requirements before conditions can be imposed on a right:

    - interference must be lawful;
    - it must serve a legitimate purpose;
    - it must be necessary in a democratic society;
    - it must not be discriminatory.

3. The Convention is a "living instrument", which means that the older a decision, the less value it may have as a guide to construction.

The Court has held that the Convention, not the domestic court, determines whether proceedings are civil or criminal. In *R. (on the application of McCann) v Manchester Crown Court* [2002] UKHL 39, their Lordships held that proceedings for anti-social behaviour orders under Crime and Disorder Act 1998, s.1 were civil proceedings and did not involve a criminal charge under Art.6 of the Convention. The applicable standard of proof was the criminal standard but hearsay evidence was allowed, as civil evidence rules applied. Lord Steyn's starting point was that the Crown Prosecution Service was not involved and "an extensive interpretation of what is a criminal charge under Art.6(1) would, by rendering the injunctive process ineffectual, prejudice the freedom of liberal democracies to maintain the rule of law by the use of civil injunctions.

In *Georgiou v UK* (2001) the ECtHR held that penalty assessments for VAT were criminal matters. The Chancery Division held that the same applied to determinations of the tax commissioners to penalise defaulting taxpayers.

5. Examples of the Convention's Application in English Law

It should be understood that cases against *any* State before the ECtHR are of equal value to the English and Welsh courts in assisting them to apply the Convention. Below, I list just a few cases, most of which involved the UK as a respondent, as well as some in our courts. This is only a sample, not a comprehensive list so the reader can start to understand the impact of Convention law on English law.

4–014

Article 2 Right to Life

Assassination by the state

In 1995, the Court found a violation of the right to life in the notorious "Death on the Rock" case, where the SAS had shot dead three IRA members in Gibraltar, suspected of having planted a car bomb. This ruling provoked a hostile reaction from Michael Heseltine, a Conservative Minister (see above). For a full account see *The Guardian* and other newspapers of September 28, 1995.

4–015

The right to die

In *Pretty v UK* (2002) the dying Diane Pretty took her case to the ECtHR in Strasbourg, after the House of Lords refused to rule that the Director of Public Prosecutions (DPP) should be told by the courts to grant her husband immunity from prosecution in assisting her planned suicide. Her application was unanimously declared inadmissible. The Court took the opportunity to restate the scope of certain articles. Article 2, right to life, did not extend to a right to die. Article 3 imposed positive and negative obligations on states to avoid "inhuman and degrading treatment and punishment" but this did not extend to condemning the DPP's refusal to grant her husband immunity from prosecution, because it took "treatment" beyond its ordinary meaning. Article 8 (private and family life) was engaged because under it, notions of the quality of life took on significance but there was no violation of Art.8, because, in regulating behaviour for the protection of public morals, the state's "margin of appreciation" was particularly in evidence (in other words, the state had a lot of discretion) so the Suicide Act did not amount to a disproportionate interference with the applicant's right. Mrs Pretty died a few days later.

4–016

Coroners' juries and inquests into deaths in custody

In *R. (Middleton) v West Somerset Coroner* [2004] UKHL 10, the House of Lords held that the State's procedural obligation to investigate a death which might have violated the right to life (Art.2),

4–017

because it was a death in custody, required an inquest jury to draw conclusions on the central factual issues of the case. Their Lordships examined previous actions against the UK in the ECtHR, involving deaths in custody and ruled that the word "how" in the Coroners Act 1988 and the Coroners' Rules should be interpreted as meaning not simply "by what means" but also "in what circumstances" the person died.

On the same day, they ruled that this did not apply retrospectively, to inquests held before the Human Rights Act came into force. It was now settled, as a general proposition, that the Human Rights Act was not retrospective: *In Re McKerr* [2004] UKHL 12.

The House ruled in 2003, that where a death in custody occurs, the State has a duty to ensure a reasonably prompt, effective investigation before an independent body with an opportunity for the relatives of the deceased to participate: *R. v SS for the Home Dept Ex p. Amin* [2003] UKHL 51. In this case, where the victim had been killed by his cellmate in Feltham Young Offender Institution, there had been an investigation into the death by the Prison Service, the police and the Commission for Racial Equality but the Minister had refused the family's request for an independent public inquiry. It was held that the Minister had not met minimum standards set down by the ECtHR in other cases involving deaths in custody in the UK. One of these was *Edwards v UK* (2002), in which the ECtHR had held that there had been a violation of Art.2 and Art.13. The applicants complained that the relevant authorities had failed to protect the life of their son who was stamped on and kicked to death whilst sharing a cell at Colchester police station. Article 2 placed a positive obligation on the Home Secretary to take appropriate steps to safeguard lives and the screening process for risky prisoners was inadequate.

These decisions have caused changes in detention practices as well as changes in the conduct of inquiries and inquests, following deaths in custody. The coronial system is being restructured, as explained in Chapter 6 on civil courts, below. These cases also engage Art.8, by requiring that the family be involved and informed.

Article 3 Inhuman and Degrading Treatment

The State's duty to protect children

4–018   The UK's failure to provide children with protection against serious long-term neglect and abuse was a breach: *Z v UK* (2001, ECtHR).

Minimum standards of treatment in custody

4–019   Where a prisoner committed suicide, after manifesting suicidal tendencies, the Court found a breach because of lack of medical records of the detainee's mental state and treatment by a doctor who lacked specialist psychiatric knowledge. Further, the imposition of an additional sentence, close to his release date, was incompatible with the required standard of treatment in respect of the mentally ill: *Keenan v UK* (2001, ECtHR).

In *Price v UK* (2001, ECtHR), the applicant was severely disabled and suffered from recurring kidney problems. In the course of civil proceedings, she was committed to seven days' imprisonment for contempt for refusing to answer questions. She was detained in a police station, then a prison. She was forced to sleep in a wheelchair, was too cold and was not given appropriate help to use the toilet or to remain dressed in a dignified manner. She was refused legal aid. The ECtHR found there was a violation of Art.3, although it was not deliberate.

In *McGlinchey v UK* (2003, ECtHR) A heroin addict and asthmatic collapsed and died in prison. In failing to monitor her condition, the prison authority had ill-treated her, contrary to Art.3.

Asylum seekers

A breach of Art.3, in relation to asylum seekers, was found by the CA in *R.(Q) v SS for the Home* [2003] EWCA Civ 364. The Court upheld the controversial decision of Andrew Collins J., which had provoked a vicious personal attack upon him and upon judges in general by Home Secretary Blunkett (discussed in Chapter 14 on judges, below). The Nationality Immigration and Asylum Act 2002, s.55 provided that the Home Secretary could not support an asylum seeker unless he was satisfied that the claim was made as soon as practicable on arrival in the UK so asylum seekers who made their way to London before approaching the Home Office were denied any help. The Court did not find any breach of the Convention in s.55, but in the unfair procedure used by the Home Secretary to determine whether asylum seekers had made their claims as soon as reasonably practicable.

4–020

Article 5 Liberty and Security

See Chapter 10 on criminal procedure, in addition to the cases outlined below.

4–021

Detention without a review of its lawfulness

In *Hussain v UK, Singh v UK* (1996, ECtHR) the treatment of the applicants, sentenced indeterminately "at Her Majesty's pleasure", as juveniles, was a breach, since, after the expiry of the fixed "tariff" part of their sentence, they were unable to have the lawfulness of their continued detention reviewed by a court. For instance, the Parole Board had considered and recommended the release of one

4–022

applicant but the Home Secretary informed the applicant that he had not accepted the recommendation. The lack of adversarial proceedings prevented it from being a court or court-like body. Similarly, the 15-year tariff set by the child killers of Jamie Bulger was later declared to breach the Convention.

In *Stafford v UK* (2002) the ECtHR sat as a Grand Chamber of 17 judges, signifying the importance of the decision. The Home Secretary's decision to keep S in prison longer than recommended by the Parole Board was held to be a breach of Art.5. The fact that a politician rather than a judge kept S in prison went against the "spirit of the Convention" as too arbitrary. (Note: Home Secretary David Blunkett expressed disappointment.) This was one of a series of cases diminishing the power of the Home Secretary over sentencing. No other country in the Council of Europe allows a Government minister to determine sentence length for individuals. The case was cited and followed by the ECtHR again in 2004 in *Hill v UK*. The applicant was awarded damages on the grounds that his detention was only reviewed by the Parole Board, a body without the power to release him.

In *Waite v UK* (ECtHR, 2002) the denial of an oral hearing by the Parole Board violated Art.5(4) and the lack of compensation for this violated Art.5(5). There was a very similar decision by the House of Lords in *R. v Parole Board Ex p. West* [2005] UKHL 1. In some cases, procedural fairness at common law required an oral hearing. A prisoner should have the benefit of a procedure that reflected the importance to him, as well as to society. If this had been provided, there would have been no violation of Art.5.

4–023   In *Reid v UK* (ECtHR, 2003) it was held that placing the burden of proof on R to establish that his continued detention in a mental hospital did not satisfy conditions of lawfulness was not compatible with Art.5(4) and the long delay (application 1994, appeal to the HL, 1998) had breached Art.5(4). One of several cases in which English procedure was shown to be in breach of the separation of powers was *Benjamin and Wilson v UK* (2002, ECtHR). The Court held that there was a violation of Art.5, where lifers were detained in top security mental hospital and whose detention was renewed by a mental health review tribunal. The tribunal could only make recommendations to the Home Secretary as to release. It had no power to order release itself. It was unacceptable that release should be decided on by a member of the executive, a government minister. (See similar problems exposed by Art.6, below).

Part of the Mental Health Act 1983 was declared incompatible with the Convention Art.5(4) by the Court of Appeal. The Act allowed a mental patient to apply to a mental health review tribunal to have their detention reviewed but made no provision for applicants like this one, who were incapable of applying: *In Re (MH) v The Health Secretary* [2004] EWCA Civ 1609.

Detention of asylum seekers

The House of Lords held, in *R. (Saadi and others) v SS for the Home Dept* [2002] UKHL 41, that detaining asylum seekers while their claims were determined was not a breach of Art.5. The State had a right to control entry and until it had authorized entry, entry is unauthorized. Oakington Reception Centre provided reasonable conditions.

4–024

Lawful arrest

A person arrested on reasonable suspicion of having committed a crime could not claim his right to liberty and security of the person had been breached: *O'Hara v UK* (2001, ECtHR).

4–025

Indefinite internment

December 2004 saw an unusual panel of nine Law Lords taking a radical decision on a very controversial piece of legislation in a case which Lord Hoffman said was one of the most important in recent years: *A (FC) and others v SS for the Home Dept* [2004] UKHL 56. The appellants challenged the lawfulness of their indefinite detention under the Anti-Terrorism, Crime and Security Act 2001, an Act passed swiftly after the terrorist destruction of the New York World Trade Centre on September 11, 2001, which enabled the internment without trial of foreign nationals whom the Home Secretary suspected were terrorists. There were no similar powers over British citizens. The Act had always been opposed by civil libertarians. The Government had derogated from (opted out of) its obligations under Art.5, as provided for by the Convention where there is "a public emergency threatening the life of the nation". No other European country had done this in the wake of "9/11". Seven Law Lords ruled that indefinite detention without trial was unlawful because it was a disproportionate inter-ference with liberty (Art.5) and equality (Art.14). Lord Hoffman went further, claiming the nation was not under threat, as required for dero-gation. Like seven of his fellow Law Lords, he saw the Act as offen-sive to fundamental constitutional principles:

4–026

> "The real threat to the life of the nation, in the sense of a people living in accordance with its traditional laws and political values, comes not from terrorism but from laws such as these. That is the true measure of what terrorism may achieve. It is for Parliament to decide whether to give the terrorists such a victory."

Baroness Hale said "We have always taken it for granted that we cannot be locked up in this country without trial or explanation".

Lord Hope said it was impossible to overstate the importance of liberty in a democracy. Lord Scott said "Indefinite imprisonment, on grounds not disclosed, is the stuff of nightmares, associated with . . . Soviet Russia in the Stalinist era."

They were not persuaded by the Attorney-General's argument, on behalf of the Government, that the Act did not offend against Art.5 because it allowed for review by the Special Immigration Appeals Commission, which could hear the evidence against the accused (too sensitive to be admitted in a court) and overrule the Home Secretary. Nor were they at all impressed by the Attorney's argument that they, the Law Lords, were an unelected and undemocratic body who should not second guess ministers. This had been a favourite argument of Home Secretary Blunkett in his repeated attacks on the judges. Their Lordships made a ruling of incompatibility.

4–027   In the ensuing days, the Government were faced with what much of the media portrayed as a constitutional crisis. The new Home Secretary declined to release the suspects but announced he would await a decision by Parliament on the legislation, due for its annual renewal in spring 2005. This caused some of the special Government-appointed advocates for the detainees to threaten to resign and caused some backbenchers to threaten trouble. In March 2005, Parliament passed the Prevention of Terrorism Act to replace the offending 2001 Act but it was ferociously debated. Opponents of the Bill, including all civil liberties groups, did not cite the Convention so much as ancient liberties fundamental to the British constitution, such as habeas corpus, laid down in Magna Carta. The Act again derogates from the requirements of the Convention. It allows British and foreign terrorist suspects to be placed under a control order (meaning house arrest), by the Home Secretary. Although this will be reviewed by a judge, it does not satisfy critics that it amounts to detention without trial. They asked why we are the only country in Europe which considers it necessary to do this. Other countries' laws permit the admission of evidence obtained by surveillance, such as telephone tapping so such suspects can be tried for say, incitement or conspiracy to commit terrorist offences. The reader might also like to consider this: the conditions of detention under a control order are much more draconian than those of house arrest under the old apartheid regime in South Africa.

Defaulters in the Magistrates' Court

4–028   Magistrates who jailed fine defaulters or council tax defaulters breached Arts 5 and 6: *Beet v UK* (2005, ECtHR). Legal aid had not been available in these cases before 1997.

Article 6 Fair Trial

Per Lord Steyn in *Kebilene* (1999) "when article 6 of the Convention   4–029
becomes part of our law, it will be the prism through which other
aspects of our criminal law may have to be re-examined". The
biggest cluster of cases and legislative changes generated by the
Human Rights Act have been those on criminal procedure, mostly
Art.6. Some are dealt with here and the rest in Chapter 10, below.

Nevertheless, the most dramatic impact of Art.6 was that it necessitated wholesale constitutional reform to the office of Lord
Chancellor and the position of the Law Lords, explained below.

Remember that the Convention, not the national court, determines whether proceedings are civil or criminal and our courts have
sometimes been reluctant to accept this.

Courts martial—appearance of bias

The ECtHR has repeatedly found against the UK in relation to   4–030
courts-martial proceedings and systems of military adjudication
which had been in place for over 600 years have had to be altered.
For instance, in *Findlay v UK* (1997); *Coyne v UK* (1997). Since a
defendant's commanding officer and other officers participated in
proceedings, they were insufficiently independent. In response to
Findlay, the Conservative Government had introduced the Armed
Forces Bill (later Act) of 1996 but it was inadequate to remedy the
defect. The Armed Forces Discipline Act 2000 was an attempt to
make the system compliant with the Convention but in 2002 the
system had to be suspended and investigated further. At the time
of the *Findlay* case, there were 50 others outstanding, which are
costing millions of pounds to settle and cases are still going
through the ECtHR, such as *Cooper v UK* (2004) and *Grieves v UK*
(2003). See discussion of courts martial by Alex Wade.

Crown immunity

Matthews v MOD [2003] UKHL 4: Armed forces' Crown immunity   4–031
was not incompatible with Art.6. Lord Bingham felt himself bound
by the common law, in ruling that no claim could be made in tort
against the armed forces. The claimant had wanted to bring an
action for damages, having suffered the effects of exposure to
asbestos, during his naval career.

Delay

The ECtHR has frequently found a breach of Art.6 in cases where   4–032
it takes a long time to bring proceedings to a conclusion. They delivered 248 judgments against Italy in the first eight months of 2000.
The Art.6 requirement that justice be reasonably swift applies to civil
as well as criminal proceedings. This should be assessed in the light

of all the circumstances of the case. Where an applicant's companies had gone into receivership, proceedings against him lasted nine years. Much of the delay was his own fault but the Court was satisfied proceedings against him had not been pursued with due diligence and he was awarded damages: *Eastaway v UK* (2004, ECtHR). Similarly, a 13 year delay relating to a tax penalty was found to breach Art.6 in *King v UK* (2005).

Open justice

4–033   The denial of a public hearing and public pronouncement of judgment in child custody proceedings was not a breach: *B v UK, P v UK* (2001, ECtHR). This case was cited in *Allen v Clibbery* [2002] EWCA Civ 45 discussed in Chapter 6 on the civil courts, under the section on open justice, below.

Legal aid—equality of arms

4–034   *McVicar v UK* (2002): Linford Christie sued the applicant journalist for defamation in alleging that he used performance-enhancing drugs. The Court held that the unavailability of legal aid for the defendant did not violate Arts 6 or 10, as a well educated journalist was capable of forming a cogent argument. Defamation law was not so complex as to require representation.

The same issue, denial of legal aid, arose in an application made by the two defendants in the famous "McLibel case", the longest trial in English legal history, lasting 313 days in 1994–6. The saga was finally resolved in the ECtHR in 2005: *Steel and Morris v UK*. The Court held that there had been a breach of Art.6 because the applicants were denied legal aid, in defending themselves against a defamation action by McDonalds, after distributing leaflets attacking the fast food chain. The Court recalled that the Convention was intended to guarantee practical and effective rights. That was particularly so of the right of access to courts, in view of the prominent place of the right to fair trial in a democratic society.

It was central to the concept of a fair trial, civil or criminal, that a litigant was not denied the opportunity to present his or her case effectively before the court and that he or she was able to enjoy equality of arms with the opposing side. The question whether legal aid was necessary was to be determined on the facts. It depended on what was at stake for the applicant, the complexity of law and procedure and the capacity of the applicants to represent themselves. The applicants argued they were severely hampered by lack of resources, such as note-taking and photocopying, not just legal advice. The facts were complex, involving 40,000 pages of documentary evidence. Nor was the law straightforward. Extensive legal and procedural issues had to be resolved even before the trial started. Although the applicants were articulate and they had some help from *pro bono* (free) lawyers, they mainly acted alone. The trial length was a testament to their lack of skill and experience. They had been deprived of the opportunity to present their case effectively and there was inequality of arms. See also Art.10. There is more material on the Convention's requirements for access to a lawyer in criminal proceedings in Chapter 10 on criminal procedure, below.

The privilege against self-incrimination

The Road Traffic Act 1988, s.172, which required a registered **4–035** owner to reveal the identity of the driver of a car was not a breach of the privilege against self-incrimination: *Brown (Margaret Anderson) v Stott* (2000, PC). This case put an end to hundreds of speeding drivers thinking they could get away with not responding after being caught on speed cameras. See Chapter 10, below.

Covert surveillance

Allan v UK (2002, ECtHR): the use of covert audio and video **4–036** recording devices in his cell and the visiting area and on another prisoner breached A's Art.8 rights and the use of an informer to elicit incriminating statements breached his Art.6 right to silence.

The presumption of innocence—retrospectivity

Very importantly, the House of Lords ruled in *R. v Lambert* [2001] **4–037** UKHL 37, that the presumption of innocence in Art.6(2) did not apply retrospectively in appeals against convictions secured in trials conducted before the HRA came fully into effect. In *R. v Kansal (No.2)* [2001] UKHL 62, a 3/2 majority of Law Lords expressed the view that this decision was a mistake but declined to apply the 1966 Practice Statement to overrule themselves in *Lambert*. They repeated their refusal in *R. v Benjafield* [2002] UKHL 2.

Interpreter

In *Cuscani v UK* (2002) the Court held there had been a breach of **4–038** Art.6 in failing to provide an interpreter at a sentencing hearing.

Separation of powers: judges must determine sentences, not ministers

In *R. (on the application of Anderson) v SS for the Home Dept* [2002] **4–039** UKHL 46, the Home Secretary's power to determine the length of a life sentence was incompatible with Art.6. Following previous ECtHR case law, the House of seven Law Lords held that the Secretary of State's role was objectionable because he was not independent of the executive. The European Court had been right to describe the complete functional separation of the judiciary from the executive as "fundamental", since the rule of law depended on it. Home Secretary David Blunkett promised the Government would establish a clear set of principles to fix minimum tariffs and a new judicial authority would consider tariffs for current lifers. Similarly, in *Easterbrook v UK* (ECtHR, 2003), the Court found a violation of Art.6 where the minimum period of detention, 16 years, was set by the Home Secretary and not the trial judge. The fact that a member of the executive government performed this judicial function caused the breach of Art.6. Note similar rulings where lack of separation of powers offended against Art.5, above.

In *Ezeh and Connors v UK* (2002) the ECtHR found a breach of Art.6(3) where prisoners were denied legal aid or advice before a disciplinary hearing which could have resulted in an extra 42 days' detention. The UK asked for the case to be referred to the Grand Chamber. They affirmed the decision and held that, in determining whether proceedings were criminal, it was necessary to take into account the legal classification of the offence in national law, the nature of the offence and the nature and degree of severity of the penalty.

The separation of powers in planning decisions

4–040   The domestic planning process ground to a halt by February 2001, because of so many challenges in the High Court that it breached Art.6. Some of those challenges had been upheld by the High Court and all planning appeals were suspended while cases were hastily sent up to the House of Lords using the leapfrog procedure. The House of Lords put paid to all such claims by upholding the Secretary of State's appeals in joined cases in *Alconbury* [2001] UKHL 23. The Minister's powers under the Town and Country Planning Act were not incompatible with the Art.6(1) right to have civil rights determined by an independent and impartial tribunal. Lord Slynn relied on previous decisions by the ECtHR which recognised that some administrative law decisions which affected civil rights were taken by Ministers answerable to elected bodies.

The judicial approach in judicial review proceedings

4–041   The nature of judicial review proceedings which restricted the court to examining the quality of the decision-making process rather than the merits of the decision meant that an applicant alleging bias had not had a fair hearing: *Kingsley v UK* (2001, ECtHR). Here, the problem was that the CA had held that the Gaming Board of GB had taken a biased decision but had no power to remit it to the Board. The HRA 1998 has had a profound effect on the judicial approach in cases of judicial review, as I discuss below.

Can civil litigants be forced into ADR?

Forcing litigating parties into alternative dispute resolution 4–042
(ADR) was an unacceptable constraint on their right of access to the
courts: *Halsey v Milton Keynes General NHS Trust* [2004] EWCA Civ
576. See Chapter 12 on ADR, below.

Damages for breach of Article 6

A finding of breach of Art.6 was normally "just satisfaction" in 4–043
itself. Damages would only be awarded in exceptional circumstances: *R. (Greenfield) v SS for the Home Department* [2005] UKHL 14.

Article 7 No Punishment Without Law

Sex Offenders Register

The Court found inadmissible an action under Arts 7 and 8 chal- 4–044
lenging the Sex Offenders Register. Registration was not a "penalty"
but aimed at preventing re-offending and was not severe. The
measure pursued legitimate aims. Taking into account the gravity
of the harm that could be done to victims, the requirement to register was not disproportionate: *Adamson v UK* (ECtHR, 1999).

Release on licence

In *R. (Uttley) v SS for the Home Dept* [2003] EWCA Civ 1130, the CA 4–045
accepted that an offender's release on licence at the end of his sentence
was a harsher sentence than that originally imposed, when the regime
in place at that earlier date would have resulted in an automatic, full
remission of sentence. The CA made a declaration of incompatibility
against the offending sections of the Criminal Justice Act 1991.

Article 8 Private and Family Life

Gays in the Armed Forces

The Court considered that military investigations into the sexual- 4–046
ity of gay members of the armed forces and their subsequent dismissal were grave breaches: *Lustig-Prean and Becket v UK* and joined
applications (1999).

Transsexuals' rights

In gender reassignment cases, where applicants born as males 4–047
sought to be re-registered as females, the Court held that the
Government was under no positive duty to amend its system of
birth registration: *Sheffield and Horsham v UK* (1998) but in 2002, in *I
v U, Goodwin v UK* (ECtHR), a Grand Chamber of the Court took a
different approach, perhaps illustrating that the Convention is
organic—its interpretation will change over the years and in different circumstances. Where G had undergone gender re-assignment

surgery, it was a breach of Art.8 for the State not to recognise a change of legal gender. Since the surgery was provided by the State, this was illogical. The very essence of the Convention was respect for human dignity and freedom. It was unsatisfactory for post-operative transsexuals to live in an intermediate zone. A Home Office Report of 2000 had said that problems in a change in the law could be overcome but the UK Government had not acted on it. Since 1986, the Court had emphasised the importance of keeping the need for appropriate legal measures under review, having regard to scientific and societal developments.

There had also been a breach of Arts 8 and 12, in denying the applicants a right to marry someone the opposite of their new sex. Just because a minority of states permitted this it did not mean this fell within the margin of appreciation. The State could not bar a right to marry. This was followed in 2004 by a case attacking the NHS pension scheme, in which the ECtHR made the same point: *KB v NHS Pensions Agency*. States could prescribe the conditions for legal recognition of transsexual marriage. See also Art.12, below.

Gross indecency in private

4–048   A conviction for gross indecency under the Sexual Offences Act 1956 constituted an unnecessary interference with the right to respect for private life. Following a search of his premises, police had seized photos and videos of the applicant and other consenting men engaging in oral sex and mutual masturbation. The acts took place in the applicant's home and did not involve physical harm. There was no evidence the tapes were available for wider distribution: *ADT v UK* (ECtHR, 2000). The opposite and somewhat surprising, result was reached by a nine-judge court in *Laskey, Jaggard and Brown v UK* (1997). This involved another consenting group of homosexuals who, in private, engaged in sado-masochistic maltreatment of the genitals with nettles and staples, ritualistic beating and branding. They had been convicted under the Offences Against the Person Act 1861, which, it was agreed, was an interference in their right to respect for private life but it was carried out "in accordance with the law" and pursued a legitimate aim of "protection of health or morals". The only issue before the Court was whether the interference was "necessary in a democratic society". The Court observed that there was a significant degree of injury and wounding and the State authorities were entitled to consider the potential harm to health.

Prison correspondence

4–049   A policy that prisoners must be absent when privileged legal correspondence held in their cells was examined by prison officers was unlawful. The House of Lords reached this conclusion by applying the common law but it was supported by the Art.8(1) right to respect for correspondence: *R. v SS for the Home Dept Ex p. Daly* [2001] UKHL 26. This case is very important as the House ruled that the courts must apply a proportionality test in judicial review cases, including Human Rights cases, as proportionality is a principle of English law.

Covert surveillance

Covert surveillance of the accused, at home and in police cells, while he was suspected of planning an armed robbery, was a violation of Arts 8 and 13: *PG and JH v UK* (ECtHR, 2001). Covert surveillance is now regulated by statute.

4–050

Giving CCTV images to the media

Peck v UK (ECtHR, 2003): the disclosure to the media by Brentwood CC of closed circuit TV footage of P with a knife, without masking his face, was a breach of his Art.8 right to private life. It portrayed him as a threat in an anti-crime advertising campaign and did not show that this was, indeed, a suicide attempt. Also, the Broadcasting Standards Council, the ITC and judicial review left P without an effective remedy. Invoking Art.41, the Court awarded over 20,000 Euros in damages and costs.

4–051

Deaths in custody

The series of cases involving deaths in custody, described above, show that Art.8 is engaged, in requiring families to be fully informed and involved, in any inquest or inquiry.

4–052

Care and adoption proceedings

The 2002 case of *P, C and S v UK* involved care and adoption proceedings brought by a local authority when a mother was suspected of harming her daughter. There was a breach of Art.6 because of insufficient reasons and inadequate legal representation and a violation of Art.8, in that the applicants were prevented from effective involvement in the decisions on care and freeing for adoption.

4–053

Enforced medical treatment

Article 8 embraces the right to physical and moral integrity. In *Glass v UK* (2004), the ECtHR was satisfied that the decision of medical staff to administer diomorphine to the applicant's son, despite her objections, gave rise to an interference with his right to respect for private life and, in particular, the right to bodily integrity.

4–054

Prison visitors

The House of Lords, in *Wainwright v Home Office* [2003] UKHL 53 took a restrictive approach to the issue of privacy. Prison visitors had been strip searched in 1997 because the authorities suspected

4–055

that their relative, the prisoner, had been dealing in drugs in prison. This was a very important case, as the House held that there was no general tort of invasion of privacy at common law and Art.8 did not guarantee a right to privacy, as such. Lord Hoffman said there was nothing in the jurisprudence of the ECtHR which suggested the adoption of some high-level right of privacy.

Supermodel in rehab

4–056   The House did not depart from this principle in *Campbell v MGN* [2004] UKHL 22. This case arose from the *Daily Mirror's* disclosure that, despite her denials, supermodel Naomi Campbell was secretly attending meetings of Narcotics Anonymous. The House was split 3/2 on the result, because they differed on how to apply the law to the facts but they agreed on the law and the correct approach. "Put crudely," said Baroness Hale, "it is a prima donna celebrity against a celebrity-exploiting tabloid newspaper." Where Art.8 was engaged, the court must carry out a carefully focused and penetrating balancing exercise to reconcile the restrictions that the Art.8 and Art.10 rights impose on one another, applying the principle of proportionality. In media cases where both articles were engaged, it was necessary to conduct a parallel analysis, looking at the comparative importance of the rights being claimed in the individual case and at the justifications for interfering with or restricting each right, and applying the proportionality test to each. The majority held that, on the facts, The *Mirror* had gone too far in the details they had published.

Protecting the child of a defendant

4–057   The same reasoning was applied by the Law Lords in *In Re S (a child)* [2004] UKHL 47. They held that the press should not be restrained from publishing the identity of a defendant in a murder trial in order to protect the privacy of his child.

Publicising ASBOs

4–058   In publicising anti-social behaviour orders, publicity should be confined to what is reasonable and proportionate: *R. (on the application of Stanley, Marshall and Kelly) v Metropolitan Police Commissioner* [2004] EWHC 2229.

Gypsies

4–059   In *Chichester DC v First Secretary of State* [2004] EWCA Civ 1248, the CA ruled that the planning authority's issuing of enforcement notices requiring the removal by gypsies of mobile homes on land they had bought constituted a disproportionate interference in the gypsies' Art.8 rights.

In *Price v Leeds City Council* [2005] EWCA Civ 289, a case involving evicting gypsies from a football pitch, the CA was faced with conflicting decisions of the House of Lords and ECtHR. The CA held that that inferior courts were bound to follow the House of Lords decision. If the lower courts started following Strasbourg jurisprudence (the ECtHR) instead, chaos would follow. Pending the House of Lords hearing, councils throughout the UK left 4,000 travellers in illegal encampments.

Article 9 Freedom of Thought, Conscience and Religion

Islamic dress

The ECtHR held there to be no breach of Art.9 in a ban placed   4–060
on Islamic headscarves by the University of Istanbul. Turkey's Constitutional Court guaranteed democratic values, including the freedom of religion but restrictions could be placed on this freedom if necessary, to defend other values and principles, including secularism and equality: *Leyla Sahin v Turkey* (2004).

The CA reached the opposite conclusion in *R. (on the application of Begum) v Governors of Denbigh High School* [2005] EWCA Civ 199. The appellant, a Muslim in a school which was 79 per cent Muslim, won her right to wear a jilbab, in contravention of school uniform, which permitted pupils to wear a shalwar kameeze. The CA held that the right approach was for a school, as an emanation of the state, to start from the premise that they are limiting the pupil's rights to freedom of religion and then to consider whether the limitation was justifiable. The issue was whether it was necessary in a democratic society to place a restriction on those Muslim girls who sincerely believed they should cover themselves more comprehensively.

Corporal punishment

Although the statutory ban on corporal punishment in UK   4–061
schools was capable of interfering with Art.9 rights, Parliament was entitled to take the view that the ban was necessary in a democratic society to protect children. The claimants were parents and teachers at four independent Christian Fellowship schools: *R. (Williamson) v SS for Education and Employment* [2005] UKHL 15.

Article 10 Freedom of Expression

Government spook spilling the beans

R. v Shayler [2002] UKHL 11. The key question before the House of   4–062
Lords was whether prosecution under the Official Secrets Act complied with Art.10(2) freedom of expression. The ban on disclosures was not absolute, said the Lord Bingham, as a former member of the MI5 could make disclosures to others—the staff counsellor, a higher

113

ranking former civil servant, or the Attorney-General, police or DPP if unlawfulness was alleged. If misbehaviour or maladministration was alleged, concern could be expressed to Government ministers, or two Parliamentary committees, or one of three other security commissioners.

S argued all of these mechanisms were ineffective in practice. Lord Bingham accepted that possibility. In that case, the MI5 officer could seek authorisation to disclose to a wider audience. And whoever is called on to grant authorisation should not treat the decision as a routine or mechanical process. They should bear in mind the importance attached to the right of freedom of expression and the need for any restriction to be "necessary, responsive to a pressing social need and proportionate." If a refusal to allow disclosure were unjustified, the officer could seek judicial review.

The House relied on changes to the nature of judicial review since the HRA came into force, explained below. John Wadham, for Liberty, commented on the decision as "a real step forward".

The tension between freedom of expression and protection from defamation

4–063   In *Steel and Morris v UK*, the successful appeal by the McLibel two, discussed above, the ECtHR said the central issue on an Art.10 application was whether the interference with freedom of speech was necessary in a democratic society. The Court distinguished fact from value judgments. The Court had long held that political expression, including expression on matters of public interest required a high level of protection. In a democratic society even small and informal campaign groups, like London Greenpeace, to which the pair belonged, had to be able to carry on their activities effectively. In a campaign leaflet, a certain degree of exaggeration could be tolerated but in this case the allegations made against McDonalds were very serious and were presented as statements of fact rather than value judgments. The fact that the burden of proof was on the defendants to prove the truth of their allegations was not incompatible with Art.10. Even a large multinational had a right to defend itself and it had a competing interest in protecting its commercial success. The state was free under the margin of appreciation to provide such a remedy to the corporation but lack of procedural fairness gave rise to a breach of Art.10. Also, the damages were disproportionate.

Article 12 Right to Marry

Transsexuals
4–064   In *Bellinger v Bellinger* [2003] UKHL 21 the House of Lords ruled that a transsexual could not legally be recognised in her new gender

so her marriage was void under the Matrimonial Causes Act 1973. The House was bound by this UK statute but declared UK law to be incompatible with the Convention, Arts 8 and 12. The Government promised a Bill to give transsexuals legal recognition. This was done via the Gender Recognition Act 2004. The Human Rights Unit pages of the DCA website explain the implications of this for those affected.

Article 13 Effective Remedy

Deaths in custody again

In a number of the cases above, such as those arising out of deaths   **4–065** in custody, the European Court also held there was a breach of this article, because the inquests held were an ineffective remedy.

Article 14 Prohibition against Discrimination

Widowers

Bereaved fathers were equally entitled to the "widowed mother's   **4–066** allowance", conceded the UK, in *Cornwell v UK* (ECtHR, 2000). In the long term, the Government dealt with this problem by introducing the Welfare Reform and Pensions Act 1999.

6. The Approach of English Courts to Convention Rights and Interpretation of Domestic Law

Does the Convention Allow Judges to Make Law?

Prior to the implementation of the HRA 1998, the Government   **4–067** sought to stop fears that the courts would be swamped with claims by pointing out that the Convention had been in force in Scotland since May 1999 and 98 per cent of challenges had failed. There was a great deal of speculation in the Parliamentary debates on the Human Rights Bill in 1998 and in law journals as to how the courts might or should approach the Convention.

Emmerson is reported as predicting "a major shift of power from Parliament to judges. They will, in effect, be able to rewrite sections of Acts by reading into them words that are not there and by massaging away any potential conflicts with the Constitution." (*The Times*, November 26, 1998). Nevertheless, in 1999, the House of Lords was swift to point out, in *Kebilene*, that the Convention gave way to Parliamentary sovereignty. In the words of Lord Steyn:

"It is crystal clear that the carefully and subtly drafted Human Rights Act 1998 preserves the principle of Parliamentary sovereignty. In a case of incompatibility, which cannot be avoided by interpretation under section 3 (1), the courts may not disapply legislation. The court may merely issue a declaration of incompatibility which then gives rise to a power to take remedial action: see section 10."

As for common law remedies, Lord Chancellor Irvine said in Parliament:

"In my view, the courts may not act as legislators and grant new remedies for infringement of Convention rights unless the common law itself enables them to develop new rights and remedies. I believe that the true view is that the courts will be able to develop the common law by relying on the existing domestic principles of trespass, nuisance, copyright, confidence and the like, to fashion a common law right to privacy."

4–068   A clear exposition of the approach of the courts in the years immediately following the importation of Convention rights in 2000 was set out by Aileen Kavanagh in 2004. She made the following observations, which I paraphrase here:

1. Section 3 does not require any ambiguity before it comes into operation: *R. v Lambert* [2001] UKHL 37.
2. It is only a rule of interpretation, not legislation, according to many judges.
3. She argues that s.3 does require judicial law-making but it is much more limited in scope and effect than law-making by the legislature.
4. The way judges interpret s.3 and the word "possible" will affect their interpretive approach.
5. The interpretive issues posed by the Convention cannot be resolved linguistically. For instance, there is no point in using a dictionary to determine whether the right to life in Art.2 includes a right to death. Lord Bingham said in *HM AG for Scotland v Brown* (PC, 2000) that the ECtHR had shown a willingness to imply terms into the Convention when necessary.
6. If judges merely declared the law, all they could do in some cases was to say that the HRA is indeterminate on the matter.
7. Broad evaluative terms in the Convention necessitate the judges engaging in moral reasoning—about what is fair, for instance, under Art.6.
8. Interpretation combines applying and making the law.
9. Where there is no previous case law on the point, judges are required to make the law.
10. Judges are also under a duty to arrive at a just decision in the instant case.

116

11. HRA case law shows that even where judges are engaged in innovative decision-making, they are still concerned to preserve continuity, authority and stability to the greatest possible degree.
12. When judges make law under s.3, they do so by interpretive reasoning.
13. Legislators, on the other hand, are entitled to create new frameworks or radically alter existing ones.
14. Much judicial law-making is by way of filling in the gaps in legislation and they will read in words in order to make legislation Convention compliant but they cannot rewrite a whole statute.
15. The fact that judicial law-making is incremental places limits on the ability or willingness of the judges to reform the law, as in *Bellinger v Bellinger*, above, where Lord Nicholls said the recognition of gender assignment for the purposes of marriage is part of a wider problem which should be considered as a whole so it was preferable to leave this to Parliament.
16. Judges are trained to resolve legal issues and are ill-equipped to make decisions about general policy.
17. A "possible" meaning of legislation is not necessarily its ordinary meaning, nor is it unlimited.
18. Where there is an outright contradiction between the words of a statute and Convention rights, then judges cannot "read or give effect" to those terms. Lord Steyn, in *R. v A*, below, pointed out that Parliament rejected the New Zealand legislative model whereby judges find a "reasonable interpretation."

An Example from 2001 and a 2004 Case

By May 2001, the House of Lords was already asked to construe a new statute which appeared to conflict with Convention rights. This is a landmark precedent because it demonstrated how the House was prepared to interpret and apply their own duty under s.3 of the HRA. The case was *R. v A* [2001] UKHL 25. The House had to construe s.41 of the Youth Justice and Criminal Evidence Act 1999, restricting evidence and questioning about the victim's sexual history. In this case, a man accused of rape wanted to bring evidence of his previous sexual relationship with the complainant, to support his defence that she had consented. In a pre-trial ruling, the judge had ruled this out because of the 1999 Act but considered that his ruling breached Art.6. The law lords applied their interpretive duty under s.3 of the HRA and gave proper regard to the protection of the complainant but effectively "read into" the statute protection for the accused under Art.6. They told the trial judge he could proceed with the case in the light of their ruling—in other words, telling him

4–069

to make a bold interpretation and allow this evidence in for the sake of protecting the accused under Art.6. I shall analyse Lord Steyn's interpretive methods sequentially, with my explanations italicised. It is well worth reading his judgment. Like all reports of the Law Lords' judgments, is available, free on the Parliament website. Click on "judicial business" then "judgments".

1. *He plunged straight into a purposive construction of the 1999 Act*: in the criminal courts, outmoded beliefs about women and sexual matters lingered on. *Referring to approaches in another common law country*, in Canadian jurisprudence, they had been referred to as discredited twin myths "that unchaste women were more likely to consent to intercourse and in any event, were less worthy of belief".

2. *Statement of moral principle*: "such generalised, stereotyped and unfounded prejudices ought to have no place in our legal system". It resulted in an absurdly low conviction rate in rape cases. The Sexual Offences (Amendment) Act 1976 did not achieve its object.

3. *Conclusion on purpose of the 1999 Act*: "(t)here was a serious mischief to be corrected".

4. *Statement of problem before the House*: the blanket exclusion of prior sexual history between the complainant and the accused posed an acute problem of proportionality.

5. *Applying what he called* "common sense": a prior relationship between accused and accuser might be relevant to the issue of consent in rape.

6. *Statement of principle of interpretive duty, based on his interpretation of the court's duty under the HRA 1998*: when a question arose as to whether, in a criminal statute, Parliament had adopted a legislative scheme which made an excessive inroad into the right to a fair trial, the court was qualified to make its own judgment and had to do so.

7. *Application of ECtHR jurisprudence*: it was well established that the guarantee of a fair trial under Art.6 was absolute. A conviction obtained in breach could not stand. The only balancing permitted was in respect of what the concept of a fair trial entailed. Applying proportionality, in determining whether a limitation was arbitrary or excessive, a court should ask itself whether:

   (i) the legislative objective was sufficiently important to justify limiting a fundamental right;
   (ii) the measures designed to meet that objective were rationally connected to it, and

> (iii) the means used to impair the right or freedom were no more than necessary to accomplish the objective.

8. Two processes of interpretation had to be distinguished.

> 1. Ordinary (traditional, English) methods of purposive and contextual interpretation might yield ways of minimising the "exorbitant breadth" of the section, ie the blanket ban on questioning a woman about her sexual history.
> 2. The interpretative obligation of HRA, s.3(1). (*i.e.*, so far as possible, primary legislation had to be given effect in a way compatible with the Convention).

9. *He applied the first method, looked at the wording of the section and relevant domestic cases on evidence prior to the 1998 Act and concluded this could not solve the problem.*

10. *Interpreting s.3 of the 1998 Act:* he cited *Kebilene* (1999). The HRA s.3 obligation went far beyond the rule which enabled the courts to take the Convention into account in resolving any ambiguity in a legislative provision. Parliament specifically rejected the legislative model requiring a reasonable interpretation. It placed on a court a duty to strive to find a possible interpretation compatible with Convention rights. It was much more radical than the ordinary method of interpretation which permitted a departure from language of an Act to avoid absurd consequences. In accordance with the will of Parliament, *in enacting the HRA*, it would sometimes be necessary to adopt an interpretation which linguistically might appear strained. The techniques to be used would not only involve the reading down of express language in a statute but also the implication of provisions.

11. *Interpreting s.4 of the HRA 1998*: a declaration of incompatibility was a measure of last resort.

12. *Conclusion, implying Parliamentary intent*: the legislature, if alerted to the problem, would not have wished to deny the accused the right to put forward a full defence by advancing probative material. It was possible to read into s.41 of the 1999 Act the implied provision that evidence or questioning required to ensure a fair trial under Art.6 should not be inadmissible.

13. *Implications for future trials*: sometimes logically relevant evidence of sexual experience might be admitted but where the line was to be drawn was up to the trial judge.

The same bold approach, demonstrating that the courts are prepared to read words into a statute, effecting quite substantial   **4–070** rewriting, was adopted by the CA and then the House of Lords in *Ghaidan v Godin-Mendoza* [2001] EWCA Civ 1533 and [2004] UKHL 30. M., the homosexual partner of the deceased tenant of a flat, appealed from a decision that he could not be awarded a statutory tenancy under the Rent Act 1977. He could not qualify as a "spouse" under the Act and thus did not enjoy the benefit granted to an unmarried heterosexual partner in the same position. The Court held that, in cases involving Art.14, four questions must be asked:

1. Do the facts fall within the ambit of one or more of the substantive rights under the Convention?
2. If so, was there different treatment as respects that right between a complainant and other persons put forward for comparison?
3. Were the chosen comparators in an analogous situation to the complainant's situation?
4. If so, did the difference have an objective and reasonable justification? Did it pursue a legitimate aim and bear a reasonable relationship of proportionality to the aim sought to be achieved?

Deference to Parliament has a minor role to play, said the Court of Appeal, where issues of constitutional importance, such as discrimination, arise. Discrimination on grounds of sexual orientation was now an impermissible ground on the same level as any others under Art.14, and s.3 of the Human Rights Act required that words should be read into the Rent Act. The words defining "spouse" as "his or her wife or husband" should be read to mean "as if they were his or her wife or husband". In the House of Lords, it was held that s.3 was the core remedy provided by the HRA and the s.4 declaration of incompatibility should only be a last resort. As long as it did not go against the grain of the legislative measure, there was no limit to the words that could be read in or out of a legislative measure.

The House of Lords ruling is very important, since it is the latest case, at my time of writing, 2005, to set down guidelines on interpretation. Notice that the House seems to balk at the idea of the courts laying down an entire legal framework. Where the CA had effectively created a whole new scheme of "starred milestones" in local authority care plans in child care cases, the House overruled them. This judicial innovation passed well beyond the boundaries of interpreting the Children Act 1989. Such a scheme would have had far reaching ramifications for local authorities and their care of children. It was likely to have ramifications for the allocation of scarce resources. These were matters for Parliament: *In Re S, In Re W and others* [2002] UKHL 10.

The Impact of the Convention on the Judicial Approach in Judicial Review Cases

Notice that the new approach that the courts are required to take, of evaluating *proportionality* of the State's action's replaces the test of "reasonableness" in judicial review cases. This was made clear by the House of Lords in *Daly* [2001] UKHL 26. The High Court's traditional power to review the legality of executive action and decisions of the lower courts was developed and refined by the courts in the twentieth century. The courts declined to examine the merits of a decision, provided it had been taken procedurally correctly and provided the decision-maker had taken account of all relevant factors and decided rationally. This was known as the *Wednesbury* test of irrationality or unreasonableness, based on the test laid down in *Associated Provincial Picture Houses v Wednesbury Corporation* (1948). In *Kingsley v UK* (2001), the ECtHR held that this was inadequate. The reviewing court should not confine itself to examining the quality of the decision making process and not the merits. In *Daly* and many other cases, the House of Lords has made it clear that the required test for judicial review, since the HRA has been in force is one of proportionality. The reviewing court must ask itself whether:

4–071

1. the objective is sufficiently important to justify limiting a fundamental right;
2. the measures designed to meet the objective are rationally connected to it and
3. the means used are no more than necessary to accomplish the objective.

Other Points on Interpretation

Pepper v Hart

In *Wilson v SS for Trade and Industry* [2003] UKHL 40, the House of Lords held that when the court was require to evaluate legislation under the HRA, it was entitled to look at ministerial statements to determine the policy behind an Act. Lord Nicholls applied *Pepper v Hart*, saying that it removed from the law an irrational self-imposed judicial rule against consulting parliamentary material as an external aid to interpretation.

4–072

The Human Rights Act is not retrospective

In the 2004 case of *In Re McKerr*, which is discussed above, under Art.2, the House held that it was now settled that the Human Rights

4–073

Act was not retrospective. Some earlier cases had failed to distinguish between rights created by the Convention and rights created by the Act by reference to the Convention. The former were not part of this country's law. The latter were. See the discussion of case law on the presumption of innocence, under Art.6, above.

The impact on judges' approach to non-Convention cases

4–074   The language and concepts of the Convention have entered some judges' thinking in statutory interpretation in cases which have nothing to do with Human Rights, in the same way that Community law has affected interpretation in non-Community cases. For instance in *Warborough Investments Ltd v S Robinson & Sons (Holdings) Ltd* [2003] EWCA Civ 751, discussed in Chapter 12 on alternatives, below, Parker L.J. used the phrase "margin of appreciation" to mean degree of latitude, in allowing discretion to an arbitrator. The phrase comes from the Convention, referring to the degree of freedom allowed to a domestic state in applying the Convention.

7. Who Can Bring an Action and Against Whom Can Actions be Brought?

Who Can Join in?

4–075   The White Paper proposing the Human Rights Act suggested "bringing rights home" to enable people to enforce their rights in our courts, rather than having to go to the ECtHR in Strasbourg, as they had to do until 2000. Naturally the person deprived of their right can bring an action, usually in the High Court, for judicial review, but other interest groups and pressure groups would like to join in on public interest test cases. This point was made by a JUSTICE/Public Law Project working party in 1996. The Civil Procedure Rules were amended to enable "any person" to apply to file evidence or make representations at the judicial review hearing. In *Re Northern Ireland Human Rights Commission* [2002] UKHL 25 the House of Lords welcomed third party intervention where such a body could assist the court or there was a danger that an important principle of law had not been brought to the attention of the court. The Commission was allowed to intervene in *Amin* (2003), discussed above, under Art.2, as was Stonewall, the gay rights group, in *Ghaidan v Mendoza* (2002), above. It was accepted by the House of Lords in *R. (Rusbridger) v Attorney-General* [2003] UKHL 38 that the courts were prepared to grant a declaration, to clarify the law, where no wrong had been alleged.

Does the Human Rights Act have a "Horizontal" Effect?

As for the persons against whom an action can be taken, the Act   4–076
does not explain "public bodies" but it includes central and local
government departments, non-departmental public bodies and the
courts and tribunals. Section 6(3)(b) of the Act provides that it shall
be unlawful for a private person exercising a public function to act
in a way incompatible with a Convention right. There have been
many weighty academic articles on whether the Act provides rights
against private bodies. This debate is fuelled by the ambiguous and
cryptic nature of the Act itself. If you read the wording of the statute
you can see this for yourself. On the one hand, as I pointed out
above, s.3 requires primary and subordinate legislation to be read
as far as possible in a way which is compatible with Convention
rights but this instruction is not limited to public authorities or just
the courts. It appears to apply to all of us. Under s.2, courts and tribunals must take into account ECtHR jurisprudence. The
Government could have specifically excluded private parties from
the scope of the Act, as other jurisdictions have done but did not.
On the other hand, ss.6 and 7 only allow challenge to actions of
public authorities, generally, with the exception of any person exercising "functions of a public nature". We are not helped by the statements made by the Lord Chancellor who sponsored the Bill through
the House of Lords. In the second reading, on the illegality of contravening a Convention right he said:

> "We decided first of all that a provision of this kind should apply
> only to public authorities . . . and not to private individuals . . .
> The Convention had its origins in a desire to protect people from
> the misuse of power by the State, rather than from the actions of
> private individuals."

On the other hand he said:

> "We have taken the view that . . . excluding Convention consid-
> erations altogether from cases between individuals . . . would
> have to be justified. We do not think that would be justifiable; nor
> indeed do we think that it would be practicable" (cited in a
> JUSTICE bulletin, autumn 1998).

Dawn Oliver points out that, by 2004, the case law on this point
is very confusing. She criticises the approach taken in some cases
and acknowledges that there are academics who differ from her
view. Nevertheless, she rightly points out that "public functions",
the phrase used in some cases and articles, do not equate to

"functions of a public nature". Public authorities are bound by the Act in all that they do, even when performing acts of a private nature. What is much more unclear and rendered worse by the courts is whether liability arises when a private contractor is carrying out work contracted for by a public authority, such as gardening or cleaning. These, she suggests, are functions of a private nature. The private contractors enjoy Convention rights of their own which have to be balanced against the rights of the recipients of those services. The ECtHR gives governments a wide margin of appreciation on these matters and so does not help in interpretation. She argues that a broad interpretation could encourage litigation between private parties. It would create legal uncertainty and have negative implications for many charitable or not-for-profit organisations, providing services for disadvantaged people, such as the disabled, the elderly and the homeless. For these reasons, she is diametrically opposed to the suggestion in the seventh report of the Joint Parliamentary Committee on Human Rights (2003–4) that a broader approach should be taken by the courts. Many academics have expressed opinions on the broader issue of whether Convention rights apply "horizontally" between private parties. At one extreme was the late Sir William Wade. He took the view that the individual only had to plead that their Convention right had been violated and if the court agreed, it had a duty to enforce those rights. On the other hand Sir Richard Buxton argued that the Act did nothing to create private rights. A full examination of these academic opinions is beyond the scope of this text on the English legal system. Wider discussion can be found in textbooks and articles on public law.

8. Evaluations of the Act's Impact

4–077   Lord Irvine, in a November 2002 speech, said the courts had not dissolved into chaos; there was not a politicised judiciary or the inauguration of the rule of lawyers. We had developed a domestic "margin of appreciation". The courts recognised that, in some areas, Parliament and the Government are better placed to make judgments. The Convention had reinvigorated the common law and "legal reasoning applied here carries weight in Stasbourg–as we hoped it would when drafting the Bill."

John Wadham and Rachel Taylor, of Liberty, thought our courts had, however, been too reticent. They left it to the ECtHR to develop Convention jurisprudence, as indicated by the number of domestic judgments reversed by the Court. Nevertheless, since they wrote this in 2002, Liberty has welcomed decisions such as *A (FC) v SS for the*

Home [2004] UKHL 56, on terrorist suspects, described under Art.5, above.

Lord Chief Justice Woolf, in a 2002 speech said of those who found the Act intrinsically objectionable, that if they rejected its values, they were rejecting the standards of Western society. "I find their attitude unacceptable in the 21st century". Speaking at the ECtHR in January 2003, he said the Convention had had a "remarkably smooth transition into English law". English lawyers and judges felt "instinctively at home with Strasbourg jurisprudence . . . On the framework provided by the Articles of the Convention, it appeared to our judges that the judges of the Strasbourg Court by their decisions had been extremely creative in very much a common law manner: developing the law by giving pragmatic decisions on the facts of the cases that came before them."

LCD sponsored research, by John Raine and Clive Walker, pub- **4–078** lished in October 2002, showed that, in the first 18 months, anticipated problems, such as a large increase in court business, had not materialised. The requirement for magistrates to give reasons had added an average of 15 minutes onto a case. (The LCD is now the Department for Constitutional Affairs).

The Human Rights pages on the DCA website disclose that over 10 declarations of incompatibility had been made by 2004. It explains the outcomes. A further five had been made and overturned on appeal. Of course, there have been many outcomes of the decisions of the ECtHR, as can be seen from the analysis of case law above.

On the other hand, politicians, according to Danny Nicol, do not share the view of some judges, typified by Sir John Laws, that the Convention embodies "values which no democratic politician could honestly contest". Parliamentary debates on such controversial areas as terrorism and asylum, during 2000–3 demonstrate that "the more 'fundamental' the rights at stake, the fiercer the desire of politicians to preserve their right to have the final say". They were far from being willing participants in nurturing the rights culture.

Nevertheless, the Joint Committee on Human Rights has been **4–079** very proactive in drawing parliamentarians' attention to human rights issues. It decided to scrutinise all Bills. The Committee's legal adviser, Professor David Feldman told the Statute Law Society, in January 2003, that the concept of human rights was gaining influence at the policy and drafting stages. Fewer Bills lacked safeguards than in 2001 and government departments were better able to respond the questions on human rights.

On the negative side, however, the Audit Commission reported that by October 2003, more than half of all public bodies in England

and Wales had still not adopted a strategy for human rights. DCA Minister, David Lammy reacted impatiently, in 2004 "It is tragic and pathetic that some public authorities see human rights as a matter for their legal departments and no-one else".

In May 2004, the Government published a White Paper proposing a Commission for Equality and Human Rights (CEHR). The CEHR will be responsible for challenging discrimination across society and for promoting human rights. This followed a call for such a national commission by the UN Human Rights Committee, in 2001.

9. The Dramatic Effect of Article 6: Repositioning the Judiciary in the UK Constitution

4–080   The most radical consequence of the importation of the Convention into UK law was, however, constitutional reform to the role of Lord Chancellor, the Law Lords and the rest of the judiciary, effected by the Constitutional Reform Act 2005. The Act originated in a 2003 announcement by the New Labour Government that they intended to make sweeping constitutional reforms. They announced that they would abolish the 1400 year old office of Lord Chancellor, convert the Law Lords into a Supreme Court, reform the system of judicial appointments and consider abolishing Queen's Counsel. Interested parties, including the judiciary were, to say the least, taken aback by such radical announcements because they were presented as decisions, as a *fait accompli*, without prior consultation, or any forewarning. The architect of previous constitutional reforms, the HRA 1998 and the reconstruction of the House of Lords, Lord Chancellor Irvine, had recently dismissed suggestions for these further reforms so he had to go. On the same day as the announcement, Cabinet was reshuffled and Lord Falconer replaced Lord Irvine as Lord Chancellor, his Department being renamed the Department of Constitutional Affairs.

For those of us who had watched politics very closely, however, the announcements seemed to be an acceptance of the inevitable, rather than a threatening shock. It had become apparent that tripartite role of Lord Chancellor, holding significant power in all three organs of government, was untenable, in the context of the Convention. A series of cases had made it clear that it was unacceptable, under Art.6 (fair trial) for a member of the executive (government) to sit as a judge, casting severe doubt over the Lord Chancellor's position. Academics were swift to draw this inference (and some of us had lectured for decades on the problematic concentration of governmental power in the hands of the Lord Chancellor). Then two outspoken Law Lords, Bingham and Steyn, repeatedly said in well-publicised speeches and in writing, that the Lord Chancellor's position was an unacceptable breach of the separation of powers, under the Convention and that the Law Lords should move out of Parliament and into a Supreme Court. It seemed to me that the writing was on the wall for the office of Lord Chancellor in spring 2003, when the Council of Europe made it crystal clear that it was a flagrant breach of Art.6.

To tell the story in a little more detail, the first crucial Art.6 case, as Lord Bingham saw it, was *Findlay v UK*, described above, in relation to courts-martial. In his 2002 speech, he cited the ECtHR:

> "In order to establish whether a tribunal can be considered as "independent" regard must be had inter alia to the manner of appointment of its members and their term of office, the existence of guarantees against outside pressures and the question whether the body presents an appearance of independence".

Applying this reasoning, the role of a Scottish temporary sheriff was successfully challenged before the Judicial Committee of the Privy Council, in *Starrs v Ruxton* (2000). Lord Reed said that the importation of the Convention had effected "a very important shift in thinking about the constitution". It was inadequate for Convention rights to depend on political convention (habit). "The Convention guarantees the protection of those rights through legal processes, rather than political processes." As a consequence of this Scottish case, Lord Chancellor Irvine felt obliged to abolish the position of assistant recorder in the English legal system.

Crucially, the dual role of the Bailiff of Guernsey, as legislator and judge, was successfully challenged before the ECtHR in *McGonnell v UK* (2000). The Bailiff's role was directly paralleled by the Lord Chancellor so at this point it became clear to academic and other human rights lawyers that his problematic role would have to be scrutinised, as would the position of the law lords in Parliament. The ECtHR reaffirmed the same principle in *Kleyn v Netherlands*, in May 2003, the month before the government's announcement on constitutional reform. *McGonnell* was cited extensively in the Scottish Court of Session judgment in *Davidson v Scottish Ministers* (*No.2*) [2004] UKHL 34. The issue here was the legality of a Scottish decision of a panel of judges which included a member of the House of Lords who had been directly involved in the passage of the legislation central to the decision. The decision was overturned. Notice also that the separation of powers has moved increasingly

4–081

to the forefront of Convention challenges to institutions in the English legal system, such as the Parole Board, as can be seen in the case law outlined above. Note especially the observations of the House of Lords in the 2002 case of *Anderson*, above.

Advocating a Supreme Court in May 2002, an argument he had already made in a 2001 speech and elsewhere, the senior Law Lord, Lord Bingham set out his reasons and the various alternative models for a new court. I examine these in Chapter 6, on civil courts, below. Also speaking in 2002, another Law Lord, Johan Steyn, was much more strident. Most of his attack was directed to the Lord Chancellor's position, although his speech was entitled "The Case for a Supreme Court." Lord Steyn, a South African, took a comparative view, examining the functional separation of powers, or lack of it, in the UK, in the context of the rest of the democratic world.

"In insulating the judicial function from the legislative and executive functions separation of powers in turn rests of the principles of judicial independence and the rule of law . . . But nowhere outside Britain, even in democracies with the weakest forms of separation of powers, is the independence of the judiciary potentially compromised in the eyes of citizens by relegating the status of the highest court to the position of a subordinate part of the legislature. And nowhere outside Britain is the independence of the judiciary potentially compromised in the eyes of citizens by permitting a serving politician to sit as a judge, let alone in the highest court which fulfils constitutional functions."

He examined in some depth the concept of separation of powers and the reasons for it, dismissing British defences of the status quo. His brilliant exposition of the concept and the problematic confusion of powers in the UK is well worth reading and explains elegantly and in detail why the Government were forced to attempt to unravel some of those powers, in the Constitutional Reform Act 2005.

"Justice Brandeis said that the separation of powers serves, not to promote efficiency but to prevent the exercise of arbitrary power. . . . For protection, citizens must look to the courts. Tensions between these ideals arise from time to time. The executive and the judiciary are not on the same side. The stability of democratic institutions ultimately depends on public confidence"

4–082   Within a year of these two powerful Law Lords expressing highly publicised disquiet, so did the Parliamentary Assembly of the Council of Europe. They published a report called *Office of the Lord*

Chancellor in the constitutional system of the United Kingdom (Doc. 9798, a report to their Committee on Legal Affairs and Human Rights), in April 2003 saying,

"Whilst the office of Lord Chancellor may be venerable and as yet remain unchallenged before the European Court of Human Rights, continuation of the current system creates real problems of lack of transparency and thus of lack of respect for the rule of law".

In the previous month, the author of this report, Erik Jurgens, Rapporteur to that committee, had appeared before the newly formed House of Commons Committee on the Lord Chancellor's Department. He was polite enough not to use the word hypocrisy and recognised that the ancient British constitution was venerated but his evidence shows exasperation at the British failure to understand the requirements of the separation of powers.

"Every day in my Council of Europe work I am in confrontation with new democracies from central and Eastern Europe, who I tell they should not do certain things, and they say, 'What about the British? They have these appointed Members of Parliament in the upper House. They have a Lord Chancellor' . . . I think it would be very good to show we are not only making remarks about the new democracies from Eastern Europe but also willing to look at our own systems and see if they really are functioning in a proper way . . . (and he responded to committee members who defended the Lord Chancellor's position in government and judiciary): . . . If you say he is a link between the Cabinet and the judges I think you are saying something very dangerous. In both directions it is dangerous. I do not think judges should say anything to the Cabinet except in public and I do not think the Cabinet should say anything to the judges except in public because transparency is just about the most important point of the whole thing. I do not like the idea of a Lord Chancellor or any other member of the Cabinet speaking to judges privately and if that is happening then it should stop immediately . . . The thing we are trying to fight for in all of Europe is the transparency of the difference between the judicature, the judiciary and the executive."

He pointed out that countries who had been on the other side in World War II had made great efforts to develop new constitutions in compliance with the Convention. It was time to review the old, unchanged constitutions. Mr Jurgens' evidence was broadcast on the media. On hearing his words, I realised the Lord Chancellor's role would have to be dismantled. Only three years earlier, New

Labour had imported the Convention. They could hardly be seen to be ignoring its very guardian, the Council of Europe. Ironically, the minister who had overseen importation of the Convention via the Human Rights Act was the Lord Chancellor himself. As he was not persuaded of the need to give away his powers, Prime Minister Blair had no alternative but to replace him.

I examine the consequences for the Law Lords in Chapter 6 on the civil courts and the consequences for the Lord Chancellor and judiciary in Chapter 14 on judges, below.

BIBLIOGRAPHY

4–083   G. Bindman, "Contempt of the European Court", *New Statesman*, November 15, 1996.

Lord Bingham of Cornhill, "A New Supreme Court for the United Kingdom", May 1, 2003, The Constitution Unit, University College, London, *http://www.ucl.ac.uk/constitution-unit* and see his 2001 speech "The Evolving Constitution", Law Society, Chancery Lane, London Thursday, October 4, 2001.

The Court's judgments: *www.echr.coe.int*

DCA press release 59/04, *Lammy's human rights wakeup call to public authorities*.

S. Fredman, "Judging Democracy: The role of the Judiciary under the HRA 1998" (2000) 53 C.L.P. 98.

R. Hudson, (1996) 146 N.L.J. 1029.

A. Kavanagh, "The Elusive Divide between Interpretation and Legislation under the Human Rights Act 1998" (2004) 24 (2) *Oxford Journal of Legal Studies* 259.

Lord Chancellor Irvine's 1999 Paul Sieghart lecture is on the DCA website *www.dca.gov.uk* under "publications" and "ministers' speeches".

Lord Irvine, "The Human Rights Act Two Years On: An Analysis", speech delivered on November 1, 2002, reproduced at [2003] P. L. 308 (also available on *Westlaw*).

R. Masterman, "*A Supreme Court for the United Kingdom*: two steps forward, but one step back for judicial independence" [2004] P.L. 48 (also on *Westlaw*). See now his 2004 book, *Democracy Through Law*.

D. Nicol, "The Human Rights Act and the politicians" (2004) 24 *Legal Studies* 451.

D. Oliver, "Functions of a Public Nature under the Human Rights Act" [2004] P.L. 329, also on *Westlaw*.

A. O'Neill, "Judicial Politics and the Judicial Committee: the Devolution Jurisprudence of the Privy Council" (2001) 64 M.L.R 603.

A. T. H. Smith, "The Human Rights Act and the Criminal Lawyer: The Constitutional Context" [1999] Crim. L.R. 251 and see other articles in the same issue.

K. Starmer and others, articles in *The Times*, October 2, 2001, reviewing the Act's first year.

(Lord) Johan Steyn, "The Case for a Supreme Court" (2002) 118 L.Q.R. 392 (also on *Westlaw*).

A. Wade, "Forces need final push to match civil justice", *The Times*, January 25, 2005.

J. Wadham and R. Taylor, "The Human Rights Act two years on" (2002) 152 N.L.J. 1485.

Supplements to *The Times*, September 26, 2000 and October 2, 2001.

R. White, *The English Legal System in Action*, (1999).

Lord Woolf, "Human Rights: Have the Public Benefited?", speech, October 15, 2002.

FURTHER READING AND SOURCES FOR UPDATING THIS CHAPTER

Online updates to this book: *http://www.sweetandmaxwell.co.uk/academic/updates/darbyshire/index.html*

The Department of Constitutional Affairs: *www.dca.gov.uk*. See People's Rights/Human Rights and press releases.   **4–084**

European Court of Human Rights: *www.echr.coe.int*. See Annual Report, press releases and judgments.

Regular updates on human rights in *Legal Action* and the *New Law Journal* (N.L.J. is also on *Lexis*).

The European Human Rights Law Review (which is also on *Westlaw*).

5. Law Reform and the Changing Legal System

1. The Inevitability of Change

The one certainty in the study of any area of law is that it will be **5–001** characterised by change. New governments want to make their mark and a government with a powerful majority like New Labour will succeed in having most of the Bills implementing their policy passed by Parliament. Every branch of the law, together with the legal system which lies behind it, is constantly undergoing change. Indeed, in recent years, the complaint has been made that Parliament is choking with the sheer volume of legislation it is expected to scrutinise. This makes life difficult for the rest of us, keeping up with change. As can be seen from a comparison of this book with the 1996 edition, most of it has been rewritten.

To the piles of domestic legislation we can barely digest, we have to add Community legislation: Treaties and Regulations over which the UK Parliament has no control but bind all of us and Directives, most of which the UK Parliament enacts through statutory instrument.

Equally, the higher courts develop the common law and change the law. Judges in the House of Lords and Court of Appeal have, for instance, been forced to change their approach to statutory interpretation and become much more proactive, by the Human Rights Act 1998 and our membership of the EU, as can be seen from the previous two chapters. There are today more judges and more cases to be tried, than ever before. Inevitably, the more complex the society, the more complex the law and the more complicated the cases which arise.

There is substantial and constant campaigning by pressure **5–002** groups like JUSTICE, Liberty, the Statute Law Reform Society and the Legal Action Group, as well as the Bar Council, the Law Society and specialised interest groups, for changes in the legal system.

Lord Justice Carnwarth said, "Everyone nowadays regards law reform as 'a good thing'. It was not always so. It was a proud boast of Lord Bathurst the 18th century Lord Chancellor, that when he left office, he had left English law exactly as he had found it". How much easier the lawyer's life must have been in those days.

2. Methods of Law Reform

Parliament

5–003   Most Acts result from Government Bills, sponsored by the relevant Minister. The Minister, in turn, will be under pressure from government colleagues. Education legislation, for example, will be introduced by the Secretary of State for Education and will have been prepared initially by that department. Only a very few private Members of Parliament succeed each year in getting a Public Act on to the Statute Book. This is because parliamentary time is so valuable that the Government tends to demand almost all of it. Often the pressure for the legislation has come from interest groups, unions or pressure groups. Some, like the CBI, are very powerful organisations with wide national support but sometimes pressure from a small organisation can have the desired effect.

Very often legislation will be introduced following the report of a Royal Commission or an ad hoc review body. Royal Commissions may be established to consider law reform in a specific field and they are given limited terms of reference. They are disbanded once they have reported. For example, the Royal Commission on Criminal Justice (1991–3) and Lord Woolf's scrutiny of civil procedure resulted in significant changes in civil and criminal procedure, as we can see from Chapters 9 and 10, below. The report of a lone civil servant, Martin Narey, in his 1997 *Review of Delay in the Criminal Justice System* resulted in the enactment of large chunks of the Crime and Disorder Act 1998. Reforms of the court structure and criminal procedure are coming into effect as I write this book, in 2005, as a result of Lord Justice Auld's *Review of the Criminal Courts of England and Wales* (2001). There are many more examples throughout this book.

The Judiciary

5–004   Judges, whilst being bound by precedent, can nevertheless effect quite dramatic changes in the law through the medium of statutory interpretation and reinterpretation of the common law. This happened in 1991 when the lower courts and finally the House of Lords abolished the rule that a husband cannot be guilty of raping his wife: *R. v R.* As I have tried to demonstrate in Chapter 4, above, by reading words into statutes and boldly extending the ambit of statutory interpretation, the House of Lords has extended people's Convention rights.

Ostensibly, judges are not concerned with law reform but it is not uncommon for them to draw attention to anomalies and to call for change and I gave examples of this in examining case law, in Chapter 2, above. An example occurred in *R. v Kai-Whitewind* [2005] EWCA Crim 1092, where the CA highlighted defects in the law on infanticide and complained that it was unsatisfactory and outdated. Also, the Law Lords, retired Law Lords, the Lord Chief Justice and other senior judges make public speeches calling for reform of the law or the legal system. Many of these are available on the website of the Department of Constitutional Affairs. Senior judges have often spoken in law reform debates in the House of Lords. As well as contributing to the debates on constitutional reform, from 2003, they turned out in force in the debate on the Human Rights Bill. In the debate on the Crime and Disorder Bill 1998, Lord Chief Justice Bingham made a powerful speech on justices' clerks' powers, which made the Government think again. In the late 1980s, Lord Chief Justice Lane and others made provocative speeches opposing Lord Chancellor Mackay's proposals to take away the Bar's monopoly on rights of audience. This and the famous judges' "strike", in 1989 resulted in such a watering down of the Courts and Legal Services Act 1990 that almost no progress was made in opening up rights of audience in court in the 1990s, a situation which in turn was deplored by Lord Chancellor Irvine in a 1998 consultation paper on rights of audience. Judges also have the Judges' Council as a vehicle for discussion of administrative and legislative proposals. For example, they submitted comments on the consultation papers on constitutional reform, published in 2003.

The Law Commission—a Story of Frustration and Wasted Taxpayers' Money

The Law Commission is an independent body established in 1965   **5–005** to keep the law of England and Wales under review "with a view to its systematic development and reform, including in particular the codification of such law, the elimination of anomalies, the repeal of obsolete and unnecessary enactments, the reduction of the number of separate enactments and generally the simplification and modernisation of the law".

The commissioners are distinguished lawyers seconded full-time from their employment for a five-year period. The chairperson is always a senior judge. The others are barristers, solicitors, judges or academics. Despite criticism, there are no laypeople. They have a secretary and about 20 members of the Government Legal Service, four or five Parliamentary Counsel, to draft Bills for them, 15 research assistants (highly qualified new law graduates), a librarian and administrative staff.

They conduct 20–30 projects at any one time. They research an area of law, which has been criticised by judges, lawyers, government departments or the public, to identify defects then issue proposals in a consultation paper, which they publish in hard copy and on their website. Once responses have been considered, they publish a report, usually with a draft Bill appended. Uncontentious law reform measures can be speeded through Parliament in the "Jellicoe" procedure which allows the use of a Special Public Bill Committee, without using parliamentary time allocated to normal Bills. The procedure was used for the Public International Law Act 1994 which implemented three Law Commission reports. Full lists of their consultation papers and reports appear on their website, as do a description of their work and their annual reports.

5–006   One of their jobs is consolidation of statutes and they have achieved this in a number of instances. Another job is statute law revision. Good progress has been made in the repeal of obsolete statutes. By means of Statute Law (Repeals) Acts, they have repealed over 5,000 redundant Acts since 1965.

Codification is inevitably a long-term plan, since in each case the ultimate objective is a single self-contained code, which will be "the statement of all the relevant law in a logical and coherent form" but, until the 1990s, they were especially frustrated in their lack of progress in persuading governments to allocate parliamentary time to Bills designed to enact their Draft Criminal Code, which they published in 1989.

In the white paper published by the Labour Government in advance of the introduction of the Law Commissions Bill, the point was made that there was an urgent need for a review body. This was substantiated by the fact that there were said to exist some 3,000 Acts of Parliament dating from 1234, many volumes of delegated legislation and some 300,000 reported case decisions.

5–007   The annual report of the Law Commission, on their website, shows which of their recommendations have been implemented. In 2004, they reported that seven of their recent reports had been implemented in the previous year, a further 17 had been accepted by Government and 15 awaited attention. This is a much better success rate than in the past. In the 1990s, successive chairmen of the Commission complained bitterly at the log-jam of their reports ignored by governments. Only four were implemented in 1990–1994. The 1994 Annual Report complained of "serious unease among many people" that the work of the Commission was being neglected. In a 1994 interview, the then Chairman Sir Henry Brooke said there were 36 reports "stuck in the log-jam" and he was anxious to publicise this and put it to an end.

The Jellicoe procedure for speeding Bills through was introduced in 1994 and Hudson commented "(h)ow it can have taken until now to devise such an obvious procedure beggars belief" ((1994) 144 N.L.J. 1668). Disappointingly, the next chairman, Dame Mary Arden, commented in 1998 "the procedure has not worked quite as had been hoped as it makes very heavy demands on the time of members of the committee and of ministers and their officials". In the 1996 Annual Report, in an open letter to the Conservative Lord Chancellor, she accused the Government of wasting taxpayers' money by delaying implementation of law reforms. One of the reports ignored was on conspiracy to defraud, noting defects in the law. In *Preddy* (1996), the House of Lords ruled that mortgage fraud was not covered by the law of theft. Eleven prosecutions had to be dropped and many others were not brought. Another scandal relates to the state of offences against the person, embodied in the decrepit, inappropriate, contradictory and archaically-worded Offences Against the Person Act 1861, upon which the Commission reported in 1993. Commissioner Stephen Silber QC complained of inaction in 1996. He illustrated it with the example of stalking. Had their proposals been implemented, there would have been none of the uncertainty that arose in the courts as to whether it was a criminal offence. Still, in 2005, eighty thousand cases per year are being prosecuted under this anachronistic Act.

One would think the Commission's work so uncontroversial that it would provoke no criticism but in 1995, *The Daily Mail* launched a campaign against its Family Violence Bill, calling the Commission a "trendy, left-wing academic quango" of "(l)egal commissars subverting family values" (quoted by Cretney). The Bill was introduced by the Jellicoe procedure but proved far from uncontroversial and was dropped. Conservative Lady Olga Maitland said the Commissioners were "living on another planet".

The Commission's website contains its consultation papers, final reports, annual reports and details of its current work. During 2003–4 they published law reform reports on such topics as non-accidental death and injury to children; land valuation and housing; partnership; housing tenure and compensation for compulsory purchase. They published consultation papers on partial defences to murder and forfeiture and intestacy. The law reform teams at the Commission currently cover criminal law and evidence, public law, property and trust law and commercial law and common law. In March 2003, the Department of Constituional Affairs (DCA) published the *Quinquennial Review of the Law Commission*. John Halliday, its author, recommended strengthening its relationships with

5–008

government. The aim should be to maximise public benefits derived from law reform. Performance would be at its best, he said, when:

- the projects selected were those most likely to result in public benefits through successful law reform;
- government committed itself in advance to act on the outcomes;
- projects were managed to the highest standards, with regular reviews to ensure timeliness;
- links between the Commission and its stakeholders (mainly Government departments) were strong;
- the Commission's internal systems and systems for managing the relationship with Government were strong; and
- the Commission and the DCA had the necessary vision, commitment, skills and resources.

He made a number of recommendations to improve the work and organisation of the Commission and its links with government and the public. Most of these had been implemented by 2005.

Advisory Committees

5–009 For ensuring that improvements are made in the law as circumstances demand, certain standing committees have been set up with responsibility for reporting on particular matters in need of reform.

Royal Commissions

5–010 These are appointed ad hoc, to conduct major reviews of the law or legal system. For instance, the Royal Commission on Assizes and Quarter Sessions (1969) recommended the creation of the Crown Court. The Royal Commission on Criminal Procedure (1980) produced recommendations which led to the passing of the Police and Criminal Evidence Act 1984 (PACE). The Royal Commission on Legal Services (1979) was singularly unsuccessful, in that many of its recommendations have been ignored. In 1991 the Home Secretary and Lord Chancellor established the Royal Commission on Criminal Justice, at the height of public concern over famous miscarriages of justice. It reported in 1993 and some of its recommendations have been followed, such as those on appeals, in the Criminal Appeal Act 1995. Others have been ignored, such as those on the right to silence.

Other Bodies

5–011 The Lord Chancellor, in particular, is advised by several standing and many ad hoc committees. One of the most obvious standing committees is the Legal Services Commission, discussed in Chapter 17, below. In addition, he currently has working parties considering various topics and the Research Secretariat of the Department sets an agenda for future research, which you can read on the DCA website, and funds projects conducted by academics which fit into its agenda. In the last decade, two judges and a senior lawyer were appointed to report on reforming the work and organisation of the civil courts (Lord Woolf), the criminal courts (Lord Justice Auld) and tribunals (Sir Andrew Leggatt). Their reports and the outcomes are discussed in Chapters 9, 10 and 12, below.

Green Papers and White Papers

All government departments may publish green papers setting   5–012
out their proposals for legislative change. These are open invitations for comment by the interested public at large. Once gathered in, these responses help to modify final legislative proposals which are set out in a white paper. The DCA does not work through green papers so much as consultation papers, available in electronic form, which you can see in their dozens on the DCA website. It produces just about too many consultation papers for one person to keep up with.

Statute Law Revision

Dame Mary Arden provides an interesting account of this. The   5–013
Renton Committee on the Preparation of Legislation, in 1995, made detailed recommendations on the drafting of statutes, parliamentary procedure and statutory interpretation. In 1992 the Hansard Commission reported on the legislative process. Dame Mary quoted a 1987 Report of the Law Reform Commission of Victoria:

- Badly drafted legislation encouraged litigation and was, therefore, expensive.
- Unclear legislation transferred the power to determine the law from an elected legislature to the courts.
- It is a fundamental civil liberty that people should be able to know and understand the laws that govern them.

She told the story of the Tax Law Rewrite. In 1995, the Inland Revenue published two documents listing criticisms of the 6,000 pages of tax legislation, including:

- Tax legislation suffered from complicated syntax, long sentences and archaic or ambiguous language.
- The principles underlying the rules were not apparent. This forced the courts to interpret strictly according to wording.
- There was too much detail, covering every conceivable situation.
- Many sections could not be understood in isolation.

- Some rules were wide and, therefore, uncertain.
- It was difficult to find all the rules.
- Definitions were inconsistent and spread throughout different statutes.
- There was an imbalance between primary and secondary legislation.
- There was a lack of consultation and openness in drafting statutes.

The Inland Revenue decided to organise a project themselves, a five-year plain English rewrite, consulting representative bodies and taxpayers and employing 40 lawyers. A special joint committee of the Lords and Commons would scrutinise Bills.

Consolidation and Codification

5–014   The work of the Law Commission and other reforming bodies leads on to a consideration of the actual process by which legislation is simplified. Under the Consolidation of Enactments (Procedure) Act 1949, a system was introduced by Parliament under which, where the bringing together of separate statutory provisions, known as "consolidation", was deemed to be desirable, the Lord Chancellor could arrange to have prepared a memorandum showing how these various provisions would take effect in the proposed consolidating Act. Thus, for example, the whole of the legislation concerned with tribunals and inquiries was brought together and updated in the Tribunals and Inquiries Act 1992.

The consolidating procedure is not possible where the Bill involves changes of substance in the law, known as "codification". A codifying measure brings together the existing statute and case law, in an attempt to produce a full statement as it relates to that particular branch of law. The main examples of successful codification date from the end of the nineteenth century when the following four statutes were passed: the Bills of Exchange Act 1882, the Partnership Act 1890, the Sale of Goods Act 1893 and the Marine Insurance Act 1906. The Bills of Exchange Act 1882, which was prepared by Sir M. D. Chalmers, involved the consideration of 17 existing statutes and some 2,500 decided cases. These were compressed to make a statute 100 sections long. After these Acts were passed, there was no more codifying legislation until the Theft Act 1968. The codification of arbitration law in the Arbitration Act 1996 was discussed in Chapter 2 on sources, above. It was partly codifying and partly consolidating and was subject to a special Jellicoe procedure, described above and in Chapter 2.

The difference between consolidation and codification is classically illustrated by the modern example of the Powers of Criminal

Courts (Sentencing) Act 2000, designed to pull together all the legislative strands of sentencing, which has been such a struggle in
application for judges and an even greater struggle for justices'
clerks and other magistrates' legal advisers. The problem is,
however, that this neat fabric was already unravelling, with a new
statute in 2001 and has been further unwound annually, by later
statutes. Doubtless, the Government will never resist the temptation to pick away at sentencing and criminal procedure as it does
every year, usually in more than one statute. What the Law
Commission, Lord Chief Justices and academics are clamouring for
is a proper criminal code, which would include all substantive
criminal statute law, criminal procedure and sentencing, like the
California Penal Code and that of every other US state. Then all we
need do is to buy or download the latest version every year. When
the Government is tempted to pick away at procedure, it will have
to weave its amendments into the existing cloth of such a code,
instead of unravelling it and confusing everybody by adding a new
statute.

The Law Commission, frustrated at inaction on a criminal code,   5–015
pointed out on its website in 2001 that we are almost the only
country in the world without one. Lord Chief Justice Bingham told
this pathetic history of English criminal law in exasperated tones.
"The plea for such a code cannot, I fear, startle by its novelty":

- 1818, both houses petitioned the Prince Regent to establish a
  Law Commission to consolidate statute law.
- 1831, Commission established to inquire into codifying criminal law.
- 1835–1845, it produced eight reports, culminating in a
  Criminal Law Code Bill, ultimately dropped.
- 1879, Royal Commission recommended code containing 550
  clauses.
- 1844–1882, Lord Brougham and others made eight parliamentary attempts to enact a code.
- 1965, Law Commission established.
- Criminal Code Team established including Professor Sir John
  Smith "the outstanding criminal lawyer of our time"
  (Bingham).
- Code published 1985, revised and expanded 1989.

Lord Bingham concluded:

"even the most breathless admirer of the common law must
regard it as a reproach that after 700 years of judicial decision-
making our highest tribunal should have been called upon time

and again in recent years to consider the mental ingredients of murder, the oldest and most serious of crimes" (at p.695).

Cambridge Professor J. R. Spencer added a plea for a code of criminal procedure, because in this context English inaction looks even more pathetic in the face of a 1995 Scottish code:

"... the sources are at present in a shocking mess, as a result of which the law is not readily accessible to those who have reason to discover it ... dispersed among ... some 150 statutes ... even the modern ones are mainly messy and unsystematic and hard for the user to find his way around: a succession of Criminal Justice Acts, each a disparate jumble of new rules, or of new amendments to old ones" (at p.520).

He added that almost all the law of evidence was uncodified and our haphazard way of creating rules resulted in "all sorts of astonishing contradictions". He, the Law Commission and others were, doubtless, pleasantly surprised by the government announcement, in their 2001 white paper, *Criminal Justice: The Way Ahead* that they intended to introduce a criminal code. This was reiterated in the July 2002 white paper *Justice for All*. Quickly taking advantage of government interest in codification, the Law Commission is currently engaged in updating its 1989 Draft Criminal Code. It has employed two outside experts to help in this and, when new sections are ready, circulates them, by email, to interested parties, such as practising and academic lawyers' groups.

As explained in Chapter 10 on criminal procedure, below, the bold step has finally been taken, in 2005, of reducing all the rules of criminal procedure to one set: the Criminal Procedure Rules. They have now been set out in one place but are still a hopeless mishmash. The newly established Criminal Procedure Rule Committee now has the awful task of organising them into some sensible form and rewriting them in plain English.

3. Change and the English Legal System

5–016   The period since 1980 has seen the most upheaval in the English legal system since the Supreme Court of Judicature Acts of the 1880s merged law and equity and created the Supreme Court.

In the criminal justice system, the 1980s started with the work of the Royal Commission on Criminal Procedure which resulted in several pieces of legislation. Most notable was PACE in 1984, strengthening the rights of suspected persons. The Prosecution of

Offences Act 1985 created a national prosecution service, the Crown Prosecution Service. The spate of miscarriages of justice which came to light in the late 1980s and early 1990s, notably the Guildford Four and Birmingham Six cases, provoked the establishment of the Royal Commission on Criminal Justice, whose terms of reference charged it with the astonishingly bold task of assessing the desirability of importing inquisitorial elements of procedure from civil law countries. It produced a highly controversial report in 1993 which resulted in some sections of the Criminal Justice and Public Order Act 1994, the Criminal Appeal Act 1995 and the Criminal Procedure and Investigations Act 1996. 2001 saw the publication of Lord Justice Auld's *Review of the Criminal Courts*, resulting in the restructuring of court management, in the Courts Act 2003 and considerable changes to the rules of evidence and criminal procedure, in the Criminal Justice Act 2003 and other statutes.

As far as civil procedure is concerned, equally radical changes have taken place. The Civil Justice Review of 1988 raised the question of whether a redistribution of civil work and a change in pretrial procedure and the costs regime could cut out undesirable facets of English civil procedure, notably cost and delay in the High Court. Its recommendations led to Part I of the Courts and Legal Services Act 1990, which gave county courts almost the same jurisdiction as the High Court, allowing for a very significant shift of work down into the county court. The Heilbron-Hodge Report then the Woolf report of 1996 effected very significant changes in civil practice, then the Civil Procedure Rules 1998.

As for the court structure, the Children Act of 1989 gave parallel   **5–017** jurisdiction, in matters affecting children, to the three first instance courts, the county court, magistrates' court and High Court. Lord Chancellor Mackay said he saw this Act as paving the way towards a family court. The 1980s saw a massive growth in applications for judicial review to the High Court, following a simplification of procedure, and the practice of their being listed in the Crown Office list. By 2000, this list had transformed into the Administrative Court.

As far as members of the legal profession are concerned, they are still to feel the real impact of the Government's attack on their monopolies. The Administration of Justice Act 1985 effectively destroyed the solicitors' conveyancing monopoly by establishing a system of licensed conveyancers. This, however, posed no serious threat, in comparison with the Courts and Legal Services Act 1990, which empowered the Lord Chancellor to open up competition to banks and building societies. Neither has the other side of the profession been spared from threat. Again, the Courts and Legal Services Act 1990 destroys the barristers' monopoly over rights of audience in the higher courts, effectively allowing anyone to apply to be licensed for rights of audience in the various levels of court. As a corollary of this, judicial and other similar appointments are no longer limited to barristers and the Courts and Legal Services Act substitutes rights of audience as the qualification. It had not had much impact, however, by 1998, so the new Lord Chancellor Irvine introduced the Access to Justice Act 1999, which finally abolished the restrictive practices of the Bar. Nevertheless, thanks largely to the misgivings by the Law Society and the tenacious attitude of the Bar in protecting its organisational structure and restrictive practices, much of the 1990 Act was never implemented and the rest of it had limited effect so the work and organisation of the two sides of the legal profession remains largely as it was in 1970 and this structure including the QC system has been under scrutiny yet again, in 2003–5, as explained in Chapter 13 on the legal profession, below.

The Legal Aid Act 1988 took the administration of civil legal aid out of the hands of the Law Society and gave it to a new Legal Aid Board. It allowed the Lord Chancellor wide and controversial powers to establish a franchising system for the provision of legal advice. Throughout the 1990s, the legal aid system came under increasing scrutiny. Lord Chancellor Mackay wanted to reform it but his successor, Lord Irvine scrapped it and replaced it with a radically new structure provided for in the Access to Justice Act 1999, which took a holistic approach to the funding of and distribution of all legal services, not just those provided by lawyers in private practice.

BIBLIOGRAPHY

5–018 Dame Mary Arden, "Modernising Legislation" [1998] P.L. 65.

Rt. Hon. Lord Bingham of Cornhill LCJ, "A Criminal Code: Must We Wait for Ever?" [1998] Crim. L.R. 694 (*Public Law* (P.L.) and *The Criminal Law Review* (Crim. L.R.) are on *Westlaw*).

Interview with Sir Henry Brooke, *The Magistrate*, February 1994.

Lord Justice Carnwarth, "The art of the possible" *Counsel*, February 2002, p.20.

S. M. Cretney, "The Law Commission: True Dawns and False Dawns" (1996) 59 M.L.R. 631 (historical).

Law Commission website: *www.lawcom.gov.uk*. Contains information on the LC, Annual Reports, consultation papers and reports.

J. R. Spencer, "The Case for a Code of Criminal Procedure" [2000] Crim. L.R. 519.

Part II: Institutions

THE COURT STRUCTURE

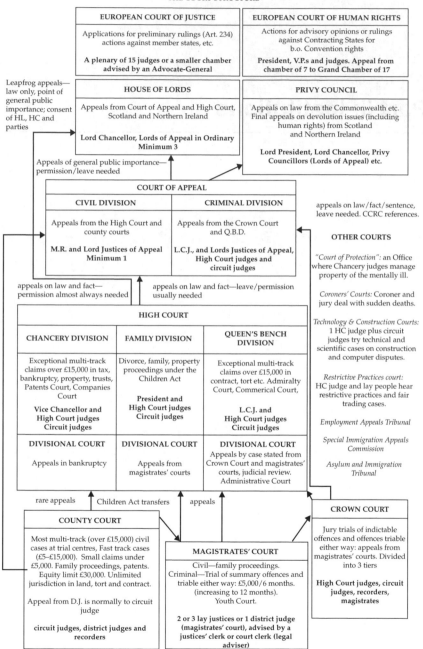

EUROPEAN COURT OF JUSTICE

Applications for preliminary rulings (Art. 234) actions against member states, etc.

A plenary of 15 judges or a smaller chamber advised by an Advocate-General

EUROPEAN COURT OF HUMAN RIGHTS

Actions for advisory opinions or rulings against Contracting States for b.o. Convention rights

President, V.P.s and judges. Appeal from chamber of 7 to Grand Chamber of 17

Leapfrog appeals—law only, point of general public importance; consent of HL, HC and parties

HOUSE OF LORDS

Appeals from Court of Appeal and High Court, Scotland and Northern Ireland

Lord Chancellor, Lords of Appeal in Ordinary Minimum 3

PRIVY COUNCIL

Appeals on law from the Commonwealth etc. Final appeals on devolution issues (including human rights) from Scotland and Northern Ireland

Lord President, Lord Chancellor, Privy Councillors (Lords of Appeal) etc.

Appeals of general public importance—permission/leave needed

COURT OF APPEAL

CIVIL DIVISION	CRIMINAL DIVISION
Appeals from the High Court and county courts	Appeals from the Crown Court and Q.B.D.
M.R. and Lord Justices of Appeal Minimum 1	**L.C.J., and Lords Justices of Appeal, High Court judges and circuit judges**

appeals on law/fact/sentence, leave needed. CCRC references.

OTHER COURTS

"Court of Protection": an Office where Chancery judges manage property of the mentally ill.

Coroners' Courts: Coroner and jury deal with sudden deaths.

Technology & Construction Courts: 1 HC judge plus circuit judges try technical and scientific cases on construction and computer disputes.

Restrictive Practices court: HC judge and lay people hear restrictive practices and fair trading cases.

Employment Appeals Tribunal

Special Immigration Appeals Commission

Asylum and Immigration Tribunal

appeals on law and fact—permission almost always needed

appeals on law and fact—leave/permission usually needed

HIGH COURT

CHANCERY DIVISION	FAMILY DIVISION	QUEEN'S BENCH DIVISION
Exceptional multi-track claims over £15,000 in tax, bankruptcy, property, trusts, Patents Court, Companies Court	Divorce, family, property proceedings under the Children Act	Exceptional multi-track claims over £15,000 in contract, tort etc. Admiralty Court, Commerical Court,
Vice Chancellor and High Court judges Circuit judges	**President and High Court judges Circuit judges**	**L.C.J. and High Court judges Circuit judges**
DIVISIONAL COURT	DIVISIONAL COURT	DIVISIONAL COURT
Appeals in bankruptcy	Appeals from magistrates' courts	Appeals by case stated from Crown Court and magistrates' courts, judicial review. Administrative Court

rare appeals   Children Act transfers   appeals

COUNTY COURT

Most multi-track (over £15,000) civil cases at trial centres, Fast track cases (£5–£15,000). Small claims under £5,000. Family proceedings, patents. Equity limit £30,000. Unlimited jurisdiction in land, tort and contract.

Appeal from D.J. is normally to circuit judge

circuit judges, district judges and recorders

MAGISTRATES' COURT

Civil—family proceedings. Criminal—Trial of summary offences and triable either way: £5,000/6 months. (increasing to 12 months). Youth Court.

2 or 3 lay justices or 1 district judge (magistrates' court), advised by a justices' clerk or court clerk (legal adviser)

CROWN COURT

Jury trials of indictable offences and offences triable either way: appeals from magistrates' courts. Divided into 3 tiers

High Court judges, circuit judges, recorders, magistrates

6. Civil Courts

"I don't give a fuck whether we're peers or not" (Senior Law Lord, Lord Bingham, on being asked by Boris Johnson MP whether he would not miss being in "the best club in London" if the Law Lords moved out of Parliament, *The Spectator*, May 2002.)

As with the rest of the legal system, the work and jurisdiction of the civil courts has recently been through a massive upheaval. Thankfully, things have settled down, since around 2002. Following the recommendations of the Civil Justice Review (1988), the Lord Chancellor was given sweeping powers under the Courts and Legal Services Act 1990 to reorganise the civil business of the High Court and the county courts. The Review recommended a significant shift of work down to the county courts, as it found that the High Court was clogged up with trivial cases. The Woolf Report, *Access to Justice* was published in 1996 and recommended a radical overhaul of civil procedure. Lord Woolf's recommendations were implemented by the Civil Procedure Rules 1998, which came into effect in 1999. From 2005, the big development at the pinnacle of the criminal and civil court structure is the creation of a Supreme Court.

Details of the courts' work are provided in the annual *Judicial Statistics*, on the website of the Department for Constitutional Affairs (DCA). Not only does it provide statistics, for instance, on how many trial days occupied full-time judges and how many occupied deputies, but the report also gives very straightforward and useful descriptions of each court. Most courts are now administered by Her Majesty's Courts Service, which is an independent government agency, which came into being on April 1, 2005.

6–001

1. Magistrates' Courts

6–002   Lay magistrates usually sit in threes, or sometimes as a pair. District judges (magistrates' courts) sit alone or, rarely, with two lay justices (see Chapter 15 on magistrates, below). Under the 1989 Children Act, implemented in October 1991, the domestic proceedings courts were renamed "family proceedings courts" and the specially trained magistrates who adjudicate are selected from "the family panel". They can make and enforce financial provisions following a family breakdown and can make orders protecting adults and children. Unlike the county courts and High Court, they cannot grant divorces. Under the 1989 Act, they share jurisdiction in children cases with the High Court and county courts and those cases are allocated according to complexity. They can make a range of orders relating to children, including care and supervision orders, adoption orders and contact and residence orders. After 2005, family panels may be dismantled, as a result of the Courts Act 2003.

Other civil work includes Council Tax and VAT enforcement. In 2005, the magistrates lost their work in the administration of liquor licensing, to local authorities. This was a logical change. Magistrates used to carry out all local government functions until the passing of the Local Government Act 1888 created separate local councils and licensing was a relic of this administrative work.

2. County Courts

6–003   Since their establishment by the County Courts Act 1846, they have provided a local and relatively inexpensive alternative to the High Court for the trial of civil cases. They do not follow county boundaries. Their name is historical. In 2005 there were 218 county courts in England and Wales, each with at least one circuit judge and one district judge. Circuit judges can hear all types of case and hear the more important work. District judges' jurisdiction to assess damages is now unlimited, unless otherwise directed. They preside over the small claims court, where the limit is £5,000. They are procedural judges so they deal with pre-trial case management and they deal with 80 per cent of the contested trials in the county courts. Circuit judges generally hear matters where over £15,000 is claimed. They also exercise case management powers. Recorders are lawyers who sit part time and their jurisdiction is similar to that of circuit judges. Deputy district judges are barristers or solicitors who sit part time. All types of judge sit alone although circuit judges and recorders may sit with a jury of eight, in categories of case described in Chapter 16 on the jury, below. The Lord Chancellor nominates, "tickets", a number of all these types of judge to sit in proceedings under the Children Act 1989. There are some specialist circuit judges. These include those in the mercantile courts, Designated Civil Judges who are responsible for judicial management of civil judges in their area and Designated Family Judges who sit at care centres and are responsible for the judicial management of the centres' work.

County Court Jurisdiction

Under the Courts and Legal Services Act 1990, s.3 the county court was given almost all the powers of the High Court, with some restrictions. Nevertheless, county courts try the vast bulk of civil cases, such as tort, contract, property, insolvency and bankruptcy with the High Court reserved for a few special cases, in accordance with the recommendations of the Civil Justice Review 1988 and the Woolf Report 1996. In over three quarters of county court claims, the amount claimed is less than £3,000 or unspecified. Some county courts have the jurisdiction to hear "equity" cases on trusts and contested probate up to the value of £30,000. Under the Civil Procedure Rules 1998, cases are divided into small claims, fast track and multi-track and the county courts hear all small claims, virtually all fast track claims and most multi-track claims. Virtually all divorces are heard in county courts and very few are heard in the High Court. County courts share jurisdiction under the Children Act 1989 with the magistrates' courts and the High Court. Public law care cases involve parties other than just the parents, such as the local authority and are heard at certain special county courts called care centres. Family hearing centres hear private family proceedings, where only the parents and children are involved. County Courts include five specialist mercantile courts (the provincial equivalent of the Commercial Court) and a patents county court, all of which have specialist circuit judges. A few circuit judges have special jurisdiction to hear cases under the Race Relations Act 1976.

In 2005, the DCA consulted on whether we should have a single civil court, discussed below.

6–004

3. The High Court of Justice

The High Court of Justice and the Court of Appeal (CA) were brought into being as the Supreme Court of Judicature under the Judicature Acts 1873–1875. At that time, the High Court consisted of five Divisions, the Queen's Bench, Chancery, Probate, Divorce and Admiralty, Exchequer and Common Pleas. The last two Divisions were merged in the Queen's Bench Division (QBD) in 1880 and the

6–005

remaining three Divisions continued unaltered from then until the Administration of Justice Act 1970 redistributed the functions of the Probate, Divorce and Admiralty Division and created the Family Division.

The High Court sits at the Royal Courts of Justice in the Strand and, for the convenience of litigants and their solicitors, there are a number of district registries and trial centres in the larger cities in England and Wales. There are 107 High Court judges appointed to the three Divisions, 17 in Chancery, 18 Family Division judges and 72 in the Queen's Bench. Trials are also conducted by deputy High Court judges (retired judges or specially appointed practitioners who the Lord Chancellor is testing out) and circuit judges authorised ("ticketed") under the Supreme Court Act by the Lord Chancellor to sit part time in the High Court. The annual *Judicial Statistics* on the DCA website provide information on what proportion of the case-load is heard by different types of judge.

The Queen's Bench Division

6–006   This, the great common law court, takes its name from the fact that the early royal judges sat on "the bench", "*en banc*", at Westminster. This Court absorbed the whole common law jurisdiction, when the High Court was reformed, as described. The present jurisdiction of the Division is thus both civil and criminal, original and appellate and the QBD is much larger than the other two Divisions.

In terms of its civil jurisdiction, most cases are contract or tort. Cases are heard in the Royal Courts of Justice or at provincial district registries of the High Court, located at county court centres. Interlocutory hearings (case management) are held by Masters of the High Court in London (in a part of the Royal Courts of Justice called "the Bear Garden") and by district judges outside London. The Division contains the Commercial Court and the Admiralty Court. In the Admiralty Court, one judge and registrars hear cases relating to ships, such as shipping collisions and damage to cargo. Most cases are disposed of in London but some are heard in district registries with specialist jurisdiction. This court has a long history. A "commercial list" was established in the High Court in 1895. The 11 judges who sit in the Commercial Court hear cases on shipping and aviation and contracts relating to shipping, commerce, insurance, banking, international credit and questions arising from arbitrations. A specialist Administrative Court was added in 2000. The QBD administers the Technology and Construction Court (TCC) (formerly Official Referees Court) which hears such things as technical construction disputes, computer and sale of goods litigation, torts relating to the occupation of land and questions arising from arbitrations in building and engineering disputes. Seven fulltime TCC circuit judges sit in London, supervised by a High Court judge and around 50 provincial circuit judges and recorders are nominated, "ticketed" to hear TCC cases in the TCC and elsewhere. Except for the specialists, Most QBD judges spend half their time sitting on circuit hearing serious Crown Court cases or civil cases heard outside London. Specialist QBD judges also sit in the Restrictive Practices Court and the Employment Appeal Tribunal. Judges generally sit alone, with the exception of certain judicial review cases and commercial arbitrations. Jury trial is permitted in five torts and at the discretion of the judge but is very rare in other cases. The most common and well publicised jury trials are defamation actions.

The Divisional Court of the Queen's Bench Division

In its appellate jurisdiction, the Queen's Bench, like the other two 6–007 Divisions, has what is rather confusingly called a Divisional Court. This is, in most instances, an appeal court. In the Queen's Bench Division its jurisdiction includes such matters as follows.

- appeals on a point of law by way of case stated from magistrates' courts, tribunals and the Crown Court;
- the supervisory jurisdiction of the High Court over inferior courts and tribunals and, most importantly, over governmental and other public bodies. Specialist judges of the Administrative Court, created in 2000, hear applications for judicial review. For instance, challenging the closure of a hospital, or a refusal to grant asylum, or a decision to evict gypsies from public land, or allocate a child to a particular school. The Administrative Court also sits in Cardiff, to hear judicial review cases from Wales. Planning appeals and appeals from magistrates' courts can also be held in Wales;
- applications for habeas corpus (challenging the legality of detention); and
- appeals and applications on planning matters.

The judicial review work of the Administrative Court was expected to expand significantly as actions have been brought, from 2001, to test the boundaries of the Human Rights Act 1998 and the practical meaning of the Convention in English law. The Convention became part of English law in October 2000. Accordingly, the Lord Chancellor asked Parliament to create some extra QBD judicial posts, to cope with the workload. There are currently 37 High Court judges nominated ("ticketed") to hear these judicial review cases, including family and chancery judges. In *A (A Patient) v A Health Authority* [2002] EWHC 18, it was held that cases involving the welfare of children or incompetent adults should be litigated by way of judicial review, where they only invoked public law points. Other such cases belonged in the family division. Some matters are heard by a single judge, such as applications for leave to apply for judicial review (on paper or in person) and others must be heard by at least two judges in a Divisional Court, usually a High Court judge and a Lord Justice of Appeal. More details are provided on the Administrative Court's website.

The Chancery Division

6–008   This Division is the direct descendant of the Lord Chancellor's equity jurisdiction, and it is thus substantially concerned with those matters which, before the Judicature Acts 1873–1875, belonged to the Court of Chancery. It has also had allocated to it by statute the responsibility for such matters as the winding-up of companies and revenue cases. Its 17 specialist judges are headed by the Vice-Chancellor. The Lord Chancellor also has jurisdiction but never sits. Interlocutory matters are heard by High Court Masters in London and district judges outside. Some trials are heard by deputy High Court judges. Its jurisdiction can be summarised as:

- disputed intellectual property, copyright or patents;
- the execution or declaration of trusts;
- the redemption and foreclosure of mortgages;
- conveyancing and land law matters;
- partnership actions and other business and industrial disputes;
- the administration of the estates of deceased persons (contested probate);
- revenue issues, *i.e.* taxation cases;
- insolvency;
- professional negligence claims against solicitors, accountants surveyors and others.

It also contains two specialist courts: the Patents Court, dealing with patents and registered designs and the Companies Court, which deals mainly with company insolvency. It has administrative responsibility for the Restrictive Practices Court. The Chancery Division sits at the Royal Courts of Justice and eight provincial High Court centres. Most of the substantial work in the provinces is handled by circuit judges "ticketed" for High Court Chancery work. The Divisional Court of the Chancery Division hears tax appeals from the Commissioners of Taxes and from the county courts in bankruptcy cases. Because of its intellectual property and copyright jurisdiction, the litigants we are most likely to hear of in Chancery are pop and rock stars, such as the Spice Girls, Bruce

Springstein and George Michael. In a 2001 case, in which Arsenal Football Club claimed a company was infringing the clothing trademarks, Laddie J. could not resist waving an Arsenal scarf above his head and offering to decorate his colleagues' rooms with Arsenal wallpaper.

The Family Division

This Division shares family jurisdiction with the magistrates' court and the county court. Its 18 specialist judges are headed by a President. The main responsibilities of the Family Division are as follows:

6–009

- complex defended divorce cases, either in London or district registries with divorce jurisdiction;
- complex applications relating to children, under the Children Act 1989: for instance applications for care orders, adoptions, wardship, residence and contact orders, where the contest is acrimonious or complex or one or more parties lives outside England and Wales. Jurisdiction under the Children Act is concurrent with that of the county court and magistrates' court. Cases may be transferred. Only this court may deal with wardship applications, in which the court orders a child to be made a ward of court and subject to its control; and
- the grant of probate or letters of administration to authorise the disposal of a decreased person's estate where the matter is uncontested. This work is done at the Principal Registry in London and 11 District Probate Registries in England and Wales.

The Divisional Court of the Family Division hears appeals from decisions of magistrates in a wide variety of domestic matters including orders made under the Children Act. It also deals with judicial review of family issues, as illustrated by the Diane Blood case, described in Chapter 2 on sources, above. 1998 saw a sudden increase in the work of the Probate Service of the Family Division, supplying copies of the will of the late Diana, Princess of Wales.

In 1989, Lord Chancellor Mackay introduced the Children Bill, claiming that it was the first step towards a unified family court. There had been pressure for such a court for decades previously. Lord Justice Thorpe was quoted in *The Times*, in January 2005, as saying that a new unified family court was coming into being in 2006. This is an exaggeration. In 2004, a new Family Procedure Rule Committee was appointed, under the Courts Act 2003, to create a unified set of rules applicable in all family proceedings. At the same time, the Family Justice Council (FJC) was created, "to promote an inter-disciplinary approach to the needs of family justice, and through consultation and research, to monitor the effectiveness of the system and advise on reforms necessary for continuous improvement" (FJC website). Sadly, there are no plans for a unified family court and these proceedings remain divided between the magistrates' courts, the county courts and the High Court.

4. The Court of Appeal (Civil Division)

6–010   The Court of Appeal (CA) was created by the Judicature Acts 1873–1875, together with the High Court of Justice, to form the Supreme Court of Judicature. (This is not to be confused with the forthcoming new Supreme Court, which will replace the Law Lords, described below). It was at first intended that the CA should be the final appeal court, but a change of plan led to the Appellate Jurisdiction Act 1876, under which the House of Lords in its judicial capacity was retained as the highest appeal court.

Thirty-five Lords Justices sit in the CA. The Master of the Rolls heads the Civil Division of the CA and the President of the Family Division and the Vice-Chancellor sit occasionally. It hears appeals on fact and law from the High Court, including divisional courts, the county courts and certain tribunals. Until recently, the Court was composed of three Lords Justices but, after the Access to Justice Act 1999, s.54, the Court may be composed of one or more judges, depending on the importance and complexity of the case. The rationale behind this was "proportionality and efficiency", explained in the 1998 Government white paper *Modernising Justice*, the same as the principles underlying the Civil Procedure Rules 1998. In a case of great importance (see *Ward v James* (1966)) a "full court" of five judges is convened. It sits in the Royal Courts of Justice in the Strand but sat in Cardiff for the first time in 1999 and will sit in Wales at regular intervals. The Lord Chief Justice, Lord Woolf has a habit of sitting in the Civil Division to hear important cases interpreting the Civil Procedure Rules 1998, since it was he who devised them and oversaw their implementation, as Master of the Rolls. An example is *Callery v Gray (No.1)* [2001] EWCA Civ 1117, discussed in Chapter 17 on legal services, below.

5. The House of Lords Transforms into the Supreme Court

6–011   As I write, in 2005, the Appellate Committee of the House of Lords is the final court of appeal in civil matters from all courts in

England, Wales and Northern Ireland and Scotland. It assumed its present jurisdiction under the Appellate Jurisdiction Act 1876. There is now a maximum of 12 Lords of Appeal in Ordinary, known as the "Law Lords". At least two of the judges will be from Scotland and one from Northern Ireland. In addition to the Lords of Appeal in Ordinary, other judges who can take part in the work of the House are the Lord Chancellor, ex-Lord Chancellors, the Master of the Rolls, the Lord Chief Justice, foreign appeal judges and peers who have held high judicial office. They are also called Lords of Appeal and sometimes called Law Lords. By constitutional convention, peers who are not judges do not take part in the hearing of appeals.

Normally, five judges hear an appeal. If a case is exceptionally important, such as the 2004 case on indefinite detention of foreigners suspected of being terrorists, discussed in Chapter 4 on human rights, above, nine Law Lords may sit. The cases are heard in two committee rooms of the House of Lords in the Palace of Westminster, or, occasionally, in the chamber. The judges wear lounge suits, although the advocates are robed, and the atmosphere is comparatively informal. The cases heard always raise a point of law of general public importance, which is the sole ground for obtaining leave to appeal to the House of Lords. In English appeals, leave may be granted by the court below. This may be the CA or the Queen's Bench Divisional Court. If leave is refused by the court below, it is still possible for a party wishing to appeal to ask the Appeal Committee of the House of Lords itself to give leave to appeal. Under the Administration of Justice Act 1969, it is possible for an appeal to "leapfrog" the CA and go direct to the House of Lords provided:

(i)   the trial judge is prepared to grant a certificate;
(ii) the parties agree to this course;
(iii) a point of law of general public importance is involved, which relates wholly or mainly to the construction of a statute or statutory instrument; or the judge was bound by a previous decision of the CA or the House of Lords; and
(iv) the House of Lords grants leave.

In view of these stringent conditions not many successful leapfrog applications are made (nine in 2003, all civil).

Their Lordships, after hearing the appeal, will take time to prepare their "opinions", or "speeches" as their Lordships' judgments are called. It is open to all five judges to give individual opinions and then the majority view prevails. The Court finally gives notice of its decision to the House of Lords itself, in the chamber. Judgments of the House of Lords are almost always reported, because every one adds some new principle to, or clarifies some existing principle of, law. The decisions of the Law Lords are binding on all lower courts, and they thus form the most important precedents in domestic law. There are only around 60 such decisions in civil cases per year.

A New Supreme Court for the UK

> **"It seems unlikely that any person or body of people consciously decided to devolve the ultimate judicial authority within the country formerly vested in a personal monarch on this chamber of the legislature".** (Lord Bingham, 2002, speaking of the Law Lords.)

6–012   At the time of writing, 2005, the Constitutional Reform Act has just been passed. This will eventually replace the House of Lords with a Supreme Court. As explained in Chapter 4 on human rights, above, this Act results from the Government announcement in 2003 that it was determined to reform the constitution, by abolishing the Lord Chancellor, reforming judicial appointments and moving the Law Lords into a Supreme Court. Their aim was, according to the new Lord Chancellor, Lord Falconer, to "put the relationship between Parliament, the Government and judges on a modern footing. We will have a proper separation of powers and we will further strengthen the independence of the judiciary . . .. The time has come to cease asking the law lords to try to fulfil two increasingly incompatible roles."

The problem with the Law Lords, apart from their inclusion of the Lord Chancellor, which I discuss in Chapter 14 on judges, below, was their place in the legislature and consequent danger that they could be involved in debates on Bills which they might later have to have to interpret and apply in court. Further, despite the constitutional convention that Law Lords should not take part in political debates in the House of Lords chamber, some Law Lords had done so. Both in reality and in appearances, the Law Lords breached the separation of judicial and legislative power required by the European Convention on Human Rights. Senior Law Lord Tom Bingham and his eminent colleague Johan Steyn had both advocated the establishment of a Supreme Court in prominent 2002 speeches and elsewhere.

Although they acknowledged that they were in a minority of Law Lords, the Government was persuaded by their arguments. Lord Steyn invoked the words of the famous constitutionalist Walter Bagehot, that the "the Supreme Court of the English people. . . . ought not to be hidden beneath the robes of a legislative assembly". He was alarmed at the confusion of functions in the eyes of the public and foreign observers, reminding us that when the Law Lords delivered their judgements in the first *Pinochet* case, in the Lords' chamber, foreign television viewers thought Lady Thatcher was part of the dissenting minority, opposing the extradition of General Pinochet in 1998. Acknowledging that Law Lords now seldom spoke in House of Lords debates, he argued that their privilege to do so was no longer defensible. We needed an independent Supreme Court which would "in the eyes of the public carry a badge of independence and neutrality. . . . a potent symbol of the rule of law". He examined the requirements for judicial independence under Art.6 of the Convention (discussed in Chapter 4, above), the United Nations General Assembly, the Council of Europe's Charter of the Statute for Judges and the Universal Charter of the Judge.

Responding to Lord Chancellor Irvine's 2001 dismissal of a proposed Supreme Court on the ground that other new court buildings took priority, he said lack of a building should not be used as a pretext for delay, "There is no legitimate excuse for procrastination." **6–013**

In his equally important 2002 speech, Lord Bingham examined the history of the Law Lords, remarking that it was unlikely that anyone had consciously decided to give ultimate judicial authority to this chamber of the legislature. Although it had been mooted, as recently as the 1960s, that the Law Lords should be abolished, leaving the CA as the final appellate body, that argument was rarely heard now. Nevertheless, we will pause a moment to examine this issue. Stevens has pointed out, in various of his works, cited in Chapter 14 on judges, below, that the 1873 Judicature Act abolished appeals to the House of Lords and set up "the Imperial Court of Appeals", sitting in the Strand. It was only a group of Tory mavericks that led it back to the House of Lords, three years later, for the purpose of "dignity", said Stevens. In the comment examined below. Baroness Hale examined the option of abolishing the final court of appeal altogether.

The reasons for questioning the future of the Law Lords were, said Lord Bingham, the recent reforms of the House of Lords as a parliamentary chamber, the Human Rights Act and the new role of the Privy Council in devolution issues. The last development raised the issue of whether the Law Lords and Judicial Committee of the Privy Council should be merged. He examined the four different models for a Supreme Court, as he saw them:

1. An amalgamated Appellate Committee and Privy Council Judicial Committee acting as the Supreme Court of the UK.
2. A new constitutional court, operating alongside courts in the three UK jurisdictions (Northern Ireland, Scotland and England and Wales).

3. A "Luxembourg model", modelled on the ECJ, giving authoritative rulings on points of law referred to it by other courts (as under the Art.234 procedure described in Chapter 3, above).
4. The Appellate Committee severed from the legislature, re-housed and renamed but with its powers unchanged and with the PC Judicial Committee continuing alongside.

He preferred the fourth option, properly staffed and resourced for litigants, staff and judges. He was not in favour of enhancing the powers of the Law Lords, or changing the existing leave procedures or power to deliver separate opinions.

6–014   The following year, in June 2003, after coming under pressure from the Council of Europe, as described in Chapter 4, above, the Government announced their intention to form a Supreme Court. In the consultation paper which followed, canvassing views on such a court's powers and constitution, they relied heavily on Lord Bingham's ideas: *Constitutional Reform: a Supreme Court for the United Kingdom* (DCA). Below, I paraphrase and summarise the main questions it raised and the responses. Note that the Government did not ask *whether* there should be a Supreme Court. "The Government *will* legislate to abolish the jurisdiction of the House of Lords" (my emphasis) but they emphasised that they had no intention of creating a US style supreme court, with the power to strike down legislation:

> "We do not see any place for a Supreme Court on the United States model, able to strike down legislation. Parliament is supreme in our constitution and must remain so. Nor, in the absence of a codified, clearly delineated body of constitutional law, do we see a role for a Constitutional Court" (DCA Press Release 296/03).

The consultation paper asked the following questions:

1. *Should its jurisdiction include the devolution cases dealt with by the Judicial Committee of the Privy Council (explained below).*
   86 per cent of respondents were in favour. While the Judges' Council agreed, the Law Lords did not agree.
2. *Do you agree that its members should remain at 12, with access to a supplementary panel?*
   74 per cent agreed, including the Law Lords and Judges' Council but JUSTICE felt the number should be increased to 15.
3. *Should retired Supreme Court members be appointed to the House of Lords (i.e. the upper House of Parliament)?*

68 per cent agreed but 32 per cent favoured complete severance. The Law Lords felt this might be appropriate, provided
such peers were beyond retiring age or had announced they
would no longer sit as judges. 78 per cent of respondents
favoured a bar on sitting and voting in the House of Lords and
this should be extended to all holders of high judicial office,
such as the Lord Chief Justice. The Judges' Council disagreed
and the Law Lords held mixed views.

4. *Should the court sit in panels, as the Law Lords did, or should every
   member sit on every case (as in the US Supreme Court)?*
   69 per cent of respondents thought the Court should sit in
   panels, with the remainder favouring the second option. The
   Law Lords felt that sitting *en banc*, as a whole group, was
   impracticable, save on rare occasions, because of the case
   load demands of sitting in both this court and the Privy
   Council and several respondents cited Lord Bingham's
   concern that if all members of the court decided all cases, the
   appointing authority might try and influence decision
   making when filling vacancies.

5. *Should the Court decide for itself which appeals it hears?*
   64 per cent felt the position should remain unchanged from
   the procedure I describe above, in relation to the Law Lords.

6. *What should its members be called?*
   Suggestions varied. The consultation paper proposed
   "Justices of the Supreme Court".

In the Law Lords' response, they emphasised that, while three agreed
with Lord Bingham, six considered the proposed change unnecessary and harmful. They believed the Law Lords' presence in
Parliament to be beneficial to the Law Lords, the house and litigants.
The cost would outweigh any benefit. It should be noted, however,
that, the following year, two of the opponents were replaced by new
Law Lords. One of these was the outspoken Brenda Hale, for whom
the planned Supreme Court was not radical enough (see below). All
Law Lords were agreed that a Supreme Court should be properly
accommodated and resourced in a building that reflected "the importance of the rule of law in a modern democracy". It should enjoy an
independent budget. They noted that no business plan had been
attached to the consultation paper. The Government's plans provoked some outspoken opposition among individual Law Lords and
the Lord Chief Justice. New Zealand judge and former Lord of
Appeal Lord Cooke, considered that in the British constitution,
mixing powers "works in a way envied outside Britain". He detailed
examples of the ways in which Parliamentary Committee work and
debates in the chamber had benefited from the contribution of

serving and former Law Lords. Lord Bingham's own maiden speech, on the European Convention, cited in Chapter 4, above, was a perfect model of such a contribution. Citing Lord Wilberforce, a retired Law Lord and intellectual giant of the twentieth century, he thought no instance could be cited of a Law Lord's participation in legislation having affected his judgment. The suggestion that the Law Lords violated the European Convention was, he thought "a figment in the imagination of a controversialist" and no solid evidence of public perception of a lack of independence had been forthcoming. Retired Lord of Appeal, Lord Lloyd, made the same point. He referred to the proposed reforms as "constitutional vandalism".

6–015   The most outspoken critic was, however, Lord Chief Justice Woolf. Concerned at plans to replace the Lord Chancellor with a different type of minister, he announced that he was delaying retirement to stay and fight for the independence of the judiciary. In a 2004 speech in Cambridge, he remarked that the proposed court would be a "poor relation" of the world's other supreme courts, because of its more limited role:

> "We will be exchanging a first class Final Court of Appeal for a second class Supreme Court. . . . Separating the House of Lords in its legislative capacity from its activities as the Final Court of Appeal could act as a catalyst causing the new court to be more proactive than its predecessor. This could lead to tensions. Although the Law Lords involvement in the legislative chamber is limited, the very fact that they are members of the legislature does provide them with an insight and understanding of the workings of Parliament to a greater extent than will be possible if they are no longer part of the House of Lords." (DCA website)

Lord Chancellor Falconer responded in the House of Lords, four days later, when introducing the Constitutional Reform Bill for its second reading:

> "The Law Lords are appointed to the final Court of Appeal, not the legislature. They are judges. We. . . . believe in the supremacy of Parliament. Ultimately, laws must be made by Parliament. The judges, in accordance with law, must construe and interpret those laws. However, unlike systems such as that in the United States of America, we do not want policy issues such as capital punishment, abortion or racial discrimination to be decided by judges. . . . That most certainly does not make our system any worse or better than that in the United States of America; it is simply different. . . . It will not make our new Supreme Court in any sense second rate." (Hansard, March 7, 2004)

In this second reading, opposition was led by Lord Lloyd, the retired Law Lord, taking advantage of his position in the legislature. The Bill was almost defeated but the Government rescued it by promising that it could be scrutinised by a Parliamentary select committee. It was delayed and, unusually, carried over to the next Parliamentary session, in the autumn. The committee made 400 amendments. By the autumn, Lord Chief Justice Woolf, placated by the Government's promise of £45 million to fund the new building, was prepared to support the Bill. Peers defeated Lord Lloyd's attempt to have the Supreme Court jettisoned from the Bill. By Christmas 2004, it was clear there would be a separate Supreme Court and the only outstanding issue was to find a building prestigious enough to house it.

Lord Lloyd dismissed as "nonsense" the argument that there was a breach of the separation of powers in the Law Lords, sitting in the Upper House and speaking on Bills. A 2002 policy paper by JUSTICE had revealed that, in 2003, Law Lords had spoken in debates on asylum, proceeds of crime, the European Arrest Warrant and the Hunting Bill. Opponents of their removal from the Upper House pointed to their valuable and well-informed contribution to debate. On the other hand, those who favoured removal pointed out that retired Law Lords, if they were appointed peers, could satisfy that need, provided they had withdrawn from sitting as judges entirely.

Some academics and others interested in the constitutional anomaly that was the Law Lords had advocated a supreme court for years. To all critics, the reforms were too hasty and ill-thought-through. This group were frustrated that the proposals for the Supreme Court did not go far enough. Robert Stevens considered the Government's reasoning to be *Alice in Wonderland* "if we say often enough that our judges are apolitical they will be." The consultation paper emphasised the supremacy of Parliament, yet the reality was that the Human Rights Act and the European Communities Act had required the Law Lords to apply a fundamental law and act as a type of constitutional court.

Baroness Hale of Richmond (Brenda Hale), sometime academic, **6–016** who was appointed as the first ever woman Lord of Appeal in 2004, had frequently articulated her views on the judiciary. She gave us an interesting insight into the practical background to some of the issues raised by the questions in the consultation paper. She carefully examined the ramifications of abolishing the Law Lords and not replacing them with another court. This was an option ignored by most other commentators so her analysis is worth reading.

Examining the criteria for appeals being heard by their Lordships, she argued that, whereas civil appellants lower down the court structure had to demonstrate "a real prospect of success," the Law

Lords' real criterion in accepting a case was "whether it is something important that they fancy doing". For instance, Diane Pretty's case on the right to life, under Art.2 of the Convention (see Chapter 4, above) had no prospect of success but it raised issues upon which the Law Lords wanted to have their say. The main argument for retaining the new court's jurisdiction over ordinary civil cases was uniformity of approach (in England and Wales, Scotland and Northern Ireland) but she was cynical about that. The opportunity for correction in such cases only arose rarely and randomly, dependent on whether one of the parties wanted to appeal. Anyway, few lawyers appearing before the Law Lords did any comparative research. On the other hand, one argument for retaining a final appellate court rested on the deficiencies of the Court of Appeal, which worked under a great deal of pressure and was heavily dependent on the quality of the arguments prepared before it.

Finally, she asked, "If we are to have all the upheaval this will entail, is it not worth contemplating doing something a little more radical?" She argued that a supreme court was there to bridge the gap between law and society and to protect democracy. Ordinary civil and criminal cases could be removed, leaving them to the courts of appeal in Scotland, Northern Ireland, England and Wales, leaving the Supreme Court for cases of constitutional importance, on human rights, devolution, Europe, international treaties and perhaps adding in those ordinary cases where a serious inconsistency had arisen between the UK's jurisdictions. The new court could choose which cases it took. Such a change would raise an argument for fundamental change in composition. It was commonplace for members of other supreme courts to come from much wider professional backgrounds than the Law Lords. As a consequence, the style of judgments might change: to an informed and intelligent non-lawyer, the judgments of the ECtHR were much easier to read and understand than those of the Law Lords.

6–017   Professor John Bell complained that there had been no attempt at strategic thinking in the consultation papers, "It is constitutional reform by way of incremental change". Comparing ours with continental supreme courts, he raised these questions, which I paraphrase:

1. Why have a *single* Supreme Court? European courts have specialist panels and some jurisdictions have separate courts to apply and interpret administrative law. Do we need a larger range of expertise and is there a case for a specialist reporting judge, as on the continent?
2. How should it act as authoritative interpreter of the law? The principal role of other supreme courts is to quash, rather than

re-decide, wrongly decided cases. The suggestion of a referral for a preliminary ruling on a point of law was dismissed
in the consultation paper without discussion but this might
be a more efficient way of securing decisions on significant
points of law. If the court is limited to difficult or important
points of law, should these not be paid for by public funding?
3. Is it a constitutional court? Under the devolution legislation,
abstract review of legislation is permitted. On the other hand,
the European Convention is pervasive. It might be difficult to
separate out constitutional cases.
4. Should it give advisory opinions? Some European supreme
courts do. The concept is not alien to our courts, as they can
give declaratory rulings.
5. How does it relate institutionally to law reform? The Swedish
Supreme Court can make suggestions for law reform, technically scrutinise Bills and comment on proposed reforms. The
annual reports of French supreme courts make suggestions
for law reform.
6. What is its place within the judiciary? European supreme
courts use younger judges as judicial assistants, helping them
to learn judicial technique.

Many opinions were expressed on the composition of the new UK
Supreme Court and selection of judges. I come back to this issue in
Chapter 14 on judges, below.

The Supreme Court, established by the Constitutional Reform Act 2005

Part 3 of the Constitutional Reform Act 2005 provides for a new   6–018
Supreme Court, and transfers to it the judicial functions of the appellate committee of the House of Lords and the devolution jurisdiction
of the Judicial Committee of the Privy Council. The Supreme Court is
expected to come into being in 2008. The Court consists of 12 judges
appointed by her Majesty, under letters patent. The number can be
increased by Order in Council. The Court will have a President and
Deputy President and the others are to be called Justices of the
Supreme Court. The Act provides that the existing Lords of Appeal,
Law Lords, will be the first Justices of the Supreme Court. Selection
and appointment of new Justices is provided for in some detail, in Part
3 of the Act and this is discussed in Chapter 14 on judges, below. The
Court should generally consist of an uneven number of judges and a
minimum of three. Acting judges may be appointed, to supplement
the permanent Justices, drawn from the CA or equivalent in Scotland
and Northern Ireland and from a supplementary panel consisting
effectively of the same people who could have sat as Lords of Appeal.

The Court may appoint and hear from a special adviser. The Court's rules are to be made by the President, with a view to securing that the Court is "accessible fair and efficient" and they must be "both simple and simply expressed". The Lord Chancellor must appoint a Chief Executive, in consultation with the President of the Supreme Court and the President may appoint other staff. The Lord Chancellor is responsible for providing an appropriate buildings and resources.

The Act lays down the rules as to precedent. An appeal from one jurisdiction in the UK will not be binding on the courts of another UK jurisdiction so a Scottish appeal would not be binding on England and Wales. In devolution proceedings, however, all cases are binding throughout the UK, except on the Court itself.

As a final reminder, it is important to understand that this is not a Supreme Court like that of the US, with power to strike down unconstitutional legislation, although some of the Court's decisions in Community law and human rights will inevitably have that effect, as has been explained in relation to some of the Law Lords' decisions, in Chapters 3 and 4 of this book, above.

6. The European Court of Justice

6–019   The ECJ is described in Chapter 3 on Community law, above. It consists of one judge per Member State of the EU, 25 in 2005. Each must be qualified to hold the highest judicial office in their own country, appointed for a six-year term by the governments of the Member States. The judges are assisted by eight advocates-general who prepare reasoned conclusions on the cases submitted to the Court. Judges sit in odd number chambers with the most important cases being heard by a Grand Chamber. The ECJ's job is to ensure that Community law is interpreted and applied consistently in each member state. The Court is not bound by judicial precedent and has a flexible approach to the interpretation of the Treaties.

There is a European Court of First Instance (CFI), created in 1989, to help the ECJ cope with its caseload. For detail, see Chapter 3, above.

7. The European Court of Human Rights

6–020   This court is described in Chapter 4 on the European Convention on Human Rights, above. It was set up in Strasbourg by the Council of Europe Member States in 1959 to deal with alleged violations of the 1950 European Convention on Human Rights. Since 1998 it has sat as a full-time court. It is composed of a President, Vice President and judges elected by the Parliamentary Assembly of the Council of Europe and nominated by the member states of the Council of Europe, for a six-year period. Judges are allocated to one of the court's four sections, which are geographically and gender balanced. The Court sits in Chambers of 7 judges or, in exceptional cases, as a Grand Chamber of 17 judges. The Committee of Ministers of the Council of Europe supervises the execution of the Court's judgments. Since 2000, in the UK, litigants must exhaust all their remedies through our courts before petitioning the ECtHR. For more detail, see Chapter 4, above.

8. The Judicial Committee of the Privy Council

This Committee was established in 1833, by the Judicial Committee   **6–021** Act, which, as amended, remains the basic statute. It is composed of Privy Councillors who have held or now hold high judicial office, mostly the Law Lords. It sits in Downing Street. Its primary job is as the ultimate appeal court from some Commonwealth countries and from certain of the independent Commonwealth states which have retained this form of appeal (around 26 in total). In 2003, New Zealand legislated to withdraw from the Privy Council's jurisdiction and create its own supreme court, having debated it for 100 years. As Richard Cornes commented:

"For a New Zealander one of the odder tourist experiences available in London—and soon to disappear—was to go to the top of Downing Street . . . to watch a hearing of the highest court of (though not actually in) New Zealand. . . . Clearly a court, the majority of whose members are selected by the British government, from British judges, can never be a link between the New Zealand government and the people of New Zealand." (2004, pp.210 and 214).

The Committee also hears appeals from Jersey, Guernsey and the Isle of Man and from certain domestic tribunals in England and Wales, such as the Disciplinary Committee of the Royal College of Veterinary Surgeons. Until 2003, appeal also lay from other professional disciplinary bodies, such as the General Medical Council but appeal now lies to the High Court. It recently acquired a new significant jurisdiction over devolution issues under the Scotland Act 1998, the Northern Ireland Act 1998 and the Government of Wales Act 1998 but it will lose that jurisdiction to the new Supreme Court, from its creation in about 2006. It decides on the competences and functions of the legislative and executive authorities established in Scotland

and Northern Ireland and questions as to the competence and functions of the Welsh Assembly. The Privy Council (PC) made it clear in *Hoekstra v HM Advocate (No.5)* (2000) that it only has jurisdiction over devolution issues and has not been given a general power to review the proceedings of the High Court of Justiciary in Scotland but devolution issues include human rights issues. In the debate on the Scotland Bill 1998, some peers called for a proper constitutional court. They thought the Judicial Committee of the Privy Council was inappropriate to review decisions from Scotland, because it is geographically imbalanced, consisting mainly of English Law Lords. The PC's jurisdiction is derived from statute but its history derives from its medieval role as the body of the monarch's closest advisers.

Each case must be heard by a board of not more than five and not less than three members of the Committee, although one group of exceptional cases in 2004, on the constitutionality of the Jamaican death penalty, was decided by a board of nine. In practice, the Court usually consists of five Lords of Appeal in Ordinary, sometimes assisted by a senior judge from the country concerned. The civil work of the Judicial Committee is varied. Recently it has included cases on commercial arbitration, banking, employment, revenue, land disputes, juries and matrimonial matters.

6–022   Its criminal jurisdiction is controversial. Over the last decade, the Judicial Committee has provoked the impatience of the governments of independent Caribbean countries who send appeals to it in death penalty cases. The Committee frequently allows appeals against conviction, where the death penalty has been imposed (*e.g. Boodram v State of Trinidad and Tobago* [2001] UKPC 20, or against the imposition of the death penalty. In one decision in 2000, (*Lewis*) it ruled that hundreds of death row prisoners in the Caribbean should be given a stay of execution. Similarly, in *Reyes v The Queen* ([2002] UKPC 11) and two other murder appeals, in 2002, the Judicial Committee ruled that the imposition of the mandatory death penalty was unconstitutional, in seven Caribbean countries. Its automatic imposition for some crimes was held by the PC to be inhuman or degrading treatment, offending against international standards of human rights. A similar decision was reached on the unconstitutionality of the death penalty of Jamaica, by a nine judge Judicial Committee, in *Watson v The Queen* [2004] UKPC 34. On two cases decided on the same day, however, their Lordships felt constrained by the wording of the constitutions of Barbados and Trinidad and Tobago. "The language and purpose of [the relevant constitutional provisions] are so clear that whatever may be their Lordships' views about the morality or efficacy of the death penalty, they are bound as a court of law to give effect to it", said Lord Hoffman, in giving the majority judgment in *Boyce and Joseph v The Queen* [2004] UKPC 32.

These death penalty cases are argued by the *pro bono* (meaning working without charge) units of large London law firms and English human rights barristers. They have had a very high success rate since the mid-1990s. Consequently governments and some judges in Caribbean countries see the PC as a group of unduly liberal judges who undermine their efforts to tackle high murder and violence rates and drug trafficking on their islands. They have long debated whether to abolish the PC's jurisdiction and replace it with a regional court of appeal. In 1970, at the Sixth Heads of Government Conference in Jamaica, the home delegation proposed the establishment of a Caribbean Supreme Court. In 2001 an agreement was signed to establish it and a building was set aside in Trinidad. It is obvious that as a consequence of its formation, many people now waiting on death row will be executed. In a 2005 ruling of great constitutional significance, *Independent Jamaica Council for Human Rights v Marshall–Burnett*, however, the Judicial Committee ruled that three Acts of the Jamaican Parliament, designed to give effect to the agreement to establishment of the Caribbean Court of Justice were not enacted in accordance with the procedure laid down in Jamaica's constitution and were thus void. Lord Bingham started the judgment by giving an assurance that the judges had no interest of their own in the outcome of the case. They merely existed in that capacity to serve the wishes of the people of Jamaica. If and when the people of Jamaica decided that they no longer did so, they were fully entitled to end the role of the PC.

The jurisdiction of the PC was again debated recently, since the proposal to abolish the appellate committee of the House of Lords was announced, in 2003. Of course it did not provoke anything like the mountains of comment and strong opinions on the proposals for the Supreme Court, the Lord Chancellor and judicial appointments. The Constitutional Reform Act 2005 Act does what the government originally proposed in 2003 and gives the PC's devolution jurisdiction to the new Supreme Court.

Surprisingly Sir Thomas Legg has expressed a fairly singular view: **6–023**

"I have never fully bought the argument that we are somehow bound to provide an elegant court and very senior judges to determine cases for the benefit of other independent and self-governing nations, just because they want us to. The historical basis is now very ancient history indeed, and the judge-power requirements of the judicial committee impinge seriously on those of Britain's highest court, which must be our main concern. I personally favour a polite declaration of independence." (2004, p.45).

I find his comment surprising. The reason for this jurisdiction is not just historic. It is one of moral obligation. The British went round the world grabbing land to add to their empire and colonising those places with the English language, English cultural values and, most importantly here, baby versions of the mother English legal system, applying English common law and a statutory framework remarkably like our own. We provided the final court of appeal so as to impose central control, located, funnily enough, for *our* convenience in London. Of course many of those nations would love to replace the PC with their own court, as New Zealand did, but until now the problem has been that they simply did not enjoy the necessary wealth and resources. To cut them off from access to the PC would, I suggest, be shirking our legacy of colonial responsibilities.

9. Other Civil Courts

Ecclesiastical Courts

6–024   These courts at the present time exercise control over clergy of the Church of England. In each diocese there is a consistory court, or equivalent with a different name, the judge of which is a barrister or a judge appointed by the bishop, and known as the Chancellor. Appeal lies from the consistory court to, depending on the diocese, the Arches Court of Canterbury or the Chancery Court of York, and from either court a further appeal is possible to the Judicial Committee of the PC.

Court of Protection

6–025   A judge of the Chancery Division can sit as a Court of Protection to administer the estate of a person suffering from mental disability. This "court" is a misnomer as it is, in law, an office of the Supreme Court.

The Coroner's Court

6–026   The Coroner's Court is used to inquire (by an inquest) into unexplained deaths. Its proceedings are inquisitorial, unlike those of a court. The coroner may, and sometimes must, call a jury of from seven to 11 persons to return a verdict as to the cause of death. The coroner must be legally or medically qualified. Coroners' courts are the responsibility of the DCA, since May 2005. In 2003 the Government published a fundamental review of the coronial system and in 2004 started a programme of reform. Human rights lawyers are hoping that this will take account of case law on coroners' proceedings which has arisen under the Convention and is described in Chapter 4 on human rights, above. The Review recommended:

- all coroners should be legally qualified;
- public inquests should be held into deaths in custody, trau-matic workplace deaths, public transport crashes and certain deaths of children and other cases should be investigated administratively;
- exceptionally complex or contentious inquests should be conducted by a circuit judge or High Court judge;
- the outcome of an inquest should be a factual account of the cause and circumstances of death and an analysis of whether there were systemic failings;
- coroners should report their findings swiftly to any relevant body;
- families should have a right to meet the investigator and be kept informed;
- juries should be used in most cases where Art.2 of the Convention is engaged, such as where someone is compulso-rily held by the state.

By January 2005, the new system for these penetrating, inquiry-like inquests was in use. It was announced that a retired High Court judge would be conducting an inquest, lasting some months, into the deaths of over 30 patients at one institution run by the Derbyshire Mental Health Trust. The fact that certain staff had been suspended since 1997 demonstrates the inadequacy of investigation provided under the old system.

The Employment Appeal Tribunal

6–027
This court was established by the Employment Protection Act 1975 to hear appeals from decisions of Industrial Tribunals (now employ-ment tribunals), in particular those relating to unfair dismissal, equal pay and redundancy. The composition of the court for a hearing is one High Court judge, or a "ticketed" circuit judge, sitting with two lay people who have specialised knowledge of industrial relations. It is a superior court of record, equivalent to the High Court. This means its decisions are not subject to judicial review and appeals on points of law go direct to the Court of Appeal.

Offices of the Supreme Court

6–028
These include the Official Solicitor's Department, whose job it is to protect the interests of minors and mental patients under a legal disability; the Tipstaff who delivers people to court or prison on the order of a Supreme Court judge and the Public Guardianship Office (formerly Public Trust Office), which holds private money held in court pending a case and handles the private money of some men-tally disabled persons incapable of handling their own affairs.

10. Court Management

6–029   The system of court management has been fundamentally restructured in 2005, under the Courts Act 2003, following the recommendations of the 2001 *Review of the Criminal Courts of England and Wales* (the Auld Review). The Lord Chancellor and his department, the DCA, run the courts, their staff and buildings. Under the Courts Act 2003, he is under "a duty to ensure that there is an efficient and effective system to support" the running of the courts. A new unified courts agency, Her Majesty's Courts Service is being established from April 2005, under this Act, to administer the day to day running of the courts. This replaces the Court Service and the local magistrates' courts committees, committees of magistrates who were responsible for running their courts. In 2004–5, the Lord Chancellor has established 42 local courts boards under s.4 of the Courts Act. Under s.5, they have the function of scrutinising, reviewing and making recommendations about the way the Lord Chancellor is running the local Crown Court, county courts and magistrates' courts. The Lord Chancellor issues them with guidance as to how they should carry out their functions and must give due consideration to their recommendations. Each courts board consists of seven people—one judge, two magistrates, two people with knowledge and experience of how the courts operate in their area (such as lawyers, or victim support) and two people representative of the area.

Judges of the civil courts are increasingly critical of the government's reluctance to spend money. They consider that civil justice is treated as a poor relation, so that when money is spent on information technology or other improvements it is directed to the criminal courts. In a speech against the increase in court fees, in 1997, Vice-Chancellor Sir Richard Scott said the idea the civil courts should be self-financing was "indefensible from a constitutional point of view". They are frustrated that their IT provision does not begin to equate with that recommended by Lord Woolf in his 1996 review of civil procedure, *Access to Justice*. In February 2003, the Master of the Rolls, head of the Court of Appeal (Civil Division), warned that without enough funding for new technology, the civil justice system was in danger of seizing up. He claimed that £300 million was required to upgrade the system and that only £200m had been allocated. In addition, a paper to the Lord Chancellor from the Civil Justice Council, chaired by him, argued that a large number of courts should be exempt from general taxation. He and the Civil Justice Council and other civil judges are very critical of the Government's stated aim to make the civil courts self-funding. They consider that the courts should be run as a public service. In

July 2002, Lord Chief Justice Woolf accused the Government of "flawed thinking" over their proposal that the civil courts could fund themselves. The policy was "self-evidently nonsense". No other country in the world had such a policy and its effects were "pernicious and dangerous". In October 2003, Lord Justice Mance said the Government must face the fact that civil justice would never pay for itself. He said that in other Commonwealth countries, New Zealand and Australia, fee income paid for less than half the cost of civil and family courts. High fees put people off bringing their cases to court and would mean that commercial cases would subsidise family cases.

Lawyers' groups, such as the Legal Action Group joined the judges in their opposition to the plan for "full costs recovery". The June 2004 editorial of *Legal Action* expressed alarm at the plan to raise income from High Court and CA fees by 108 per cent. The last round of court fee increases had cost the Community Legal Service (CLS) Fund (civil legal aid) £7 million a year and any further increase, without compensating the CLS fund was short-sighted and hypocritical of the Government.

One typical judicial speech, in November 2004, was that of Lord **6–030** Justice Brooke, Vice-President of the Civil Division of the Court of Appeal. He had spent 19 years promoting IT in the courts. He complained of "chronic underfunding" in the civil courts. Things were getting worse, with an inadequate IT infrastructure and very poor pay in the court service, leading to a high turnover of staff. Lawyers were just as critical. In the sixth Woolf survey carried out by the Law Society in 2003, solicitors complained of administrative problems. 40 per cent complained that inefficient administration of court offices had impacted on their clients' ability to pursue claims. A third had had clients who had been discouraged from proceeding because of cost, especially in the High Court.

There are long-standing complaints that London's commercial courts: the Commercial Court, the Admiralty Court and the Technology and Construction Court have inadequate facilities and this risks losing commercial court business from London to foreign destinations. The Lord Chancellor's Department, predecessor to the DCA, published a consultation paper in 2002 but nothing has been done. The commercial court sits in office blocks around the Royal Courts of Justice and in St. Dunstan's house, nearby, described by one judge as "a public disgrace", because of its cramped courtrooms and lack of waiting and consultation facilities. Detailed plans have been drawn up for a replacement to Queen's Building in the Royal Courts of Justice, which would accommodate the commercial and chancery courts but, again, nothing has been done. The London business community share the judges' frustration. They are well aware that the civil courts' IT systems are extremely poor, compared with those of large London law firms. The Commercial Court is important in attracting foreigners in to use London's legal services, which feed the Treasury with at least £850 million a year in taxes. In around 70 per cent of Commercial Court cases, one litigant is foreign. In over 40 per cent, both sides are foreign so the fear of losing work to foreign jurisdictions is a real one. Lord Phillips M.R., head of the civil courts said in 2005 that the number of trials had recently dropped by one third and this was a reflection on better commercial court facilities in Amsterdam, Dublin and elsewhere.

At the lower levels of the court structure, judges complain that court closures reduce public access to justice. By concentrating courts in a few larger centres, it is increasingly difficult and expensive for parties, witnesses, lawyers and other court users to get to the few remaining courts. Since one of the advantages of lay justices used to be their familiarity with their locality, this problem has an added dimension in the context of the widespread closure of magistrates' courts since the 1980s. In 2002, John Killah, writing in *the Times*, complained that 110 local courts had closed in the previous 10 years. These were decisions of local magistrates' courts committees, keen to achieve value for money. He pointed out that it was already difficult enough to get witnesses to turn up to court, without making it worse. Kingston people, after a vigorous campaign, managed to fend off plans to close their magistrates' court, which has sat in Kingston since 1230. Also concerned with access to justice, in 2002, judges and Court Service staff objected to plans to reduce fully serviced county courts from 218 to 93. At the same time, courts of all types have been closing and been replaced with modern combined court centres. This is because the old buildings lack adequate facilities, such as access for the disabled and consultation rooms. The problem is that some of the grand old courthouses are listed buildings, where even the interiors are listed and cannot be altered. The tendency has been to close these and let them rot, rather than attempt to adapt them. They are of no use to developers, because of their listed status. This has been of great concern to judges, court users, architects and all those concerned with our legal and architectural heritage. One such group is SAVE Britain's Heritage. They reported on the problem in 2004, in *Silence in Court, the future of the UK's historic law courts*. They pointed out that 800 law courts had closed since 1945.

6–031   New courts vary in design and there have been recent examples of design defects which have delayed court openings or irritated court users, such as in South Wales in 2004–5. Guidelines were issued in 2004, in the Court Standards Design Guide. They follow a key recommendation of the Auld Review on modernising justice. All new Crown Courts, county courts and magistrates' courts will now have a standard layout. The guide will also ensure better access for all users including the disabled and mothers with young children and it recommends separate waiting areas for witnesses and defendants. Court designers and architects will be expected to incorporate IT such as video links, video conferencing, email, in-court intranet and public display screens in their designs.

Details of the progress, or lack of it, of the modernisation programme for the civil courts can be found on the Her Majesty's Courts Service website, in its Annual Reports.

11. Should we have a Single Civil Court?

The DCA launched a consultation paper in 2005 on *A Single Civil Court?* It asked the questions:

6–032

1. Would a single civil court benefit users and the judiciary?
2. Should there be a single family court that hears all family cases, combining the family jurisdiction of the county court, High Court and the magistrates' court?
3. Would creating a single civil court and removing geographical restrictions improve access to civil justice?
4. Should the existing judicial structure remain the same in a single civil court?

Launching the paper, Minister David Lammy said:

"We want to see how reducing the complexity of the court system, creating a more modern structure for court users, could improve access to justice and see, for example, whether there could be savings. Would it be easier to manage cases, ensure that disputes are resolved more quickly and at reduced cost?"

The Master of the Rolls (head of the civil courts) and Lord Chief Justice, head of the criminal courts, had already announced support for the idea in 2004. Lord Phillips M.R. remarked that the fewer structural barriers there were, the better. He considered it the logical conclusion to the Woolf reforms, which divided civil work into three tracks and created one set of rules for the High Court and county court. Unification would lend flexibility in matching cases to judges. It would stop different divisions of the High Court having different rules. He acknowledged that some judges were apprehensive that it meant abolishing High Court judges. He said we did not need any more High Court judges. There had been a steady creep in their numbers while civil cases were declining. High Court judges were very expensive. All the Heads of Division are currently discussing whether they can use High Court judges more flexibly, as there are too few of them. He said you could have specialist courts, like the existing Commercial Court but within a unified court.

12. Open Justice?

6–033 There has been increasing pressure in recent years for the courts to be more open and approachable. In a democracy, government, including the judiciary, derives its authority from the people. Members of the public should, therefore, have a right to attend court. After all, justice is administered on their behalf and paid for by the taxpayer. Public scrutiny is an incentive for judges and other court professionals to behave politely, fairly and competently. It should encourage consistency in the conduct of proceedings and in the decisions made, such as sentencing. Openness and approachability should encourage civil litigants to take their cases to court, thus enhancing access to justice. In criminal cases, if the apprehension, conviction and sentencing of offenders is to have any generally deterrent effect then criminal cases must be reported, locally and nationally.

Further, most international judicial instruments emphasise that the right to a public trial is the right of a litigant. Of course, a civil litigant may not want publicity, hence the popularity of arbitration and other forms of alternative dispute resolution, described in Chapter 12, below.

In any event, Art.6(1) of the Convention (right to a fair trial) provides:

"In the determination of his civil rights and obligations or of any criminal charge against him, everyone is entitled to a fair and public hearing within a reasonable time by an independent and impartial tribunal established by law. Judgment shall be pronounced publicly but the press and public may be excluded from all or part of the trial in the interests of morals, public order or national security in a democratic society, where the interests of juveniles or the protection of the private life of the parties so require, or to the extent strictly necessary in the opinion of the court in special circumstances where publicity would prejudice the interests of justice."

Under present practice, in 2005, there are some proceedings which are routinely closed to the public and/or unreported and some of these are problematic. Where a defendant is refused bail by magistrates and applies to the Crown Court, he appears before a judge in chambers. Proceedings are tape recorded but unreported by the press. Reporting restrictions are regularly imposed, under the Contempt of Court Act 1981, in other Crown Court proceedings. The youth court, in the magistrates' court, is closed to ordinary members of the public, to protect the young person. Proceedings may be reported but the youngster will not be named, unless the judge or justices make an exception to permit this.

The procedure in all civil courts is now regulated by the Civil Procedure Rules 1998 (CPR). The general rule for hearings in court is set out in CPR 39.2: This states that "(1)The general rule is that a hearing is to be in public". Under (3), a hearing, or any part of it, may be in private if publicity would defeat its object, or it involves national security, or confidential information or it is necessary to protect a patient or child, or for various other reasons, or where the court considers it necessary, "in the interests of justice". The Rules direct the civil judge to Art.6 of the Convetion, above. The importation of Art.6 had a big impact on civil judges. Bearing in mind that small claims and most other proceedings are heard by district judges in the county court, in the judge's own room ("chambers"), these all took place behind closed doors until 1999. They have now had to be opened up to the public, because this is required by Art.6 and the CPR. I would add the comment that the present position is far from satisfactory, however. Most civil district judges have key coded security doors on their chambers so a member of the public is likely to be deterred from asking if they could watch proceedings, even if they were aware that they are open to the public. I have been engaged in researching the judiciary during 2003–5 and have yet to see any member of the public watching these civil proceedings. 6–034

One of the greatest anomalies relates to family proceedings, the closed nature of which has become very contentious, since 2000. While these are open in the magistrates' court, identical cases in the county courts and High Court are closed to the public and unreported. This is a reversal of the position in the early twentieth century, when the newspapers would print salacious details exposed in divorce cases. Hewson explained that the judges of the time thought such cases ought to be open, as a matter of principle. In 1936, in *McPherson v McPherson*, the PC said that a divorce pronounced in private was voidable, because the judge had denied the public their right to be present. Lord Blansbourgh said "publicity is the authentic hallmark of judicial, as distinct from administrative procedure". In *Ambard v Attorney-General for Trinidad and*

Tobago (1936, PC) Lord Atkin remarked "Justice is not a cloistered virtue". The history of publicity in family cases and present position are described at length in the judgments of the President of the Family Division and Thorpe L.J. in *Allan v Clibbery* [2002] EWCA Civ 45. Uncontested divorces are dealt with without any hearing at all, in the county court, other than the formal pronouncement of decrees nisi en bloc. Contested divorces in open court are almost unknown. Most complex cases involve proceedings under the Children Act 1989 or to ancillary relief proceedings (disputes about money and assets after a relationship breaks down). Applications for ancillary relief are almost invariably heard in chambers. The public is almost always excluded from children proceedings which invariably remain confidential, subject to judgments, made suitably anonymous. The judges recognized in this and other cases that the courts have to effect a balancing exercise between the right to respect for family life and privacy in Art.8 and the right to freedom of expression in Art.10. They remarked that it is widely recognised in European jurisprudence that the balance in children cases is in favour of confidentiality, see *B v UK, P v UK* (2001, ECtHR). In *Allan v Clibbery*, Allan, described as a prominent businessman, lost his appeal against his former mistress being permitted to disclose to the *Daily Mail* and Hong Kong media, the details of their private lives that came to light in the property dispute that arose after their relationship broke down. It had become apparent at the hearing that she was one of several mistresses and the appellant claimed to have paid her to be at his disposal, for sex. In 2004, in *Blunkett v Quinn* [2004] EWHC 2816 (Fam), Ryder J. decided to deliver in open court his judgment in a case involving the then Home Secretary, David Blunkett and his ex-lover and her child. He said he did this in order to correct false information already in the public domain, in the ferocious publicity surrounding the case.

In 2004–5, many fathers' groups, such as the aggressive Fathers 4 Justice, represented by Spiderman, Batman and other demonstrators, argued that more family proceedings should be open to the public. They were aggrieved at what they saw as the courts' failure to enforce contact orders allowing them to see their children where a mother disobeys court orders. They considered that publicity would expose the unreasonableness, as they saw it, of disobedient mothers and ineffectual judges. Some judges also argued for greater publicity, for different reasons. For example, Lord Justice Thorpe was quoted by Gibb, in January 2005, as considering that it would be "healthy" to remove privacy. Exposing the system to public scrutiny would reveal the family justice system to be in good condition. He reminded us that in Scotland, family proceedings have always been in public. "Campaigners say that the judges have a vested interest in maintaining privacy because it enables them to carry on making these 'wicked' decisions in private".

The courts are a source of free, public entertainment and educa- **6–035** tion. Until the late twentieth century, public galleries were routinely populated by people who were interested in court proceedings in general, especially those with time on their hands. Now that TV and DVD are more fun, courts are rarely visited, with exceptions such as the Old Bailey and certain cases in the Royal Courts of Justice, such as the Sally Clark murder appeal and various defamation actions. In the 1980s, the Bar Council campaigned to televise court proceedings. They gave up. In 1994, Sir Thomas Bingham, then Master of the Rolls and now a Law Lord, spoke in favour of an experiment in televising. During that period, an experiment was being conducted in televising trials in Scotland. In 2002, the Lockerbie Appeal, involving a Scottish court sitting in the Netherlands, was televised. In November 2004, Lord Chancellor Falconer launched a consultation paper on televising the courts and at the same time, an experiment started in recording the proceedings of the CA (Civil Division). Footage was not broadcast but used for evaluation. It is currently illegal to take photographs or record proceedings in court, or even to make drawings. Court artists, whose depictions appear in the media, have to leave the courtroom and sketch from memory. Mohammed Zahir, who used his mobile phone to take pictures of defendants in the dock of Birmingham Crown Court, was jailed for 9 months in 2004. In the USA, all 50 states permit cameras in some courts and 39 allow them into trial courts. *Court TV* broadcasts high profile trials. Some of these are broadcast internationally, such as the Rodney King beatings trials and the O.J. Simpson trial in the 1990s but Lord Chancellor Falconer remarked, in November 2004, "We don't want our courts turning into US-style media circuses. . . . Justice should be seen to be done but our priority must be that justice is done." Lord Justice Judge, Deputy Chief Justice, took part in a seminar debating broadcasting the courts in January 2005. He said he was deeply committed to open justice but he was worried witnesses would be deterred and for that reason, he distinguished televising the courts from televising Parliament.

Interestingly, the Constitutional Reform Act 2005 exempts the new Supreme Court from the ban on photography. In the meantime, courts have been holding open days to try and attract the public back into court. The initiative started in the magistrates' courts and has spread to the Crown Court and combined court centres. Visitors can explore the courtrooms and prison vans and participate in mock sentencing exercises.

BIBLIOGRAPHY

6–036 Speeches by Lords Bingham and Steyn are referenced in Chapter 4.

I. Caplin, "Chief Justice rises to the supreme challenge", *The Times*, September 14, 2004 (on the NZ Supreme Court).

R. Cooke, "The Law Lords; An Endangered Heritage" (2003) 119 L.Q.R. 49. The LQR is available in hard copy and on *Westlaw*.

R. Cornes, "Appealing to history: the New Zealand Supreme Court debate" (2004) 24 *Legal Studies* 210.

Department for Constitutional Affairs, *Constitutional Reform: a Supreme Court for the United Kingdom*, CP 11/03 July 2003 and responses on the DCA website: *www.dca.gov.uk* and Lord Falconer's press release 296/03.

The Law Lords' response to the Government's consultation paper on Constitutional reform: a Supreme Court for the United Kingdom, July 2003, Parliament website, under Judicial Work: *www.parliament.uk*

F. Gibb and J. Killah, "Magistrates will be packaged off to vast justice factories in large urban centres", *The Times*, July 2, 2002.

F. Gibb, "Radical in a roll-neck sweater has judicial mission to reform", (interview with the M.R. on a unified civil court),*The Times*, March 2, 2005.

F. Gibb, "Fathers winning battle to have custody hearings in public." *The Times*, January 10, 2005.

B. Henson, "Why have secrecy in the family courts?" (2003) 153 N.L.J. 369.

H. Schleiff, "Cameras in courts" (2004) 154 N.L.J. 1745 (also available on *LexisNexis*).

Sir Richard Scott's 1997 speech is quoted at (1997) 147 N.L.J. 750.

Lord Woolf C.J., Squire Centenary Lecture, March 4, 2004, Cambridge, "The Rule of Law and a Change in the Constitution", televised. The transcript is on the judges' speeches section of the DCA website: *www.dca.gov.uk*

The articles by Professor Robert Stevens, Baroness Hale, Sir Thomas Legg and Professor John Bell all appear in a special issue of *Legal Studies*, on the proposed Supreme Court, Vol.24, March 2004.

FURTHER READING AND SOURCES FOR UPDATING THIS
6–037 CHAPTER

Online updates to this book: *http://www.sweetandmaxwell.co.uk/academic/updates/darbyshire/index.html*. This site also contains a self-guided tour of legal London, with pictures.

Annual *Judicial Statistics*, DCA website: *www.dca.gov.uk*. The report used in the preparation of this chapter was the 2003 report and more detail, including recent case statistics, can be found in those annual reports.

The Administrative Court website, part of the Her Majesty's Courts
  Service website: *www.hmcourts-service.gov.uk*
Civil Justice Council: *www.civiljusticecouncil.gov.uk*
Family Justice Council: *www.family-justice-council.org.uk*
For more detail on the Law Lords and their judgments, see the UK
  Parliament website: *www.parliament.uk* (click on "Judicial Work").
In 2005, the website of the European Court of Justice, containing more
  detailed information and judgments: *http://europa.eu.int/institu-*
  tions/court/index_en.htm
European Court of Human Rights, information, press releases and
  judgments: *www.echr.coe.int/Eng/General.htm*
Judicial Committee of the Privy Council, information and judgments: *www.privy-council.org.uk*
For details of coroners and updates on the reform of coroners'
  courts, see the "Coroner reform" pages of the Home Office
  website: *www.homeoffice.gov.uk*. (These will eventually be moved
  to the DCA website).
Judges' speeches are on the DCA website.
For those interested in our legal architectural heritage: *www.savebri-*
  tainsheritage.org. Their 2004 report is summarised in *Counsel*, June
  2004, p.32.

7. Criminal Courts

There are two criminal trial courts (courts of original jurisdiction) 7–001
in England and Wales and all criminal cases are heard in one of these
two, the magistrates' court or the Crown Court. Lord Justice Auld,
in his *Review of the Criminal Courts of England and Wales* (2001) recommended the development of a third middle tier but most respondents to the *Review* were opposed to this and the Government
rejected the idea. He recommended a unified criminal court divided
into three tiers, or failing this, a unified courts administration. This
last recommendation has been carried out and Her Majesty's Courts
Service has been created, as explained below.

Part 7 of the Courts Act 2003 defines criminal courts (s.68) and
provides for a Criminal Procedure Rules Committee to make one
coordinated set of rules for the criminal courts. As explained in
Chapter 10 on criminal procedure, below, the very first set of criminal procedure rules was published and applicable from April 2005.
This also follows a recommendation of Lord Justice Auld. His
Review has a dedicated website. It also contains a summary and
some of the responses made by interested individuals and groups.
On the website accompanying this book, there is a summary of the
main recommendations and a commentary.

Most of his recommendations related to criminal procedure and
they, and their outcomes, are explained in Chapter 10, below. The
most obvious outcomes are the Courts Act 2003 and the Criminal
Justice Act 2003, which are being brought into force during the lifetime of this book.

1. Summary Proceedings in the Magistrates' Court

There are hundreds of magistrates' courts spread throughout 7–002
England and Wales, although their numbers have diminished

because of court closures and bench amalgamations since the 1980s, as explained in the previous chapter. Over 95 per cent of criminal cases begin and end at the magistrates' court. Until 1949 they were known as police courts and many magistrates' courts are situated close to police stations. This is unfortunate since it conveys the impression that the court sits at the convenience of the police to distribute punishment in accordance with police evidence. As the police inevitably figure prominently in the magistrates' court, it is not surprising that the public has tended to think of it as the police court (see Darbyshire, "Concern", 1997, cited below). Happily, there are not so many uniformed police officers in today's courts as there were prior to 1985. The Prosecution of Offences Act 1985 replaced police prosecutors with Crown Prosecutors and the 1990s saw private security officers replacing police court security officers. For most people who appear in a criminal court, as a defendant, witness or victim, the court involved will be the magistrates' court. All summary offences are statutorily defined. They include the vast bulk of traffic offences, the most trivial of which many people wrongly assume not to be normal criminal offences. Even a parking offence is a criminal offence, in English law. We do not have a third species of law, "violations", as they do in the US. Common assault is a summary offence, as are many regulatory offences, prosecuted by government departments.

The category of offences of medium seriousness is called "triable either way" and most are tried in the magistrates' court. Here, the defendant may elect trial in the magistrates' court or in the Crown Court, unless the magistrates insist on a Crown Court trial. Most defendants opt for summary trial in the magistrates' court. The procedure is described more fully in Chapter 10 on criminal procedure.

Magistrates' jurisdiction is statutory. They can send an offender to prison for up to six months, or a maximum of 12 for more than one offence and/or impose a fine of up to £5,000 (fixed by the Powers of the Criminal Courts (Sentencing) Act 2000) but when the Criminal Justice Act 2003, s.154 comes into force, magistrates' sentencing powers will double to one year's imprisonment. If, after conviction, the bench feel their powers of sentence are inadequate, they may commit to the Crown Court for sentencing. A district judge (magistrates' court) sitting alone generally has the same powers as a bench of two or three lay justices. At the hearing of any case, the bench is assisted by the justices' clerk or, more usually, a court clerk (sometimes called legal adviser). The former is legally qualified. The magistrates' clerk may advise the magistrates on the law. Magistrates and their clerks are discussed more fully in Chapter 15, below.

7–003   Throughout the nineteenth and twentieth centuries, more and more work has been shifted down onto the shoulders of the magistrates, by reclassifying offences as summary only or by shifting them out of the indictable category into the triable either way category. The result is that magistrates deal with over 95 per cent of all criminal cases and 95 per cent of all sentencing. It is a big mistake, therefore, to think of this court as dealing with trivia. Of course, intention is that, when the Criminal Justice Act 2003 comes into force, even more work will shift out of the Crown Court and into the magistrates' court. For discussion see Darbyshire ("Importance and Neglect", 1997).

The Crown Court

This court is discussed more fully below. The Crown Court hears   7–004
appeals against conviction and/or sentence from those convicted in the magistrates' court. Appeals are usually heard by a circuit judge and two magistrates. The Crown Court also sentences defendants who have been committed for sentencing by magistrates, after having been summarily convicted of an either-way offence.

The Divisional Court of the Queen's Bench Division

This court hears prosecution and defence appeals by way of case   7–005
stated on points of law from the magistrates' courts and conducts judicial reviews of the legality of proceedings in magistrates' courts. In doing this it is exercising the High Court's prerogative power to review the legality of proceedings in inferior tribunals. These procedures are discussed more fully in the previous chapter. As explained there, an Administrative Court was created in 2000.

House of Lords

Where the case stated raises a point of law of general public   7–006
importance, provided leave is given by the Divisional Court or by the Appeal Committee of the House of Lords, the prosecution or defence may appeal to the House, bypassing the Court of Appeal. This is known as a "leapfrog" appeal, described in Chapter 6 on civil courts, above. The House, and its replacement with a Supreme Court, has also been described in Chapter 6.

2. Trial on Indictment

Indictable offences are recognised at common law, or by statute,   7–007
and are the more serious forms of crime. As well as indictable offences, "triable either way" offences can also be tried at the Crown Court. Criminal procedure is described in Chapter 10, below.

The Crown Court

The Courts Act 1971, which abolished the courts of quarter   7–008
sessions and assizes, created in their place one unified Crown Court.

It forms part of the Supreme Court and under the 1971 Courts Act, England and Wales are divided into six circuits based in London, Bristol, Birmingham, Manchester, Cardiff and Leeds. There are 78 Crown Court Centres of three types. *First tier* centres are visited by High Court judges for serious Crown Court work and High Court civil business. *Second tier* centres are visited by High Court judges for Crown Court criminal business only. *Third tier* centres are not normally visited by a High Court judge. Circuit judges and recorders sit at all three. Two presiding High Court judges are appointed to each circuit and are responsible for the organisational arrangements of the Crown Court. By Practice Direction, the Lord Chief Justice directs that offences should be classified into one of four categories and should be tried accordingly:

Class 1: The most serious offences are generally tried by a High Court judge, unless released by the presiding judge to a circuit judge. They include treason and murder.

Class 2: These are generally also tried by a High Court judge unless released to a circuit judge or a recorder. They include manslaughter and rape.

Class 3: These may be listed for a High Court judge but shifted to a circuit judge or authorised, trained recorder, if the listing officer, with general or particular directions by the presiding judge, so decides. They include all indictable offences other than those falling within classes 1, 2 and 4, for example, affray, aggravated burglary, kidnapping and causing death by dangerous driving.

Class 4: These offences are normally tried by a circuit judge or recorder but can be tried by a High Court judge, with the consent of that judge or the presiding judge. This class includes all "triable either way" offences and certain others, for example conspiracy, robbery, grievous bodily harm.

The most famous Crown Court Centre is the Old Bailey in the City of London. It has a fascinating and gruesome history over several centuries and is a world famous tourist attraction. It deals with the most serious offences from London and the south of England. About 95 per cent of its workload is heard at other Crown Court Centres, such as Kingston so it is left with only the most serious cases of murder, fraud, terrorism, rape and so on. The Old Bailey is described on the website accompanying this book, as it forms part of my illustrated self-guided tour of legal London (see note on Online Updates at the front of this book).

The Court of Appeal (Criminal Division)

The CA (Criminal Division) was established under the provisions   7–009
of the Criminal Appeal Act 1966 to replace the former Court of
Criminal Appeal. The Court's jurisdiction is contained in the
Criminal Appeal Act 1968, as amended by the Criminal Appeal Act
1995, and the Criminal Justice Act 2003. Its work is fully described
in Chapter 10 on criminal procedure, below.

It usually sits only in the Royal Courts of Justice in the Strand but
in 1999, Lord Chief Justice Bingham took it to sit in Liverpool and
in Bristol and it sat at Snaresbrook in 2002. (The Royal Courts of
Justice also feature in my legal London tour, on this book's website).
The Court is made up of the Lord Chief Justice, the Vice-President
of the Criminal Division, Lords Justices of Appeal, the judges of the
Queen's Bench Division and a number of circuit judges specially
nominated by the Lord Chief Justice. It normally sits as a bench of
three: one Lord Justice of Appeal and two High Court judges, or one
Lord Justice of Appeal, one High Court judge and a circuit judge.
The jurisdiction of the CACD, as it is known is:

(i)   to hear appeals against conviction on indictment with the
        leave of the CA or if the trial judge certifies that the case is fit
        for appeal (Criminal Appeal Act 1995, s.1);
(ii)   to hear appeals against sentence pronounced by the Crown
        Court provided that the sentence is not one fixed by law and
        provided that the court grants leave. An application for
        leave may be determined by a single judge, but if leave is
        refused, the appellant can require a full court, *i.e.* two or
        more judges to determine the matter;
(iii)   to hear appeals referred to it by the Criminal Cases Review
        Commission, under the Criminal Appeal Act 1995;
(iv)   to hear appeals against a verdict of "not guilty by reason of
        insanity" or against findings of fitness and unfitness to plead;
(v)   to hear an appeal by the prosecution against an acquittal on
        a point of law at the trial in the Crown Court. This provision
        involves an application by the Attorney-General for the
        opinion of the Court on the point of law and is known as an
        "Attorney-General's Reference". The result cannot affect the
        acquittal and the defendant is not named in the appeal;
(vi)   to hear an appeal by the prosecutor, again as an "Attorney-
        General's Reference" against a lenient sentence. In this case
        the Court will set out sentencing guidelines for the future
        but may also increase the actual sentence imposed; and
(vii)   to hear prosecution appeals against judge's rulings, under
        the Criminal Justice Act 2003, as described in Chapter 10 on
        criminal procedure, below.

The CACD publishes an annual report, providing statistical details of its caseload. It can be downloaded from the Her Majesty's Courts Service website.

The CACD has a massive case load and the judges who sit in it are under enormous pressure to deal with long lists of appeals very swiftly. It is normal for a bench of three judges to deal with a mixed list of sentencing appeals and applications for leave to appeal all morning (eight cases or more) and a substantive appeal in the afternoon. High Court judges normally sit in the court for a maximum shift of three weeks at a time, as the pressure of work is so great, usually requiring the judges to work long hours into the night and at weekends, reading papers and writing judgements. Bear that in mind the next time you read the law report of a criminal appeal.

House of Lords

7–010   This, and its proposed replacement by a Supreme Court, are described in Chapter 6, above. This hears appeals from the CA and those which have leapfrogged from the High Court. Either prosecutor or defendant may appeal, provided the CA certifies that a point of law of general public importance is involved and that either court feels that the point should be considered by the House and grants leave. The House, in disposing of the appeal, may exercise any of the powers of the CA, or remit the case to it (Criminal Appeal Act 1968.)

The European Court of Justice and the European Court of Human Rights

7–011   These are described in Chapters 3 and 4, above.

3. The Youth Court

7–012   In the UK, the age of criminal responsibility is 10. Ten to 17-year-olds are almost all tried in the Youth Court, which is a special court within the magistrates' court. This is a very important court, since the peak age of offending in England and Wales is around 17–18 (source: *Annual Criminal Statistics*), although the majority of young offenders are diverted from the criminal process by the official cautioning scheme, put on a statutory basis by the Crime and Disorder Act 1998. As explained in the Magistrates' Chapter, the bench comprises specially trained lay magistrates, who usually sit in mixed gender threesomes, or a district judge (magistrates' court). The predecessor of the court, the juvenile court, was formed in 1908, by the Juvenile Offences Act. It was thought desirable to keep adult

defendants separate from juveniles. Ideally, the Act's progenito
would have liked to have seen a separate system of courts for
young offenders. Separate courts have never been developed,
except in large cities like London, Nottingham, Birmingham and
elsewhere, where the caseload warranted it. Instead, it became the
habit at smaller courts to convene the juvenile court on a separate
day from the adult court. Eventually, this was whittled down to an
hour's gap between adult and juvenile courts but this was abandoned. The Court originally dealt with the "deprived" as well as
the "depraved". In other words, it heard civil applications, often
from the local authority, to take the child into care for its own
welfare. This work was given away to the family proceedings
court when the youth court was created by the Children Act 1989
so it now has a purely criminal jurisdiction. Importantly, the public
are excluded from the youth court and procedure is more informal
than that of the adult court. The youth court has a variety of
powers. For example, as well as fining the child and/or parent, it
can impose a supervision order, which is like a probation order for
children, or order detention and training for up to two years so
magistrates are more powerful in this court than in the adult court.

Only those youngsters who commit very serious crimes or those
tried with an adult are meant to be sent up for trial in the Crown
Court. This means something like murder or rape. Jamie Bulger's
killers, Thompson and Venables, were tried in the Crown Court.
Lord Justice Auld recommended, in his *Review of the Criminal Courts*,
that serious crimes should be heard in a youth court composed of a
judge and two youth panel magistrates. In the Courts Act 2003, all
judges were given the jurisdiction to sit in the magistrates' court but
there are no current plans to carry out Lord Justice Auld's suggestion and remove children from the Crown Court altogether. For more
details of the guidelines magistrates have been given by the courts
on determining which cases should be sent up from the youth court
to the Crown Court, see Thompson, 2004. The criteria are now very
complex.

4. The Community Justice Centre—a New Type of Criminal Court

In December 2004, a pilot project commenced, establishing a   7–013
Community Justice Centre in North Liverpool. The aim of the
Department of Constitutional Affairs (DCA) in establishing it is to
engage the local community in finding solutions to anti-social
behaviour, social exclusion and crime. It was modelled on the Red

Hook Project in New York. The court will start with the jurisdiction of the magistrates' court and its remit will later be expanded. It will act as an outreach centre for the local community, using the court building for community activities. It is accompanied by a programme of community consultation and engagement. One of its themes is restorative justice. Its first judge has been newly appointed as a circuit judge. He was a district judge in the magistrates' court prior to this appointment. He is a graduate of Liverpool University. He will monitor the progress of sentences he passes. For more details of the Red Hook project and other models, see Brimacombe.

5. The Special Immigration Appeals Commission

7–014   Although this is classed as a tribunal, it is a superior court of record and is both an appellate administrative tribunal and has a criminal jurisdiction. It was established by the Special Immigration Appeals Commission Act 1997 to hear such cases as appeals from deportation orders but it achieved notoriety as the last route of appeal for foreign nationals detained on the grounds of being terrorist suspects, under the Anti-Terrorism, Crime and Security Act 2001, the Act which fell foul of the Convention, in the 2004 House of Lords case *A (FC) and others v SS for the Home Dept* described in Chapter 4, above. Suspects who appeared before it and risked being detained in prison indefinitely, were represented by special advocates, appointed by the Government. During the successful challenge of the Act's legality, several of them resigned.

6. Court Management and Modernisation

7–015   Departmental responsibility for resourcing and managing all courts is that of the DCA and ministerial responsibility is taken by the Lord Chancellor and junior ministers in the DCA. As explained in Chapter 15 on magistrates, below, they used to run their own courts via committees called magistrates' courts committees. These have been replaced by local Courts Boards, which are responsible for running all local courts and are described in the previous chapter. The Court Service, which ran the Crown Court and courts other than magistrates' courts, has been replaced from 2005 with Her Majesty's Courts Service (HMCS) which is an independent agency, running all the courts. Again, this follows a recommendation in the 2001 Auld Review that we should have a unified courts agency.

The best source of information on running the courts are the Annual reports of the Court Service/HMCS. The 2003–4 report explains that as part of its Modernising Justice programme, which commenced in 2001, it is about halfway through installing a new IT infrastructure called LINK, intended for the use of the judiciary and staff in all Crown Court Centres. New computers are being installed which will allow secure email access to all criminal justice agencies and criminal lawyers. It will allow access to case management software and the courts' diaries.

This system has been piloted in several areas already and I know from my research on judges in 2003–4 that, while barristers are prepared to cooperate with this system, firms of defence solicitors have not been persuaded to participate, despite the fact that the government is prepared to install the relevant hardware and software in their offices. The software enables the effective trial management programme to operate as intended. This new plan for efficiency in criminal cases is described in Chapter 10 on criminal procedure, below.

As part of the modernisation programme the Crown Court is being **7–016** linked to prison service video conferencing facilities so that prisoners can "appear" from secure conditions in preliminary hearings without having to transport them to court, which is notoriously expensive and the cause of frustrating delays. The same new technology allows vulnerable witnesses to give evidence from outside the courtroom.

Another part of the programme is the installation of XHIBIT which allows all trial participants to track the progress of a case through modern technology, using the internet and texting to mobile phones and pagers. Witnesses and police officers will not need to hang around waiting in court but will be able to come when needed. The DCA estimates 80,000 policing days per year will be freed up in this way.

During the 1990s the courts have been endeavouring to make themselves more user-friendly, to court users and visitors. A Courts Charter has been published and is available from the HMCS website. The Charter Mark is awarded to courts who satisfy these criteria:

1. set standards for service;
2. are open and provide full information;
3. consult and involve;
4. encourage access and the promotion of choice;
5. treat all fairly;
6. put things right when they go wrong;
7. use resources effectively;
8. innovate and improve;

9. work with other providers; and
10. satisfy their customers.

Details of how courts have provided better facilities for users are listed in the press releases on the DCA website when it is announced that another court has been granted a charter mark. Examples include: training staff in sign language; sending court staff into solicitors' offices to learn how the court could improve its service; providing consulting rooms and dedicated Witness Support suites with separate entrances.

7–017   Her Majesty's Courts Service Annual Report updates us on the modernisation programme, including the piloting of electronic advice kiosks and video conferencing. An increasing number of courts have their own websites, accessed via the HMCS website.

7. Justice for All 2002

7–018   This white paper sets out the Government's response to the Auld recommendations and the comments thereon and explains the Government's plans for criminal justice, much of which they are now putting into effect, especially via the Courts Act 2003 and the Criminal Justice Act 2003.

One of the Government's promises was to "integrate the management of the courts within a single courts administration and allow the Crown Court judges to conduct trials in magistrates' courts" (Executive Summary, 0.12). Under the heading "Joining up the CJS" they resolved, "we must bring the component parts of the CJS together to form a coherent whole". This required joining up criminal justice agencies and "linking up the targets, delivery objectives, strategic plans, IT systems and the daily work of every individual in each criminal justice agency". They said they had already:

- established a cabinet committee chaired by the Home Secretary, including the Lord Chancellor and Attorney-General;
- appointed a Minister for Justice Systems Information Technology; and
- established a new criminal justice IT organisation.

They proposed to:

- invest £600m in IT;
- establish a new National Criminal Justice Board, chaired by the Permanent Secretary of the Home Office, including the Permanent Secretary of the Lord Chancellor's Department, the

DPP, the Chief Executives of the CJS agencies, the President of ACPO and a senior judge. It would support a new cabinet committee and be responsible for overall CJS delivery;
- establish a Criminal Justice Council that would improve on consultative mechanisms;
- set up 42 Criminal Justice Boards in 2002-3, accountable to the new Criminal Justice Board, "with accompanying advisory and consultative machinery";
- ensure secure email by 2003;
- ensure electronic exchange of case file information by 2005; and
- ensure victims may track case progress by 2005.
(Executive Summary, 0.26 to 0.29).

Lord Justice Auld's *Review of the Criminal Courts of England and Wales* (2001) had recommended most of these improvements. He recommended Criminal Justice Boards, in the hope of making the management of criminal justice much more coherent. Virtually all of this has been put into operation by 2005, as explained in this chapter and Chapter 10 on criminal procedure, below.

FURTHER READING AND SOURCES FOR UPDATING THIS CHAPTER

Online updates to this book: *http://www.sweetandmaxwell.co.uk/* **7–019**
academic/updates/darbyshire/index.html. That website also includes a self-guided legal London tour, taking the visitor to the Old Bailey, the most important Crown Court centre, the Royal Courts of Justice and the Inns of Court.
Information on the courts' jurisdiction and statistics on their workload are contained in the Annual *Judicial Statistics,* DCA website: *www.dca.gov.uk*
Annual Reports of the Court Service/Her Majesty's Courts Service: *www.hmcourts-service.gov.uk*
Lord Justice Auld, *Review of the Criminal Courts of England and Wales* (2001): *www.criminal-courts-review.org.uk*
Justice for All, July 2002 and the Government's response: *www.cjson-line. gov.uk*
H. Brimacombe, "Bringing justice closer to the community", *Legal Action*, December 2004, p.10.
P. Darbyshire, "An Essay on the Importance and Neglect of the Magistracy" [1997] Crim. L.R. 627.
P. Darbyshire, "For the New Lord Chancellor—Some Causes of Concern About Magistrates" [1997] Crim. L.R. 861.
R. Thompson, "Lost in Translation: Determining Jurisdiction in the Youth Court" (2004) 168 *Justice of the Peace* 388.

8. History

1. Continuity

The UK's system of government, and the legal institutions which   8–001
form part of it, are only explicable in terms of their long history.

One important factor is that whereas most continental legal
systems rely heavily on legal principles derived from Roman Law,
the English legal system has remained comparatively uninfluenced
by this source. The reasons for is the unbroken historical development of the system in England, where at no time was it felt necessary to look outside the principles of common law or equity for
assistance. Inevitably, through the ecclesiastical courts in particular,
some Roman Law influence can be traced but in general terms this
is very limited, and especially when comparison is made with
systems elsewhere. Indeed, the reason why England resisted the
"invasion" of Roman Law, which forms the base of European civil
law systems, was that a unified common law system was already
growing in strength from the period prior to the Norman Conquest.

2. Early History

Anglo-Saxon Laws

The earliest English laws of which there is documentary evidence   8–002
date from the Anglo-Saxon period of English history before the
Norman Conquest. These laws are not strictly English laws; more
accurately they are the laws relating to a particular tribal area such
as Kent, Wessex or Mercia. In practice these laws are based on what
seems to have been the original customs of the local settlers. Not
unnaturally there are marked discrepancies in the details of the laws
remaining from the different areas. They clearly derive from the
time before England emerged as a national unit.

The Norman Conquest (1066)

8–003   The Anglo-Saxon divisions were just giving way to a national entity when the Norman invasion of England occurred. The result of the Battle of Hastings in 1066 led to William the Conqueror ascending the English throne determined on a process of centralisation. William's tactics were to impose strong national government and this he did by causing his Norman followers to become the major land-owners throughout the country. The system used was "subinfeudation" under which all land belonged to the monarch and was by him granted to his followers on certain conditions. In turn they could grant their land to their tenants. Again subject to conditions, those tenants could make similar grants and so on, down the ladder. This method of granting land created the complete feudal system under which tenants owed duties to their lord, whilst he in turn owed duties to his lord and so on up to the monarch, as the supreme point of the feudal pyramid. However, the system never became as firmly entrenched in this country as it did, for instance, in France.

Feudal Courts

8–004   In the development of the feudal system a characteristic benefit to the feudal lord was the right to hold his own court. From the holding of this court he would obtain financial benefits, whilst at the same time it gave him effective power over the locality. So far as the ordinary individual was concerned this local manor court was the one which affected him most. Bearing in mind that the concept of central authority in law and government was still comparatively new, it was to take a long time before the royal courts were able to exercise control over these local courts. Although the passage of centuries did see the transfer of real power from local to national courts, these feudal courts remained in being in many instances down to the property legislation of 1925. Until 1925 there was a tenure of property called "copyhold", which involved the registration of the transaction in the local court roll so that the person held the land by "copy" of the court roll. This was a survival of a feudal court responsibility.

Royal Courts

8–005   Following the Norman Conquest, succeeding monarchs soon realised that besides the need for strong national government there was also a need for the development of a system of national law and order. To this end the closest advisers of the monarch—the "*curia regis*", or "King's council", as it was called—encouraged, over a period of time, the establishment of three separate royal courts which sat at Westminster. These were:

(i) the Court of Exchequer, which as the name applies was mainly concerned with cases affecting the royal revenue, but which also had a limited civil jurisdiction;

(ii) the Court of King's Bench, which taking its name from the original concept of the monarch sitting with his judges "*en banc*"—on the bench—at Westminster, dealt with both civil and criminal cases in which the King had an interest; and

(iii) the Court of Common Pleas, which was established to hear civil cases brought by one individual against another.

Each of the courts had its own judges. In the Court of Exchequer sat judges called Barons, with a presiding judge known as the Chief Baron. This Court appears to be the oldest of the three, emerging in recognisable form in the early thirteenth century having developed out of the financial organisation responsible for the royal revenues. The Court of King's Bench had its own Chief Justice and separate judges, and was closely linked with the monarch and the Great Council for a very long time. This was due, in particular, to the original understanding that this was the court which followed the King's person. The Court of Common Pleas had its own Chief Justice and judges and left records from the early thirteenth century.

All three courts seem to have been required by the monarch— Stow in his survey of London says in 1224—to make their base in Westminster Hall and there arose continuing conflicts between them over jurisdiction. The importance of getting more and more work was largely brought about by the fact that the judges were paid out of the court fees. At any rate these three royal courts, later added to by the introduction of a Court of Chancery, survived five centuries before being reconstructed into the present High Court of Justice in the Judicature Acts 1873–1875. The ultimate merger of Exchequer and Common Pleas into the Queen's Bench Division came about in 1880.

3. The Common Law

Origin

As a centralised system of law and order gradually developed, so it became necessary for the various customary laws of the different regions to give way to national laws. This national law came to be known as the common law. It was called "common" because it was common to the whole country, as opposed to the local customs which had previously predominated in the different regions. Since inevitably the different customs at times turned out to be in conflict, the decisions of the judges, absorbing certain of these customs and

8–006

rejecting others, came to be of first-rate importance. They were creating "the law of the realm". Consequently, a feature of the original establishment of the common law is that it was derived entirely from case law.

Development

8–007   The Norman Kings, in attempting to weld the country together, made use of royal commissioners to travel the country to deal with governmental matters of one kind and another. The production of the "Domesday Book", as a property and financial survey, is the best known example of this system. The extension of these activities to the judicial field seems to have arisen not long after the Conquest, when the King would appoint judges as royal commissioners, charged with certain royal powers, to travel different parts of the country to deal with civil and criminal matters in the locality in which they arose.

The sending of judges, or, as they were originally called, "itinerant justices in Eyre", around the country, dates from not long after the Conquest; but the assize system, as later developed, really dates from the reign of Henry II (1154–89). The assize system only came to an end with the passing of the Courts Act 1971.

It was an important part of the work of these judges to formulate the common law. A task which over a lengthy period of time they did, by meeting together formally and informally to resolve problems which had arisen in the cases coming before them. The principles of law thus laid down, once accepted and developed, formed the common law. As these judges were linked with the courts meeting in Westminster Hall, the building up of a national system grew apace. However, the common law never completely abolished local custom. In fact, as we have seen in the chapter on Sources, custom has remained a source of law to the present time, even though it rarely applies today.

Forms of Action

8–008   In addition to settling principles of law which were to be followed nationally, the courts also began to establish formal rules relating to the procedure to be adopted in cases coming before them. These rules laid down early that actions were to be begun by the issue of a royal writ, and that the claim made was to be set out in an accepted fashion. This was called a form of action and over a period of time the system took on rigidity in that the judges came to take the view that unless a claimant could find an appropriate form of action their claim was not one known to the law. The court officials responsible for the issue of writs tried initially to satisfy the demands of claimants by drawing up a new form of action, but the judges frowned on this course and the practice was stopped by the Provisions of Oxford 1258. So great was the resulting dissatisfaction that 30 years later by the Statute of Westminster 1285 this strict approach was slightly relaxed, so that the officials could issue a new writ, where the new situation was closely related to that covered by an existing writ. The new writs so issued became known as writs *"in consimili casu"*. The effect which the writ system had on the development of the legal system is seen below in the section concerning Equity.

Common law remains in being today in that the decisions of judges are still adding to it and in theory the legislation produced by Parliament is supplementing it. Every development in the system operates on the basis that its foundation is the common law. Some confusion has arisen because there are several different meanings attaching to the term:

(i) In the historical sense which has already been examined, common law refers to the national law of this country as opposed to local law or custom. It is the law "common" to England and Wales.

(ii) Sometimes the term is used to mean the law as made by the judges, in contrast to the law as made by Parliament. In this context, common law is limited to case decisions or precedents coming from the courts of common law and equity and so does not include legislation. It must not be overlooked that, as a result of the doctrine of parliamentary supremacy, legislation can always change or overrule the common law.

(iii) As the next section will show, there were, for centuries in England and Wales, two parallel systems of law, one known as the common law and the other as equity. In some contexts the term common law does not include the law derived from the courts of equity.

(iv) Finally the term common law may be used to draw a contrast with systems of foreign law. Here common law takes in both equity and legislation in that it means the complete law of England and Wales. When referring to an overseas country which has derived its legal system from England and Wales the term common law system or jurisdiction is used. This explains why sometimes an English judge will find case decisions from such countries contain persuasive arguments.

4. Equity

Origin

The difficulty which was experienced in the common law courts in relation to the use of writs and the forms of action led to

8–009

increasing dissatisfaction with the system. Litigants who were unable to get satisfaction from the courts turned to the monarch and petitioned him to do justice to his subjects and provide them with a remedy. The monarch handed these petitions on to the Lord Chancellor, who, as Keeper of the King's Conscience and an ecclesiastic, seemed to be a suitable person to deal with them. He set up his own Court of Chancery where he, or his representative, would sit to dispose of these petitions. In doing this work the Lord Chancellor would be guided by equity, or fairness, in coming to his decisions. Consequently, the legal decisions which succeeding Lord Chancellors made came to be known collectively as equity. The system seems to have become well established in the course of the fifteenth century.

Because of the rapid increase in the judicial nature of the work, it was soon found necessary to have a lawyer as Lord Chancellor. The discretion vested in early Lord Chancellors gradually gave way to a system of judicial precedent in equity, but it was a long time before the common law joke died, about equity being as long as the Chancellor's foot. In practice both common law and equity came to operate as parallel systems, with each set of courts regarding itself as bound by its own judicial precedents.

Development

8–010   Having once begun to remedy the wrongs brought about by the rigidity and technicality of the common law system, equity soon found itself establishing a jurisdiction over matters where the common law had failed, and continued to fail, to recognise legal rights and duties. The law relating to trusts, for example, was entirely based on decisions of the Court of Chancery. Nonetheless equity was always a "gloss" on the common law; it always presumed the existence of the common law and simply supplemented it where necessary. That it continued to exist for some five centuries is an indication of the unchanging nature of English legal institutions, as well as of the important contribution which equity made to the development of English law.

Examples of new rights

8–011   The whole of the law of trusts, which was to become an important aspect of property law, owed its existence entirely to the willingness of equity to recognise and enforce the obligation of a trustee to a beneficiary.

Equity accepted the use of the mortgage as a method of borrowing money against the security of real property, when the common law took a literal view of the obligation undertaken by the borrower. It introduced the "equity of redemption" to enable a borrower to retain the property which was the security for the loan, even where there was default under the strict terms of the mortgage deed.

Examples of new remedies

At common law the only remedy for breach of contract was damages, a money payment as compensation for the loss suffered. Equity realised that in some cases damages was not an adequate remedy, and therefore proceeded to introduce the equitable remedies of injunction and specific performance. An injunction is used to prevent a party from acting in breach of their legal obligations; a decree of specific performance is used to order a party to carry out their side of a contract. These remedies mean that a party to a contract cannot just decide to break it and pay damages.

8–012

Other equitable remedies are the declaratory order or judgment; the right to have a deed corrected by the process known as rectification; and the right to rescind (withdraw from) a contract. The willingness of equity to intervene where fraud was proven and its preparedness to deal with detailed accounts in the law of trusts and the administration of estates, also gained it wide jurisdiction. The appointment of a receiver is another solution to the problem of the management of certain financial matters, and was introduced by equity.

Examples of new procedures

In contrast to the rigid system of common law remedies equity favoured a flexibility of approach. Consequently it was prepared, by a *"subpoena"*, to order witnesses to attend, to have them examined and cross-examined orally, to require relevant documents to be produced, known as discovery of documents, to insist on relevant questions being answered, by the use of interrogatories, and to have the case heard in English, where the common law for centuries used Latin. In the event of a failure to comply with an order, equity was prepared to impose immediate sanctions for this contempt of court.

8–013

Another classification sometimes employed is to define the jurisdiction of equity as exclusive, concurrent and auxiliary. In the exclusive jurisdiction sense, equity recognised actions, as in trusts and mortgages, where the common law would provide no remedy; in the concurrent jurisdiction sense equity would add to the remedies provided by the common law, as by the introduction of the injunction and the decree of specific performance; in the auxiliary jurisdiction sense equity employed a more flexible procedure than the common law. It will be seen that these three terms simply emphasise the ways in which equity can be seen to be related to, but to be different from, common law.

Maxims of Equity

8–014   As a result of its supplemental role, it became possible over the years for an observer to point to certain characteristics of equity. These became so well known as to be called the maxims of equity. Among the most famous are:

> He who comes to equity must come with clean hands;
> Equity will not suffer a wrong to be without remedy;
> Delay defeats equity; and
> Equity looks to the intent rather than to the form.

The maxims emphasise that equity, being based in its origins on fairness and natural justice, attempted to maintain this approach throughout its later history. Certainly, the judges retained their personal discretion so that equitable remedies were not, and are not, obtainable as of right. It is very important to understand that, whereas the litigant has a right to a remedy, at common law, once she has proven her case, this is not so with equity. All equitable remedies are discretionary.

Relationship between Common Law and Equity

Early history

8–015   Naturally, as might be presumed, in the early stages of their respective development relations between the two systems were comparatively strained. The common law lawyers regarded equity as an interloper, lacking the firmly-based legal principles with which they were familiar. They were unable, unlike the modern observer with the advantage of hindsight, to see that equity was invaluable in remedying deficiencies in the common law and in encouraging the latter to develop its substantive law and procedure.

As the Court of Chancery built up its jurisdiction and the two systems could be seen to be operating on a parallel basis, inevitably the question arose, what was to happen in the unusual instance when there was a conflict? This problem was solved by James I, in the *Earl of Oxford's* case (1615), by a ruling that where there was a such a conflict, the rules of equity were to prevail.

The later history of equity was dogged in the eighteenth and nineteenth centuries by the courts of Chancery becoming overburdened with work, with increasing reliance being placed on judicial precedent and consequent delays. Dickens' attack in his novel, *Bleak House*, on the delays and costs in the system, seems to have to been thoroughly justified, with some examples of cases awaiting judgment dragging on for scores of years until both parties were dead.

Parliament in the 1850s endeavoured by legislation—the Common Law Procedure Acts 1852–1854 and the Chancery (Amendment) Act 1858—to ease the position, but the dual systems continued in being, to the sometimes substantial detriment of litigants, until the Supreme Court of Judicature Acts 1873–1875.

5. Nineteenth Century Developments

The Supreme Court of Judicature Acts 1873–1875

This legislation reorganised the existing court structures com- **8–016**
pletely and, in the process, formally brought together the common law courts and the courts of Chancery. In the Supreme Court of Judicature set up by the Acts, the three original royal courts became three divisions of the new High Court of Justice. the Court of Chancery which administered equity became the fourth division, *i.e.* the Chancery Division of the High Court, and a fifth division, dealing with those matters not within common law or equity, namely Probate, Divorce and Admiralty, completed the new arrangements. By Order in Council in 1880, the three royal courts were merged to form the Queen's Bench Division, thus leaving the three Divisions of the High Court—Queen's Bench, Chancery and Probate, Divorce and Admiralty—which were then to remain unchanged for 90 years.

The Judicature Acts 1873–1875 placed on a statutory basis the old rule that where common law and equity conflict, equity shall prevail. At the same time, it gave power to all the courts to administer the principles of common law and equity and to grant the remedies of both, as circumstances in a case demanded. Consequently, the old conflict no longer arises, although common law and equity principles still exist.

By bringing the two systems together administratively, and allowing the High Court judge to exercise the principles, procedures and remedies of common law and equity in a single case in the one court, it seemed to many people that the two systems had merged. That this was somewhat superficial is borne out by the exclusive jurisdictions left to the Queen's Bench and Chancery Divisions. In practice the work formerly done by the Court of Chancery is exactly that dealt with in the Chancery Division; equally it has its own judges selected from those advocates practising in Chancery. A Chancery case remains something quite unlike a common law case, and the same can be said of the procedure.

The whole of the legislation has now been consolidated in the Supreme Court Act 1981.

Probate, Divorce and Admiralty Jurisdiction

The Supreme Court of Judicature Acts 1873–1875 in their reconstruction of the court system established a separate Division of the High Court of Justice called the Probate, Divorce and Admiralty Division. Why was it that these three branches of the law merited a division of their own?

The answer is that these three important legal topics fell neither within the common law nor equity jurisdictions, since Probate (which is concerned with wills) and divorce were, for centuries, treated as ecclesiastical matters, and there was a separate Admiralty Court inevitably influenced by international shipping practices.

Probate and divorce were transferred from the ecclesiastical courts to the ordinary civil courts in 1857 by the setting up of a Court of Probate and a separate Divorce Court.

The High Court of Admiralty although of great age historically gradually lost its widest jurisdiction to the common law courts, but it retained powers over collisions at sea, salvage and prize cases. All other aspects of the law merchant, that is the law affecting traders, had over the centuries been transferred to the common law courts.

Appeal Courts

8–018   The Supreme Court of Judicature Acts 1873–1875, in creating a Court of Appeal alongside the new High Court of Justice, had intended that this Court with its specially designated Lords Justices of Appeal should be the final appellate court for civil matters. Political considerations intervened, however and the proposal to remove judicial functions from the House of Lords was shelved. The Appellate Jurisdiction Act 1876 provided for the retention of the House of Lords as the final appeal court in civil cases and for the creation of special judges, Lords of Appeal in Ordinary, as life peers to staff the court.

6. Twentieth Century Developments

Criminal Courts

8–019   In 1907, the Criminal Appeal Act established the Court of Criminal Appeal to provide for the first time a general right of appeal for persons convicted and sentenced in indictable criminal cases. A further appeal in matters of general public importance lay to the House of Lords. The Court of Criminal Appeal became the Court of Appeal (Criminal Division) by the Criminal Appeal Act 1966.

The role of the Queen's Bench Divisional Court in ruling on points of law arising by way of case stated in summary criminal cases was amended by the Administration of Justice Act 1960. This Act enabled an appeal in a case of general public importance to be taken to the House of Lords if the divisional court grants a certificate to that effect and leave is obtained from the divisional court or the appeal committee of the House of Lords.

The court structure for trying indictable criminal cases was substantially changed by the Courts Act 1971 which abolished the historically derived Court of Quarter Sessions and Assizes and replaced them with a court called the Crown Court. The Crown Court was to be organised on a six circuit basis so as to achieve a much needed flexibility to lead to the prompt trial of indictable criminal cases.

Civil Courts

The Administration of Justice Act 1970 created a Family Division   8–020
of the High Court and amended the jurisdiction of the Queen's Bench and Chancery divisions, redistributing the functions of the former Probate Divorce and Admiralty Division. One novel change in appeal provisions was the introduction by the Administration of Justice Act 1969 of a possible "leapfrog" appeal from the High Court to the House of Lords, bypassing the Court of Appeal. The procedure was, however, made subject to stringent conditions which in practice limit its use.

The Courts and Legal Services Act 1990 gave concurrent jurisdiction in civil matters to the high court and the county court, with the exception of judicial review, an exercise of prerogative power vested in the High Court.

Part III: Procedures

9. Civil Procedure

"English institutions have tended to reflect the traditions and values of upper class England. English civil procedure has always reflected the values and traditions of the English sport of cricket most markedly in the adversary system of justice, and not only in the sense that both are slow and boring. In summary, each side prepares its team for the contest. One side in turn goes into bat (i.e. address the court and call its witnesses) and faces the bowling of the other side (i.e. the cross-examination of its witnesses); then the other side takes its turn at the wicket, calling its witnesses. Each side then has the opportunity in final speeches to make its case and unmake that of its opponent. Throughout, an independent third party umpire, selected on grounds of his relative expertise and experience, watches, listens, and enforces the rules, and at the end of the game gives his decision to the winner.

The adversary system has a number of disturbing features for those who are more interested in the achievement of justice than in the playing of the game." (The Hon. Mr Justice Lightman, of the High Court, Chancery Division in the Edward Bramley Memorial Lecture University of Sheffield, April 4, 2003.)

9–001 Procedure, or the way a case is brought to court and put through the system, is very important in the English legal system, as anyone commencing training as a barrister or solicitor rapidly finds out.

This chapter explains civil procedure, normally activated when one private citizen or enterprise seeks to bring another to court for a civil wrong against them, such as a breach of contract, or a tort. Remember, it is up to the claimant to bring a case, not the State and the State has no interest in the outcome of the case, unless it happens to be one of the litigants. It just provides the courts to enable resolution of a private dispute. At the end of this chapter we examine a procedure that can be used in civil or criminal cases, judicial review, where an aggrieved person may challenge the procedural legality or decision of an inferior court, or public body.

In the next chapter we then go on to examine criminal procedure, where a case is normally prosecuted by the State, the Crown, but may be brought by a private person. Here, the State, charged with controlling crime, does have an interest in the outcome so these courts are empowered to impose punishment on behalf of the public. In the following chapter, we next examine the adversarial process.

9–002   Before we examine the formal rules for taking a civil action through the courts, we have to bear in mind that the vast majority of people who could have a civil law remedy to their problem do not take it to court or even to any alternative forum. Civil disputes resolved through trial are and have been for centuries, only a tiny fraction of those where proceedings are issued. In turn, all of these are the tip of a much bigger iceberg of cases settled between solicitors but even then, most people do not get round even to seeing a solicitor. All this was well known even before its confirmation by Genn's *Paths to Justice*. This has led Michael Zander to conclude that most people simply cannot be bothered to go to court, however much you simplify procedure and make the courts more accessible:

> "When a dispute occurs, most people are prepared to complain and many are prepared to go so far as to take advice, but on the whole, for a great variety of understandable reasons, they show little interest in using any of the forms of civil justice.
>
> I believe that this is not to be regarded as necessarily a bad thing, there is probably very little that can be done to change the situation." (2000, p.38).

1. Civil Procedure after "the Woolf Reforms"

> "There was a time when there was a premium on ambush and taking your opponent by surprise: litigation was a sport and the outcome turned very much on who you could afford to instruct as your advocate and champion." (Lightman J., 1999).

9–003   Thankfully, after centuries of complaint that English civil litigation was an embarrassment, conducted as a lawyers' Dickensian game and was slow, expensive and complex, the Civil Procedure Rules 1998 were passed, in the hope that one simplified set of rules for the High Court and county courts, drafted in plain English and introducing judicial case management, would rid us of some of these problems. The Rules were drafted according to the recommendations of Lord Woolf, in his famous 1996 report, *Access to Justice*. The Civil Procedure Rules 1998 and over 50 practice directions replaced two separate sets of rules for the High Court and county court, in April 1999. They embodied a radically different approach to civil procedure from what had gone before. The background to this "new scenario", the Woolf reforms, is explained below, along with an evaluation of how the reforms are working in practice, after the description of the new procedure. One of the major problems with the old system is that an adversarial system, where the parties are left to battle it out, uncontrolled by the court, is inherently unfair, where the parties are not equally matched in terms of resources, information or wealth, such as where a patient who suffered negligent surgery sues a health authority or a consumer sues a large company.

2. Civil Procedure Act 1997

Section 1 provided for one set of practice rules for the Court of **9–004** Appeal (CA), High Court and county courts, "with a view to securing that the civil justice system is accessible, fair and efficient".

Section 2 provided a Civil Court Rule Committee to include people "with experience in and knowledge of" consumer affairs and lay advice.

Section 6 established a Civil Justice Council comprising the Master of the Rolls (which, in 1999, was Lord Woolf), judges, lawyers, consumer/lay advice and litigant representatives, to keep the civil justice system under review (including alternative dispute resolution (ADR) and tribunals), advise the Lord Chancellor and suggest research.

3. The 1998 Rules and the New Regime: The Civil Procedure Rules 1998 (CPR)

The Overriding Objective
The overriding objective is set out in Rule 1.1:   **9–005**
 The rules enable the court to deal with a case justly—

 a. ensuring the parties are on an equal footing;
 b. saving expense;
 c. dealing with the case in a way which is proportionate:

   • to the amount of money involved;
   • to the importance of the case;

- to the complexity of the issues;
- to the financial position of parties;

d. ensuring that it is dealt with expeditiously and fairly; and
e. allotting to it an appropriate share of the court's resources.

The court must apply the objective in interpreting the rules and exercising their powers.

The overriding objective is not waffly sentiment. It has repeatedly been applied by the Court of Appeal. In *Hertsmere Primary Care Trust v Rabindra–Anandh* [2005] EWHC 320, the High Court held that the overriding objective means that parties are duty bound to co-operate with each other. The CA has held that there is no need to refer to Art.6 of the Convention because of the court's obligation in the Rules to deal with cases justly: (*Daniels v Walker*, 2000).

> "To the outsider these objectives of a civilised legal system would appear self-evident, and the surprise lies, not in their statement in the CPR, but in the need to state them and their absence prior to implementation of the reforms" (Lightman J., 2003.)

Pre-action Protocols

9–006   The guidelines have been issued for personal injury litigation and clinical disputes, construction and engineering, professional negligence, defamation, disease and illness, housing disrepair, judicial review and many other topics of litigation. These are statements of best practice in negotiation, encouraging exchange of information and putting the parties into a position to settle fairly. To see that negotiations are conducted fairly at this stage is very important because only a small fraction (under 20 per cent) of civil disputes are ever brought to court (see Genn, 1999; Zander, 2000). If one party behaves obstructively in negotiations, they can be penalized in costs, if the action later comes to court.

Starting Proceedings

9–007   The claimant (formerly plaintiff) or court issues and serves the claim on the defendant. This must include particulars of the claim (statement of case) or they must be served within four months. They may include points of law, witness lists and documents and must include statements of truth and value and specify the remedy sought. The 2001 Court Service consultation paper *Modernising the Civil Courts*, proposed that people should soon be able to issue a claim online, by telephone or digital TV. By 2005, money claims can be issued and defended online and a number of other documents can be emailed to some courts. All forms are meant to be in plain English and can be found on the Her Majesty's Courts Service website. The claimant then has four months to serve the claim form on the defendant.

The defendant must, within 14 days:

- admit the claim or
- file a defence (statement of case) or
- acknowledge.

If he files a defence, the case is automatically transferred to his home court. If not, the claimant may request a *default judgment* (Part 12). This means asking the court to grant his claim as the defendant has not entered a defence. Most cases end at this point. Over three quarters of county court claims are "default actions" where the claimant, usually a company, is collecting a debt from a customer and, in the absence of a defence, judgment is automatically issued, without the involvement of a judge. Most are bulk claims issued at the centralised Claims Production Centre in Northampton, by claimants such as banks, credit/store card issuers, mail order catalogues and utilities. Most are then enforced by warrants issued at the County Court Bulk Centre.

The defendant may issue a claim against a co-defendant or third party or make a counterclaim (Part 20, CPR). The claimant may reply and defend. The parties may write direct to others requesting further information (formerly known as "further and better particulars", now Part 18 CPR).

Procedural judges

They manage cases. This means masters in the Royal Courts of **9–008** Justice and district judges in the county court and High Court district registries. Hearings may be by telephone. By 2004, some courts had introduced email facilities, enabling various documents to be filed by email, such as questionnaires, requests for judgment in default, defences, expert reports, skeleton arguments and summaries.

Allocation

Defended claims are allocated to one of three tracks, once the defendant has completed the allocation questionnaire. The judge may transfer a case to another court.

Small claims

For most actions under £5,000, except:

- personal injuries over £1,000;
- disrepair over £1,000;

211

- landlord harassment or unlawful eviction; and
- allegations of dishonesty.

Claims over £5,000 may be allocated to the small claims procedure, by consent.

Fast track

9–009   For most cases £5–15,000, which can be tried in a day. Oral expert evidence is limited to two fields and one expert per field.

Multi-track

Claims over £15,000 or over one day's trial. The High Court can only hear claims exceeding £15,000 or, in personal injury claims, over £50,000.

Claims with no monetary value

These, such as applications for injunctions, are allocated where the judge considers they will be dealt with most justly.

Discretionary factors

9–010   The procedural judge must have regard to:

- the nature of the remedy sought;
- the complexity of facts, law and evidence;
- the number of parties;
- the value of the counterclaim;
- oral evidence;
- the importance of the claim to non-parties;
- the parties' views;
- the circumstances of the parties.

The Woolf Report suggested the following cases for the multi-track:

- those of public importance (an example of such a case was that of a dyslexic suing her local education authority for failure to diagnose her condition: *Phelps v Hillingdon LBC* (1998, CA);
- test cases: an example was successful negligence litigation by ex-miners, suffering from respiratory diseases against British coal, which encouraged many others to claim compensation, in 1998;
- clinical disputes (formerly medical negligence);
- cases with the right to jury trial.

Multi-track cases

These will normally be transferred out to trial centres but some must stay in the Royal Courts of Justice, *e.g.*:

212

- specialist cases;
- defamation;
- fraud;
- contentious probate;
- claims against the police (remember that many of these are jury trials).

The Court's Duty to Manage Cases

This duty had already been introduced, as a matter of good prac-   9–011
tice, from 1994 in Practice Directions. It included timetabling, the
requirement for skeleton arguments and limitation of oral argument. The duty now includes:

- encouraging parties to co-operate;
- identifying issues at an early stage;
- deciding promptly which issues can be disposed of summarily;
- deciding the order of issues;
- encouraging ADR;
- helping parties settle;
- fixing timetables;
- considering cost benefit;
- grouping issues;
- dealing with a case in the absence of one or more parties;
- making use of IT;
- directing the trial process quickly and efficiently.

Sanctions for failure to comply with case management

These include striking out, costs and debarring part of a case or
evidence. Trials will only be postponed as a last resort. Sanctions
should be designed to prevent rather than punish non-compliance
with rules and timetables. The CA suggested there are more flexible
ways of controlling claimants' default and delay rather than a draconian strike-out: *Biguzzi* (1999).

Interim Orders

The parties may apply for the interim orders listed below. This   9–012
should be less necessary than before 1999, because of case management—the court may now act on its own initiative. There is an
obligation to apply early.

- Pre-action remedies if urgent.
- Applications without notice (formerly called *ex parte*).
- Extensions or shortening of time.
- Requiring attendance.

213

- Separating or consolidating issues or excluding issues.
- Deciding the order of issues.
- Staying (pausing) all or part of the case, hoping for settlement.
- Interim injunctions/declarations.
- Freezing injunctions (formerly called *Mareva* injunctions), which can also be made against a third party and search orders (formerly *Anton Piller* orders) may only be ordered by a High Court judge or authorised judge.
- Pre-action disclosure (formerly discovery) or inspection, including against non-parties.
- Interim payments and payments into court.
- A summary assessment of costs.

Other Points

Summary judgment

9–013   This may be initiated by the claimant, defendant or court, where the claim or defence "has no real prospect of success". The court may enter judgment, dismiss the case, strike out a claim, or make a conditional order.

District judges

These have unlimited jurisdiction to assess damages, unless otherwise directed. They should not deal with complex cases: *Sandry v Jones* (2000, CA).

Group litigation order

This may be made (Civil Procedure Amendment Rule 19) to allow for case management in multi-party actions.

Basic Procedure in Defended Cases

Small claims procedure

9–014   The claimant completes the simple claim form, online, or from a county court office. Circuit Judge Nic Madge, who had a wealth of experience in handling small claims as a district judge, reported (2004) that "litigants in person", people conducting their own cases, had little difficulty in preparing them. Once a claim has been allocated to this track, standard procedural directions, such as requiring the exchange of documents, will be issued. Hearings are meant to be in public (Convention, Art.6, fair trial) but will normally be held in the district judges' chambers. The public very rarely observe these proceedings and are probably unaware that they are open. Costs are low and fixed so, however much the litigant spends on her side of the case, she cannot expect to recoup extravagant expenses. The rules require the parties to help the court in furthering the overriding objective. It is rare for evidence to be taken on oath.

The district judge may adopt any procedure she considers fair, including hearing lay representatives. Baldwin's research indicated differences in procedure from one judge to another. Immediately after Baldwin's research, in 1996 I shadowed a number of district judges. I too found that they all had idiosyncratic ways of conducting small claims. They were all aware of Baldwin's research and sensitive about whether their way of doing things was the "correct" one. Judges may follow traditional adversarial procedure, with speeches and examination of witnesses in the traditional trial order, or may adopt a more inquisitorial approach. Judge Madge observed "An interventionist approach . . . is effective in eliciting evidence from litigants in person. It is seen by unrepresented parties as a "helping hand" . . . By discussing the facts of the case, judges find what common ground does exist between the parties . . .". He felt the key judicial skills were maintaining a balance between informality and fairness, and ensuring a level playing field. Judges give formal judgments, applying the law, and state their reasons orally.

Incidentally, the first small claims courts were developed outside the court system, in London and Manchester, in 1971, primarily to deal with small consumer complaints, for which county court procedure was too elaborate and expensive. Although they were thus a type of privately accessible ADR (alternative dispute resolution), they proved so popular that they were absorbed into the county court system, which developed the small claims procedure. It has remained important for costs to be low and fixed so litigants will know in advance the cost of bringing an action. Procedure has always been kept simple, with district judges permitted great leeway to assist the parties so that people can represent themselves. The vast majority of litigants are unrepresented and so what was meant to provide cheap DIY justice seems to have succeeded. For this reason, the Legal Services Commission generally refuses public funding for legal representation in the small claims track.

Prior to the reforms, in 1997, Baldwin found that at least three **9–015** quarters of small claims litigants were contented with the way their cases had been handled in court, whereas, of those involved in formal, county court open court trials, 40 per cent considered them inappropriate and disproportionately expensive for this kind of dispute. Baldwin found small claims tended to be used by professional people or businesses and had not provided the poor with an avenue for redress. He continued to research the effects of increasing the small claims limit to £5,000 and litigants' levels of satisfaction with small claims. This report was published in 2002. He advised against raising the small claims limit again as there was some evidence that, in larger claims, litigants needed more advice and benefited from representation.

Judge Madge presented a snapshot of the types of case he had heard in the first six months of 2002. 44 per cent were business debts, 22 per cent landlord and tenant disputes, 16 per cent road traffic claims and 10 per cent complaints about services, such as work by builders or plumbers. 42 per cent were for less than £1000. Half the litigants were individuals and the other half companies or firms. Fewer than one in five were represented. The time between issuing the claim and final hearing was less than six months, in 70 per cent of cases. Permission to appeal was sought in only six per cent of cases but not granted.

Fast track procedure

9–016   The intention is for the court to maintain "proportionality", which means limiting the costs recoverable from the unsuccessful party. For instance, where counsel is briefed, the court cannot normally order costs for a solicitor to accompany her. The aim is to increase access to justice by removing uncertainty. The fast track aims to help the parties to obtain justice speedily. The court directs the timetable and fixes the trial date no more than 30 weeks ahead. The intention is to provide little scope for either party to create extra work to gain a tactical advantage. Lord Woolf said it was important for the court to protect the weaker party against oppressive or unreasonable behaviour by a powerful party. Standard directions now include disclosure, the exchange of witness statements, expert evidence, and fixing the trial date. Parties are encouraged to use a single expert, or a court-appointed expert. The standard timetable is nine months from the issue of proceedings to trial. An indexed, paginated bundle must be produced to the court three to seven days pre-trial and may include an agreed case summary. The judge pre-reads the bundle. Judges may be given time off for pre-reading. Trial costs are fixed according to the amount recovered. Other costs are assessed summarily by the judge after the trial. See below.

Multi-track procedure

9–017   This varies. Simple cases are treated like fast track ones. Complex ones may have several directions hearings:

1. a case management conference attended by lawyers familiar with the case, which may require a 500-word case summary;
2. a pre-trial review of the statement of issues;
3. other directions hearings.

Practice directions require the exchange of skeleton arguments and bundles of documents pre-trial, as well as their submission to the court. There is no sanction for breach of a practice direction, as it is not part of the rules but if these documents are delivered too late for the court or the other party to read, the court might decide not to admit them.

Disclosure (formerly known as discovery)

Lord Woolf thought one of two major generators of unnecessary cost was uncontrolled discovery so the automatic obligation to disclose documents is replaced by standard disclosure which requires only documents on which a party relies and documents which:

9–018

- adversely affect his case;
- adversely affect another party's case;
- support another party's case;
- are required by a practice direction.

The court's power to control evidence (Rule 32)

The court has power to control the issues, the nature of the evidence and its delivery: whether it is prepared to hear oral, hearsay, or written evidence, etc. The court has a great deal of control over what evidence it is prepared to hear and the format in which it is prepared to hear witnesses. Lord Woolf was of the strong opinion that over use of expert witnesses by both sides had made litigation costly and unduly adversarial. He denounced the development of the "large litigation support industry. . . . This goes against all principles of proportionality and access to justice." (Final Report). The assumption is now that one witness will do or, if more than one is permitted, that they will agree a statement pre-trial. Under Part 35, the expert's duty is to help the court and no party may call an expert or use a report without the court's permission.

9–019

Offers to settle (Part 36)

This procedure encourages the parties to settle by financial incentive. It extends the system of pre-1999 payments into court and Calderbank letters. Under the old rules, the defendant could make a payment into court and force the plaintiff to take a gamble: take the money or proceed to trial and risk paying both sides' costs since the time of the payment in, which could be a Pyrrhic victory for a winning plaintiff. This happened to Albert Reynolds, former Irish Prime Minister, in 1996 when he won a libel action against the *Sunday Times* but had to pay over £1 million in costs. The intention of the new rules is that allowing the claimant to make an offer to settle alters the balance of power. It includes pre-action formal offers, the claimant's

9–020

or defendant's offer to settle and the defendant's Part 36 payments into court. Where the offer is the same as or better than that ordered by the judge, the offeror is rewarded by having the judge order that the other side will pay both sides' costs since the date of expiry of the offer. The CA has held that the same applies to an offer made by an NHS Trust, even where they did not pay the money into court: *Crouch v King's Healthcare NHS Trust* [2004] EWCA Civ 1332. Incidentally, the trial judge knows nothing of the payment in, or offer, otherwise the gamble would not work. The money is looked after by the Public Guardianship Office (formerly Public Trust Office).

Basic trial procedure

9–021   In fast track and multi-track trials procedure is as follows:

1. The claimant/claimant's advocate makes her opening speech.
2. The claimant's first witness is examined by the claimant or advocate and then the defendant or her advocate. Where expert witnesses are used, their reports, delivered pre-trial, generally stand as their evidence-in-chief so they only go into the witness box to be cross-examined. If there is a single joint expert, whose evidence is agreed, it may not be necessary to call him to appear in court. Witnesses may appear via video conferencing links.
3. Each subsequent witness for the claimant is so examined.
4. The defendant or defence advocate may make a submission of "no case to answer", arguing that, if the judge heard no more, she would not have heard sufficient evidence to find the case proven.
5. The defendant or defence advocate makes his opening speech.
6. Each defence witness is examined and cross-examined, in turn. Expert's reports are dealt with as above.
7. Closing speeches are made by the claimant, or her advocate, and defendant, or advocate.
8. The judge decides whether the claimant has proven her case to his satisfaction. The quantum of proof in a criminal case is "proof on the balance of probabilities", which is a much lower quantum or standard of proof than in a criminal case, which has to be proven "beyond reasonable doubt". The judge delivers judgment, or, if a jury is present, he sums up the evidence to them and they deliver their verdict, again applying the civil standard of proof. The judge usually makes an order.
9. The judge hears arguments on costs then makes an order as to costs.
10. The judge then hears any application for permission to appeal. The whole trial will have been recorded (and the same

applies to small claims) so that a transcript may be requested if one of the parties is considering an appeal or if they need it for any other reason.

Costs

Under the old regime, in most cases costs would "follow" the 9–022 event so the outcome would amount to "winner takes all". Under the new rules, the judge must assess costs in accordance with which party won different issues and the judge's view as to how reasonably the parties behaved. The court may make a wasted costs order against a representative if she has acted improperly, unreasonably or negligently and her conduct has caused unnecessary costs to the other party. Throughout the proceedings, costs must be kept down to a proportionate level. In *Lownds v SS for the Home Dept* [2002] EWCA Civ 365, the CA held that, when assessing costs, the court should firstly consider whether the total sum claimed was proportionate and then conduct an item by item assessment. If the sum claimed was proportionate, all that was required was that each item should have been reasonably incurred for a reasonable amount but if the sum claimed was disproportionate, the court would have to be satisfied that the work in relation to each item was necessary and that the amount incurred was reasonable.

General Points

The reforms were intended to cut the length of trial. Suitable cases 9–023 may be disposed without a hearing (Rule 1.4(2)). The statutory right to jury trial is unaffected in deceit, libel, slander, malicious prosecution and false imprisonment cases. Generally, hearings must be in open court. Practice Direction 39 refers to the ECHR. There are exceptions where hearings may be in private (formerly known as "*in camera*", "in chambers"), such as mortgage possession cases and proceedings involving children.

Witness statements count as evidence-in-chief in the trial. Supplementary questions may be asked only for "good reason". Money judgments must be complied with within 14 days.

Interpretation of the CPR

Despite the fact that the Rules are written in plain English and 9–024 meant to be understandable to ordinary litigants, it has been necessary for the courts to interpret them. The main interpreting court is, not surprisingly the Civil Division of the CA. They held in *Morgan EST (Scotland) Ltd v Hanson Concrete Products Ltd* [2005] EWCA Civ 134 that the case law under the old pre-1999 rules was not applicable in interpreting the CPR.

Judicial behaviour

9–025   Judicial bias is a ground of appeal. If a judge interferes too much in the presentation of the case, he risks breaching the common rules of "natural justice", or fairness and, consequently, Art.6 of the Convention (fair trial). The CA had to consider what level of intervention and irritability is tolerable in a judge, in *Alpha Lettings Ltd v Neptune Research and Development Inc* [2003] EWCA Civ 704. The trial judge had shown irritability with the defendant's witnesses and the defendant's counsel and made numerous interventions. They remarked that one part of the trial had been "depressing to hear on the tape" and "depressing to read on the transcript". They rejected the defendant's argument, however, because the judge had not at any time prevented the witnesses from giving evidence nor had he prevented the advocates from eliciting that evidence. He had occasionally expressed surprise at certain answers but had never betrayed a refusal to be persuaded of any factual proposition. They approved the words of Sir Thomas Bingham M.R. in *Arab Monetary Fund v Hashim* (1993):

> "In some jurisdictions the forensic tradition is that judges sit mute, listening to the advocates without interruption, asking no question, voicing no opinion, until they break their silence to give judgment. That is a perfectly respectable tradition but it is not ours . . . The English tradition sanctions and even encourages a measure of disclosure by the judge of his current thinking . . . An expression of scepticism is not suggestive of bias unless the judge conveys an unwillingness to be persuaded of a factual proposition whatever the evidence may be".

Advocate to the court

9–026   Formerly known as an *amicus curiae*, such an advocate may be appointed by the Attorney-General, at the court's request, where there is a danger of an important and difficult point of law being decided without the court hearing relevant argument. The Advocate represents no-one and will not normally lead evidence, cross-examine witnesses or investigate the facts. A request for an Advocate may be made to the Official Solicitor or CAFCASS, on behalf of a child or an adult with disabilities. The Official Solicitor himself may appear.

Technical errors

9–027   The overriding objective means that technical errors should not be regarded as incurable: *Law v St Margaret's Insurances Ltd* [2001] EWCA Civ 30. The courts will not be rigid where an injustice would be caused. The CA, in *Goode v Martin* [2001] EWCA Civ 1899 allowed a claimant to amend her statement of claim in an action for damages for personal injury, when a strict interpretation of the CPR would not have permitted it. They held that in interpreting the language of a rule of court, the Human Rights Act provided the court with an extra tool for interpretation so as to produce a just result and avoid any question of the violation of a litigant's right to a fair trial under Art.6 of the Convention.

"No case to answer"

The defendant may submit to the court there is "no case to answer" at the end of the claimant's evidence in the trial, where he considers the claimant's case has no real prospect of success. If the court agrees, it will uphold that submission.

9–028

Reasons

The judge has a duty to give reasons, which is a function of due process. Parties should know why they had won or lost; the losing party would know whether there was a ground of appeal; giving reasons concentrates the mind so the decision is more likely to be soundly based on the evidence. *Flannery v Halifax Estate Agencies Ltd* (1999, CA).

9–029

Res judicata

The doctrine of *res judicata* imposes the principle that there should be finality in litigation. An adjudication by a court in a case will bar a second claim *Henderson v Henderson* (1843), unless there is ignorance of the first claim or an agreement between the parties or for various other reasons. The doctrine was applied by the CA in *Lennon v Birmingham City Council* [2001] EWCA Civ 435. An employee brought proceedings against her employer before a tribunal which were dismissed on her withdrawal. She was estopped from bringing the same proceedings in the county court.

9–030

Advocates duties

Advocates have a common law duty not to mislead the court: *Vernon v Bosley* (1997, CA) and a duty to keep up-to-date with recent law reports: *Copeland v Smith* (2000, CA).

9–031

Expert witnesses

The 1990s also saw the massive growth in the use of expert witnesses. A judge is entitled to reject an expert's version of events, where he prefers the honest evidence of a claimant: *Armstrong v First York Ltd* [2005] EWCA Civ 277. The court can make a costs order against an expert who has caused significant expense and has done so in flagrant reckless disregard of his duties to the court: *Phillips v Symes* [2004] EWHC 2330 (Ch).

9–032

221

Civil jury trial

9–033 Jury trial is available in six torts. See Chapter 16 on the jury, below. In *Tate v Safeway* (2000), the CA ruled that the 1998 procedural rules could not be used to deprive a libel defendant of his right to jury trial.

Authorities produced by the judge

9–034 In the adversarial procedure of England and Wales, the parties are expected to bring all relevant evidence, authorities and legal argument to the court. The court has no duty to research the law for itself but, where a judge does find a case that he considers relevant, he should give the parties the opportunity to address him on it: Not to do so may amount to a breach of the rules of natural justice (fairness): *Silva v Albion Hotel (Freshwater) Ltd* [2002] EWCA Civ 1784.

Litigants in Person, McKenzie Friends, Lay Representatives, Litigation Friends and Vexatious Litigants

9–035 I have added this section, in 2005, because my observation of civil judges over the last two years has shown me that every civil judge, including those of the CA, *frequently* has litigants in person (people representing themselves (LIPs)) appearing before them. This affects Chancery High Court judges, family judges and those in the Technology and Construction Court (TCC) equally. If the case is factually and/or legally complex, say in the TCC, and there are litigants in person on both sides, then the judge has really got her work cut out. Much judicial time and energy is spent in helping people to argue their cases. Outside the courtroom, much of the time and resources of court staff and volunteers is devoted to helping them. The treatment of this group is a yardstick by which to measure whether New Labour has achieved its professed aim of enhancing access to justice by reforming civil procedure and redirecting funds spent on legal services. Moorhead remarked, in 2004, that the case law on LIPs and their helpers reflected three competing values: access to justice, court efficiency and the interests of regulated legal service providers. People representing themselves are at an inherent disadvantage in our adversarial system, which requires each party to bring all relevant argument and information to the court and requires the adduction of evidence through examination and cross-examination. Very few lay people can cope with this and they become dependent on the court to help them through the process, as I pointed out in relation to unrepresented parties in magistrates' courts, in my 1984 book, *The Magistrates' Clerk*.

There is an almost unrestricted right to represent oneself and in small claims, up to £5,000, meaning most civil claims, the procedure is meant to be simple enough for people to argue their case without legal help. Generally, public funding for representation will not be granted.

In 1997, Applebey remarked on the recent "explosion" of litigants in person but, by 2005, numbers have risen even more dramatically. One judge, quoted in the PSU report, 2003, below, remarked on the "massive influx" of LIPs since 1999. There are several reasons for this:

1. Whereas, in 1979, government claimed that 80 per cent of households were eligible for legal aid, the 1980s and 90s saw legal aid decline to the extent that even those on state benefits were above the financial limit for eligibility. (See the Chapter 17 on legal services, below).
2. The small claims limit has increased from £100 in 1973 to £5,000 so this has meant an automatic increase in LIPs.
3. Lawyers are very expensive, especially in the UK. Often people are going to court to recover money, or defending themselves over money claims, or are appearing because they have been made bankrupt and they can ill afford the court fees, let alone legal representation.
4. There are many appellants who, although they were represented in the lower court, have had their public funding (legal aid) withdrawn after losing their case or cannot afford a lawyer at this stage, even though they were represented before.
5. Some LIPs choose to represent themselves, even though they could afford a lawyer. The Civil Procedure Rules 1998 are drafted in plain English, available to the public on the DCA website and meant to be simple.

The 1990s saw England's longest ever trial, which became known as "the McLibel Trial". Two unrepresented people defended themselves against McDonalds, in a defamation action (it is described in Chapter 4 on human rights, above). Trials such as this, where the presence of unrepresented parties massively slowed litigation and expended much judicial time, caused the Judges' Council to establish a working party, chaired by Lord Justice Otton. They reported in 1995, on the sharp rise of LIPs in the Royal Courts of Justice (RCJ). These were occupying a disproportionate amount of time and resources, including court staff. LIPs could be "seriously disadvantaged", compared with those who were represented. Some had no case; others could not cope with the complexity of proceedings. They lacked objectivity and the advocacy skills. The Otton report recommended strengthening the resources of the Citizens Advice Bureau in the RCJ and

9–036

encouraging court staff to recommend that LIPs should seek their legal advice. At the same time, High Court judges were given a pool of judicial assistants on whom they could call for legal assistance, where one or both parties were incapable of researching the law involved in a case.

Lord Woolf, reporting in 1996, in *Access to Justice*, considered that courts should be more pro-active in helping LIPs, with information and advice provided via people, leaflets (in English and other languages), kiosks and IT. Judges should be interventionist, in helping LIPs to understand procedure, present their case and test the evidence. They should treat them with respect and not give priority to lawyers. Much of what Woolf and Otton recommended has been achieved. The Rules have been simplified and are in plain English; Latin has been eliminated; the courts have developed user guides, simplified forms and leaflets in many languages. Legal advice and other support is provided for LIPs in the RCJ but remains patchy elsewhere, however.

The Citizens Advice Bureau (CAB) in the RCJ was described by Lord Justice Mummery in a 2004 *Times* interview, as "a kind of legal casualty department". It employs solicitors and 250 volunteer legal advisers, from almost 60 city firms of solicitors. It helps 11,000 people and deals with 14,000 inquiries per year, which gives an idea of the scale of support needed by LIPs. In some cases, the CAB can arrange free representation from the Bar *Pro Bono* Unit. Mummery L.J. drew attention to recent important precedents in which the CAB had acted. He remarked on how much CA judges appreciated the help of the CAB. In 2004, the CAB enjoyed its 25 year anniversary but this has been supplemented, since 2001, by the Personal Support Unit in the RCJ. Its volunteers help LIPs, witnesses, victims and family members with advice on court procedure, and accompany people in court to provide emotional support but not legal advice. The Personal Support Unit remarked in their 2003 report, that LIPs can behave in an unrestrained manner, are often obsessional and usually stressed. Frequently, their behaviour causes stress in court staff and judges. The report contains quotations from judges praising the work of the Personal Support Unit for improving court efficiency and enhancing access to justice.

9–037   Naturally, judges have to be very patient and sensitive, in handling litigants in person and they must take care to ensure that the LIP's rights to a fair trial are upheld, according to the common law rules of natural justice and Art.6 of the Convention. Recognising the problems of LIPs, the law provides them with some rights to help in court:

1. A "litigation friend" may represent a child or mental patient, under Part 21 of the CPR.

2. A "McKenzie Friend" may accompany the LIP in court, to support and take notes but has no right to speak.
3. A lay representative is permitted to represent an LIP in a small claim, under s.27 of the Courts and Legal Services Act 1990 but the LIP must be present. The court has a general discretion to hear anyone.
4. A lawyer with appropriate rights of audience may represent the individual without charging (*pro bono*).

While earlier case law gave an almost unlimited right to be accompanied in court, one leading authority is more restrictive. In *R. v Bow County Court Ex p. Pelling* (1999) Dr Pelling, a member of Families Need Fathers, had been refused permission to accompany a fellow member of the group in court, Mr Greenwood, as a McKenzie friend. Lord Woolf M.R., in the CA found that Mr Greenwood could not have been prejudiced in any way. His application was straightforward and he was familiar with court procedure, having himself acted as Dr Pelling's McKenzie friend. Moorhead examines case law decided by the family judges of the CA: Thorpe L.J., Ward L.J. and President Butler-Sloss, which takes a more sympathetic view of the need of LIPs for McKenzie friends. Moorhead concludes that the case law is contradictory.

A McKenzie friend, unless they are a lawyer with rights of audience, or appearing in a small claim, has no right to speak in court but the court has a discretion to permit them to do so. Judges and staff in the RCJ (High Court and CA) are well aware that there is a growing industry of people who are prepared to act as lay representatives and charge money for it. It is not unusual for the courts to allow them to argue a case for an LIP. There are competing values and uneven results here, as Moorhead observed. On the one hand, the judges sympathise with LIPs who cannot obtain publicly funded services and they permit such representatives as a means of enhancing access to justice. On the other hand, they have to protect the legal profession's rights of audience. Practically, some courts have observed, in their judgments, how useful a lay representative can be (*Izzo v Philip Ross & Co Ltd* (2002)) but in other cases, incompetent McKenzie friends can be a nuisance. Moorhead described the cases of *Paragon Finance Plc v Noueiri* [2001] EWCA Civ 1402. In this group of cases, the McKenzie friend was an experienced LIP. He submitted futile appeals and told the LIP he would win £250,000 and that he wanted 20 per cent of that. The CA was satisfied that he was practicing advocacy in the RCJ as an unqualified person and that he must be stopped, in the public interest. He was incompetent, took hopeless points and advanced futile arguments. The CA made an order banning him acting on anyone else's behalf in the RCJ, except with a judge's permission, and they gave general guidance on McKenzie friends.

For some litigants in person, their litigation becomes a fulltime pursuit. I spent many working days, shadowing judges in the RCJ in 2004 and was told by judges' clerks and judges of litigants who virtually "live" in the RCJ. When litigants in person become obsessive, attempting to persecute one or more parties or making multiple hopeless applications, they may become classed as "vexatious litigants" and can be banned from initiating proceedings. In the cases of *Bhamjee v Forsdick* [2003] EWCA Civ 1113 and *R. (Mahajan) v Central London County Court* [2004] EWCA Civ 946, the CA set out guidelines as to the court's duties and power when faced with such pests. The first LIP, as can be seen from the case law, had acted against a number of defendants and was attempting to sue five barristers. The second LIP was involved in numerous civil claims in the county court, High Court and CA. In a third case, *HM Attorney-General v Chitolie* [2004] EWHC 1943 (Admin), Mr. Chitolie was found to be a vexatious litigant after involvement in 18 civil actions. These cases were followed, in October 2004, by a new Rule (3.11) setting out the courts' powers to make a civil restraint order (CRO) against a vexatious litigant. The court may respond to an application or act of its own motion. Where a statement of case or application is struck out or dismissed and is totally without merit, the court order *must* specify that fact and the court *must* consider whether to make a CRO. A limited CRO, for up to two years, can be made where a party has made two or more applications "totally without merit". Any application made by the litigant will automatically be dismissed, unless they have the permission of an identified judge. An extended CRO can be made where the litigant has persistently made applications which are totally without merit and this can be made to cover any court, if made by a CA judge. A general CRO is the most severe and will only be issued where a party has tried to ignore an extended CRO. For some, vexatious litigation is a disease, known elsewhere in Europe as De Clerambault's syndrome. Naturally, vexatious litigants often try to sue their lawyers, the judges and the courts. In the period 1997–2003, the Lord Chancellor's Department (now DCA) spent £3 million defending itself from such actions.

4. Appeals from the High Court and County Court from 2000

9–038   The Government explained the rationale behind the new appeals regime, Part 52 of the CPR 1998, in its 1998 white paper, *Modernising*

Justice. The resulting procedure is contained in the Access to Justice Act 1999, in the Civil Procedure Rules 1998, the amended Rules of the Supreme Court and in various practice directions. The whole regime was explained by the CA (Civil Division) in *Tanfern Ltd v Cameron-Macdonald* (2000). The Government explained, in *Modernising Justice*, that they planned to achieve their objectives of proportionality and efficiency (the same as in the rest of civil procedure) by:

- diverting from the CA those cases which, by their nature, do not require the attention of the most senior judges in the country; and
- making various changes to the working methods of the Court, "which will enable it to deploy its resources more efficiently and effectively", to enable the Court to deal with the increased workload which would result from the Human Rights Act 1998 (brought into force in 2000).

Their guiding principles are now:

- Permission to appeal will only be given where the court considers that an appeal would have a real prospect of success.
- In normal circumstances, more than one appeal cannot be justified.
- There should be no automatic right to appeal. Leave (now called permission) is required in virtually all appeals to the CA.

Jurisdiction

The Government, after consultation, decided routes of appeal should be as follows.   9–039

- In fast track cases heard by a district judge, appeal lies to a circuit judge.
- In fast track cases heard by a circuit judge, appeal lies to a High Court judge.
- In multi-track cases, appeals against *final orders* lie to the CA, regardless of the original judge.
- In multi-track cases, appeals against a *procedural decision* of a district judge will be to a circuit judge; decisions by a master or circuit judge lie to a High Court judge and from procedural decisions of a High Court judge lie to the CA.
- Exceptional cases involving important points of principle or which affect a number of litigants may go straight to the CA.

Composition

9–040   Changes to the composition, procedures, working methods and management of the CA (Civil Division) are designed to help it operate more efficiently. Under the Access to Justice Act 1999, the CA can now consist of any number of judges, according to the importance and complexity of the case. If there are two judges and they cannot agree, the case may have to be re-argued before a new court of three or the original two plus a third: *Farley* (2000).

Procedure (set down in Practice Directions)

9–041   Trial judges should routinely ask parties if they want permission to appeal but if in any doubt whether the appeal would have a real prospect of success or involves a general point of principle, should decline permission and let the litigant seek it from the CA. Permission can be granted if, though there is no real prospect of success, there is a public interest issue. On a point of law, permission should not be granted unless the judge thinks there is a real prospect of the CA coming to a different conclusion on a point of law which will materially affect the outcome of the case. A point of law includes an appeal on the ground that there was no evidence to support the finding. On an appeal on a question of fact, the CA will rarely interfere with a decision based on the judge's evaluation of oral evidence but permission is more appropriate where a party challenges the judge's inference from primary facts or where the judge has not benefited from seeing witnesses. Where there is a lot of evidence, the judge should give reasons for refusing permission. Skeleton arguments should be submitted.

The CA has been attempting to cut down delays and the length of hearings since about 1994. The judges work at a very fast rate, as I am finding in my observations of judges' work 2003–5. They have vast amounts of papers to read, in preparing for appeals. They normally sit in court four days a week so have to fit in judgment writing and all this reading into their one reading day, plus evenings and weekends. They do not have the time to read irrelevant material or to deal with skeleton arguments or document bundles which come in late. Exasperated with practitioners who do not seem to understand this, they amended the appeal Practice Direction (PD52) in 2004. The CA explained these changes in *Scribes West Ltd v Relsa Anstalt (No.1)* [2004] EWCA Civ 835. They complained bitterly of a "proliferation of bundles . . . (and) widespread ignorance of provisions . . . which were designed to assist the court but did not succeed in their object." (*per* Brooke L.J.). The Direction requires the exclusion of all extraneous documents, with a costs penalty for unnecessary copying or incomplete bundles. The appellant must file a skeleton argument 14 days in advance and the respondent a week in advance or the court may refuse to hear an argument. The Direction is strict but its purpose is to support the CA's determination to streamline its work and prevent this being defeated by inefficient lawyers. Reflective of that determination is their decision in *Babbings v Kirklees Metropolitan Council* (2004) that where counsel is due to present a short application and would have to travel some distance, they should consider using the video link for a hearing. They warned that, in future they might have regard to this, in assessing costs.

Approach

Generally, every appeal is limited to a review of the decision of the   9–042
lower court, unless Practice Direction provides otherwise or the court considered that in the circumstances of an individual appeal, it would be in the interests of justice to hold a rehearing.

Grounds

The appeal court will only allow an appeal where the lower court   9–043
was wrong (in substance) or where it was unjust because of a serious procedural or other irregularity. Under the new procedure, the decision of the lower court attracts a much greater significance.

Recording decisions

The new emphasis on the importance of the first instance decision   9–044
makes it all the more important for decisions to be recorded accurately.

Powers

The general rule is that an appeal court has all the powers of the   9–045
lower court. It also has the power to affirm, set aside or vary any order or judgment of the lower court, to refer any claim or issue for determination by the lower court, to order a new trial or hearing and to make a costs order. The CA is very reluctant to overturn a trial judge's findings of fact, because she has seen the witnesses or their statements and they consider her to be in a better position than themselves. They are even more reluctant to overturn a jury's decision. As we can see from the quotation from *R. v McIlkenny* (1991), in the Criminal Division, cited in Chapter 10 on criminal procedure, below, this is mainly because judges accord juries a special constitutional position, which they are reluctant to usurp, as a matter of principle. Also, as juries do not give reasons, that makes it all the more difficult to draft an appeal or reconsider their findings of fact.

The last word and binding House of Lords precedent on the conditions in which the CA will overturn a *civil* jury's decision is in the leading authority. In *Grobbelaar v News Group Newspapers* [2001] EWCA Civ 33, the CA overturned an £85,000 damages award to a former Liverpool goalkeeper for a defamation action in which the jury were persuaded that he had been falsely accused of match fixing, despite strong video and audio-taped evidence (repeatedly shown on TV) of his taking bribes and boasting of a previous conspiracy. Simon Brown L.J. warned: "the court must inevitably be reluctant to find a jury's verdict perverse and anxious not to usurp their function" but he was satisfied that the CA had the jurisdiction to entertain an appeal on the ground of perversity, if the verdict, on all the evidence, was not properly and reasonably open to the jury. A lengthy and detailed examination of the facts led the court "inexorably to the view that Mr Grobbelaar's story is, quite simply, incredible. All logic, common sense and reason compel one to that conclusion." Mr Grobbelaar appealed to the House of Lords. While they allowed his appeal, because they *could* find a rational explanation for the jury's verdict, on an examination of the facts, they agreed with Simon Brown's reasoning on appellate courts' reluctance to overturn a jury verdict: [2002] UKHL 40. Lord Bingham set out the position of an appellate court in examining a civil jury verdict:

> "The oracular utterance of the jury contains no reasoning, no elaboration. But it is not immune from review. The jury is a judicial decision-maker of a very special kind, but it is a judicial decision-maker nonetheless. While speculation about the jury's reasoning and train of thought is impermissible, the drawing of inevitable or proper inferences from the jury's decision is not, and is indeed inherent in the process of review. . . . it is a very serious thing to stigmatise as perverse the unanimous finding of jurors who have solemnly sworn to return a true verdict according to the evidence. A jury may, of course, from time to time act in a wholly irrational way, but that is not a conclusion to be reached lightly or if any alternative explanation not involving perversity presents itself"

The House nevertheless reduced the damages to a nominal £1, or "derisory damages" as Lord Millett called them, Lord Bingham explaining that the appellant "acted in a way in which no decent or honest footballer would act".

In exceptional cases, the CA has power to re-open an appeal already determined. This was done on grounds of alleged bias, in *Taylor v Lawrence* [2001] EWCA Civ 119. Lord Woolf CJ said it had implicit powers to do that which was necessary to achieve the dual objectives of an appellate court (the private objective, of correcting wrong decisions so as to ensure justice between the litigants and the public objective, to ensure confidence in the administration of justice by clarifying and developing the law). This could be done only where the CA was satisfied that leave to appeal would not be given by the House of Lords. This is a very important decision of a five judge court, headed by the Lord Chief Justice and Master of the Rolls.

Second Appeals

The CA in *Tanfern* said Parliament had made it clear in the Access 9–046 to Justice Act 1999 that second appeals would now be a rarity. The decision of the first appeal court should be given primacy, unless the CA itself considered that the appeal would raise an important point of principle or practice, or that there was some other compelling reason for it to hear a second appeal. Only the CA can grant permission for a second appeal from the county court or High Court: *Clark v Perks* (2000, CA). In *Uphill v BRB (Residuary) Ltd* [2005] EWCA Civ 60, the CA gave guidance on permission to appeal for a second time:

1. The reference to "an important point of principle" in the CPR meant an important point of principle or practice that had not already been decided.
2. Permission is unlikely to be granted unless the court considers the prospects of success to be very high.
3. That will not be enough to provide a "compelling reason" for an appeal. All the circumstances will need to be examined.
4. There may be a "compelling reason" to permit an appeal even where the prospects of success are not very high. An example would be where the court is satisfied other proceedings were tainted.

Appeals from Small Claims Hearings from 2000

An appellant must obtain permission to appeal but grounds are 9–047 not restricted, as they used to be. Appeal lies to a circuit judge and there is a guarantee of an oral hearing, which is a review, not a rehearing.

5. The Background to the Woolf Reforms

The problems of English civil procedure have been the subject of 9–048 scrutiny for centuries. Prior to the Civil Justice Review 1988, there had been 63 reports, since 1900. With tedious and frustrating repetition, they all identified the same core problems so that the opening words of Chapter 2 of Lord Woolf's interim report, 1995, gave commentators a frisson of déjà vu: "The process is too expensive, too slow and too complex." His Lordship said these problems militated against the provision of an accessible system of civil courts which is necessary for people to enforce their rights. Indeed, the very title of the Woolf report, *Access to Justice*, seems like an ironic cliché, after years of concern over the lack of it.

The Civil Justice Review was remarkable for the breadth and depth of its scrutiny of the system, its radical approach and its success rate, in that many of its recommendations were soon translated into law, in the Courts and Legal Services Act 1990 and subsequent delegated legislation. It recommended merging the jurisdiction of the county court and High Court and enabling the Lord Chancellor to make rules allowing for flexible distribution of the caseload between them. This was done, as was the shifting down into the county court of most cases, leaving the High Court for procedurally or evidentially complex cases and judicial review. Yet, despite the fact that its reforms were potentially the most radical since the Judicature Acts of 1893–1895, they did not satisfy critics. The two sides of the legal profession swiftly produced a 1993 report (Heilbron-Hodge) on the continuing problems of civil justice and their proposals for dealing with them so the Lord Chancellor commissioned Lord Woolf to carry out yet another scrutiny. In the meantime, the Heads of Division (Master of the Rolls, Lord Chief Justice and Vice-Chancellor) took matters into their own hands by issuing new and fairly radical Practice Directions for the conduct of litigation in the High Court. Listed below are some of reviews and reforms which preceded and, indeed, pre-empted the Woolf reforms.

The Heilbron-Hodge Report 1993

9–049   The report started with the working premise that:

> "It is axiomatic that in any free and democratic society all citizens should be equal before the law. This means that all litigants, rich and poor, however large or however small is the subject matter of their litigation, should have access to a fair and impartial system of disputes resolution."

They complained that:

- "An air of Dickensian antiquity pervades the civil process";
- "Procedures are unnecessarily technical, inflexible, rule-ridden, formalistic and often incomprehensible to the ordinary litigant for whom they are ultimately designed";
- lawyers and judges were reluctant to change;
- progress of actions lay with the parties and their lawyers rather than the courts; causing avoidable delay;
- fear of costs of litigation deterred people from using the courts;

- most people wanted their dispute resolved rather than their "day in court".

The principles underlying their recommendations were:

- litigation should encourage the early settlement of disputes;
- litigants should have imposed upon them sensible procedural time-frames;
- judges should adopt a more interventionist role to ensure that issues are limited, delays are reduced and court time is not wasted;
- since court time is costly, a balance should be struck between the written and oral word and what can be achieved out of court rather than in court;
- justice should, where possible, be brought to the people;
- a widespread introduction of technology is urgently required;
- facilities for the litigant urgently need improving;
- additional resources must be found to improve the system.

Here are some of their main recommendations. Some reforms were effected by the 1994/5 Practice Directions. My comments are bracketed:

1. Merger of QBD and Chancery (not accepted but now under reconsideration in 2005).
2. High Court listing should be computerised (done).
3. Common procedural rules for the High Court and county court (repeating the Civil Justice Review; done in the Woolf Reforms, from 1999).
4. Judicial review cases to be heard on circuit and more specialist county court trial centres (now Welsh cases can be heard in Wales, since devolution).
5. Revival of an ethos of public service amongst court staff and assistance to litigants (done: courts are now awarded a Charter Mark if they demonstrate how well they serve the public—see Chapter 7, above).
6. Plain English court documents (done).
7. A more interventionist approach by judges at trial and on appeal (already existed in small claims; now done where the litigant is in person and generally required by the court's duty to manage cases under the CPR).
8. Limits on discovery of documents; provision of skeleton arguments and bundles to the court and opposing parties (done since the 1994–5 Practice Directions were issued).

9. Judicial intervention at trial to avoid time wasting (now required by the CPR).
10. Promotion of alternative dispute resolution (ADR) (now included in the CPR).

The 1994/1995 Practice Directions

9–050   The Heilbron-Hodge Report doubtless prompted these Practice Directions and the 1994 establishment of Lord Woolf's scrutiny of civil procedure, reporting in *Access to Justice* (1996). Directions were issued for all three High Court divisions. They emphasised the importance of reducing cost and delay and threatened that "failure by practitioners to conduct cases economically will be visited by appropriate orders for costs". The court should limit discovery of documents, oral submissions, examination of witnesses, the issues on which it wishes to be addressed and reading aloud from documents and authorities. Witness statements would generally stand as evidence-in-chief and the parties should, pre-trial, limit the issues. Bundled, photocopied documents and skeleton arguments were to be lodged in court pre-trial. Opening speeches were to be succinct and, where appropriate, lawyers had to verify that they have considered the possibility of ADR with their client. These Directions had a significant impact on the shape of the civil trial. The parties and the judge now read most of the arguments and documentation in advance of trial, thus departing radically from the oral tradition characteristic of the common law, adversarial procedure. The Directions also encouraged the judge to control the nature and content of the cases presented to her, again signifying a departure from the traditional judge's role as a non-interfering umpire.

The Interim Woolf Report 1995

9–051   This repeated many of the recommendations of its predecessors, the Civil Justice Review and the Heilbron-Hodge Report. Amongst Lord Woolf's main recommendations were these:

1. An effective system of case management by the court, instead of allowing the parties to flout rules and run the cases.
2. An expanded small claims jurisdiction of £3,000 (introduced, in 1996, then expanded to £5,000) and a fast track for cases up to £10,000.
3. Judicial, tailored case management for cases over £10,000.
4. Encouragement of early settlement, assisted by enabling either party to make an offer to settle, replacing the system of payment into court.
5. The creation of a new Head of Civil Justice.
6. A single set of High Court/county court rules.

7. Court appointment of single, neutral expert witnesses.
8. Promotion of the use of IT for case management by judges and use of video and telephone conferencing.

Almost all of this was repeated in the final report, *Access to Justice* in 1996, then translated into the law, in the 1997 Act and 1998 CPR and Practice Directions, as set out above. There were some amendments, as you can see. For example, on point 7, the court does not appoint experts but normally requires the parties to agree on a single expert. As can be seen below, point 8 of Woolf's plan has not been fulfilled. Progress on IT in the civil courts is worse than dismal, by 2005.

6. Reactions to the Woolf Report

Zander (1995) said the overwhelming majority of cases settled so did not need management; "we have virtually no information about either delays or costs" and Woolf had not commissioned research on his proposals; they had been trying to reform the system in the US for 20 years without success; English judges had no familiarity with case management; many studies showed pre-trial hearings designed to make trials shorter made them longer and added to cost; US research showed litigants were interested in an unbiased, careful hearing, not informal hearings. Zander (1996) feared increasing judicial discretionary powers of case management would create inconsistent decisions, making the process arbitrary and unpredictable: "My own view is that training can do little to deal with the problem because inconsistency stems from legitimate differences in philosophy as to how a judge should go about the business of judging". He also said lawyers would be unable to stick to time-limits. Case management was a common theme throughout Canada, the US and Australia. Zander (1997) cited a 1997 study of 10,000 US cases by the Rand Corporation which found that some US judges considered case management an attack on judicial independence and believed it emphasised speed and efficiency at the expense of justice. The study also found case management added to costs because lawyers spent an extra 20 hours responding to court directions, even in cases which would have settled anyway. Costs would become front-loaded. Lord Woolf called Zander's criticisms "strident . . . misleading and inaccurate" (1997). Zander defended himself in a lecture to the Chancery Bar Association and later, in 2000.

A Law Society survey of litigation solicitors found only one third considered litigation too adversarial and a third thought case management would improve litigation. 62 per cent thought judges

9–052

should encourage earlier settlements (Law Society's *Gazette*, May 21, 1997).

Zuckerman (1996) argued that the cause of excessive cost lay not in the complexity of procedure but in the incentives lawyers had to complicate litigation. Much of what he said applied to the old legal aid system, since abolished.

7. Developments from 2001

9–053   In 1998, the Lord Chancellor admitted that what many critics were saying was true—the courts would not be ready to cope fully with the Woolf reforms of 1999, because they did not have the technology in place but the Court Service published a consultation paper, in January 2001, *Modernising the Civil Courts*. It built on the reforms already made and expanded on plans announced in *Modernising Justice*, the 1998 white paper. Much of it was about IT: the "virtual court", issue of claims and enforcement procedures online or from a digital TV; "Court on Call", enabling court processes to be dealt with over the telephone; "gateway partnerships" between advice agencies and court staff, enabling the client to access the court and advice at the same time. Once this was done and they centralise information and advice via the Internet, call centres and advice kiosks, the Court Service planned (and still plans) to cut the county courts down to a network of hearing centres. They planned to rationalise their estate (buildings) and share more courts with magistrates. In July 2000, the programme of reform started, with video conferencing from Cardiff, Leeds or a private VC suite, to the CA in the Royal Courts of Justice, London, for civil applications for permission to appeal. Further, people involved in any civil case at the pilot courts are able to choose to give evidence or make submissions via video link. The Cardiff and Leeds courts also tested the use of video conferencing in civil and criminal matters and tribunal cases but moving on from these pilots to all county courts has been very slow or nonexistent in some cases. Most of the above remains a very distant aspiration, in 2005—see discussion below.

8. Evaluating the Woolf Reforms: Research, Surveys and Comments since 1999

Research and Surveys
9–054   The first national consumer satisfaction survey of court users, in 2001, found 79 per cent were satisfied with the overall level of

service. Eighty-six per cent were happy with the counter service, leaflets and forms and telephone responses

A survey of heads of legal departments of UK companies by Eversheds, lawyers, found 54 per cent of respondents considered civil litigation improved in 1999–2000. Fifty-two per cent found litigation quicker but only 22 per cent considered it cheaper. Forty-three per cent were settling cases earlier. Clients no longer sought aggressive, uncompromising lawyers. Disputes were handled differently and 41 per cent had used ADR. Only 24 per cent thought litigants were getting better justice. Forty-four per cent said they were not. Nineteen per cent said costs had risen.

A MORI survey of 180 firms after the first year of the reforms, found that 76 per cent said there had been faster settlements and less litigation, although most respondents thought the outcome would have been the same under the old system. The early-settlement offer, bringing heavy penalties to those refusing to settle, had had the biggest impact on litigation, according to two thirds of private practice lawyers. Mediation had significantly increased (see Chapter 12 on alternatives to the civil courts, below). The Civil Justice Audit, comprised of this and a CEDR survey of 30 civil judges found: 80 per cent of lawyers were satisfied with the CPR; 36 per cent believed litigation had decreased; 47 per cent reported settling cases faster; 60 per cent thought judges should initiate settlement discussion; 58 per cent thought cases should be stayed for mediation and 78 per cent of in-house lawyers thought mediation should be required before a business dispute went to court ((2000) 150 N.L.J. 531).

Another survey by Wragge & Co of in-house commercial lawyers   **9–055**
found 81 per cent of respondents thought courts did not have enough resources. Eighty-nine per cent liked the changes and found litigation quicker, 41 per cent found costs cut and 80 per cent found ADR had proved popular. (Both surveys are summarised in *The Times*, May 2, 2000.)

In August 2002, the Lord Chancellor's Department published an updated evaluation of the Woolf reforms, confirming their "broad success". Claims had dropped. The use of pre-action protocols and offers to settle had diverted cases from litigation. About eight per cent settled at the court door and 70 settled earlier. Time from issue to trial had dropped from 639 days in 1997, to 498 in 2000–2001. There had been a levelling off in the use of ADR: "Civil Justice Reform Evaluation—Further Findings".

A 2002 Court Service survey of court users showed 20 per cent of lawyers found court procedures difficult to understand but 45 per cent of professionals thought the Woolf reforms had simplified procedures.

9–056   A 2001 survey of 130 solicitors by the Law Society showed they were concerned that the assessment of costs was arbitrary and unpredictable, often causing them to make a loss over litigation. They thought there was an unwillingness to apply sanctions and a lack of judicial consistency. New procedures (frontloading) were not cheaper for clients and led to more work. Most respondents considered the use of joint experts inappropriate in multi-track cases.

Lord Phillips M.R., at the Law Society's Civil Litigation Conference 2002, said case management had reduced the average length of time for a case to come to trial from 600 days to 520 days and for claims over £5,000 from 750 to 450 days. Nevertheless, there was a lot of anecdotal evidence to the effect that the Woolf Reforms had increased the cost of litigation in relation to cases that go the whole way.

A 2002 joint Law Society/Civil Justice Council report by Goriely and others was the first detailed piece of research on the success rate of the Woolf reforms. The team examined the impact of the Woolf Reforms on pre-action behaviour. 54 lawyers, insurers and claims managers were interviewed, specialising in clinical disputes, personal injury and housing and 150 pre- and post-Woolf case files were inspected. The research concluded that the Woolf Reforms had enhanced access to justice. Early disclosure had led to more settlements at the pre-action stage and they were based on better information. Most practitioners regarded the reforms as a success, citing clearer structure and greater certainty in the fast track. They praised the invention of claimants' Part 36 offers and considered that pre-action protocols enabled informed settlement. They complained of a lack of sanctions for breach, however. Expert evidence continued to be problematic, although the instruction of agreed experts had almost eradicated the concept of an expert owned by one side. Many felt that the courts were inefficient in listing, because they were under-resourced. Problems caused by lack of IT were well known (see Civil Justice Council website).

In February 2004, the Legal Services Research Centre published a major survey into civil justice problems. This is discussed in Chapter 17 on legal services, below.

Comments
9–057   Robert Turner, Senior Master in the High Court, and head of the masters who manage civil QBD cases pre-trial, welcomed the new rules ((2000) 150 N.L.J. 49). The pervading adversarial approach had gone and been replaced by a degree of co-operation. Settlements were achieved earlier, procedures were defining the real issues between the parties and solicitors would find the quicker rate of disposal allowed them to do more work. In the short

term, however, the new rules had not succeeded in attacking cost, delay and complexity because the new system was costly at the commencement of the action ("front loaded"); the new procedures with pre-action protocols, allocation and listing questionnaires and case management conferences, etc. were more complex and many county courts were struggling with implementation so delays were occurring.

Master John Leslie commented on "a new spirit of co-operation abroad". He found around 50 per cent of cases stayed for a settlement attempt did settle. He too complained of a lack of IT, though (*Counsel*, 2000).

Zander, in 2000, described the Woolf reforms in a more tempered way than before, praising some elements but he reiterated his criticism of front loading of costs, in the manner of "I told you so" and penalties for non-compliance and the inconsistent approach of judges when given discretion.

Suzanne Burn, an experienced civil litigator, wrote a very useful article in 2003, summarising many evaluations of Woolf and adding in comments from her own experience as a practitioner and that of her colleagues (she was later appointed a District Judge, in 2005). She said there had been very limited research into the impact of the reforms. It was difficult to isolate the impact of the Woolf reforms because of the complicating factors: **9–058**

- the withdrawal of public funding (formerly legal aid) from many types of civil claim and the widened scope of conditional fees;
- the introduction of tougher quality standards for legal service providers; and
- the implementation of the Human Rights Act 1998 in 2000.

As she rightly observes, measuring the success of such broad aims as Lord Woolf's is very difficult.

Lightman J. (2003) drew the following conclusions, from his 32 years at the Bar and nine as a High Court judge:

1. Although the pre-action protocols had front-loaded costs they had substantially reduced the number of actions launched and led to a reduction in civil business.
2. Summary orders for costs had led to parties "feeling the pain" earlier and so they were more cautious and sensible. Unnecessary court business was avoided.
3. The assumption by the court of full case management powers should and often did enable the court to ensure the interlocutory stages and delay were minimised.

4. The severe limitation on expert witnesses had removed a drain on resources and court time.
5. Small claims provided a public service of inestimable value.

The total volume of litigation

9–059   This has fallen since the implementation of the Woolf reforms in 1999 but this is the continuation of a previous trend. The rate of settlement between issue and trial has increased. In my ongoing research on judges, I have found that High Court and CA judges consider this a cause for concern but I routinely point out that one of Woolf's aims was to require managing judges to encourage early settlement. His reforms were supposed to put parties on an equal footing and the encourage *fair* settlements. Whether the increasing volumes of settlements are for fair amounts of damages is almost impossible to quantify. Qureshi points out that Woolf considered that individuals had a constitutional right to an accessible and effective system of civil litigation, via the courts, yet, in 1998–2002, there had been a 500 per cent reduction of proceedings commenced in the Queen's Bench Division. My reaction to this would be to point out that parties may be resorting to alternative dispute resolution (ADR) and Qureshi acknowledges that this may be one reason. I would add that we can never measure this, because ADR is unquantifiable. It is mostly not court-controlled. It is unregulated and operated as a multitude of private enterprises, whose statistics are not always made public. If ADR is increasing then this can be seen as a success of the Woolf reforms, not a failure, since Woolf wanted to encourage ADR and the CPR place a duty on judges to encourage ADR where possible and ensure that lawyers have discussed the possibility with their clients. The case law, which Qureshi discusses, reinforces this in the context of costs.

I would also add, in response to Qureshi, that the mischief of the Courts and Legal Services Act 1990 was to shift the civil case load onto the county courts, reserving the High Court for complex or unusual cases and the 1998 Rules continue this aspiration so if the QBD has lost work that is a success. One needs to examine the total civil case load. Examining the county court workload as well, in the Judicial Statistics (DCA website), we can see that county court claims have diminished too, from over 2,245,000 in 1998, to over 1,571,000 in 2003 *but* Burn is correct that this is just a continuation of a previous trend, as in 1990 there were over 3,311,000 claims.

Making the process simpler

9–060   It is arguable whether this has been achieved. While the Rules and forms are simple and in plain English, Burn points out that there are over 500 forms and the Rules and Practice Directions are longer than the old rules. Amendments are published almost monthly.

The impact on costs

As Burn pointed out, this is very difficult to quantify. A true assessment of the cost to the litigant would require access to files in law firms, insurers and clients.

9–061

Has there been a culture change?

Lord Woolf hoped for a significant change in the way lawyers and litigants approach civil disputes away from adversarialism, the battle approach. Burn considers that lawyers are now more careful about sending deliberately aggressive letters to the opposition and "tactical" applications are less frequent but the "costs war" on conditional fees (see below) shows that adversarial behaviour is "far from dead".

9–062

Pre-action protocols as a culture change

Burn says concerns have been expressed in all surveys that these frontload costs. In support of Burn, I would add that of the 73 judges I have so far interviewed in my current research, most have expressed a view on the Woolf reforms and virtually all of them considered the Woolf reforms to be a success but remarked on the increased expense of civil cases, especially caused by the frontloading of costs. This is because the pre-action protocols require a lot of work from solicitors *before* a claim is issued, in investigating their client's case and disclosing information to the other side. Another complaint is that the courts rarely penalize parties for non-compliance with a protocol. These comments were reaffirmed at the judges' Technology and Construction Court annual conference I attended in 2004, when a users survey manifested the complaint that parties were not penalised for non-compliance with the TCC pre-action protocol.

9–063

Small claims

See Baldwin's research, above. The volume of small claims has dropped significantly, despite the limit's increasing from £3,000 to £5,000.

9–064

Case management

Burn concludes that "There seems to be no consensus about the value of judicial case management". Plotnikoff and Woolfson found that most district judges and masters were comfortable in the role of case manager but some practitioners, says Burn, complain that judges do not read the case papers in advance. Case management

9–065

241

conferences vary considerably from court to court. I can support this. In researching judges, I discovered that whereas in one part of the Western circuit, judges insist that the lawyers and their parties appear at case management conferences, because their statistics show that this encourages settlement, judges elsewhere expect to be able to conduct CMCs by telephone conference. Burn remarks that:

> "the one great advantage of CPR case management over the old-style laissez-faire approach is that cases no longer drift–there is always a return date to ensure judges keep an eye on progress . . . Many practitioners, sadly, are their own worst enemies if they wish to minimize judicial 'interference'. (She remarks on failure to complete forms correctly and disproportionate costs estimates) . . . a casual attitude to case management".

From spending several weeks in 2002–3, looking over the shoulders of eight district judges, I can verify this. District judges frequently showed me that papers sent in to them by solicitors were a "dog's breakfast" and showed me how they were routinely referring cases back to solicitors for forms to be correctly completed or items to be properly explained.

Sanctions and cost penalties

9–066 Burn said that relatively few cases are struck out under the CPR for non-compliance with court directions and orders. She concludes that dealing with cases "justly", rather than by the rule book is working well.

Offers to settle

9–067 "Definitely one of the successes of the CPR", says Burn.

9–068 **Outstanding problems** remain, in ADR, expert witnesses, costs and IT. The Civil Justice Council, established by the Civil Procedure Act 1997, has the job of keeping civil justice under review. It is chaired by the Master of the Rolls, Lord Phillips of Worth Matravers and head of civil justice, whose deputy is Lord Justice Dyson. Both are energetic and dynamic forward-thinking judges who do this job on top of their day job of deciding heavy duty cases in the CA. The Council has a number of committees. Its annual reports appear on its website. Lord Phillips writes the introductions, in which he comments on the Council's current concerns. The 2002 report was preoccupied with the "costs war", which he and the Council made it their mission to resolve, acting in a pro-active manner to bring together the different "sides" in this war. In the 2003 Annual Report, Lord Phillips reported on the successes they had achieved in this. I discuss this in the next section.

9. Problems Outstanding in 2005—and Solutions

The "Costs War"

Conditional fee agreements (CFAs) were Lord Chancellor Irvine's **9–069** alternative solution for claimants who could not afford to litigate, after he withdrew legal aid from some of them, following the Access to Justice Act 1999. All this is explained in Chapter 17 on legal services, below. A CFA means a "no win, no fee" contract between such a private client and a solicitor. The client takes out insurance against losing, because he will then be liable to pay the winner's costs. The client also agrees to pay a success fee to the solicitor, a percentage of the costs, if he wins. This has to be paid by the loser of the case. The success fee enables the solicitor to build up funds to finance the cases he loses. Of course, clients do not mind what level of success fee they agree to, because they know they will pay nothing at all, whether they win or lose the case. A problem arose because litigants who lost cases, often insurance companies, felt solicitors were profiteering by charging unreasonable percentages as success fees and satellite litigation, arguing about these amounts, had bedevilled the civil courts after 2000. In *Callery v Gray* [2002] UKHL 28, the success fee had been agreed at 60 per cent and was reduced by the district judge to 40 per cent. The CA thought 20 per cent was reasonable. The House of Lords thought this was too generous but felt that regulating civil litigation was the CA's business and declined to interfere. Lord Hoffman thought fee level should be regulated by law. After a series of test cases in May 2003, defendant insurers continued to bring technical challenges to CFAs and the CA ran out of patience. They awarded costs against the defendants and said such litigants should "stop all this nonsense".

In the meantime, the Civil Justice Council commissioned research, in 2003, on how to calculate the reasonableness of a success fee and the Master of the Rolls, leader of the CA and the Civil Justice Council, decided to mediate a settlement between the two sides in the costs war. He called interested parties together in a house party in December 2002 to agree on a fixed costs scheme in out-of-court settlements in cases arising out of road traffic accidents. Another agreement was reached in employers' liability claims, in 2004. In the 2002 Annual Report of the Civil Justice Council, he complained that costs were the "Achilles heel" of the (Woolf) reforms" and in the 2003 Report he said that costs law had "dominated our (meaning the CA's) worksheets in 2003" so it was not an overstatement that these new agreements heralded "a revolution in legal costs". CPR 45 now fixes success fees for different types of case, since October

2003. Introducing the new rules, minister David Lammy said fixed success fees would "help ensure that justice is delivered at a reasonable and proportionate cost". Nevertheless, in 2004, 13 media organisations, including the BBC, complained that high fees in CFAs were severely damaging press freedom in privacy and libel cases. They were forced to settle cases even when they felt the claims were weak. Claimant's lawyers were charging disproportionate fees. Naomi Campbell took a case against the *Daily Mirror* to the House of Lords under a "no win, no fee" contract (described in Chapter 4 on Human Rights, above). Alastair Brett, of News International complained of "a revolting state of affairs with some lawyers displaying a greed unparalleled in any other profession".

Unregulated Experts

9–070   Lord Woolf called the uncontrolled use of experts one of the biggest generators of costs under the old civil justice regime, before his reforms. Wealthy litigants would line up an array of them to try and defeat the opposition. All that is now gone, as parties are expected to agree to a single joint expert, in most cases. The outstanding problem is, however, the unregulated "industry" of experts that the old pre-1999 regime generated, making money out of lawyers' willingness to hire them. Anyone can claim to be an expert. The two bodies representing experts have failed to agree on how to regulate them. Worse, the system is open to fraud, as demonstrated by the conviction of Barian Baluchi, in 2005. An ex-taxi driver, he had posed as a psychiatrist and gained registration by the General Medical Council in 1998 by stealing the identity of a Madrid psychiatrist. He bought a PhD from a "distance learning" college and gave evidence on over 2000 asylum seekers, 1,000 of whom were allowed to stay in the UK. His name appeared in the 2002 Expert Witness Directory, endorsed by the Law Society. The Civil Justice Council has set up a committee on experts which the Master of the Rolls hopes will lead to a code of guidance. In 2004, the Legal Services Commission proposed that experts regularly providing forensic services should be quality-assured and hired on fixed fees.

Court Fees

9–071   As I described in Chapter 6 on civil courts, above, there is a continuing argument between the Civil Justice Council and the judges, led by the Master of the Rolls, and the Government. The latter is determined to make the civil courts pay for themselves and the judges think increases in court fees deny people access to justice. They, and lawyers, think the courts should be viewed as a public service, as they are in other countries. Civil court fees rose by up to 150 per cent in January 2005. In December 2004, the Association of

Personal Injury Lawyers said that, in the previous 24 years court fees had risen by up to 4,150 per cent. Commercial lawyers are concerned at competition from foreign courts. Adrian Jack pointed out that a high value five day case in the High Court would cost £6,100 here but only £2,300 in Germany. The Treasury complained that the courts were running at a loss. That was partly because it insisted on charging the Court Service interest on assets it already owned, such as the Royal Courts of Justice.

The Failure to Enforce Judgments

If people cannot get their damages payments from defendants **9–072** after winning their case, there is no point in their having gone to court in the first place and no access to justice. There is no point in making civil procedure simpler and encouraging people to take their claims to court if they cannot get their winnings. They will have expended extra money in court fees and will be even worse off. In 2003, Baldwin published research funded by the Lord Chancellor's Department. He examined civil claims ending in a "default judgement". This means, as described above, where the defendant fails to enter a defence so the claimant gets judgment in his favour automatically.

He found that only a small proportion of county court and High Court claimants received full payment within the time ordered by the court. He and Cunnington argued, in 2004 that where the courts' enforcement mechanisms are ineffective, there is a breach of the claimant's human rights, under both Art.6 of the Convention (fair trial) and Art.1 of Protocol 1 (right to respect for possessions), as the judgments of the ECtHR demonstrate. They alluded to an enforcement review, then in progress, which was established by the present government in 1998. They considered that it was being conducted in an "information vacuum", as little was known about which type of defendant paid up or which was the most effective type of enforcement. They found that "Very many defendants were highly elusive". Only 13.3 per cent of the High Court claimants surveyed had received full payment and some had had to go to considerable lengths to get it. The more money was at stake, the less likely claimants were to be paid. The futility of the court process led to feelings of "bitterness, frustration, cynicism, anger, disenchantment and powerlessness". Some ensured that recalcitrant defendants were bankrupted or blacklisted for credit, by being entered on the register of county court judgments. The authors acknowledged the DCA's white paper (2003) on enforcement but concluded that "it is unlikely that any workable and fair system of enforcement will be capable of producing more than moderate rates of payment". The courts, they argued, could not be expected to assume responsibility for debt recovery that fell on lenders and "Since the interests of creditors and debtors are often quire irreconcilable, no system of enforcement could be devised that would achieve even a satisfactory balance between them". The 2003 paper announced the Government intention to introduce data disclosure orders, allowing courts to obtain information from such third parties as banks, the Inland Revenue and credit reference agencies, to facilitate decision making as to effective enforcement action.

Do we have a Compensation Culture?

9–073   Teachers, businesses, insurers, local authorities and public bodies, notably the NHS, have all made claims, in the 1990s that they are suffering from a compensation culture and they consider that this is fuelled by the claimants' ability to obtain the no win no fee services of solicitors or claims handling companies. Lawyers who represent claimants, such as the Association of Personal Injury Lawyers, have retorted that the compensation culture is a myth. Prior to the 1990s, citizens of England and Wales were, allegedly, very reluctant to litigate compared with Americans and Germans, who were considered overly litigious. When organising the civil justice system and access to legal services, the Government needs to balance the competing interests of access to justice and combating social exclusion on the one hand and greed and profiteering on the other. In 2003, The Law Society and the Federation of Small Businesses sought action from the Lord Chancellor over the growth of "ambulance chasers", blamed for increasing insurance liability premiums by encouraging employees to sue for accidents in the workplace under no win no fee arrangements. The groups were calling for the creation of a regulatory body to monitor these companies with the power to discipline those found guilty of acting unethically.

By 2003, the chief medical officer, Sir Liam Donaldson was expressing alarm at the slow and cumbersome process of clinical negligence litigation which was costing the NHS double what it had in 1998. He proposed setting up an NHS run fast track redress scheme. Since healthcare for Wales is run separately, Wales already has a scheme for mediating even very large clinical disputes.

In December 2004, Dominic Clayden, of the insurers, Norwich Union, complained that "Claims management companies and solicitors have exploited the public's expectations in terms of what is compensatable, and the amounts that might be achieved". The Law Society refuted this but, in the same month, the Bar Council said the reforms recommended by Sir David Clementi (see Chapter 13, below), known as "Tesco law" would encourage a compensation culture.

The Better Regulation Task Force published "Better Routes to   **9–074**
Redress" in 2004, commissioned by the Government, to try to give
an objective view on whether a compensation culture existed:
www.brtf.gov.uk. Their report concluded that there was no compensation culture but the perception that there was caused a fear of litigation. This, I suggest, rather contradicts the evidence presented in
their report. Giving examples of the amounts paid out by public
bodies in compensation claims, they mentioned one highway
authority that spent £2 million of its £22 million budget settling
compensation claims. The report correctly pointed out that the
news media were fond of reporting outlandish claims but neglected
to report their outcome—that they often got nowhere. They
acknowledged that the emergence of the no win no fee contract and
claims management companies had encouraged more claims but
some claims were well founded and made public authorities and
others better at managing risk.

On the negative side, the "have a go" culture drained public
resources, made organisations cautious, contributed to higher
insurance premiums and clogged up the system for meritorious
claimants. They recommended:

- better regulation of claims companies;
- consumer advice;
- restrictions on advertising in hospitals and surgeries;
- raising the small claims limit in personal injuries;
- examining the overlap between ombudsmen;
- more encouragement of mediation;
- researching the possibility of contingency fees;
- promoting NHS rehabilitation, risk management.

Lord Chancellor Falconer initially announced that claims firms
should regulate themselves but, in March 2005, he announced that he
was disappointed. They had not done so and it was time to take firm
action. He warned that a "front-line regulator" would be imposed.

IT

As is very well known, the Woolf reforms were launched   **9–075**
without the supporting IT systems in place that Lord Woolf had
envisaged. This has caused frustration to judges, problems for the
court staff and frustration to court users who could not email large
documents into the commercial court, or even email most courts
(*Court of Appeal (Civil Division) Review of the Year 2004*). Only in
2005 is progress commencing on the sort of electronic communication between parties and courts that was envisaged by Lord
Woolf. Even now, the civil courts are having to take second place

far behind the LINK communication and case management system currently being installed in the criminal courts and criminal justice agencies so no end is in sight. The Master of the Rolls has never missed an opportunity to draw attention to the inadequacy of civil courts' IT systems. As he said in his *Court of Appeal (Civil Division) Review of the Year 2002–3,*

> "Continued IT modernisation is essential if we are to provide the type of modern court services both professionals and citizens are coming to expect, and I continue to press Government to ensure that adequate funding is made available to continue this reform".

10. Judicial Review

9–076 Historically, a person aggrieved with an error of law or the procedure of an inferior court could petition the monarch to refer the proceedings for examination in the High Court. The High Court now exercises this residuary monarchical prerogative, in judicial review proceedings. The procedure is available in civil and criminal cases. Procedure is determined by CPR Part 54 and a Practice Direction, both of which came into force in October 2000. The claim is made in the Administrative Court, in the QBD, or the Administrative Court for Wales, at Cardiff. The question of permission is normally considered without a hearing. At the substantive hearing, the judge examines the legality and procedural correctness of the decision of the lower court or tribunal and whether the body has acted within its powers or *ultra vires.* The court may impose a quashing order on a defective decision (formerly *certiorari*), or make a mandatory order that a public body carry out its duty (formerly *mandamus*) or declare the law or order an injunction, preventing an illegality. The judge has no concern with substituting a new finding of fact. Guidance was given by Lord Steyn in *R. v SS for the Home Dept Ex p. Daly* [2001] UKHL 26. Lord Steyn emphasised the difference between proportionality, under the Convention and traditional grounds for review, despite the overlap. He said:

> "the doctrine of proportionality may require the reviewing court to assess the balance which the decision maker has struck, not merely whether it is in the range of rational or reasonable decisions. . . . The proportionality test may go further than the traditional grounds of review in as much as it may require attention to be directed to the relative weight accorded to interests and considerations."

Since the 1960s and especially since the procedure was made easier in 1981, there has been a massive growth in judicial review cases and most of them have been challenges to the legality of public bodies' decisions, mostly local or central government. Challenges have been made to a broad list of such decisions: planning, hospital closure, policing tactics, benefits which apply differently to men and women, decisions relating to the National Lottery and so on. It was thought that this court would be very busy with challenges under the Human Rights Act and this has occurred to a certain extent, although the courts were not swamped, as it was predicted they would be.

11. Family Procedure

Family procedure is the subject of a special set of rules, not   9–077
covered by this book. The Courts Act 2003, Part 7 provides for a new Family Procedure Rule Committee and allows the President of the Family Division to issue Practice Directions, with the concurrence of the Lord Chancellor, which bind magistrates' courts and the county courts as well as the High Court. The Civil Procedure Rules do not apply to most family proceedings but there are certain exceptions. For instance, the cost rules do apply. It is sometimes said that elements of the CPR were copied from existing family procedure. Family judges were well aware already of the need to keep costs and delay down and experts were only used with the court's permission. Nevertheless, Lord Justice Thorpe, now Deputy Head of Family Justice, complained in *Allan v Clibbery* [2002] EWCA Civ 45:

"In recent years the family justice system has seemed something of a Cinderella. In reality the reforms as to access and reporting introduced in the wake of civil justice reforms have not been replicated in the family justice system . . . That state of affairs only heightens the case for the resumption of the rolling programme for the reform of family law and practice".

BIBLIOGRAPHY
Note that the *New Law Journal* is available in hard copy from most   9–078
   law libraries and is available electronically, on the subscriber database, *Lexis*. The *Civil Justice Quarterly* is available in hard copy and on the subscriber database *Westlaw*.
G. Applebey, "The Growth of Litigants in Person in English Criminal Proceedings" (1997) 16 C.J.Q. 127.

J. Baldwin, "Monitoring the Rise of the Small Claims Limit: Litigants' Experiences of Different Forms of Adjudication" LCD Research Series 1/97, DCA website: *www.dca. gov.uk*

J. Baldwin, *Small Claims in the County Court in England and Wales: The Bargain Basement of Civil Justice* (1997).

J. Baldwin, "Small Claims Hearings: The 'Interventionist' Role Played by District Judges" (1998) 17 C.J.Q. 20.

J. Baldwin, "Increasing the Small Claims Limit" (1998) 148 N.L.J. 274.

J. Baldwin, "Lay and judicial perspectives on the expansion of the small claims regime" LCD Research Series 8/02, available on the DCA website: *www.dca.gov.uk*

J. Baldwin, "Evaluating the Effectiveness of Enforcement Procedures in Undefended Claims in the Civil Courts" DCA Research Study 3/2003: *www.dca.gov.uk*

J. Baldwin and R. Cunnington, "The Crisis in Enforcement of Civil Judgments in England and Wales" (2004) 23 C.J.Q. 305, also on *Westlaw*.

S. Burn, "The Woolf Reforms in Retrospect", *Legal Action*, July 2003, p.8.

P. Darbyshire, *The Magistrates' Clerk* (1984).

H. Genn, *Paths to Justice* (1999).

A. Jack, "Court fees: the new stealth tax?" (2004) 154 N.L.J. 909 (also on *LexisNexis*).

Mr Justice Lightman, "The case for judicial intervention" (1999) 149 N.L.J. 1819 (an excellent brief account of how civil litigation used to be, prior to the Woolf Reforms).

Sir Gavin Lightman's 2003 speech is reproduced as The Hon. Mr Justice Lightman, "The Civil Justice System and Legal Profession—The Challenges Ahead" (2003) 22 C.J.Q. 235, also available on *Westlaw*.

N. Madge, "Small Claims in the County Court" (2004) 23 C.J.Q. 201.

R. Moorhead, "Access or Aggravation? Litigants in Person, McKenzie Friends and Lay Representation" (2003) 22 C.J.Q. 133.

J. Plotnikoff and R. Woolfson "Judges' Case Management Perspectives: the Views of Opinion Formers and Case Managers" LCD Research Series 3/02, DCA website: *www.dca.gov.uk.*

M. Zander on the Woolf report: (1995) 145 N.L.J. 154; (1996) 146 N.L.J. 1590; (1997) 147 N.L.J. 353 and 539; Woolf on Zander (1997) 147 N.L.J. 751; Zander defends himself: (1997) 147 N.L.J. 768 and *Civil Justice Quarterly*. See responses to Zander and other critics by Greenslade at (1996) 146 N.L.J. 1147. Zander had the last word in *The State of Justice* (2000), Chapter 2.

FURTHER READING ON CIVIL PROCEDURE AND SOURCES FOR UPDATING THIS CHAPTER

Online updates to this book: *http://www.sweetandmaxwell.co.uk/ academic/updates/darbyshire/index.html*   **9–079**

Times law reports.

New Law Journal available in hard copy and on *Lexis.*

Mr Justice Lightman's 2003 speech, referenced above, is an invaluable critique. I strongly recommend it.

Summary of Lord Woolf's final report *Access to Justice,* 1996, in the Law Society's *Gazette,* August 2, 1996.

Civil Procedure Rules, DCA website: *www.dca.gov.uk*

Civil Justice Council annual reports and reviews: *www.open.gov.uk/ civjustice*

Civil Justice Quarterly for updates, commentary, research and academic analysis. It is in hard copy and on *Westlaw.*

Her Majesty's Courts Service: *www.hmcourts-service.gov.uk*

A.A.S. Zuckerman and R. Cranston (eds), *Reform of Civil Procedure— Essays on Access to Justice* (1995).

For a practical guide, any of the following books. Use the latest edition only:

Grainger & M. Fealy with M. Spencer, *The Civil Procedure Rules in Action,* and *Introduction to the New Civil Procedure Rules.*

J. O'Hare & K. Browne, *Civil Litigation.*

R. N. Hill, *A Practical Guide to Civil Litigation.*

10. Criminal Procedure

"Having a Criminal Justice Bill before Parliament is like having a skip outside your house overnight. People take your rejected junk and other people stuff their junk into it." (Cambridge Professor John Spencer, 1996, quoting an anonymous contributor to the Justices' Clerks' Society Conference that year.)

"The criminal justice system and public confidence in it are readily susceptible to damage by disjointed, sporadic and precipitate change." (Lord Justice Auld, *Review of the Criminal Courts of England and Wales* (2001).)

Since the 1980s, criminal procedure and the criminal courts seem **10–001** to be under continual and fundamental review and consequent restructuring. Much of this has been well thought through and long overdue. Added to this though and for the sake of a sound bite demonstrating he is tough on crime, each Home Secretary cannot resist making a list of statutory alterations *every* year. The result is a complex mish-mash of statutes amended by sets of other statutes which is a nightmare to apply for judges, magistrates' clerks and practising lawyers. Apart from the uncertainty of knowing which sections of new statutes are in force, there is often a problem that one statutory provision has barely been implemented before another supersedes it. Magistrates' clerks (legal advisers) work at the chalk face, their courts dealing with the bulk of criminal cases. They are the first to discover that a new bit of "junk" does not fit in to the rest, as they struggle to make sense of the latest whim of a Home Secretary in an endeavour to explain it to their lay justices. Circuit judges in the Crown Court, determined to assert their independence, simply ignore many of the changes that they disapprove of, provided that they can get away with it without being appealed. In the meantime, criminal lawyers, demoralised by being paid one less peanut every year (see Chapter 17, below) cannot be bothered with the masochism of mastering the latest statute. In 2005 they are leaving criminal practice more quickly than dentists abandoned the NHS.

Procedure has been scrutinised by the Royal Commission on Criminal Procedure 1981, which resulted in the Police and Criminal Evidence Act 1984 (PACE) and the creation of the Crown Prosecution Service; then the Royal Commission on Criminal Justice 1993, which resulted in the Criminal Justice and Public Order Act 1994, the Criminal Appeal Act 1995 and the Criminal Procedure and Investigations Act 1996 and then the Narey Report 1997 (*Review of Delay in the Criminal Justice System*), which resulted in the Crime and Disorder Act 1998.

On top of this, there has been a long list of white papers, especially on young offenders. These resulted in a wholly new youth justice scheme, set up by the 1998 Act.

10–002   In 2000, the Human Rights Act 1998 came into effect and has had and will in future have a profound impact on criminal procedure, especially through Arts 5 and 6, as described below, via the case law of the ECtHR and our own courts. Many statutory changes have had to be made, to render our procedure compatible with the Convention.

In case we were in danger of becoming complacent, Lord Justice Auld was asked to conduct the Criminal Courts Review, performing a similar scrutiny of the criminal courts and procedure to that of Lord Woolf on the civil courts, discussed in the previous chapter. Lord Justice Auld reported in October 2001. His *Review of the Criminal Courts in England and Wales* made sweeping proposals for a unified three tier criminal court system and major changes to criminal procedure and the rules of evidence. His *Review* proved controversial and provoked a great deal of debate. The Government's legislative plans responding to all this were set out in the white paper, *Justice for All* (2002). Although his suggestion for a third and middle tier of criminal court was not accepted, many of his other proposals, such as restructuring court management, widening jury participation, streamlining criminal procedure rules and making changes to disclosure and evidence have been enacted in the Courts Act 2003 and the Criminal Justice Act 2003 (CJA 2003). At my time of writing, 2005, some parts of these Acts have been brought into force.

Added to all of these major changes, there has been a battery of statutes on specific aspects of procedure and policing and sentencing. This chapter does not deal with police powers, evidence or sentencing, or I would have even more cause to moan.

10–003   To ease the misery of every criminal practitioner, student and judge, Spencer called for a unified Code of Criminal Procedure and this recommendation was reiterated by Auld L.J. At last, this is being done and the first set of Criminal Procedure Rules was published in 2005.

We start this chapter at the point of prosecution but first we need to understand some fundamental principles, newly articulated, at least in this form, in the English legal system.

1. European Convention on Human Rights, Articles 5 and 6

The HRA 1998 brought Convention rights into English law in 2000. **10–004** The fundamental rights contained in Arts 5 and 6 have become the yardstick against which all statute and case law on English criminal procedure must now be measured. The text of the Convention Articles is appended to the HRA 1998 and the Government's Human Rights Unit website is worth visiting for links and up to date information on changes in the law and new cases. The text of Art.6 is as follows.

Right to a Fair Trial

1. In the determination of his civil rights and obligations and of **10–005** any criminal charge against him, everyone is entitled to a fair and public hearing within a reasonable time by an independent and impartial tribunal established by law. Judgment shall be pronounced publicly but the press and public may be excluded from all or part of the trial in the interests of morals, public order or national security in a democratic society, where the interests of juveniles or the private life of the parties so require, or to the extent strictly necessary in the opinion of the court in special circumstances where publicity would prejudice the interests of justice.
2. Everyone charged with a criminal offence shall be presumed innocent until proved guilty according to the law.
3. Everyone charged with a criminal offence has the following minimum rights:

   (a) to be informed promptly, in a language which he understands and in detail, of the nature and cause of the accusation against him;

   (b) to have adequate time and facilities for the preparation of his defence;

   (c) to defend himself in person or through legal assistance of his own choosing or, if he has not sufficient means to pay for legal assistance, to be given it free if the interests of justice so require;

(d) to examine or have examined witnesses against him and to obtain the attendance and examination of witnesses on his behalf under the same conditions as witnesses against him;

(e) to have the free assistance of an interpreter if he cannot understand or speak the language used in court.

Here is a paraphrase of Art.5. It appears in full, with the other Convention rights, appended as a Schedule to the HRA 1998.

Right to Liberty and Security

10–006
1. Everyone has the right to liberty and security of person. No one shall be deprived of his liberty save in the following cases and in accordance with a procedure prescribed by law:

   - lawful detention after conviction;
   - lawful arrest or detention for non-compliance with a court order or to secure fulfilment of a legal obligation;
   - lawful arrest or detention, effected to bring someone before a competent legal authority on reasonable suspicion of having committed an offence or when it is reasonably considered necessary to prevent his committing an offence or fleeing after having done so;
   - detention of a minor by lawful order for the purpose of educational supervision or lawful detention to bring him before a competent legal authority;
   - lawful detention to prevent spread of infectious diseases, of persons of unsound mind, alcoholics or drug addicts or vagrants;
   - lawful arrest or detention to prevent unauthorised entry into the country, or for extradition or deportation.

2. Everyone who is arrested shall be informed promptly, in a language which he understands, of the reasons for his arrest and of any charge against him.
3. Everyone arrested . . . shall be brought before a judge or other authorised officer to exercise judicial power and shall be entitled to trial within a reasonable time or to release pending trial. Release may be conditioned by guarantees to appear for trial.
4. Everyone who is deprived of his liberty by arrest or detention shall be entitled to take proceedings by which the lawfulness of his detention shall be decided speedily by a court and his release ordered if the detention is not lawful.
5. Everyone who has been the victim of arrest or detention in contravention of the provisions of this Article shall have an enforceable right to compensation.

In the text below, I examine how these two articles have already been used in interpreting the main elements of English criminal procedure. I come back to the Convention at the end of this chapter.

2. The Criminal Procedure Rules 2005

Lord Justice Auld, in his *Review of the Criminal Courts in England and Wales* agreed with Spencer about developing a criminal code. What was needed, he said was a concise and simply expressed statement of the current statutory and common law procedural rules and the product of the current overlay of practice directions, codes of guidance and the like. The new single code should be laid out in such a way that it could be readily amended, without recourse to statute, he said, so the plan is to revise the rules twice a year "to help introduce certainty", as the Department of Constitutional Affairs (DCA) website claims.

10–007

As a reward for this insight, in 2004 Auld L.J. was given the hard task, on top of his demanding day job as a judge in the Court of Appeal (CA), of helping to devise such a code. The Lord Chief Justice chairs the new Criminal Procedure Rules Committee, which is comprised of judges at every level of the criminal courts including Auld L.J., a justices' clerk, the DPP, criminal lawyers and representatives of other elements of the criminal justice system. Their central task was to reduce into 78 parts, in simple English, the chaos that is English criminal procedure. Each part brings together the separate rules applicable in the magistrates' court and Crown Court. The principled aim behind this is not just to consolidate but to make the law more accessible to ordinary people, as the 1998 Civil Procedure Rules aim to do in the civil context. Now this first step has been done, just writing all the rules down in one place, the next aim will be to review the rules to check that they are accessible, fair and efficient and to rewrite them so they are "simple and simply expressed".

The Rules Committee was also a suggestion of Auld L.J. and replaces the plethora of similar bodies that had developed over the years and this one new Code replaces 50 sets of rules. His 2001 recommendations for the Committee and the new Code were accepted by the Government in their white paper, *Justice for All* (2002) and the Committee is established by Part 7 of the CJA 2003, ss.69–73. Section 69 confirms that, when making Rules, the Committee should give due attention to securing that:

"(a) the criminal justice system is accessible, fair and efficient, and
(b) the rules are both simple and simply expressed" (s.69).

10–008   Also on the level of principle in an erstwhile unprincipled system, the Rules introduce a new overriding objective and detailed rules of case management, imposing duties even on defence lawyers and bringing about "a culture change", according to Lord Chief Justice Woolf and Lord Chancellor Falconer. In all these respects, the new rules mirror the principles of the Civil Procedure Rules 1998, described in the last chapter. Lord Woolf was the architect of the latter and now presides over the criminal justice system and the development of these new rules.

The Criminal Procedure Rules 2005 came into force in April 2005 and are on the HMSO website: *www.legislation.hmso.gov.uk*. This first version is SI 2005/384.

The Overriding Objective

Rule 1.1

10–009   "The overriding objective of this new code is that criminal cases be dealt with justly."

This includes (1.2)

"(a) acquitting the innocent and convicting the guilty;
(b) dealing with the prosecution and the defence fairly;
(c) recognising the rights of a defendant, particularly under Art 6 of the European Convention on Human Rights;
(d) respecting the interests of witnesses, victims and jurors and keeping them informed of the progress of the case;
(e) dealing with the case efficiently and expeditiously;
(f) ensuring that appropriate information is available to the court when bail and sentence are considered; and
(g) dealing with the case in ways that take into account:

(i)   the gravity of the offence alleged,
(ii)   the complexity of what is in issue,
(iii) the severity of the consequences for the defendant and others affected, and
(iv) the needs of other cases".

Critique

10–010   Consider:

1. Under (a), is convicting the guilty meant to be as important as acquitting the innocent? The rhetoric of the English legal system has traditionally asserted that convicting the innocent is a much graver fault than acquitting the guilty and been prepared to acquit some guilty people in the endeavour to protect

the accused's due process rights to minimize the risk of convicting an innocent. Blackstone, in the eighteenth century, set the ratio of risk as 1:10: but other writers have set it as 1:20 or as high as 1:100, in Bentham's case. Given the power of Blackstone's rhetoric over our thinking in the English legal system, we mostly seem to have settled for his 1:10 ratio. Auld L.J. gave considerable thought to the principles underlying the criminal justice system, in his *Review*, Chapter 1. The Lord Chief Justice, when introducing the new Rules emphasised the presumption of innocence and it is, of course, guaranteed by Art.6 of the Convention but some were surprised that it was not articulated in the Overriding Objective.

2. The last subsection, (g), seems to import the civil procedural concept of proportionality but is that appropriate in criminal cases? Does it mean trivial cases should be accorded less time and attention? That may suit the system and recognise how most cases are speeded through the magistrates' court following a guilty plea but does it recognise the seriousness to the accused of even a minor conviction of, say, theft?

3. Every case participant is under a duty to further the overriding objective, copying the same duty in civil proceedings but is this appropriate in criminal proceedings? Whereas the law assumes civil litigants to be on an equal footing, the defence in a criminal case can never be on an equal footing with the prosecutor where, as in most cases, the prosecutor is the Crown. The Crown represents the full might of the State, with all the resources of the police and prosecuting authorities so there is an inherent massive imbalance, which English law has traditionally recognised by giving many protective rules to the defendant. At common law, while the prosecutor's duty is to the court, the defence lawyer's duty is to his client. Is (g) compatible with this and, if not, is this satisfied by (c)?

Active Case Management under Part 3

Criminal courts are placed under a duty to further the overriding **10–011** objective by actively managing the case. This includes (I paraphrase):

(a) early identification of issues;
(b) early identification of the needs of witnesses;
(c) achieving certainty as to who is to do what, by timetabling;
(d) monitoring progress and compliance with directions;
(e) ensuring evidence is presented in the shortest and clearest way;
(f) discouraging delay and avoiding unnecessary hearings;
(g) encouraging cooperation;
(h) making use of technology.

Case progression

10–012   Rule 3.4 requires a court officer to be appointed as a case progression officer, whose job it will be to "progress the case", monitor compliance with directions and keep the court informed. She should be readily contactable. Under Rule 3.5 the court may nominate a judge, magistrate or clerk to manage a case. Directions can be made by the court without a hearing and communication can be made by telephone or email. A magistrates' court may give directions as to how the case is to proceed in the Crown Court, if that is its destination. Under Rule 3.10, in order to manage a trial, the court may require a party to give information on which witnesses he intends to call, what arrangements need to be made for their giving of evidence, what points of law will be raised and what timetable he proposes.

Penalties

10–013   Very controversially, in Rule 3.5 the court is given powers to "specify the consequences of failing to comply with a direction". These have not yet been spelled out but defence lawyers fear they will suffer financial penalties from their already meagre remuneration. At the mere suggestion of this, when such a proposal was made in 2003, some judges were disturbed at the prospect of being expected to fine lawyers. Rule 3.9 permits the court to require a certificate of readiness from the parties.

Spending a day in a busy court would demonstrate to an observer that it is frequently the police or prosecution that is ill-prepared. Will they be penalised by the dismissal of a prosecution? This seems highly unlikely. Defence solicitors in magistrates' courts are routinely delayed by their disorganised clients' failure to turn up to appointments to take instructions. What will be the penalty there? Delays are frequently caused by prison vans being late to court or court technology failing, or, in London, by reports not being ready because the probation service is overworked and underfunded. What then?

Pilot results

10–014   Despite these misgivings, judges, the Attorney-General and the DCA have expressed enthusiasm over the results of the pilots of the Effective Trial Management Programme, which commenced in December 2003. By July 2004, the DCA reported that at one Crown Court alone, 700 witnesses had been spared attendance and ineffective trials had been cut to 12.8 per cent. At the same time, prosecutors piloted a witness care scheme called "no witness no justice" and this had enhanced attendance so that eight out of ten witnesses now appeared when expected.

All of this is part of a longer term efficiency drive. The new Office for Criminal Justice Reform reported in 2005 that ineffective trials had been reduced from 12,000 a year in 2001–2 to 8000 in 2003–4. They publish quarterly statistics on their website. In March 2005, the Lord Chief Justice published a new Practice Direction on case management to accompany the new Rules.

Case collapse

As part of the same drastic efficiency drive, new rules were passed in September 2004 to penalise any third party with a wasted costs order if, through "serious misconduct" they caused a trial to collapse. This is provided for in s.93 of the Courts Act 2003. This could be applied, for instance, to a newspaper that prejudicially reports a trial so it has to be abandoned, or to someone who intimidates a witness or to someone who, despite a warning, tells a juror prejudicial information about the accused. Attorney-General Lord Goldsmith placed guidance on his website for the media wishing to report high profile trials. This was prompted by trials collapsing because of adverse media publicity.

10–015

Background

The background to this is a 2002 Audit Commission Report, *Route to Justice*. It identified reforms necessary to make the criminal process more efficient, including the co-ordination of agencies, better information management and more logical incentives but the media latched onto one suggestion–that the present fee structure could be seen as an incentive for lawyers to prolong cases. Although the Government press release made nothing of this criticism, Home Office minister, as he then was, Lord Falconer told *The Guardian* that a "culture change " was needed. There should be no advantage for lawyers "in stretching things out for long enough so that their client's case might slip through the cracks."

10–016

> ### "Inefficiency hampers legal system"
> Sir, Recently I attended a Crown Court in London to represent the Crown in a criminal case. The defendant, a man with a history of mental illness, had been convicted of serious offences and remanded in custody for the preparation of a pre-sentence report (by the Probation Service) and a psychiatric report (by the prison medical team), both to be considered prior to sentencing.
>
> In the event, neither report had been completed. The Probation Service is apparently understaffed and experiencing difficulties in obtaining appointments to see prisoners. The prison medical team has had funding withdrawn, as a result of which it cannot provide reports for the court.

10–017

The case was not heard for an hour after it had been listed. The company that has recently been awarded the contract for delivering prisoners to court was late in delivering the defendant; it then transpired that there were no dock officers available to provide security during the hearing. When the matter finally proceeded, nothing could be done save to remand the defendant back into custody while further attempts were made to secure reports upon his condition . . .

Those charged with the political responsibility for criminal justice would do well to address the chronic shortages in funding and human resources at the most fundamental levels, before turning their minds to the ever-increasing barrage of legislation to which we are subjected.

Yours faithfully, MARK SIMEON JONES.

(Letter to *The Times*, February 21, 2005.)

3. The Prosecutors

10–018   The Attorney-General is a Government minister in charge of the prosecution process in England and Wales. He is appointed by the Prime Minister and so may change when the Government changes. The present Attorney-General is a friend of Tony Blair's, Lord Peter Goldsmith QC. Since New Labour were elected in 1997, Attorney-Generals have been appointed from the Lords but prior to that they were normally MPs, sitting in the House of Commons.

His department is called the Law Officers' Department. His deputy is the Solicitor General. The Attorney is in overall charge of the prosecution process and answerable to Parliament for decisions to prosecute or not to prosecute. The Director of Public Prosecutions (DPP) is in charge of the specialist Serious Fraud Office (SFO), the new Serious Organised Crime Agency (SOCA) and the Crown Prosecution Service (CPS). The DPP's appointment is non-political. The present DPP is Ken Macdonald QC who is keen to emphasise the independence of the CPS. His own background as a defence barrister includes defending Irish and Middle Eastern terrorist suspects.

SOCA will commence work in 2006 and will incorporate officers from the National Crime Squad, the National Criminal Intelligence Service and part of customs and it will work with CPS and Inland

Revenue lawyers on such crimes as drug trafficking, money laundering and racketeering. The media have already likened it to the FBI.

The CPS is a national prosecution service, created by the Prosecution of Offences Act 1985 and it now undertakes most prosecutions. Many others are initiated by those government departments (central or local) and government agencies with statutory powers of prosecution. For instance, if you are caught polluting a river, you may be prosecuted by the National Rivers Authority. Private citizens retain their right to prosecute, unlike in Scotland. The most serious offences, such as those under the Official Secrets Act, may only be prosecuted by the Attorney-General but it is rare for him to appear in court. He is normally represented by counsel. An example of Peter Goldsmith appearing in court occurred in December 2004, in the House of Lords appeal relating to detention of foreign terrorist suspects, described in Chapter 4 on human rights, above. His attempt to persuade the Law Lords that they were an undemocratic set of judges with no right to overturn the Anti-Terrorism, Crime & Security Act 2001 fell on deaf and very hostile ears.

10–019

The Decision to Charge

The CJA 2003 has given the CPS a new power to charge suspects, in all but the most trivial of offences. This was justified on the basis that the police, not being lawyers, made mistakes as to charge. Students of criminal law will not be surprised at this. The procedural change, which was a key recommendation of the Auld *Review* in 2001, follows concerns that too many prosecutions end in acquittal and it is hoped it will increase the number of successful prosecutions as well as reducing costs and delays. The reform was being piloted in a six month project in five towns from 2002.

10–020

This change has been criticised, however, on the ground that it will involve prosecutors being located in police stations, when the very reason for creating the CPS was to provide prosecutors who were independent of the police, who were formerly responsible for prosecuting most offences. It is important to understand, however, that unlike their Continental European counterparts, our prosecutors do not have the power to direct police investigations. This charging scheme was introduced in 2004 after pilot schemes resulted in a 40 per cent increase in early guilty pleas and a decrease of up to 90 per cent in discontinued, ineffective or changed cases. The 2004 Code for Crown prosecutors sets out a "threshold test" for charging. The Crown Prosecutor decides whether there is a reasonable suspicion and whether it is in the public interest to charge. Under the CJA 2003, the police Custody Officer is given a new power to bail a person, without charge, to enable the DPP to decide whether to charge.

The Decision to Prosecute

10–021   There is no obligation on a Crown Prosecutor to prosecute all offences. This is classically expressed in Lord Shawcross's 1951 statement in the House of Commons:

> "It never has been the rule in this country—I hope it never will be—that criminal offences must automatically be the subject of prosecution."

For instance, most young offenders (10–17) are cautioned for the offences they admit. The practice of official cautioning for juveniles was developed and administered in different ways by various police forces during the course of the twentieth century and only placed on a statutory basis and thus regularised into a scheme of reprimands and final warnings, in the 1998 Crime and Disorder Act. This has now been extended to adults, following a recommendation in the Auld Review. They may be given a simple or conditional caution by the police, following a decision by a Crown Prosecutor that it is in the public interest to divert the offender from prosecution. The CJA 2003 permits the CPS to issue a conditional caution, where there is sufficient evidence to charge a suspect with an offence which he or she admits, and the suspect agrees. If the suspect fails to comply with the conditions, he may be prosecuted for the offence. A restorative justice process has been piloted from 2004 to 2006. Offenders and victims agree on what reparations the offender should make to the victim or the wider community, instead of being prosecuted.

In deciding whether to prosecute, CPS prosecutors review the file of evidence they receive from the police and apply the *Code for Crown Prosecutors 2004*, which requires a two-stage test. The prosecutor must first decide on the sufficiency of the evidence to provide a realistic prospect of conviction and then, only if that test is satisfied, ask whether it is in the public interest to go ahead with the prosecution. The Code is written in plain English and appears on the CPS website. A new statement on independence opens the 2004 Code:

> "Although the Crown Prosecution Service works closely with the police, it is independent of them. The independence of Crown Prosecutors is of fundamental constitutional importance. Casework decisions taken with fairness, impartiality and integrity help deliver justice for victims, witnesses, defendants and the public."

This was obviously considered to be a necessary reassurance, in response to concerns about Crown Prosecutors becoming too pally with police officers, now they are installed in police stations.

The evidential stage

The Crown Prosecutor must be satisfied that there is enough evidence to provide a realistic prospect of conviction, They need to be satisfied that the evidence is legally admissible and reliable, taking account of the witnesses.

10–022

The public interest stage

Once the evidential test is satisfied, prosecutors must take account of public interest factors for and against prosecution but there is a presumption in favour of prosecution. The more serious the offence, the more likely it is to be prosecuted. Factors in favour include use of a weapon, premeditation, vulnerable victim and so on. Factors against include likelihood of a minor penalty; the defendant having made reparation, and so on. The prosecutor must keep the decision under constant review.

10–023

A decision not to prosecute is not ordinarily judicially reviewable. In *R. v DPP Ex p. Kebilene* (1999, HL), the House confirmed that, "absent *mala fides* or an exceptional circumstance, the decision of the Director (to consent to a prosecution) is not amenable to judicial review" (*per* Lord Steyn). A decision to prosecute can be challenged before the trial judge as an abuse of process, or form a ground of appeal, he said. By 2004 it seems that the Administrative Court was weary of wasting time dismissing fruitless applications for judicial review of decisions to prosecute. The Senior Presiding Judge, Lord Justice Thomas warned the Legal Services Commission, which funded these applications, that applications should not be made, save in exceptional circumstances: *R. (Pepushi) v CPS* [2004] EWHC 798 (Admin).

The ECtHR has held, in a group of cases heard against the UK in 2001: *Jordan, McKerr, Kelly and Shanaghan*, that in certain exceptional instances, where parties might reasonably expect a prosecution, that the DPP must give reasons for not prosecuting.

Getting the case into court

Following the issue of a written charge by the police or prosecutor, the defendant is issued with a requisition to appear in court, under s.29 of the CJA 2003, again following a recommendation of the Auld *Review*. This will replace the "summons", under the old law.

10–024

The Prosecutor's Duty

In *Randall v R.* [2002] UKPC 19, the Privy Council set out clear guidelines for fair trial, including a reiteration of the rule that the duty of prosecuting counsel was not to obtain a conviction at all costs but to act as a minister for justice and the jury's attention must

10–025

not be distracted from its central task of deciding on guilt, to the required standard.

The Crown Prosecution Service

10–026   Ever since the CPS was created, in 1985, there have been allegations that it is underfunded and that Crown Prosecutors are consequently overworked and too many cases are dropped or lost through lack of preparation. A 2000 survey of the CPS exposed their lack of morale yet again and the issue was discussed in Parliament in December 2000. A statutory CPS inspectorate was created in 2000 and the Government announced new funding. The CPS was restructured into 42 areas by the Access to Justice Act 1999 and has developed criminal justice units and trial units, following the recommendations of the Glidewell report on the CPS, to work closely with the police in preparing cases for the magistrates' court. A 2001 report by Denman found extensive racism within the CPS and the DPP acknowledged the service was "institutionally racist" and announced a review of CPS case decisions for racism and sexism. The CPS established a Diversity Monitoring Project and an independent report *Race for Justice* was published in 2003. The researchers examined 13,000 files for evidence race or gender discrimination and discovered various inconsistencies. Prosecutors were more likely to oppose bail for black and Asian men. It recommended the use of specialist prosecutors for racist and religious crimes.

Victims

10–027   The DPP is empowered to stop a prosecution. Victims can ask for judicial review of a decision to discontinue a prosecution *R. (on the application of Joseph) v DPP* (2000, DC) but the courts are loath to interfere. The DPP is not obliged to follow the victim's wishes but there have been repeated complaints by victims that they are not kept informed. The Government promised in its 2001 white paper *Criminal Justice: The Way Ahead* that by 2005 a victim would be able to track the progress of their case online and this is now possible at many courts, thanks to XHIBIT, the new software explained in Chapter 7 on the criminal courts, above.

The Code emphasises that the CPS does not act for victims but prosecutors should take account of their wishes in deciding whether to prosecute. A 2001 Practice Direction on Victim Personal Statements was issued by Lord Woolf C.J. When giving a statement to the police, the victim will be given the opportunity to make one and can update it at any time. It should be taken into account by the court in passing sentence, along with any supporting evidence. It must be in proper form, such as a s.9 statement or an expert's report and served on the defence. The opinions of the victim or close relatives as to what the sentence should be are not relevant.

Prosecution Witnesses

There has traditionally been a ban in prosecutors interviewing wit-   **10–028** nesses prior to their court appearance and English law has generally frowned on the American practice of coaching witnesses. This means the CPS has no means of testing the reliability of witnesses and there is a risk that the case will collapse if prosecution witnesses proves to be lying or unconvincing in the witness box. As a result of the Damilola Taylor murder case, the Attorney-General proposed that prosecutors should interview all witnesses (not just the vulnerable) face to face, instead of relying on signed witness statements. Until the 1970s, the DPP used to be able to test the reliability of prosecution witnesses by requesting an old style full committal in the magistrates' court. This meant that the whole of the prosecution case would be presented to the examining magistrates and prosecution witnesses would be examined and cross-examined in exactly the same way as they would be when the trial later occurred in the Crown Court.

By 2005, it has become popular to hire private training companies to prepare prosecution witnesses and this has resulted in defence appeals. The CA set out in *R. v Momodou* [2005] EWCA Crim 177 what is permitted for prosecution and defence: witness coaching is prohibited and always has been in English law. There should be no discussion of the proceedings. It was permissible to engage in witness familiarisation so that witnesses understood the layout of the courtroom and likely sequence of events. It was solicitors' and advocates' professional duty to inform the trial judge if any familiarisation process had taken place, using outside agencies.

Where children give evidence in criminal proceedings alleging violence or sex offences, they are interviewed in advance of the trial, on video, by specialists. This video of the initial statement is played to the court. They then "appear" at trial by live video link and can be examined and cross-examined. There is a presumption, under the Youth Justice and Criminal Evidence Act 1999 that they will give evidence in this way. Special measures to protect other vulnerable witnesses were enacted in the Special Measures Directions etc Rules 2002. These rules implement a paper called *Speaking up for Justice*, July 2002 and the 2002 *Justice for All* white paper. Measures include the ability to give evidence via live TV links, video recordings, or screens around the witness box. Trials may be conducted without wigs and gowns, and without people in the public gallery. Pilot projects commenced in 2002, to examine the possibility of allowing intermediaries to assist witnesses with communication difficulties, and the use of video recorded pre-trial cross- examination. These measures have been piloted for several years and are now in place.

10–029   The measures are a response to the concern that many prosecutions failed because witnesses failed to turn up to court or failed to perform as expected, in the witness box. More than 30,000 cases were abandoned in 2001, as witnesses and victims refused or failed to give evidence: see G. Langdon-Down, "A voice for the weak in court trials", *The Times*, July 16, 2002. A Home Office Report, *Narrowing the Justice Gap*, in October 2002, made the same point. Of 5.17 million recorded crimes, only 1.02 million were punished, less than 20 per cent. Despite reforms, a joint report by the NSPCC and Witness Support, in 2004, found that young witnesses suffered almost a year's delay before their cases came to court and this exacerbated their fear and trauma. Half the respondents could not understand some of the questioning or found it confusing and one third still found the experience upsetting, despite the video link: *In their Own Words*. The Government is now reviewing these special measures. See also a 2003 Audit Commission report, *Victims and Witnesses* (2003).

The CJA 2003, s.116 goes even further, allowing the admission of statements from witnesses who are too frightened to testify. Of course, when prosecution witnesses are heavily protected, defence lawyers will allege that the accused has suffered an unfair trial, in breach of Art.6 of the Convention. This is exactly what has happened in a 2005 murder trial. Two young women victims had been killed in cross-fire in a gangland revenge attack and it proved extremely difficult to persuade witnesses to come forward. The accused were eventually brought to trial using heavily protected witnesses. They were given false names and various protective devices in court. The defence team immediately threatened to appeal the murder convictions but the DPP defended these unprecedented measures, saying it was the *only* way the case could be brought to trial, such was the local fear of these gangs. On appeal, the courts will need to consider whether the interference with the accused's Art.6 rights was proportionate. The proportionality test is explained in Chapter 4 on human rights, above. In *R. (D) v Camberwell Green Youth Court* [2005] UKHL 4, it was held that the taking of evidence from a child witness by a video link did not breach Art.6. It was not a breach of the principle of equality of arms that the child defendants were not accorded the same facility.

4. Bail

10–030   Most offenders who are arrested by the police are bailed by them for a court appearance at the next available court sitting of the magistrates' court. The police may grant bail at the police station and the CJA 2003 enables "street bail" from the scene of the arrest.

Bail may include conditions, such as a curfew, or specified residence, or exclusion from the environs of the victim's home, or surrendering of a passport and a surety (money guarantee) may be required. Bail may be renewed by the clerk or magistrates, if the defendant is not dealt with at the first court appearance. The offender has a right to bail under the Bail Act 1976, which reversed the common law presumption against bail so, if the police oppose bail and the offender contests this, a contested bail hearing will take place at the magistrates' court. Indeed, the court (magistrates' or Crown Court) must consider whether bail should be granted at each appearance. Where a court or constable grants or refuses bail or imposes conditions, they must give written reasons to the defendant (s.5). The defendant accused or convicted of an imprisonable offence need not be granted bail if the court is satisfied that there are substantial grounds for believing that the defendant, if released on bail, would:

- fail to surrender to custody; or
- commit an offence; or
- interfere with witnesses.

The defendant need not be granted bail if the offence is indictable or triable either way and he was already on bail for another offence, or if the court is satisfied he should be kept in custody for his own protection or (child) welfare, or he is serving a custodial sentence, or if there has not been time to obtain sufficient information to decided on bail, or if he has been arrested whilst on bail, or he is being remanded for a report and it would be impractical to make inquiries without keeping him in custody. The CJA 2003 introduced a presumption against bail for an offender who had previously failed to surrender to custody ("jumped bail"). There is also a new presumption against bail for certain class A drug users. Where the defendant is accused of a non-imprisonable offence, acceptable reasons for refusing bail are more limited.

Those convicted of or charged with manslaughter, murder, **10–031** attempted murder, rape or attempted rape lost their right to bail under the Criminal Justice and Public Order Act 1994 but since the Crime and Disorder Act 1998 came into force, they may be granted bail in exceptional circumstances. This amendment was made by the 1998 Act, in order to satisfy the requirements of Art.5 of the Convention (liberty and security of the person). The Article provides that no one shall be deprived of his liberty save in specified cases, in accordance with a procedure prescribed by law. Article 5(3) limits pre-trial detention because a person shall be released pending trial unless the State can show "relevant and sufficient" reasons to justify continued detention, which requires the exercise of judicial discretion. This 1994 Act, abolishing bail for certain offenders, was in breach of the Convention, which the UK Government accepted in *Caballero v UK* (2000, ECtHR).

The impact of Art.5 on bail has been the subject of a number of ECtHR and domestic cases. In *R. v Havering Magistrates' Court Ex p. DPP* (2000, QBD), the applicant argued that Art.5 had been breached at his hearing for breach of bail conditions, when the magistrates heard hearsay evidence. The Court held:

- If the process conformed with Art.5, it did not have to conform to Art.6 as well.
- The ECtHR case law simply underlined that the defendant could not be deprived of his liberty without a fair opportunity to answer the basis on which the order was sought.
- In doing so it was essential to bear in mind the nature and purpose of the proceedings.
- A magistrate was required to come to a fair and rational opinion based on the material put before him.
- In doing so he must bear in mind the consequences to the defendant—loss of liberty (in the context of presumption of innocence).
- Article 5 did not require facts to be proven to the criminal standard of proof.
- The magistrate was not restricted to legally admissible evidence—it could be hearsay—so long as he took account of the quality of the evidence.
- The defendant had to be given a full and fair opportunity to comment on that material and to give oral evidence.

The defendant may renew his application for bail, if the magistrates refuse it, or appeal to a judge in chambers. Under the Bail Amendment Act 1993, the prosecution may appeal against a grant of bail by magistrates, to a judge in the Crown Court.

5. The Right to Silence

10–032   Until the Criminal Justice and Public Order Act 1994, the defendant had a virtually unqualified two-stage right to silence, both in the police station and at trial. In court, this extended to the right not to be asked questions and the judge could comment on a defendant's exercise of the right but not adversely. The right was considered by the Criminal Law Revision Committee, in 1972, the Royal Commission on Criminal Procedure, 1981, and the Royal Commission on Criminal Justice, 1993, and it has long been a subject of controversy.

Proponents hail it as a major safeguard of the English legal system that the defendant cannot convict himself out of his own mouth. It leaves the burden of proof entirely on the prosecution. Opponents criticise it as a rule protecting the guilty. They believe it encourages the police to intimidate suspects into confessing and some have said that it is sentimental to argue that the accused should not be allowed to convict himself.

In 1987, the Conservative Home Secretary set up a working party to examine the effects of abolishing the right to silence but this was quietly disbanded at the peak of public concern over wrongful convictions, such as those of the Guildford Four and, in 1991, Birmingham Six. The 1993 Royal Commission considered the value and operation of the right to silence. The majority recommended that adverse inferences should not be drawn from silence at the police station and recommended retaining the existing caution (that is, the warning given by police before questioning by them). Only when the prosecution's case had been fully disclosed should the defendant be required to offer an answer to the charges made against him, at the risk of adverse comment at trial on any new defence he then discloses or any departure from a previously disclosed defence (in other words, in the event of an "ambush defence").

The Criminal Justice and Public Order Act 1994 went much further than this and, critics would say, effectively vitiates both stages of the right to silence. Sections 34–39 allow the court to draw "such inferences as appear proper" from the accused's failure to mention, under police questioning, any fact which he could have been expected to mention, or failure, under questioning, to account for any objects, marks or substances, or failure, under questioning, to account for his presence at a particular place, or failure to give evidence or answer questions at trial.   **10–033**

The provisions on silence in the 1994 Act are one of the most heavily criticised and discussed areas of a provocative statute. The operation of the sections in practice has been the subject of critical comment. It is said that the sections offer no protection to the mentally disordered suspect and that the re-drafted police caution is so lengthy and complex that it is only fully understood by a minority of suspects. The CA had already ruled, in October 1995, in three appeals against conviction on the grounds that trial judges had wrongly directed the jury on the effects of these sections. The CA held (*R. v Cowan* (1996)) that the trial judge was required to remind the jury of certain rules still protecting the defendant, for instance, that the burden of proof lay on the prosecution, that the defendant was entitled to remain silent, that an inference drawn from silence could not on its own prove guilt, that the jury had to be satisfied that the prosecution had established a case to answer before drawing any inferences from the defendant's silence and, finally, that if they concluded that his silence could only sensibly be attributed to the defendant's having no answer or none that would stand up to cross-examination, they could then draw an adverse inference. The Judicial Studies Board issued a specimen direction to juries for the use of judges in future trials (all such specimen directions can be read on the JSB website). It is confusing and complex.

Those who criticised these sections as being a breach of Art.6 of the Convention were disappointed by the case of *Murray v UK* (1996), in which the ECtHR ruled, in respect of a similar provision in Northern Ireland, that there was no such thing as an absolute right of silence and it was only a matter of common sense to permit the drawing of adverse inferences where a defendant said nothing in the face of overwhelming evidence. The ECtHR, nevertheless, considered legal advice crucial to a defendant who exercised his right to silence. The Attorney-General swiftly issued guidance in the light of this ruling and the Youth Justice and Criminal Evidence Act 1999 disapplies s.34 in cases where the suspect has not been allowed the opportunity to consult a solicitor prior to questioning.

10–034   The application of the 1994 Act's provisions on silence have continued to give rise to a stream of appeals to the CA, not least because the relevant sections are so difficult to apply, in practice, that judges quite often mistakenly permit the jury to draw an adverse inference in cases where it is not applicable. This glut of cases has led Birch to argue that, on a cost-benefit analysis, s.34 should be repealed because it is "too expensive". It consumes too much judicial time at trial and on appeal. It "is a headache for the conscientious jury and a tool with which the slapdash, incompetent jury may wreak injustice" and "the gains in terms of cogent evidence are likely to be slight". In many appeals, the prosecution had a strong case at trial, without silence. The danger in these cases is, if s.34 is wrongly applied, it may result in the quashing of an otherwise respectable conviction. On the other hand, some appeals have demonstrated that its application has persuaded some juries to attach considerable, misplaced significance to silence. She restates some "obvious" features of the section. For instance, if no facts are advanced at trial, the section has no application. Also, the section does not necessarily contemplate a silent interviewee, just one who refuses to answer some of the interviewer's questions. Then she explains some of the problems of interpreting and applying the section. The section permits the jury to draw "such inferences as appear proper" but what this means is not explained. (I would remind the reader that this applies to magistrates as well as juries.) Similarly undefined are what is a fact and what is relevant in terms of evidence relied on. Birch's article, incidentally, gives an excellent explanation of the moral and practical arguments surrounding the right of silence, as well as the history of s.34. In research on the effects of a similar provision on silence in Northern Ireland, in 1990–1995, Jackson found that the change of law had resulted in a large decrease in cases where the defendant refused to testify. Nevertheless, there had, ironically, been a marked decline in the conviction rate.

Despite Birch's article, nothing has been done to rid the courts of this menace of a statutory provision. Any observer of the CA (Criminal Division) can watch the court, week in week out, quashing convictions of people who are probably guilty but whose trial has been found to be defective because the trial judge misapplied this incomprehensible set of sections and their equally incomprehensible specimen direction in her or his directions to the jury. Judges are well aware of the amount of public money wasted on such appeals, but then they have no power over the law makers. In practice, where a defendant exercises his right of silence, it is usually a partial exercise. He chooses to answer some questions and not others. These common cases pose especial difficulties for trial judges in directing juries. In my current research on the judiciary, which involves shadowing circuit judges and High Court judges in their work, I have found that the experienced judges often disapprove of the provisions on silence and for that reason, or because of the fear of giving a misdirection and being appealed, they steer clear and decline to remark on the accused's partial exercise of the right of silence.

Consider this: juries and magistrates are not, generally, idiots. They will draw whatever conclusions they see fit from the accused's failure to answer questions or account for the evidence, whatever the law tells them to do, in the case of magistrates, or whatever the trial judge tells them to do, in the case of juries. Section 34 is pointless, confusing to judges and juries, time wasting and wasteful of the resources of the CA and I have no doubt that it causes unnecessary retrials and causes convictions of the some of the genuinely guilty to be quashed.

An important ruling on silence was *Condron v UK* (2000, ECtHR), **10–035** the first case in which the ECtHR pronounced on the validity of s.34. See Ashworth's comment on the report in 2000 and Jennings, Ashworth and Emmerson and see cases in which it has been applied (*e.g. Betts and Hall* (2000, CA)). In this case, the applicants had stood trial in 1995 on charges of supplying heroin and possession with intent to supply. On the advice of their solicitor, they did not respond to questioning as they were suffering withdrawal symptoms. The judge permitted the jury to draw an adverse inference under s.34. The ECtHR found a violation of Art.6(1) of the Convention because the judge had left the jury at liberty to draw an adverse inference, even if they had been satisfied that the applicants remained silent for good reason on the advice of their solicitor. The CA had no means of knowing whether an adverse inference had played a significant role in the decision to convict. Four days later, the ECtHR delivered their judgment in *Averill v UK* (2000). In this Northern Irish terrorist case, the applicant was denied legal advice during the first 24 hours of his detention, which the Court held to be a violation of Art.6(1) of the Czbut, following *Murray*, held there was no violation of Art.6(2) just because the judge had drawn an adverse inference from silence. They held that, while it would be incompatible with the right to a fair trial to base a conviction solely or mainly on an accused's silence, in appropriate circumstances silence could be taken into account when assessing the persuasiveness of other prosecution evidence. The Court noted that the trial judge was not obliged to draw inferences from silence but did so in the exercise of his discretion and provided detailed reasons for his decision. Further, the CA scrupulously reviewed the reasons given by the trial judge and endorsed his decision. Jennings *et al.* draw the following conclusions from these cases:

- Legal advice is fundamentally important, especially where there is a possibility of adverse inferences.
- There may be other good reasons for remaining silent, apart from legal advice.
- A trial was not rendered unfair where adverse inferences were drawn from silence if the only reason was a professed policy of not speaking to the police.
- Adverse inferences may properly be drawn from silence where the situation clearly calls for an explanation. For instance, in *Averill*, his failure to account for his presence near the scene of a double murder and his failure to account for fibres on his clothing and in his hair justified such inferences.

See also, *Magee v UK* (2000), where the ECtHR found that depriving the applicant of legal advice during the early stages of police interrogation was a violation of Art.6. It was only after he signed a confession that he was allowed to see a solicitor. From *R. v Ali* [2001] EWCA Crim 863 it appears that the defendant satisfies s.34 if he prepares a statement containing all the facts he relies on at trial. Where D relies on a pre-prepared statement at his police interview, the jury should be directed to compare it with the defence's evidence at trial to see if he relied on a fact not mentioned in his statement: *R. v Turner* [2003] EWCA Crim 3108. In *Webber* [2004] UKHL 1 the HL held that a positive suggestion put by a witness by or on behalf of a defendant may amount to a fact relied on by the defence, under s.34. In *R. v Johnson, R. v Hind* [2005] EWCA Crim 971, the CA held that s.34 could not be constructed broadly, to allow the drawing of an adverse inference from a defendant's refusal to leave this cell, in order to be interviewed.

Betts and Hall resulted in the specimen jury direction being rewritten but it was recently considered to be too favourable to the accused. In *R. v Howell* [2003] EWCA Crim 1, the CA, *per* Laws L.J., held that "the public interest that inheres in reasonable disclosure by a suspected person of what he has to say when faced with a set of facts which accuse him, is thwarted if currency is given to the belief that if a suspect remains silent on legal advice he may systematically avoid adverse comment at his trial." The absence of a written statement from the complainant at the time of the interview was not a good enough reason to remain silent. The victim was in hospital with life threatening injuries at the time.

The jury instruction is therefore being rewritten again, as a result of **10–036** *Beckles* [2004] EWCA Crim 2766. The CA reviewed all the authorities, including *Betts and Hall* and *Howell* that were said to be incompatible with the resultant specimen direction. They held that where a solicitor's advice was relied on, the ultimate question for the jury under s.34 remained whether the facts relied on at trial were facts which the defendant could *reasonably* have been expected to mention at interview. if they were not, that is the end of the matter. It may still not have been *reasonable* for him to rely on the advice, or the advice may not have been the true explanation for his silence. Under the revised direction, the jury will be asked to consider whether the defendant *genuinely and reasonably* relied on the advice to remain silent.

The Privilege against Self-Incrimination

The privilege is not spelled out in Art.6 of the Convention but is **10–037** a developed element of ECtHR jurisprudence. At the moment, there seem to be two sets of conflicting decisions of the Court on procedures which fall foul of the rule and they are commented on by Ashworth in "The Self-Incrimination Saga", *Archbold News*, June 27, 2001 and in a comment on *Henney and McGuinness v Ireland* [2001] Crim. L.R. 481.

The Privy Council, on appeal in a Scottish case, *Brown v Stott* (2000), held that s.172(2) of the Road Traffic Act, which required a registered vehicle owner to disclose who was the driver of a car in which she had travelled, did not breach the privilege because only a simple question is put, in the interests of public safety. (They suspected she had been drinking). This was a relief to prosecuting authorities, in view of the number of drivers caught for speeding who had started claiming a defence under Art.6. This was applied by the Divisional Court in *DPP v Wilson* [2001] EWHC Admin 198 confirming that an admission in answer to the statutory question may be used in evidence in a subsequent prosecution. Ashworth expressed concern about the correctness of these decisions, especially that the latter case did not cite the ECtHR decisions in *Heaney and McGuinness v Ireland* and *Quinn v Ireland*, handed down after *Brown* in December 2000. In the former, the applicants had been convicted of a refusal to give police an account of their movements under Irish terrorist legislation. This was held to have been a breach of the privilege. The Court accepted that the privilege against self-incrimination was not absolute but held that the threat of imprisonment "destroyed the very essence of the right". The Court approved of *Funke v France* (1993), where the sanction was only a fine. Another relevant decision was *JB v Switzerland* (2001), which ruled there was a breach by the tax authorities in requiring the applicant to furnish information about the source of income on pain of fines. Ashworth remarks on the strange distinction between these cases and the ECtHR's attitude to the requirement to submit to blood and urine tests, which they have held does not breach the privilege.

Commentators consider that another 2001 decision by the ECtHR manifests the same illogical reasoning. In *PG and JH v UK*, the police obtained speech samples from the suspects' bugged cells which were used to match with speech evidence of a conspiracy to rob, and the defendants, identified by the speech matches, were convicted. The Court held that the manner in which the speech samples were obtained, secretly, was not in breach of Art 6. Voice samples which did not include incriminating statements might be regarded as akin to blood, hair or other physical or objective specimens used in forensic analysis and to which the privilege against self-incrimination did not apply. They distinguished the decision in *Saunders v UK* (1997) which held that where someone was compelled to provide answers, as Saunders was to the Department of Trade and Industry, these answers could not be used against him at his trial, as this breached the privilege against self-incrimination. Evidence obtained by methods of coercion or oppression in defiance of the will of the accused was inadmissible. This did not extend to evidence obtained from the accused by compulsory powers which had an existence independent of the will of the accused, such as documents and samples of breath, blood, urine and bodily tissue for DNA testing.

10–038   The latest case on this, applying the same reasoning as *Saunders*, was *Kansal v UK* (2004), also discussed in Chapter 4 on the European Convention on Human Rights, above. In this case,

Kansal's company, which operated chemists shops, went into liquidation and he was questioned by the Official Receiver. Had he failed to comply, without reasonable excuse, he would have been guilty of contempt of court. He was subsequently tried on criminal charges and the prosecution used the transcript of his interview with the Official Receiver as evidence against him. As explained, in Chapter 4, the House of Lords reluctantly held that he could not rely on the HRA 1998, as his trial, in 1992, took place before the Act came into force (2000). The ECtHR held there was a breach of Art.6.1, in the same way as in *Saunders*. There had been an infringement of the right not to incriminate himself so his trial had been unfair. The Court reminded him that they had already dismissed his claim that he had been deprived of an effective remedy.

6. Disclosure of Evidence

By 2005 the rules governing the disclosure of evidence are very **10–039** complex. They are now contained in the Criminal Procedure and Investigations Act 1996, as amended by the CJA 2003, the Convention, Arts 5 and 6, considerable recent ECtHR and English case law applying the Convention to the Act and the Attorney-General's Guidelines on Disclosure (2000) and appended Commentary. The complexity of disclosure rules is hardly surprising since they provide the very fulcrum on which the scales of justice swing, balancing the interests of all of us, represented by the State, in securing the conviction of the guilty, and the interests of a civilised democracy in ensuring that the innocent accused are acquitted, hence the case law and masses of surrounding commentary. As the Attorney-General says in his guidelines "(a) failure to take action leading to proper disclosure may result in a wrongful conviction. It may alternatively lead to a successful abuse of process argument or an acquittal against the weight of the evidence".

One of the most controversial elements of the 1996 Act was its introduction of a requirement for pre-trial disclosure by the accused. This new requirement on the defence to disclose an outline of their story before hearing the prosecution's entire case (or risk the court's drawing adverse inferences) was criticised by many as a breach of the presumption of innocence. Defence lawyers also objected that the Act curtailed disclosure requirements on the prosecution, which had been governed by case law. The Conservative Government had set out its proposals for the Act in a consultation document, *Disclosure*, in 1995. They were concerned by the findings of the Royal Commission on Criminal Justice, 1993, that the defence were gaining an unfair advantage over the prosecution by disclosure requirements which had become unduly onerous, following recent case law reacting to famous miscarriages of justice, such as the Birmingham Six, Guildford Four, Maguires, Kisko and Judith Ward. Defence lawyers could delay trial and put obstacles in the way of a prosecution by requiring the disclosure of more and more evidence yet the accused was still in the position of being able to ambush them with a surprise defence, at trial, thus securing an unwarranted acquittal.

The Act was immediately attacked as unfair on the defence and a potential breach of the Convention, which was not then binding in English law. Since it came into force in 1997, its contentiousness has increased, as defence lawyers have made repeated challenges to the Act or practice under the Convention and there were widespread allegations of prosecution non-disclosure (see *The Times*, May 4, 1999) and an increasing number of prosecutions stopped by judges. One of the worst was a 2000 £5 million trial alleging police corruption and drug smuggling, in which the judge said the CPS disclosure certificate had "all the intellectual content of a fax sheet cover". The Attorney-General, in his commentary, explained that his guidelines were a response to these concerns and an interim measure, pending a review of disclosure in the light of research commenced in 2000 to evaluate the working of the 1996 Act.

10–040   The CJA 2003 completely reorganised the disclosure procedure, following recommendations by Auld L.J. in his 2001 *Review of the Criminal Courts*. From December 2005, the 2003 Act replaces the old two stage test with a new objective single test, requiring the prosecutor to disclose prosecution material that has not previously been disclosed and which might reasonably be considered capable of undermining the case for the prosecution against the accused, or of assisting the case for the accused. It replaces the secondary disclosure stage with a revised continuing duty on the prosecutor to disclose material that meets the new test. The prosecutor is specifically required to review the prosecution material on receipt of the defence statement and to make further disclosure if required under the continuing duty.

Corker comments that this change was made because the 1996 Act never worked as intended. Under-resourced prosecutors, fearful of causing miscarriages of justice, never had the time to comply with the two stages so just gave all non-sensitive material to the accused.

The 2003 Act also amends the defence disclosure requirements, requiring the accused to provide a more detailed defence statement, setting out the nature of his defence including any particular defences on which he intends to rely and indicating any points of law he wishes to take, including any points as to the admissibility of evidence or abuse of process. Again, this is because the 1996 Act had not persuaded defendants to be forthcoming. Defence statements usually amounted to a couple of useless lines and judges were reluctant to penalise defence non-disclosure.

Other new provisions are a requirement for the judge to warn the **10–041** accused about any failure to comply with the defence statement requirements. An updated defence statement may be required, to assist the management of the trial, requiring the accused to serve details of his witnesses and experts, which will give the police a new power to interview defence witnesses prior to trial. This will be accompanied by a code of practice. The judge has the discretion to disclose the defence statement to the jury.

If the defence fails to comply with these statutory requirements, the court or any other party can make such comments as appear appropriate and the magistrates or jury can draw such inferences as appear proper.

There was always a doubt over whether the 1996 Act satisfied the requirements of the Convention. The leading case of *Rowe v UK* (2000) said:

> "It is a fundamental aspect of the right to a fair trial that criminal proceedings, including the elements of such proceedings that relate to procedure, should be adversarial and that there should be equality of arms between the prosecution and defence. The right to an adversarial trial means, in a criminal case, that both prosecution and defence must be given the opportunity to have knowledge of and comment on the observations filed and the evidence adduced by the other party. . . . In addition, Article 6(1) requires, as indeed does English law . . . that the prosecution authorities should disclose to the defence all material evidence in their possession for or against the accused . . ."

The ECtHR warned, however, that "entitlement to disclosure of **10–042** relevant evidence is not an absolute right". There are three competing interests that might lead to the withholding of evidence—national security, protection of witnesses, and preserving secrecy in police investigations. This was applied when the case came back to the CA decision in *R. v Davies, Johnson and Rowe* (2000). In 2001, in his *Review* Auld L.J. suggested simplifying the disclosure tests and regime, hence the changes introduced in the 2003 Act. In the meantime, the CPS and police have drawn up Joint Operational Instructions on disclosure (*www.cps.gov.uk*), in response to a review by the CPS Inspectorate, in 2000.

Particular problems have arisen in relation to claims of public interest immunity by the prosecution, where they seek the judge's permission to withhold evidence from the defence on the grounds of its sensitivity, such as the national interest or, more usually, that they sought to protect the identity of a police informer. Where this application is made there is a pre-trial hearing by the judge and special counsel may be appointed to represent the interests of the accused. In *R. v H, R. v C* [2004] UKHL 3, the House of Lords held that appointing special counsel to represent the defendant in an ordinary criminal trial, in a PII hearing should be a course of last resort.

- If D could not be tried fairly, he should not be tried at all.
- Save in exceptional circumstances, the judge was not a factual decision-maker.
- Appointment of special counsel raised ethical issues.
- There was no dissonance between domestic legislation and Strasbourg jurisprudence, interpreting *Edwards and Lewis v UK* (2003, ECtHR).
- The ECtHR did not lay down rigid rules. It declared principles and applied them on a case by case basis.

7. Plea Bargaining and Sentencing Discounts

10–043   At any time prior to or during a criminal trial, it is common for a defendant to change his plea from "not guilty" to "guilty" to one or more counts. This results in what has become known as a "cracked trial". This wastes court time and public resources and, in relation to trial on indictment, was one of the concerns of the Royal Commission on Criminal Justice, 1993. It usually results from plea negotiations between prosecution or defence, which may be initiated by either side, commonly known as "plea bargaining". This means the defendant agrees to plead guilty in exchange for a concession by the prosecutor, such as a reduced charge (charge-bargaining) or a concession that the facts of the crime were not so serious as originally alleged (fact-bargaining). The defendant may also plead guilty in the hope of a reduced sentence. The CA has long sanctioned a system of a 25–30 per cent "sentence discount", rewarding the defendant for pleading guilty but the case of *Turner* (1970) prohibited the trial judge becoming involved in a plea bargain to assure the defendant of a specific sentence discount. This prevented the development of a full-blown system of legally enforceable plea bargains, conducted in special hearings, before a judge, which exists in most of the US.

The Royal Commission said nothing about such pre-trial negotiations involving the judge but, in order to try and obviate the occurrence of cracked trials, recommended a "sentencing canvass", offering the defendant a graduated system of sentencing discounts: the earlier the plea, the greater the discount. Whilst acknowledging the danger that this might induce innocent people to plead guilty, the Commission, heavily influenced by the Bar Council's Seabrook Report (1992), concluded that this risk would not be increased by "clearer articulation of the long accepted principle" of sentencing discounts. Section 48 of the Criminal Justice and Public Order Act 1994 (now Powers of Criminal Courts (Sentencing) Act 2000) gave statutory recognition to the system of informal sentencing discounts and, indeed, made it mandatory, by requiring the sentencing judge to take into account the timing and circumstances of a guilty plea and, if the punishment is accordingly reduced, to state so in open court.

According to *Turner*, advocates are not meant to pressurise clients into pleading guilty and judges are not meant to offer specific discounts but cases decided by the CA expose the frequency of breaches of these rules by judges and counsel doing secret pre-trial deals in chambers. One such case was *R. v Dossetter* (1999), where the CA reminded advocates that plea bargaining "forms no part of English criminal jurisprudence". Another was *Nazham and Nazham* [2004] EWCA Crim 491. Here counsel had seen the judge in his chambers and the judge had remarked "this has got plea written all over it and bags of credit". The CA declined to quash the convictions because they found the defendants' freedom of choice had not been inhibited but observed that the judge should not have made his remarks. They observed that, since there are now sentencing guidelines for guilty pleas, there is no reason why a judge should not give an indication of sentencing parameters in open court.

In cases from the late 1990s, the courts have moved towards **10–044** enforcing promises held out to defendants. In *Attorney General's References (Nos 80 and 81 of 1999) (R. v Thompson and Rodgers)* (1999) and *R. v Peverett* (2000), while the CA deprecated the unsuitably light sentences the offenders had received, nevertheless refused the Attorney-General leave to refer them to the CA as unduly lenient. Where the prosecutor (CPS) had made representations to the defendant on which he was entitled to rely and had acted to his detriment by pleading guilty, this could properly be regarded as having given rise to a legitimate expectation that the Crown (represented by the Attorney-General) would not subsequently seek to resile from those representations. In other words, the Court enforced the plea bargains, in fairness to the defendant, despite warning that it had long set its face against plea bargaining. See also *Jackson* (2000) where the judge had promised a sentence discount so the CA felt obliged to enforce it, despite the defendant's "appalling" driving record. The second was swiftly followed by the *Attorney-General's Guidelines on the Acceptance of Pleas* (2000), in which the Attorney reminded prosecutors that justice should be transparent. He goes so far as to say that where the case is not exceptional, it is the duty of the advocate to remind the judge of the CA's decisions and disassociate himself from sentence discussions. This reflects concern over the number of Crown Court judges who flout *Turner*, let alone counsel. The guidelines have recently been amended to require a written record of the basis of plea.

The Bar has long advocated the formalisation of the system of plea bargaining, by offering these graduated sentencing discounts and they spelled this out in their 1992 Seabrook Report, mentioned above. My view is diametrically opposed. I do not want to see the English legal system going down this American route. I set out a long list of reasons, in 2000. Not least of my objections are these.

1. Every piece of research into defendants discloses a subset who plead guilty while maintaining innocence, often induced to do so by the temptation of a lighter sentence.
2. Rewarding someone for pleading guilty is morally repugnant and hypocritical, since it punishes those who exercise their right to trial.
3. Before the 1994 Act, magistrates, who do 95 per cent of sentencing, managed without discounts so I cannot see why they should be expected to give them now.
4. Scottish judges traditionally considered sentencing discounts immoral and inappropriate and spoke out against them.
5. Research by Henham found that the application of the discount is erratic in both the Crown Court and in magistrates' courts.

In his 2001 *Review of the Criminal Courts*, Auld L.J. reiterated the Royal Commission's call for a formalised system of graduated sentencing discounts for guilty pleas, coupled with a system of advanced indication of sentence. The Government responded, in *Justice for All* (2002) that it intended to introduce a clearer tariff of sentence discount. This is not incorporated in the CJA 2003 but was announced by Lord Chancellor Falconer in 2003, as part of the Case Preparation Project (see below) and has now been published by the Sentencing Guidelines Council. The 2003 Act, s.144 requires the sentencing court to take account of the timing and circumstances of the guilty plea. Interestingly, the Act provides that, where the accused has been given an indication of sentence by magistrates, as explained below, no court may impose a custodial sentence but provides that apart from this a sentence indication is not binding on a court and will not provide grounds of appeal. This reverses the common law, since a series of CA cases in the 1990s, discussed above, allowed appeals by defendants who had received harsher sentences than they had been led to believe by the court, pre-trial.

In accordance with Auld L.J.'s recommendations, the newly **10–045** created Sentencing Guidelines Council (SGC) published guidance on a graduated discount structure for guilty pleas, to be applied by all courts from January 2005 (s.172, CJA 2003). The Guidelines are on the SGC website (*www.sentencing-guidelines.gov.uk*). In brief, the main elements are as follows.

1. The court considers remorse and any other mitigating factors and calculates the appropriate sentence. It also takes into consideration any other admitted offences (TICs).
2. The court discounts the sentence in accordance with a sliding scale: a maximum of one third for a plea at the first reasonable opportunity (in the police station); a maximum of one quarter discount after the trial date is set or a one tenth discount if the accused changes his plea to guilty at the court door or at trial.
3. Of course there is no discount if the accused is found guilty after trial.
4. The sliding scale applies even if the accused is caught red handed.

In *R. v Goodyear* [2005] EWCA Crim 888, a five judge CA laid down **10–046** guidelines on what judges should now do in the light of this "different culture". Re-emphasising the principle that the defendant's plea must be made voluntarily and free from any improper pressure, they could not see that this precluded a defendant's seeking an advance indication of sentence. They laid down the following guidelines: the judge should confine himself to indicating the maximum sentence for a plea of guilty at that point and could only act at the request of the defendant, not on his own initiative or that of the defence lawyer. The judge could refuse an indication but, once given, it was binding on him or any other judge who became responsible for the case. An indication should not be sought on the basis of hypothetical facts. The judge should never be invited to give an indication on the basis of a plea bargain. He should not be asked to indicate levels of sentence dependent on different pleas. The defence advocate was personally responsible for ensuring that his client fully appreciated that he should not plead guilty unless he was guilty and that any indication remained subject to the Attorney-General's right to appeal against an unduly lenient sentence. Any agreed basis of plea should be reduced into writing before an indication was sought. If there were no agreement about the basis of plea, there should be a hearing on the disputed facts, in front of the judge (called a *Newton* hearing). Any sentence

lication should normally be given at a case management hearing
1 should be in open court and recorded. As for magistrates'
courts, it would be wise to see how these new arrangements settled
in at the Crown Court before copying the procedure.

Although the guidelines warn judges against taking part in any
apparent plea bargain, these graduated sentencing discounts are
designed to encourage early guilty pleas and will encourage bargaining between prosecution and defence. Those of us who oppose
plea bargaining have irretrievably lost the battle. In support of the
system, sentencing discounts at least have the virtue of transparency—to offenders, judges, magistrates, victims and the public—
on the SGC website. The new scheme is highly unlikely, however, to
produce consistency in sentencing, because sentencers will differ, as
research shows they have done, in deciding on the starting point: the
appropriate full, undiscounted sentence. In 2005 the Attorney-
General is expected to issue guidelines on the acceptance of pleas
and the role of the prosecutor in sentencing.

8. Cases Heard in the Magistrates' Court

10–047   The Criminal Law Act 1977 divided offences into three categories:
first, offences triable only on indictment in the Crown Court; secondly, offences triable only summarily in the magistrates' court; and
thirdly, offences triable either way. The Criminal Justice Act 1988
added a fourth category, summary offences triable on indictment.

As I pointed out in 1997, in "An Essay on the Importance and Neglect
of the Magistracy", in the twentieth century Parliament repeatedly
downgraded indictable offences to triable either way and triable
either way offences to summary offences, thus shifting criminal
business down onto the shoulders of the magistrates. Also, when
new offences are created they tend to be summary or triable either
way, thus guaranteeing that all of the first category and most of the
second will be heard by magistrates. They now deal with over 95
per cent of criminal business from start to finish. It should be
obvious from that statistic that magistrates' work is not all trivial,
although many people imagine this to be the case, including, unfortunately, many judges and lawyers.

The most obvious summary offences are almost all Road Traffic
Act offences; drunk and disorderly behaviour; assaults such as
common assault; minor criminal damage cases and cases prosecuted
by government departments or agencies. A summary case is usually
begun by an information being laid before a Justice of the Peace
requesting that they issue a summons to the person accused. The
summons will require that person to appear at a named magistrates'

court, at a time stipulated, so that the case against him may be heard. As explained previously, this is being replaced by a system of requisitions. The Road Traffic Act allows defendants to motoring offences to plead "guilty" by post, avoiding a court appearance.

Duty solicitors, private practitioners now funded by the Criminal Defence Service, are meant to be available, at each magistrates' court.

Speeding Cases through the Court

The Home Office *Review of Delay in the Criminal Justice System* **10–048** (1997) "the Narey report", recommended various measures to speed criminal cases through the courts, responding to a concern that an "adjournment culture" pervaded most magistrates' courts, where magistrates would readily accede to all requests to adjourn the case, thus causing multiple appearances and consequent delay in most cases. Consequent upon the recommendations of its author, Martin Narey, sections of the Crime and Disorder Act 1998 are designed as time-saving measures. Under s.43, time limits may be set for different types of case. Section 46 provides that where a person is bailed (by the police) to appear before a magistrates' court, the date set for his appearance should be the next available court sitting. This means someone arrested on a Thursday night can now expect to find themselves before the court on Friday morning. If they plead guilty, the expectation behind the Act is that they should normally be sentenced there and then. If they are likely to plead not guilty, their first appearance may take the form of an early administrative hearing, under s.50 of the Act, at which the defendant's eligibility for criminal defence may be determined. Such hearings may be conducted by the single justice or a justices' clerk, or a legal adviser (court clerk) acting under powers delegated by the justices' clerk. Section 49 lists powers that may be exercised by a single justice or clerk. These include a lot of judicial trial management powers which are likely to be exercised at a later hearing called a pre-trial review. For instance, at an EAH or pre-trial review, a clerk may renew bail on conditions previously imposed. I have expressed concern about giving these new judicial powers to clerks (see Chapter 15 on magistrates, below).

The Courts Act 2003, s.45, places on a statutory basis pre-trial hearings which have been held since the 1970s in magistrates' courts, as a matter of practice. Case management decisions as provided for in the new Criminal Procedure Rules 2005 can be made at such hearings.

A speedy first appearance is also required by Art.5 of the Convention, discussed above. Article 5(3) says everyone who is arrested or detained shall be brought promptly before a judge and shall be entitled to trial within a reasonable time or to release pending trial.

The Guilty Plea

10–049   When the accused appears before the court, he is asked if he pleads guilty or not guilty. The vast majority of offenders plead guilty (see annual *Criminal Statistics*). If he pleads guilty, he may be convicted and sentenced immediately, unless the magistrates require more information on the defendant, in which case they will adjourn for the preparation of a medical or psychiatric report or a pre-sentence report, prepared by a probation officer or social worker. The Crime and Disorder Act 1998, s.53 provides that a member of the CPS staff who is not a Crown Prosecutor may prosecute guilty pleas in the magistrates' court.

The Not Guilty Plea and Trial

10–050   If a plea of not guilty is entered, the prosecutor will outline the case against the accused, then call witnesses to substantiate that accusation. They may be cross-examined by the defence. As in all criminal trials in England and Wales, the *onus of proof* is on the prosecution to prove the case against the person accused. The *quantum of proof*, sometimes called the *standard of proof* required is "proof beyond reasonable doubt". If the magistrates are left with a reasonable doubt they must acquit the defendant, since he is entitled to the benefit of any doubt.

Crimes with a reverse burden of proof

10–051   The onus is always on the prosecution to prove guilt. In some offences, however, the accused may be acquitted if he can disprove an element of the evidence. The fairness of such "reverse burdens" was considered in *Sheldrake v DPP* [2004] UKHL 43. In this case S was convicted of being in charge of a car whilst over the alcohol limit. Under the Road Traffic Act 1988, he had a defence, if he could prove, on the balance of probabilities, that there was no likelihood of his driving the car. S contended that this offended against the presumption of innocence in Art.6. The appeal went up to the House of Lords, via the Divisional Court of the QBD and the CA. The House took the opportunity to thoroughly examine this issue. Lord Bingham, giving the lead judgment held:

1. An evidential burden is not a burden of proof. It is a burden of raising an issue on the evidence for the consideration of the tribunal of fact. It is then for the prosecutor to prove beyond reasonable doubt that it does not avail the defendant.

2. Our courts must look to the jurisprudence of the ECtHR under Art.6. The now defunct European Commission on Human Rights had held several times that these reverse burdens do not breach Art 6.
3. Where some infringement of the presumption of innocence is justified, it should not be greater than necessary to achieve its legitimate objective.
4. In this drink driving offence, the obvious risk was causing death or injury so the burden placed on the accused was not unreasonable or arbitrary.

No case to answer

As the onus to prove guilt is on the prosecution, it follows that at the conclusion of the prosecution case, the defendant, or his legal representative, may submit to the magistrates that there is "no case to answer". This submission means, simply, that the evidence produced by the prosecution does not prove that the defendant has committed the offence with which he is charged. It is up to the prosecution to establish his guilt, not for him to convict himself out of his own mouth. If the magistrates uphold that submission the case is dismissed forthwith. If not, the full case for the defence is then presented to the court. Defence witnesses will be called, the prosecutor may cross-examine them and the magistrates will decide whether or not the evidence is sufficient for them to convict. If so, they may sentence the defendant. If they are considering custody or one of the alternatives, they will adjourn for a pre-sentence report. If they decide to acquit, the case is dismissed.

10–052

Magistrates can call for the assistance of their court clerk (legal adviser) if the case raises issues of law or mixed fact and law and they can ask her advice on sentencing. This is explained in greater depth in the chapter on magistrates. The maximum penalty open to the magistrates, unless a specific statute provides otherwise, is six months' imprisonment, and/or a £5,000 fine. If a defendant is convicted of two or more offences at the same hearing the magistrates have power to send him to prison for 12 months. They may send a convicted defendant to the Crown Court for sentencing, if they feel their powers are inadequate. When the CJA 2003 comes into force, it will double the magistrates' maximum sentencing power to one year's custody for a single offence. Magistrates who were the subject of doctoral research by Andrew Herbert were opposed to this change. Many felt they were already being asked to handle cases at the extreme of their ability.

Appeals

If magistrates discover they have made a mistake, they may re-open a case to vary a sentence or order where it appears to be in

10–053

the interests of justice to do so (Magistrates' Courts Act 1980, as amended). The convicted defendant has the right to appeal to the Crown Court on fact and/or sentence if he pleaded not guilty, or sentence only if he pleaded guilty. Disagreements between witnesses as to the story are disputes of fact. An appeal on a point of law may be made by the prosecution or defence "by way of case stated" to the Divisional Court of the Queen's Bench Division. For a summary appeal, the Crown Court is composed of either a circuit judge or a recorder accompanied by two magistrates. The decision of the court is by a majority and the judge has a second and casting vote if the members are equally divided. The magistrates must accept the judge's pronouncements on matters of law.

In its appeal court role, the Crown Court conducts a complete rehearing of the case. This means that a second trial takes place, since the parties and the witnesses will give their evidence again. The Crown Court then reaches its own independent conclusion. No jury is used in these appeal cases and there is no further appeal possible on fact in a summary case from the Crown Court. The Crown Court has a duty to give reasons for its decision on the appeal unless the reasons are obvious or the case is simple: *R. v Kingston Crown Court Ex p. Bell* (2000, QBD) and see *R. v Snaresbrook CC Ex p. Input Management Ltd* (1999, QBD). If on the appeal a point of law is argued before the court, the court may, having given its decision, agree to state a case for the consideration of the Queen's Bench Divisional Court.

The Divisional Court of the Queen's Bench Division

10–054   As has just been seen, an appeal on a point of law from the magistrates' court's decision or the decision of the Crown Court is heard here. The appeal is by way of "case stated". This means that the prosecution, or convicted person, or legal representative, asks the magistrates, or judge in the Crown Court to state a case for the consideration of the Divisional Court. This case is then prepared in writing by the judge or magistrates' clerk setting out the point of law which was raised, the decision of the magistrates and the reason why they decided it as they did. As magistrates' courts are not courts of record, this used to involve the clerk in composing reasons some months after trial, from his and the magistrates' memories but, as magistrates have been giving reasons since the HRA 1998 imported into English law the requirement for a reasoned judgment, stating a case will be a lot easier now.

If the Divisional Court decides that the magistrates were wrong, it has three options: (i) it may reverse, affirm or amend the magistrates' decision; (ii) it may remit the case to the magistrates requiring them either to continue hearing the case, or to discharge or convict the accused, as appropriate; (iii) it may make such order as it thinks fit (Supreme Court Act 1981). Note that the prosecution has equal right of appeal here and may succeed in having the case sent back for the magistrates to convict.

The Queen's Bench Divisional Court also exercises the High Court's supervisory jurisdiction over the functioning of magistrates' courts and the Crown Court in their dealings with summary cases. The judicial review of a case is so similar to an appeal by way of case stated that I have seen a High Court judge ask, two days into a hearing, which type of case he was hearing. The QBD has stated that it would prefer that convictions were challenged by way of case stated than by judicial review: *Chester v Gloucester Crown Court* (1998). Judicial review proceedings are not appropriate for sentencing appeals: *Allen v West Yorkshire Probation Service* [2001] EWHC Admin 2 but the existence of a right of appeal to the Crown Court does not preclude a person convicted of offences by magistrates seeking judicial review where the complaint raised was of procedural impropriety, unfairness or bias: *R. v Hereford Magistrates' Court Ex p. Rowlands* (1997, CA). A further appeal, subject to leave being obtained, is possible to the House of Lords. Such cases are rare. One example is *Sheldrake*, discussed above, on reverse burdens of proof. There is inconsistency between types of appeal available from the two courts of first instance (Crown and Magistrates'). Auld L.J. recommended harmonisation.

Post Appeal

The Criminal Appeal Act 1995 gives the Criminal Cases Review Commission (described below) an unconditional power to refer a conviction or sentence imposed by magistrates to the Crown Court, to be treated as an appeal.

10–055

9. Offences Triable Either Way—Mode of Trial, "Case Allocation"

Where the accused is charged with an "either way" offence, a decision must be taken whether to allocate it to summary trial in the magistrates' court or trial on indictment in the Crown Court. Under the Magistrates' Courts Act 1980, the magistrates can send the case up to the Crown Court if they consider it too serious or complex for them but in most instances, they are content to accept jurisdiction. In this event, the accused is then given the choice as to mode of trial. The CJA 2003, Sch.3 introduced provisions to change the mode of trial decision-making procedure yet again, with a view to making

10–056

289

magistrates' and the accused's decision-making on mode of trial better informed. These followed the recommendations of Auld L.J. in the *Review of the Criminal Courts*. The Act provides that, before deciding on mode of trial, the magistrates should be told of the accused's previous convictions. They must give prosecution and defence a chance to air their views and take account of the allocation guidelines issued by the new Sentencing Guidelines Council. If the court decides the case is suitable for summary trial, they must explain so, in ordinary language, to the accused and tell him he can choose a Crown Court trial but that, if the charge is of a certain violent or sexual offence, they can still commit him to the Crown Court for sentence if, having tried the case, they think their sentencing powers are too low.

The accused can then request an indication of the sentence he might get if he were to plead guilty in the magistrates' court but the court is not obliged to provide this. If they do, they must allow the accused an opportunity to reconsider his plea, which he will have entered in the plea before venue procedure, below. If the accused does not change his plea, the CJA 2003 makes it clear that any sentence indication is not binding on a later court. If the magistrates decide to send him to the Crown Court or the accused elects a Crown Court trial, they must send him direct, under s.51 of the Crime and Disorder Act 1998, without a committal. New guidelines will be issued on this procedure.

Experience has shown that the vast majority of defendants who have an option choose to have the case tried by magistrates and the new amendments to the allocation procedure are designed to provide more information to the magistrates and the accused, in the hope of persuading magistrates to keep more cases in their court and persuading even more defendants to choose summary trial in the magistrates' court.

10–057   As Home Secretary, Jack Straw twice introduced Bills designed to remove the accused's right to choose the mode of trial but they were both rejected by the House of Lords. The story of these Bills and their background is told in Chapter 16 on the jury, below. As I explain in that chapter, his Conservative predecessor, recognising the sentimental attachment of the English to jury trial in criminal cases, decided it would be politically inexpedient to remove the defendant's right to opt for jury trial in all triable either way cases.

The Plea before Venue Procedure

10–058   Instead, he sponsored what is now s.49 of the Criminal Procedure and Investigations Act 1996 which requires the magistrates, *before* determining mode of trial in triable either way cases, to ascertain the accused's plea. Where he indicates a not guilty plea, they must proceed to deal with the case summarily. Where the accused pleads not guilty, as explained above, they may choose to send the case up to the Crown Court or, where they decline to do so, they must still give the defendant the option of summary trial or trial on indictment at the Crown Court. In other words, if the defendant expresses an intention to plead guilty, he loses the right to opt for the Crown Court. The magistrates must hear the case but retain the right to send it up to the Crown Court for sentence, where they feel their own sentencing powers are too low. There is of course, nothing to prevent the accused from indicating a not guilty plea at this stage, then changing his plea to guilty at the Crown Court. In such cases, the section fails to achieve its desired objective, hence the introduction of the graduated sentencing discount to induce early guilty pleas, described above.

The Committal—now Abolished

Where the justices choose to send the accused for trial in the Crown Court, or he so elects, he used to be "committed" for trial there in committal proceedings. This inquiry was an impartial investigation of the prosecution case. Written statements were submitted to the examining magistrates. In effect this was committal by consent. The accused was thus made fully aware of the case which he had to meet at trial. Committals in either way cases were abolished by the CJA 2003 which extended s.51 of the 1998 Act, below.

10–059

10. The Trial of Young Offenders

Most young offenders, 10–17, are tried in the youth court, which is part of the magistrates' court. Young offenders will only be sent to the Crown Court for trial if certain conditions are satisfied under Sch.3 to the CJA 2003, or other statutes. D. A. Thomas endeavoured to explain the complex rules now applicable, from 2005. He commented "It might be possible to devise a more convoluted scheme than this, but only with great difficulty."

10–060

1. A defendant under 18 must be sent to the Crown Court if he is charged with homicide (murder or manslaughter), or has committed certain firearms offences.
2. He must be sent if charged jointly with an adult and the court considers sending him in to be in the interests of justice, or if charged with a serious or complex fraud that should be managed by the Crown Court, or if a child has been called as a witness and the case should be taken over by the Crown Court to avoid prejudicing the interests of the child.

3. If none of these conditions is satisfied but the offence is one to which s.91 of the Powers of Criminal Courts (Sentencing) Act 2000 applies, the court must follow the plea before venue procedure set out below. If he pleads not guilty and the court considers that, if convicted, it ought to be possible to sentence him to detention under s.91 or if the offence is a specified offence, then he should be sent to the Crown Court. In all other cases he must be tried summarily.
4. If he has pleaded guilty and been convicted in the magistrates' court, he may be sent to the Crown Court for sentencing under certain circumstances and the court feels the Crown Court has the power to sentence to detention. This power does not apply to a young person who has been found guilty after trial.
5. He should be sent to the Crown Court if he has committed a "specified offence" and the court considers he qualifies for a sentence of detention for public protection or an extended sentence of detention. (I have oversimplified the procedure for the sake of brevity but Thomas should be consulted for a better explanation.)

Thomas and Venables, who killed toddler Jamie Bulger when they were 10, were tried in the Crown Court. In *T and V v UK* (1999) the Court agreed that the formality and ritual of the Crown Court trial must have been intimidating and incomprehensible to 11-year-old children, as the defendants then were, and so their Art.6 Convention rights to a fair trial had been violated. Consequently, in 2000, the Lord Chief Justice issued a Practice Direction requiring that youth trials should take account of the age, maturity and development of the defendant. For instance, robes, wigs and police uniform should not normally be worn; participants should be on the same level; the young defendant should be able to sit near the family or guardians and they should be given regular breaks. The court is not open to members of the public. The victim may wish to attend. Ball *et al.* cite research demonstrating that young offenders and their families can be confused as to court personnel and observe that good practice requires the chairman to explain their functions but, in my observation of two city youth courts in 2004, proceedings are conducted too swiftly to allow for this.

As a result of *SC v UK* (2004, ECtHR) it has been suggested that the Practice Direction is inadequate to satisfy the fair trial requirements of Art.6. This trial of an 11-year-old took place before the Direction was issued. Because of his long history of offending, he was sent to the Crown Court for trial. Reports showed him to have learning difficulties and his level of understanding was more like that of an eight-year-old. On appeal, new evidence suggested he had had little understanding of trial or its consequences. Commenting on this case Andrew Ashworth suggests it implies that the Practice Direction does not go far enough and where the defendant is very young and there is evidence of mental impairment, it may be necessary to convene what the ECtHR calls a "specialist tribunal".

"In most European countries it would not be possible to prosecute a child of 11, and it is no surprise that the European Court of Human Rights insists on high standards for effective participation and on special arrangements if such cases do go ahead." (2004)

As required by the United Nations Convention on the Rights of the Child, Art.3.1, the child has a right to respect of his privacy so there are restrictions on the reporting of proceedings and Art.6.1 of the European Convention on Human Rights provides that the press and public can be excluded in the interests of the juvenile. The Children and Young Persons Act 1933, as amended, provides that nothing may be published which is likely to lead members of the public to identify a person (victim/witness/defendant) under 18. This may require preventing the naming of adults involved, for instance, as defendants.

11. Indictable Offences

Committal Abolished—Section 51 of the Crime and Disorder Act 1998

After previous failed statutory attempts, this section removed committal proceedings for indictable offences, from 2001. It had been recommended by the Narey Report on delay, 1997, as well by the Royal Commission on Criminal Justice 1993. Narey found that indictable cases wasted much of their time in the magistrates' court. The pilot schemes proved successful, with an average reduction of seven weeks per case. Since 2001 there is a simple preliminary hearing in the magistrates' court, before two or three justices. Its purpose is to decide the defendant's remand status and deal with legal representation. Magistrates will usually hear a full bail application at such a hearing and may adjourn the hearing if there is insufficient information before them. It might also be adjourned at the prosecution's request if they seek to produce co-defendants.

10–061

The Plea and Directions Hearing/Case Management Hearings

At the Crown Court, the defendant (except in cases of fraud) has been required, since the mid 1990s, to appear at a proceeding called

10–062

a "plea and directions hearing", designed to prepare for trial and fix the trial date. In all class one or serious or complex cases the prosecution provides a summary, identifying issues of law and fact and estimating trial length. The arraignment takes place at the hearing: the defendant enters a plea of guilty or not guilty to each of the charges. Following a not guilty plea, the parties are expected to inform the court of such matters as: witnesses, defence witnesses whose written statements are accepted, admitted facts, any alibi, points of law and special requirements for the trial (for example, live video links for child witnesses) and these requirements are now embodied in the case management and progression rules of the new 2005 Criminal Procedure Rules.

If the plea is "guilty", the judge should, if possible, proceed to sentence the defendant, after hearing his plea in mitigation. This is a plea for leniency, allowing the defendant to argue any partial excuses or explanation for his admitted offences. If the judge or recorder is considering imposing a custodial sentence or non-custodial alternative, she may require a pre-sentence report to be prepared, or, where appropriate, a medical or psychiatric report. Since 1999–2000 various Crown Court centres have been abandoning oral plea and directions hearings (PDHs) in small class 4 cases and the issues are dealt with in writing. Virtual plea and directions hearings, via a secure internal website, have been piloted at in the Crown Court in Manchester for over two years.

Preparatory hearings are held before serious fraud trials and may be ordered in complex and lengthy cases, under the Criminal Procedure and Investigations Act 1996. The prosecution may appeal against a judge's ruling. Auld L.J. recommended a move away from pre-trial hearings towards standard timetables and co-operation between the parties. As explained above, the 2005 Procedure Rules and the Effective Trial Management Programme will now dispose of the need for PDHs in many cases because it will be up to the Case Progression Officer to monitor trial preparation in most cases and she can communicate via telephone or email with the parties, keeping the court abreast of timetable developments. It will be up to the lawyers involved to certify the readiness of the case for trial. PDHs are to be renamed Case Management Hearings.

Trial on Indictment

Arguments on points of law and acquittals by the judge—the new power to appeal

10–063   One of the big advantages to the defendant of a trial in the Crown Court, over summary trial in the magistrates' court, is that the pre-trial legal argument stage provides a very realistic opportunity for the case to be dismissed on the order of the trial judge, in an ordered or directed acquittal. Indeed, over half of Crown Court acquittals occur before or during the trial, without a jury's ever being given an opportunity to bring in a verdict. This is one of the elements which contribute to the acquittal rate in the Crown Court being significantly higher than that in the magistrates' court. When the prosecution appear at court and offer no evidence, the judge orders an acquittal and one of the biggest factors causing this is the non-appearance of a crucial witness, or their retraction of evidence. Baldwin found that this was foreseeable in many such collapsed cases and the prosecution could have been withdrawn at an earlier stage. It was doubtless research such as this which prompted the new special measures for vulnerable witnesses, described above.

A judge may direct an acquittal during the trial. Mostly, this happens at the close of the prosecution case when the defence have successfully invited the judge to find that there is not a sufficient case to convict the defendant, in a submission of "no case to answer". This may be decided on a point of law, or an assessment of the sufficiency of the evidence. The Law Commission Report, *Double Jeopardy and Prosecution Appeals* (No.267, 2001) recommended that where the judge acquits at this point on a point of law, the prosecution should have a right of appeal against an acquittal. This was accepted by the Government and appeared as a proposal in the 2001 white paper, *Criminal Justice: The Way Ahead*. Where a judge wrongly rejects a submission of "no case", the conviction will be regarded as unsafe by the CA: *R. v Smith* (1999, CA).

Also, legal argument may take place at any time in the trial, where the judge is asked to rule on a point of law or evidence in the absence of the jury, in a *"voir dire"* hearing (a trial within a trial). When the prosecution depends on poor quality, unsupported identification evidence, the judge must direct an acquittal. Otherwise, the judge's task is to consider, without usurping the jury's function, whether there is evidence upon which a reasonable jury could convict. Directed acquittals are again caused mainly by inadequate or untrustworthy witnesses but also by legal problems and evidential insufficiency (Baldwin). In *R. v Brown* [2001] EWCA Crim 961, the CA held that the judge is under a duty to keep under review whether to direct an acquittal, such power to be sparingly exercised, and should do so if satisfied that no jury on the evidence could safely convict. What a judge may not do is prevent the prosecution bringing their case because he thinks the defendant's defence is likely to be believed by the jury: *Attorney General's Ref No.2 of 2000* (2001, CA). If the judge upholds the defence submission and directs an acquittal, the prosecution did not have the power to appeal and the Law Commission recommended that this should not change (see *Prosecution Appeals against Judges' Rulings* (C.P. 158, 2000). Pattenden powerfully argued that this meant that any wrongfully directed acquittal (and the numbers were found to be significant, by Block, Corbett and Peay) by the judge must go unchallenged, which is unfair for the victim, witnesses and public. Prosecutors had much more extensive rights of appeal in some common law and European civil law jurisdictions. The Law Commission's final report (No.267), published in 2001, confirmed their recommendations in the consultation paper, for which they received a high degree of support.

10–064   Consequently the CJA 2003, Part 9, introduces a prosecution right of appeal, in certain serious offences, to the CA against a judge's evidentiary ruling which has terminated the trial (thus acquitting the accused) before a jury has been convened or during the prosecution case, or as a result of a submission of "no case to answer" by the defence, at the conclusion of the prosecution case. The Act also introduces a prosecution right to appeal against a judge's ruling which has been made at any time before the close of the prosecution case. In both instances, the prosecution must obtain leave from the trial judge or the CA. The CA may affirm the ruling and acquit the defendant, remit the case to the trial court for the trial to continue or order a retrial, where they think it is in the interests of justice to do so. The grounds for overturning a trial judge's ruling are if it was wrong in law, involved an error of law or principle, or was unreasonable.

A judge may stop a trial at any time, if he thinks adverse publicity may endanger the impartiality of the jury. This happened very controversially in 2001, to the trial of Leeds United footballers Lee Bowyer and Jonathan Woodgate, accused of beating an Asian student unconscious. The jury had already deliberated for 21 hours at the end of a nine-week trial, costing £8 million, when the *Sunday Mirror* published an interview with the victim's father, alleging that it was a racist attack. The judge reported the newspaper to the Attorney-General, who alone has the power to prosecute them for contempt.

Jury trial

10–065   If the plea is "not guilty" the court proceeds to swear in 12 jurors, who will be responsible at the end of the trial for deciding whether the accused is guilty or not guilty. Once the jury is sworn in, the prosecution will open the case by outlining the facts and then calling the prosecution witnesses to give evidence to prove those facts. The defence can cross-examine all such witnesses. Undisputed evidence can be admitted by written statement. At the close of the prosecution case the defence counsel has the same right, as described above in the magistrates' court, to submit "no case to answer", *i.e.* to argue that there is insufficient evidence upon which the jury can convict. Only the judge can invite the jury to acquit at this point: *R. v Speechley* [2004] EWCA Crim 307.

Unless such a submission is successful, the defence advocate presents the defence case and calls witnesses for the defence, possibly including the defendant. These witnesses too can be cross-examined on their evidence. The accused is not required to give evidence. This rule is called the right to silence and is discussed above.

When the final speeches by the prosecution and defence advocate have been made, the judge normally "sums up" the evidence for the benefit of the jury. This summing-up and the judge's direction on law is the last speech which the jury hear before they retire to consider their verdict. In it the judge has to balance the arguments of the prosecution and the defence, but leave the jury to decide on the issue of guilt, beyond reasonable doubt, of the accused.

As a result of the abolition of the requirement for a unanimous verdict by the Criminal Justice Act 1967, it is possible for the judge to accept a majority verdict of the jury, provided that there are not more than two in the minority. If there are three or more in the minority this is known as a "hung jury" and the trial is abandoned. It is then up to the prosecution whether to request a retrial. The judge will only stop this if he considers it an abuse of process. Normally prosecutions are abandoned after two juries have hung but there is nothing in law stopping a retrial.

10–066

If the jury has dropped to 11 or ten in number there can be a majority verdict if there is not more than one dissenter. Every effort is made, however, to obtain a unanimous verdict and the jury must have been out for at least two hours before the judge is able to accept a majority verdict. If the verdict is "not guilty" the accused is immediately discharged; if the verdict is "guilty", after a plea in mitigation by his counsel, he will be sentenced by the judge. I return to the jury in Chapter 16, below. I made a series of recommendations for restructuring jury trial in a 2001 report for Auld L.J. in his *Criminal Courts Review*. It is obtainable from the CCR website.

Trial by Judge Alone

Following recommendations by Auld L.J., the Criminal Justice Bill 2003 aimed to introduce a procedure for trial by judge alone, in certain circumstances. Prior to the Bill, now the 2003 Act, all Crown Court trials had to be conducted by a judge and jury. The Bill would have permitted the defendant to apply to be tried by judge alone but this clause was highly controversial and not enacted.

10–067

Under s.43 of the CJA 2003, the judge may, in future, grant a prosecution application for trial by judge alone, in serious and complex frauds. He may only do this with the consent of the Lord Chief Justice or nominated judge. Certain conditions apply. The trial must be likely to be so long, or complex, or both, as to make it so burdensome on the jury that the interests of justice require that serious consideration should be given to the question of whether the trial should be conducted without a jury. In deciding to make such an order, the judge must have regard to any steps that can be made to reduce the length or complexity of the trial so long as that does not seriously disadvantage the prosecution.

10–068   Section 44 of the 2003 Act allows the judge to direct a judge-only trial where there is a danger of jury tampering. The judge must be satisfied that there is a "real and present danger that jury tampering would take place". The second condition is that, notwithstanding any steps that could be taken, such as police protection, the likelihood of tampering is so great as to make it necessary in the interests of justice for the trial to be conducted without a jury. The section gives examples of cases where there is a real and present danger of jury tampering: where the trial is a retrial because of previous case involving jury tampering; where the defendant or defendants have previously been involved in a case where there has been jury tampering, or where there has been intimidation or attempted intimidation of witnesses.

Section 43 on fraud trials is not yet in force because, in order to get these two clauses passed through Parliament, the Government promised not to implement s.43 without further consideration. As I explain in Chapter 16 on the jury, below, in March 2005 a two year £60 million corruption trial collapsed at the Old Bailey, after one juror was removed for suspected benefit fraud and two others said they could not go on. This was the type of trial Auld L.J. undoubtedly had in mind when he suggested the option of judge only trials in serious and complex cases.

In 2002, the Law Commission suggested a two stage procedure to prosecute multiple offences. Sample counts would be used to prosecute an offender before a judge and jury and, if convicted, he would be tried by judge alone for linked offences. The Commission's work on fraud highlighted the difficulty of prosecuting multiple fraud offences: *www.lawcom.gov.uk: The Effective Prosecution of Multiple Offending* (Report 277). This suggestion resulted in s.13 of the Domestic Violence, Crime and Victims Act 2004. This permits the prosecution to apply for trial by jury of sample counts on an indictment where there are so many counts that trial by jury of all of them would be impracticable. If the jury convicts on a sample count, the other counts may be triad by judge alone.

Appeals by the Convicted Defendant

10–069   A convicted person may appeal from the Crown Court to the CA (Criminal Division), with leave of the CA or if the trial judge grants a certificate that the case is fit for appeal (Criminal Appeal Act 1968, s.1

as simplified by the Criminal Appeal Act 1995, s.1). He may appeal against sentence, with leave of the CA (1968 Act, ss.9–11). Applications for leave to the CA are normally considered on paper, by a High Court judge. If she refuses leave, the application may be re-heard by the CA in open court. Many unmeritorious applications are made because prisoners have plenty of spare time. In *R. v Kuimba* (2005) the CA, led by the Lord Chief Justice said it should make more use of its power to order that time spent in custody, pending the outcome of such an application should not be credited towards the sentence. An appeal by way of case stated on a point of law may be made to the High Court (QBD Divisional Court). An application for judicial review is precluded "in matters relating to trial on indictment" but not in relation to other matters: Supreme Court Act 1981, s. 29(3).

New—Prosecution Applications for Retrial following Acquittal

The 2003 Act, Part 10 also made a controversial exception to the double jeopardy rule, which protects a person from being tried twice for the same offence. With the DPP's consent, a prosecutor may apply to the CA to quash an acquittal (here or abroad) and order a retrial. This can be done following trial on indictment or a successful appeal. If the CA is satisfied that there is "new and compelling evidence" ("reliable" and "substantial") against the person, in relation to the offence and that it is in the interests of justice to do so, they must quash the acquittal and order a retrial. In determining the interests of justice, the CA must take into account, among other things, whether a fair retrial is likely and the length of time since the alleged offence was committed.

10–070

The provision applies only to serious offences such as kidnapping, terrorist offences, rape, armed robbery, certain Class A drugs offences and murder and manslaughter. This enactment follows a recommendation of Auld L.J. in the *Review of the Criminal Courts* (Chapter 12). He, in turn, was influenced by this suggestion in the Macpherson Report on the Stephen Lawrence Inquiry, a recommendation of the House of Commons Home Affairs Select Committee and the Law Commission Report, *Double Jeopardy and Prosecution Appeals* (No.267).

12. Powers of the Court of Appeal in Appeals against Conviction

Grounds

Section 2(1) of the Criminal Appeal Act 1995 amends the Criminal Appeal Act 1968 to set out simplified grounds upon which the CA may allow a criminal appeal. The CA:

10–071

"(a) shall allow an appeal against conviction if they think that the conviction is unsafe; and

(b) shall dismiss such an appeal in any other case."

Receiving Fresh Evidence

10–072   The CA may "receive any evidence which was not adduced in the proceedings from which the appeal lies" where it is necessary or expedient in the interests of justice to do so (Criminal Appeal Act 1968, as amended by the 1995 Act, s.4). The Court must, in considering whether to receive any evidence, have regard in particular to:

(a) whether the evidence appears to the Court to be capable of belief;

(b) whether it appears to the Court that the evidence may afford any ground for allowing the appeal;

(c) whether the evidence would have been admissible at the trial;

(d) whether there is a reasonable explanation for the failure to adduce the evidence at trial.

(Criminal Appeal Act 1968, s.23(2), as amended by s.4 of the 1995 Act, paraphrased). They are free to admit evidence irrespective of these criteria, however: *Bowler* (Reference by the Home Secretary) [1997] EWCA Crim 1957.

In *Craven* (2000, CA), the Court held that, empowered as it was to receive fresh evidence and taking account of all the evidence before it, including evidence to which the jury might not have had access, they should uphold a conviction, if they considered it safe. Thus a defect at trial, rendering it unfair, could be cured by a fair and proper consideration of the evidence on appeal. They applied the ECtHR case of *Edwards v UK* (1993). The same principle was applied in *Hanratty* [2002] EWCA Crim 1141. The CA heard an appeal that put an end to one of the longest "miscarriage of justice" sagas in English legal history. Hanratty had been hanged for the A6 murders in the 1960s. So much had been written about the case, including books, that generations had grown up assuming H to be innocent. The family members leading his campaign had not even been born at the time of his hanging. They took it for granted that once the CA admitted DNA evidence from Hanratty's exhumed body this would prove his innocence, (DNA techniques had obviously not been discovered at his time of trial). On the contrary, the DNA results confirmed his guilt. The CA held that the overriding consideration for the Court in deciding whether fresh evidence should be admitted was whether the evidence would assist the court to achieve justice. Justice could equally be achieved by upholding a conviction if it was safe or setting it aside if it was unsafe. Accordingly, fresh evidence may be admitted when tendered by the prosecution, even where it was not relevant to a specific ground of appeal, but rather to the guilt or innocence of the appellant at large.

As Duff (below) points out, a common reason for non-referral by the Criminal Cases Review Commission (CCRC) of a case to the CA is that, although fresh evidence has come to light, there is no reasonable explanation why it was not adduced at trial (*CCRC Annual Report 1999–2000*). The prosecution are entitled to take account of new evidence at trial and can change their allegations: *Mercer* [2001] EWCA Crim 638.

In *Pendleton* [2001] UKHL 66, the leading case in this context, the   **10–073** House of Lords confirmed that the correct test for the CA to apply in determining an appeal related to the effect of the fresh evidence on the minds of the members of the court, not the effect it would have had on a jury. The question was whether the conviction was unsafe, not whether the accused was guilty. The CA should remind itself:

> "it is not and never should become the primary decision-maker
> . . . The Court of Appeal can make its assessment of the evidence
> it has heard, but save in a clear case it is at a disadvantage in
> seeking to relate that evidence to the rest of the evidence which
> the jury heard. For these reasons it will usually be wise for the
> Court of Appeal, in a case of any difficulty, to test their own pro-
> visional view by asking whether the evidence, if given at trial,
> might reasonably have affected the decision of the trial jury to
> convict. If it might, the conviction must be thought to be unsafe."

In *Hakala* (2002), Judge L.J. added that, where fresh evidence is disputed the Court must decide to what extent it can be accepted and must evaluate it relative to the remaining material that was before the jury at trial. It may serve to affirm rather than undermine the safety of a conviction.

Referral to the CCRC

Section 5 of the 1995 Act gives the CA a power to direct the CCRC   **10–074** (which the Act created) to investigate and report on any specified matter relevant to the determination of an appeal against conviction, where such an investigation is likely to result in the Court being able to resolve the appeal and where the matter cannot be resolved by the Court without such a reference.

Comment

10–075   The 1995 amendments to the CA's powers all result from the recommendations of the Royal Commission on Criminal Justice, 1993.
These were a culmination of years of criticism from JUSTICE (1989,
etc.), the House of Commons Select Committee on Home Affairs
(1981), academics, MPs and many others. It was repeatedly said that
the grounds of appeal in the 1968 Act were narrow and ambiguous,
that the CA interpreted their powers too narrowly, that they were
too ready to uphold a conviction, even where they accepted there
had been an irregularity at trial, and that they were too reluctant to
admit fresh evidence.

The Act was designed to simplify the grounds of appeal so, for
instance, it was decided in s.2 to make the ground for quashing an
appeal simply a determination that it was "unsafe", instead of
"unsafe or unsatisfactory", as the 1968 Act had read. The other list
of grounds in the unamended Act were deleted, as it was thought
that "unsafe" was a comprehensive enough term to cover all types
of miscarriage of justice which should be quashed. Indeed, the
Home Secretary and Minister of State, in introducing the Bill,
assured Parliament that the new ground simply restated the existing practice of the CA. All this is explained by Sir John Smith, in the
Criminal Law Review. He warned in it, as he had Parliament, that
"unsafe" needed clarification. He regretted that the Government
was not persuaded by his argument.

Judicial Interpretation of "Unsafe"

10–076   Since then, the CA has provoked more regret, by producing a
series of contradictory cases on what errors at trial can render a conviction unsafe enough to merit quashing. Sir John explains the confusing result in his comment on *Rajcoomar* (1999, CA). In this case,
where the defendant pleaded guilty after the judge wrongly
rejected an abuse of process objection, the Court declined to quash
the conviction, following *Chalkley* (1998), where they had held that
their amended grounds for quashing were narrower than under the
old law. The Court distinguished *Mullen* (1999), where they had
held that "for a conviction to be safe, it must be lawful and, if it
results from a trial which should never have taken place, it can
hardly be regarded as safe". Sir John, commenting in the *Criminal
Law Review* on these two and other cases, submitted there is no
proper ground for a distinction. In each case, it was assumed that
there was no doubt the defendant committed the offence charged
but there was a fundamental procedural flaw so the conviction
should have been quashed. Indeed the Court in *Mullen* considered
the meaning of "unsafe" sufficiently ambiguous for them to apply
Pepper v Hart, to permit themselves to look at *Hansard* (parliamen-

tary proceedings) to see what was the intention behind the amendment. We encountered this case in Chapter 2 on sources, above.

Unfortunately, there seem to be inconsistencies in the increasing batch of cases where the CA has had to determine the meaning of "unsafe" in the context of the fair trial requirement under Art.6. When the CA in *R. v Togher, R. v Doran, R. v Parsons* (2000) took into account (their words) the ECtHR's judgment in *R. v Davis, Johnson and Rowe* (2000) on disclosure, cited above, they held that they were required by the HRA 1998 to interpret the domestic legislation in a way compatible with the Convention, where possible. Although *Chalkley* suggested the safety of a conviction was to be considered irrespective of the trial process, they, in *Togher*, preferred the approach in *Mullen*. If a defendant had been had been denied a fair trial, it would almost be inevitable that the conviction would be regarded as unsafe. These cases were not mentioned by the CA in *R. v Williams* (2001). Here, the Court held that a mis- or non-direction must be significant in order to render a conviction unsafe. It leaves the problem of determining when a misdirection or non-direction is "significant". These precedents were, nevertheless mentioned in *R. v Craven* (2001, CA), which held that whether there was such unfairness as to render a conviction unsafe depended on the vice which was said to constitute unfairness. If the verdict of the jury would not have been different then the trial was not unfair and the conviction not unsafe. If a defect at trial was cured on appeal then the defendant had received a fair trial under Art.6. In *R. v Francom* [2000] UKHL 25, the CA held they should approach the issue of safety of a conviction in the same way as the ECtHR. *R. v A* [2001] UKHL 25, discussed in depth in Chapter 4 on human rights, above, went further than these cases. The House of Lords held that a breach of Art.6 will *always* result in a conviction being unsafe.

The Nature of an Appeal to the Court of Appeal

It is important to understand that the CA does not provide a **10–077** rehearing in criminal cases, unlike an appeal from a magistrates' court to the Crown Court. The limited powers of the CA were spelt out in the successful appeal of the Birmingham Six in 1991, *R. v McIlkenny and others*, in a judgment read out by the judges in turn:

"Nothing in section 2 of the Act, or anywhere else obliges or entitles us to say whether we think that the appellant is innocent. This is a point of great constitutional importance. The task of deciding whether a man is innocent or guilty falls on the jury. We are concerned solely with the question whether the verdict of the jury can stand. Rightly or wrongly (we think rightly) trial by jury is the foundation of our criminal justice system . . . The primacy of the jury in the criminal justice system is well illustrated by the difference between the Criminal and Civil Divisions of the Court of Appeal . . . A civil appeal is by way of rehearing of the whole case. So the court is concerned with fact as well as law . . . It follows that in a civil case the Court of Appeal may take a different view of the facts from the court below. In a criminal case this is not possible . . . the Criminal Division is perhaps more accurately described as a court of review."

Further, the CA may substitute a conviction for an alternative offence, or order a retrial, where it feels this is required by the interests of justice.

Retrials

10–078
A retrial has only been available since 1964. There are arguments for and against retrials. A retrial is preferable for the accused over an outright dismissal of his appeal. At least he gets another chance. On the other hand it is said retrials may be tainted by publicity, as the jury may have developed their own opinions over the first trial or appeal in a high profile case. This was unsuccessfully argued as inherently unsafe, in *Stone* (2001, CA). The CA held that, following the successful appeal against conviction by Michael Stone for the highly publicised murder of Lin and Megan Russell, the question whether a retrial should be ordered where there had been extensive publicity had to be decided on a balance of probabilities: whether he would suffer serious prejudice to the extent that no fair trial could be held. Stone was retried in 2001 and convicted by a second jury.

Also, the witnesses' memories will have faded and the element of surprise in cross-examination will be lost, as all witnesses will have become familiar with all the evidence. A retrial gives both prosecution and defence the opportunity to strengthen their case. One omission from the Act is that the power to order retrials under the 1968 Criminal Appeal Act, s.7 is left untouched, despite considerable debate, in the Royal Commission and elsewhere, over the circumstances in which it is appropriate to order a retrial. See Smith, 1995.

Attorney-General's References

10–079
The Attorney-General may, under the Criminal Justice Act 1972, refer a point of law to the CA, on behalf of the prosecution, following an acquittal. The CA simply clarifies the law for the future, leaving the acquittal verdict untouched. The point may then be referred to the House of Lords.

Appeals on sentence

10–080
The defendant may appeal against the sentence imposed by the Crown Court to the CA who may substitute any other sentence or

order within the powers of the Crown Court, provided it is not more severe than originally. The Criminal Justice Act 1988, s.36 gives the Attorney-General new prosecutorial power to refer any "unduly lenient" Crown Court sentence to the CA, who then have the power to quash it and substitute any sentence within the Crown Court's powers. This applies to indictable and some either way offences. The Attorney may then refer any such decision of the CA up to the House of Lords.

Shute published an analysis of these appeals in 1989–1997 which disclosed that a disproportionate percentage of reviewed sentences had been imposed at the Old Bailey. The Old Bailey (Central Criminal Court) deals with some of the most notorious offenders in England and Wales.

Appeals to the House of Lords

A further appeal to the House of Lords is possible by the prosecu-   **10–081** tion or the defence but only if the CA certifies that the case reveals a point of law of general public importance and either that court or the House of Lords grants leave (permission). There are very few criminal appeals heard by the House of Lords each year. In 2001, Auld L.J. suggested reconstituting the CA and improving its procedures.

13. Post-Appeal: Resolving Miscarriages of Justice

Until 1996, the Home Secretary had power to refer cases to the CA   **10–082** but would not normally do this unless all avenues of appeal had been exhausted and there was fresh evidence upon which the CA might decide that the conviction was unsafe and unsatisfactory (Criminal Appeal Act 1968 s.17). For example, this power was used in 1987 to refer the convictions of the Birmingham Six to the CA and again in 1991.

The Royal Commission on Criminal Justice 1993, paying heed to the multitude of critics who complained that the Home Secretary was too reluctant to use his power to refer, recommended that it should be replaced by that of a criminal cases review authority, whose job it would be to investigate miscarriages of justice in cases referred to them by the CA, or drawn to their attention in other ways. Following this recommendation, s.17 was duly repealed in the Criminal Appeal Act 1995, which created a Criminal Cases Review Commission (CCRC) (ss.8–25). The Commission is a body corporate, independent of Government, whose 11 members are appointed by the Crown on the advice of the Prime Minister. One third of them must be lawyers and two thirds must be experienced in the criminal justice system.

Under s.9, they have a very broad power to refer any conviction or sentence at any time after an unsuccessful appeal or a refusal of leave, to the CA. The condition for their making a reference is that they "consider there is a real possibility that the conviction, verdict, finding or sentence would not be upheld" because of an argument or evidence not raised in the convicting court or an argument, point of law or information not raised prior to sentence. Section 13(2) provides an even wider power to refer any case which does not satisfy those conditions, in exceptional circumstances. When deciding whether to refer, the Commission has a duty to take account of representations made to them and they have wide investigatory powers. They may seek the CA's opinion, direct an investigation by the police or any other relevant public body, require the production of documents, reports or opinions or undertake any inquiry they consider appropriate.

10–083   In 1999, the Administrative Court, led by Lord Woolf C.J., gave guidance on the CCRC's exercise of its powers, in *Pearson*. They emphasised the uniqueness of the CCRC's predictive function and stressed the broad discretion accorded to it by Parliament. They considered that, in new evidence cases, the CCRC was correct to try and predict whether the CA would be likely to exercise its powers to admit fresh evidence. This means the CCRC applies the same criteria as the CA is required to do in admitting fresh evidence.

Intriguingly, *R. v Smith* [2002] EWCA Crim 2907 was one of those cases where the CA reluctantly felt itself bound by a literal interpretation of statute. Section 14(5) of the Criminal Appeal Act 1995 seemed to say that once the CCRC, on whatever grounds, had made a reference to the court, the appellant might add any further grounds, including those expressly rejected by the CCRC. Their Lordships were "very surprised indeed" at this and respectfully suggested an amendment.

In *Bentley* (2001), below, the CA held that although it could cause difficulties in some cases, they had no difficulty in this case in applying changes in the common law and modern standards of fairness to hold that Bentley was wrongfully hanged.

10–084   In *Mills and Poole* [2003] EWCA Crim 1753, the applicants had already appealed unsuccessfully to the CA with new evidence that a police officer had persuaded a witness who would have given evidence supporting the accused to change his account. The CCRC refused to refer the case to the CA again, on the grounds that the new material added virtually nothing to the grounds used in the unsuccessful appeal. The CCRC's decision was upheld in judicial review proceedings but Lord Woolf C.J. commented that new material might not be significant but it could still tip the balance in favour of allowing the appeal.

The 1995 Act preserves the prerogative power to pardon a convicted individual. This is a residual monarchical prerogative, exercised traditionally by the Home Secretary and s.16 gives him the power to refer any case under his consideration to the Commission for their opinion.

Identifying the Causes of Miscarriages of Justice and the work of the CCRC

Laurence Elks, a member of the CCRC provided a useful review of its work in 2004.

10–085

Historic cases

Three cases from the 1950s where the convicted person had been hanged were quashed by the CA: *Mattan*, in 1998 and *Kelly* [2003] EWCA Crim 1752, both on new evidence and non-disclosure, and *Bentley*, in 2001, on the grounds of an unfair trial. In 2004, the CCRC decided not to refer the case of Timothy Evans, wrongly hanged for murdering his baby daughter, in 1950. John Christie later confessed to this and other murders and was hanged. The case, like Bentley's, had been one of the most notorious miscarriages of justice in English legal history. It had been the subject of a book, *Ten Rillington Place*, by Ludovik Kennedy and a film starring Richard Attenborough. The CCRC declined to refer the case to the CA as Evans had been given a posthumous royal pardon in 1966, on the recommendation of the Home Secretary. In judicial review proceedings, the High Court upheld the CCRC's refusal but publicly declared Evans to be innocent. One notorious cases referred by the Board was that of the A6 murderer James Hanratty (above), hanged in 1962, whose body was exhumed in 2000 for DNA tests.

10–086

Some other references by the CCRC have involved very old convictions, which took place before the Police and Criminal Evidence Act 1984 offered protection to the accused and rendered confessions obtained in oppressive circumstances inadmissible. One such case was that of Stephen Downing, sentenced for murder in 1973, as a semi-literate 17-year-old, with a very low mental age. The saddest aspect of this case is that although his sentencing judge set a 17 year tariff, he spent a further ten years in prison because of his refusal to admit the offence: [2002] EWCA Crim 263. In this group of cases, defects identified by the CCRC include oppressive questioning, failure to protect mentally vulnerable suspects, like Downing, failure to caution, or "verballing", meaning the attribution of false statements to the accused.

Also in this group are cases involving police malpractice, reminiscent of the famous miscarriages of justice, such as the Birmingham Six and Guildford Four, the first of which prompted the establishment of the Royal Commission on Criminal Justice, whose recommendations led to the establishment of the CCRC. One such case was that of Robert Brown, freed on appeal in 2002, after serving 25 years in prison, the longest wrongful imprisonment served by any miscarriage of justice victim. On his arrest in 1977, Brown was a 19 year old, with one conviction for stealing a pair of shoes from a shop he broke into, who was arrested for non-payment of his fine. He was questioned over the death of a woman near his home, despite eyewitness evidence of a suspect in his thirties. In the police station, he was interrogated by two police officers, Butler and Bethell. Neither took notes. Butler punched him. They took his clothes and, while he was naked, they made him do step-ups and assaulted him. After two days' humiliation and abuse, he signed a confession. He refused to plead guilty, despite the offer of a plea bargain for a guilty plea to manslaughter. Two appeals failed before the CCRC examined the case and reported to the CA that Bethell had rewritten forensic evidence that might have established Brown's innocence. Because Brown was an uncooperative prisoner, who went on hunger strikes and refused to work, he was ineligible for parole and so, like Stephen Downing, he spent many extra years in prison. (See the account by Petty).

Non-disclosure

10–087   Yet another man who was refused parole for protesting his innocence was the second longest-serving victim of wrongful imprisonment in Britain, Patrick Nicholls, freed with an apology by the CA in 1998, 23 years after being wrongfully convicted of the murder of a woman who almost certainly died of natural causes. Nicholls had found the body of the 74 year old, Gladys Heath, at the bottom of her stairs and was convicted on flawed pathology evidence. The CA found that medical and police notes that raised the possibility that no murder had taken place were not passed to counsel for the Crown or to Nicholls.

Elks usefully comments that, although it was widely predicted that there would be a flood of applications to the CCRC resulting from the disclosure regime in the CPIA 1996, described above, this did not occur. Critics of the Act feared hat prosecutors would wrongly withhold significant material, causing miscarriages of justice. This supports Corker's comment, above, on disclosure under the 1996 Act, that prosecutors did not have the time or resources to sift evidence into that required for primary and secondary disclosure so gave everything to the defence.

Elks recounts cases of non-disclosure by bodies other than the CPS which have caused miscarriages of justice. In C [2003] EWCA Crim 1246, the applicant had been convicted of raping a child but the CCRC's investigations of social services' material supported his story that it could not have been him, at the relevant time.

Note, incidentally, that Sally Clark's second and successful appeal rested on non-disclosure by a prosecution witness, her babies' pathologist, as explained below, but this was not a failure to disclose on the part of the CPS under the 1996 Act.

Expert evidence

Nicholls' case, above, is also an example of a conviction obtained **10–088** by expert evidence which was later proven to be flawed. Two pathologists, both dead by the time of his appeal, had concluded that Mrs Heath had been suffocated and beaten about the face. The CA heard new evidence from an Irish state pathologist that her facial injuries were trivial and probably caused by a fall. In prison, Nicholls taught himself law, to advise others who protested their innocence. He befriended Paddy Hill, of the Birmingham Six, who campaigned for Nicholls after his own release.

Note that when people like this are released following appeal, they are given none of the help or rehabilitation of other released prisoners. Nicholls was freed with £85 in cash and a holdall of personal possessions. He was not allowed to take with him the medication he needed as a stroke victim, nor his squeeze ball which aided recuperation. This was prison property. He was put alone in a taxi and left to catch the Isle of Wight ferry for the mainland. When Paddy Hill met him there, he was shaking, confused and blue around the lips. When Robert Brown was freed, he was given £40, a train ticket to his native Glasgow and a box of legal documents marked HMP (Her Majesty's Prisons). Both were eligible for compensation but this takes some time to secure and is not available to everyone who has been wrongfully convicted, as explained below.

Another person who was wrongly convicted of murder, on flawed expert evidence was Mark Dallagher, freed in 2004, pending a retrial ordered by the CA (not on a CCRC reference). He was convicted on erroneous earprint evidence. His trial had included evidence from a Dutch police inspector, supposedly an expert, who had examined an earprint at the crime scene and claimed it was an exact match to Dallagher's. In 2002, the CA found that this type of evidence was unreliable and ordered a retrial but in the meantime the police began an investigation and found that a DNA sample from the earprint proved that it could not have been Dallagher's.

The most famous contemporary case of a wrongful conviction **10–089** involving a litany of flawed expert evidence was that of solicitor

Sally Clark, who was convicted and given two life sentences, in 1999, for murdering her sons, who she claimed were victims of cot deaths. She lost her first appeal but her husband, Stephen, and others waged a high-publicity campaign, supported by the Law Society. An eminent professor, Sir Roy Meadow, had given evidence to her trial jury that there was a one in 73 million chance of both of her sons dying in cot deaths. At that time, he was famous for "Meadow's law", that "one cot death is a tragedy, two is suspicious and three is murder". He reiterated this to Sally Clarks's jury and to the jury at Angela Cannings' trial, below. By the time of Sally Clark's second appeal, in 2003, his theory was discredited, with other experts asserting that the chances of two cot deaths were more like one in sixty, and Sir Roy had admitted his statistics were mistaken.

The success of Sally Clark's second appeal however, rested on the discovery of misconduct by yet another expert at her trial, the pathologist of her two dead babies, Alan Williams. In 1998, he received evidence of a potentially fatal infection in the second baby, Harry's spinal fluid but had failed to disclose it. It was found by the vigilance of Sally Clark's husband, hidden in the file on the other baby. Dr Williams had initially concluded Harry had died from being shaken, then changed his mind to claim smothering. Two years earlier, a manslaughter trial (quite unconnected) had ended when Williams admitted making an error. By 2005 Dr Williams was appearing before a General Medical Council disciplinary panel, on a charge of serious professional misconduct.

As if two unreliable experts were not enough, it almost defies belief that a third decided to involve himself in falsely accusing Stephen Clark of being the real murderer. Professor David Southall, then regarded as one of the country's foremost paediatricians, made the accusation after watching a TV programme showing Stephen Clark describing the baby's illness. Without having even examined the medical files on the babies, he contacted the police and told them Stephen Clark should be investigated for murder. He said their third and remaining child should be taken into care and, given Professor Southall's eminence, the local authority seriously considered doing this. In 2004, Professor Southall was also answering charges before the General Medical Council and was found guilty of serious professional misconduct.

10–090   Following Sally Clark's successful appeal, in January 2003 [2003] EWCA Crim 1020, the evidence of Professor Sir Roy Meadow became suspicious. He had been one of the first UK experts to write about Munchausen's syndrome by proxy, wherein parents injure their children in order to draw attention to themselves. Parents have been filmed doing this but Sir Roy was too ready to offer this explanation in cases of multiple infant deaths, thus effectively reversing the burden of proof, obliging the parents to find an innocent explanation for their children's deaths.

In this context, it became predictable that the CA would overturn the conviction of Angela Cannings, on January 19, 2004 [2004] EWCA Crim 01, as she had also been convicted on his evidence, and his "Meadows' Law", of murdering her two sons, in 2002. Note that the 2004 appeal was Cannings' first appeal, not a reference from the CCRC so does not meet most definitions of "miscarriage of justice". The CA took the opportunity to lay down guidelines in such cases. Where there were two or more unexplained infant deaths in a family, no cogent evidence and serious disagreement between expert witnesses, then the parents should not be prosecuted for murder.

1. The experts had taken the wrong starting point: assuming that lightning does not strike twice and therefore assuming abuse. Experts should start with an open mind and look at each episode (each child death) separately.
2. The exclusion of currently known natural causes of infant death does not establish that the deaths resulted from deliberate infliction of harm.
3. Experts must not be over-dogmatic in their approach.
4. The court must pay sufficient regard to the progress of scientific knowledge.
5. Where there is a serious disagreement among reputable experts, then the prosecuting authorities should be slow to commence or continue a prosecution.

The CA added, in *R. v Kai-Whitewind* [2005] EWCA Crim 1092 that this did not automatically mean a prosecution should not be brought. It was for the jury to decide in a dispute between experts. There was ample evidence here to justify the guilty verdict.

Of course medical experts are used in cases of alleged child abuse, where a local authority applies to the family courts to take a child or children into care, for their own protection. Sir Roy Meadow and those who followed his theories had given evidence at hundreds of such hearings, which are held in private. The CA (Civil Division) ruled in *Re LU and Re LB (a child)* [2004] EWCA Civ that the principles laid down in *Cannings* should apply to these public law children cases but where there is a disagreement between experts, social services should bring a case to court and it was the judge's duty to resolve such a disagreement.

After *Clark*, Attorney-General Lord Goldsmith announced a **10–091** review of 258 convictions in the previous 10 years, priority being given to 50 cases where the parent was still in prison. As a result of this, 28 people had their convictions referred to the CCRC and six of these asked for their convictions to be referred back to the CA.

Care cases were also reviewed, since there were many where Professor Meadows had given evidence, after which a child was taken into local authority care. Only one care order was changed on review, however.

Also as a result of the widespread concern prompted by these cases, a group of agencies involved in sudden infant deaths established a working group, chaired by Baroness Kennedy. Its recommendations will have a wider impact than on infant deaths alone.

1. Prosecution medical experts must disclose scientific data favourable to the defence.
2. They have a duty to ensure their evidence is sound and based on peer reviewed research. Medical experts should not use the courtroom to "fly their personal kites".
3. They must ensure they are independent and doctors should not give expert evidence on their own patients.
4. Doctors should be trained in the principles applied by the courts and the difference between civil and criminal courts.
5. Care should be taken in selecting the correct expert.
6. Doctors should be willing to say "I don't know".
7. Judges have a proactive duty to ensure these high standards are followed.
8. There should be a pre-trial meeting of experts.

For further detail, see the report *Sudden Unexpected Death in Infancy: A Multi-Agency Protocol for Care and Investigation* (*www.rcpath.org*) and the article by Rowe.

10–092   Naturally, the public were scandalised by the fact that these convictions rested on the dogmatic and sometimes controversial beliefs of experts who were regarded as eminent in their field and who were later exposed as over-zealously applying their own over-generalised theories. Uncontrolled use of expert evidence had resulted in restrictions on its use in civil cases, as we have seen, in the Woolf reforms and Auld L.J., in the 2001 *Review of the Criminal Courts* had expressed concern that there was no single system of accreditation of expert witnesses and no requirement for them to have any qualifications. He thought there should be a single body with the following attributes: independence; verifiable standards of current competence; a code of conduct and disciplinary powers of removal. Keogh commented that, by 2004, the Council for the Registration of Forensic Practitioners seemed to be satisfying these needs.

New techniques

Thankfully, the Forensic Science Service usually keeps the 10–093
exhibits from old trials, usually. Retesting them with new DNA
techniques has provided exculpatory evidence in a number of cases,
such as that of Dallagher, above—not forgetting that in Hanratty's
case it confirmed his guilt, of course.

False confessions

In addition to the many old pre-PACE miscarriages of justice of 10–094
justice caused by false confession, such as Downing, above, there have
been successful appeals of post-PACE convictions, where confessions
have been obtained from unprotected vulnerable suspects. Many of
these have been demonstrated as false by Professor Gisli Gudjonsson,
the world expert in the phenomenon of false confessions (see *The
Psychology of Interrogations & Confessions: A Handbook*, 2002).

Critiques of the CCRC

When the CCRC was created, concern was expressed over the fact 10–095
that it would be using the police to investigate miscarriages of
justice, some of which will have been caused by police malpractice
but there is no evidence that this has caused a problem. Different
criticisms have been made over the years and, since the CCRC's
approach to its job has changed and developed since its creation, it
makes sense to examine the most recent analysis, which is that of
Nobles and Schiff in 2005.

The Commission reports on its work annually and the report can
be obtained from its website. The Commission's first cases were 280
transferred from the Home Office and Northern Ireland Office when
it started work in 1997 but it was rapidly swamped with over 3,000
in the next four years. Despite an expansion from extra funding in
1998 its backlog increased. Eventually it stabilised and fell by 75 per
cent by 2003 but the waiting time is currently (2005) about 27 months
for those at liberty and 15 months for those in prison. The
Commission has to consider about 900 cases a year and only refers
about 40, or four per cent, back to the CA. For the latest statistics on
caseload, cases referred and outcome from the CA, see their Annual
Report on their website. The present chairman, Graham Zellick, is
keen to publicise and open up the work of the Commission.

The most common critique of the statutory powers of the
Commission, since its creation is that it is limited to referring cases
where there is a "real possibility" the CA will find the conviction
unsafe. This seems to place the Commission in "an essentially
dependent position" (Duff, 2001) and require them to apply "a par-
asitic standard" (Nobles and Schiff, 2001, 2005). The impact of this
restriction is demonstrated in *R. v CCRC Ex p. Porter* (1999, QBD).

The applicant sought judicial review of a determination by the CCRC not to refer her case to the CA because they considered it unlikely the Court would admit fresh evidence or quash her murder conviction. She argued that the Commission had sought to usurp the CA's functions. In deciding on her case, and trying to predict whether the Court would be prepared to receive her fresh evidence, the Commission had reviewed a considerable number of CA cases.

10–096   A Divisional Court led by Lord Bingham C.J. refused her application, because applications to call fresh evidence depended on their peculiar facts and the CCRC had given detailed reasons for its view. Duff said this case showed the Commission was diverted from its principal task of investigating alleged miscarriages of justice into detailed analyses of the jurisprudence of the CA in order to try and second guess its likely determination of a case, because of its anxiety to establish a "real possibility" that they will quash the conviction. Duff, a member of the Scottish CCRC, demonstrated, through hypothetical scenarios, just how difficult it can be for the Commission to decide on a reference. He was concerned at the over-legalistic approach of the English Commission, arguing that the members cannot have been expected to assess cases like lawyers, in, for instance, assessing the admissibility of evidence, because of the requirement that some of them be laypeople. He suggested, for example, that where there is convincing *inadmissible* evidence of a miscarriage of justice, the CCRC should readily refer a case to the Home Secretary in the hope that he will apply the prerogative of mercy.

Historic cases

10–097   Given the enormous backlog, it has always concerned some of us that precious resources have been prioritised towards clearing up wrongful hangings of those long dead, such as Derek Bentley, hanged in 1952, while possible innocents wait in prison for years. In some capital cases where convictions were upheld by the CA, the Court doubted the value of the CCRC's efforts: *R. v Ellis* [2003] EWCA Crim 3556, the case involving the last woman to be hanged in Britain, in 1955 and *Knighton* [2002] EWCA Crim 2227. In its annual reports, the CCRC has defended this practice.

Relationship with the Court of Appeal

10–098   The CCRC's interaction with the CA is very usefully examined by Nobles and Schiff, in 2005. *Some* of the points they make can be summarised as below.

1. Critics such as the Miscarriages of Justice organisation consider the CCRC fails to refer sufficient numbers of cases to the

CA. The present chairman of the CCRC defends them, saying they have to take account of the CA's approach. To refer too many cases would raise expectations and cause confusion and would not serve the public interest. In a *Times* interview (see F. Gibb, 2004) he said the CA quash 70 per cent of CCRC referrals, which he considered about right:

> "we don't think there is any point sending cases doomed to failure, wasting public resources and clogging up the hugely overwhelmed CA, raising expectations that won't be met."

2. Nevertheless the task of second guessing what the CA might do with a case is made more difficult by the need for both bodies to take account of exceptional circumstances so the CCRC has to take account of the CA's power to depart from its normal restrictions, in say, admitting fresh evidence, as described above.

3. In its first three years, the CCRC's referrals were at triple the rate referred before, by the Home Office. The CCRC's caseload represents a potential threat to the workload of the CA so the CA has expressed some concerns over the approach of the CCRC.

4. Since 1983, the CA has been prepared to accept new grounds of appeal added after a case has been referred to them. This is understandable, because once an applicant gets public funding for an appeal, the defence lawyers will probably reinvestigate the case and discover new grounds of appeal but such grounds have gone way beyond those set out by the CCRC in some cases and the CA has sought some means of control. This was provided in the CJA 2003. An appellant now needs leave to appeal on grounds beyond those set out by the CCRC. Nobles and Schiff consider this will make more work for the CCRC in ensuring they do not omit any possible ground of appeal. The CA has added even more work for the CCRC by asking it to discuss cases with the original defence team, where an appeal raises issues on the conduct of the trial.

5. The CA has suggested the CCRC should not reinterview witnesses in some case. While this may seem like common sense, Nobles and Schiff are concerned that this may cause an injustice in a case where a conviction could have been shown by this to be unsafe.

6. The CA has asked the CCRC not to refer sentence cases where it would result in the appellant spending more time in prison. This happens because the Parole Board (PB) declines

315

to consider cases which may go on appeal. Nobles and Schiff consider this troubling because there is a significant legal difference between having your sentence shortened (by the CA) and being released on licence by the PB.

7. The question of how the CCRC should respond to cases where the law has changed in the applicant's favour present a major difficulty because there is no time limit to a reference so there is often a significant time gap between trial and referral. When the courts at first interpreted the HRA 1998 as retrospective, the CA were worried about being swamped. Since then, the House of Lords decisions in such cases as *R. v Lambert* [2001] UKHL 37 have ruled that the HRA is not retrospective. Nevertheless, the CA has been prepared to give the benefit of a change in the law to the appellant such as in one case where his convictions, prior to a House of Lords ruling on the point, caused him to be declared bankrupt.

8. The CA has criticised the CCRC for referring cases out of time where there has been no appeal and has used the difficulties in assessing the safety of old convictions as a reason for declining to examine the safety of a conviction. This is contradictory, argue Nobles and Schiff, because the CA has been prepared to overturn a sexual abuse conviction where the trial process could not be faulted, on the grounds that they considered the conviction to be unsafe. The CCRC's reaction was that this left them with no option but to review all similar sexual abuse cases.

9. The CCRC could play safe and only refer cases where there is genuine new evidence but it would then deprive the CA of relaxing its conservative attitude in exceptional cases.

The Royal Prerogative of Mercy

10–099   As explained above, the 1995 Act preserved this power, exercised by the Home Secretary, to release a sentenced prisoner. Jack Straw did this in 2000, where a prisoner in transit saved a life in a road accident.

Compensating Miscarriages of Justice

10–100   The two routes to compensation and the two leading authorities, both in the House of Lords in 2004, are explained in Ferguson's article and that of Robins. An application may be made to the Home Secretary, acting under his prerogative powers, for en *ex gratia* payment. His decision is final unless it is found on judicial review to be irrational or taken unfairly: *In Re McFarland* [2004] UKHL 17. The amount is fixed by an independent assessor whose decision is binding. Payments may be made in exceptional cases where an applicant has spent time in custody because of a serious default by a public authority. Angela Cannings did not qualify for compensation because her wrongful conviction was caused by a mistaken expert, not, for instance, a corrupt police officer. The expert was a privately hired independent contractor, not employed to participate in the trial as part of a public employment.

The other source is statutory. An application may be made under s.133 of the Criminal Justice Act 1988, which was enacted to comply with the UK's obligation under the International Covenant on Civil and Political Rights 1966, Art.14(6), which the UK ratified in 1976. Case law has specified that the conviction must have been quashed, without substitution of a lesser conviction. The quashing must be based on a newly discovered fact that was unknown at trial and on appeal. New or newly discovered evidence relating to an issue of fact which had been before the trial court does not count, nor does a new legal ruling on facts which were known all along. In *Mullen's* case (1999), above, the prosecution should never have been brought. *Mullen* [2004] UKHL 18 added:

1. The section only applies to a failure in the trial process (not, say an abuse of process, as occurred to Mullen).
2. Miscarriage of justice is not a term of art. People who should not have been convicted could be included in the term, whether they were guilty or not.
3. Whatever meaning the ECtHR attached to the relevant provision of the Convention, it was irrelevant to interpretation of the UK's obligations under the ICCPR. The signatory states to the IC were not bound by the view of the ECtHR.
4. Appeal courts are not required to decide whether an appellant was innocent and in practice rarely do.

Ferguson considers this to be an unsatisfactory decision—see his critique. Note the restriction to something going wrong at the trial process and consider whether most people's definitions of "miscarriage of justice" would be confined to the trial process. This leaves ineligible those who should never have been prosecuted in the first place, such as Mullen.

14. More Effects of the Convention

Use of the Convention

Defendants can use the Convention to challenge substantive law **10–101** as a defence, as an argument for a stay of proceedings as an abuse of process, to apply to quash an indictment and to found a submission of no case to answer and they can use breach of Convention rights as a ground of appeal. The issue of whether Art.6, fair trial, applied retrospectively caused a great deal of confusion in appeals until the House of Lords held in *R. v Lambert* (above) that Art.6(2) the presumption of innocence, did not apply to a conviction before the HRA 1998 Act came into force (October 2, 2000).

It was envisaged that the Convention would have the biggest impact in magistrates' courts. The LCD (now DCA) established a fast track group in 2002, to identify cases around the country which raised an important point. Justices' clerks and other legal advisers also have access to a human rights intranet. A group of defence lawyers has been formed to monitor human rights issues. It includes several lawyers' groups. The Law Officers set up an equivalent group for prosecutors.

Examples

Bugging

10–102   On electronic surveillance, telephone tapping and bugging, Art.8, guaranteeing the right to respect for private life, allows interference by the State only in limited circumstances, such as national security. The interference must be necessary and proportionate. This is why British human rights groups such as Liberty are arguing, in 2005, that such techniques could be used to gather evidence from those suspected of plotting terrorist offences, to bring them to criminal trial in court, rather than using the draconian power granted to the Home Secretary to place the suspects under house arrest, under the highly controversial Prevention of Terrorism Act 2005. This is discussed in Chapter 4 on human rights, above, and, as I pointed out in that chapter, all other European countries have chosen to use surveillance evidence to deal with terrorists in a proper trial. We are the only people to use house arrest.

Delay

10–103   In *Howarth v UK* (2000), the ECtHR found there had been a breach of the "reasonable time" requirement of Art.6(1), when proceedings lasted four years from arrest to sentencing appeal. This does not apply to delay between the commission of the crime and the prosecution, as can be seen from the multitude of child abuse cases since 1990, whose facts occurred in the 1970s or before. Also, rape trials are sometimes brought nowadays on events in the 1970s or earlier where new DNA techniques can be used on old evidential exhibits. In *Attorney General's Ref (No.2 of 2001)* [2003] UKHL 68, the House of Lords held that time started to run from when the defendant was charged or summonsed.

Lawyer client communications

On lawyer-client communications, the ECtHR has held that the 10–104 right to communicate in confidence is a basic right of Art.6(3)(c). This means police stations must allow detainees to speak to their lawyers in private over the telephone. In *Brennan v UK* (2001, ECtHR) the Court found a violation of Art.6 when a police officer was present during the applicant's first consultation with his solicitor after arrest.

Our courts must consider how this affects seating arrangements in the courtroom and waiting areas in the court building. When you next visit a trial, especially in the Crown Court with a secure glass dock, observe how difficult it is for the accused to communicate with his lawyers or even attract their attention from his position at the back of the courtroom.

Legal representation

Article 6 requires legal representation where it is necessary in the 10–105 interests of justice. The ECtHR looks at the articulacy of the defendant and the complexity of defending themselves: see Chapter 1 on human rights, above, (the story of the McLibel case) and Chapter 17 on legal services, below. The right to a fair trial is breached in advance of trial if the accused is detained without access to a lawyer for a long period. Here the accused was detained for over 24 hours before being given access to a lawyer: *Magee v UK* (2000, ECtHR). The Convention principle of equality of arms did not mean that if the Crown instructed a QC in a criminal trial a defendant who was being defended at public expense should also be entitled to be defended by leading counsel: *R. v Lea* [2002] EWCA Crim 215.

Trial in the absence of the accused

Where the accused had absconded, the trial judge had the discre- 10–106 tion to commence his trial for robbery. There was no breach of Art.6: *R. v Jones* [2002] UKHL 5.

Public Hearing

A hearing should be in public, unless there are pressing reasons 10–107 to the contrary: *Riepan v Austria* (2000). Judgment is to be pronounced publicly and this right is unqualified. This means judgment has to be read in open court and publicly available: *Preto v Italy* (1983, ECtHR).

Handcuffs

English judges are now extremely reluctant to accede to prosecu- 10–108 tion requests for the defendant to be handcuffed: Art.3 (Prohibition of Torture: inhuman or degrading treatment).

Victims' rights

10–109   The Convention offers no specific rights. The Commission has held that it is not appropriate to recognise any role for a victim's family in sentencing a murderer, as they are not "impartial".

Witness Protection

10–110   The Youth Justice and Criminal Evidence Act 1999 was successfully challenged in the CA within days of its coming into force. Section 41, which restricted the right of a rape defendant to question the sexual history of his alleged victim was found to be in breach of Art.6. On appeal to the House of Lords, their Lordships held that it was for the trial judge in each case to decide whether the proposed evidence and questioning were relevant and necessary for fairness: see lengthy analysis of this case, *R. v A* [2001] UKHL 25 in Chapter 4, above. Incidentally, the same Act bans unrepresented defendants in rape cases from questioning victims. This has not been challenged.

Written statements

10–111   In *Arnold* [2004] EWCA 1293, the CA held that very great care must be taken in each case to comply with the letter and spirit of Art.6.

Jury deliberations

10–112   In *Gregory v UK* (1997) the ECtHR held that the secrecy of jury deliberations did not render a trial unfair under Art.6. In this case, the jury had handed a note to the judge alleging that "racial overtones" had been shown by one of their members. The judge consulted both counsel and redirected the jury. The Court held that, in the absence of proof of actual or subjective bias, they had to consider the actions of the experienced trial judge who had observed the jury. The redirection had been sufficiently forceful, detailed and carefully worded to ensure the impartiality of the jury and dispel objective doubts.

Costs

10–113   The refusal to order costs to a successful defendant violates the presumption of innocence in Art.6(2).

Sentencing

10–114   The Convention has had a significant impact on sentencing, some of which is discussed in Chapter 4 on human rights, above. Controversy arose in 2001, when the Parole Board released on licence the killers of toddler Jamie Bulger. This followed their application to the ECtHR under Art.6 (*T and V v UK* (1999)). Their trial judge, in 1993, fixed their sentence tariff at eight years, which was subsequently increased by the Home Secretary, Michael Howard to fifteen, because of "public concern". This was quashed in the High Court on judicial review but the now defunct European Commission on Human Rights said the Home Secretary was not an "impartial" sentencer so this role was switched to the Lord Chief Justice, who fixed the tariff at eight years. For further discussion of the problem of lack of separation of powers in sentencing tariffs and review, see Chapter 4, above.

Reasons

Because of the duty to give reasons, magistrates, whose courts are **10–115** not courts of record, started to give reasons for all their decisions before the HRA 1998 came into force. They also recognised that these must specifically explain their decision. Tick-box reasons will not suffice. The High Court said that, in giving reasons for a conviction, all magistrates needed to do to satisfy the HRA and Art.6 was to inform the defendant why and that could usually be done in a few simple sentences: *McGovern v Brent* (2001, HC). Also, the QBD held in *Moran v DPP* [2002] EWHC 89, that magistrates did not need to give reasons for rejecting a submission of no case to answer.

R. v Denton (2000, CA) held that a Crown Court judge should have given reasons. That had been a rule of English law for many years and was simply given added emphasis by Art.6.

15. Reform of Criminal Procedure

The Royal Commission on Criminal Procedure 1981

A Royal Commission on Criminal Procedure reported in 1981 and **10–116** many of its recommendations have been enacted. The Prosecution of Offences Act 1985 instituted the Crown Prosecution Service in place of prosecution by the police and the Police and Criminal Evidence Act 1984 (PACE) introduced a comprehensive code of police powers and practices in the investigation of crime and amended the rules of evidence in criminal proceedings in certain respects.

Royal Commission on Criminal Justice 1993

This was established in 1991, in response to public anxiety over a **10–117** well-publicised series of miscarriages of justice, overturned by the CA, including the cases of "The Guildford Four", "The Birmingham Six", the Maguires and others. Its terms of reference were to examine the effectiveness of the criminal justice system in securing the conviction of the guilty and the acquittal of the innocent and to examine in particular:

1. the supervision by senior officers of police investigations;
2. the role of the prosecutor in supervising the gathering of evidence and arrangements for its disclosure to the defence;

3. the role of experts and the forensic science services;
4. access to experts and legal services by the defence;
5. the accused's opportunities to state his case;
6. the powers of the courts in directing proceedings, including the possibility of their having an investigative role during and pre-trial; uncorroborated confession evidence;
7. the role of the CA;
8. arrangements for investigating miscarriages of justice when appeal rights have been exhausted.

The Commission decided against importing inquisitorial elements from foreign systems. They commissioned a great deal of research into the workings of the English and foreign criminal processes and examined many aspects of our system, from the point of police investigations, to the post appeal process. They made 352 recommendations, too many to summarise here, although most of the recommendations relevant to this book are discussed above. Critics pointed out that, ironically, most of its recommendations would strengthen prosecution powers. Many recommendations have already provoked legislation, although not always in line with the Commission's wishes. Examples of this are certain sections of the Criminal Justice and Public Order Act 1994, the Criminal Appeal Act 1995 and the Criminal Procedure and Investigations Act 1996. Changes in practice have also followed, such as those required by the practice directions on plea and directions hearings. All of these are discussed above.

The Human Rights Act 1998
10–118   This has had the biggest impact of any recent reform of criminal procedure as should be obvious from this chapter and the Chapter 4 on human rights, above.

Modernising the Crown Court
10–119   The Court Service, the independent agency which administers the Crown Court, now replaced by Her Majesty's Courts Service, produced a consultation paper in 1999, *Transforming the Crown Court*, with proposals to streamline Crown Court business and hearings. One of the stated aims was to carry out 100 per cent of court service functions electronically, where possible, by 2008. It promised that the courtroom will be revolutionised by IT to support the oral presentation of evidence on screen and by video links and by the electronic recording of proceedings. As an effort to enhance "customer service", information and services would be increasingly available online and via call centres 24 hours a day and technology would be used to reduce the stress of court appearances for defendants and

witnesses. The new central summoning system for jurors is part of these reforms (see Chapter 16 on the jury, below). The reforms aimed to reduce the unit cost of a Crown Court case and reduce the time taken from transfer to the Crown Court to disposal, by improving case management. As explained in Chapter 7 on the criminal courts, above, new IT systems were piloted at the Crown Court at Kingston from 2001 to 2005 and by 2005 have been installed in most Crown Court centres. The progress of this planned modernisation is reported annually in the Court Service annual report, on their website. It is also discussed in Chapter 7, above.

Some fraud trials are now being conducted as paperless trials, with all documentation scanned in and displayed electronically. The most famous example was the Maxwell trial, which took place in the special fraud trial suite of the Old Bailey in Chichester Rents, Chancery Lane.

The *Review of the Criminal Courts* and *Criminal Justice: The Way Ahead*

As described in the chapter on criminal courts, Lord Justice **10–120** Auld was given the task in 2000–2001, of reviewing the structure and procedures of the criminal courts. His 2001 report appears on the *Review* website: *www.criminal-courts-review.org.uk*. There are also responses and a summary on the website. Another summary of the main points and commentary appears on the website accompanying this book (see note on Online Updates at the front of this book).

Justice for All 2002

This white paper was the Government's response to the Auld **10–121** Report and the Halliday Report on sentencing. The Government published a companion document, noting where it agreed with or departed from these reports' recommendations. Most importantly, the Government had finally abandoned its controversial plans to abolish the right to elect trial by jury and rejected Lord Justice Auld's "middle tier" of criminal courts. The white paper explains the mischief of the Courts Act 2003, the CJA 2003 and other related statutes. Its contents are too long to list here but as most of them have been put into practice or law their results are discussed in this chapter. See the Executive Summary. The paper is downloadable from *www.cjsonline.org.uk*. Here are some more of its proposals, covering evidence and procedure and, as can be seen above, almost all of them have been achieved. My comments are bracketed:

- co-locating police and CPS in criminal justice units (CJA 2003);

- allowing the CPS to determine charges (CJA 2003);
- investing in IT (Lord Chief Justice Woolf had publicly demanded this, in June 2002—see report on progress in Chapter 7, above);
- giving sentence indications to encourage early pleas (implemented by 2005, as described above);
- increasing magistrates' sentencing powers to 12 months (enacted but not yet in force—see above);
- allowing police to impose pre-charge bail conditions (CJA 2003—see street bail, above);
- extending the prosecution's right of appeal against bail;
- piloting a presumption against bail for some class A drug offenders (CJA 2003);
- increasing incentives to comply with disclosure rules (CJA 2003, discussed above);
- allowing more hearsay evidence (see under witnesses above);
- allowing for trial by judge alone in serious and complex trials or where there is a risk of jury intimidation (CJA 2003—see judge-only trials, above);
- extending the use of preparatory hearings (CJA 2003);
- allowing previous misconduct evidence in some cases (CJA 2003);
- removing double jeopardy for serious cases if compelling new evidence arises (CJA 2003);
- giving witnesses greater access to their original statements at trial;
- giving the prosecution a right to appeal against judicial acquittals (CJA 2003);
- increasing jury eligibility (done—see Chapter 16 on the jury, below);
- introducing a Sentencing Guidelines Council to enhance uniformity (done, see above);

When Lord Falconer introduced the paper to the press, he explained that the Government's aim was to tilt the scales of justice towards the victim. Naturally, lawyers have been provoked by the overt crime control tenor of the paper: "Far too many offenders escape justice, creating a `justice gap' between the numbers of crimes recorded by he police and the number where an offender is brought to justice". Comments include the newspapers at the time and M. Zander, "What to make of Mr Blunkett's package of reforms?" (2002) 152 N.L.J. 1141. Interestingly, Lord Falconer soon admitted that, because of lack of money, the plans could not be implemented immediately but were "a blueprint for the next five to ten years".

BIBLIOGRAPHY

The Criminal Law Review (Crim. L.R.) is on *Westlaw* and the *New Law*   **10–122**
Journal (N.L.J. is on *Lexis*).

A. J. Ashworth, comments on *Rowe and Davis v UK* and *Jasper v UK*;
Fitt v UK [2000] Crim. L.R. 584.

A. J. Ashworth, comment on *R. v Davis, Johnson and Rowe* [2000]
Crim. L.R. 1012.

A. J. Ashworth, comment on *SC v UK* [2004] Crim. L.R. 130.

Condron v UK [2000] Crim. L.R. 679 and *Averill v UK* [2000] Crim.
L.R. 682 and Ashworth's comments thereon.

J. Baldwin, "Understanding Judge Ordered and Judge Directed
Acquittals" [1997] Crim. L.R. 536.

C. Ball, K. McCormac & N. Stone, *Young Offenders: Law Policy and
Practice* (2nd ed., 2001).

M. Berlins, "Do We Need Two Appeal Courts" 1 *Poly Law Review* 1.

D. Birch, "Suffering in Silence: A Cost–Benefit Analysis of s.34 of the
Criminal Justice and Public Order Act 1994" [1999] Crim. L.R. 769.

B. Block, etc., "Ordered and Directed Acquittals in the Crown Court:
A Time of Change" [1993] Crim.L. R. 971.

M. Burton, "Reviewing Crown Prosecution Service decisions not to
prosecute" [2001] Crim. L.R. 374.

The Code for Crown Prosecutors: www.cps.org.uk

D. Corker, "A step too far", on the 2004 Home Office white paper,
One Step Ahead and SOCA, (2004) 154 N.L.J. 896.

Criminal Justice: The Way Ahead (2001). See DCA website: *www.dca.
gov.uk*

P. Darbyshire, "The Mischief of Plea Bargaining and Sentencing
Rewards" [2000] Crim. L.R. 895.

P. Duff, "Criminal Cases Review Commissions and Deference to the
Courts: The Evaluation of the Evidence and Evidentiary Rules"
[2001] Crim. L.R. 341, examining the arguments of Nobles and
Schiff at (1995) 58 M.L.R. 299.

L. Elks, "The Criminal Cases Review Commission—Lessons from   **10–125**
Experience" *Archbold News*, March 8, 2004, issue 2.

B. Emmerson and A. Ashworth, *Human Rights and Criminal
Proceedings* (1999).

P. Ferguson, "Compensating miscarriages of justice" (2004) 154
N.L.J. 842.

F. Gibb, "Justice's quality controller" on the CCRC, *The Times*,
November 23, 2004.

F. Gibb, "Macdonald's mission to supercharge the CPS", *The Times*,
July 13, 2004.

Herbert's research on the increase in magistrates' sentencing
powers: see synopsis by Zander at (2003) 153 N.L.J. 689 and full

report by A. Herbert, "Mode of Trial and Magistrates' Sentencing Powers" [2003] Crim. L.R. 314.

Home Office, *Review of Delay in the Criminal Justice System*, 1997 (The Narey Report) See Home Office website: *www.homeoffice.gov.uk*.

A. James, N. Taylor and C. Walker, "The Criminal Cases Review Commission: Economy, Effectiveness and Justice" [2000] Crim. L.R. 140.

A. Jennings, A. Ashworth and B. Emmerson, "Silence and Safety: The Impact of Human Rights Law" [2000] Crim. L.R. 879.

JUSTICE, *Miscarriages of Justice* (1989).

A. Keogh, "Experts in the dock" (2004) 154 N.L.J. 1762.

K. Macdonald QC, "The new *Code for Crown Prosecutors*", (2005) 155 N.L.J. 12. (Ken Macdonald is the DPP).

M. McConville and L. Bridges (eds), *Criminal Justice in Crisis* (1994): the fullest and best collection of critiques of the Royal Commission on Criminal Justice.

R. Nobles and D. Schiff, "The Criminal Cases Review Commission: Reporting Success?" (2001) 64 M.L.R. 280.

R. Nobles and D. Schiff, "The Right to Appeal and Workable Systems of Justice" (2002) 65 M.L.R. 676.

R. Nobles and D. Schiff, "The Criminal Cases Review Commission: Establishing a Workable Relationship with the Court of Appeal" [2005] Crim. L.R. 173.

N. Padfield, "Plea Before Venue" (1997) 147 N.L.J. 1369.

R. Pattenden, "Prosecution Appeals Against Judges' Rulings" [2000] Crim. L.R. 971, discussing Law Commission Consultation Paper No.158 (2000).

P. Plowden, "Make do and mend or a cultural revolution" (2005) 155 N.L.J. 328 and "Case management and the Criminal Procedure Rules (2005) 155 N.L.J. 416.

P. Plowden and K. Kerrigan, (2001) 151 N.L.J. 735, on disclosure.

R. v Criminal Cases Review Commission Ex p. Pearson [1999] Crim. L.R. 732, including comment by Sir John Smith.

J. Robins, "Cannings case shows need for a fair system of redress", *The Times*, January 25, 2005.

J. Rowe, "Expert Evidence and sudden infant deaths: where next?" (2004) 154 N.L.J. 1757.

The Royal Commission on Criminal Justice Report, Cm. 2263 (1993).

Lord Shawcross's statement is taken from *Hansard* and quoted in the Code for Crown Prosecutors.

S. Shute, "Who Passes Unduly Lenient Sentences?" [1999] Crim. L.R. 603.

J. C. Smith, "The Criminal Appeal Act 1995: (1) Appeals Against Conviction" [1995] Crim. L.R. 920. Also, comment on *Rajcoomar* [1999] Crim. L.R. 728. and see his comments on *Chalkley* (1999) and *Mullen* (1999).

J. R. Spencer, "The Case for a Code of Criminal Procedure" [2000] Crim. L.R. 519, which also gives a great potted history of trial procedure and references to excellent historical sources.

S. Tendler, "FBI-style gangbusters will stop criminals living off hidden loot" (on SOCA, the Serious and Organized Crime Agency) *The Times*, November 25, 2004.

D. A. Thomas, comment on *R. (on the application of H, A and O) v Southampton Youth Court* [2005] Crim. L.R. 398.

N. Walker, "What does fairness mean in a criminal trial?" (2001) 151 N.L.J. 1240.

M. Zander, "Silence in Northern Ireland" (2001) 151 N.L.J. 138, on Jackson's research.

FURTHER READING AND SOURCES FOR UPDATING THIS CHAPTER

Online updates to this book: *http://www.sweetandmaxwell.co.uk/* **10–123** *academic/updates/darbyshire/index.html*

Archbold, published by Sweet and Maxwell, annually. This is probably the most comprehensive practitioner's manual on criminal procedure. See also *Archbold's Magistrates' Courts Criminal Practice*, annually.

Archbold News.

Criminal Cases Review Commission: *www.ccrc.gov.uk*

Lord Justice Auld, *Review of the Criminal Courts of England and Wales* (2001): *www.criminal-courts-review.org.uk*

Criminal Justice System website (see annual reports): *www. criminal-justice-system.gov.uk*

Criminal Law Review in hard copy and on *Westlaw*.

Crown Prosecution Service, information 020 7796 8442, website: *www.cps.gov.uk*

Judicial Studies Board website, includes all specimen directions to juries: *www.jsboard.co.uk*

New Law Journal in hard copy and on *Lexis*.

Times law reports.

FURTHER MATERIAL ON MISCARRIAGES OF JUSTICE

On individuals:
(1994) 144 N.L.J. 634; (1996) 146 N.L.J. 1552; (1999) 149 N.L.J. 1017; **10–124** (1998) 148 N.L.J. 667; (1998) 148 N.L.J. 1028; Woffinden, *The Times*, June 2, 1998; D. Jessel, *The Guardian*, November 19, 1996.

On Derek Bentley: D. Pannick, *The Times*, February 11, 1997.

On the Birmingham Six: *Counsel*, April 1991, p.8; (1990) 140 N.L.J. 160; L. Blom-Cooper, *The Birmingham Six and Other Cases* (1997, resulting in libel actions by the Birmingham Six).

The Bridgewater Three: *The Times*, February 22, 1997 and other newspapers; *R. v Home Secretary Ex p. Hickey* (1997).

On Robert Brown: M. Petty, "They Took my Life . . . Now I Long for Peace", *The Times*, July 22, 2004.

On Angela Cannings' conviction: J. Bale, "Mother who killed sons jailed for life", *The Times*, April 17, 2002 and other newspapers on that date.

On Sally Clark, newspaper reports of January 30, 2003, J. Batt, *Stolen Innocence: The Sally Clark Story—A Mother's Fight for Justice* (2004).

On Mark Dallagher, "Court frees man jailed for murder by 'earprint'", *The Times*, January 23, 2004.

On Stephen Downing, (2000) 164 *Justice of the Peace* 909 and newspaper reports in 2000.

Guildford Four: *Legal Action*, December 1989, p. 7; (1989) 139 N.L.J. 1441; (1989) 139 N.L.J. 1449.

On Hanratty: Law Report, as above; *HANRATTY—The Whole Truth* Channel 4, May 2, 2002; newspaper reports of week beginning April 15, 2002.

The Maguires: *The Times*, July 17, 1990 and other press coverage.

Stephan Kisko: *The Times*, February 18, 1992.

On Patrick Nicholls: D. Kennedy, "Court clears man of murder after 23 years in jail", *The Times*, June 13, 1998.

The Winchester Three: (1990) 140 N.L.J. 164.

On miscarriages of justice generally:

The best contemporary source is the Criminal Cases Review Commission: *www.ccrc.gov.uk*

INNOCENT: *www.innocent.org.uk*

R. Buxton, "Miscarriages of Justice and the Court of Appeal" (1993) 109 L.Q.R. 66.

J. J. Eddleston, *Blind Justice* (2000) (written by an excellent story teller, with pictures).

B. Forst, *Errors of Justice* (2004).

D. Jessel, *Trial and Error* (1994).

JUSTICE, *Miscarriages of Justice*, (1989); *Remedying Miscarriages of Justice*.

R. Kee, *Trial and Error: The Maguires, the Guildford Pub Bombings and British Justice* (1989).

J. Kirkby, *Miscarriages of Justice—Our Lamentable Failure?* (1991, Child and Co. lecture, Inns of Court School of Law).

R. Nobles and D. Schiff, *Understanding Miscarriages of Justice* (2001).

B. Woffinden, *Miscarriages of Justice* (1989).

Dates of books are not given. Ensure you read the latest edition. Check on *www.amazon.co.uk*

11. The Adversarial Process

A contrast used to be drawn between the English legal system as **11–001** "adversarial" and continental European systems, mostly daughters of the French legal system as "inquisitorial". As we shall see, that comparison is far too crude and is now inaccurate. Nevertheless, our type of procedure is accurately described as adversarial. Many historians and sociologists attribute the rise of the adversarial procedure to the rise of lawyers, in the eighteenth century. The adversarial model of procedure, in its purest form incorporates the following elements.

1. The Judge as Unbiased Umpire

It used to be said that the essence of the role of the English judge, **11–002** or magistrate, is that she acts as an unbiased umpire whose job it is to listen to evidence presented by both sides, without interfering in the trial process. This was often contrasted with the role of the *juge d'instruction*, the French first instance judge who performs an inquisitorial role in some trials, directing criminal investigations, cross-examining the defendant and compiling a dossier of evidence for the trial court. There is no comparable English equivalent. The court takes a much greater role in compiling the evidence and is involved at an earlier stage in the process. Similarly, the role of the German judge is to take an active part in the assembling of evidence and the questioning of witnesses, before and at trial. This is a rather crude comparison, not least because the European Convention on Human Rights provides that a fair trial must be adversarial and continental European jurisdictions have embraced the Convention in their law much longer than the UK. It used to be said that the English judge's role, in the civil and criminal trial, as a non-interfering umpire, is a reflection of the English sense of fair play: each side has an equal opportunity to win the litigation "game" by convincing the judge of the merits of their argument, collecting good evidence and citing favourable case authorities. The judge does not interfere in the presentation of evidence by examining and cross-examining witnesses. This is left to the parties or their advocates. The role of the judge was set down clearly by Lord Denning M.R. in *Jones v National Coal Board* (1957, CA) and can be summarised thus. He should:

1. listen to all the evidence, only interfering to clarify neglected or obscure points;
2. see that advocates behave and stick to the rules;
3. exclude irrelevancies and discourage repetition;
4. make sure he understands the advocates' points;
5. at the end, make up his mind where the truth lies.

If the judge interferes unduly in the advocates' speeches or adduction of evidence, it may constitute a ground of appeal. For a statement on the judicial role in criminal cases, see *R. v Tuegal* (2000, CA).

The Parties Control the Evidence

11–003   Prior to the 1990s the parties brought whatever evidence they saw fit to prove their case. The court would seldom limit it. Similarly, the parties would decide which and how many witnesses to call. The parties were able to "keep their cards close to their chest" pre-trial, which was sometimes likened to "trial by ambush". This, plus the complexity of English procedural rules, plus the rigid adduction of evidence by examination and cross-examination, meant that unrepresented parties were at a disadvantage and it was often the case that the best lawyer won. All of this is explained in graphic detail by Mr Justice Lightman, in the 2003 lecture cited in Chapter 9 on civil procedure, above.

The Best Case Wins

11–004   It is the court's job to determine the relative strength of the parties' cases, not to determine where the truth lies. Having said that, the Court of Appeal (CA) has sometimes said in recent cases that its job is to do justice, as can be seen in Chapter 10 on criminal procedure, above.

The Principle of Orality

11–005   Most cases were argued by word of mouth, from start to finish. This was a relic of jury trial but was elevated to the level of principle.

2. Criticism of the Adversarial System

11–006   Mr Justice Lightman's 2003 criticisms of the adversarial nature of English civil procedure are typical:

1. Success turns very much on the performance on the day. If a party or witness underperforms or counsel lets him down, there is no chance of a replay.
2. Performance at trial turns on investment in the litigation "money talks loud and clear." Cases are won or lost by the quality of representation.
3. The limitation on the role of the judge means his search for truth is confined to the evidence placed before him by the parties.
4. The adversarial system is expensive and time-consuming. He attacked the silk system—the high fees paid to QCs, as can be seen from the quotations in Chapter 13 on the legal profession, below.
5. The deficiencies of the adversary system are aggravated by the case law system: "judges are increasingly . . . bombarded . . . with torrents of authorities. The judges make too little efforts to keep their judgments as brief as the reasoning requires."

Added to this, is the problem that it is left to the parties to select witnesses. This means that there may be a witness who could give damming evidence against both sides so the court does not get to know of their existence. The courts very rarely use their power to call witnesses.

The plight of the unrepresented in criminal cases has been well documented in socio-legal research (Dell (1971); Carlen (1976); Darbyshire (1984)). Lay people find it very difficult to present their "story" to the court by means of examining witnesses. To add to this problem, they are often very nervous and in unfamiliar surroundings. Where a defendant is unrepresented, mostly in the magistrates' courts, he is wholly dependent on the goodwill and expertise of the bench or, more realistically, the clerk, to help him put his case and examine witnesses and explain what is being asked of him, for example, choice of venue in a triable-either-way offence. Some clerks are much more prepared and skilled to help than others. The same problem occurs in a civil case where one or both sides is a litigant in person. The increasing numbers of litigants in person have crated difficulties for judges, in our adversarial process, as explained in Chapter 9, above.

3. Erosion of the Adversarial Process

The last quarter of the twentieth century saw an erosion of this archetype at work in the English legal system: **11–007**

- During 1991–1993, The Royal Commission on Criminal Justice considered whether the court should have an investigative role before and during the criminal trial. They did not recommend this but that:

  "Wherever practicable in complex cases judges should take on responsibility for managing the progress of a case, securing its passage through the various stages of pre-trial discussion to preparatory hearing and trial and making sure that the parties have fulfilled their obligations both to each other and to the court."

  Recommendation 254 and the 1995 Practice Direction on Plea and Directions Hearings in the Crown Court, described above, goes some way towards this aim. As explained Chapter 10, above, from 2005, judges' trial management powers in criminal cases have been emphasised and enhanced.
- The Heilbron–Hodge Committee (1993) and Lord Woolf (1996) recommended an interventionist role for the civil trial judge and active case management is now the hallmark of civil procedure, with the judge controlling the speed and length of the civil case, limiting the evidence presented. For an excellent and entertaining analysis of the implications of this change in the judicial role see Lightman J. at (1999) 149 N.L.J. 1819.
- The interim report of the Civil Justice Review (1986) prompted the courts to require, by Practice Directions, that the parties exchanged witness statements, forcing them to lay some of their cards on the table. Openness was massively enhanced by the requirement for skeleton arguments and document bundles to be exchanged pre-trial and presented to the court.
- Skeleton arguments, bundles and use of witness statements have made a massive shift from oral case argument to arguments on paper with the judges and opposition reading pre-trial. No longer can a student observe court proceedings and expect to be entertained to a full story being told to the court. Oral argument has been limited in the US since 1849 but until the 1990s, advocates in England and Wales dictated the length of trials by simply giving an estimate to the court. The CA first introduced a requirement for skeleton arguments in 1989. See the comparative account of Leggatt L.J.
- In civil cases, since the 1998 Rules have been in force, parties frequently share a single expert. Nevertheless, a judge (and jury) will still frequently find themselves having to decide

between two experts in a criminal case (for example on psychiatric or forensic evidence).
- Jolowicz considers that most judges want to do substantive justice in the case (get to the truth), not just procedural justice and that the Woolf reforms will help them to realise that objective, which is to be welcomed ((1996) C.J.Q. 198).
- Small claims in the county court have always been an exception to the adversarial stereotype. Research by Applebey (1978) showed some registrars (now called district judges) employed an inquisitorial technique. Many of those who appear are unrepresented and, therefore, the progress of the case depends on the district judge being somewhat interventionist. This was explored and confirmed by Baldwin's research, cited in Chapter 9, above. The Civil Justice Review (1998) recommended that registrars (now district judges, since 1990) adopt a more standardised inquisitorial role in small claims.

BIBLIOGRAPHY AND FURTHER READING

J. H. Langbein, *The Origins of the Adversary Criminal Trial*, 2003.   **11–008**

Leggatt L.J., "The Future of the Oral Tradition in the Court of Appeal" [1995] C.J.Q. 1.

Sir Gavin Lightman's 2003 lecture at Sheffield University is reproduced as The Hon. Mr Justice Lightman, "The Civil Justice System and Legal Profession—The Challenges Ahead" (2003) 22 C.J.Q. 235, also available on *Westlaw*.

12. Alternatives to the Civil Courts: Institutions and Procedures

"Having spent years in court reading the papers for cases only to be told at the last minute that the parties have come to terms, I am persuaded that alternative dispute resolution is something that people ought to try first." (Lord Browne-Wilkinson, ex-Law Lord turned mediator, quoted in *The Times*, March 16, 2005.)

This chapter deals with alternative hearings for civil disputes, outside the court system. There is a big difference between the two sets of alternatives, however. With tribunal systems, Parliament has decided that certain disputes will not go to court but to an alternative forum. The litigant has no choice. With arbitration and Alternative Dispute Resolution (ADR), on the other hand, it is generally the litigants who have chosen to use a private alternative.

12–001

1. Tribunals

The Special Commissioners of Income Tax celebrate their 200th birthday in 2005. Income tax, intended as a temporary measure, was introduced by Pitt the Younger to raise funds to fight the Napoleonic wars. (Source: *Counsel*, February 2005.)

12–002

Function

Outside the court system, 130 bodies and sets of tribunals adjudicate on specialist civil disputes. They have a much greater caseload than the civil courts. The largest hears over 300,000 cases a year. Lord Chancellor Irvine said, in a 2000 speech they have "a colossal impact on the lives of well over 470,000 people every year." They are

12–003

sometimes referred to as "administrative tribunals", because many of them hear appeals by the citizen against an administrative decision, or, like the Civil Aviation Authority, they take the initial decision.

As the State grew throughout the twentieth century it created statutory schemes of administration to confer benefits or regulate people's activities in more and more ways. The same statutes created individual systems of tribunals to adjudicate in disputes arising out of those schemes, between citizen and State. Tribunal systems exist to deal with agriculture, (*e.g.* Agricultural Lands Tribunal), regulating competition and financial services, (*e.g.* The Competition Appeal Tribunal, The Financial Services and Markets Tribunal), education, (*e.g.* Admission Appeal Panels, Special Educational Needs and Disability Tribunal), employment, (*e.g.* Employment Tribunals), land, (*e.g.* Lands Tribunal), social security and pensions, (*e.g.* The Appeals Service, Pensions Appeal Tribunals), health, (*e.g.* Mental Health Review Tribunals, The Care Standards Tribunal) and taxation, (*e.g.* General Commissioners of Income Tax) and many other matters.

Some of them deal with disputes between private citizens. Employment Tribunals hear employees' claims against employers, relating to unfair dismissal, redundancy and discrimination and Rent Assessment Panels hear landlord-tenant disputes. These are more like court-substitutes and there is no logical reason why the county court should not have been given this jurisdiction.

Characteristics

12–004 *Creation*

All tribunals are creatures of statute. They were decided by the Franks Committee (1957) to be "machinery for adjudication", in other words, court-like bodies, not part of the administrative set-up. The Franks Report said they should be run according to the principles of "openness, fairness and impartiality". Some appellate bodies are superior courts of record: the Employment Appeal Tribunal, the Asylum and Immigration Tribunal and the controversial Special Immigration Appeals Commission, the court that hears appeals from terrorist suspects facing deportation from the UK.

12–005 *Composition varies*

Some are composed of a lawyer alone and some have a lawyer chair (now renamed "tribunal judge") and two laypeople. Characteristics can change as has recently been the case with those dealing with immigration and asylum and social security. Where laypeople are used, they normally represent certain interests, such as employers at large, and employees, in the employment tribunals; or they provide expertise, such as tribunals which include doctors, psychiatrists (Mental Health Review Tribunals) or accountants. Appointments are often made by the relevant department but the Lord Chancellor appoints the legally qualified chairmen of over 14 tribunals and the lay members of some. All this is about to change, as can be seen below. The tribunal committee of the Judicial Studies Board provides training.

Procedure

Some have procedural rules. The Council on Tribunals, below, publishes a model. Others have none. The Employment Tribunals, in 2001, imported the overriding objective of the Civil Procedure Rules into their new rules. Again, this is about to change as tribunals will eventually be placed under a unified set of rules. Case loads vary enormously. Whereas the Appeal Tribunals under the Social Security Act 1998 hear over 100,000 cases a year, the Sea Fish Licence Tribunal and the Antarctic Act Tribunal usually hear none.   12–006

Organisation

Originally, they were all administered separately. Tribunals concerned with tax, state benefits and health problems were organised on a national basis but those which hardly ever sit tend to be central. Some tribunals have never been constituted. For instance, no Mines and Quarries Tribunal has ever been convened, since provision was made for it in 1954. In some cases, the relevant government department is responsible for administration. The Department for Constitutional Affairs (DCA) has responsibility for several. Again, this will change with centralised administration, described below.   12–007

Appeal

From most tribunals, there is no appeal on fact, except from those with an appellate level. For instance, appeal lies from employment tribunals to the Employment Appeal Tribunal, a superior court of record. The Court of Appeal (CA) held, in *P v SS of the Home Dept* [2004] EWCA Civ 1640 that an appellate tribunal should not determine the facts afresh. They should accept the facts found by the lower tribunal unless it was shown that the evidence did not support the findings made, or the findings were clearly wrong.   12–008

Appeal on a point of law lies to the High Court or CA from the decisions of some tribunals under various statutes. If a tribunal acts outside its powers (*ultra vires*) procedurally or by taking an unreasonable decision, an aggrieved party can apply for judicial review, described in Chapter 9 on civil procedure, above.

The Council on Tribunals

This supervisory body was created in 1958, on the recommendation of the Franks Committee. It consists of 10 to 15 part-time lay   12–009 members and has to report annually to Parliament on the operation of tribunals and inquiries. If the Council wishes, it can submit a special report to Parliament at any time. It investigates complaints from members of the public, instigates its own examination of the way in which the system is working and assists the central government departments which are responsible for the membership of tribunals and for the procedural rules under which tribunals and inquiries are held.

Advantages and Disadvantages

12–010   The early tribunal systems were established by Labour and Liberal governments to keep disputes out of the courts and the grasp of Conservative or conservative judges who they distrusted. Now, however, both Labour and Conservative governments have continued creating new tribunals with increasing frequency, in the second half of the twentieth century and in this century. An example is the Gender Recognition Panel, created by the Gender Recognition Act 2004.

Professor Wade, in his authoritative text *Administrative Law*, claimed they were cheap, speedier and more accessible than the courts. Harlow, 2001, below, challenges the claim to these advantages as partially inaccurate. More specifically, benefits were said to be these: the costs are negligible; there are no court fees and people can *supposedly* manage without lawyers; tribunals can give a fixed date for the hearing in contrast to courts; procedure is meant to be informal; tribunal members can assist the parties; their jurisdiction is limited so members become specialists, compared with a civil judge, and they involve laypeople as adjudicators. They are not bound by precedent but those tribunals with an appeal level, such as employment and immigration, have developed their own specialist sets of law reports, which effectively act as precedents.

Critics of tribunals point to their informality, lack of visibility, lack of precedent and consequent unpredictability as endangering a fair hearing. Worse, legal aid (now called legal help and legal representation) had only been made available for applicants to four tribunals until 2000 (Commons Commissioners, Lands Tribunal, Mental Health Review Tribunals, Employment Appeal Tribunal) so in most cases people have to pay for a lawyer privately or represent themselves. This is unfair in those tribunals which have become very like courts, because of the frequent use of private lawyers and because they have developed their own case law, such as Employment Tribunals. Research (*e.g.* Genn and Genn, 1989) showed that being represented at a tribunal enhanced the appellant's chances of success. The Citizens' Advice Bureaux complained, in 1995, that tribunals were neither expeditious nor free from technicality, as proponents claimed. The Human Rights Act 1998 prompted Lord Chancellor Irvine to authorise the Legal Services Commission to extend publicly funded legal representation to more tribunals. In 2000, it was extended to hearings before the immigration adjudicators and Immigration Appellate Authority (now Asylum and Immigration Tribunal) and in 2001, he announced an extension to proceedings before the VAT and Duties Tribunal, the General and Special Commissioners of Income Tax and the Protection of Children Act Tribunal. The Lord Chancellor explained to the House of Lords, "where a tribunal is dealing with penalties which the courts have decided are criminal, within the terms of the European Convention on Human Rights, or where the appellant reasonably argues that the penalties are criminal, provision for legal assistance will be provided, where the interests of justice require it". See Harlow, cited below.

Ironically, some tribunals have become so courtlike that they have **12–011** lost any advantage over the courts so arbitration is starting to be offered as an alternative. For instance, from 2001, parties can opt out of the overcrowded employment tribunals and into a new ACAS arbitration scheme for simple unfair dismissal claims. Formal pleadings, jurisdictional arguments, complex legal issues and cross-examination are banned and lawyers have no special status. Interestingly, in response to some of these concerns, the rules of employment tribunals were changed in 2001, with the insertion of the overriding objective, the extension of case management powers, and power to penalise an advocate with a costs order, all ideas borrowed from the Woolf reforms to civil procedure, described in Chapter 9, above.

It was often pointed out that tribunal administration and their clerks were usually from the department whose decision was being appealed against so they appeared to lack independence.

Many critics condemned as cost-saving measures the reorganisation of social security tribunals in the Social Security Act 1998. Oral hearings were reduced, despite government statistics which showed the applicant's chances of success were greater with an oral hearing. Three-person tribunals were cut down, meaning the elimination of laypeople (see Adler). Many more criticisms were articulated in 2000–2001.

The Leggatt Review of Tribunals

Tribunals have developed piecemeal and numbers increased sig- **12–012** nificantly since 1960. Governments have created new ones rather than add jurisdiction to an existing one. Their growth was questioned by the Committee on Ministers' Powers (1932) and the Franks Committee on Administrative Tribunals and Enquiries

(1957) and they were under review in 2000–2001 by the *Review of Tribunals* (Leggatt Committee). The Franks Report led to the 1958 Tribunals and Inquiries Act, consolidated in the 1992 Act. The 1958 Act, as well as setting up the Council on Tribunals, ensured reasoned decisions, provided for appeals on points of law to the High Court and ensured that chairmen of most tribunals should be drawn from a panel of lawyers and that, wherever possible, procedural rules should apply.

The Leggatt Review was prompted by what Lord Chancellor Irvine called, at its launch, "haphazard growth of tribunals, complex routes of appeal and the need for mechanisms to ensure coherent development of the law". The Review's terms of reference (paraphrased) were to ensure that:

- there are fair, timely, proportionate and effective arrangements for handling disputes, within a framework that encourages systematic development of the law and forms a coherent structure, with the superior courts, for the delivery of administrative justice;
- arrangements conform with the Convention;
- there are adequate arrangements for improving people's understanding of their rights;
- arrangements for funding and management are efficient and pay due regard to judicial independence;
- performance standards are effectively applied and monitored.

The Review body proposed a series of benchmarks against which the achievement of fairness should be tested: independence from departments; accessible and supportive systems; suitable jurisdiction; simple procedures; effective and suitable decision-making process; proportionate remedies; speed; authority and expertise and cost effectiveness. They invited comments on these in the contexts of the Convention, devolution and the Government's *Modernising Government* programme (white paper, 1999). Responses are on the website and, below, I discuss the comments of experienced commentators.

Adler and Bradley (in Partington, 2001) identified these problems:

1. No appeal was provided from some administrative decisions.
2. The manner in which new tribunals were established and existing ones changed for short-term administrative or political reasons and the inability of the Council on Tribunals (COT) to stop this.

3. The poor resources of those with small caseloads for such activities as selection, monitoring and training of chairmen and members.
4. The weakness of the COT compared with government departments. With their small secretariat, no research capacity, inability to produce complete statistics and sporadic pre-announced visits to a handful of tribunal hearings, they were ill-equipped to fulfil their statutory duty to "keep under review the constitution and workings of tribunals" (Tribunals and Inquiries Act 1992).

They examined various proposals for reform and described two **12–013** models of unified tribunal systems from Australia and Quebec. Robson had proposed to the Franks Committee (1957) an Administrative Appeal Tribunal, which could generate a set of general principles, enabling the system to be more simple and coherent. Similarly, the Whyatt Report (1961) proposed a general tribunal, modelled on a Swedish one, to deal with complaints where there was no specialist tribunal. The JUSTICE-All Souls Report (1988) had, however, rejected an administrative appeal tribunal, because of the sheer volume of work. Adler and Bradley examined the Australian Administrative Review Tribunal, two-tiered, with the first comprising a number of specialist review tribunals and the second a specialist panel to review first tier decisions raising substantial questions of law or mixed fact and law. They also examined the Administrative Tribunal of Quebec.

They then set out their proposals for a Unified Appeal Tribunal (UAT) consisting of ten specialist divisions. Existing tribunals would be brought into its framework and any future tribunals would be added. There would be a right of appeal from all government discretionary decisions. Panels would always comprise a legally qualified person and laypeople or specialists. Standard procedural rules would apply. Selection and training would be unified. The UAT would require accommodation in all centres of population. Common services, such as clerking, IT and publicity would be provided in the tribunal building. The UAT would be able to commission research. Appeal should be available on a point of law to the courts from the upper tier of the UAT. They concluded:

"Those who consider our proposal as altogether too ambitious and too radical might stop briefly to consider what the state of the ordinary courts would be like if there were as many specialised courts as there are tribunals and if, every time Parliament created some new private law rights or new regulatory offences, a new civil or criminal court were to be created."

Professor Carol Harlow (in Partington, 2001) examined the implications of the Convention and Community law for tribunals. She argued that the requirements of the 1957 Franks Report, (openness, fairness, impartiality, reasons) differed little from Art.6(1) of the Convention. She examined in some depth whether various different tribunals were likely to be required by Art.6 to provide publicly funded representation, remarking that the ECtHR had not been generous in its attitude to legal aid. She considered English administrative justice to possess an advantage over the continental model of specialist administrative courts. French administrative court procedures had been found to be in breach of the Convention on a number of occasions, with the adjudicators held to be insufficiently independent of the executive. An Independent Tribunal Service would strengthen the independence of the system and make it less vulnerable to challenge.

Sir Andrew Leggatt's Report of the Review of Tribunals, *Tribunals for Users One System, One Service* was published in 2001. The full version and the summary are on the website. It has become known as the Leggatt Report.

Leggatt Report and Recommendations

12–014   The Review concentrated on "statutory bodies which provide a specialised machinery for the adjudication of cases that would otherwise be decided by the civil courts" (Leggatt, para.1.6), which numbered 70. Leggatt considered regulatory or investigatory bodies to be outside his remit.

Tribunals or courts?

12–015   Leggatt suggested three tests as indicators that tribunals rather than courts should decide cases:

- Users should, with help, be able to prepare and present their own cases (but he found most tribunals did not currently satisfy this aim).
- Where expertise, or accessibility to users, is a major issue in the resolution of disputes.
- Where a tribunal can be effective in dealing with the mixture of fact and law.

Judicial review should not be the citizen's only recourse. "(We) want the results of this Review to be a renewed sense among tribunals and their staff that they are there to do different things from the courts, and in different ways, but with equal independence." (Leggatt, para.1.14).

Identifiable problems with tribunals in 2001

"The most striking feature of tribunals is their isolation. This is a   **12–016**
serious problem. Apart from the narrowness of outlook which it
engenders, it leads to duplication of effort. Each tribunal invents its
own IT, its own internal processes, and its own service standards,
though not all of them do have such standards. There is under-
investment in training in many tribunals. The bigger tribunals have
good accommodation, frequently under-used; the smaller ones are
scratching around for suitable venues for hearings. The Appeals
Service has invested in relatively up-to-date IT; most other tribunals' IT is much more primitive and is years behind the systems
we found in Australia. Most tribunals find it difficult to retain suitable staff, especially in London, because of the limited career
prospects they can offer. In most cases, tribunals feel that they are
at the back of the queue for resources." (Leggatt, para.1.18).

The relationship with departments

"There is also an uneasy relationship between most tribunals and
the departments on whose decisions they are adjudicating. In   **12–017**
those tribunals which are paid for by the sponsoring departments,
the chairmen and members feel that they cannot be seen as independent . . . At the same time, paradoxically, many tribunals do
not enter into the appropriate dialogue which would enable
departments to learn from adverse tribunal decisions and thereby
to improve their primary decision-making." (Leggatt, para.1.19).

The relationship with users
Sometimes there were unacceptable delays, because of inefficient
document-handling, poor listing, too many adjournments and so   **12–018**
on. Tribunals' communications with users were sometimes terse
and impersonal. "Users frequently feel in the dark . . . " (Leggatt,
para.1.22).

Procedures

"In some tribunals, proceedings are informal. In others, they are at   **12–019**
least as formal as those of the courts . . . The MORI research study
found that approaches sometimes differ within the same tribunal."
(Leggatt, para.1.24).

"Perhaps the biggest challenge for tribunals is to enable users
who feel that they have been unfairly treated to come to the

tribunal without undue apprehension, and to leave feeling that they have been given a fair opportunity to put their case." (Leggatt, para.1.25).

A more independent system

12–020   Most respondents to the consultation thought tribunals were not perceived to be independent from government departments. Although Leggatt examined the separate system of administrative courts existing in the major European systems, he concluded that adopting such a system would be wholly disproportionate to identified problems. The Report quoted the philosophy of the Franks Report 1957: "We consider that tribunals should properly be regarded as machinery provided by Parliament for adjudication rather than as part of the machinery of administration." (Leggatt, para.2.6).

On the European Convention, he concluded that Art.6(1) (fair trial) did not apply to some tribunals but the "equality of arms" principle had implications for Mental Health Review Tribunals and immigration tribunals. He interpreted the Convention case law as requiring "institutional and structural impartiality" and that should guide the operation of tribunals in the future (para.2.25). The most obvious impact of Art.6(1) was to require all those who adjudicate and participate in hearings to be independent and impartial. He reproduced some telling quotations from the tribunal users' survey to illustrate the perception that tribunal hearings were not impartial, such as "obviously it is on their (the Government department's) side, they are paying for everybody, aren't they?" (para.2.16). The "one guiding principle" said Leggatt, was that tribunals must demonstrate similar qualities of independence and impartiality to the courts (para.2.18). There was no question of Government attempting to influence individual decisions but it could not be said that they were *demonstrably* independent.

The only way that users could be satisfied that tribunals were truly independent was by developing a clear separation between ministers and other authorities whose decisions are tested by tribunals and the minister who appoints and supports them. Tribunals should be formed into a coherent system to sit alongside the ordinary courts, with administrative support provided by the Lord Chancellor's Department (now the Department of Constitutional Affairs (DCA)) (para.2.25). This would have the further advantage of facilitating administrative and procedural reform (para.2.27).

A more coherent system

12–021   Leggatt recommended that there should be a single tribunals system which would include all tribunals, including all of those run by local authorities and tribunals dealing with disputes between parties. Not only were tribunal users confused by the different requirements of tribunals but so were their solicitors and other advisers. Without a single system, existing tribunals would be hard pressed to satisfy the Government's aims to effect radical reform, for instance to make all services available electronically by 2005. A single system would enable the citizen to submit an appeal in the knowledge that it would be allocated to the correct tribunal. It would also provide a clearer and simpler system for developing the law. The Tribunals Service should be an executive agency of the Lord Chancellor's Department (now DCA).

As for tribunals which adjudicated between private parties, these were more adversarial than those where the citizen was challenging the state but Leggatt rejected the suggestion that they should become courts. That would be a retrograde step. They benefited from having a lawyer in the chair plus wing members who brought experience of both sides of industry. The increasing complexity of the law had made it difficult for users to represent themselves but the Review suggested a package of measures to improve services.

The Woolf reforms to civil justice should be quickly adapted for tribunals, to ensure that procedures are speedy, proportionate and cheap.

On land, property and housing, there were confusing overlaps between courts and tribunals as well as between tribunals. A comprehensive solution should be worked out, to remove overlaps and prevent forum-shopping (Leggatt, Chapter 3).

A more user-friendly system

Users should be given information on how to start a case, prepare and present it. They should be able to do this for themselves. The investment must be made in this, in order to comply with the Convention. Information should be designed by experts and be available in a range of media and formats. There should be designated customer service points. The Community Legal Service contract scheme should be extended to key advice organisations and used to assure quality advice. **12–022**

There should be a procedure or code specifying that decision-makers should provide information on what the appellant's statutory entitlement was, what had been decided in the case, the reasons and whether or not there was a right of appeal. The Community Legal Service should include representation in more tribunals but on a case-by-case basis (Leggatt, Chapter 4).

Structure and powers

The Tribunals System should be divided by subject-matter into eight divisions, one of which should deal with disputes between **12–023** citizens and the rest disputes between citizen and state. There should be a single route of appeal to a single appellate division. Generally, there should be a right of appeal on a point of law from first-tier to second-tier tribunals and from second-tier to the CA. The appellate body should have power to uphold the appeal, quash the decision or remit it for reconsideration, or grant declaratory relief (this means, declare what they law is). Appeal should remain to the CA from certain expert tribunals which deal with exceptionally complex cases. (Leggatt, paras.6.1–6.15).

Precedent

12–024   "First tier tribunals should continue to consider each case on its merits and decide it as the public interest may require. Their decisions should not set binding precedents" (para.6.19) but a system of designating binding cases, as currently used by the Social Security Commissioners and IAT, should be adopted throughout the appellate division.

Judicial review

12–025   Leggatt recommended that the second tier (appeals) tribunals should be statutorily excluded from judicial review (JR) and that JR from first-tier tribunals should be precluded unless all rights of appeal had been exhausted. He quoted Sir Jeffery Bowman's review of the Crown Office (JR cases). Bowman had found the complex and haphazard growth of tribunals and appeal routes had increased the volume and complexity of JR cases, of which immigration and asylum cases were around two thirds (Leggatt, para.6.27). Leggatt thought his recommendations would provide a comprehensive right of appeal from first-tier tribunals. Users would benefit from an expert appeal body with a High Court judge. The aim of the new appellate Division would be to develop, by its general expertise and selective identification of binding precedents, a coherent approach to the law. The Senior President and other Presidents would be High Court judges so it would be inappropriate to subject them to JR by another equal status judge.

Presidents

12–026   The Tribunals System should be headed by a Senior President, who should be a High Court judge sitting in one of the appellate tribunals. There should be Presidents for the Immigration, Social Security and Pensions, Land and Valuation, Financial and Employment appellate Divisions. Some of the Presidents should be High Court judges. They should co-ordinate consistency in decision-making and uniformity of practice and procedure and should hear the most difficult, novel or complex cases (Leggatt, Chapters 6 and 7).

A Tribunals Board

The system should be directed by a Board, consisting of the **12–027** Presidents and others, which would oversee the appointment of members, co-ordinate their training, investigate complaints against them and recommend changes in procedural rules.

The conduct of tribunals

Tribunal members should do all they could to try to understand **12–028** the point of view of the citizen. Their approach should be an enabling one, "giving the parties confidence in their ability to participate, and in the tribunal's capacity to compensate for any lack of skills or knowledge" (para.7.5). Chairmen should identify parties who found difficulty with tribunal procedures and in seeing what could properly be done to assist them. Advertisements for chairmen and members should emphasise the need for interpersonal skills. Their training should be improved and include core competencies, such as interpersonal skills peculiar to the distinctive approach to tribunals. Chairmen should be specially trained in competencies needed to help them overcome communication, language and literacy difficulties of some users. The Judicial Studies Board should provide training. All should be subject to performance appraisal and continuing training. A Judicial Appointments Commissioner should supervise appointment of the lawyers and another the non-lawyers.

The Council on Tribunals should fulfil important new roles, monitoring the development of the new system. Their primary duty should be the championing of users' causes and they should include members with the experience and perspective of users. Their reports should be published more widely and the Government should reply formally. The COT should comment on draft legislation. In the longer term, it should be made responsible for upholding administrative justice and keeping it under review, for monitoring developments in administrative law and for recommending improvements to the Lord Chancellor. It should be able to commission research (Leggatt, Chapter 7).

Active case management

The recommendations here have similar aims to case manage- **12–029** ment under the Civil Procedure Rules 1998, described in Chapter 9 of this book, above. Cases should be moved along; IT should monitor case progress; Practice Directions should be issued. The registrar should consider whether the case was suitable for ADR and the President of each Division should be responsible for exploring ADR (Leggatt, Chapter 8).

Relationship with departments

12–030   Government departments should consider introducing internal review procedures to establish that their side of the case is correct in fact and law, that contesting the appeal was the only realistic action and that opposing the appeal was a justifiable use of public funds. The reviewing officer should be empowered to remedy obvious errors. Departments should adopt a central capacity for scrutinising tribunal decisions and disseminating lessons learned. Tribunals should be able to identify systemic problems and suggest remedies (Leggatt, Chapter 9).

Government Response to Leggatt

12–031   In March 2003, The Lord Chancellor announced the launch of a new unified Tribunals Service. The Service will formerly come into operation in 2006 and Government promises it will form the basis of future Government policy designed to increase tribunal accessibility, raise service standards, and improve administration in the tribunals administered by Government, responsible for 90 per cent of tribunal cases.

In 2004, a white paper was issued by the DCA, *Transforming Public Services: Complaints, Redress and Tribunals* (it is on the DCA website). The summary claims that the programme of reform it announces

"goes further than just looking at tribunals—it looks at the administrative justice system as a whole and sets out proposals to improve the whole end to end dispute resolution process . . . This means helping to improve standards of decision making across government and, where things do go wrong, promoting quicker and more effective means of dispute resolution, so that fewer cases come before tribunals . . . This approach to proportionate dispute resolution is the first manifestation of the department's new strategy for helping users of the justice system resolve issues without recourse to formal hearings . . . the new (Unified Tribunals Service) will be more than just a federation of existing tribunals. It will be a new organisation and a new type of organisation. It will have two central pillars: administrative justice appeals and employment cases. Its mission will be to help prevent and resolve disputes, using any appropriate method and working with its partners in and out of government, and to help improve administrative justice and justice in the workplace, so that the need for dispute is reduced".

Notice the language here and the breadth of vision. Government seems to be recognizing the need to prevent disputes arising in the first place and that the whole system by which citizens' complaints about government are handled needs restructuring. It is also a formal acknowledgement of the irony I pointed out above, that tribunals, originally established as informal, cheap and quick alternatives to the courts have themselves become so elaborate and complex that ADR is used to avoid a tribunal hearing. The white paper's main points are as follows.

- The creation of a Senior President of Tribunals. Lord Justice Carnwath has already been appointed.
- A unified and cohesive system of deployment for those sitting in first-tier tribunals and another for those sitting in appellate tribunals.
- The renaming of legal members of tribunals as "Tribunal Judge" and "Tribunal Appellate Judge" respectively.
- Simplifying the arrangements whereby panel members can sit in more than one jurisdiction while safeguarding necessary expertise.
- Further improving arrangements for training and appraisal.

Structural changes include:

- a statutory tribunals rule committee;
- a more coherent structure of appeals and reviews;
- a unified tax appeals system; and
- a new and enhanced role for the Council on Tribunals, which will in time evolve into an Administrative Justice Council.

All of this will take years to achieve, beyond 2005. An example of structural rationalisation came in 2003, when the eight tribunals dealing with land, property and valuation were restructured.

2. Arbitration

Arbitration was the nineteenth century merchants' alternative to the expense and delay of the High Court. Arbitration is classified by some as a form of ADR but, as it is more formal and results in a legally binding decision, most specialist ADR writers exclude it. It means the reference of a dispute to a third party or parties to decide according to law but outside the confines of normal courtrooms or procedure. The parties pay privately for the arbitration.   **12–032**

Arbitration may arise in one of three ways:

1. *By reference from a court*
   A judge of the commercial court may refer a suitable case to arbitration or herself act as arbitrator. The Lands Tribunal has a statutory power to act as arbitrator by consent.

2. *By agreement after a dispute has arisen*
For instance, if a contract has broken down, the parties might agree to refer their dispute to an arbitrator.

3. *By contract*
Contracting parties may agree that, in the event of a dispute arising under the contract, they will refer it to an arbitrator to be appointed by, say, the Chartered Institute of Arbitrators, or the Bar Council, or the International Chamber of Commerce. Such clauses are common in commercial contracts and insurance. Examine your own household or vehicle insurance policy if you want to see an example of an arbitration clause to which you are, unwittingly, a party.

Arbitrations are usually conducted by one or three people. An arbitrator may be a specialist lawyer or, more likely, a technical expert in the subject in dispute. The Chartered Institute of Arbitrators has around 10,500 members in 2005, mostly non-lawyers. It provides training leading to qualification.

12–033   Arbitrations are governed by the Arbitration Act 1996. Section 1(a) states that the object of arbitration is "the fair resolution of disputes by an impartial tribunal without unnecessary delay or expense". Section 1(b) continues that "the parties should be free to agree how their disputes are resolved, subject only to such safeguards as are necessary in the public interest". Section 33 imposes a general duty on an arbitrator to act fairly. The arbitrator has both the right and the duty to devise and adopt suitable procedures to minimise delay and expense. Section 34 gives her absolute power over procedure. An arbitration agreement may incorporate specific rules of arbitration but if it does not, the default provisions of the Act apply. An arbitration will normally follow essentially the same stages as civil litigation, described in Chapter 9, above: exchanging documents, factual and expert evidence and then a hearing but frequently, issues are dealt with by written submissions and then a telephone hearing. Often, there is not a general duty of disclosure, as in the courts, but only an obligation to identify the documents relied on by the party. Most arbitral rules permit the arbitrator to act inquisitorially and the Act provides that the arbitration is not bound by the strict rules of evidence. Unlike civil litigation, where the court is bound to decide according to the law, the arbitrator may decide the dispute in accordance with "such other considerations as are agreed by (the parties) or determined by the tribunal" (s.46). This means that an equity clause may be agreed, requiring the arbitrator to decide according to equity and good conscience.

Once parties have voluntarily and validly submitted to arbitration, the courts will not normally entertain one party if they try and ignore this agreement and make a court claim. The court will normally order a stay or stop of proceedings, under s.9. The arbitrator gives a reasoned decision which is enforceable in court. There are three grounds on which an award may be challenged in court: jurisdiction; serious irregularity; or on a point of law. The question must be one of general public importance and the decision of the arbitrators should be at least open to serious doubt: *CMA v Beteiligungs-Kommanditgesellschaft* [2002] EWCA Civ 1878. The Act has been subject to considerable interpretation in case law. For example, in *Warborough Investments Ltd v S Robinson & Sons (Holdings) Ltd* [2003] EWCA Civ 751, the CA held that the pursuit of the object of arbitration, under s.1 required the courts to accord to arbitrators a reasonably wide discretion in the discharge of their duties. The courts can act as an appointing authority of last resort, where the parties cannot agree on an arbitrator. They can compel the production of evidence and enforce an arbitration award. Because many foreign arbitrations are conducted in London, difficult issues of private international law can arise. Case law on arbitration has also been - generated in the European Court of Justice, such as *Van Uden* (1998).

Most disputes in shipping or aviation are referred to arbitration, as are those of multinational corporations. They are common in oil, gas, banking, commodities, insurance and securities and international trade. Arbitrations are very big, lucrative business to London's lawyers and accompany the use of London as an international commercial centre. Many cross-border disputes arose through the construction of the channel tunnel, for instance, a £1 billion claim by Eurotunnel against Trans Manche Link, but they were often resolved by arbitration conducted through the International Chamber of Commerce in Paris. Other international arbitration bodies include the London Court of International Arbitration, the London Maritime Arbitrators Association as well as centres in New York, Geneva, Stockholm and Hong Kong. It is estimated that Paris has the most international arbitrations but, since the nature of arbitration is private, there are no statistics.

Domestically, a number of specialist schemes exist, such as **12–034** Professional Arbitration on Court Terms, run by the Law Society and Royal Institute of Chartered Surveyors as an alternative to courts determining lease renewal terms and commercial rents and the Personal Insurance Arbitration Scheme, one of over 80 small claims schemes administered by the Chartered Institute of Arbitrators, to provide arbitration under domestic insurance contracts such as holiday or car insurance. Under this scheme, the insurer is bound by the arbitrator's award but if the insured does not like it, he can have a second bite of the cherry by making a claim in the courts. Some barristers are trained as arbitrators and offer their services on a commercial basis. In 1999, the Chartered Institute of Arbitrators launched the London Arbitration Scheme, with an attempt to keep the cost proportionate (20 per cent) to the subject of dispute. An example of a scheme run by the Institute commenced in 2004. The London Borough of Hackney launched an independent arbitration service aimed at curbing costly no-win, no-fee claims (solicitors acting under conditional fees—see discussion in Chapters 9 and 17). The service is administered by the Chartered Institute of Arbitrators and saves about £1 million per year. Tenants are offered £500 to pay for their legal costs and the arbitrator makes a decision within eight weeks. Litigating housing cases through the courts had cost £7,500 per case and could take two years. Three other councils already had similar schemes by 2004.

Arbitration became popular because it had the advantages of being swift, arranged at a date to suit the parties, cheaper than court proceedings and more private. Obviously, this is desirable where time is of the essence, (*e.g.* a dispute about liability for damage to a perishable cargo) or the parties do not want their commercial secrets exposed in the courtroom. Sampson (1997), however, argues that, because of lawyer domination, arbitration has become "a mirror image of litigation", with complex parallel procedures to civil litigation. He quotes Sir Thomas Bingham M.R.:

> "the arbitration process, by mimicking the processes of the courts and becoming over-legalistic and overlawyered has betrayed its birthright by allowing itself to become as slow, as expensive and almost as formal as the court proceedings from which it was intended to offer escape".

The 1996 Act was meant to reverse this process, by giving powers to enable arbitrators to force the pace of arbitration. The advantages offered by civil litigation in the courts are: if one party believes the other's case has no substance, she can ask for summary judgment; further parties can be added if necessary; the arbitrator has no power to consolidate arbitrations in a multi-party action.

Is Arbitration Moving Out of London?

12–035   As I mentioned above, the very nature of arbitration is that it is a private proceeding so there are no official statistics, nationally or internationally. It seems to me then, that claims that London used to be the "arbitration capital of the world" or that "arbitration is moving out of London" to foreign competitors are extremely difficult to substantiate. Nevertheless, in 2003, the then Lord Mayor of London, barrister Gavyn Arthur, staged a conference in London, to ask why arbitrations were going to Paris. This is reported on by Smulian, who observes that London's advantages are its financial and commercial power, its position in international time zones, the respect accorded to English law and its use in foreign contracts, which are also written in English. I would add that London is, historically, an international insurance and maritime law centre and London is now used by large American law firms as a springboard into Europe. The disadvantages of arbitrating in London, as opposed to foreign jurisdictions are, according to experienced practitioners cited by Smulian:

- expense, caused by labour intensive emphasis on document disclosure and examination of witnesses;
- longer hearings than those conducted by European civil lawyers;
- the cultural arrogance of English lawyers, convinced, like American lawyers, that their systems and methods are innately superior;
- the use of barristers and retired judges as arbitrators, who attempt to replicate court procedure.

I would again warn, however, that it is very difficult to demonstrate that arbitration is, indeed declining and, if it is, what is not borne in mind, is that parties may simply be resorting to ADR instead which is, again, a *private* procedure and thus unquantifiable.

3. Alternative Dispute Resolution

This has been the fashionable development of the 1990s. Many British lawyers, most notably the Conservative Lord Chancellor Mackay, who favoured public funding for family mediation, then Labour's Lord Chancellor Irvine took a very active interest in this American import, as a means of avoiding the public and private expense and the private pain of litigation.   12–036

ADR can be defined as any method of resolving a legal problem without resorting to the legal process. Experts consider that any subject can be referred to ADR but advisability depends on the parties' attitudes. Below are some of the alternatives to conventional litigation:

Types of ADR

ACAS (The Advisory, Conciliation and Arbitration Service)
This body was set up in 1974 to trouble shoot employment disputes and keep potential complaints out of employment tribunals.   12–037

Adjudication

This is a quick dispute resolution process designed for the construction industry, to make sure work is not unduly delayed. It was created by the Housing Grants, Construction and Regeneration Act 1996.

Conciliation

The conciliator takes a more interventionist role than a mediator, in bringing the two parties together and suggesting solutions to help achieve a settlement. Incidentally, mediation and conciliation have been used in China for centuries. The United Nations Commission on International Trade Law provides a set of model rules.

Early neutral evaluation

12–038   A neutral professional, often a lawyer or judge, hears a summary of each party's case and gives a non-binding assessment of the merits, which can be used as a basis for settlement or negotiation. Since a 1996 Practice Statement, the Commercial Court judges can offer this to parties appearing before them.

Expert determination

An independent expert is appointed to decide and her decision is binding. It is not caught by the Arbitration Act and thus not elaborate and has no right of appeal. An example is the use of a surveyor at a rent review.

Formalised settlement conference

Described at (1995) 145 N.L.J. 383.

Mediation

12–039   A mediator helps both sides to come to an agreement which they can accept. It can be evaluative, where the mediator assesses the legal strength of a case or facilitative, where the mediator concentrates on assisting the parties to define the issues. If an agreement is reached it can be written down and forms a legally binding contract, unless the parties state otherwise. If not, traditional civil litigation is still open so proponents consider it a "no lose" option for a lawyer. Usually, the mediator acts as a go-between, negotiating with each party in their separate private rooms.

Med-arb

This is a combination of mediation and arbitration, where the parties agree to mediate but if no settlement is reached, the dispute is referred to arbitration. The mediator may turn into an arbitrator.

Mini Trial

The means the hiring of an independent person to give a non-binding decision on the issue. Hiring retired judges to do this is common in the US. The *Judge Judy* television programme is a somewhat crude example.

Neutral fact finding

This is a non-binding procedure used for complex technical   12–040
issues. A neutral expert is appointed to investigate the facts and evaluate the merits of the dispute. It can form the basis of settlement or negotiation.

Online dispute resolution

There are a number of websites offering this, predominantly American. They are usually used for low-value disputes.

ADR is not suitable for every claim. For instance, where the   12–041
parties refuse to speak to one another, or where, as in most cases, the defendant is silent and judgment is ordered in default to the claimant. It is ideal where the parties must continue in a relationship, such as neighbours or businesses. Also, it can save years of nit-picking argument, generating thousands of pounds of costs in multi-party commercial disputes.

Examples of ADR

Family mediation

The most popular form of ADR is mediation. Family mediation   12–042
services have been offered, at least since the 1980s, by local authorities, charities and, by the mid-1990s, by lawyers and others trained for the job and sometimes government funded. By 1996, Lord Woolf became the patron of the British Association of Lawyer Mediators, the founders of which had recognised a new market, which they did not want to let slip out of lawyers' hands. Notice, again, the judicial encouragement of ADR. Hundreds of lawyers attended mediation courses. Even specialist barristers' chambers started offering mediation direct to the public. Under the Family Law Act 1996 attending a mediation information meeting can be compulsory, in certain circumstances. A family judge can order mediation but there are no sanctions for failing to attend.

In 1997–1999, 14 pilot schemes were launched and over 7,500 people attended information meetings on mediation but monitoring by Professor Gwynn Davies showed disappointing results. Although 90 per cent of attendees found the meetings useful, only seven per cent went on to mediation and 39 per cent reported that the meeting made them more likely to seek legal advice. Most people attended alone, yet many of the options described required the commitment of both spouses. In 2004, a report by the Newcastle Centre for Family Studies describes a study of 1,000 people who participated in pilot information meetings. Only 10 per cent of respondents chose to attend mediation. Of those who attended mediation, one third said they did so because their solicitor suggested it. One quarter of those who had mediated reported that it resolved issues. The report concluded that many people were using it when it was not appropriate. In the meantime, family resolution pilots were commenced in three areas, to try to keep child contact disputes out of court. A green paper was published in 2004, *Parental Separation: Children's Needs and Parental Responsibilities* (DCA website). It proposes to put this type of ADR on a statutory footing. Judges will have power to direct parents to in-court conciliation and mediation, although they will not be compulsory. Lord Falconer said, in January 2005, that research had shown that compulsion would breed resentment. The Legal Services Commission (LSC) is prepared to pay for family mediation. The number of mediation sessions funded by the LSC has risen from 400 in 1997 to 1,400 in 2003. It is strongly in favour of encouraging ADR and runs the Family Advice and Information Service. There is a UK college of family mediators.

By 2005, more than 250 family lawyers had been trained in collaborative law, a no-court divorce scheme that originated in the USA. Parties get a signed guarantee that lawyers will not let things escalate or insist on going to court.

Commercial Court

12–043   Some of the Commercial Court judges are very keen on encouraging ADR in commercial cases. They established a working party to examine the scope for applying pressure on litigants to use ADR. Coleman J. enforced a mediation clause in a commercial contract in *Cable & Wireless Plc v IBM UK Ltd* [2002] EWHC 2059.

NHS

12–044   After reports by the National Audit Office that clinical disputes could cost £4.4 billion per year, the NHS set up a pilot project to help resolve claims quickly. An example of a large group mediation was that involving the parents of children whose organs were wrongly retained, after death, at the Alder Hey Children's Hospital. After the mediation, in 2003, each set of parents received a sum of money, an apology and a pledge to erect a plaque to commemorate the children. £100,000 was donated to charity. Discussions with a representative focus group of the parents established that what they really wanted was an apology. In 2005, a Speedy Resolution Scheme for some publicly funded clinical disputes involving Welsh NHS trusts was piloted. The Trusts will set out an accident plan in each case, to prevent future accidents, as well as offering an apology and explanation, where appropriate. Cases will be resolved without resorting to litigation.

Government contractual disputes

In the meantime, the Government announced, in 2001, that it would be using ADR in its disputes. Evaluating this shift in policy, the DCA reported that, in the financial year up to March 2003, ADR had been used or attempted in 617 disputes across Government. Where ADR was used, it was successful in 89 per cent of cases. Departments estimated savings had been £6 million. Departments now include ADR clauses in their standard procurement contracts.

12–045

Public Funding for ADR

Public funding, formerly known as legal aid, is discussed in Chapter 17, on legal services, below. It can be provided for early neutral evaluation, mediation and arbitration. If ADR fails, the Community Legal Service, the provider, usually requires an explanation from the funded client's legal representative. In 2005, the Government announced a restructuring of legal aid to promote the resolution of disputes out of court, as explained in Chapter 17.

12–046

In March 2005, the Government launched a National Mediation helpline, to put callers in touch with an accredited independent mediator. For claims up to £50,000 costs will be fixed (and are very low). Legally aided clients will be able to claim reasonable costs. In March 2005, DCA Minister David Lammy announced measures to refocus the civil legal aid scheme to encourage early resolution of disputes and the use of ADR. Eligibility for legal representation was reduced and eligibility for help, such as advice would be increased. Funding for family cases was restructured to encourage early settlement out of court. To discourage unnecessary litigation, in clinical negligence cases and actions against the police most applicants will now be expected to pursue any available complaints system before they are funded to take proceedings. This will give the potential defendant public body the opportunity to respond to the matters raised and provide an explanation or apology if appropriate. These changes followed a 2004 Legal Services Commission consultation paper "A new focus for civil legal aid—encouraging early resolution; discouraging unnecessary litigation".

Will the Courts Enforce ADR?

In *Frank Cowl & others v Plymouth City Council* [2001] EWCA Civ 1935, Lord Woolf C.J. said

12–047

"insufficient attention is paid to the paramount importance of avoiding litigation whenever this is possible . . . both sides must by now be acutely aware of the contribution alternative dispute resolution can make to resolving disputes in a manner which both meets the needs of the parties and the public and saves expense and stress" (para.1).

This case involved a judicial review of the closure of a care home, with residents complaining that there had been insufficient consultation and a violation of their Convention rights, under Arts 2, 3 and 8. Under pressure from the CA, the parties agreed to an ADR process. Lord Woolf said courts should take a pro-active approach to ADR. Parties should be asked why a complaints procedure has not been used. The courts should not permit judicial review proceedings, except for good reason, where a significant part of the issues could be resolved outside the litigation process. Lord Woolf asked that the LSC co-operate in this approach and they have done so, expecting applicants for public funding to give detail of alternatives to litigation. The issue will be whether a private paying client would go to court rather than seeking to pursue alternatives, taking into account the likely effectiveness of alternatives, the attitude of the opponent and all other circumstances.

In April 2002, the CA held, in *Dunnett v Railtrack* [2002] EWCA Civ 303 that a party to litigation who turned down ADR when suggested by the court might suffer uncomfortable consequences in costs. Brooke L.J. reminded the parties that they had a duty to further the overriding objective of the Civil Procedure Rules (see Chapter 9, above). There have been a number of cases since then where this precedent has been applied and successful parties have had their costs refused or reduced. In October 2002, the Commercial Court gave a strong endorsement to ADR in *Cable & Wireless Plc v IBM UK Ltd* (above) Colman J. held that a contractual term providing for mandatory ADR should not generally be held void for uncertainty. For the courts to decline to enforce contractual references to ADR on the grounds of intrinsic uncertainty would be to fly in the face of public policy. Even where there was an unqualified reference to ADR, a sufficiently certain and definable minimum duty of participation should not be hard to find. Further, an ADR clause was analogous to an arbitration agreement ancillary to the main contract and enforceable by a stay of proceedings or by an injunction. He remarked that the making of an ADR order in the Commercial Court had become commonplace, even where one or both parties objected. This case was applied by Blackburne J. in *Shirayama Shokusan Co Ltd and others v Danovo Ltd* [2003] EWHC 3006 (Ch). He decided he had the power to order ADR in the face of repeated refusals by the claimants to accept the defendants' offers to mediate. He was persuaded by the defendants that the parties had a shared interest in mediating as they were likely to continue in a long-term relationship.

The courts have recently backtracked, however, on their view that unwilling parties could be forced into ADR, in a very important CA ruling. In *Halsey v Milton Keynes General NHS Trust* [2004] EWCA Civ 576, the CA heard arguments from four (extra) interested parties, the Law Society, the Civil Mediation Centre, the ADR Group and the Centre for Effective Dispute Resolution. The court produced a definitive set of guidelines on two points: the courts powers to order ADR and whether a party who refuses to participate in ADR should be penalised in costs:

> "It is one thing to encourage the parties to agree to mediation, even to encourage them in the strongest terms. It is another to order them to do so. . . . It seems to us likely that compulsion of ADR would be regarded as an unacceptable constraint on the right of access to the court and, therefore, a violation of article 6 . . . the court's role is to encourage, not to compel. The form of encouragement may be robust . . . mediation and other ADR processes do not offer a panacea, and can have disadvantages as well as advantages . . . " (para.9)

The question whether a party has acted unreasonably in refusing ADR must be determined having regard to all the circumstances of the particular case: (a) the nature of the dispute; (b) the merits of the case; (c) the extent to which other settlement methods have been attempted; (d) whether the costs of the ADR would be disproportionately high; (e) whether any delay in setting up and attending the ADR would have been prejudicial; and (f) whether the ADR had a reasonable prospect of success. These factors should not be regarded as an exhaustive check-list. This precedent has been applied in *Reed Executive Plc v Reed Business Information Ltd* [2004] EWCA Civ 887, *McMillan Williams v Range* [2004] EWCA Civ 294 and *Burchell v Bullard* [2005] EWCA Civ 358. See discussion by Sautter, 2005.

In the meantime, the courts have been keen to establish court- **12–048** based mediation schemes and many county courts have renamed themselves "Civil Justice Centres" to reflect the fact that they offer ADR as well as litigation in court. For example, a March 2004 evaluation of a small claims mediation scheme at Exeter, reported on the Civil Justice Council website, showed that a high proportion of small claims referred to mediation settled. Parties generally found mediation useful. They thought the proceeding was more informal and the mediator a better listener than a judge. It was more likely to be successful between business parties than those in personal relationships or emotionally-charged disputes. 90 per cent thought they would use mediation again. A major advantage was that, even if the case failed, parties benefited from hearing the other side and receiving directions from the judge.

Following the mediation experiment in Central London County Court, commencing in 1996 and reported below, Central London County Court was renamed Central London Civil Justice Centre. In 2004, it started a new scheme of automatic referral, copied from Ontario. Under this, about 20 random cases per week are automatically referred to mediation. This applies to cases of personal injury, trade or housing debts above the small claims limit. If one or both of the parties objects to mediation, they have to give reasons. A district judge decides whether the case should be referred to mediation or proceed through court. If a party still declines to mediate, for reasons unsatisfactory to the judge, they risk being liable to pay costs. If mediation is unsuccessful or only partially successful, they are free to continue with court proceedings. Manchester County Court introduced a free mediation adviser in 2004.

The Slow Growth of ADR

Lawyers were slow to catch on

12–049　　The slow development of ADR in the last 15 years shows that judges were much faster to learn about it and promote it than practising lawyers and the quotations from the case law above express judges' frustration with lawyers. By 1989, ADR was highly developed in the US. By 1992, the Law Society announced it was a priority in their continuing education scheme and it was favoured in the 1993 Heilbron– Hodge report on civil litigation and the Woolf Report 1996 and was promoted by Lord Chancellor Mackay in all his speeches and his green and white papers on legal aid in 1995 and 1996. Nevertheless, although it was much discussed in law journals from 1989 and, from 1990, firms started offering it commercially, many lawyers had still not heard of it even by 1997. Also, lawyers were hostile to it, (Shapiro, 1997 and Genn's survey of Central London County Court, below). Big commercial solicitors' firms were the first lawyers to catch on to ADR, with a 1997 survey of the 200 top property law firms showing that 70 per cent regarded mediation as effective. ADR trainers found that most people wishing to be trained as mediators were lawyers but they had to drop the adversarial habit of aggressive confrontation (*Gazette*, 1997).

The courts promoted ADR

12–050　　Since lawyers were slow to use ADR, it was left to the judges to devise schemes for it. In 1993, the Commercial Court announced in a Practice Note that the judges would encourage ADR in suitable cases and from 1996 permitted a judge to stay (suspend) a case to enable the parties to try ADR. From 1995, High Court Practice Directions required the parties' solicitors to certify whether they had considered resolving the dispute by ADR and discussed this with their client. From 1996, the London Patents County Court offered litigants the alternatives of expert arbitration or fast-track mediation. From 1997, legal aid was available for the Central London County Court mediation pilot scheme and a court-linked mediation scheme was commenced in Bristol. Following the Woolf reforms, the Civil Procedure Rules 1998, Rule 1, placed a duty on the court, as part of its active case management, to encourage the parties to use ADR, if the court considered it appropriate. The CA set up an ADR scheme, whereby invitations to participate in the scheme were sent out in almost all final appeals.

Acceptance of voluntary, court-annexed schemes was initially disappointing. From November 1998 to March 1999, parties in 250 CA cases were offered mediation but both sides agreed to mediate in only 12. A mediation scheme was offered, virtually cost-free, at Central London County Court from 1996. Hazel Genn evaluated the scheme after two years. She found that in only about five per cent of cases both parties accepted mediation. The joint demand for mediation was lowest where both parties were legally represented. Interviews with solicitors revealed:

- widespread ignorance of mediation among lawyers;
- apprehension about showing weakness;
- litigant resistance to compromise.

Of those who mediated, 62 per cent settled and the settlement rate was highest where neither party was legally represented. Average settlement amounts were £2,000 lower than non-mediated settlements. Solicitors felt mediation had saved time but there was a common view that failure to settle at mediation increased costs. Some of the most successful mediators were barristers. Another report by Hazel Genn (2002) reviewed the Commercial Court's ADR scheme and the voluntary Court of Appeal ADR scheme, in 1996–2000. She concluded that voluntary take-up of ADR schemes remained "at a modest level" and, outside commercial practice, "the profession remains very cautious about the use of ADR". In November 2002, Lord Chief Justice Woolf said he felt we had not gone "nearly far enough" with ADR. The fact that it was not compulsory was delaying things.

In 1999, a survey of the top 500 companies in the North West, 52 per cent of respondents said their solicitors had not discussed with them the possibility of resolving a dispute through mediation

(Goriely and Williams, 1997). The same year, concerned at the lack of uptake of ADR, the Lord Chancellor's Department (now DCA) published a discussion paper to try and ascertain why. Respondents said it was not easy to find out about different ADR services. There was no central register. Levels of awareness of ADR were low. Fifty-one per cent of respondents had found benefits of ADR in time, cost or convenience. Benefits cited were: preserving or rebuilding relationships between disputants, privacy, flexibility, informality, stress reduction, the enabling of a win-win scenario, innovative solutions, greater client participation and the ownership of the process. Most thought that government should do more to promote ADR but that it should not be obligatory. The Civil Justice Council responded, warning that Article 6 of the Convention meant that access to the courts could not be excluded. They urged "a major educational push" to attract a wider public to the benefits of ADR and they gave an account of the Canadian Disputes Resolution Fund.

12–051   At last, by the late 1990s a critical core of big law firms had been attracted to mediation, the most popular form of ADR, in non-family cases. S.J. Berwin offered ADR to their clients from 1997. A break-through came in 1998, when a case funded by the Law Society and ADR group successfully challenged the Legal Aid Board's refusal to fund non-family mediation. Now mediation can be funded by the Legal Services Commission, the LAB's successor. Nevertheless, the biggest boost to ADR, especially mediation, is bound to come from its promotion by Rule 1 of the CPR, as explained above. A 2000 MORI survey of 180 law firms showed that, since the rules had come into force the previous year, 54 per cent said they were more likely to have been involved in mediation.

Contemporary statistics from private ADR firms now show show a big rise in mediation. For instance, the Centre for Effective Dispute Resolution statistics demonstrate a significant increase in mediation after the Civil Procedure Rules came into force in 1999. There was then a slight decline until 2002, when the case of *Dunnett v Railtrack* (above) showed that the courts were prepared to penalise even winning parties in costs if they refused to mediate. The 2004 statistics from the Centre for Effective Dispute Resolution confirm mediation growth with an overall increase of 35 per cent in 2003 and eight per cent in 2004, to an all time high of 693 cases. Most of these mediations lasted just one day with 75 per cent of cases settling on the day or shortly after. The reader will find the latest statistics in the articles in the library section of the CEDR website.

A 2003 article by Jackie Lewis, in the Law Society's *Gazette* gave an interesting insight into why solicitors in big law firms now use ADR. One observed that clients were now thinking about it as a first option and there was much more awareness of it. Another attributed the growth of ADR to the civil procedure pre-action protocols in his field, construction and engineering, which require the parties to state why they do not consider ADR appropriate in their case.

By way of contrast, social welfare lawyers have remained remarkably resistant to ADR. In 2002, Helen Carr addressed this. She said they were concerned at the imbalance of power between their clients and the opposite party, whether a private employer or the State. They argued that mediation could disguise the fundamental causes of certain problems and that some social welfare problems, such as racial harassment or domestic violence were not amenable to mediation. There was an underlying fear in such lawyers that the real purpose of advocating ADR in social welfare cases was a cost cutting exercise by the State. Challenging their views, she argued that courts do not necessarily deliver justice, nor do legal rights of themselves solve the problems of social exclusion. The Government acknowledged that inadequate housing was a major cause of social exclusion but it was not suggesting legal rights were a solution to the problem. She said the role of community mediation had been critical in an increased appreciation of what ADR could offer to address social exclusion. Tensions between neighbours in areas of social exclusion could easily escalate. There was further potential for mediation in landlord-tenant disputes. **12–052**

In a 2004 conference organised by the Public Law Project , Lord Justice Maurice Kay, sometime head of the Administrative Court, said ADR had the greatest potential in housing, community care and education cases where there was an ongoing relationship between the claimant and a public body. The Administrative Court was trying to promote use of ADR. While lawyers acting for the socially disadvantaged in public law judicial review cases had been wary of ADR, experienced mediators pointed out the advantages. ADR could increase parties' sense of ownership of the case and the solution, in contrast with the limited remedies available in judicial review that did not address the real grievance. The grievance could be addressed directly. This reduced acrimony and promoted a continuing working relationship. It got away from the idea of winners and losers and focused on practical solutions. Even if mediation did not succeed, it could focus issues for the court. Public interest lawyers were concerned that there was a tension between Government's desire to save costs on judicial review and the difficulty of finding competent and experienced mediators.

BIBLIOGRAPHY ON TRIBUNALS
Adler (1999) 6 *Journal of Social Security Law* 99 and *Legal Action*, September 1997. **12–053**

H. Genn and Y. Genn, *The Effectiveness of Representation at Tribunals* (1989).

M. Partington (ed.), *The Leggatt Review of Tribunals: Academic Seminar Papers* (University of Bristol, 2001).

Review of Tribunals (2000), LCD Consultation Paper, *www.tribunals-review.org.uk* and final report *Tribunals for Users One System, One Services* by Sir Andew Leggatt, 2001, on same website.

BIBLIOGRAPHY ON ARBITRATION

12–054 T. Sampson, "Arbitration Act 1996—a fresh start?" (1997) 147 N.L.J. 261.

M. Smulian, "City feels the heat", Law Society's *Gazette*, June 19, 2003.

BIBLIOGRAPHY ON ADR

12–055 V Bondy, "Who Needs ADR?" (article on the 2004 Public Law Project conference on ADR in judicial review cases), *Legal Action*, September 2004, p.6.

H. Carr, "Alternative routes to justice", *Legal Action*, March 2002, p.1.

CEDR Solve Mediation Statistics 2004: *www.cedr.co.uk*

DCA Press Notice, March 2, 2005 "More Advice—Less Litigation", on encouraging ADR by reconstructing legal aid eligibility.

H. Genn, "The Central London County Court Pilot Mediation Scheme Evaluation Report", LCD Research Report 5/98 (1998) and "Court-Based ADR Initiatives for Non-Family Civil Disputes: the Commercial Court and the CA", LCD Research Report 1/02 (2002), archived on the DCA website: *www.dca.gov.uk*

T. Goriely and T. Williams, "Resolving Civil Disputes: Choosing Between Out-of-Court Schemes and Litigation—A Review of the Literature", LCD Research Report 3/97 (1997).

J. Lewis, "Meet the Middleman", Law Society's *Gazette*, May 9, 2003.

Lord Chancellor's Department, "Alternative Dispute Resolution: A Discussion Paper", 1999 and "Summary of Responses", archived on the DCA website.

Lord Mackay of Clashfern, *The Administration of Justice* (1994), Chapter 4.

J. Michaelson, "The A–Z of ADR" (2003) 153 N.L.J. 101, 146, 181, 232.

E. Sautter, "*Halsey*—mediation one year on" (2005) ISS N.L.J. 730.

D. Shapiro, 147 N.L.J. (1997) 426.

M. Zander, *The State of Justice* (2000), pp.35–38.

Several authors, Law Society's *Gazette*, November 5, 1997.

Various items from the *New Law Journal*.

FURTHER SOURCES FOR UPDATING THIS CHAPTER AND FURTHER INFORMATION

Online updates to this book: *http://www.sweetandmaxwell.co.uk/*   **12–056**
academic/updates/darbyshire/index.html

Department of Constitutional Affairs: *www.dca.gov.uk* (try press notices, consultation papers, the legal system, legal policy and so on).

The New Law Journal, also available on *Lexis*, a subscriber database used by many UK universities.

The Law Society's *Gazette*, available free, online: *www.lawgazette.co.uk*

On Tribunals

The Council on Tribunals: *www.council-on-tribunals.gov.uk*

On ADR

The Centre for Effective Dispute Resolution, an independent non-profit organisation, promoting ADR, supported by professional bodies: *www.cedr.co.uk* (browse through LIBRARY and NEWS (see toolbar at top of home page) to find articles and statistics)

Civil Justice Council website: *www.civiljusticecouncil.gov.uk*

Part IV: Professionals in the Law

13. The Legal Profession

"I do not believe that many of the restrictive practices under which lawyers work can still be justified in the public interest ... I am not satisfied that the main frontline bodies have put the interests of the consumer and the public in front of their own interests" (Sir David Clementi, *Review of the Regulatory Framework for Legal Services in England and Wales*, December 2004.)

"The quality of solicitors and counsel varies as does the quality of wine from 'unfit to drink' to vintage. Vintage tends to be very expensive beyond the means of the ordinary litigant. Most must be satisfied with 'plonk'." (The Hon. Mr Justice Lightman, "The Civil Justice System and Legal Profession—The Challenges Ahead" (2003) 22 C.J.Q. 235.)

1. Barristers and Solicitors

The main characteristic of the English legal profession is that it is **13–001** divided into two, barristers and solicitors. This makes it unusual but not unique, in world-wide terms. For centuries, each side has enjoyed certain protected monopolies in legal services but, since 1985, most of these have been abolished by degrees. This and the significant changes in the structure of legal services, wrought by the Access to Justice Act 1999 and threatened by the 2004 Clementi Review, have left some members of the legal profession feeling insecure.

The barrister is usually thought of primarily as an advocate. Until 1990, barristers had virtually exclusive rights of audience as advocates before all the superior courts. They are known as "counsel". In total there were, in 2003, around 11,000 barristers in independent practice. Senior judges in the English legal system are, with very few exceptions, drawn exclusively from the ranks of experienced counsel.

The solicitor can be an advocate in the magistrates' court and county court and may, since the Courts and Legal Services Act 1990 (CLSA), apply for rights of audience at all levels but she is more familiar to the public in her role as a general legal adviser. In 2003, there were over 116,000 solicitors, of whom around 92,000 held practising certificates.

13–002   Members of the public are able to call at a solicitor's office and seek advice, whereas a barrister could, until 2004, only be consulted indirectly through a solicitor, except by specified clients. The solicitor is sometimes likened to a general practitioner and the barrister to a consultant.

The analogy must not be taken too far, however, since the legal knowledge of the newly qualified barrister will not equal that of the senior partners of a firm of solicitors. Often, the solicitor is more of a specialist than the barrister.

Apart from the barristers and solicitors in private practice, a large number of lawyers are employed in large solicitors' firms, in central and local government, in commerce and industry and in education. For instance, in 2003, there were 2,700 employed barristers.

Barristers' attachment to wearing a lump of horsehair on their heads is ferocious. In the 18th century, wigs were regarded as a ridiculous Regency affectation, a fad. Even Lord Denman forbade his own son to wear one.

---

2. Training, Entry and Diversity

Barristers

13–003   A would-be barrister must first register as a student member of one of the four Inns of Court, Gray's Inn, Lincoln's Inn, Inner Temple and Middle Temple. They are close to the Royal Courts of Justice in London. The Inns, to one of which every barrister must belong, originated as colleges teaching the common law to advocates.

Detailed regulations govern entry to the profession. The general pattern is for the student to obtain a law degree and thereafter to undergo the one-year Bar Vocational Course (BVC). On satisfactory completion of the vocational course, students are called to the Bar by their Inn of Court. Graduates who do not have a law degree have to pass a one-year course, the Common Professional Examination or Postgraduate Diploma in Law, before proceeding to the BVC. Curiously, students are required to attend their Inn of Court to dine. This is a relic of the Inns' collegiate function. However brilliant the student, she cannot be called to the Bar unless she has eaten all of her 12 dinners, or completed the alternative, such as residential weekends.

After call to the Bar, the student has to undergo an apprenticeship known as pupillage. This involves understudying a junior counsel in day-to-day practice for a period of 12 months. Students entering employment may undergo pupillage as an employee. From 2001 all barristers are required to undertake continuing professional development.

Solicitors

The usual method of entry is a law degree and then a one-year **13–004** Legal Practice Course (LPC), or by taking a four year qualifying law degree, currently offered only at Northumbria. Provision is made, however, for non-law graduates and mature students to qualify as solicitors by undergoing a one-year educational stage before the Legal Practice Course. After this, the student must serve as a trainee in a firm of solicitors for two years. When the student has completed the training contract he may be "admitted" by the Master of the Rolls formally adding his name to the roll of officers of the Supreme Court. (The Master of the Rolls (M.R.) is the head of civil justice and heads the Court of Appeal (Civil Division)). He may not practice without an annual practising certificate individually issued by the Law Society. In order to obtain a practising certificate the solicitor has to comply with very detailed regulations governing solicitors' accounts and be insured through a managing general agency or approved insurer. All solicitors must, since 1998, undergo regular "continuing professional development" by attending non-examined training. The Law Society has statutory powers to regulate solicitors' training. Following consultation, in 2004, they approved the first courses geared to the needs of individual big firms, such as Linklaters and Clifford Chance.

Entering the Legal Profession: Numbers, Diversity and Cost

Entry to the profession is expensive and, historically, has been dif- **13–005** ficult for disadvantaged groups. The latest Bar and Law Society statistics, available in 2005 are, however, more encouraging.

Numbers

Law graduates escalated in the 1990s, to over 9,500 per year. Of **13–006** the 11,000 law students commencing in 2002, 63 per cent were female and 25 per cent were ethnic minority. 9,200 people graduated with a straight law degree, of whom 5,700 were women. Women were more likely than men to graduate with a first class or upper second class law degree. A further 3,500–4,000 students are

371

estimated to have graduated with a mixed degree which would qualify them for the academic stage of legal education. In 2002–3, 9,000 would-be solicitors enrolled with the Law Society, of whom 62 per cent were women and 22 per cent were non-white. In 2003, 7,200 sat the LPC examinations with a pass rate of around 80 per cent. Around 5,650 new traineeships were registered that year so, as can be seen, that means around 110 fewer traineeships were available than students eligible to enter a training contract. This is a significant improvement on 1999, when 6,285 students enrolled on an LPC course and only 4,827 new traineeships were registered. Research for the Law Society's Strategic Research Unit in 2003 exposed a "real problem" for small firms in recruiting and retaining solicitors.

In 2002–3, 17.9 per cent of trainee solicitors were non-white. Again, this compares favourably with statistics from four years earlier. Research conducted by the Policy Studies Institute for the Law Society, tracking the progress of 4,000 law degree and CPE graduates from 1993, showed that, by 1997, 25 per cent of LPC graduates still did not have training contracts. They found a bias against women, ethnic minority applicants, those from new universities and from less privileged backgrounds, irrespective of academic performance. City recruits were 16 times more likely to have graduated from Oxbridge than a new university, (*The Law Student Cohort Study*, Law Society's Strategic Research Unit). Non-whites had to make more applications than their white counterparts. The slow progress of ethnic minorities was caused by difficulties in entering the profession. Of those entering the LPC in 1998, 75 per cent of whites but only 45 per cent of minorities obtained a training contract. Attitudes of the profession were attacked as favouring white males, by Cherie Booth and senior minority solicitors, in 2000. Discriminatory attitudes were exposed in 2000 by Phil Thomas, in *Discriminating Lawyers*. In 2001, a scheme was launched by the Law Society, a charity and law firms to help ethnic minority students find training places and in 2002, the Law Society launched an *Equality and Diversity Framework for Action*. In 2003, the Law Society launched a Diversity Access Scheme to provide scholarships to law students from disadvantaged backgrounds. The Society encouraged solicitors' firms to provide work placements and mentoring schemes. By 2003, 7.9 per cent of solicitors with practising certificates were minority, compared with 5.5 per cent in 1999 and 3.1 per cent in 1993.

A 2005 Law Society Research Report, *Equality, Diversity and the Legal Practice Course*, compared success rates of whites and minorities on the LPC. There was a significant difference in performance between whites and non-whites but when other factors were controlled for, such as A level points, class of degree and whether a training contract had been obtained, there was no difference.

Women as a percentage of solicitors have increased throughout the   **13–007**
1990s and by 2003 they accounted for 39.7 per cent of solicitors with
practising certificates, compared with 27.6 per cent in 1993. The Law
Society was, nevertheless, concerned to find out why so many
women left the profession after ten years in practice. They commissioned research in 2004. Women who had taken a career break or left
were interviewed. They felt very strongly that the profession was
losing valuable talent due to rigid work practices, such as long hours,
perceived lack of career progression for women and little value being
attributed to women solicitors. This made little economic sense,
given the expenditure on training.

In 2004, the Law Society revised their Anti-Discrimination Rule,
which goes beyond current anti-discrimination legislation. They
are currently (in 2005) considering whether equality and diversity
training should be part of continuing professional education for
solicitors.

Entry to the Bar is more difficult. It is overcrowded, with many
forced out of practice. The workload of the criminal Bar (half the
Bar) declined in the 1990s and the Bar feared a reduction in civil
work because of the Access to Justice Act 1999. In 2003, there were
711 pupils, representing a reduction in pupillages available in the
1990s. 51.5 per cent of these were women and 19.5 per cent minority. There was a further reduction in 2004, with around 1,400 new
BVC graduates chasing 600 pupillages. Generally, only a fraction of
pupils are taken on as practising tenants. Fewer than three per cent
of those graduating with a law degree or the CPE will secure a
tenancy, meaning a permanent place as a barrister, after pupillage.
Discriminating Lawyers found that while 66 per cent of male
Oxbridge graduates secured pupillage, only ten per cent from new
universities did.

Women as a percentage of practising barristers have increased   **13–008**
throughout the 1990s, as with solicitors. In 2003, 29 per cent of independent barristers and 43 per cent of employed barristers were
women. This compares with 1997, when 25.4 per cent of practising
barristers were women.

In a Sheffield University survey by Joanna Shapland and Angela
Sorsby, nearly half the non-white junior Bar claimed to have experienced discrimination. Over a third of women claimed to have suffered sex discrimination.

In 2004, the Fawcett Society published a 12-month study of
women's experiences in the criminal justice system. Findings were
that women represented:

- 1 of 12 Law Lords.
- 5 of 43 chief constables.

- 18 of 42 chief probation officers.
- 7 of 42 chief Crown Prosecutors.
- 31 of 138 prison governors.

They drew attention to pyramid of women in the legal profession and judiciary. Seven per cent of High Court judges were women (all barristers), compared with 59 per cent of law graduates.

13–009   At a 2002 meeting of the Council of the Inns of Court, following an inquiry by Thorpe L.J., the Inns agreed to a package of 48 measures to try to eliminate sex and race discrimination. The report found that the Inns' benchers were overwhelmingly white and male, 66 of 1028, in 1999, were female. There was also a systematic bias in favour of whites in the award of scholarships and bursaries by the Inns. In 1999, 56.9 per cent of white applicants and 25.6 per cent of minority applicants were successful but 2000 figures showed a "sharp improvement".

As with solicitors, there is a large attrition rate of women from practice and the Bar Council is now (2005) surveying those who have left in the last three years. In 2004, the Bar Council approved a revised *Equality and Diversity Code for the Bar*. It emphasizes the importance of giving pupils and junior tenants (new barristers) access to good quality work. The Bar Code of conduct now requires each set of chambers to have an equality policy and one member must take responsibility for equality and diversity issues. Diversity training is being incorporated into barristers' continuing education.

Cost

13–010   In 2005, the fee for the LPC or BVC was £8–10,000. Many lawyers carry large debts by the time they qualify. Ironically, the 2000 report of the PSI *Cohort* study found that professional sponsorship was most likely to go to those from well-off families. Seventy-four per cent of Oxbridge graduates received LPC funding, compared with 3 per cent from new universities. Sixty per cent of trainees were paid below the Law Society minimum, with the disabled, non-Oxbridge graduates and those from state schools paid the least. In November 2004, a Department of Constitutional Affairs (DCA) minister urged city law firms to stop discriminating in favour of Oxbridge law graduates, saying they were 16 times more likely to find jobs in the city than those from new universities. Graduates from new universities include more ethnic minorities and those from disadvantaged backgrounds.

At the Bar, things are worse. Local authority discretionary grants, which used to fund many through the Bar exams (80 per cent of students in 1987) have dried up. One 1970s recipient, from a poor background, was Cherie Booth who said the current expense of going to the Bar discriminates against the poor (1997 Bar Conference). In 2003, the Bar Council established a task force on funding entry to the Bar. It recommended monitoring entry, disseminating more information about entry to the Bar and raising more funds to target support for needy students. In October 2004, the Attorney-General, addressing the Young Bar Conference, said the Bar risked "going back to being the preserve of the privileged and wealthy".

Many new barristers cannot survive, because their earnings are less than their chambers rent. Hence, many drop out of the Bar within the first five years, with large debts. In 2001, the Bar Council voted to introduce compulsory financial awards to pupils of £10,000 per year. For new lawyers, work can be hard. The PSI *Cohort* study showed a third of trainee solicitors regularly worked over 50 hours a week.

3. Organisation and Regulation

The organisation of the two branches of the legal profession is the responsibility of two quite independent sets of governing bodies. 13–011

Barristers

The Inns of Court
The Inns are administered by their senior members, Benchers. The student is called to the Bar at her Inn. The Inns, historically, had a collegiate function in training new barristers. They now provide the dining system and own and administer valuable property in the Temple area from which most of London's practising barristers rent their chambers. The Inns are included and depicted in my self-guided walking tour on the Sweet and Maxwell website (see note on Online Updates at the front of this book). 13–012

The General Council of the Bar (known as "the Bar Council")
This is the professional governing body of the Bar. It comprises elected barristers and those representing the Inns, circuits and specialist Bar Associations. The Bar Council performs similar professional functions to the Law Society. It lays down the Bar's Code of Conduct and administers the system for disciplining errant barristers and it represents the bar as a trade union. In addition, the six court circuits have their own Bar Associations, as do specialist barristers. The Council's informative website explains all aspects of the organisation and the profession. 13–013

Junior Counsel and Queen's Counsel ("Silks")

> "As I said in . . . 1998 . . . in the public perception the grant of silk is a licence to print money . . . informed advisers wisely recommend prospective litigants . . . to sue on the Continent . . . In those countries at least equal justice is obtainable at a fraction of the cost." (The Hon. Mr Justice Lightman, "The Civil Justice System and Legal Profession—The Challenges Ahead" (2003) 22 C.J.Q. 235.)

13–014   All practising barristers, however old, are junior counsel unless they have been designated Queen's Counsel (QC). At the time of writing, 2005, there are 1244 QCs, of whom 103 are women. The status, first recognised in the sixteenth century, was not created by statute. It is bestowed by the Queen, exercising her royal prerogative power on the advice of the Lord Chancellor. Until 2003, the Lord Chancellor held an annual competition. The change of status is, financially, something of a speculation. Once appointed, the Queen's Counsel is expected to appear only in the most complex and/or important cases. She is known as a "leader" because she is often accompanied by one, and sometimes two, junior counsel. There used to be a rule called the Two Counsel Rule whereby a QC had to pay a junior to appear as an assistant in court. This was abolished in 1977, following criticism by the Monopolies and Mergers Commission but it is still widely followed in practice. The practice has been the subject of repeated criticism and scrutiny and regulations on public funding have made inroads into it. Becoming a QC is called "taking silk", since the status entitles the barrister to wear a silk gown, rather than a junior barrister's stuff gown. QCs enjoy other privileges. Apart from being paid significantly higher fees, even in publicly funded cases, they are entitled to sit in the front row of the courtroom. Indeed, in the old courtrooms in the Royal Courts of Justice, a gate separates that row from those behind. Apart from sitting closest to the judge, they also have the formal right to address her before any other advocate.

The appointment system for silks has been under scrutiny by Lord Chancellor Falconer in 2003–4, following years of criticism. The old criteria required candidates to have practised for ten years, with at least five years' advocacy experience in the higher courts. This meant that solicitor-advocates (still only a handful) were not considered suitable until about 1999. The Lord Chancellor's criteria included outstanding ability as an advocate; high professional standing and respect; a high quality practice based on demanding cases and there used to be a requirement that the applicant could demonstrate high earnings. The Lord Chancellor made "consultations" with the judiciary and the profession, in the selection process. Statistics revealed that very few women and ethnic minorities applied. In 2000, of 506 applicants, only 53 were women and 24 ethnic minority.

The Adam Smith Institute published a strong attack on the silk system, in Reeves' 1998 report, *Silk Cut*. They recommended silks should be abolished, for these reasons:

- The term "junior" for other barristers is misleading.
- The annual "silk round" occupies seven civil servants.
- Those employed in local authorities, the Crown Prosecution Service (CPS) and industry are not eligible.
- Very competent barristers may seldom appear before the consultant judges.
- Silks are about ten per cent of the Bar. This keeps able juniors out.
- The office has become the route to extremely high earnings. Clients are lured into extra expense because they think that employing a silk will enhance their chances of success.
- Ireland is the only other EU Member State with a silk system.
- Judges have criticised the waste of public money in using silks.
- Despite the abolition of the Two Counsel Rule, silks rarely appear alone.
- Although silks are meant to be selected for their outstanding competence as advocates, the European Court of Justice has criticised the written submissions of British lawyers as unduly long and repetitive.
- Without silk, a free market in advocacy would prevail, with reputations dependent on competence.
- An archaic and misleading title is bestowed upon relatively few practitioners, which does nothing to enhance legal services.

In February 1999, over 100 MPs, led by Andrew Dismore, **13–015** started campaigning for the abolition of silk. At the 1999 silk ceremony, Lord Chancellor Irvine defended the award of silk as "the kite-mark of quality", enabling lawyers and clients to identify the leading members of the profession and to identify likely candidates for the Bench. In April 2000, when no solicitor-advocate of the six who applied was granted silk, the Law Society President condemned the rank of QC as a perk for barristers. Since 1996, when they could first apply, only eight solicitor-advocates had been awarded the rank. In his speech at the 2001 silk ceremony,

Lord Irvine insisted the appointment process was fair and open but, unexpectedly, in the Bar's October 2000 annual conference, they voted overwhelmingly to reform it.

Since 1995, there has been increasing concern expressed in the press over the earnings of silks, especially those funded by the State for criminal defence, as I explain in Chapter 17 on legal services, below—"fat cats". Judges have joined in this criticism. Mr Justice Lightman, speaking to the Chancery Bar in 1998, said "it must be a matter of grave concern if leaders of the first rank charge fees beyond the range reasonably affordable by ordinary litigants but fees which their wealthy and powerful opponents can afford. There is then no equality before the law." A 2000 survey of barristers' earnings found 26 silks earned over a million pounds a year and in 2001, *The Lawyer* published a survey showing silks lost as many cases as they won, in 2000.

Bearing in mind that the mischief of the Courts and Legal Services Act 1990 and the Access to Justice Act 1999 was to demolish the profession's restrictive practices, as explained below, it is remarkable how swiftly the whole issue was reopened by the Office of Fair Trading, in 2001. In July 2002, the Lord Chancellor's Department (now DCA) published a consultation paper called *In the public interest?* This was provoked by a 2001 report, *Competition in the Professions*, by the Director General of Fair Trading, which questioned the competitiveness of the silk system.

13–016   The LCD consulted on the regulation of legal services, including possible changes to the QC system to improve its value to consumers. In its response, the Office of Fair Trading insisted that the QC system was anti-competitive, lacked quality control and was of little use to customers. The appointments system hindered competition because the earning power and competitive position of barristers was enhanced but little extra value was offered to clients. It lacked quality control because the title QC was not removed from a barrister if standards dropped. The Bar Council rejected these comments, arguing that the appointments system had been modernised and was "much fairer and more transparent" and there was no barrier to competition but the Law Society, which had long opposed the QC system, considered it inappropriate for the Queen to confer on members of a single private profession a public honour and rank which accorded them precedence. There was no logical reason why outstanding doctors or dentists should not be so honoured. Solicitors did not find the QC rank of use in selecting an advocate of guaranteed quality. Critics objected to the rank's being a reward for advocacy, when in litigation nowadays there was an emphasis on seeking an early settlement, usually effected by solicitors. They also objected to the selection process, based on consultations with judges and lawyers, rather than evidence. The judiciary considered that the QC rank was helpful in identifying candidates for judicial appointments but the Bar considered this inappropriate.

In 2003, Lord Chancellor Falconer (himself a QC, married to a QC) published yet another consultation paper, *Constitutional reform: the future of Queen's Counsel*, which most commentators assumed signalled New Labour's intention to abolish the rank. This new paper raised a long list of questions. It is archived, with responses, on the DCA website (*www.dca.gov.uk*). To summarise, the paper asked whether the QC rank should continue or be restructured and if so upon what criteria; whether Government involvement was appropriate; what were the benefits of the QC system; whether it should be restricted to advocates and if there were to be a replacement quality mark, by what mechanism should it be awarded.

Not surprisingly, the biggest group of respondents were QCs, comprising 93 of the 376. Another 110 respondents were judges, barristers or their representative bodies. Almost half of respondents thought the rank should be retained and half of them thought it should be reformed. Of those who thought it should be abolished, three quarters would replace it with another quality mark. The majority of respondents considered it appropriate for the state to award a professional rank. Most thought the public interest would not suffer if Government was not directly responsible for the selection process. Most considered that a Minister could make recommendations after guidance from another body and that individuals should not be subject to reappraisal. Most thought, if the rank were to be discontinued then the Government should not be involved in a replacement quality mark. Most respondents considered that the public benefited from the rank of QC and that the mark should be confined to advocates. Interestingly, one group of strong proponents of retention of the QC title were black lawyers, who argued that, just as they were poised to enter the rank, the opportunity might be snatched away from them.

Lord Chancellor Falconer announced his decision in May 2004. He **13–017** did not express an intention to abolish the system but he declined to continue his ministerial involvement in selection. He instead asked the Bar and Law Society to develop new schemes for accrediting advocates. Kitemarking must serve consumers' interests by identifying excellence. He would retain responsibility for making recommendations to the Queen. The consultation process demonstrated the need for (*yet another*) wider review of information available to consumers of legal services so he would establish a longer term market study and in the meantime, leave it to the Bar and Law Society to devise an interim scheme, using the term QC. This caused the Law

Society to express disappointment. By November 2004, the profession had agreed on such a scheme. The new process is designed to improve fairness and transparency. The consultation system, or "secret soundings", as critics called it, will be replaced by a system with structured references from judges and practitioners. The applicant will undergo an interview with a human resources professional, to test personal skills and understanding of diversity issues. Selection will be made by a panel of judges, lawyers and lay people. Poorly performing silks may have their title revoked by the selection panel.

Treasury Counsel

13–018   An elite group of barristers, known as Treasury Counsel, are briefed to appear for the Government in public law cases and for the prosecution in top criminal cases in the Old Bailey. In recent years this system has suffered two accusations. The first was a complaint that the selection system was secretive and discriminatory, favouring white males from a limited background and the second was that Treasury Counsel were overpaid. A former circuit judge, in a report to the Attorney-General in 2000, said they were often paid twice as much as the judges before whom they appeared.

The Barrister's Clerk

13–019   It is normal for a "set" of barristers in chambers to share a clerk as a business manager and it is said that the clerk, or practice manager, can make or break, the barrister. The barrister's clerk arranges work and negotiates the fee unless it is a publicly funded case paid for by the Community Legal Service Fund or Criminal Defence Service. There is an Institute of Barristers' Clerks, which represents clerks' interests. In October 2000, *The Independent* reported that some clerks earned up to £350,000, far more than most barristers.

Solicitors

13–020   ### The Law Society
Solicitors are, by statute, professionally regulated by the Law Society which is controlled by an elected body consisting of a Council and President and they are assisted by a full-time Chief Executive and a large Secretariat. For non-statutory purposes, membership of the Law Society is voluntary. The Society publishes the Law Society's *Gazette*. The mechanism for handling client's complaints is described on the Law Society's website.

The Law Society's hopeless struggle to regulate the profession and respond to consumer complaints satisfactorily is almost too painful to describe. Since the 1979 Royal Commission on Legal Services (RCLS) Report, there has been growing governmental concern over the ability of the solicitors' profession to regulate themselves. Independent surveys exposed poor quality work. A 1995 Consumers' Association survey tested the quality of advice given to researchers posing as clients. In a variety of legal problems, only a small minority of solicitors gave the correct advice. A 2000 Consumers' Association survey found many vulnerable people felt they received a second class service and again in 2001, they criticised solicitors' services. In 2004, the Consumers' Association reported on shoddy service yet again. They found solicitors had not improved since a survey three years earlier. Excessive delay was the commonest complaint, followed by negligence, failure to respond to letters or telephone calls and lack of respect.

In the meantime, the Law Society was failing to cope with a mounting backlog of complaints. In 1996, it replaced the discredited Solicitors' Complaints Bureau with the Office for the Supervision of Solicitors (OSS) but this had no effect. It in turn was replaced, again to no avail. In 1999, the Legal Services Ombudsman, appointed under the Courts and Legal Services Act 1990 to oversee the complaints process, described complaints handling as "spiralling out of control". In 1998, Lord Chancellor Irvine warned the Law Society that he would ask Parliament for statutory power to take over the regulation of solicitors from the Law Society and this was granted in the Access to Justice Act 1999. In 1999, in a speech to the Law Society conference he described their handling of complaints as "lamentable". In January 2001, LCD Minister David Lock gave a final written warning to the Law Society that it would lose its "privilege" of self-regulation if it did not radically improve matters by the summer but, by July 2001, the Legal Services Ombudsman repeated this warning. She was satisfied with the handling of complaints in only 57 per cent of cases. In 2003, she again reported that Law Society complaints handling was "unacceptable". In 2004, Lord Chancellor Falconer gave her the additional job of Legal Services Complaints Commissioner and the power to fine the Law Society £1 million if it failed to deal adequately with complaints. In May 2005 she again reported on poor service and delays in Law Society complaints handling.

The Law Society Practice Rules require solicitors' firms to provide **13–021** an in-house complaints procedure. Research by a Bristol University team in 1998 found 80 per cent of clients sampled had not been told of such a procedure, as required, and the procedure was seldom, if ever, used and the operation of the process was criticised by other researchers in 2000. Another academic, Avrom Sherr, produced a damning report on the solicitors' complaints procedures in 1999 (*Willing Blindness?—Complaints Handling Procedures*). In 1998, a Channel 4 *Dispatches* programme uncovered various dishonest solicitors who had been found guilty by the Solicitors' Disciplinary

Tribunal of fraud or mishandling clients' money and who continued to practice. The 2004 CA survey, quoted above, reported that more than 40 per cent of their survey respondents who received poor service failed to complain, thinking there was no point. Of those who did complain, almost all were dissatisfied with complaints handling. One person described the Law Society as "a body drinking at the same waterhole as the legal hyenas it purports to be checking up on".

The Institute of Legal Executives
13–022   The body which represents over 22,000 qualified "para-legals" employed in solicitors' offices is the Institute of Legal Executives, which has its own examination system for admission as an Associate or a Fellow of the Institute. The routine work of a solicitor's office is largely carried out by legal executives and they are significant fee earners in many practices.

Clementi on Complaints and Regulation
13–023   Doubtless through exasperation with solicitors' inability to regulate themselves, but also because of the attacks on the profession by the Office of Fair Trading, Lord Chancellor Falconer established *The Review of the Regulatory Framework for Legal Services in England and Wales*, carried out in 2003–4 by David Clementi. He was appointed to examine what form of regulation would be best to promote competition and innovation, serve consumer interests and make lawyers more accountable.

In December 2004, he produced his *Review*. He considered that existing arrangements did not prioritise the public interest. He complained of the "absolute cat's cradle" of 22 existing regulatory bodies for lawyers. Unsurprisingly, he suggested abolishing the legal profession's right to self-regulation. There should be a new regulator, a Legal Services Board, chaired by a non-lawyer and accountable to Parliament. Its statutory objectives would include upholding the rule of law, promoting access to justice, protecting consumer interests and promoting competition. The Board would have the power to exercise all regulatory functions but would normally delegate these to the professional bodies. It would assess their rules, in consultation with the Office of Fair Trading. The Bar and Law Society would have to separate their regulatory functions from their trade union functions. The Law Society had already resolved to do that, in anticipation of his report and by March 2005 the Bar had proposed a Bar Standards Board which would include laypeople. All complaints would be made to an Office for Legal Complaints, independent of the professions. Its aim would be to provide "quick and fair redress to consumers". It would have the power to investigate complaints, mediate between client and lawyers and make binding orders for consumer redress. It would not get involved with discipline, as executed by the Solicitors' Disciplinary Tribunal. Clementi refused to agree that the Bar should continue to regulate themselves. The outgoing Bar chairman grumbled at this, justifiably protesting that the Bar's track-record on complaints handling had been a good one. He retorted "We have a right to expect earned autonomy in our affairs". Lord Chancellor Falconer responded that the Government broadly accepted Clementi's recommendations, promising a white paper in 2005, then legislation. Below, I discuss Clementi's recommendations on legal practice and reactions to his report.

4. Work of Barristers and Solicitors

Barristers

Most barristers are professional advocates. As such, a barrister   13–024
must be capable of prosecuting in a criminal case one day and defending an accused person the next; or of preparing a skeleton argument and taking the case for a claimant in a civil action one day and doing the same for a defendant the next. In this way barristers claim to attain a real degree of objectivity and independence, becoming specialists in advocacy.

In practice there is a great deal of paperwork involved in the pre-trial stages of a case, particularly where skeleton arguments have to be prepared. Additionally, barristers will often be asked, by solicitors or other professionals, to give written advice on a particular legal matter. This is known as "taking counsel's opinion". Indeed, some barristers who specialise in planning law, tax law or employment law may do most of their work from their offices (chambers), or home, in documentary form, and only occasionally appear in court. Over half of practising barristers work in London. The remainder operate from around 60 provincial centres.

Until the recommendations of the Clementi report are fully implemented, barristers are not allowed to form partnerships, other than overseas, but may share the same set of chambers and also frequently share a clerk. It often happens that court hearings overlap or are fixed for the same day and then another barrister usually in the same chambers, has to take the case at short notice. This is called a "late brief" and is discussed below.

From a low point of 1,919 barristers in 1960, the Bar has increased   13–025
in size each year and does not seem to have been affected by enhancing solicitors' rights of audience, because so few have chosen to qualify, as described below. Their work has diversified in parallel with solicitors' work. The enforcement of the Human Rights Act in

2000 has provided a substantial opportunity for a new and broad field of specialist advice which is much in demand.

The Access to Justice Act 1999, while seen as threatening some publicly funded work, has permitted quality civil rights chambers to gain legal services contracts for the first time, with the Legal Services Commission, in the same way as firms of solicitors. Like solicitors, the Bar have developed their own *pro bono* scheme, some of which is directed to working with Community Legal Service volunteers on welfare law advice, as explained in Chapter 17, on legal services, below.

In 2000, the Bar launched BarMark, its own quality assurance standard, granted by the Bar Council and certified by the British Standards Institution.

Solicitors

13–026   The trend is towards having several solicitors in partnership or, since 1992, incorporated companies, and towards ever larger firms or consortia of firms and this trend will increase, because of the requirement for contracts for legal services, explained in Chapter 17, below. This gives them the opportunity to specialise to some extent so that whilst one partner may spend all his time on family work, another will deal with litigation, another with probate and trusts and so on. In some of the larger London firms there are more than 100 partners who are highly specialised. Solicitors' main specialisms are as follows:

Commercial work

13–027   City solicitors advise on company formation and organisation, taxation, insolvency, intellectual property, pensions, insurance, contracts and financial regulation. Most large London firms are now multi-national partnerships. Solicitors export a significant element of their services to foreign clients. A 1999 Law Society survey showed legal services contributed £791m to the UK's invisible earnings.

Domestic conveyancing

This means transferring the legal title to property. The 1979 Royal Commission on Legal Studies found this to be the "bread and butter" fee earner of many firms, especially as solicitors enjoyed a monopoly, at that time. The financial recession from 1989 forced solicitors to look for other work, however.

Selling property

As solicitors saw some of their conveyancing work disappear to estate agents and institutions, some started selling property, during the 1980s.

Family law

The divorce rate and growth in legal aid caused an expansion of this work since 1980. The Children Act 1989 permitted children to be legally aided and thus separately represented from each of their parents and any involved local authority.

13–028

Probate

There has been a decline, since 1989, in the number of solicitors involved in the administration of deceased persons' property. Solicitors' monopoly over probate work was abolished by the Courts and Legal Services Act 1990 but rules to fully open the market to non-lawyers were only implemented in 2004.

Employment

Surveys have shown this to be a growth area in the 1990s.

Social welfare

Solicitors have been notoriously poor in providing advice on welfare law, such as housing and state benefits. The RCLS 1979, criticised this gap in provision. Now, solicitors' firms who seek a Community Legal Service contract must show they can provide advice in welfare benefits.

13–029

Criminal law

This was another big growth area in legally aided work since 1980, with the expansion of the duty solicitor schemes into magistrates' courts and police stations. As explained in Chapter 17, below, the stated aim of the Criminal Defence Service is to concentrate publicly funded representation into fewer larger firms of solicitors and exclude the "dabblers", who will still be entitled to represent privately paying clients.

Accidents and personal injury

Specialist litigators have developed since 1980, sometimes involving multi-party actions, with multiple claimants, such as industrial disasters or the negligent release of new drugs.

Consumer protection

Although the small claims civil track is designed to be used by the litigant in person, many parties choose to be privately represented.

13–030

Individual financial advice

This relates to investments, insurance and pensions. The 1997 survey showed that one sixth of practitioners regularly conducted personal bankruptcy and debt work. Many are registered under the Financial Services Act.

Pro bono work

This means providing legal services free of charge. The Solicitors *Pro Bono* Group was formed in 1997, with funds donated by big city law firms, several of whom had established *pro bono* units. Solicitors employed in some of these units concentrate on big human rights cases and on representing appellants against the death penalty, in appeals from the Caribbean. A 2003 survey showed that around half of solicitors surveyed had done *pro bono* work in the last twelve months. Small firms were more likely to have offered such services than large ones. Lord Chief Justice Woolf, who has for years tried to eliminate legal Latin, wanted to replace the term with "law for free" but no-one seems to have taken any notice.

International practice

13–031   English law firms have offices in around 40 foreign countries. The Rights of Establishment Directive 98/51 (implemented in 2000) makes it easy for solicitors to open up offices in other Member States of the EU. After three years they will have the right to acquire the title of lawyer in the foreign state.

Advocacy

Solicitors all have rights of audience before magistrates' courts and county courts. Additionally, they may qualify for an advocacy certificate in the higher courts.

Multi Disciplinary Partnerships

By 2005, solicitors were still banned from forming a partnership with a member of another profession. The 1979 RCLS supported the ban. The Conservative government's green paper, *The Work and Organisation of the Legal Profession* (Cm 570, 1989) viewed this as an unnecessary restriction on competition and s.66 of the Courts and Legal Services Act 1990 removed the statutory prohibition. The Law Society nevertheless maintained its opposition, arguing that Multi Disciplinary Partnerships (MDPs) would undermine the network of solicitors' firms, threaten client confidentiality and create conflicts of interest. The 1997 survey showed that over half of solicitors thought that MDPs were inevitable.

5. Professional Etiquette

13–032   The judiciary and the legal profession is organised in a rigid hierarchical system which is symbolised in the layout of the court-room and was historically supported by the professions' monopolies and rules of etiquette and dress. The judge sits on a raised dais. In old courtrooms such as Chester, this is many feet above the Bar. High Court judges have five different sets of gowns and two types of wig, for ceremony, different types of case and red letter days (saints' days). Until the 1980s, advocates addressed them in grovelling language and some still do "May it please your lordship . . . ". Queen's Counsel sit nearest to the judge, on the front row. They wear a special wig, a long court coat and a silk gown. Lesser advocates, known as junior barristers, sit behind them, wearing a different horsehair wig and stuff gown. On the back of their gown is a pocket, where the barrister's fee would be inserted by a grateful client, as this "gentlemen's profession" could not be seen to soil their hands with money. If a solicitor qualifies to sit in these rows, as a solicitor-advocate, he is not permitted to wear a wig. Behind the barristers sit the solicitors or representatives, who have done most of the work in preparing the case. It used to be the case that barristers would address one another in court as "my learned friend" and solicitors as "my friend". An outsider could be forgiven for thinking that barristers are the superior profession, more learned, people who have passed more difficult exams and that QCs are the very crème of the intellectual crème of the law.

Both barristers and solicitors are closely restricted in their professional conduct by the supervision of their respective governing bodies. Generally, except under the BarDIRECT scheme, a barrister only meets the lay client when the solicitor, or solicitor's representative, is present, so building up the isolation, as well as the objectivity, of the barrister. In order to prevent barristers gaining unfair advantage by cultivating the friendship of solicitors, there used to be a rule which prevented a solicitor and barrister in a case from having lunch together. Separate dining rooms were created even in the court buildings of the 1980s.

In a 2000 vote, most barristers chose to retain wigs, as enhancing the dignity and solemnity of court proceedings and a formal sign of the advocate's status and importance in the courtroom. This is despite the fact that Lord Chief Justice Woolf thinks they are outmoded and Lord Chancellor Irvine expressed his distaste for wigs in civil disputes and dispensed with all his ceremonial garb for his appearances as speaker of the House of Lords. In 2003, Lord Chancellor Falconer published a consultation paper on court dress but nothing has come of it.

Solicitors, of course, regard all this as so much snobbery. They **13–033** expressed disappointment at Lord Falconer's decision in 2004, not to abolish QCs. Even employed barristers complained to Sir David Clementi that they felt like second class citizens compared with the independent bar.

There used to be a rule, articulated in the 1969 case of *Rondel v Worsley* (HL) that barristers could not be sued for negligent work in court, or in preparation of court work. In *Arthur JS Hall & Co v Simons* (2000), the House of Lords abolished this protection as no longer in accord with public policy and being out of line with the liability of other professions, such as doctors, and with lawyers in other EU states. It would end the anomalous exception to the basic premise that there should be a remedy for a wrong. There was no reason to fear a flood of actions against barristers. It tended to erode confidence in the legal system if advocates, alone among professional men, were immune from liability for negligence.

A corollary of this immunity was the rule that barristers did not sue for their fees because, historically, barristers were not contractually bound to solicitors but were paid an *honorarium*, or gift for services rendered. The Courts and Legal Services Act 1990, s.61, permitted barristers to enter into binding contracts. Nevertheless, the slowness of solicitors in paying fees still puts new barristers under a severe financial strain.

Finally, one result of the division of the legal profession is that no one can practise as both a barrister and a solicitor at the same time although it is now possible to be doubly qualified. Provision has, however, been made for transfer from one profession to the other and it has become easier over the years, especially since the Access to Justice Act 1999.

6. The Abolition of the Professions' Monopolies: Bar Wars

13–034   Since the mid-1970s, people have questioned the desirability of allowing the legal profession to preserve its ancient monopolies. In the eyes of others, they are restrictive practices, limiting competition and consumer choice and allowing lawyers to overcharge. Margaret Thatcher assumed all monopolies and restrictive practices to be anti-competitive. Her Scottish Lord Chancellor, Lord Mackay, worshipped no sacred cows in the English legal system but if lawyers imagined that New Labour would be any more supportive of their monopolies, then they were mistaken. In 2003, European Commissioner Mario Monti warned professions to stop acting in an anti-competitive manner and urged them to modernise practice rules. He warned that the European Commission would take a member state to the ECJ if it permitted unjustified restraints on competition or protected them by law.

Notice, from the following story, what a slow struggle it has been to dismantle lawyers' restrictive practices and how both sides of the profession have passionately defended their monopolies on the ground that they best serve the public interest.

The Abolition of the Solicitors' Conveyancing Monopoly

The conveyancing monopoly was one of the reasons for the   13–035
establishment of the RCLS, 1976–1979. Under the Solicitors Act
1922, unqualified persons were prohibited from conveyancing for
gain. The RCLS found most solicitors' practices derived 40 to 60 per
cent of their gross fee income from it. Critics complained that it
allowed solicitors to overcharge. They operated a scale of fees
which meant that, for conveying an expensive property, however
simple the work, they earned a large fee. Solicitors defended their
monopoly by claiming that their training, professional ethics and
compulsory indemnity insurance all protected the public.

The Commission disappointed all critics by recommending the
preservation of the monopoly but the Consumers' Association promoted Austin Mitchell MP's House Buyers' Bill, in 1983, designed
to abolish it. He withdrew the Bill in 1984, when the Thatcher government assured him they would introduce similar legislation. To
Thatcher's cabinet, monopolies were all undesirable, as stifling
competition in the free market and thus limiting consumer choice.
The Farrand Committee was established, to examine the system of
conveyancing. They recommended a system of licensed conveyancers and this was enacted in the Administration of Justice Act
1985.

Solicitors perceived a much greater threat from conveyancing by
banks and building societies. The Building Societies Act 1986 gave
the Lord Chancellor the power to permit this but it remained
unimplemented throughout the 1980s. The Law Society complained that such a practice would create conflicts of interest.
Conservative Lord Chancellor Mackay addressed this question in
one of his three 1989 green papers, *Conveyancing By Authorised
Practitioners*. It proposed a simplified framework, replacing the
1986 Act. The paper denied solicitors' allegations that the public
would be unprotected. Solicitors continued to argue that the
public would suffer from conflicts of interest, being persuaded to
have their conveyancing done by their mortgage lender, who
probably also sold them their house. They claimed that "unfair
competition" from banks and building societies would extinguish
most firms of high street solicitors, thus denying the public easy
access to legal services. The Government refined its plans in a 1989
white paper, *Legal Services: A Framework for the Future*. They

proposed to add further safeguards for the public against conflicts of interest. This resulted in the Courts and Legal Services Act 1990, ss.34–53, which provides the regulatory machinery for licensed conveyancers.

13–036 Most importantly, s.17(1) articulates the Conservative philosophy enacted in their reforms of legal services and abolition of lawyers' monopolies: the statutory objective of the Act.

"The development of legal services in England and Wales (and in particular the development of advocacy, litigation, conveyancing and probate services) by making provision for new or better ways of providing such services and a wider choice of persons providing them, while maintaining the proper and efficient administration of justice."

Consequences of the abolition

13–037 Solicitors relaxed their advertising ban. Conveyancing costs fell dramatically. Solicitors began selling houses, getting their own back on estate agents. The Law Society developed the practice of identifying and promoting new areas of work for solicitors. The profession has expanded each year, contrary to the Law Society's prediction that this was the death knell of the high street solicitor. Most significantly, solicitors attacked the Bar's monopoly over rights of audience in the higher courts.

Abolition of the Probate and Litigation Monopolies

13–038 Solicitors' monopolies over probate and litigation work (negotiation and case management prior to trial) were protected by the Solicitors' Act 1922. They were abolished, in a similar way, by the Courts and Legal Services Act 1990, which permitted institutions and legal executives to offer probate services.

As for litigation, solicitors did not fuss about the abolition of this restrictive practice. The Bar has been contemplating for decades whether ordinary clients should be permitted to directly access a barrister, who would then conduct all the litigation and not just the advocacy element. They have progressively permitted barristers to access certain groups of clients direct. This scheme is now called BarDIRECT and in July 2004, it was radically extended to all cases except criminal, family and immigration work. A rule of non-discrimination applies and barristers must be trained. Barristers are still not allowed to conduct litigation, however. The Access to Justice Act 1999 permitted the Bar Council to authorise this so the only barrier to barristers conducting litigation is now the Bar Council itself.

Abolishing the Bar's Monopoly over Rights of Audience

Since county courts were created by the County Courts Act 1846, **13–039** solicitors have had rights of audience before them. In magistrates' courts, the vast majority of advocates are solicitors. Solicitors may also appear in tribunals, as may laypeople, such as Citizens' Advice Bureaux workers and other charity workers. Others who have rights of audience include employees of central and local government and other public bodies. Additionally, individuals have a right to represent themselves. This is thought of as an important civil right.

Solicitors, then, are by far the most prolific of advocates but the public's image of the typical advocate has always been the robed and bewigged barrister because, until 1990, they had a monopoly over rights of audience in the Crown Court and all superior courts, with certain exceptions. The cases dealt with in the superior courts are, generally, more complex, time consuming and, importantly, lucrative.

The Royal Commission on Legal Services (1976–1979)

Solicitors asked the RCLS to extend their rights of audience to the **13–040** Crown Court (at the very least). To the Bar's relief, the Commission concluded that an extension would be against the public interest. Their reasons are worth studying because they are still argued now, in defence of a separate Bar:

- It would destroy the livelihood of the junior Bar (90 per cent of the Bar), who derived 30–50 per cent of their income from criminal work.
- If it resulted in the development of substantial solicitors' advocacy practices, prosecuting or defending, this would lead to the loss of independence.
- If solicitors were given general rights, it might lead to the development of large, specialist firms, which would be against the public interest.
- County court trials, which solicitors were used to conducting, could not be compared with jury trials, which required the skills of public speaking, a detailed knowledge of the law of evidence and the ability to cross-examine.
- The majority of solicitors' practices were not geared to providing advocacy services. Most solicitors could not absent themselves from their offices for most of the working day, sometimes for days on end.
- Even if solicitors were only given the right to appear in guilty pleas in the Crown Court, this could still threaten the livelihood of the young criminal Bar. Also, the "offender requires

391

the highest possible standard of representation which can only be provided by a specialist advocate".

- Such a change would be a step nearer to a fused legal profession, which the Commission did not favour.

Thatcherite attack on restrictive practices

13–041 In the very week that the Government announced a review of their conveyancing monopoly, the Law Society retaliated by launching an attack on the Bar, a campaign for rights of audience in all courts. To the scandalised amusement of the press, the two sides of the profession waged a bitter public debate.

The Marre Report

13–042 To take the heat out of the atmosphere, the two sides established the Committee on the Future of the Legal Profession, (the Marre Committee) in 1986. They recommended extending solicitors' rights of audience to the Crown Court, organised by a licensing system.

The green papers

13–043 The next significant watershed was the Lord Chancellor's publication, in 1989, of three green papers. The paper on *The Work and Organisation of the Legal Profession* acknowledged the Bar's case for restricting rights of audience:

- Judges work without legal assistance, therefore rely on the strength and adequacy of advocacy.
- Judges need to trust advocates not to mislead the court.
- Judgments create precedents. Judges look to advocates to cite all relevant authorities. "The presentation of cogent legal argument is a highly skilled task requiring not only a knowledge of the law but also constant practice in advocacy."

Therefore, rights of audience should be restricted to those who are properly trained, suitably experienced and subject to codes of conduct which maintain standards.

Then Lord Chancellor Mackay dropped his bombshell, making himself the instant enemy of judges and the Bar:

"The basic premise is that the satisfaction of such requirements should, for the future, alone be the test for granting rights of audience; and not whether an advocate happened by initial qualification to be a lawyer, whether a barrister or a solicitor, and whether in private practice or employed." (para.5.8)

A system of advocacy certificates, general and limited would be established, with professional bodies determining whether candidates had satisfied the relevant requirements, such as passing exams. The Lord Chancellor, after consulting the judges, would determine which professional bodies would have the power to grant rights.

Judicial hysteria

13–044 The Bar and judiciary were deeply affronted. Judges considered it their exclusive prerogative to decide who could appear before them. They launched verbal open warfare on Lord Mackay. The Bar Chairman said "the proposals will remove the control of justice from the judges and entrust it to civil servants". This would give rise to "grave constitutional dangers". Predictably, he argued "the general public will be the loser and so will justice."

Judges warned of an imminent constitutional collapse. Lord Chief Justice Lane called the green paper "one of the most sinister documents ever to emanate from government". He warned, famously, "Oppression does not stand on the doorstep with a toothbrush moustache and a swastika armband". Lord Donaldson added, in similar vein "Get your tanks off my lawn!" Judges threatened a one-day strike if Lord Chancellor Mackay would not allow them extra time to respond. High Court judges called the proposals "a grave breach of the doctrine of the separation of powers". The long-term effect might be to "impair the competence, integrity and trustworthiness of advocates and, as a result, significantly damage the quality of justice in this country."

Solicitors retorted that judges were using a double standard, forgetting that solicitors were already advocates in the lower courts.

The Courts and Legal Services Act 1990

13–045 A version of the Lord Chancellor's proposals was enacted in the Courts and Legal Services Act 1990 which established a new system for granting rights of audience. What was enacted was a watered down version of what Lord Mackay wanted. He had been forced to capitulate to the judges' demands. (This, according to Lord Chancellor Irvine, in 1998, proved to be the scheme's downfall.) While s.27 provided that "appropriate authorised bodies" could grant rights of audience, s.29 required them to be subjected to such a cumbersome machinery for approval, as to be almost unworkable. Further, they had to gain approval for the tiniest alterations to their codes of conduct, if these affected rights of audience. The Lord Chancellor was statutorily compelled to seek the advice of the Lord Chancellor's Advisory Committee on Legal Education and Conduct and of the Director General of Fair Trading, before taking a decision jointly with the four "designated judges". Each of the judges could veto a proposed rule change.

Effects of the 1990 Act: solicitor-advocates

13–046   By 1994, only 15 solicitors had applied for qualification. By 1998, there were only 624 solicitor-advocates, out of 70,000 and there are still very few (see below). This could be because of the cost and palaver of taking the course and exams. Some solicitors, with many years' advocacy experience in the magistrates' court could see little point in making this effort which would place them in no better position than a newly qualified barrister.

Research by teams from the Universities of Westminster and Bristol found:

- Most solicitors with higher court rights qualified through being former barristers.
- Of all solicitor-advocates, few had appeared in the superior courts.
- Several factors inhibited Crown Court advocacy: lack of certainty over trial dates, the low volume of work, length of trials and remuneration.
- Small criminal litigation firms could not afford to develop in-house advocacy practices.
- Personal injury and professional negligence solicitors did not believe in-house advocacy would improve the service to their clients.
- Solicitors regularly exercised their county court rights, where the limit was already £50,000 so extended rights of audience were an irrelevance.
- Specialist family lawyers already conducted their own advocacy as a matter of routine. High Court appearances in family cases were extremely rare.
- Solicitors did not like being stigmatised as abnormal advocates, by, for example, not being allowed to wear wigs. (See G. Davis, 1997.)

In the meantime, by 1993, work for the youngest barristers was dropping, because of a reduction in case load of the criminal courts and competition in the magistrates' courts from freelance solicitor-advocates (especially in London) who acted as agents for other solicitors. Solicitors preferred to use them because, unlike the Bar, they were prepared to guarantee an appearance and would not return a brief at the last moment. Experienced solicitors were more skilful than new barristers and solicitors understood legal aid forms.

Rather surprisingly, given the judicial backlash over audience rights in the higher courts, not much fuss was made when the Crime and Disorder Act 1998 granted audience rights to laypeople employed by the Crown Prosecution Service (CPS) in the magistrates' court.

The "sorry saga" of employed lawyers

The 1990s saw the Law Society and the CPS in a frustrating strug- **13–047**
gle to gain higher court rights of audience for employed solicitors
and for barristers employed by the CPS. To cut a six-year long story
short, proponents argued that it was bizarre to deny rights of audience to someone like the Director of Public Prosecutions, who had
formerly been an eminent QC in independent practice. CPS
employees and employed solicitors were acceptable advocates in
the lower courts so why not allow them higher court rights?

The Bar argued that it was against the public interest to allow
prosecutions to be undertaken by state prosecutors, the CPS. The
interest of justice would benefit from the use of independent,
private practice solicitors and counsel, hired ad hoc by the CPS,
because they took independent decisions, unconstrained by CPS
instructions. CPS lawyers would be determined to enhance their
conviction rates.

Labour's disgust with the "sorry saga"

In June 1998, Lord Chancellor Irvine produced a consultation **13–048**
paper, *Rights of Audience and Rights to Conduct Litigation in England
and Wales*. If his predecessor's 1989 green papers were a bombshell,
then this and its accompanying package of reforms were a rocket,
designed to propel the legal profession from the Dickensian era to
the modern day. The language of his foreword to the paper betrays
his exasperation over the failure of the 1990 Act to achieve Lord
Mackay's objective of opening up rights of audience:

"there remain features of the way the [legal] profession is organised which the Government believes stifle innovation and maintain rigid structures, limiting consumer choice and increasing the
expense of going to law. One particular example is the restriction
on the right to appear in the higher courts as an advocate;
members of the public often complain that they are required to
hire two lawyers, where one would do. . . . The 1990 Act was
intended to allow solicitors to obtain the right to appear in any
court, thus increasing the public's choice of advocate; it was also
intended to allow employed lawyers, such as Crown Prosecutors,
to appear in the higher courts. However, there has been continuing opposition to these changes, both before and after the Act was
passed, with the result that the Act has achieved virtually
nothing. Eight years on, nearly all advocates in the higher courts
are barristers in private practice.

The failure of the Act's good intentions and the inadequacy of
the mechanisms it put in place to extend rights of audience are
best illustrated by the sorry saga of the Law Society's attempt to

obtain rights of audience in the higher courts for employed solicitors, which is set out in this paper. After a prolonged gestation of
six years to-ing and fro-ing, advice and counter-advice, referrals
backwards and forwards, a Byzantine procedure produced a
mouse of reform: employed solicitors were allowed to appear in
substantive proceedings in the higher courts, provided they were
led by a lawyer in private practice.

The Government is not satisfied that the present state of affairs
is in the public interest . . . Our view is that all qualified barristers and qualified solicitors should in principle have the right to
appear in any court."

This extract neatly summarises the argument of the consultation
paper. Additional arguments were:

- Rights of audience needed to be restricted because the consequence of using an untrained advocate might be to adversely
  affect the client, any other party involved in the case and the
  wider public, as tax payer.
- It was irrational that barristers lost their rights of audience on
  becoming employed and regained them when they returned
  to private practice.
- As for the argument that barristers provided high quality
  advocacy, there were already concerns about the standard
  of private barristers' advocacy. The Public Accounts
  Committee survey showed that, at some Crown Court
  Centres, 75 per cent of CPS instructions had been returned.
  In a third of these cases, there was concern about the experience level of the new barrister who handled the case.
- The argument that junior barristers must be allowed to cut
  their teeth prosecuting in the Crown Court was inconsistent
  with arguments that the independent Bar provided uni-
  formly high quality advocacy.
- The Government believed that barristers should be
  employed because of their merits, not because they had a
  monopoly.
- Rights of audience should be portable. Once a person has
  qualified, he should carry that qualification to any other
  branch of the profession.

The Lord Chancellor crystallised his plans in his 1998 white paper,
Modernising Justice, which accompanied the Access to Justice Bill
(now the 1999 Act) and explained its background. Predictably, the
Bar and judges reacted with the same arguments with which they
had attacked Lord Mackay's green papers. Allowing a minister to

regulate rights of audience was a breach of the separation of powers. This was a judicial prerogative dating back to 1280. David Pannick QC dismissed this:

"[p]arliament can and does intervene to regulate the administration of justice in all other respects. It does so because the public interest is most effectively, and democratically assessed by those we elect rather than by barristers who have been appointed to the bench . . . judges have no right to decide, and no expertise that qualifies them to decide, what the public interest requires in a policy context where there are competing considerations. . . . The special pleading of judges and barristers has had no persuasive effect on laypeople, save to reinforce their low opinion of the legal profession." (*The Times*, 1998).

The Access to Justice Act 1999

Unmoved by the protestations of the Bar and judiciary and backed by the Office of Fair Trading, Lord Irvine introduced his Access to Justice Bill in December 1998. Part III of the Act introduced the following scheme: 13–049

Section 36 grants rights of audience to every barrister and solicitor in all proceedings, subject only to the qualification regulations and rules of conduct imposed by their professional bodies.

Section 37 prohibits any restriction on the rights of audience of employed advocates, including lawyers employed by the CPS and s.38 provides the same protection for employees of the Legal Services Commission.

Section 39 makes advocacy rights portable so a barrister, for example, no longer has to give up audience rights on converting to be a solicitor.

Progress Since the 1999 Act

Both the Law Society and the Bar Council were forced to change their rules by July 2000 to comply with the Act and permit higher court audience rights to employed barristers and the Law Society produced a new scheme designed to make it much easier for solicitors to train for higher court audience rights. Even trainee solicitors can begin working for advocacy certificates. Nevertheless, by 2005 there were still under 2000 solicitor-advocates (out of 116,000 solicitors), very few of whom had full audience rights.   13–050

The Clementi Review—"Tesco Law"

Lord Chancellor Falconer, in 2003, announced proposals to allow banks, building societies and insurance companies to handle probate and this was permitted from 2004. He suggested supermarkets   13–051 and other retailers to provide legal services, when he established the Clementi Review, appointing Sir David Clementi, former deputy governor of the Bank of England to conduct it. Commentators branded this as "Tesco law". In December 2005, he produced his report: *Review of the Regulatory Framework for Legal Services in England and Wales*. It had become obvious from his consultation paper that Sir David was not contemplating recommending anything as radical as many lawyers feared—such as fusion of the professions. "The review", he said, "favours a regulatory framework which permits a high degree of choice: choice both for the consumer, in where he goes for legal services, and for the lawyer, in the type of economic unit he works for." This is what he recommended:

1. *Legal Disciplinary Practices* should be considered. Lawyers of any kind should be allowed to practice together in Legal Disciplinary Practices (LDPs). Managers could include non-lawyers, such as an existing IT manager in a big law firm. There would be a Head of Legal Practice and a Head of Finance and Administration. Non-lawyers would have to sign up to a code of practice prioritising clients. There should be a majority of lawyers in the management group but these could include any lawyers, including legal executives and licensed conveyancers.
2. *Investment in LDPs* could come from outside owners (*e.g.* Tesco) but they would need to be "fit to own" and there should be no conflict of interest. An insurance company could not own, say, a personal injury firm. The benefit of such investors would include fresh ideas, better attention to customer service than lawyers and competition, thus lower prices.
3. *Multi Disciplinary Partnerships* might be considered, once LDPs had been tested.

Reactions to Clementi

13–052 *Consumer Bodies* such as the Office of Fair Trading were enthusiastic.

The Department of Constitutional Affairs indicated strong support, promising a white paper in 2005 then legislation.

The Law Society welcomed the proposals, especially for LDPs. They said they had recommended these back in 1989. President Edward Nally said Tesco law was not a threat. Statistics showed that many solicitors already found private practice a less attractive option than they did a few years ago. For most consumers the development of supermarkets had been a good thing.

13–053 *The Bar Chairman* welcomed competition but the said the Bar Council were concerned about the ethics of non-lawyers running a legal practice. They warned that Tesco law could encourage a compensation culture. The Bar Council was very hostile to MDPs, saying they led to conflicts of interest. A previous chairman had said he would fight these plans "tooth and claw". The newest Chairman, Guy Mansfield said lawyers belonged to a profession but Clementi talked of "the legal service industry". There was a danger of over-commercialising the law. A lawyer owed a duty not simply to his client but to the court. He said the Bar were not Luddites but no country in the world favoured MDPs.

LAG, the Legal Action Group of lawyers said Sir David had addressed many of their concerns on regulating LDPs.

The Legal Services Commission welcomed the proposals, saying a single independent regulator would better serve the needs of the vulnerable and socially excluded. It considered the existing professional bodies did not meet the best interests of consumers.

Tesco, in the meantime has started offering DIY kits on some areas of the law. . .

7. Fusion: Do We Need Two Professions?

The legal profession in England and Wales is unusual in world-wide terms, the two sides of the profession being characterised and preserved by their respective monopolies and restrictive practices. Because those have been torn down since 1985 this again raises the question of whether the two sides of the profession will eventually merge and, if so whether a single profession would better serve the public interest. Barristers have always argued that giving rights of audience to solicitors will sound the death knell to the Bar. As we have seen, Lord Mackay took no notice of this argument and endeavoured to open up rights of audience in the 1990 Act. As Lord Irvine pointed out, in 1998, however, civilisation as we know it has not ended in the 1990s. Indeed, numbers of independently practising barristers have increased every year since 1990. The RCLS and many other individuals have discussed the feasibility and desirability of a fused profession. Here are the pros and cons but these points are obviously supplemented by the facts and arguments examined throughout this chapter. 13–054

Arguments Against a Divided Profession

Expense to the client
Why should the client pay for one or two barristers to argue his case in court, accompanied by a solicitor's representative? Why not 13–055

just let the client hire one lawyer to do everything, instead of paying for three "taxi meters" clocking up a huge bill, hour by hour? Professor Michael Zander provoked the establishment of the RCLS in 1976 by famously making this argument, fully explored in his book, *Lawyers and the Public Interest* (1968).

Inefficiency, failures in communication

Some witnesses suggested to the RCLS that the present structure caused this because of the distance between barristers and solicitors. Written instructions sent to counsel were often inadequate. Barristers were reluctant to complain.

Returned briefs

13–056   Very frequently, a solicitor sends a brief to chambers marked for a named barrister. At the last minute, the brief is returned because the barrister is otherwise occupied. The solicitor then has to find another barrister or permit the brief to be passed on to another barrister in the same chambers who may be a stranger to him or the client. This causes frustration to the solicitor, denied the choice of original barrister, and may destroy the client's confidence (see Mackenzie at (1990) 150 N.L.J. 512). The solicitor may have reassured the client of the best of service from the named barrister yet the client is faced with a stranger at the doors of the court. Many defendants complained of the shoddy service they received after meeting their barrister on the morning of trial, in Bottoms and McClean's *Defendants in the Criminal Process* (1976) and *Standing Accused* (1994) by Mike McConville *et al.*

Zander and Henderson's *Crown Court Study* for the Royal Commission on Criminal Justice (RCCJ) 1993 provided statistics which illustrated how bad the problem is. In 66 per cent of contested cases, the CPS said the barrister who appeared at trial was not the barrister originally instructed. In most cases, the CPS learned of the change of barrister at the last minute. In eight per cent of cases where there was a change of barrister it was said to cause a problem. As for defence barristers, in 48 per cent of cases, the barrister at trial was not the one originally instructed and in the majority of such cases, the solicitor was informed on the day before, or on the day of hearing. In 60 per cent of cases, the defendant either saw no barrister or a different one before trial. In 17 per cent of cases, the solicitor said the original barrister would have been better than the substitute.

In 1997, research by the National Audit Office showed that CPS briefs had been returned in 75 per cent of the cases sampled and new counsel was judged to be inappropriate in almost a third of these. In 1998, the CPS inspectorate published a report on child witnesses, heavily critical that briefs were returned in half of all child abuse cases.

The Legal Action Group, in evidence to the RCCJ, argued that the "detachment" which the Bar claims to be an advantage is seen by the client as ignorance of his case and circumstances. Public confidence in the legal system suffers.

Arguments Against Fusion

Free from interruptions by clients

Barristers can concentrate on the specialist matters, benefiting from the fact that another lawyer has already identified the issues and sifted out the relevant facts.   13–057

Jury advocacy

This is a specialist type of advocacy, requiring special skills akin to those involved in public speaking. These skills require regular practice. There may be grave consequences to the client. Emotions run high. The barrister is accustomed to this environment and can provide the necessary detachment.

Loss of choice

If the profession were fused, leading barristers would join large firms of solicitors and so the ability to brief them would be lost to all other solicitors. Under the present system, clients in the remotest areas or with the most complex problems still have access to the best barristers. Solicitors under a fused profession would not readily refer a client to another firm. Access to advocates would be reduced. Most firms of solicitors have few partners. They could not absent themselves from the office for days on end appearing in court. It is therefore important that solicitors have access to barristers to provide services which they could not.

Advocacy

In a fused system, there would be a drop in quality of advocacy, which would damage not just the interests of the client but the administration of justice. Standards would decline because the specialist knowledge of the Bar would be diluted. Specialisms need regular practice. The Bar can fairly claim to be specialist advocates.   13–058

Cost effectiveness

The present system is more cost effective. Under a fused system, it would be more expensive to have a solicitor to represent the client as solicitors' overheads are larger.

Orality

English practice rests on the principle of oral hearing, which demands well prepared, experienced practitioners. (This point, like those below, was made by Mann). It is no longer as valid as it then was. Now, skeleton arguments must be prepared in all civil cases and most appeals.

Procedure
13–059   English procedure requires a single and continuous hearing, which requires time and undivided attention that few solicitors could afford.

Judicial unpreparedness
In England and Wales the principle of *curia novit legem* applies. This means that counsel submits the law to the court, which is assumed to know nothing. Counsel has a duty not to mislead the court. Such a system requires specialist knowledge and experience, intensive preparation and much training. If we required judges to research and prepare the law in each case, we would require many more judges.

Comment
13–060   These are good points in relation to advocacy in the higher courts but firstly, they ignore the fact that most advocates are solicitors and, since Mann wrote, the county court deals with some very important civil cases, where solicitors have rights of audience. Really Mann's arguments support the existence of specialist advocates, not a divided profession, bolstered by all the monopolies and restrictive practices lawyers enjoyed in his day.

Further, the notion that solicitors generally choose the best advocate for the job, from amongst the pool of barristers sounds great in theory but, as we have seen, in the routine of the Crown Court, both prosecution and defence briefs end up, more often than not, with a barrister who was not the one originally selected.

8. Race and Gender Discrimination

13–061   There is not the space in this book to recount the sad litany of race and gender discrimination in the legal profession but see the website accompanying this book (see note on Online Updates at the front of this book). See also Thomas, *Discriminating Lawyers*.

BIBLIOGRAPHY
13–062   A. E. Bottoms and J. D. McClean, *Defendants in the Criminal Process* (1976).

Sir David Clementi, *Review of the Regulatory Framework for Legal Services in England and Wales*, December 2004 (*www.legal-services-review.org.uk*)

Articles on Clementi: M. Zander (2005) 155 N.L.J. 41; S. Young (2005) 155 NLJ 45; E. Nally (2004) 154 N.L.J. 1461.

Constitutional reform: the future of Queen's Counsel, 2003, DCA website: *www.dca.gov.uk* in the consultation papers archive. Responses are on the same site.

G. Davis, etc., (1998) 148 N.L.J. 832, on solicitors' in-house complaints procedures and on the Bristol and Westminster research on solicitor-advocates, (1997) 147 N.L.J. 212.

L. Duff and L. Webley, *Equality and Diversity, Women Solicitors*, Law Society Research Study 48, Vol.II, 2004.

The Fawcett Society: *www.fawcettsociety.org.uk*

F. Gibb, "Solicitors 'still give shoddy service'", *The Times*, June 30, 2004.

F. Gibb, "This is a profession, not an industry" (interview with the Bar Council Chairman on Clementi), *The Times*, December 14, 2004.

F. A. Mann on fusion (1977) 98 L.Q.R. 367

M. McConville *et al.*, *Standing Accused* (1994).

P. Reeves, *Silk Cut* (1998) for the Adam Smith Institute.

Sheffield University Publications are listed on *www.sheff.ac.uk*

D. Pannick, "Will lawyers become reformed characters?", *The Times*, November 3, 1998, p.41.

A. Sherr, *Willing Blindness?—Complaints Handling Procedures* (1999).

P. Thomas, *Discriminating Lawyers* (2000).

T. Williams and T. Goriely, *Recruitment and Retention of Solicitors in Small Firms*, Law Society Research Study 44, 2003.   **13–063**

M. Zander and P. Henderson, *Crown Court Study* (1993, HMSO).

FURTHER READING AND SOURCES FOR UPDATING THIS CHAPTER

Online updates to this book: http://*www.sweetandmaxwell.co.uk/acdemic/updates/darbyshire/index.html*

I also used the following general sources, which the reader can use for updating the information in this chapter:

The Bar Council: *www.barcouncil.org.uk*

The Bar's Legal Education website: *www.legaleducation.org.uk*

Counsel, the Bar's in-house magazine.

The Institute of Legal Executives: *www.ilex.org.uk*

The Law Society: *www.lawsociety.org.uk* (especially the Annual Statistical Report).

The Law Society's Strategic Research Unit: *www.research.lawsociety.org.uk*

The Law Society's *Gazette*, distributed to all members of the Law Society: *www.lawgazette.co.uk*

The *New Law Journal* is in most law libraries and on *Lexis*.

Further reading on silks: L. Tsang, "The 400-year-old Queen's Counsel system is on trial. Both sides present their case", *The Times*, October 7, 2003 (gives a *vox pop* from 18 lawyers).

14. Judges

PD "Are you at the Bar, then?
LH "No, I'm a Law Lord"
PD "Ooh, sorry!"
LH "That's OK. I'm one of the old, white, male geezers".
(The author meets Lord Lennie Hoffman, 1996.)

1. The Constitutional Reform Act 2005— A New Constitutional Framework

> "It is a sad comment on our democracy that there has been little argument in the press, or on television about these issues, even in the broadsheet press or the serious political programmes. They are self-evidently, one would have thought, *fundamental* issues, the resolution of which is likely to affect our public life for decades and possibly centuries to come." (Lord Justice Keene, 2004.)

The Lord Chancellor and the Lord Chief Justice

As explained in Chapter 4 on human rights, above, this Act results 14–001 from the Government announcement in 2003 that it was determined to reform the constitution, by dismantling much of the role of the Lord Chancellor, reforming judicial appointments and moving the Law Lords into a Supreme Court. Their aim was, according to the new Lord Chancellor, Lord Falconer, to "put the relationship between Parliament, the Government and judges on a modern footing. We will have a proper separation of powers and we will further strengthen the independence of the judiciary". As I explained in Chapter 4, it became apparent that the Lord

405

Chancellor's tripartite role, as a member of all three organs of government: legislature (as speaker in the House of Lords), executive government (as a minister) and head of judiciary, was unacceptable under Art.6 of the Convention. This is the fair trial provision, which requires that a judge must be independent of the government. Similarly, the Council of Europe made it clear to the government that the Law Lords' position similarly breached the separation of powers, because, as judges, they were also peers in Parliament, entitled to speak in debate and sit on committees.

Accordingly, the Act effectively replaces his office as head of the judiciary with the Lord Chief Justice. It creates a new Judicial Appointments Commission and a Supreme Court. Part 2 of the Act shares judiciary related functions between the reformed ministerial office of Lord Chancellor and the Lord Chief Justice.

The Lord Chancellor

14–002   The Act places great emphasis on judicial independence. Section 1 states that the Act does not adversely affect the constitutional principle of the rule of law or the Lord Chancellor's role in relation to it. The Act requires the Lord Chancellor to be qualified by experience. He is not required to be a judge or a member of the House of Lords. The Bill was amended twice, to require high judicial office, by a rebellious House of Lords, in the face of Government wishes but the Government re-amended it twice. The Lord Chancellor and other ministers are under a duty to uphold judicial independence in matters relating to the judiciary or administration of justice. Specifically, they must not seek to influence judicial decisions, through any "special access". The Lord Chancellor must "have regard to" the support judges need to carry out their functions and he must have regard to the need for the public interest to be represented in matters relating to the judiciary or administration of justice. This (s.3) should be read in conjunction with Part 1 of the Courts Act 2003, which sets out the duty of the Lord Chancellor to ensure that there is an efficient and effective system to support the carrying on of the business of the courts of England and Wales.

The Act provides for the Lord Chancellor's judicial appointment functions to be transferred to the monarch and for many of his functions, judicial and non-judicial, to be disposed of. Because the Lord Chancellor will no longer be a judge, it has been agreed that the judges will be represented by a senior judge on the Board of Her Majesty's Court Service, the new non-executive agency which now manages the courts and came into being on April 1, 2005.

These functions remain the statutory responsibility of the Lord Chancellor:

- The framework of the court system, including jurisdictional and geographical boundaries.
- Providing and allocating money and resources for the administration of justice.
- Judges' pay, terms and conditions; resources for training.
- Determining the overall number of judges and allocating business between the courts.

"I do swear that in the office of Lord High Chancellor of Great Britain I will respect the rule of law, defend the independence of the judiciary and discharge my duty to ensure the provision of resources for the efficient and effective support of the courts for which I am responsible. So help me God". (The 2005 Act requires a Lord Chancellor to swear this new oath.)

The Lord Chief Justice

The Act declares that the Lord Chief Justice holds office as President of the Courts of England and Wales and is Head of the Judiciary for England and Wales. He is given the responsibility of representing judges' views to Parliament and government; for judicial welfare, training and guidance and for deployment of the judiciary and allocation of work within the courts. The Lord Chancellor's rule making powers are transferred to him, as are powers to make Practice Directions. He is entitled to lay before Parliament a written representation on any matter of importance to the judiciary or administration of justice.

14–003

The following statutory responsibilities are transferred from the Lord Chancellor to the Lord Chief Justice:

- Posts for individual judges.
- Making rules for deploying magistrates.
- Authorising judges (colloquially known as "ticketing" (for example, deciding which circuit judges will have "murder tickets" and "serious sex tickets")).
- Allocating work within the courts of one level (*e.g.* between divisions of the High Court).
- Appointing judges to specific posts, such as Presiding Judge.
- Appointing judges to committees and boards, though the framework for these appointments will be the Lord Chancellor's responsibility.

- Appointing judges to rule-making committees. Non-judges will be appointed by the Lord Chancellor.

Other judges

14–004   The Lord Chief Justice is declared Head of Criminal Justice and may appoint a Deputy. The Act creates a new post of Head of Family Justice, to be held by the President of the Family Division. The Lord Chief Justice may appoint a Deputy Head of Family Justice and this was done in January 2005, while the Act was still a Bill. The creation of these new posts mirrors the existing statutory posts of Head and Deputy Head of Civil Justice, established by s.62 of the Courts Act 2003. The Lord Chief Justice may, and no doubt will, delegate to the heads of civil, criminal and family justice the power to make practice directions on procedure.

The Vice-Chancellor, head of the Chancery Division and so-called as he was the Lord Chancellor's deputy becomes the "Chancellor of the High Court". A new post of President of the Queen's Bench Division is created and that will be held by the Lord Chief Justice.

The Background to this Part of the Act—the Unacceptable Role of the Lord Chancellor in all Three Organs of Government

14–005   The UK has never had a real separation of powers but the Lord Chancellor's role constituted the most spectacular breach, as he was a key member of all three organs of government: judiciary, executive and legislature. He was not only a judge but the head of the judiciary. He was not only a minister but the most important of Cabinet ministers, on nine crucial Cabinet committees and chairing four of them. The incumbent until 2003, Lord Irvine likened himself to Tony Blair's "Cardinal Wolsey". He was not only a member of the legislature but the very speaker of the House of Lords and, unlike the Commons speaker, free to participate in political debate.

In the last section of Chapter 4 on human rights, above , I explained why, by 2003, the Government were embarrassed by the European Court of Human Rights and the Council of Europe, into dismantling the Lord Chancellor's role and removing the Law Lords from Parliament.

I explained that the government's decision was preceded by attacks on the status quo by two Law Lords, Bingham and Steyn. I quoted Lord Steyn's 2002 speech in that chapter and in Chapter 6, in the section on the Supreme Court. Most of his speech was, however, reserved for a strident attack on the office of Lord Chancellor. He listed all the ways in which it breached the separation of powers and he demolished, one by one, the arguments raised in its defence, especially by Lord Chancellor Irvine. To explain the problem, I can do no better than quote him at length:

"And nowhere outside Britain is the independence of the judiciary potentially compromised in the eyes of citizens by permitting a serving politician to sit as a judge at any level, let alone in the highest court which fulfils constitutional functions . . . The major obstacle to creating a Supreme Court is the privilege of the Lord Chancellor of sitting in the Appellate Committee of the House of Lords. I will argue that the Lord Chancellor's participation in judicial business in the highest court no longer serves a useful purpose and is contrary to the public interest . . . The fog surrounding the figure of the Lord Chancellor, so vividly described in 1853 by Dickens in *Bleak House*, has not entirely lifted . . . By convention the Lord Chancellor is a Cabinet Minister, and he is in charge of a large spending government department. For a long time the Lord Chancellor's predominantly political role has raised questions about the propriety of his subsidiary judicial role. In her important book *The Office of the Lord Chancellor* (2001) Professor Woodhouse has shown why these questions became more acute during the Lord Chancellorship of Lord Mackay of Clashfern (1989–1996) and even more so during the period in office of Lord Irvine of Lairg (1997 to date). She attributes this to the increasing politicisation of the office. She has described in detail the vast increase in the nature and extent of the present Lord Chancellor's executive responsibilities. He is responsible for formulating and implementing policies affecting the administration of justice, which are often a matter of party political debate. In addition he chairs Cabinet committees over a large range of policy issues beyond his departmental responsibility. He is at the centre of political power in a party political sense. In all these respects he is bound by the doctrine of collective responsibility. In his legislative role he assumes some of the functions of the Speaker in the House of Commons; he takes part in debates; he speaks for the Government; and he votes . . . under the Appellate Jurisdiction Act 1876 he may and does sit in the Appellate Committee of the House of Lords, and in the Privy Council. When he sits the Lord Chancellor automatically presides, with the attendant influence of doing so. He swears an oath to act impartially when he sits judicially. In England he is the head of the judiciary. His task is to protect the independence of the judiciary wherever the onslaughts on it may come from . . . He asserts an absolute right in his unfettered discretion to decide when to sit. It is . . . an astonishing proposition that a member of the executive claims to this day to have the right to decide who among the Law Lords should sit on a particular case. It is, however, by no means a theoretical point. If the Lord Chancellor has the legal power to dictate in a given case the composition of the highest court in the land, he will be entitled to exercise it and nobody will in practice know when the power has been exercised directly or indirectly. Not much legal certainty and transparency there"

14–006   Lord Steyn went on to say that Lord Irvine had sat in eight appeals with the Law Lords, two of which were considerably important and involved the relationship between the executive and citizens. Lord Irvine's role in them was criticized in the House of Lords chamber. There was another case from which he was asked to stand down, involving a death in custody. It would be unthinkable for him to sit in any of the major cases coming before the Law Lords on constitutional law, devolution, human rights. Secondly, he did not make a significant contribution to the Law Lords' work. "There will not be a ripple in the pond if he ceases to sit" and

> "The practice of the Lord Chancellor and his predecessors of sitting in the Appellate Committee is not consistent with even the weakest principle of separation of powers or the most tolerant interpretation of the constitutional principles of judicial independence or rule of law. In *Hinds v The Queen*, in the context of the relationship between the legislature and the judiciary under the constitution of Jamaica, the Privy Council held "that the British Constitution is firmly based on the separation of powers between the legislature, the executive and judiciary". In *Duport Steels Ltd v Sirs*, again in the setting of the relationship between the legislature and the courts, the House of Lords reiterated "that it cannot be too strongly emphasised that the British constitution, although largely unwritten, is firmly based on the separation of powers". The same necessarily applies to the relationship between the executive and the courts. Initially Lord Irvine of Lairg took the same view. In office he has become dismissive of the principle: his theme became "we are pragmatists, not purists"."

Lord Steyn then went on to deal with Lord Irvine's defence of his tripartite role as useful because he could represent the judiciary when he sat in Cabinet and the Cabinet had a representative in the judiciary. One might ask, said Lord Steyn how this could be effective when he sat so little with the Law Lords and, anyway, it was a vice, not a virtue, to assume that it was proper to inform the judiciary of the Government's wishes. "The judiciary does not need a 'representative' in the cabinet. In no other constitutional democracy does the judiciary have a 'representative' in cabinet". He concluded

"By gracefully accepting the inevitable, the Lord Chancellor, a principle architect of the Human Rights Act 1998, will render another great service to our law".

Unfortunately, Lord Chancellor Irvine chose not to accept the inevitable so the following year, 2003, his close friend, Prime Minister Blair removed him, replaced him with another friend, Lord Falconer, and announced on the same day that his government would be dismantling the 1400 year old office of Lord Chancellor, replacing the Law Lords with a Supreme Court and reforming the system of judicial appointments. All this came as a big shock to some judges, most of the Law Lords and the media but, as I explained in Chapter 4, above, for those of us who had understood the implications of Art.6 of the Convention and had noticed that a key member of the Council of Europe had visited Parliament to tell us how embarrassing it was trying to explain the British constitutional setup to the emergent democracies of eastern Europe, we knew the writing was on the wall for the Lord Chancellor and the Law Lords. Lord Irvine had been hoist by his own petard, the Human Rights Act 1998.

Attacks on the role of Lord Chancellor were not new. The lawyers' pressure group, JUSTICE, had called for reform for more than 20 years. Academics had frequently drawn attention to the anomalous role. Real pressure was placed directly on the Government, however, in May 2001, when the Parliamentary Assembly of the Council of Europe called on the British Government to review the office of Lord Chancellor. Even Lord Irvine had conceded that he would not prescribe the office of Lord Chancellor to emergent democracies but he famously defended the office "We have never been a nation of purists but pragmatists". This was his response to the attack on his office by the Council of Europe, described in Chapter 4. As for Lord Steyn, Irvine dismissed him as being in a minority of one.

Nevertheless, there was a furore when the Government made its dramatic announcements. Given the extent of the constitutional reforms and the fact that they were announced as a decision, not a proposal, commentators criticized the Government's failure to inform the Queen and some members of the judiciary were aggrieved that they had not been consulted.

Most importantly, Lord Chief Justice Woolf voiced his disquiet at **14–007** the determination to abolish the Lord Chancellor. On appointment, it was announced that Charlie Falconer was to be the last Lord Chancellor. He was also appointed Secretary of State for

Constitutional Affairs and the Lord Chancellor's Department was renamed the Department for Constitutional Affairs (DCA). He announced that he would not be sitting as a judge. The Lord Chief Justice stated publicly that he would postpone his pending retirement to stay and fight for judicial independence because of the loss of the Lord Chancellor, the defender of the judiciary in the cabinet, as he saw it. Indeed, he voiced his concerns so frequently, in and out of Parliament, that he could only be appeased by a January 2004 *Concordat*, an agreement between him and the Government, guaranteeing judicial independence, making the Lord Chief Justice the Head of the Judiciary, guaranteeing that judicial appointments would be free from political interference and detailing how responsibilities for judicial appointments and the administration of justice were to be shared between the Lord Chief Justice and government ministers. This *Concordat* is published on the DCA website and, as can be seen, the guarantees secured by the Lord Chief Justice were all spelled out in the Constitutional Reform Act.

In the meantime, in 2003, the Government published several consultation papers, on judicial and silk appointments, the Supreme Court and the Lord Chancellor's non-judicial functions. They were consulting, of course, not on *whether* these massive constitutional reforms were to take place but *how*. On the day that the *Concordat* was published so was another consultation paper, very belatedly, on the judiciary-related functions of the Lord Chancellor, curiously absent from the earlier set.

Many others shared the Lord Chief Justice's concern. "If the Lord Chancellor goes, who will fight the Treasury for legal aid, which carries few votes? Who will have ultimate authority over the legal profession?" asked lawyer, Lord Alexander. Lord Mackay, the last Conservative Lord Chancellor said many times that, from his experience, the Lord Chancellor's presence did have a real restraining effect. While the Lord Chancellor had held a high position in the Cabinet hierarchy, the replacement Secretary of State for Constitutional Affairs was placed at the very bottom of the Cabinet list in *Hansard*. The Law Lords had responded to the consultation papers by emphasising the Lord Chancellor's importance in safeguarding the rule of law and the independence of the judiciary. "The Government's proposals to place all these responsibilities on an overtly political Secretary of State pose a threat to the independence of the judicial process." In response, the new and, supposedly, last Lord Chancellor, Lord Falconer said that he was not just there to represent the views of the judiciary. "Like all Cabinet ministers I am there to ensure the public interest is served." This remark is very telling, as it illustrates starkly the problem of the Lord Chancellor's dual role. As radical QC

Baroness Helena Kennedy put it in *The Times*, "When the talk in Cabinet is of law and order, the Home Secretary might be the voice of 'order' in the political firmament, but the Lord Chancellor has to speak for 'law' and justice". She was not the only person to point out that Lord Irvine had clung onto office, not out of stubbornness but out of a genuine anxiety to defend the rule of law and judicial independence against the increasingly unrestrained attacks of his Cabinet colleague, Home Secretary Blunkett. I come back to this point below, under judicial independence.

The *Concordat* may have pacified the Lord Chief Justice but it did not satisfy other peers. He became a supporter of the Bill and anxious that it should not be delayed, as he wanted judicial appointments reformed and was now a convert to a Supreme Court but he was outvoted. Peers, led by former Law Lords, defeated the Bill. In March 2004, the Government gave in to a demand that the Bill be referred to a select committee, in exchange for being allowed to carry it over into the 2004–5 Parliamentary session. The Committee made 400 amendments to the Bill. They supported the *Concordat* and agreed on a number of other points now in the Act but crucially, they voted 240 to 208 to retain the title of Lord Chancellor. The whole debate on the Bill was reopened in October 2004, with ex law lords even more vociferous. "What is the greatest legal office in the world? . . . the Lord Chancellor", asked Lord Cooke of Thorndon, ex Law Lord. Lord Lloyd, another former Law Lord spoke for the opposition in Parliament. While he understood that it was wrong for the Lord Chancellor to sit in Cabinet and be a judge, the proposed alternative of putting all ministers under a duty to uphold judicial independence was "nothing but a form of words".

By October 2004, the Government was getting desperate to salvage the Bill from its savaging by ex Law Lords and other attackers in the House of Lords. They surprisingly accepted "the will of the House" and amended the Bill to preserve the title Lord Chancellor. Although Lord Falconer grumbled that he could not see why such a post had to be held by a lawyer, he conceded this point too and that requirement appears in the Act. This followed widespread and vociferous protests that a non-lawyer could not defend the judiciary.

In all the heated debate on constitutional reform in 2003–5, there was, then, much talk of "judicial independence" and claims that the Lord Chancellor in Cabinet was its ancient and only guardian. It was left to the eminent academic Robert Stevens to quietly remind us that the Lord Chancellor had only become the champion of judicial independence in 1880 and in any event, the separation of powers and independence of the judiciary were, in the UK context, considerably flaky concepts.

14–008

14–009   The idea of a ministry of justice was mooted in the nineteenth century and it was judicial panic about that prospect which led to the Lord Chancellor becoming head of the judiciary in cabinet. This idea has not been much discussed in the debate on constitutional reform, since 1993 but was Labour party policy when they were in opposition. Some believe that such a ministry, headed by a Cabinet minister from the House of Commons, would have provided a counterweight to the power of the Home Office.

2. Just What is Meant by the Independence of the Judiciary?

> "With the Executive sitting in the legislature, English discussions of the separation of powers and judicial independence have a slightly unreal quality." (Robert Stevens, 2004.)

The Independence of the Judiciary

14–010   It is appropriate at this point to examine these uncertain concepts. Constitutional theorists, notably Locke in the seventeenth century and Montesquieu in the eighteenth, praised the separation of powers as a guarantee of democracy. The concentration of governmental power of more than one type—legislative, executive and judicial—in the hands of one person or body is considered dangerous. It is notable that that when a dictator or an extreme regime takes power, they dismiss judges who will not do their bidding. This was happening in 2003 in Malaysia. Some written constitutions try to guard against this. In the British constitution there is no point in looking for a separation of powers. When I discovered the concept as a first year law student, I was amazed to read claims like that of Lord Diplock, quoted by Lord Steyn, above, that our constitution pretended to have such a separation. How could that be, with the Cabinet government sitting in the legislature? All we can hope for in the UK is a system of checks and balances that allows one organ of government to be kept in check by the others.

Stevens, in *The Independence of the Judiciary* (1993) attributed to Blackstone (*Commentaries*, 1765) the concept of the judiciary as one of the three organs of government which needed independence from the other elements, though he reminded us that from 1701 to 1832, the judges were an integral part of the ruling oligarchy. "Nothing underlines the atheoretical nature of the British Constitution more than the casualness with which it approaches the separation of powers" (1993). It is a constitutional myth, he has often said, that there is independence of the judiciary in England (1994). All the Act of Settlement 1700 provided for was independence for individual judges, not for the independence of the judiciary as a whole, as a co-equal branch of government, in Montesquieu's sense, as they are meant to be in the US. Judges simply moved from being "lions under the throne" to lions under the Parliamentary mace.

As Dicey pointed out in the nineteenth century, the rule of law was dependent on the supremacy of Parliament so the task of judges was to carry out the will of Parliament. Our judges do not have the power to judicially review primary legislation and declare it to be unconstitutional, as does the US Supreme Court. The only exceptions to this have come in the 1972 European Communities Act, which gave the judges power to declare a UK Act to be incompatible with Community law (see Chapter 3, above) and the Human Rights Act 1998 (see Chapter 4, above). The latter has made them considerably more powerful, since 2000.

Nor did our judges have control over an independent budget and **14–011** court service. As Professor Scott pointed out, since the Beeching reforms in the Courts Act 1971, judicial administration in England has not been "judiciary-based" but "executive-based", unlike the USA and the Australian courts, at Federal level. I might comment at this point that Scott and other constitutional lawyers forget the one exception to this—magistrates. They controlled their own budget, decided on the deployment of their own buildings and resources and hired and fired their own staff until 2005, via magistrates' courts committees. During the Beeching reforms, the judges argued that their collective independence required them to be in control of the courts but they lost the argument. Again, the answer they received was that they could rely on their champion in the Cabinet, the Lord Chancellor. Increasingly, governments have sought to increase executive control over court management and expenditure and judges have been publicly objecting to this, often in hysterical terms, throughout the late 1980s and 1990s. They were fond of quoting early American constitutionalist, Alexander Hamilton, writing in *The Federalist* (No.78), who described the judiciary as the weakest and least dangerous department of government, although they normally omitted to attribute the quotation.

Sir Francis Purchas spoke and wrote at length of the threat to judicial independence. He likened 1980s developments to the Nazi regime. The argument had started in 1987, with Vice Chancellor Sir Nicholas Browne-Wilkinson (quoted by Stevens) complaining of the "widespread dissatisfaction amongst litigants caused by the use of county court judges and members of the Bar sitting as deputy High Court judges to try 29 per cent of all High Court civil cases in

1985." Lord Chief Justice Lane and then Lord Chief Justice Taylor publicly attacked Lord Chancellor Mackay in 1991 and 1992. Judge Harold Wilson objected to the takeover of court administration by civil servants of the Court Service.

Although it may be constitutionally desirable to have judges running the courts, for the sake of separation of powers, I have to point out that it cannot be assumed they would make a better job of it than an executive agency. Their clamour rather astonishingly harks back to the era prior to the Courts Act 1971, when the county court judges (around 90) managed their own affairs, with the help of a registrar, claiming the system had worked well. This may well have been the case at county court level but at Assize level, judicial-centred case management was archaic and producing lengthy delays. Until 1972, we had the bizarre set-up of each assize judge being followed around his circuit by all relevant paperwork, clerks and other functionaries from one Assize town to another. A day was set aside for travelling (from the days of horse drawn transport) and a day each for packing and unpacking. During this period the court was incommunicado to all court users.

14–012 Similarly, the power of magistrates to run their own courts until 2005 had many negative consequences. The abolition of magistrates' courts committees by the Courts Act 2003 resulted from a recommendation of Lord Justice Auld's *Review of the Criminal Courts*. I was one of those who urged him to get rid of them. Researching in the 1970s, I found that magistrates' training varied radically depending on the views of the local MCC, as did the quality and qualifications of their clerks (legal advisers), whom they were responsible for hiring and firing. Throughout the 1980s more and more magistrates' courts were closed, destroying local justice, and such closures were often the decisions of MCCs. By 1998, they had all acquired different computer hardware and software which could not communicate with one another or with other criminal justice agencies. Attempting to coordinate all these systems then replace them was an enormous waste of public money.

Judges of the 1980s considered that their independence was under attack when Lord Chancellor Mackay proposed to destroy the Bar's monopoly over rights of audience in the higher courts. This provoked judicial hysteria, as I described in the previous chapter. Judges called the proposals "a grave breach of the doctrine of the separation of powers". Judges sought to emphasise that they had, for centuries, enjoyed the prerogative of deciding who appeared before them. They were appalled that this power would pass to a Government minister, the Lord Chancellor. It should be pointed out though that judges and the Bar were the only group to consider this an essential element to judicial independence.

In 2003, lay justices were similarly alarmed at the Courts Bill's threat to dismantle magistrates' courts committees. To placate them, the Lord Chancellor launched a consultation on the Courts Board which would replace them from 2005. Professor Scott argued strongly that, in the context of the constitutional reforms, there was the opportunity for strengthening the separation of powers by making the superior courts "judiciary-based". It appears that the 2005 Act does just that, at least as far as the Supreme Court is concerned and it goes some way towards allowing judges much more autonomy to manage the courts. Also, while the Act was still a Bill, in March 2005, a "mini-ministry" of 60 civil servants was installed in the Royal Courts of Justice to help judges when they take over responsibility for their budget, complaints, discipline and welfare. The Lord Chief Justice, Master of the Rolls and other senior judges were given some management training.

In many ways our judiciary has grown in power and independence since 1960. Stevens pointed out that judicial review of executive (government) action has grown out of all recognition. This, I would add, was escalated by introducing a much easier judicial review procedure in 1981 and has been developed on the judges own initiative, in massively broadening the concept of what is "unreasonable", when striking down subordinate legislation and governmental decisions. Judicial review is a power the judges have taken upon themselves and the Human Rights Act 1998 has added to their tool kit of grounds for review. As Stevens said, it is exactly the sort of *droit administratif* that Dicey denied we had. Whenever a Government has tried to oust the power of the courts to judicially review executive action, the courts have avoided it. In 2004, New Labour introduced a Bill which would have abolished judicial review of decisions over asylum seekers and Lord Chief Justice Woolf attacked it in a public lecture, delivered at Cambridge. In another speech, Law Lord Lord Steyn attacked the Bill as "Contrary to the rule of law" and to the principle of "open justice for all".

14–013

An unusual and extreme example of the struggle between the judiciary and what they see as an authoritarian government's piece of primary legislation was the Law Lords' striking down of anti-terrorism legislation in December 2004 in *A (FC) v SS for the Home Dept* (2004, described in Chapter 4, above). The judges, in cases like this, see themselves as upholding the rule of law and civil liberties established centuries ago in the ancient unwritten British constitution. They see themselves as upholding the will of Parliament, which is their job under our constitution. Helena Kennedy, below, was writing in February 2004 but her words could have been about this December 2004 case.

> "Populist governments can get all manner of laws through Parliament; the whole purpose of human rights principles is that in their application they provide standards against which all law must be measured . . . A common mistake is that MPs come to equate a party political majority with 'Parliament' . . . They seem to think that, as long as a Commons majority approves of what a minister does, nothing more need be said about the legality of his or her behaviour . . . The judges are in fact asserting the supremacy of parliament rather than their own . . . If they fulfil their function properly, judges will at times upset public opinion and governments because they will protect the interests of unpopular minorities-those accused of crime, asylum-seekers, paedophiles, prisoners and probably fox-hunters". (Baroness Helena Kennedy QC, 2004.)

14–014   It is this growth in power, especially since the Human Rights Act, that has prompted Stevens (back in 1994) and others to point out that the views of the judges are a matter of public interest so maybe they should be carefully publicly examined before appointment, as they are in the US and South Africa.

As for the Lord Chancellor, explains Stevens, this is how he got his twentieth century role. The Hatherley Royal Commission on the Judicature, reporting in the late 1860s, floated the idea of a Ministry of Justice. This caused the judges to fear that their affairs might be handled by a minister who was a non-lawyer. Lord Chancellors Selborne and Cairns, the reforming Chancellors of the Gladstone and Disraeli governments "hit on an ingenious solution: the Lord Chancellor would become de facto the minister for the judges"; hence the emergence, in 1883, of the Lord Chancellor's Office." 2003, said Stevens (2004), saw history repeating itself. Judges were nervous at the threatened abolition of the Lord Chancellor because they feared a non-lawyer, such as a Secretary of State for Constitutional Affairs might be, could not protect them from the increasingly bitter and personal attacks of a powerful minister like Home Secretary David Blunkett.

Nevertheless, Stevens considered the guarantee of judicial independence in the Constitutional Reform Bill, now Act, to be meaningless.

Individual Judicial Independence

14–015   While we do not have an independent judiciary, in the American sense, we do protect the independence of individual judges. In modern times, independence and impartiality of the judiciary is a fundamental principle of the UN Basic Principles on the

Independence of the Judiciary, General Assembly Resolution 40/31 and 40/149 and the Convention, Art.6, as enacted into English law in The Human Rights Act 1998 s.1 and Sch.1. Judicial independence seems to contain these elements:

1. Security of tenure

It is thought that to make them easily removable would threaten judges' independence, subjecting them to political interference. Thus, senior judges enjoy a formidable security of tenure. Under the Act of Settlement 1700, they may only be removed following a motion by both Houses of Parliament. No English judge has been removed in this way.

Until 2005, removing and disciplining the lower judiciary (that means circuit judge and below) was the Lord Chancellor's job. Following the enactment of the 2005 Act, power of discipline is transferred to the Lord Chief Justice. With the agreement of the Lord Chancellor, he may give advice, or a warning or reprimand to any judge. Under the Courts Act 1971, the Lord Chancellor can, if he thinks fit, remove a circuit judge from office on the ground of incapacity or misbehaviour. Under the Constitutional Reform Act this can now only be done with the Lord Chief Justice's consent. Removal under the 2005 Act is dealt with at para.14–041, below. Under previous legislation, a Liverpool county court judge, William Ramshay was removed, following endless complaints and an unseemly battle with the press. Judge Keith Bruce Campbell was removed, in 1983, following his conviction for smuggling 125 litres of whisky and 9,000 cigarettes.

Judges often resign before they can be removed. Circuit Judge Angus MacArthur resigned from the Bench in 1997, shortly before being convicted for his third drink-driving offence and jailed for 28 days. He had been reprimanded by Lord Chancellor Mackay, following his second conviction, in 1993, who had warned him that he would be removed following a third offence. In 1998, commentators were critical when Lady Justice Butler-Sloss was offered retraining instead of prosecution for careless driving after a crash which left a passenger with facial injuries. The problem with cases where judges receive lenient treatment is that the public may perceive them to be above the law.

There is no statutory definition of "misbehaviour" so it was up to the interpretation of the Lord Chancellor of the time, although this may become much clearer, when the Lord Chief Justice exercises his new powers under the 2005 Act to set down disciplinary rules for judges. In 1994, Lord Chancellor Mackay wrote to the Lord Chief Justice, setting out what conduct he regarded as misbehaviour. He asked that any judge convicted of a criminal

14–016

14–017

offence, other than parking or speeding, should write to him. He said drink-driving was "so grave as to amount prima facie to misbehaviour". The same would apply to offences of violence, dishonesty or "moral turpitude". In the same letter he warned:

> "The public expects all judges to maintain at all times proper standards of courtesy and consideration. Behaviour which could cause offence, particularly on racial or religious grounds, or amounting to sexual harassment, is not consistent with the standards expected of those who hold judicial office. A substantiated complaint of conduct of that kind. . . . is capable of being regarded as misbehaviour."

Despite this, in 2000, Lord Irvine allowed a circuit judge to keep his job after a drink-drive conviction.

Concern arose after 2000, that short term judicial appointments, which the English legal system relies on, breached Art.6 of the Convention. In the Scottish case of *Starrs v Ruxton* (2000) it was held that a temporary sheriff in Scotland was insufficiently secure in his judicial role to satisfy Art.6. Consequently, the Lord Chancellor abolished the post of assistant recorder in the English judiciary in 2000. He announced that all part-time appointments would be for a period of at least five years.

2. High salaries

14–018   These are fairly high and are fixed by a non-governmental body, the Senior Salaries Review Body. A high salary was meant to protect them from corruption. Relative to 1825, when judicial salaries were fixed at £5,500, and to modern barristers' earnings, judges are not *very* highly paid. Most senior judges and many circuit judges are appointed from the ranks of Queen's Counsel, whose average earnings are over £250,000 per year. Several earn millions. Judges' salaries are on the DCA website (*www.dca.gov.uk*). From 2006, a High Court judge will be paid £155, 404 and a circuit judge £116,515. Lord Chief Justice Woolf warned, in 2005, that unless High Court salaries were kept at a level that did not undermine the status of the job, there was a risk that senior barristers would turn down the offer of a judicial post.

3. Judges cannot be MPs and should not engage in politics

14–019   It was very common in the early twentieth century for judges to have been MPs and a political career was seen as a good background for life on the bench. This seems to have died out in the latter half of the century. Lawyers were and are heavily represented in Parliament. Indeed, Parliament's hours were organised around court sittings so a lawyer could appear in court in the morning and in the House in the afternoon. Stevens (2004) observed that even in 1960, a third of judges had been MPs or Parliamentary candidates.

Having said that, it is important to recognise that some members of the lower judiciary have been local councillors, some members of the senior judiciary have been high profile "political animals" in the past (*e.g.* Sedley L.J.) and no attempt has ever been made to separate lay magistrates from politics. Magistrates deal with over 95 per cent of criminal cases and have a massive family workload and very many of them are local councillors. In the 1970s, in many towns most councillors were also magistrates.

By convention (political tradition), the Law Lords were meant to refrain from taking part in political debates in the House of Lords and meant only to debate on law reform Bills, but much recent law reform has been very politically charged, notably the debates on the Criminal Justice Bill 2003, when the Lord Chief Justice attacked the Home Secretary's plans to set jail terms for murderers. Masterman gives examples of cases in which individual Law Lords could not sit in judgments involving legislation on which they had expressed a view in Parliament.   **14–020**

Out of court, judges are meant to refrain from controversial and outspoken speeches but the rule has frequently been broken, said Stevens (1993), giving the example of Lord Chief Justice Goddard's enthusiasm for hanging and flogging, in the 1950s. Lord Denning frequently courted controversy in the 1970s and 1980s. He repeatedly gave public speeches in law schools, even during an election campaign, attacking secondary picketing, and he famously expressed racist views on jury challenge in trials involving black defendants, in 1981. He was threatened with a civil action when he repeated the comments in his book, *What Next in the Law* in 1982. He resigned over this. The Lord Chief Justice will now set out a scheme for reprimands, under the 2005 Act. In the past, letters of rebuke were sent by the Lord Chancellor.

A famous example of this was a reprimand delivered by Lord Hailsham to Mr Justice Melford Stevenson for describing the Sexual Offences Act 1967 as "a buggers' charter". A judge can expect a swift reprimand for off the cuff remarks which can be interpreted as unjust, insensitive or politically incorrect. The Judicial Appointments Annual Report 1999–2000 revealed that seven judges were reprimanded in 1999–2000. For instance, in 1999, Old Bailey Judge Graham Boal made a sexist, racist, homophobic joke in an after dinner speech at the annual dinner of the Criminal Bar Association. Lord Chancellor Irvine gave other examples of his reprimands to judges for racist remarks in his speech at the launch of the Judicial Studies Board's Equal Treatment Benchbook in 1999.

In 1988, Lord Chancellor Mackay suspended the Kilmuir Rules, which had prevented judges speaking out in public. This was   **14–021** taken advantage of by Judge James Pickles, who courted media attention at every opportunity, culminating in the development of his own chat show. One day, in 1990, he went too far. He called a press conference in a Wakefield pub, in which he discussed a (CA) case which had criticised him and called the Lord Chief Justice "an aged dinosaur". This was too much for the tolerant and mild mannered Lord Mackay. He released his letter of "serious rebuke" to the press, in which he sought loyalty to the CA and instructed the judge to stop taking substantial fees for his media appearances. After his retirement, in 1991, Pickles became *The Sun's* star columnist, styling himself "Judge Pickles", a title he was no longer permitted to use. James Pickles' books tell the story of his cat and mouse games with two Lord Chancellors in great detail.

In his campaign for the Chancellorship of Oxford in 2003, Lord Bingham "call me Tom" of Cornhill, the senior Law Lord, was very outspoken and set up his own website. He called for the legalisation of cannabis stating it "is stupid to have a law which is not doing what it is there for". He wanted all wigs and gowns banned and better pay for judges.

One controversial practice that critics say forces judges into the political arena in an undesirable manner is the use of judges, notably Law Lords, to chair public inquiries. It is also said that this is an enormous waste of judicial time. Masterman (2004) commented on this. He gave the example of Lord Saville who had been hearing the Bloody Sunday inquiry since 1999. This is ongoing as I write in 2005 and has deprived us of one of twelve Law Lords for all these years. Such involvement could, he said, influence judges' judgment in the future. He cited Lustgarten and Leigh who had demonstrated examples of this conflict of interest in relation to cases involving intelligence and national security.

14–022

> Like many law students, I read JAG Griffiths' *The Politics of the Judiciary*, which taught us how Labour governments were suspicious of judges, because of their reputation for conservatism and for undermining Labour legislation. I never thought I would see judges, during my lifetime, opposing governments from the left but since 1996 both main political parties have tried to outdo one another on being tough on crime and terrorism and asylum seekers. Judges have consistently been the voice of the liberal left, of human rights and the rule of law. The litmus test for this is that attacks on judges now come from the right wing press. The *Daily Mail* is every judge's *bête noir*.

4. Judges cannot be sued for remarks in court

5. Parliamentarians do not criticise judicial decisions

Stevens points out that this convention is set down in Erskine   **14–023**
May, *Parliamentary Practice* but comments that, while the rule about
not commenting on cases *sub judice* seems to have remained intact,
criticism of judges has been more acceptable in recent decades.

6. Politicians should refrain from criticising judges out of court

Thanks to David Blunkett, this rule seems to have flown out of the   **14–024**
window, recently. Indeed, he has been attacked by judges, in 2003–4,
for having no understanding of this convention. *In R. (Q) v SS for the
Home Dept* [2003] EWHC 195 (Admin), discussed in Chapter 4,
above), Andrew Collins J. ruled that the Government's policy of
requiring asylum seekers to register on arrival was unfair. David
Blunkett launched into an attack, supported by the *Daily Mail*, which
showed no appreciation of the separation of powers. He complained
of being "frankly fed up" with judges overturning measures
Parliament had debated. The Lord Chief Justice and other judges
defended Collins as upholding the will of Parliament. Doubtless, Mr
Blunkett was disappointed when Collins J.'s decision was upheld in
the CA. Lord Chancellor Irvine did not sympathise with his Cabinet
colleague, the Home Secretary. "Maturity requires that, when you
get a decision that favours you, you do not clap. And when you get
one that goes against you, you don't boo." This attempt to restrain
the outraged indignation of the Home Secretary illustrated very
acutely the argument of those who supported the continued presence of the Lord Chancellor in the Cabinet.

Things went from bad to worse in 2003. In May, a retired judge,
Sir Oliver Popplewell accused Blunkett of being a "whiner" and
Blunkett attacked judges for being out of touch with public views
on sentencing, in a speech to 1000 police constables. "I just want
judges that live in the same real world as the rest of us. I just like
judges who help us and help you to do the job". In the same week,
he said Mathias Kelly, chairman of the Bar, had "lost the plot", in
criticising his plans on criminal justice.

Blunkett grumbled when the courts took away his power to
determine life prisoners' release dates (see Chapter 4, above) and
Conservative Home Secretary Michael Howard behaved similarly in
the 1980s but without Blunkett's personal character assassinations.

7. The media should refrain from criticising judges

Looking at newspaper reporting over the centuries, I doubt that   **14–025**
this was ever a convention. Stevens reports that the idea that criticising a judge was a contempt of court was invented by the CA in

1900 to protect Mr Justice Darling. It is clear that by now, judge-bashing is a hobby of The *Daily Mail* and a fairly frequent indulgence of the *Evening Standard* and The *Daily Mirror*. When Lord Woolf spoke up for asylum seekers and the rule of law he was met with "loutish pummelling" in the tabloids, as *Times* columnist Anthony Howard put it. The Lord Chief Justice makes speeches attacking this behaviour but never has any impact. By now, the Deputy Chief Justice, Sir Igor Judge, has resorted to imploring them to stop unfair criticism. I have long argued that the Lord Chief Justice should have his own press office to counter such attacks and he has at last established one, in 2005.

8. Freedom from interference with decision making

14–026   It is a hallmark of dictatorships and extreme regimes that the government tells the judges how to judge. Judicial freedom in this sense includes the discretion to conduct procedures as they see fit. An attempt by Lord Mackay to persuade Sir John Wood, President of the Employment Appeal Tribunal, to drop preliminary oral hearings, in some cases, because of the backlog of cases, was very heavily criticised and illustrates the conflicts of interest that were inherent in the Lord Chancellor's position.

A lengthy spat went on in 2003–4 between Lord Chief Justice Woolf and David Blunkett, over sentencing and whether the judiciary or the executive should decide the minimum sentence for murder, for example, and who should decide when to release prisoners. The Home Secretary suffered a series of defeats before the European Court of Human Rights and the House of Lords, applying Art.6 of the Convention, which prescribes that judges, not government ministers should exercise judicial powers. The UK was the only country in the Council of Europe that permitted executive control over sentencing, something that David Blunkett could never understand was unacceptable under Art.6. Blunkett retaliated by amending the Criminal Justice Bill 2003 to introduce statutory minimum sentences. Lord Chief Justice Woolf was very outspoken in criticising this. Lord Donaldson of Lymington, a former Master of the Rolls said the Bill's provisions on sentencing revealed the Home Secretary's total misunderstanding of the judiciary in the British unwritten constitution. He explained this element of individual judicial independence, as he saw it.

"Parliament can limit the powers of judges, can indicate its view of what should be the appropriate sentences for the normal sort of offence. What it cannot do, either directly or through guideline-making bodies, is to dictate what should be the proper sentence in individual cases, the circumstances of which are infinitely variable." (House of Lords chamber, June 17, 2003).

9. The rule against bias

Individual judges are meant to conduct proceedings in a fair and **14–027** unbiased manner, without interfering in the presentation of the case. If they "step down into the arena" of the court (metaphorically) the result may be appealed or judicially reviewed. Similarly, judges must recuse themselves (stand down) if they have a connection with any of the parties or the issues. In *In Re Pinochet Ugarte (No.2)* (1999), the House of Lords extended the rule that a judge was automatically disqualified from a hearing in which he had a pecuniary interest to cases where the judge was involved personally, or as a director of a company, in promoting some cause. In this case, the Law Lords had to re-hear a case in which Lord Hoffman had failed to declare his connections with Amnesty International. In June 2000, following *Locabail* (1999, CA), the Lord Chancellor published guidance to judges on outside interests on his website. The last word and binding precedent on the bias test is set out in *In Re Medicaments and Related Classes of Goods (No.2)* (2000, CA) by Lord Phillips M.R. (as paraphrased in the *Times* law report, February 2, 2001):

"The Court first had to ascertain all the circumstances which had a bearing on the suggestion that the judge was biased. It then had to ask whether those circumstances would lead a fair-minded and informed observer to conclude that there was a real possibility, or a real danger, the two being the same, that the tribunal was biased. The material circumstances would include any explanation given by the judge under review as to his knowledge or appreciation of those circumstances. Where that explanation was accepted by the applicant for review it could be treated as accurate. Where it was not accepted, it became one further matter to be considered from the viewpoint of the fair-minded observer. The court did not have to rule whether the explanation should be accepted or rejected, rather it had to decide whether or not the fair-minded observer would consider that there was a real danger of bias notwithstanding the explanation advanced."

An allegation of bias was made in *Lawal v Northern Spirit Ltd* [2002] EWCA Civ 1218. One of the advocates sat as a part time judge of the Employment Appeal Tribunal and had sat with the lay member on the panel. The House of Lords felt the practice failed the "fair minded and informed observer" test.

As a matter of interest, French procedure interprets the necessity for protection against bias to require that the same judge will not deal with preliminary issues and the final hearing for fear of becoming partisan.

14–028 In 2004, the Judges' Council produced a *Guide to Judicial Conduct*, explaining to judges the practical implications of the requirement for independence, impartiality, propriety, equality of treatment, competence and diligence. These requirements were laid down in the *Bangalore Principles of Judicial Conduct*, initiated by the United Nations in 2001. The guide remarked that such guides have become commonplace in other jurisdictions.

All judges receive equal treatment training and a substantial equal treatment handbook. If judges behave discourteously or partially in court, they will rapidly find they may be the subject of complaint to the Lord Chancellor or an appeal. An example was *R. v Hare* in 2004, where the CA quashed convictions on the ground that a trial judge had shown a distinct lack of courtesy to counsel for one of the defendants. The CA had listened to the audiotape of the trial. Judge L.J., Deputy Chief Justice, said their Lordships expected judges to be robust, to curb time-wasting and to keep trials moving forward but this should be achieved with reasonable courtesy to counsel.

10. A politically independent appointments system

14–029 For many decades, the system of judicial appointments, in the hands of one person, the Lord Chancellor, a Government Minister and member of the House of Lords has been criticised as an affront to judicial independence and open to political abuse. Stevens' 1993 book gives ample examples of political appointments. Most notably in modern times, Lord Donaldson was appointed Master of the Rolls by Margaret Thatcher after many controversial years chairing the scourge of trade unions, the National Industrial Relations Court. He languished unpromoted during the interim Labour governments. it does not follow, however, that Prime Ministers will always select judges according to party political bias. Famously, Conservative John Major appointed Sedley J., a sometime member of the Communist Party, and some of his other senior appointments were of fairly outspoken radicals.

The danger of allowing politicians to appoint judges is illustrated by a story told in 2004 by Lord Justice Keene:

> "When Margaret Thatcher was Prime Minister, she had a conversation with one of her back benchers, who told her that the then Lord Chief Justice, Geoffrey Lane, had said something critical of government policy. Her response, as I have been told by the back-bencher in question was 'What, *my* Lord Chief Justice?' That is emphatically *not* how the system should be."

11. Impartiality

This is a close relation of independence. Individual judges are   **14–030**
meant to be impartial, hence the rule against bias but from the
1970s critics have attacked the appointment system and rules of eligibility for the judiciary on the grounds that it produces a judiciary
of "old, white, male geezers" as Lord Hoffman called himself, in
the quotation heading this chapter. Judges such as Lady Brenda
Hale and Laura Cox J. have long argued that judges who are so
demographically imbalanced cannot possibly be impartial in their
judgments over a diverse population.

3. Who Can Apply to be a Judge?

Qualifications for being a judge are all set out in statute. Historically   **14–031**
most judicial appointments were restricted to barristers, the exception
being registrars in the county court. Since solicitors have always had
rights of audience (the right to appear before the court) in county
courts, since their creation in 1846, they have been eligible for appointment as county court registrars, now called district judges. The Courts
and Legal Services Act 1990 now bases eligibility on rights of audience, as set out here. Most civil district judges (at the bottom of the
judicial hierarchy) are solicitors and most of the rest are barristers. The
selection process is discussed in more depth in Section 4, below.

Justices of the Supreme Court

When the Supreme Court is created to replace the House of
Lords Appellate Committee (see Chapter 6, above), the first
Justices of the Supreme Court will be the existing Law Lords and
their qualification will be the same, as prescribed by the
Constitutional Reform Act 2005. They will be appointed by the
Queen by letters patent. The Prime Minister still recommends
appointments but under the new Act, he has no discretion, as he
had in selecting Law Lords. He must pass on the recommendation
made to him by the Lord Chancellor. The new selection system is
described below. The Act creates posts of President and Deputy
President of the Court. The first people to hold these posts will be
the senior Law Lord, Lord Bingham, and the second senior Law
Lord. It will be possible for a person to be appointed to one of
these posts without having been a judge of the Supreme Court.

Lords of Appeal in Ordinary (colloquially known as "Law Lords"), e.g. Lord Rodger of Earlsferry

These were appointed by the Queen on the advice of the Prime
Minister, who was likely to seek the advice of the Lord Chancellor,

Law Lords and senior judges. A Law Lord was required to have held high judicial office for two years, or audience rights in the High Court and CA for 15 years, or Scottish or Northern Irish equivalent. In practice, they were generally appointed from the CA, the Scottish Court of Session or the Court of Appeal in Northern Ireland. One exception was Lord Slynn, who was a judge in the ECJ.

The Heads of Division (Master of the Rolls, Lord Chief Justice, Vice-Chancellor and President of the Family Division), e.g. The Right Honourable Lord Phillips of Worth Matravers, or Phillips M.R.

14–032   These are appointed by the Monarch on the advice of the Prime Minister. (The Queen takes no part in the choice and the Prime Minister is advised by the Lord Chancellor.) Recruits must be Lords Justices of Appeal (and most are) or qualified as such. When the new Judicial Appointments Commission starts functioning, from 2006, it will select just one candidate and that person's name must be passed onto the Prime Minister from the Lord Chancellor. They both thus lose their discretion in the selection process that they had before the Constitutional Reform Act was passed. The Lord Chancellor may only reject a candidate or ask the selection panel to reconsider if he considers the selected candidate unsuitable.

Lords Justices of Appeal, e.g. The Right Honourable Sir David Neuberger, or Neuberger L.J. or Lord Justice Neuberger

These judges sit in the CA. They are appointed by the Monarch on the advice of the Prime Minister, who receives a recommendation from the Lord Chancellor, who, in turn, will be given just one name by the Judicial Appointments Commission. They must have a ten-year "High Court qualification" or be judges of the High Court, which is the normal route.

High Court judges, e.g. The Honourable Sir David Calvert-Smith, or Calvert-Smith J., or Mr Justice Calvert-Smith

These are appointed by the Queen on the advice of the Lord Chancellor. They need to have had a High Court qualification (rights of audience) for ten years, or to have been a circuit judge for at least two years. A few appointments are made from circuit judges and the rest are mainly barristers who have practised for 20 to 30 years and are QCs. The Courts and Legal Services Act 1990 made solicitor-advocates eligible for appointment.

Deputy High Court judges

14–033   These are appointed by the Lord Chancellor, under the Supreme Court Act 1981, s.9(4). Lord Falconer continues his predecessors' policy of testing out most High Court judges by appointing them to sit part-time, as deputies.

Retired judges
The Lord Chancellor has power to authorise retired superior judges to sit part-time until their 75th birthday.

Circuit judges, e.g. Her Honour Judge Barnes
These are appointed by the Queen on the recommendation of the Lord Chancellor, under the Courts Act 1971. From 2006, they will have been selected by the Judicial Appointments Commission. They must have a ten-year county court or Crown Court qualification, meaning solicitor with a Crown Court advocacy certificate, or barrister, or be a recorder or have been in full-time office for three years in another judicial capacity, such as a district judge. The Lord Chancellor will normally consider only applicants who have sat as recorders for at least two years, although that policy is under consideration in 2005, as described below. Once appointed, circuit judges may sit at the Crown Court or county court, or both. Some sit in the specialised jurisdictions, such as chancery or mercantile cases. Experienced circuit judges may be requested to sit in the High Court (Supreme Court Act 1981) or in the Criminal Division of the CA.

Deputy Circuit judges
These are appointed by the Lord Chancellor from among retired judges.

Recorders, e.g. Cherie Booth QC
These are part-timers appointed by the Queen, on the recommendation of the Lord Chancellor for a renewable period of five years. From 2006, they will have been selected by the new Judicial Appointments Commission. Appointees must have a 10-year Crown Court or county court qualification. In other words, they must be a barrister or solicitor. They sit in the Crown Court and/or the county court, handling less serious matters than a circuit judge. They are required to sit for at least 15–30 days per year, of which at least 10 days should be in one continuous period (currently under review).

14–034

District judges, e.g. District Judge Gold
These will be appointed by the Queen, as soon as the 2005 Act comes into force and sit full-time in the county courts or district registries of the High Court, disposing of over 80 per cent of all contested civil litigation. The statutory qualification is a seven-year general qualification, meaning barrister or solicitor. The Lord

Chancellor normally only considers applicants who have been serving deputy district judges for two years but this policy is under consideration in 2005. As with all other judicial appointments, from 2006, they will be selected by the Judicial Appointments Commission. They will be appointed by the Queen, on the recommendation of the Lord Chancellor.

Deputy District judges
These are appointed by the Lord Chancellor. They sit part-time for 20–50 days per year. Their performance is appraised and helps inform the selection process of those who apply for full-time posts.

Masters and Registrars of the Supreme Court
These mainly deal with interlocutory (pre-trial) High Court work, as trial managers. Taxing masters tax costs in Supreme Court work. They are normally appointed aged 40–60, from the ranks of deputy masters and registrars. They must have a seven-year general qualification. From 2006, they will be appointed by the Queen, on the recommendation of the Lord Chancellor but selected by the Judicial Appointments Commissions (JAC).

4. The Judicial Appointments System from 2006

14–035   In this section I examine the new system and the consultation that preceded it before analysing in greater detail the arguments that provoked this reform and the defects of the old system.

The Constitutional Reform Act 2005
14–036   The Act radically altered the system of judicial appointments to meet mounting criticism of the old system, whereby most appointments were effectively in the gift of the Lord Chancellor, who consulted with the judiciary. In this section, I examine the new statutory framework and below, the background consultation and arguments. The wording of these sections and schedules of the Act is complex so I have relied heavily on the explanatory memorandum accompanying the Bill.

Selecting and appointing Supreme Court Justices
14–037   The establishment and jurisdiction of the new Supreme Court is discussed in Chapter 6 on the civil courts, above. As stated above, the first judges of the new Supreme Court will be the existing Law Lords. After this a special Selection Commission will be appointed, in accordance with the Constitutional Reform Act 2005. It will

consist of the President of the Supreme Court, the Deputy President and one member from each of three Judicial Appointments Commissions, Scotland, Northern Ireland and England and Wales. At least one of these must be a non-lawyer. Once the Lord Chancellor has accepted the selection made, the Commission will be dissolved and a new one convened when a vacancy for another Supreme Court Justice arises. Selection must be on merit. The Commission must consult senior judges and ministers from each jurisdiction. Once a selection has been made, the Lord Chancellor can accept it or ask the Commission to reconsider, or reject their selection but the Act severely curtails his discretion in doing this and limits the acceptable grounds for rejection. When the creation of the Supreme Court was announced in 2003, Law Lord, Lord Steyn commented that a small appointing commission, like this, would be appropriate,

"the new system will have to be more open and transparent than has so far been the case . . . it should be a neutral and impartial body. It must therefore be in no way identified with the government or civil service. On the other hand it should not be entirely dominated by judges." (2003).

The Act provides for "acting judges" to be used to supplement the permanent Supreme Court Justices, where the president or deputy requests it. They must be drawn from the Supplementary Panel or Courts of Appeal of the three jurisdictions of the UK. The Supplementary Panel consists of retired Supreme Court Justices, in the same way that retired Lords of Appeal in Ordinary can supplement the full-time Law Lords.

The background discussion to all of this is contained in the 2003 consultation paper, *Constitutional Reform: a Supreme Court for the United Kingdom*, which is on the DCA website, along with a summary of responses. The responses of the Judges' Council and the Law Lords are especially important. The Supreme Court was also the subject of Law Lords' speeches and many academic articles, which are discussed and listed in Chapter 6, above.

Since the massive growth of judicial review, in the 1980s and 1990s, **14–038** and especially since the passage of the Human Rights Act 1998, it has been argued that our judicial appointment process at the highest level should be much more open to public scrutiny, since judges' decisions frequently have political repercussions. Furthermore, in enforcing the Convention, the courts will become constitutional watchdogs and the Law Lords now effectively constitutes a constitutional court. For this reason, John Patten, a former Conservative Home Office Minister, argued in favour of public hearings before the appointment of a Law Lord, as occur when a new US Supreme Court

Justice is appointed (*The Times*, March 16, 1999). This argument has been reiterated many times since then, especially since the creation of the Supreme Court was announced, in 2003.

Dawn Oliver examined these arguments in 2003 but emphasised the problems. She questioned what criteria such a confirmation hearing would apply. A Parliamentary Committee would be less qualified than an appointments commission to make a decision on a candidate's suitability. A hearing was likely to be concerned with a judge's beliefs and politics, which ought not to be relevant in the UK. Ultimately it could lead to a reduction in security of tenure. Our system assumed judges were open minded and would not let their own prejudices influence them and this had generally worked, she said.

The Judicial Appointments Commission—functions

14–039   The Act creates a new independent Judicial Appointments Commission (JAC), which will assume responsibility for the process of selecting people for judicial appointments in England and Wales and for those appointments to UK-wide tribunals made by the Lord Chancellor. The JAC will select one candidate for each vacancy, or several candidates where several vacancies may arise, and report that selection to the Lord Chancellor. The Commission will make selections for appointment of the Lord Chief Justice, Heads of Division, Lords Justices of Appeal and puisne judges (High Court judges) and Sch.12 of the Act lists the offices below the High Court for which the Commission will make selections (with tribunal members being the largest group of appointments). In other words, selection of the lower judiciary (circuit judges and below) is purely a matter for the Commission.

From around 2006, when it is hoped the Commission will start work, no one may be appointed to any of these offices who has not been selected by the Commission. The Lord Chancellor will either appoint or recommend for appointment the selected candidate, or reject a candidate, once, or ask the Commission to reconsider, once. Having exhausted these options of rejection and reconsideration, the Lord Chancellor must appoint or recommend for appointment whichever candidate is selected. The Act makes special provision for the appointment of the Lord Chief Justice and Heads of Division and of Lords Justices of Appeal; in these cases the Commission will establish a selection panel of four members, consisting of two senior judges (normally including the Lord Chief Justice) and two lay members of the Commission. The appointments of Lords Justices and above will continue to be made by The Queen formally on the advice of the Prime Minister after the Commission has made a recommendation to the Lord Chancellor.

The Act requires the Commission to encourage diversity and specifies that "selection must be solely on merit" and that appointees must be of good character. This is the first time that this has been a statutory requirement. Under the old system, the Lord Chancellor's criteria specified that appointments must be made solely on merit. The Lord Chancellor will be able to issue guidance to the Commission, which they must have regard to, but subject to that it will be for them to determine the detailed appointments procedures they will follow. Guidance can only be issued after consultation with the Lord Chief Justice and after being approved in draft by both Houses of Parliament. The Commission must report on its selections and methods to the Lord Chancellor and he can, in consultation with the Lord Chief Justice, require them to make specific reports.

The Judicial Appointments Commission—composition

Schedule 12 sets out the membership of the Judicial Appointments 14–040
Commission and its powers and responsibilities, which will reflect its status as an Executive Non-Departmental Public Body. There will be a lay Chairman and five other lay members, five judicial members, two legal professionals, the holder of an office listed in Sch.12 and a Justice of the Peace. They will be supported by a Chief Executive and staff. Commissioners will be appointed for five years and can hold appointment for a maximum of 10. The Commission may delegate its functions to committees or sub-committees. The first Chairman, Sir Nigel Wicks, was appointed in April 2005.

Removal of judges

The Lord Chancellor has statutory powers to remove judicial office 14–041
holders below the High Court (including tribunal members and lay magistrates) for incapacity or misbehaviour. These powers can be exercised only with the agreement of the Lord Chief Justice. The Lord Chancellor previously exercised an informal, non-statutory power to discipline judges, considering complaints about judicial conduct and, where necessary, writing warning or admonitory letters, as can be seen above. Part 4 of the Act makes statutory provision for a disciplinary system in relation to judges, in cases falling short of removal, in which the Lord Chief Justice is given power to advise, warn or reprimand, following disciplinary proceedings, with the agreement of the Lord Chancellor. This will not affect the Lord Chief Justice's general ability to speak informally to any judge on any matter which concerns him, without having to inform or obtain the agreement of the Lord Chancellor. The Lord Chief Justice is also given a new statutory power to suspend judges from sitting in certain circumstances, with the agreement of the Lord Chancellor. The Lord Chief Justice will also have the power to make regulations and rules governing disciplinary

cases, with the agreement of the Lord Chancellor. The Judicial Appointments and Conduct Ombudsman, who must be a lawyer, will be able to consider complaints about the handling of disciplinary cases. The Ombudsman must report annually to the Lord Chancellor.

It will remain the case that judges of the High Court and above can be removed only by the Queen on an Address from both Houses of Parliament.

Background to the New Scheme: The 2003 Consultation Paper *Constitutional Reform: a new way of appointing judges* and Responses

14–042   Since the 1970s, criticism had mounted that the appointments system was unfair and drew from too narrow a pool of potential candidates. Most judges were chosen by just one man and that man was a politician, the Lord Chancellor. He appointed all lay justices, on the recommendation of local advisory committees. He selected all of the lower judiciary (circuit judges and below) and he put forward names for the senior judiciary, to be considered by the Prime Minister. He consulted widely among the existing judiciary, seeking their opinions on candidates for the judiciary. Lord Chancellors made progressive reforms, from 1994 but these did not satisfy the critics. The Bench was said to be too narrow, in terms of class, education, age, gender and ethnic background. The old scheme was repeatedly attacked, by academics, politicians, the pressure group JUSTICE, the Law Society and women and minority lawyers' groups. The most thorough exposure of these views was collected in the House of Commons Home Affairs Committee, third report for the session 1995–1996, *Judicial Appointments Procedures Volume II, Minutes of Evidence and Appendices* (1996), (abbreviated here to "JAP").

As part of the package of constitutional reforms announced in 2003, the Government proposed to reform judicial appointments and its proposals were set out in *Constitutional Reform—A New Way of Appointing Judges*. They sought views on their declared intent to create a new, independent commission for selecting judges in England and Wales, to replace the Lord Chancellor because

"In a modern democratic society it is no longer acceptable for judicial appointments to be entirely in the hands of a Government Minister . . . the appointments system must be . . . transparent . . . accountable . . . inspire public confidence . . . the current judiciary is overwhelmingly white, male and from a narrow social and educational background . . . the Government is committed to opening up the system of appointments . . . from a wider range of social backgrounds and from a wider range of legal practice." (Foreword by the newly appointed Lord Falconer L.C.)

The Lord Chancellor went on the point out that Scotland already had such an independent commission and one formed part of the Northern Ireland Agreement. The Government did not believe in a continental style career judiciary "but they do believe that new career paths should be looked at to promote other opportunities and diversity in appointments."

The paper described three possible models: 14–043

1. An appointing Commission, to take over the Lord Chancellor's role in appointing the lower judiciary and advising the monarch on senior appointments.
2. A Commission which would make recommendations to a Minister.
3. A hybrid Commission which combined the role of making junior appointments with recommending senior appointments.

The Government favoured a recommending commission, with appointments made by a Minister. The commission should work out how to attract a diverse range of candidates. Its 15 members should be appointed by competition: five judges, five lawyers and five non-lawyers. A judicial ombudsman would take over the "watchdog" role, dealing with complaints about judicial appointments.

The response of the old Commission for Judicial Appointments

This body, a watchdog for the judicial appointments processes, 14–044 described below, had a critical influence on reforming the judicial appointments process at this point. Its views on the proposed constitutional reform of the appointment system were that the majority of the new Commission should be lay persons and they should apply best practice on human resources.

The Law Society response

The Society favoured the third, hybrid model, with the 14–045 Commission, as a non-departmental body, making a single recommendation for a senior vacancy and the degree of discretion exercisable by a minister or Prime Minister kept very narrow. Appointment to the senior judiciary must be by open competition only. The executive should play no role in bringing forward or inviting candidates. "The absence of any appearance of cronyism is vital to establishing a positive public perception".

All judges should be regularly appraised by the new JAC. They supported an ombudsman to deal with grievances about the appointments process and complaints about judges.

Their proposed commission would also appoint magistrates and tribunal members. Half its members would be lay people, with a lay chair. Its establishment would make "an institutional and cultural change in the appointments process". It would be tasked with encouraging a greater diversity of applicants. Government should be required to consult the JAC on overall appointments policy. The JAC should keep selection criteria under review. Tackling the discriminatory aspects of the current appointments process, such as automatic consultation of a homogeneous pool of senior judges, should be the JAC's priority. Appointment processes should be speeded up. People should be able to enter the judiciary at any level.

The Bar Council response

14–046   Similarly, the Bar Council favoured a hybrid Commission, with a single name nominated for each senior post. In the interests of judicial independence from the executive, the Minister's discretion should be curtailed. He would have a statutory duty to protect judicial independence and he or the Prime Minister would have to give written reasons for rejecting a nomination. Senior nominations would be made by a sub-committee. Like the Law Society, they agreed that the Commission should take over the appointment of magistrates and tribunal members. Selection criteria should be set out in a statute, and detailed by the Commission. They referred to the Glidewell Report 2003 (their own report) on ways to encourage diversity. Complaints about judges should be dealt with by Heads of Division and the Lord Chief Justice. They favoured a majority membership of judges, with a lawyer in the chair.

The Judges' Council

14–047   Judges urged the Government not to underestimate the scale of changes required by abolishing the office of Lord Chancellor. Judicial independence had to be preserved in the public interest. They wanted the Lord Chief Justice to head the judiciary, with a statutory statement of responsibilities. Deploying judges should be his job and it was essential that judicial independence and duties were not hampered by a lack of resources. Any new appointments process "should reflect the need to preserve judicial independence and calibre and to increase diversity".

JUSTICE

14–048   This group of lawyers wanted to go further than the consultation proposals. The DCA should be, exclusively, a Ministry of Justice. All members of the executive (Government and civil service) should be under a duty to uphold judicial independence. The Lord Chief

Justice should speak on behalf of judges and report annually on the judiciary. The Commission should have a lay chair and six lay members. Parliament should monitor the continued high quality of the judiciary, via a joint committee monitoring the JAC. The JAC would make senior judicial appointments. They disagreed that the JAC should have a role in appointing magistrates. There should not be a separate ombudsman and grievances should be dealt with by the JAC. It should have a statutory remit to encourage diversity. Career routes should be multi-track. The Lord Chief Justice should be head of the judiciary and responsible for discipline. They referred to the *European Charter on the Statute of Judges* which guarantees judicial independence.

Various judges

Individuals gave evidence to the Constitutional Affairs Committee, a select committee of the House of Commons. These are too lengthy to be summarised, as they are reported speech, but they can be read on the Committee's pages on the Parliament website (*www.parliament.uk*).　　　　　　　　　　　　　　　　　　14–049

The Association of Women Barristers

Like the Bar, the Law Society and JUSTICE, the Association published its own documents on judicial appointments, such as K. Monaghan's "Discrimination in the appointment of the senior judiciary and silk" (*www.womenbarristers.co.uk*). There were many other responses and these were posted on the DCA website.　　　　14–050

On January 26, 2004, Lord Chancellor Falconer and Lord Chief Justice Woolf made speeches in the House of Lords announcing the details of the proposed new statutory framework for the constitutional changes. The principles set out here have become known as The *Concordat*, mentioned above.

To the undoubted relief of the Government, Lord Falconer was able to assure their Lordships that his announcement of the new arrangements had the full support of the Lord Chief Justice. In 2003, the latter had warned that the proposed changes posed the biggest threat to judicial independence for centuries. The judges were clearly annoyed that the June 2003 announcement had been made without informing them. In the meantime, there had been extensive negotiations between the Judges' Council, the senior judiciary and the Lord Chancellor. Crucially, Lord Falconer emphasised the importance of judicial independence:

> "In making changes, we must secure embedded, enduring judicial independence; good working relationships between the judiciary

and the executive; high quality judges; and high public confidence in the judiciary . . . The reforms seek to clarify and embed in statute the principle of judicial independence. Judges must enforce, impartially, the law made by Parliament. The executive must continue to guarantee security of judicial tenure and remuneration, and ensure that the judiciary is supported by an efficient and effective system of court administration. We propose that there should be a general statutory duty on the Government, all those involved in the administration of justice and all those involved in the appointment of judges to respect and maintain judicial independence. In addition, there should be a separate specific duty falling on the Secretary of State for Constitutional Affairs to defend and uphold the continuing independence of the judiciary." (*Hansard*, Column 13).

14–051   As can be seen from the contents of the Constitutional Reform Act, above, when the Government published it as a Bill, in January 2004, they responded to the results of the consultation and changed plans accordingly.

76 per cent of respondents emphasised the importance of judicial independence. The JAC's responsibilities extend to tribunal members and lay justices, as desired by the Law Society and Bar. Local advisory committees will continue to recommend names. 88 per cent of consultation respondents thought they should continue in this role.

As for membership of the JAC, 43 per cent of consultation respondents had said that there should be an even split between lay people and lawyers or judges and contrary to the proposal, the biggest group, 45 per cent, had favoured a judicial chair. Nevertheless, respondents favouring a lay chair, such as JUSTICE, felt it would ensure independence and pointed to its success elsewhere, such as in Scotland and Canada. The Judges Council had pointed out that a judge would not have time to chair the JAC.

14–052   For judicial appointments up to and including the High Court, the JAC will advertise vacancies and select candidates and, after consulting the Lord Chief Justice, will recommend a single candidate to the Lord Chancellor, giving reasons. The Lord Chancellor can accept the recommendation, or, with reasons, reject or ask the JAC to reconsider, as explained above. Notice that the Secretary of State's discretion is severely curtailed, as this was favoured by 75 per cent of respondents to the consultation. Notice this new JAC will be a *recommending* commission, despite the fact that the majority consultation respondents favoured an appointing commission, to guarantee judicial independence, or a hybrid commission. The 24 per cent favouring a recommending commission did so because it provides ministerial responsibility to Parliament and it is closest to the old appointment system.

> "To ensure proper accountability to Parliament, the final decision on whom to appoint—or whom to recommend to the Queen for appointment—should remain with the Secretary of State. However, the Secretary of State's discretion must be severely circumscribed. He should be able to appoint only candidates recommended by the commission and should have strictly limited powers to challenge those recommendations. It is not right that a political appointee (albeit one always acting in good faith) should be able to cut across the system to appoint who he or she thinks is right." (Lord Chancellor Falconer, in the *Concordat*.)

All but the senior judicial members will be appointed following open competition. As for heads of division (meaning the president of the Family Division, Master of the Rolls and so on) notice the involvement of the most senior judges. It was urged by many respondents to the consultation paper that their views were especially valuable and well-informed. Also, any appointee would have to command the respect of those colleagues.

Although 42 per cent of consultation respondents thought the JAC should have a role in discipline and complaints, the Government preferred an independent body and this coincided with the views of the Law Society, the Bar, the Judges' Council, the former Commission for Judicial Appointments and many other respondent lawyers' groups. An ombudsman will consider complaints about appointments and the handling of complaints about judges. He will report annually to Parliament. This follows the preferences of 84 per cent of the respondents to the consultation. Like the Government, they felt it was important that a body independent of the JAC should handle such complaints.

5. Problems with the Old System of Appointing Judges

Problems had been readily identified by interest groups, such as **14–053** JUSTICE and by the witnesses who appeared before the House of Commons Home Affairs Committee, quoted extensively below. The Lord Chancellor asked Sir Leonard Peach to report on the system of selecting silks (QCs) and judges and Sir Leonard reported in 1999. The system was the subject of progressive reform over the years since 1994 but not enough to satisfy critics.

The Roles of the Lord Chancellor and Prime Minister in Appointing Judges

14–054   As Griffith said, in successive editions of *The Politics of the Judiciary*, "The most remarkable fact about the appointment of judges is that it is wholly in the hands of politicians" and he traced the history of political patronage—judicial appointments as a reward for political services. Senior judicial posts were in the gift of the Lord Chancellor and, ultimately the Prime Minister, to whom the Lord Chancellor's recommendation was made. Some bodies had expressed concern about this long ago, such as a JUSTICE sub-committee in 1972 and the Bar in 1989. This point has been discussed under the heading of "Judicial Independence", above.

Nevertheless, as Drewry pointed out,

"even the sternest critics of the present arrangements would surely have to concede that any vestige of the old party political "spoils" system that prevailed until the early part of this century has been eradicated. Above all the neutrality of judges is underpinned by the strong commitment to the constitutional principle of judicial independence, which is regularly reaffirmed by politicians of all political parties as an essential pillar of the rule of law."

Anyway, he said, the debate about the political background of judges

"has been overtaken in the last couple of decades by the transformation of party political ideology and the social class structure. Even if one accepts that judicial ideology may over the years have displayed some sympathetic resonance with traditional Conservative values, many of those values were displaced or distorted in the 1980s or 1990s by New Right free market radicalism, and Margaret Thatcher's and John Major's ministers were often given a very hard time by the courts." (1998).

Critics remained concerned about the role of politicians in appointing judges, as can be seen from Lord Justice Keene's comment on Margaret Thatcher, above. Griffith said whether the Prime Minister merely accepts the Lord Chancellor's advice on senior appointments will depend on the personalities of the two but Rozenberg insisted that Margaret Thatcher vetoed some of Lord Mackay's suggestions (JAP, p.273). Brazier, in evidence to the same 1995 Select Committee, articulated the concerns of many:

- The concentration of power in the hands of one person, without the benefit of a structured system of advice, is unsatisfactory.

The present system lacks openness, relies on unstructured questions to advisers of unknown identity. There is no accountability to Parliament.

- The increasing size of both branches of the profession means the Lord Chancellor cannot have adequate knowledge of all potential candidates. (The 1992 JUSTICE report said that, some 50 years earlier, with a Bar of 1500 and under 100 judges, the Lord Chancellor was personally involved in choosing judges.)

Some modern commentators on the constitutional reforms have advocated removing the role of the Prime Minister. One such critic was Sir Thomas Legg, who had helped Lord Chancellors to select judges for many decades. Another was Sir Iain Glidewell, in his 2003 report for the Bar Council. He expressed the view that it had become constitutionally unacceptably that judges should be appointed by the Government of the day.

In 2005, the Prime Minister's role in judicial appointments was the subject of a different type of criticism. Rather than for his political bias, Tony Blair was attacked for "cronyism", not for the first time. He selected Lord Justice Potter to be the new President of the Family Division, although he had little experience of the family courts. Sir Mark Potter had been the Bar pupil master of Lord Chancellor Falconer, Tony Blair's flatmate. Of course this followed a pattern: Tony Blair had appointed his flatmate as Lord Chancellor, to replace Lord Chancellor Irvine, who in turn happened to be Blair's pupilmaster and who introduced Tony Blair to his wife Cherie.   **14–055**

Frances Gibb, Legal Editor of *The Times* commented that "The appointment caused disbelief among senior judges, who had tipped Lord Justice Thorpe". I shared that disbelief. Thorpe L.J. has dedicated his judicial life and much of his spare time to promoting the reform and development of family law and procedure on an international scale. He has personally promoted and orchestrated co-operation between judges in child proceedings on an international scale. His efforts and achievements are unparalleled by any other judge, worldwide. He was the deputy to the outgoing President. Sir Mark, on the other hand, did not know anything about family law, in an era when family law had become much more specialised and required specialist training of every family judge, even at the lowest level. Professor Stephen Cretney, the leading academic family lawyer in England and Wales remarked on the irony that this appointment was made at the very time when the Constitutional Reform Bill was before Parliament, designed to replace such blatant cronyism with a judicial appointment system that is fair, open and transparent. The new system for appointing Heads of Division, described above at paras 14–031 and 14–039, should prevent a repeat of this scandal.

The Call for Sweeping Reform—a Judicial Appointments Commission

> "We are fortunate to have a judiciary that is politically neutral, uncorrupt, and of the highest calibre, with an international standing second to none. However we intend that a Judicial Appointments Commission will insulate more the appointment of judges from politicians. It will also promote opening up appointments to some of those groups of lawyers which are under-represented in the judiciary at the moment, including women, ethnic minorities and, at the higher levels, solicitors." (Lord Chancellor Falconer, announcing the consultation papers on constitutional reform, July 2003, DCA Press Release 296/03.)

14–056   The suggestion had frequently been made that a commission of lay persons and others should either advise the Lord Chancellor in judicial appointments or replace him. This argument was made by a JUSTICE sub-committee in 1972 and reiterated by JUSTICE in 1992. They felt its powers should stretch beyond recommending appointments, to judicial training, career development of the circuit judiciary, performance standards and complaints. Their proposed Commission would comprise 13 members: seven lay persons, two judges and four lawyers. Visible and real independence from the executive and judiciary would be crucial. The proposal was designed to secure a more diverse bench.

Supporting such a Commission, the Law Society said, in evidence to the Home Affairs Committee, in 1996, that its advantages would be:

- distancing individual appointments from ministerial control;
- assisting in formalising selection procedures and criteria to reflect good recruitment practice; and
- assisting in achieving public confidence in the objectivity and even-handedness of the selection process (JAP, 237).

In their evidence to the 1996 Home Affairs Select Committee, the Judges' Council rejected such reasoning as "misguided" and introducing politics into the selection process.

The Law Society was supported by Professor Brazier. He noted that the Liberal Democrats and the Labour Party, then in opposition, favoured a Commission. The Labour Party set out its plans for a Commission in several policy documents, including *Access to Justice* (1995) and *A New Agenda for Democracy* (1997), although the proposal did not appear in the party's 1997 election manifesto. Those commentators above were disappointed when, in October

1997, Lord Chancellor Irvine announced that he had decided not to establishe a Commission. Instead, he announced some reforms of the appointment system and promised to consider establishing an ombudsman for those aggrieved by the appointments process and a system of performance appraisal.

In the meantime, two discussion papers, by Thomas and Malleson, **14–057** had been commissioned by the Lord Chancellor's Department Research Secretariat, under the joint title, *Judicial Appointments Commissions—The European and North American Experience and the possible implications for the United Kingdom* (1997). Kate Malleson reviewed US and Canadian models and found there was no strong evidence to suggest that the use of commissions as opposed to other appointment methods had any significant effect on the make-up of the judiciary in terms of competence or representativeness. A more important variable might be their approach to the appointment process. The experience in Ontario suggested that active attempts to recruit under-represented groups could have a significant effect on the type of judges appointed. She found that public confidence in the use of commissions is generally very high. Examining continental European appointment systems, Cheryl Thomas drew attention to differences in the appointment processes that explained differences in judicial composition. Women made up a significant proportion of the judiciary in most of the countries examined and at least half of incoming judges in France, the Netherlands, Germany and Italy. She explained that, as recruitment there is through public examination based on university-level knowledge of the law, women normally fare better than men. She concluded:

"Recruitment of judges later in their professional career, as occurs in common law countries, tends to bring into play social forces which reduce women's chances: family commitments and professional discrimination. Civil law, bureaucratic-style judiciaries have favourable employment conditions for women (maternity leave, flexible working hours, *etc.*,) and the judiciary is seen as a positive career choice for women law graduates." (Full paper, LCD Research Series 6/97, p.21).

She suggested that the continental practice of involving lower ranking judges in judicial appointments commissions might also encourage an increase in the appointment of women judges, minorities and other less traditional types. It shifted the criteria for appointment and lessened the influence of legal elites who tended to favour the status quo.

The Lord Chancellor commissioned Sir Leonard Peach to carry out an independent review of the appointment process. In 1999, he recommended to the Lord Chancellor that he appoint a Commissioner for Judicial Appointments and a number of Deputy Commissioners and this was done in 2001. This was not the model suggested by JUSTICE, as they did not advise on appointments but kept the appointments process under constant review and published an annual report. Critics were disappointed at Sir Leonard's suggestion and called for an appointing commission. In July 2000, Lord Steyn became the first Law Lord openly to call for a commission. The Law Society, in support of their attack on the current selection system, pointed to Hazel Genn's study, *Paths to Justice*, 1999, which revealed that the public thought that judges were old and out of touch.

The head of this first Commission was Sir Colin Campbell, a non-lawyer and he and the other commissioners had a broad experience in recruiting in commerce and industry. Remarkably and unpredictably, Sir Colin's views themselves became a catalyst for reform. From their standpoint of outsiders, the commissioners clearly found some aspects of the old appointment system shocking and indefensible and their annual reports carried highly publicised and trenchant criticisms which doubtless embarrassed the new Labour Government and strengthened their resolve to reform the judicial appointment system, as can be seen from some quotations from their reports. Doubtless the Government was horrified when the Commission for Judicial Appointments published its Annual Report for 2003, in 2004 and commented that the system of appointing judges and Queen's Counsel was rife with wide "systemic bias" against minorities, women and solicitors that infected the way the legal profession and judiciary operated. See more below, at paras 14–061–14–062.

The only real objection to selecting judges by means of a judicial appointments commission was one that has been mentioned fairly often since 2003, "the danger of leading to a bland, antiseptic bench, technically competent but 'safe'." (Stevens, 2004).

The System of "Secret Soundings"—"Comment Collection"

14–058   Traditionally, in England and Wales, aspirants did not apply for a job as a judge. They were invited to join the bench by the metaphorical "tap on the shoulder" by the Lord Chancellor, whose civil servants gathered files of fact and opinion on potential judges and kept candidates under constant review. The Bar was so small, around 1000, until 1960, that the Lord Chancellor was presumed to know all the candidates personally. By 1990, this could not work with the lower judiciary, as the Bar was so much bigger. Many candidates for recorderships and the circuit judiciary applied for the job and some were still invited but there was no standard application form, other than for district judges. In my current research on the judiciary, I have interviewed judges, now in their fifties, who claim that there was a system of seniority in certain chambers in their circuits. When barristers, in their turn, achieved sufficient seniority in chambers, the Lord Chancellor would ask if they wanted to become a circuit judge or QC so they knew to expect that their turn would come.

Lord Chancellor Hailsham endeavoured to make the recruitment and appointment system less secretive and, in the 1980s, published his selection criteria. Lord Chancellor Mackay made countless speeches urging more women and ethnic minorities to put themselves forward. In 1994–1995 he dramatically opened up the recruitment and selection system by advertising lower judicial posts (circuit judge and below) and introducing interview panels. As for the senior judiciary, by convention, until 1998, candidates did not apply.

The problem was that, despite many reforms made by Lord Chancellor Mackay and Lord Irvine, the Lord Chancellor was still heavily reliant on these "consultations" with existing judges. They were referred to by critics as "secret soundings", to the irritation of Lord Chancellor Irvine, who valued them. The Judges' Council, in their 1996 evidence to the Home Affairs Committee defended the system:

"judges see and hear most of the potential candidates before them, day in, day out, from a position in which they are uniquely well placed to assess their professional competence and personal qualities, and to compare them with competitors in the field." (JAP, p.219).

The Equal Opportunities Commission, in their evidence, expressed "a major concern" over such soundings:

"Selection for appointment should depend on an objective assessment of the applicant's skills and abilities. Given the predominance of men in the senior ranks of the judiciary, the bar and the solicitor's profession, there is an increased risk of stereotypical assumptions being made with regard to 'female' as opposed to 'male' qualities and aptitudes. It is therefore the Commission's view that the practice of canvassing opinion is certain to risk introducing impressionistic and subjective factors into the recruitment process." (JAP, p.211).

If consultation is to continue, then those consulted should at least receive training, they argued.

Most critics made the simple point that any system which relied **14–059** on the say-so of a limited group was inevitably open to members of that group selecting people like them. As Chris Mullin MP retorted:

". . . it appears to be self-perpetuating does it not? They all know each other, many of them went to school together, most of them were at university together and they have no doubt known each other all the time dining in their various Inns of Court. They are males aged between 55 and 66 on average . . . and they appear to move in very limited circles." (JAP, p.5).

The Law Centres Federation called the Bar and the judiciary "in effect a self-perpetuating oligarchy or clique" (JAP, p.227). The Association of Women Barristers urged that the system should be abolished (JAP, p.193). The Law Society said the system disadvantaged those who were not from the standard background for judges and perpetuated the weight given to advocacy skills. They wanted "soundings" replaced with a system of objective tests and interviews, such as is used in civil service recruitment (JAP, p.229). The Bar Association for Commerce, Finance and Industry (employed barristers) called the system "wholly indefensible in the 1990s" (JAP, p.204). The Association of Women Solicitors opposed the system because it disadvantaged women and solicitors who were unlikely to appear before and, consequently, be known to serving members of the judiciary and it placed undue emphasis on advocacy skills. The African, Caribbean and Asian Lawyers' Association said that the composition of the judiciary reflected neither the British population nor the legal profession.

The accusation that the system perpetuated a clique was strikingly illustrated by research undertaken on behalf of the Association of Women Barristers. Examining 104 High Court Appointments made during 1986–1996, 70 (67.3 per cent) came from a set of chambers of which at least one ex-member was a judge during the consultation period. Only 58 of 227 sets of London chambers produced judges, of which seven sets produced an astonishing 30 appointees. Of the 131 sets outside London, they produced only seven judges. The 104 appointees, from a pool of 8,800 barristers, replaced over two thirds of the judges, yet came from roughly the same chambers as those they replaced (J. Hayes, 1997).

14–060   Sir Leonard Peach (1999) suggested that each candidate should nominate three referees and this was done. They were consulted separately from the other consultees. The problem was, however, that this extensive consultation system went on alongside the use of referees, until 2005. Each of a long list of judges was sent the list of candidates applying for various judicial posts and each judge chose upon whom to comment. Apart from this suggestion, Sir Leonard expressed his confidence in the system. This disappointed all critics, especially the

Law Society, who repeated their condemnation of the "secret sound-ings" system, as they called it, as "fundamentally flawed" and an "old boys' network". Sir Leonard did, however, recommend that the consultations system be supplemented with alternative methods of evaluating an applicant's suitability, such as one-day assessment centres and psychometric and competence testing (see comment by Malleson, 2000). The Lord Chancellor, in September 2000, announced that work would commence on a pilot for an assessment centre, following recommendations by a Bar Council and Law Society working party. He also accepted the need for wider advertising, better aptitude testing and an easier route from other judicial roles.

In June 2000, Kate Malleson and Fareda Banda reported to the Lord Chancellor on *Factors affecting the decision to apply for silk and judicial office* (see the DCA website). They exposed widespread dissatisfaction with the selection process, especially among women, solicitors and minorities, who felt particularly disadvantaged by the consultations process and resented the apparent elite group of barristers' chambers who benefited from it. Many repeated the call for a Judicial Appointments Commission.

Assessment Centres were piloted in 2002 for deputy civil district judges and High Court masters. They were being used instead of traditional interviews, to identify whether the approach encouraged more applications from currently under-represented groups. Candidates had to show political correctness, awareness of other cultures, proficiency in relating to people from a diverse society and "empathy and sensitivity" in the building of positive relationships with litigants, witnesses, advocates and colleagues. The assessments include practical exercises and role-play, an interview and written examination. In 2003, they were reported to be a success and plans were made to extend the system to recorder selection.

The Commission for Judicial Appointments savages the old boys' network

In the meantime, despite these reforms the "consultations" system   14–061
continued alongside, for most judicial posts and in the selection of Queen's Counsel. The 2003 report of the Commission for Judicial Appointments (CJA) was highly condemnatory of the consultations system. They uncovered some vague and highly subjective comments that were made about applicants, which bore little relation to the professed selection criteria for judges or Queen's Counsel, such as

- "She's too primly spinsterish".
- "She's off-puttingly headmistressy".
- "She does not always dress appropriately".

- "Smug and self-satisfied and pompous".
- "Down and out scruffy".

The commissioners, all non-lawyers who had wide experience in commerce and industry, had not come across comments like them, in 20 years of experience, said Sir Colin Campbell, their out-spoken chair. He complained that there was an over-emphasis on the views of the senior judiciary. Such comments were symptomatic of a "wider systemic bias in the way that the judiciary and the legal profession operate, that affects the position of women, ethnic minority candidates and solicitors in relation to silk and judicial appointments". There was a strong case for abandoning the consultation process. He also felt that High Court appointments, which were still mainly made by the tap on the shoulder method, should all be filled by application and interview.

In their next annual report, 2004, their recommendations were more forceful. There was a need to improve fairness and transparency in the appointments process. Great weight was given to the views of the senior judiciary, collected in the consultation process and this skewed the recruitment process towards those who were visible to the senior judiciary. They had received complaints to this effect from solicitors. Consultations should be replaced with a more structured and accountable method of collecting views from the judiciary on candidates' suitability for office. "We call for much fuller audit trails of how selection decisions have been reached." Much of their negative evidence was gleaned from complaints about the process for applicants who had been turned down. Having examined 18 such complaints, they went so far as recommending an apology from the DCA in nine cases.

The CJA were very prescriptive about what needed to be done. All candidates must have an equal opportunity to demonstrate their suitability for office. All relevant evidence must be evaluated against known competencies and criteria, appropriate to the office in question. Judicial opinions could be taken account of but gleaned in a much more organised and restricted manner, concentrating on objectivity and relevance. They welcomed the extension of appraisal of part-time office holders as that could provide useful information in considering applications for fulltime posts. They noted that the Constitutional Reform Act 2005 would require appointment on merit. That could not be assessed from the candidates' personal profile without examining their capacity to do the job.

14–062 They added that the appointment process did not recognise skills demonstrated by other judicial office holders, such as tribunal chairs, who dealt with legislation and cases at least as demanding as those heard by circuit judges. This disproportionately affected women since they accounted for 24 per cent of tribunal chairs. They had received complaints from men that the system was institutionally biased against fulltime judicial office holders, who were not visible to the consultees.

They reviewed the High Court competition and were especially critical of it. They considered that the system whereby senior judges could nominate people for consideration for the High Court was unfair because this meant different information was available for nominees and applicants. This led to "serious inequalities" in their treatment. There was no information on how the Heads of Division arrived at their shortlist. Candidates were not considered according to appointment criteria but by undisclosed criteria. Under a reformed system, head hunting would be acceptable but all candidates should apply through the same route. A new working group headed by Thomas L.J. was swift to take this point on board. From 2005, all those who are to be considered for the High Court must apply in writing and include a 1,500 word self-assessment.

The 2004 report is well worth reading in full as it exposes in some detail the shortcomings of the appointment process and gives practical examples of how this has prejudiced the chances of some applicants. It makes depressing reading for those of us who were writing student essays containing identical criticisms back in the 1970s.

Restricting Judicial Appointments to those with Rights of Audience

The gist of the above criticism, that those who do not appear 14–063 before the right judges will not be selected, is compounded by the law itself (Courts and Legal Services Act 1990) which bases all judicial appointments on audience rights. This excludes most solicitors (most lawyers) from appointment directly to the High Court and all those with purely academic qualifications from all judicial appointments. The Judges' Council defended this restriction, in 1996:

"Successful advocates must develop and exhibit the ability, founded upon sound judgment, to evaluate the strengths and weaknesses of their opponent's case as thoroughly as their own. . . . In addition, the administration of justice in England and Wales depends upon lawyers who appear before the court owing their paramount duty to the interest of justice, and not advancing arguments or evidence which are improper, mendacious or corrupt." (JAP, p.219).

Certain groups have long argued that prowess as an advocate, standing in court arguing one side of a case, does not demonstrate the skills needed of a judge, to sit quiet and give an impartial hearing to both sides and fair judgment. For instance, JUSTICE has long been opposed to the restriction of judicial eligibility to advocates:

> "The best drama producers may not be the best critics; the best players do not necessarily become the best referees. In particular the strong combative or competitive streak present in many successful advocates is out of place on the bench." (*The Judiciary in England and Wales*, 1992.)

The Law Society argued that the emphasis on advocacy "actually impairs the selection of the best candidates". Full-time advocates suffered the disadvantage of a lack of experience of dealing with clients directly, or of conducting litigation, which could lead to "a rather unworldly approach". (JAP, pp.234–235).

Other jurisdictions do not limit the judiciary to practising advocates and use is made of academics as judges in the highest courts. Thinking of the qualities needed of judges in the CA and the House of Lords, they spend most of their time considering and developing points of law. Academic lawyers devote their whole careers to developing expertise in specialist areas of the law.

14–064 Lord Chancellor Irvine accepted some of these criticisms. As a result of the Peach Report and Banda and Malleson's research, he re-wrote the appointment criteria to emphasise that he did not regard advocacy experience as an essential requirement for appointment to judicial office, from 1999.

The Constitutional Reform Act 2005 did not alter the legal requirement that candidates have rights of audience as a barrister or solicitor. Most respondents to the 2003 consultation paper favoured perpetuating the restriction. This is hardly a surprise, since most respondents were barristers, solicitors, judges or their representative organisations.

6 The Resultant Problem in 2005—Lack of Diversity—and How to Solve it

Lack of Diversity on the Bench by 2005

14–065 As we have seen, critics of the old system of appointment said it produced the current lack of diversity on the Bench—the concentration of older, white males, who come from narrow social and educational backgrounds. In October 2004, Lord Chancellor Falconer published a consultation paper, *Increasing Diversity in the Judiciary*. It will be the job of the new Judicial Appointments

Commission to devise methods of securing greater diversity on the Bench but the Lord Chancellor felt he could not wait until around 2006, when it is appointed. Thanks to the efforts of Lord Chancellor's Mackay and Irvine, since 1994, the lower sections of the judiciary have become significantly more diverse but this is not enough for the present Lord Chancellor. He has doubtless been embarrassed by the criticisms of his Commission for Judicial Appointments, whose annual reports, discussed above, pull no punches and are specific in setting out what needs to be done.

Composition in 2005

- All judges are barristers or solicitors. As can be seen, the **14–066** majority of circuit judges and above are barristers but district judges are predominantly solicitors.
- As of February 1, 2005, there were 12 white Law Lords, one of whom was a woman, Baroness Hale of Richmond, the first woman to be appointed, in October 2003. All were barristers.
- Of the 37 all-white judges in the CA, two were women (5.41 per cent). None were solicitors. Of the 107 High Court judges, two were solicitors and 10 women (9.52 per cent), one of whom was non-white. She was Linda Dobbs QC, the first ever black judge to be appointed to the senior judiciary of England and Wales, in 2004.
- Of the 640 circuit judges, 67 were women (10.47 per cent) and 90 were solicitors. Only 10 circuit judges (1.56 per cent) were ethnic minority.
- Of the 433 civil and family district judges, 406 were solicitors and 84 were women. 17 (3.93 per cent) were minority.
- Of the 126 District Judges (Magistrates' Courts), 25 (19.84 per cent) were women and 83 were solicitors. Five (3.97 per cent) were minority.
- If lay and legal tribunal members were included, around 24.9 per cent of total judicial post-holders were women and 6.9 per cent were minority.
- I have not included part-timers, that is, recorders and deputy district judges.
- To update these statistics, visit the DCA website.

Does this really demonstrate a lack of diversity?

The 2004 consultation paper assumed such statistics demon- **14–067** strated a lack of diversity.

"change is needed. . . . only 15.8 per cent of judges in the courts . . . are women, and 3.4 per cent are from ethnic minorities . . . In

451

comparison, women comprise 51.3 per cent of the population of England and Wales, and ethnic minorities, 7.9 per cent." (para.1.1).

On the other hand, Adrian Jack argued that the statistics did not demonstrate a problem because:

- Judges were older than the population at large. Of 45–64 year olds in the population, only 5.1 per cent were ethnic minority and the Bar of that age had a similar ethnic profile.
- If all judicial posts were counted, including lay and lawyer tribunal members, the consultation paper acknowledged that 24.9 per cent of all judicial posts were held by women. This *overrepresented* eligible women, argued Jack, as 20 per cent of barristers and 23 per cent of solicitors in that age group were women.

He concluded that the current appointment system was already producing greater diversity and the consultation paper smacked of "false political correctness".

Lack of social diversity

14–068 The consultation paper barely mentioned the lack of social and educational diversity reflected in the judiciary but this has been criticised for decades. It was most famously attacked by J. A. G. Griffith in successive editions of his book *The Politics of the Judiciary*. Innumerable surveys are cited by him, all demonstrating that the senior judiciary is dominated by Oxbridge graduates, educated at the top public schools (fifth edition, 1997, p.18).

The Labour Research Department published regular surveys of the judiciary and in December 2002, they reported that new Labour had failed to make the judiciary any more diverse in this respect, since they came to power in 1997.

The survey, of all 774 judges sitting in English and Welsh courts, found that 67 per cent went to public school and 60 per cent attended Oxford or Cambridge universities. Under New Labour, those in the senior courts were more likely to have been public school educated; the average age of the judges was over 60.

It goes without saying that judges will always be middle class, by definition, because they are recruited from lawyers, but judges' lack of educational diversity is extreme.

Why is Lack of Diversity a Problem?

14–069 Lord Mackay did not think it was, "It is not the function of the judiciary to reflect particular sections of the community, as it is of the democratically elected legislature" (JAP, p.130). He added that he expected composition would broaden over time. J. A. G. Griffith cynically attacked this sentiment as "weasel words" (JAP, p.261). Lord Irvine appeared to take a different view from his Conservative predecessor: "I believe that the judiciary should be a microcosm of the community that it serves." (Interview on the *Today* programme, March 21, 1999) and clearly the present Lord Chancellor, Lord Falconer considers it to be an urgent problem, in 2005.

Many have argued that an imbalance in the judiciary will warp the administration of justice itself. For instance, David Pannick argued "the quality of judicial performance would be improved if more of the bench enjoyed the experience peculiar to more than half the members of our society" (*The Times*, July 30, 1996). Barbara Hewson, of the Association of Women Barristers listed examples of gender bias in judicial and tribunal decisions and advocated the research and educational work of gender bias task forces, such as exist in the US, where the National Judicial Education Program identified three types of gender bias: stereotypical thinking about the nature and roles of men and women, how society values women and men and myths about the social and economic realities of women's lives.

On her appointment as the first female Law Lord, Baroness Hale argued why the judiciary needed more women. Quoting Canadian Chief Justice Beverley McLachlin, she argued it would:

- promote public confidence;
- be symbolic, as the judiciary are required to promote equality and fairness;
- be a sound use of human resources, tapping the intellectual qualities of the missing half of the population;
- bring a different perspective to judgments.

Baroness Hale acknowledged that the last point was controversial. She said most of her judgments could have been written by a man. Nevertheless she agreed with McLachlin that jurists are informed by their background and experience. For cultural, biological, social and historic reasons, women's experience is different. She concluded:

"The Present judiciary is disadvantaged but means well. Few if any are actively misogynist or racist but they have a lamentable lack of experience of having female or ethnic minority colleagues of equal status." (Hale, 2003).

Kate Malleson has warned, however, that

"The idea that a judge can represent the interests of a group from which he or she is drawn is clearly incompatible with the notion of impartial justice." (2004).

There was no empirical evidence that women more effectively represented the views of women, she said. American research disclosed little difference between male and female judicial decision-making. One might hope that diversifying the judiciary would increase their range of skills and experience which would enhance decision-making in general but the real reason for including under-represented groups was that "the corrosive impact of their absence on the legitimacy of the judiciary is now too great to ignore."

14–070   The 2004 DCA consultation paper said:

> "Society must have confidence in that the judiciary has a real understanding of the problems facing people from all sectors of society with whom they come into contact . . . We must ensure that our judicial system benefits from the talents of the widest possible range of individuals in fairness to all potential applicants and to ensure that talent, wherever it is, is able to be appointed." (*Increasing Diversity in the Judiciary*).

It cited a 2003 MORI survey of confidence in the criminal justice system. 54 per cent of respondents were confident or fairly confident that judges were doing a good job but 43 per cent were not very or not at all confident. The media portrayed judges as elderly, male and of a narrow social class and they and the public concluded that judges were out of touch.

14–071

> For what it is worth, I consider our current judicial composition to be deeply embarrassing in an international context where most judiciaries are more diverse and some are significantly more diverse, especially in Europe. As a student of the 1970s, I was lectured by half men, half women, white and black so the judiciary looked odd and were criticised, even in those days. By 1993, women became the majority of law graduates and they graduate, on average, with higher class law degrees than men. By 2005, 75 per cent of my undergraduate pure law students were women, many of them brown or black. All this should tell us that the aptitude for law is not confined to old, white males. There is no excuse for the narrowness of our judiciary. It results from the heavy involvement of judges in the selection system and from the concentration on barristers. The Bar, like the solicitors' branch of the profession, was inherently sexist and racist until too recently. Gender and race discrimination at the Bar were not outlawed until 1990.

Reasons Why Specific Groups are Underrepresented

The exclusion of solicitors

They have long been the most persistent of critics of the judicial   **14–072**
appointment system. Bearing in mind what I said above, that the
Courts and Legal Services Act 1990 confines judicial posts to those
with rights of audience and most solicitors do not have rights of
audience in most courts, this excludes over 90 per cent of lawyers
from the bench. The route onto the bench for solicitors is to become
a recorder or district judge and seek promotion or to gain rights of
audience, which very few solicitors have done (under 2,000 of
116,000). Prior to the Courts and Legal Services Act, solicitors were
only eligible for appointment up to circuit level. This brought about
the criticisms that the system was unfair on solicitors and produced
too narrow a pool of potential judges. There are always about ten
times more solicitors than barristers and they come from more
diverse social backgrounds. The 1990 Act has made very little difference since, in 2005, there are still only two solicitors in the senior
judiciary.

In the early 1990s, the Law Society's *Gazette* carried several critical
articles and the Society published a discussion document urging that
the system be subjected to a complete overhaul. The emphasis on
advocacy meant that solicitor candidates, minorities and women
were overlooked. It was they who urged the devising of a list of judicial qualities as formal selection criteria, which Lord Mackay eventually published in 1994. Solicitors stridently opposed the consultation
system. Further, they complained that the published selection criteria still placed too much emphasis on career success and income. The
requirement for part-time sitting (as a recorder or deputy district
judge) prior to full-time appointment was too lengthy and should be
made more flexible. Short blocks of sitting were disruptive of solicitors' practices. Other judicial appointments, such as tribunal chairman, district judge and stipendiary magistrate did not seem to be a
stepping stone to the circuit bench. Appointments should be made or
recommended by a commission, from as wide a pool of candidates as
possible, who all felt equally encouraged to apply, according to selection criteria which did not unnecessarily disadvantage any group.

Both Lord Mackay and Lord Irvine remained unmoved by these
criticisms. By October 1999, solicitors had become exasperated in
the lack of progress toward reforming the judicial appointment
system and the Law Society announced they were boycotting the
"consultations" system. In other words, if solicitors were consulted
on potential candidates, they would not offer an opinion. Lord
Irvine condemned the Law Society's action as a "disservice to its
members", in his press releases, speeches and *Judicial Appointments*

Annual Report 1999–2000. In that report, he emphasised that 47 per cent of new appointments went to solicitors but acknowledged these were not the senior appointments. In October 2000, the Law Society reiterated all their criticisms in a report again calling for an independent appointments system.

The emphasis on silk

14–073   Around half of High Court judges now in office were recruited from Queen's Counsel, as were many circuit judges. This system was opposed by solicitors, women and ethnic minorities because, as explained in the Chapter on lawyers, they alleged that the selection system for silks disadvantaged them, because of the emphasis on advocacy and because appointments to silk are massively unrepresentative of such groups, the method of recruitment to silk again being based on the same "consultations" system as was used to select judges. In very recent years, Lord Irvine then Lord Falconer responded to this criticism and tried to reassure lawyers that the silk system would not be used as a passport to the judiciary.

Racial minorities—was the old appointments system discriminatory?

14–074   Geoffrey Bindman wrote a provocative article in the Law Society's *Gazette*, in 1991, suggesting that the system was indirectly discriminatory and thus illegal, under the Race Relations Act 1976. He cited the Commission for Racial Equality's code of practice for employers, which recommended against recruitment through the recommendations of the existing workforce where the workforce was predominantly from one ethnic group and the labour market multi-racial. Recruitment by word of mouth was a common cause of discrimination. Lord Mackay refuted this criticism, sending the Law Society's president counsel's opinion (a barrister's expert opinion) to the effect that the article was "wrong in law and fact". He said he could only reach his objective of increasing the number of women and minorities on the Bench if he could find a sufficient proportion of them in the practising profession of the appropriate age and standing.

His successor, Lord Irvine, appeared equally frustrated at the low numbers of minorities applying for judicial appointment. At the Minority Lawyers' Association Conference in November 1997, he reiterated Prime Minister Tony Blair's embarrassment that there were no black senior judges and only one per cent non-white circuit judges. He explained that only about one per cent of barristers of 15 years' call, the group eligible for High Court appointments, were minority. The root cause of the problem, he said, was long-term discrimination on both sides of the legal profession: "I cannot solve all the problems by myself. The professions need to ensure their houses are in order." Black lawyers remain cynical, because of the continuing lack of non-white judges. There was a reduction in the proportion of ethnic minority practitioners appointed in 1999–2000 to 4.2 per cent from 5.4 per cent but in the *Annual Report 1999–2000*, Lord Irvine pointed out that, of lawyers with over 20 years' experience, the group from which most judges are appointed, under four per cent were minority. The appointment of Linda Dobbs as the first black senior judge was welcomed, in 2004 but Lord Chancellor Falconer's announcement on the publication of the 2004 Judicial Appointments Annual Report was very misleading. A press release entitled *Continued Increase in Minority Ethnic Judicial Appointments* boasted that 14.8 per cent of judicial appointments had gone to minorities but this included lay members of tribunals. The 2005 statistics on professional judges, at para.14–066 above, speak for themselves.

The exclusion of women

Again, the statistics quoted above speak volumes. As for the circuit   **14–075**
bench, recruitment was examined by Sally Hughes for the Law Society in 1991, in *The Circuit Bench—A Woman's Place?* She challenged the excuse made, by Lord Mackay above, that the numbers of women on the Bench would naturally increase as the number in practice increased. Examining two cohorts of barristers, she found that women took longer than men to be appointed to the Bench and were recruited from a much narrower age range. Their late appointments could not be accounted for by maternity leave. Of the 173 circuit judges appointed during 1986–1990, only 4.6 per cent were women. The majority of women judges surveyed thought that, although some had suffered discrimination early in their careers, the judicial appointments system did not discriminate against women. Nevertheless, many women had had low career expectations and one third had been invited to apply to the bench, without having put themselves forward. This was consistent, said Hughes, with employment research which showed that women were less likely to apply for promotion and more inclined to accept initial rejection than men. Thus she concluded that to restrict appointments to applicants (as transpired from 1994–1995) would damage the recruitment of women.

By 1995, the Law Society reported that there had been a rapid improvement in the number of women assistant recorders but there was little sign of improvement at higher levels. This showed that the Lord Chancellor's recruitment drive was working but changes would have to be made much lower down the system to develop the careers of women and minorities, if there were to be real impact. (JAP, pp.232–233.)

The Association of Women Solicitors complained that the require-ment to sit part-time for several years was a double bind for women solicitors. They might annoy their business partners by disrupting their practice and reducing their earning capacity shortly after taking a career break or maternity leave. The judicial atmosphere was unwelcoming to women. Women were disadvantaged by the existence of male clubs, where judges and barristers lunched. The Inns of Court and freemasonry provided opportunities for male bar-risters to fraternise with judges.

14–076   Some of their recommendations, and those of other parties have since been followed, such as open advertising and reformed selec-tion criteria (partly satisfied in 1995) and the removal of obstacles to employed barristers (in the Access to Justice Act 1999).

Malleson and Banda, cited above, 2000, found that white female barristers felt the demands of practice most put them off applying for judicial office, followed by lack of confidence in being taken seri-ously. Although some cited family responsibilities as a reason for not applying, an equal number cited the compatibility of judicial work with family responsibilities as a reason *for* applying. The quo-tation below, from the UK Association of Women Judges, spells out the problem.

Gays and lesbians

14–077   Martin Bowley, then President of the Bar Lesbian and Gay Group, had a sorry personal tale of prejudice to tell the Home Affairs Committee, in 1995. He had been informed that he was not appointed to the Bench because this was against the Lord Chancellor's policy "since [homosexuals] were particularly vul-nerable to public and private pressures". This rule was dropped in 1994. The LCD judicial appointments group staged a recruitment event at the Lesbian and Gay Law Conference 2000.

Freemasons

14–078   Where a judge is suspected of being a freemason, it is sometimes alleged that he has favoured "brothers" appearing before him, as barrister, solicitor, Crown Prosecutor, police witness or one of the parties. The problem of alleged bias is exacerbated by the fact that, unlike common membership of a golf club, membership of the freemasons is much more difficult to discover. Furthermore, they have secret signals with which to greet one another. In the context of judicial appointments, there is a further concern that aspirant bar-risters who are freemasons (all male) have a special relationship with recommending judges who are also masons.

The House of Commons Home Affairs Committee reported on its investigation into *Freemasonry in the Police and the Judiciary* (Third

Report 1997). In evidence, the United Grand Lodge of England refuted all allegations of bias or corruption, especially the frequent allegation that masons owed an allegiance to their fraternal oath which overrode their professional duties or ethics and the judicial oath. The Judges' Council, in their evidence, and Lord Chancellor Mackay could see no cause for concern. It was disclosed that 32 senior freemasons were judges, in 1997, plus an unknown number of more junior freemasons. The Law Society and the Association of Women Barristers argued that judges and senior police officers should not be freemasons. In its evidence, Liberty detailed one case alleging corrupt masonic connections. They said they knew of many such instances. The Association of Women Barristers listed "a significant number" of legal masonic Lodges. As a result of all this, Lord Chancellor Irvine required all incoming judges to publicly disclose membership of the freemasons. The Lord Chancellor, in 1998, asked over 5,000 existing judges to voluntarily declare whether they were freemasons. Two hundred and forty-seven judges admitted that they were and 64 declined to answer.

What was the Response to Such Criticisms?

As I mentioned above, various reforms took place from 1994. **14–079** From that date, the Lord Chancellor experimented with advertising jobs in the lower judiciary and placed job specifications on his website, then made applications the only route to appointment. In 1998, advertisements for the High Court started appearing but about half were still recruited by the "tap on the shoulder" method. Both Lord Mackay and Lord Irvine complained that too few women and minorities applied and held events to try to encourage recruitment of all underrepresented groups. The Commission for Judicial Appointments was established. It examined the system and was heavily critical of certain aspects of it. As stated above, assessment centres replaced interviews, for deputy district judges, and these are being extended to recorder recruitment. A joint working party on equal opportunities in judicial appointments and silk was set up in 1997, consisting of representatives of the Bar Council, Law Society, and minority lawyers' groups. It reported to the Lord Chancellor in 1999, making 42 recommendations aimed at increasing numbers of women and ethnic minorities applying for silk and judicial appointment. Many of these were implemented immediately, or following the 1999 Peach report on appointments to silk and the judiciary, discussed above. A work shadowing scheme was established, to allow lawyers to sit with judges in court.

All the 1990s reforms resulted in some success and the volume of applications for judicial appointments increased, not just because of reforms but because of the perceived downturn in some areas of lawyers' work. There was around a five per cent increase in the number of women applying between 1998–9 and 2002–3 and a similar increase in the number of ethnic minorities applying and being appointed.

Attempts to Increase Diversity from 2005: *Increasing Diversity in the Judiciary*

14–080   Lord Chancellor Falconer decided he could not wait until the Constitutional Reform Act 2005 introduced the new Judicial Appointments Commission in 2006. He decided to start consulting very widely from 2004 and his departmental paper, *Increasing Diversity in the Judiciary* examined in some depth what other tactics might be used to enhance recruitment of the missing groups. The annexes to the report are very informative, as they contain comparative information on diversity of judges in other jurisdictions and diversity in other professions.

While acknowledging that the shortcomings in the old appointment process had been a major factor in causing lack of diversity, the consultation paper rightly said that there were other problems. There was a lack of diversity in the legal profession, from which the judiciary was drawn (I discussed this in Chapter 13 on lawyers, above). Statistics showed that "trickle-up" was working, since the numbers of women and minorities entering the profession was now much greater, but was working very slowly. There was indeed a "trickle out" rate, with women dropping out of the legal profession. The paper also reported that applicants delayed applying, which made the problem worse. People were applying many years after becoming eligible to apply. The paper explored how to improve communication on what judicial appointment offered as a career option; the requirements for judicial office; the working practices of the judiciary and opportunities for progression and what more might be done by the legal profession to increase diversity of the applicant pool.

Communication

14–081   The paper said that despite efforts to publicise eligibility for judicial appointments and despite staging publicity events, eligible lawyers felt there was still not enough information available in an accessible format and there was an unawareness of judicial appointment competitions. Also, people suffered from misconceptions about the application process.

Requirements for appointment to judicial office

14–082   Unusually, the consultation paper sought opinions on the statutory qualifications for the judiciary, based on rights of audience. It noted that academics and researchers were experts on the law but were excluded, unless they were also barristers or solicitors. Similarly, the requirement for several years of post-qualification experience (seven for a district judge or ten for a recorder) conflicted with an appointments process that claimed to be merit-based. (The Commission for Judicial Appointments annual report 2004, discussed above, had complained that requiring a High Court judge to have 20 years experience was indirectly discriminatory, as only 14 per cent of practitioners with that length of experience were women).

The paper asked for opinions on whether the policy requirement for people to sit as a part-timer before being considered for a full-time appointment deterred certain people and asked whether it should be relaxed, amended or abandoned. The paper articulated the rationale behind requiring people to sit part-time before appointing them full-time:

1. Full-time judicial office was unique, in being a job for life. It was essential to appoint people who were capable and would continue to be capable of doing a good job. Part-time service allowed them to demonstrate that.
2. It allowed part-timers to see if they wanted to become a judge.
3. It allowed them to build their skills and experience. This was essential for non-practitioners like academics.
4. It afforded an opportunity to appraise them, helping to develop judicial skills and provide evidence of suitability for full-time office.
5. It was a way of ensuring a high and consistent standard of full-time appointments.

On the other hand it posed a problem for people with caring responsibilities and for solicitors whose firms banned them from part-time judicial office or who were hostile to it.

The appointment process

The consultation paper pointed out that policy had already been amended to remove the upper and lower age limits on appointment; that it had been made clear that advocacy experience was not essential and that interview panel members had been retrained and now included lay people with human resources experience. Assessment centres now replaced interviews for deputy district judges and were being piloted in 2004 for recorder selection. Appraisal was used for deputy district judges and was about to be piloted for recorders.

14–083

On the controversial subject of "consultations", the paper suggested cutting this down to four judges who knew the candidate, nominated by the senior presiding judge of the applicant's circuit and the leader of the circuit Bar. The candidate could continue to nominate six consultees.

Judicial working practices

14–084   The paper pointed out that salaried part-time judicial work had been introduced in 2001 for those who could not do a full-time job. This is different from a lawyer's appointment as a deputy or recorder sitting occasionally. It is a salaried fractional appointment as a professional judge. By 2004, 40 judges worked like this, on a flexible basis. On recruiting disabled people, they admitted they had no statistics on disabled judges but were consulting on how to attract disabled applicants. The paper asked whether there should be a change to the rule that a judge could not retire and return to practice, as there was anecdotal evidence that this discouraged some potential applicants. The paper suggested it should be better publicised to existing judges that they could apply to progress through the ranks. There was a wrong perception, for instance, that you had to be a barrister or circuit judge to be a High Court judge.

The legal profession

14–085   Interestingly, the paper dealt in some detail with the attrition rate of women from the legal profession. It pointed out that women tended to leave the profession before the point at which they might be expected to apply to be a judge. Another problem was the lack of support given by the profession to those who sought judicial appointment. This was especially acute for solicitors, some of whom were forced to choose between partnership and applying to be a deputy district judge or recorder. The paper acknowledged that the profession was more diverse than the judiciary and that each side was currently trying to promote diversity. The paper complained of the cost of entering the profession, the cost of university tuition fees and a sense of bias against degrees from certain universities. See Chapter 13 on lawyers, above, for more details of diversity, or lack of it, in the legal profession. In their response to this new consultation paper, The UK Association of Women Judges spelled out the problem for women:

"The vast majority of successful candidates to the High Court Bench are drawn from the most successful members of the Bar. The majority of candidates to the Circuit Bench are drawn from practising members of the Bar. Yet the Bar is a profession in which is difficult for women to excel, and extremely difficult to excel if there are home commitments such as having and raising children or looking after elderly relatives, or supporting a partner. A successful practice at the Bar, particularly in London, is not a job, it is a way of life. It involves being available, often at short notice, to take on an urgent matter, perhaps with travel away from home, working late in the evenings and at weekends. It involves uncertainty over which days are going to be committed, and holidays being forfeit for the sake of work. There is the uncertainty of being self-employed, with the consequential lack of employment rights. There are no regular hours, or days, or places of work. It is a job which is very self-reliant (rather than being team related) and involves selfless and selfish dedication. Any woman who is trying also to run a home and family will find this daunting, however much outside assistance she can use. Many talented women give up the Bar and many allow themselves to be 'sidetracked' in chambers. This does not apply to all, of course, but the women who do manage to keep a high profile practice and run a home and family are exceptional, and they are few. Many women feel that the price paid is too high".

Additionally, even if women did manage to keep a busy practice afloat they could not afford the time for "networking" at evenings and weekends. They suggested that one solution was that all women lawyers should be trawled for judicial appointments, including employed lawyers and academics.

> As I write, in 2005, Lord Chief Justice Woolf keeps warning that moves to diversify the judiciary must not be allowed to jeopardise the standards or integrity of the Bench. My response to this is to point out that any discriminatory system deprives itself of the talents of the excluded. Until now the excluded have been most non-whites, most women and the 92 per cent of lawyers who happen to be solicitors.

A More Radical Suggestion—a Career Judiciary

Most continental civil law countries have developed a career judiciary. Modern descriptions of a sample of systems are given in Thomas's discussion paper, cited above. Generally speaking, most judges are recruited at a very young age, soon after graduating in law. They are selected like civil servants, by competitive examinations, which sometimes include psychological and fitness testing, as well as legal knowledge, which results in women being the majority of recruits. The new recruit must attend courses at judicial college

14–086

and then starts off at the bottom of the judicial ladder and may, if successful, be promoted through the ranks to the senior judiciary. It is common to require coninuing education and further examinations. Some judges are selected from amongst practising lawyers but this is the exception. A portrait of such judges in France was drawn in an article by Adam Sage, who claims that judges are young, radical and middle-class.

From time to time, it has been fashionable to suggest a career judiciary here. Most witnesses before the 1995 Home Affairs Committee, discussed above, did not mention such a radical plan but the Law Society did favour recruitment by competitive, civil service-type examinations. The Judges' Council rejected the suggestion on the basis of profound differences between common law systems and the legal systems of continental Europe.

The Committee agreed with Brazier's opinion that the judiciary was already a career, in the sense that a career path of a judge may involve sitting in courts of a progressively higher rank. Nevertheless, the Committee firmly rejected any move to a career judiciary in this country. Dawn Oliver, in 2003, examined arguments in favour of a career judiciary but pointed out that it is not on the active agenda in the UK at present, or that of any common law jurisdiction. The habit of recruiting judges from practice was "deeply embedded". The high status our judges enjoyed and respect for the rule of law in the UK relied to an extent on the seniority and successful prior careers of those appointed.

14–087 Advocates of a career judiciary generally point out that this would significantly lower the age of the judiciary and inevitably make it much more diverse. Not everyone considers the youthfulness of European career judges to be an asset. Stephen Jakobi, Director of Fair Trials Abroad has more experience than any lawyer in the comparative merits and shortcomings of the lower judiciary around Europe:

"Countries that seek to attract young people to the bench at an early age but also insist on prolonged professional training and the existence of either experienced colleagues sitting with them or lay assessors until they reach maturity (*e.g.* Germany and the Netherlands) seem to deliver a quality of justice commensurate with international standards. Those where judges start young but where one or more of these other factors are missing (*e.g.* Spain and France) do badly." (2003).

He thought the British system worked well. Kate Malleson argued ((1997) 60 M.L.R. 655) that, since 1970, the judiciary has undergone a process of formalisation which had resulted in the creation of a form of career judiciary for the following reasons: the judiciary had expanded massively; the majority of work in the criminal courts (she meant the Crown Court) was currently carried out by part-time recorders, many of whom are seeking promotion. This must have strongly influenced their behaviour. Significantly, performance appraisal had, thus far, only been introduced to monitor the suitability of part-time judges for promotion. The formalisation of training and the issue of bench books of model directions, she saw as undermining the culture of individualism that formerly thrived within the judiciary. In her 1999 book, *The New Judiciary*, she argued that the growth in size of the judiciary and the expansion of its policy-making role were leading to radical change in the role of the judiciary.

7. Training and Appraisal

We lack the systematic form of judicial training and examinations 14–088 which are a universal requirement for continental judges. It is often said that our system of recruitment direct from practising professional advocates is the antithesis of training.

The Fear of Undermining Judicial Independence

For centuries, judges have resisted the suggestion that they 14–089 undergo training on the ground that it might undermine their "judicial independence". One of the most famous books written by a judge about judging is Lord Devlin's *The Judge* (1978). In it, he delivered a 20-page tirade against a 1976 Home Office Consultative Working Paper suggesting the introduction of judicial training. Here are some extracts:

"when in 1948 I was appointed to the High Court. . . . I had never exercised any criminal jurisdiction and not since my early days at the Bar had I appeared in a criminal court. I had never been inside a prison except once in an interviewing room. Two days after I had been sworn in, I was trying crime at Newcastle Assizes . . . for centuries judicial appointments have been made on the basis that experience at the Bar is what gives a man the necessary judicial equipment . . . where the independence of the judges may be touched or appear to be touched, it is a good thing to have a protocol. Protocol should, I think, decree that in the acquisition of background information a judge should be left to his own devices" (pp.34–35).

The sentiments are typical of judges of the old school. He thought training belonged on the continent. Nevertheless, the Judicial Studies Board was established in 1979.

Malleson challenged the claim that judicial training and performance appraisal posed a threat to judicial independence ((1997) 60 M.L.R. 655). She noted that judges used the objection of threat to their independence as a sort of trump card to play when opposing any innovation in the judiciary but they failed to explain what they meant by judicial independence. Certainly, in opposing the establishment of the Board, they meant freedom from control by the executive, or interference by any outsider, such as an academic director of studies. For this reason, the Board is run by judges. Its President is always a High Court judge; its Director of Studies is a seconded circuit judge and many of its committee members and trainers are judges. The introductory statement on the website asserts:

"An essential element of the philosophy of the JSB is that the training of judges and magistrates is under judicial control and directions."

Malleson pointed out, however, that judges perform a dual function: a constitutional role as one branch of the State counterbalancing the interest of the executive and Parliament and a distinct social service role carried out in their day-to-day work in the courts. Training and performance appraisal, she said, were not matters which affected the constitutional position of the judges, "they are concerned with the way in which legal services are provided to the public" (at 660) and are much more likely to bring pressure to bear on the decision of a judge in a particular case but, as JUSTICE had said in the 1992 report cited above, "Judicial independence has never justified substandard justice. . . . Judicial independence is constrained by the principle of good administration, for which someone or some body must be accountable to Parliament" (at 4). Training and performance appraisal, she concluded, did not pose any threat, if they were confined to updating the law and questions of how judges handled cases before them (such as fair dealing between the parties and handling delicate issues sensitively).

The Current Training Regime

14–090   Here, I summarise the training regime established by the Judicial Studies Board (JSB) at the time of writing, 2005. Updated information can be obtained from the Annual Report on the JSB website.

Recorders

Before sitting in the Crown Court, a recorder is required to attend a four-day residential induction course run by the JSB, which consists of lectures, sentencing and summing-up exercises, under the supervision of a tutor judge, a mock trial and a session on equal treatment. Appointees will also visit two penal establishments, meet probation officers and undertake a period of sitting-in with a circuit judge in a Crown Court, for five to ten days. Once sitting alone, a tutor judge will observe and report on the new recorder. The Newly Appointed Recorders' Conference provides a day's training, 18 months after appointment. At the time of writing, appraisal for recorders is being piloted.

Criminal continuation seminars

These are four-day residential courses, attended every three years by circuit judges, recorders and newly appointed High Court judges. Judges who are "ticketed" to hear serious sex offences or serious fraud cases are required to attend a specialist seminar in these subjects.

Circuit sentencing conferences

These are one-day annual conferences organised by the circuit 14–091 Presiding Judges and attended by every circuit judge and recorder on the circuit.

Civil induction seminars

Before sitting in the county court, recorders are required to attend a residential four-day induction course, where judges work in small syndicates, studying topics such as damages, court practice, equal treatment and poverty. The appointee must also sit in with a circuit judge and a district judge.

Civil continuation seminars

These are attended by circuit judges and recorders, once every three years. District judges attend an annual seminar in London. Specialist continuation seminars are organised for TCC judges and recorders, mercantile judges and so on.

Family judges

Similarly, the JSB organises induction and continuation courses in 14–092 private and public family law, for nominated family law circuit, district and deputy High Court judges, who attend in three-year cycles.

Special seminars

These are organised on an *ad hoc* basis. For instance, when the Children Act 1989 was passed, a training programme was organised for all relevant judges. From 1997, all civil judges have been given access to justice seminars on such topics as case management, the civil justice reforms and ADR.

When ethnic minority awareness training was devised, all lower judges were subject to it. It is now part of equal treatment training. An Equal Treatment Bench Book was issued to all judges in 1999, the latest edition being 2004. All judges receive equal treatment training. The Human Rights Act required the JSB to launch a massive training programme for all judges and magistrates, in 1998–9. In 2004–5, all affected judges received training in the Criminal Justice Act 2003, the Courts Act 2003 and related legislation.

Senior judges' seminars

Recently, specialist seminars have been held after court hours in the Royal Courts of Justice for High Court and CA judges.

Comment

14–093   Judicial training was the subject of much criticism when it was in its infancy but is now very sophisticated and the judges organising it have responded to criticism. New recorders generally find their induction course very intensive and challenging. They find the mock trial nerve-wracking but an excellent baptism of fire for what they are to face in the Crown Court. I speak from my experience in interviewing judges (73, thus far) and observing two JSB training sessions, in 2003–5.

The Call for Judicial Performance Appraisal

14–094   Recently, critics have called for some form of performance appraisal, possibly linked with training. For instance, the Royal Commission on Criminal Justice, 1993, said: "We are, however, less satisfied that adequate monitoring arrangements are in place and find it surprising that full-time judges seldom if ever observe trials conducted by their colleagues." (para.98).

One outspoken proponent was Judge Derek Holden. He was persuaded in favour of such a scheme when he was President of the Independent Tribunal Service. The seven regional chairmen were responsible for monitoring the 1,000 legally qualified tribunal chairmen. The results, argued Judge Holden, were useful in a monitoring system, providing an important basis for promotion or the renewal of an appointment. Such a monitoring system could become part of a training exercise (*The Times*, November 9, 1993).

Judicial performance appraisal was part of Labour policy prior to their election to power in 1997. Since then, it has been extended from tribunals to the lay magistracy, since 1998, then extended to deputy district judges and, following the recommendation of Sir Leonard Peach, it is being extended to all part-time appointments. Sir Leonard also advocated self-appraisal, which the Lord

Chancellor said he supported (*Annual Report 1999–2000*). Appraisal has been piloted for recorders from 2005. Some judges and commentators are still arguing that it should be extended to all fulltime judges. For an interesting article, see Susskind 2003. Lord Justice Auld in his *Review of the Criminal Courts* (2001) recommended that appraisal should be considered for all fulltime judges. Most solicitors were well used to appraisal systems. "A trial judge's job is a solitary one", he observed. "The only judge he sees in action is himself". He acknowledged that some judges considered it a threat to independence but magistrates had coped. Appraisal could be conducted by a team of three, not all of whom need be judges or retired judges. (*Review of the Criminal Court of England and Wales*, Chapter 6)

BIBLIOGRAPHY

G. Bindman, "Is the system of judicial appointments illegal?", Law **14–095** Society's *Gazette*, February 27, 1991, p.24.

N. Browne-Wilkinson, "The Independence of the Judiciary in the 1980s" [1988] P.L. 44. Commission for Judicial Appointments: *www.cja.gov.uk*

The *Concordat* between the Lord Chancellor and Lord Chief Justice, January 2004, properly known as "Constitutional Reform—The Lord Chancellor's judiciary-related functions: Proposals", DCA website: *www.dca.gov.uk*

The Constitutional Reform Act 2005.

S. Cretney, "He may be an eminent man, but is he right for the job?", *The Times*, February 21, 2005 (comment on the appointment of Sir Mark Potter as President of the Family Division).

DCA, *Increasing Diversity in the Judiciary*, 1994, CP 25/04: *www.dca.gov.uk* (in the archived consultation papers).

G. Drewry, Comment [1998] P.L. 1.

F. Gibb, "Closing the silk route is not a done deal" (interview with Lord Chancellor Falconer), *The Times*, September 23, 2003.

F. Gibb, "Crony taunts return with job for friend of Falconer", *The Times*, January 13, 2005.

House of Commons Home Affairs Committee, Third Report, Session 1995–1996, *Judicial Appointments Procedures* Vol.II (HMSO, 1996) (abbreviated in the text to "JAP").

J. A. G. Griffith, *The Politics of the Judiciary* (5th ed., 1995).

Dame Brenda Hale, "Equality and the Judiciary: why should we want more women judges?" [2001] P.L. 489.

Brenda Hale, "Welcome to the white men's club", *The Guardian*, October 30, 2003: *www.guardian.co.uk*

J. Hayes, on the narrow pool from which judges were drawn, "Appointment by invitation" (1997) 147 N.L.J. 520

B. Hewson, on gender bias in judicial decisions, *The Times*, September 17, 1996 and (1997) 147 N.L.J. 537 and see C. McGlynn at (1998) 148 N.L.J. 813.

A. Howard, "Lord Woolf v The Home Secretary", *The Times*, March 9, 2004.

A. Jack, "Number-crunching for diversity" (2004) 154 N.L.J. 1664.

S. Jakobi, "Younger judges", letter, *The Times*, July 10, 2003.

Sir Igor Judge, "Heroes and Villains", October 13, 2003, DCA website: *www.dca.gov.uk*

Lord Justice Keene, "Changing the Constitution: the Executive, the Judiciary and the John Adams Problem", the 80 Club Lecture, Liberal Democrat Lawyers Association, June 23, 2004, reproduced in *The Legal Democrat* 2004.

Baroness Helena Kennedy, "A good brand: is that all the Lord Chancellor is?", *The Times*, February 24, 2004.

Labour Research Department Press Releases December 2002: *www.lrd.org.uk*

Sir Thomas Legg, "Brave New World–The New Supreme Court and judicial appointments" (2004) 24 *Legal Studies* (special issue), p.45.

Lord Lloyd of Berwick, "Constitutional reform or vandalism?", *The Times*, September 14, 2004.

Lord Mackay of Clashfern, "Is there to be a Lord Chancellor no more?", *The Times*, July 13, 2004.

K. Malleson, "Judicial Training and Performance Appraisal: the problem of judicial independence" (1997) 60 M.L.R. 655.

K. Malleson, "The Peach Report on Silk and Judicial Appointments" (2000) 150 N.L.J. 8.

K. Malleson and F. Banda, *Factors affecting the decision to apply for silk and judicial office* LCD Research Report No.2/2000 (2000), DCA.

K. Malleson, "Creating a Judicial Appointments Commission: Which Model Works Best?" [2004] P.L. 102.

Kate Malleson, *The New Judiciary* (1999).

R. Masterman, "*A Supreme Court for the United Kingdom*: two steps forward but one step back on judicial independence" [2004] *Public Law* 48.

D. Oliver, *Constitutional Reform in the UK* (2003), Chapter 18 on the judiciary.

An Independent Scrutiny of the Appointment Process of Judges and Queen's Counsel in England and Wales: A Report by Sir Leonard Peach (1999), DCA website: *www.dca.gov.uk*

Sir Francis Purchas wrote several items in the 1993–4 *New Law Journal* and see Judge Harold Wilson at (1994) 144 N.L.J. 1453

A. Sage, on French judges, *The Times*, December 1, 1998.

I. R. Scott, "A Supreme Court for the United Kingdom" (2003) C.J.Q. Vol. 22, 318 (also on *Westlaw*).

R. Stevens, *The Independence of the Judiciary* (1993).

R. Stevens, "On being nicer to James and the children" (on independence and countering attacks on Mackay L.C.) (1994) 144 N.L.J. 1620.

R. Stevens, "Reform in haste and repent at leisure: Iolanthe, the Lord High Executioner and *Brave New World*" (2004) 24 *Legal Studies* 1.

(Lord) Johan Steyn, "The Case for a Supreme Court" (2002) 118 L.Q.R. 392 (also on *Westlaw*).

J. Steyn (Lord Steyn), "Creating a Supreme Court", *Counsel*, October 2003, p.14.

R. Susskind, "In this modern world, should the judges themselves be judged?", July 22, 2003.

Dr Cheryl Thomas and Dr Kate Malleson, "Judicial Appointments Commissions: The European and North American Experience and the possible implications for the United Kingdom" (1997) LCD Discussion Paper 6/97, DCA website: *www.dca.gov.uk* (under "research").

The United Nations: *www.un.org*

Lord Woolf, Lord Chief Justice of England and Wales, Squire Centenary Lecture, "The Rule of Law and a Change in the Consitution", Cambridge, March 3, 2004, *www.dca.gov.uk/judicial/speeches*

Newspaper articles from 2003–4 describing the spat between the Government and the judges over sentencing, the Asylum and Immigration (Treatment of Claimants etc) Bill 2004 and constitutional reform, especially May 15, 2003, June 17, 2003, March 9, 2004, May 10, 2004.

FURTHER READING AND SOURCES FOR UPDATING THIS CHAPTER

Online updates to this book: *http://www.sweetandmaxwell.co.uk/academic/updates/darbyshire/index.html*   **14–096**

The Department for Constitutional Affairs website: *www.dca.gov.uk* (see "JUDGES" and "press releases").

The Judicial Studies Board: *www.jsboard.co.uk*

The New Law Journal

The Times Law Section on Tuesdays carries job advertisements for judges.

Legal Studies (special issue on the constitutional reforms, especially judicial appointments) Vol.24, Issues 1 and 2, March 2004.

Lord Justice Auld, *Review of the Criminal Courts in England and Wales (2001)*: *www.criminal-courts-review.org.uk*. In Chapter 6 he examines the judicial hierarchy; matching judges to cases (ticketing); judicial administration; judges' lodgings; the composition of the judiciary, including the appointments system and training and appraisal.

Sir Sidney Kentridge, "The Highest Court: Selecting the Judges" (2003) 62(1) *Cambridge Law Journal* 55.

D. Woodhouse, *The Office of Lord Chancellor* (2001).

Part V: Laypeople in the Law

15. Magistrates

"Of the minority of cases where a trial does take place, its usual forum is the unromantic and unseen magistrates' court, where McBarnet's `ideology of triviality' is daily acted out and upon which the majority of defendants must rely for the benefit of `participatory democracy' and the safeguarding of their civil liberties." (Darbyshire, 1991.)

1. Laypeople in the Legal System

The English legal system is unique, in worldwide terms, in making such extensive use of laypeople as decision-makers, as magistrates, jurors and tribunal members. This is partly the product of history but is now justified as keeping the law in touch with the public affected by it. There are over 28,000 lay magistrates and they are by far the most important judges in the English and Welsh legal system because, along with professional magistrates, district judges (magistrates' courts) (DJMCs) they deal with over 95 per cent of defendants to criminal charges, from start to finish and 95 per cent of all sentencing. They deal with almost all young offenders, in the unseen youth court. They have a powerful family jurisdiction and deal with other civil business. They also sit in the Crown Court, alongside a circuit judge, hearing appeals from the magistrates' court. The public are remarkably ignorant about magistrates. For most people, an appearance in court means an appearance before the magistrates. Despite this, most law books give the impression that magistrates' jurisdiction is trivial. Criminal procedure and the law of criminal evidence have been developed around judges' and Parliament's false assumption that most criminal cases are dealt with by judge and jury. This is a big mistake, as I have pointed out elsewhere ("Neglect", 1997).

15–001

2. Appointment and Removal

15–002   Both lay justices and DJMCs are Justices of the Peace. Lay justices are appointed by the Crown on the advice of the Lord Chancellor. The Lord Chancellor's powers of appointment and removal are now set out in ss.9 and 10 of the Courts Act 2003. Magistrates are recruited locally and were, until recently, required to live near their bench. The Courts Act 2003 abolished this requirement but local recruitment and selection will continue. Section 7 of the Courts Act replaces local commissions with one national commission of the peace for England and Wales. The Lord Chancellor receives recommendations for appointment from over 100 local advisory committees. They are composed mainly of magistrates but the Lord Chancellor now requires that a third are non-magistrates. Since 1999, committee members have received standard training. Any adult over 21 can apply to be a magistrate. Qualities required by the Lord Chancellor are "good character, understanding and communication, social awareness, maturity and sound temperament, sound judgment and commitment and reliability" ("How to become a magistrate", DCA website).

All candidates undergo a two-stage interviewing process, meant to ascertain if they possess these necessary qualities and judicial aptitude. The committee must have regard to the number of vacancies and the "the Lord Chancellor requires that each bench should broadly reflect the community it serves in terms of gender, ethnic origin, geographical spread, occupation and political affiliation" (*Lord Chancellor's Directions*, para.8.1).

Lay justices receive no remuneration. They are, however, entitled to travelling expenses and to certain subsistence payments and a loss of earnings allowance but this allowance by no means compensates those who operate small businesses. Few justices claim their allowances (Morgan and Russell, 2000).

Criticism of the Appointment System

15–003   The overwhelming problem with the magistracy is its lack of diversity. Some say that this is partly caused by the fact that magistrates select new magistrates, although the 2000 report of the Lord Chancellor's Equality Working Group refuted this (see below). Even the Magistrates' Association called this system a "self-perpetuating oligarchy" (in evidence to the House of Commons Home Affairs Select Committee in its report on *Judicial Appointments Procedures*, 1995). Advisory Committees were given no advertising budget and have only recently been trained in interviewing techniques. They advertise locally and contact local community groups for help in recruitment, as outlined in

Darbyshire, *Concern*. The Lord Chancellor ran the first national recruitment campaign for a month in 1999. It aimed to destroy the stereotype that magistrates are white and middle class, not ordinary people. Magistrates' courts organise open days to publicise their work and the Magistrates' Association runs a "Magistrates in the Community" campaign, addressing schools and local groups and they participate in a national mock trial competition, in an endeavour to demystify the magistracy and attract applicants.

The Problem of Achieving a Balanced Bench

Successive Lord Chancellors have boasted that the magistracy   15–004
represents the community. This is not the case. Like many before me, I have argued, using the support of statistics and research, that it is predominantly Conservative, white and middle class (see "Concern", 1997). Unlike others, I am also concerned that magistrates are too old and between 1997–2005, their age profile has become significantly older. At long last, the Lord Chancellor appears to be trying to address all this on a national level, by launching a *National Strategy for the Recruitment of Magistrates* in October 2003, which is still in the process of implementation. It responds to complaints of lack of diversity and recommendations made by Lord Justice Auld, in his 2001 *Review of the Criminal Courts*.

Age

"In theory, you can become a magistrate at 21. In practice nobody   15–005
is ever appointed before 27" (Rosemary Thomson, then chairman of the Magistrates' Association in evidence to the House of Commons Home Affairs Committee, 1995). I cited this in my 1997 essay on magistrates, "Concern". In February 2005, the Department of Constitutional Affairs (DCA) informed me that this is no longer the case and they are actively trying to recruit people in their twenties. In 1997, I complained that, since the peak age of offending is around 18 for males and 15 for females, magistrates' age profile makes a double generational difference between the bench and the accused. Since I wrote this, Lord Chancellor Irvine made it clear that this did not bother him. Indeed, he raised the maximum age for new magistrates from 60 to 65, in the hope of achieving a more socially balanced bench. In 1997, I complained that only 22 per cent of lay justices were under 40. To my intense disappointment, I have to report that, by 2005, the situation is very much worse. The *Judicial Appointments Annual Report* 2003–4 discloses that only four per cent of lay justices are now under 40. No fewer than 82 per cent of magistrates are over 50.

> "The Lord Chief Justice has expressed the need for magistrates of fatherly rather than grandfatherly age" (R.M. Jackson, in *The Machinery of Justice* (1st ed., 1940).)

Social class

15–006 Successive studies, cited in my 1997 article, have shown the bias towards the middle classes and towards certain occupational groups and this is confirmed by Morgan and Russell (2000), who found the magistracy to be "overwhelmingly drawn from managerial and professional ranks". Curiously, the 2003 *Recruitment Strategy* complains of "The general but erroneous view" that magistrates are middle aged and middle class. This is contradictory, since the department's own figures confirm that this is the case, nor erroneous. Indeed, that was the very reason for launching the *Strategy*. Indeed, it then goes on to say, correctly, "There is a general difficulty in attracting applications from the working public". Various reasons have been identified for this, throughout the second half of the twentieth century. People who travel in their jobs may be unavailable to sit. People who run small businesses may find the loss of earnings allowance inadequate. Insufficient blue collar workers are attracted to apply (see evidence of the Magistrates' Association and others to the Home Affairs Committee, in 1995). Despite the fact that their jobs are protected, it may be that people fear they will be sacked for taking time off to be a magistrate, or will irritate work colleagues. A story is told by one magistrate of how he had resigned from his job because his employer denied him the seven days' leave he needed to train as a new magistrate and expected him to fulfil many of his bench sittings from annual leave (*The Magistrate*, February 2001). The 2003 *Strategy* acknowledges employers need the message that magistrates acquire marketable transferable skills. The *Strategy* adds that some one-parent families cannot spare the time to undertake voluntary work and many people cannot afford to undertake voluntary unpaid work.

In November 2003, Lord Chancellor Falconer announced that voting patterns would no longer be used as a means of determining how far the local bench represents the community. They have been replaced by indicators using a mix of occupational, industrial and social groupings, matched against the 2001 census data.

Race

15–007 Historically, the lay magistracy has under-recruited minorities. According to the 2003–4 *Annual Report*, 6.4 per cent of lay justices are non-white, compared with 7.9 per cent of the population of England and Wales, according to the 2001 census. Historically, it was difficult to attract applications from minority groups. This contrast is visible in court, where non-whites are over-represented among defendants and victims. This is especially acute in areas of minority population concentration (for detail see "Concern", 1997). Recognising this, Lord Mackay, the Conservative Lord Chancellor, then New Labour's Lord Chancellors, Irvine and Falconer, have tried to compensate by appointing more non-whites than there are in the population at large, culminating in the appointment of 9.66 per cent of new justices in 2003–4 (*Annual Report*). Recruitment of non-whites has been above eight per cent every year since 1999–2000. This probably reflects the success of various recruitment drives including the Operation Black Vote shadowing scheme, described below.

In 2004, the DCA published research by Vennard and others, "Ethnic minority magistrates' experience of the role and of the court environment". It aimed to explore whether minority magistrates had experienced racism and whether they complained of this; what was the impact of perceived discrimination and racism upon their satisfaction with the role and what levels of responsibility minority magistrates achieved. 128 magistrates from 14 benches were interviewed. The findings were as follows:

1. Most respondents considered racism endemic in this country, although less overt than in the past.
2. Respondents were motivated to become magistrates from a sense of civic responsibility and a desire to put something back into the community. Others derived a personal satisfaction and some aspired to make a positive contribution in cases involving minority defendants.
3. 70 per cent had wholly favourable initial impressions of their bench and were as fully integrated as they wished to be. Thirty per cent initially felt uneasy or marginalised. A few continued to feel outsiders on a white, middle class bench.
4. 72 per cent had not encountered racist attitudes or behaviour in their fellow magistrates. Of the other 28 per cent, they typically felt they had been excluded or marginalised by a white chairman but, as only a minority of chairmen acted in this way, they nevertheless enjoyed a good relationship with most white colleagues.
5. Four of the 128 believed they had been subjected to unequal treatment.
6. Most praised their justices' clerk and her team. Eight per cent found staff had displayed racist attitudes towards others. 13 per cent recalled racist behaviour by lawyers; nine per cent by the police and 12 per cent by defendants.

7. Most were impressed by the efforts made by their court to be fair but 21 per cent had observed magistrates displaying racist attitudes towards defendants.
8. Magistrates identified a number of obstacles to recruiting minorities: financial disincentives; employers' reluctance to allow time off; the white middle class image of the magistracy and the misperception that only educated, professional people could be magistrates.
9. 20 per cent fewer minority magistrates had become bench chairmen. There was an underrepresentation of minorities in the family court.

Disability

15–008   The Equality Working Group (below) reported a shortage of applications from disabled people.

Gender

15–009   Many commentators have complained in the past that the magistracy is overwhelmingly male. This is patently not true, as I pointed out in 1997 and as can be seen at a glance from the statistics. Of the 28,029 serving magistrates in March 2004, 13,846 were women. This proportion has remained constant for years now.

Current Attempts to Enhance Diversity

15–010   In response to the report of the Stephen Lawrence Inquiry, the Lord Chancellor's Department set up an audit of its procedures to assess whether they provided equality of opportunity and supported diversity. An Equality Working Group was established to seek ways of encouraging applications from all sections of society, eliminating discrimination and producing a diverse bench. In a 2000 report, they praised the efforts of the Lord Chancellor to foster a nationally co-ordinated approach to recruiting a diverse bench in a fair way but made various recommendations, including that the department should do the following:

- Explore ways of attracting media attention to raise the magistracy's profile among underrepresented groups.
- Train committees to distinguish between positive action and positive discrimination.
- Communicate zero tolerance of discrimination.
- Copy the Territorial Army model of presenting awards to local employers who allow their staff time off to be magistrates.
- Consider how to change people's attitudes to colleagues who take time off to serve.

- Guide committees in targeting recruitment campaigns to under-represented groups.
- Develop an integrated national strategy to replace the present piecemeal one.
- Make court buildings more accessible for disabled magistrates.
- Find out why justices resign. It seems to be because they cannot fulfil the sittings required, so guide benches on how to be flexible to accommodate such justices.
- Ensure dress codes are not culturally biased.

Lord Justice Auld emphasised the value of the lay magistracy in his 2001 *Review of the Criminal Courts* but commented that there was "scope for improvement, particularly in the manner of their recruitment, so as to achieve a better reflection, nationally and locally, of the community" (p.98). He recommended:

- Reviewing community relations and educational initiatives of benches to inform the public better and attract more suitable candidates.
- Supporting local advisory committees with a National Recruitment Strategy.
- Equipping Advisory Committees with local and national demographic data.
- Reviewing ways to make service as a magistrate more attractive to a wider range of the community.
- Find a substitute for measuring diversity by political affiliation (now done in 2003, as seen above).

In 2001, the Lord Chancellor's Department and Operation Black Vote launched the magistrates' shadowing scheme, in seven regions, encouraging members of minority ethnic communities to shadow lay justices, in the hope of recruiting some of them to the Bench. The evaluation report *Judiciary For All*, was published in 2003. Lord Chancellor Irvine said the scheme had been successful in challenging participants' views of magistrates and allowing magistrates to gain an understanding of minority communities. The scheme was launched nationwide in 2004. In October 2003, Lord Falconer launched a *National Strategy for the Recruitment of Lay Magistrates*. The *Strategy* repeats some of the concerns to which I drew attention in 1997.

The Government wants to increase recruitment and retention of a diverse spectrum of the population; raise the profile of the magistracy and dispel misconceptions; encourage younger people; target ethnic minorities and the disabled and make sitting days more flexible. The annexes to the document contain its crucial substance: the concrete plans to widen the magistracy. Recruitment campaigns will be targeted at underrepresented groups, as demonstrated by local demographic data. Some plans are simple (and overdue), such as developing a recruitment leaflet and others more complex, such as educating employers that magistrates can import transferable skills useful in their jobs. They promised an extensive advertising campaign using a variety of channels. This has been done so far, on buses, nationwide.

Removal

15–011 The Lord Chancellor can remove the name of any magistrate from the Commission, under the Courts Act 2003. This is rarely done but is usually because a magistrate refuses to enforce a particular law, such as prosecutions arising from public demonstrations, or for personal indiscretion, such as conducting an obvious extra-marital affair with another magistrate. Magistrates retire at 70.

3. Training

15–012 Lay justices are non-lawyers. They need to understand basic procedure, the rules of evidence, in outline, the elements of the law they commonly apply and how to behave appropriately in court. Training is organised locally and until 2005, was the responsibility of local Magistrates' Courts Committees (MCCs) and justices' clerks. Consequently, the quality of it differed from court to court, dependent on local attitudes and how much the Committee was prepared to spend (see my book *The Magistrates' Clerk*). Under the Magistrates' New Training Initiative, developed centrally by the Judicial Studies Board (JSB), since 1998, newly appointed magistrates have been trained to achieve four basic competences: applied understanding of the framework within which magistrates operate and the abilities to follow basic law and procedure, think and act judicially and work effectively as a team member. They are assisted by a mentor and appraised by a trained appraiser. The JSB has been applying more uniformity to training. The Board has a magisterial committee.

The Courts Act 2003, s.19 provides for rules to be made (maker unspecified) about lay justices' training and appraisal. MCCs were abolished in 2005 and responsibility for training passed to the Lord Chancellor, under the 2003 Act. Following the recommendation of Lord Justice Auld, in the *Review of the Criminal Courts*, the Government promised, in its 2002 white paper, *Justice for All*, that "the JSB will have a much stronger role in magistrates' training, to ensure more consistency in standards across the country". The Magisterial Committee of the JSB is responsible for advising on, developing and monitoring the training of lay magistrates, which is delivered locally, in practice by magistrates' clerks. It also organises the training of newly elected chairmen of magistrates' Benches and induction and continuation training for DJMCs.

Lay justices' training is provided locally according to the appraised needs of the individual and organised by local bench training and development committees. After the initial induction training, usually a weekend course, and a few hours of observing court proceedings, if necessary, the justice may commence sitting, as a "winger". Under the Magistrates' New Training Initiative, a mentor is appointed for each new justice and the justice will undertake about six mentored sittings in the first two years. Training needs are assessed according to whether the justice has achieved prescribed competences and when it is thought the justice is ready, she or he will be appraised. After four or five years, she may choose to undertake chairmanship training. Those justices appointed to specialist courts, youth and/or family must undertake specialist training. All justices are offered regular refresher training and ad hoc training as the need arises, such as that provided in the Human Rights Act and new statutes. Justices are appraised every three years. The Magistrates New Training Initiative II was launched for all new justices from April 2004 and for existing justices from 2005. Details are on the JSB website. In 2004, the DCA published its proposal rules on training under the new administrative scheme. They observed that, as magistrates are all now part of a unified bench, training will need to allow them to move easily from one bench to another if, say, they move house.

4. Organisation

There are under 300 magistrates' benches. Until 2005, magistrates' **15–013** courts were administered by local magistrates' courts committees, consisting of magistrates. MCCs spent the budget allocated by central and local government on staff, administration, recruitment to the bench and training for magistrates and clerks. Since magistrates' courts have long been locally organised, outside the ambit of centralised departmental control over all other courts, one of their hallmarks has long been their individual, sometimes idiosyncratic, differences in practice, procedure and interpretation of the law. In 2001 Auld L.J. recommended that MCCs be replaced by local courts boards and a central executive agency, administering all courts.

(*Review of the Criminal Courts*). This was done in the Courts Act 2003. From 2005, magistrates lost their managerial autonomy and are now administered locally by courts boards administering all local courts. The 2003 Act, s.5, creates local courts boards which are under a duty "to scrutinise, review and make recommendations about the way in which the Lord Chancellor is discharging his general duty in relation to the courts with which the board is concerned" and to consider draft and final business plans relating to those courts. The Lord Chancellor must "give due consideration to recommendations made by the boards". Practically, it is intended that there will be 43 boards, coterminous with the local criminal justice management areas, plus London. Magistrates were opposed to the abolition of MCCs so Lord Chancellor Falconer consulted on the composition of the new boards but Sch.1 to the 2003 Act specifies that at least one member should be a judge, at least two should be lay justices, two should have knowledge or experience of the courts and at least two more should be local people.

Nationally, from 2005, all courts are administered by a Her Majesty's Courts Service, a unified agency, as suggested by Auld L.J. and implemented in the Courts Act 2003.

An Inspectorate was established in 1994, assessing quality of service at magistrates' courts and it aims to identify and disseminate good practice. The Police and Magistrates' Courts Act 1994 also provided for the appointment, by each committee, of a "justices' chief executive", who was the line manager of all the other local justices' clerks and staff. This office was abolished by the Courts Act 2003 and the Lord Chancellor was empowered to appoint a civil servant in their stead. Nationally, the Magistrates' Association speaks for the magistrates as a collective body.

Lay justices sit in pairs or groups of three (legal maximum). In the Youth Court, three justices of mixed gender sit, or one district judge, or a mixed bench. Youth justices are specially trained, as are family court magistrates but they must also hear adult criminal cases. Collectively, magistrates are known as "the Bench" and they are addressed as "Your Worships". The Chairman of the Bench is annually elected.

5. District Judges (Magistrates' Courts), Formerly Known as Stipendiary Magistrates

15–014   DJMCs are full-time professionals, with a seven-year general qualification, as defined by the Courts and Legal Services Act, s.71. According to current policy, they will normally have sat as deputies, part-time for at least two years and their performance as such will have been assessed and their sittings observed. There were, in 2005, 128 DJMCs in England and Wales and 166 deputy DJMCs. DJMCs are normally appointed in their early forties so are younger, on average than lay justices. Deputies are part-timers, normally barristers, solicitors or justices' clerks, aged 35–55. Newly appointed deputies must observe full-time DJMCs for five days and attend a brief training course. Historically, although most cases in Outer London and the provinces are heard by justices, most cases in Inner London have, for the last three centuries, been dealt with by professionals, stipendiary magistrates or "stipes" as they used to be known. They were appointed locally. In the provinces, this was to meet increased caseloads, since professionals deal with cases more speedily than justices. The Royal Commission on Criminal Justice, 1993, recommended that there should be a more systematic approach to the role of stipendiaries and a unified stipendiary bench was created by the Access to Justice Act 1999 when stipendiaries were renamed district judges.

6. Magistrates' Clerks

> "In many ways the most important person in the whole set-up of the administration of justice" (Lord Chief Justice Parker, in the House of Lords debate on the Justices of the Peace Bill 1968.)

The importance of magistrates' clerks, or legal advisers should not be underestimated. Lay justices and DJMCs are arbiters of both fact and law so, in criminal cases, they perform the functions of both judge and jury in the Crown Court. Both lay justices and DJMCs are advised by magistrates' clerks and since the lay justices are there because they are not, generally, lawyers, they are wholly dependent on their clerks for advice on law and practice. Remember that this is in the context of magistrates handling over 95 per cent of criminal business and a substantial amount of family business. **15–015**

Section 28 of the Courts Act 2003 states

> "(4) The functions of a justices' clerk include giving advice to any or all of the justices of the peace to whom he is clerk about matters of law (including procedure and practice) on questions arising in connection with the discharge of their functions, including questions arising when the clerk is not personally attending on them.

> (5) The powers of a justices' clerk include, at any time when he thinks he should do so, bringing to the attention of any or all of the justices of the peace to whom he is clerk any point of law (including procedure and practice) that is or may be involved in any question so arising."

and s.29 articulates the independence of the clerks in their advisory functions. It states that they are not subject to the direction of the Lord Chancellor or any other person.

In 1955, Glanville Williams said, that "If legal argument takes place in court, the argument is addressed to the justices, who may hardly follow a word of it; in reality, however, it is intended for the ears of the clerk". This is still the case. Indeed, the High Court has warned magistrates that they should follow their clerk's advice, in *Jones v Nicks* (1976). Williams said that the danger arising from this was that clerks could be tempted to interfere in proceedings in a way that is "theoretically unwarrantable." The only significant piece of empirical research on magistrates' clerks was my own, conducted in the 1970s and reported in *The Magistrates' Clerk* and thus too old to be of any practical application. I found examples of clerks effectively taking decision-making out of the justices' hands, especially in relation to the admissibility of evidence and I found examples of clerks who were prepared to admit to very significant influence over lay justices, especially over sentencing. I also found significant differences in approach, from clerk to clerk and court to court. Since the 1970s magistrates and legal advisors are much better trained and most legal advisors are now professionally qualified. I would expect that, if this research were to be replicated now, I would find far fewer inconsistencies in practice and that both clerks and justices would have a better sense of their proper role. I would hope not to find any if the displays of unfairness or prejudice I reported in *The Magistrates' Clerk*. Having said all this, research by McLaughlin in 1990 found that clerks did influence magistrates' decision making.

15–016   As Glanville Williams pointed out in 1955, if clerks or legal advisers retire to give advice to the justices, as they often do, it may give the impression that the clerk may exercise undue domination over the justices. He suggested that clerks give their advice in open court. In 2000, when I was asked to advise Auld L.J. on the implications of the Human Rights Act 1998 in magistrates' courts, I expressed the same opinion, drawing attention to Art.6 of the Convention, on fair trial. Since the 1990s, all clerks and legal advisers have been trained to give their advice in open court, where possible and that, where they give advice in the retiring room, that this should be repeated in open court. This has been affirmed by successive practice directions, now in the *Practice Direction (Criminal Proceedings: Consolidation)*

2002. Where advice is given in the retiring room, good practice dictates that it will be given on a provisional basis only to the justices or DJMC. Its substance should be repeated in open court, allowing the parties to make representations and then the advice will be stated in open court with amendments as required. This was reiterated by the Privy Council in 2003, in *Clark v Kelly* [2003] UKPC D1. A Privy Council decision is not binding on the English and Welsh courts but is very heavily persuasive. In applying Art.6.1 of the Convention, their lordships reiterated the requirements of the Practice Direction exactly. The Direction then, which is not law, has been reaffirmed by a heavily persuasive precedent.

The chief clerk at each court is called the justices' clerk. A justices' clerk may be in charge of more than one Bench and the nationwide trend of the last two decades has been to amalgamate Benches under one clerkship. In 2005, there were around 80 justices' clerks, all of whom were professionally qualified barristers or solicitors. Of course, since many justices' clerks are in charge of more than one court and since most courts have more than one courtroom in session at a time, the justices' clerk necessarily delegates advisory functions to her assistants. Some justices' clerks are in charge of whole counties. These assistant clerks are called court clerks, or more usually, legal advisors, of whom there are around 2,500 in 2005 and, until 2010, they need not be professionally qualified. The DCA informed me, in March 2005, that it has no statistics on their qualifications. Delegated legislation in 1980 required that, if not professionally qualified, court clerks should be law graduates or equivalent, or possess a special clerks' Home Office diploma in magisterial law, or be qualified by five years' experience before 1980.

This leads to the curious situation where, in many provincial courtrooms, the court clerk advising the lay justices is not professionally qualified. More anomalous is the fact that in Inner London, where most cases are heard by DJMCs, they are often advised by professionally qualified clerks. The nationwide situation remains patchy, dependent on whether the local MCCs have pursued a policy of recruiting professionals. In 1999, the Lord Chancellor's Department (now DCA) introduced delegated legislation, requiring that, by 2010, all court clerks should be professionally qualified as barristers or solicitors. To the disappointment of someone who had been campaigning for this for many years (see *The Magistrates' Clerk*), the over 40s were exempted, because some areas are so dependent on unqualified clerks that they would not all be able to qualify in time. More disappointingly, those who were in post 1998 have also been exempted from qualification. There remain benches where most legal advisors are not professionally qualified barristers or solicitors.

15–017   The clerks' staff, like the justices' clerks, used to be recruited and paid by local magistrates' courts committees. Justices' clerks and other legal advisers were very anxious when it became clear that they were to become part of Her Majesty's Courts Service in 2005, implementing the Courts Act 2003. Since the justices' clerk may exercise judicial functions and these are routinely delegated to other legal advisers, they pointed out that it was anomalous and a breach of the separation of powers for them to become civil servants like the clerks of other courts, who do not give legal advice or exercise judicial functions. The Justices' Clerks' Society submitted a paper to Lord Chancellor Falconer suggesting that justices' clerks should be judicial officers appointed by the Judicial Appointments Committee and accountable for the quality of justice in local magistrates' courts. The Lord Chancellor could see no problem with justices' clerks being civil servants. Justices' clerks and their staff are now appointed by the Lord Chancellor under s.27 of the Courts Act 2003. The functions of the justices' clerk are now set out under s.28 and s.29 articulates their independence from the Lord Chancellor, when exercising their judicial functions, as can be seen above.

Concern over the Clerks' Powers

15–018   In 1999, I raised the following concerns. Under the Crime and Disorder Act 1998, extensive pre-trial judicial powers may be delegated to a single justice or justices' clerk, exercisable in an early administrative hearing or pre-trial review (as suggested by the Narey Report, *Review of Delay in the Criminal Justice System*, (1997)). This means legal advisers (court clerks), in reality, because justices' clerks delegate almost all of their powers. In the Lords' debate on the Bill, Lord Chief Justice Bingham expressed the same concern: pre-trial management powers are judicial; clerks are not judges. Magistrates should be doing the judging. As a result of Lord Bingham's intervention, fewer management powers were given to clerks than they wanted. Case management powers are now set out in general terms, in the Criminal Procedure Rules 2005 but these cross-refer to the existing legislation. Justices' clerks and their assistants are, of course, listed as potential case managers.

The 1999 Access to Justice Act abolished the criminal legal aid means test because the Lord Chancellor lost patience with court clerks' inefficiency at applying it, after the Audit Commission found wide scale errors in applying the means test, for seven years running. From then on, clerks granted representation under the new criminal defence service scheme applying only the merits test. My research into clerks in the 1970s and later research showed that the merits test on criminal legal aid, now criminal defence, is open to highly subjective interpretation, resulting in different rates of grant from court to court. The means test was reinstated, as described in Chapter 17 on legal services, below, again administered by magistrates' clerks. It remains to be seen whether this will result in the same inconsistent decisions as bedevilled the pre-1999 scheme.

7. History

Most people consider that a royal proclamation in 1195, which set   **15–019**
up keepers of the peace to assist the sheriff in the maintenance of law and order, was the origin of the justice of the peace. Clearer evidence comes from statutes in 1327 and 1361 under which "good and lawful men" were to be "assigned to keep the peace", holding administrative rather than judicial authority, and like the present-day justice, not legally qualified and acting part-time. The title Justice of the Peace was first used in the 1361 statute. In 1363, a statute required four quarter sessions to be held annually, and gradually the power to deal with criminal cases was added to the administrative work. From 1496, justices were permitted to try the minor (summary) criminal cases locally at petty sessions, instead of at quarter sessions, so giving rise to magistrates' courts as courts of summary jurisdiction, as they now are. When quarter sessions were replaced by the Crown Court, magistrates retained their role, hearing appeals alongside a circuit judge. Magistrates were the local government until elected authorities were created under the Local Government Acts of 1888 and 1894. Traces of this are still in the statutory one-third membership of magistrates on local police authorities.

8. Should Lay Justices be Replaced by Professionals?

Lay Justices' Conspiracy Theory

Despite repeated assurances to the contrary by successive Lord   **15–020**
Chancellors and then by Auld L.J. in his *Review of the Criminal Courts*, lay justices have a theory that there is a conspiracy to replace them with professionals, whose numbers have steadily grown over the 1990s. This is typified by Robson's article. In 2002, she warned that this could be the point "where the lay magistracy may be launched on a long farewell". In his speech to the Magistrates' Association, The Lord Chancellor hoped the white paper *Justice for All* (2002)

"banishes the myths of a few years ago" that "the lay magistracy was an endangered species". Magistrates would become part of a unified national bench, giving them greater flexibility to be shifted to different courts. Nevertheless the Lord Chancellor assured them of the "primacy of local justice and individual availability".

Some lay justices' anxiety has not abated, despite the fact that the Criminal Justice Act 2003 doubled their sentencing powers and Lord Chancellor Falconer expressed an intention to double recruitment of lay justices in 2004–7. Even in 2004, I heard magistrates repeating the same conspiracy theory. I have found examples of the theory dating back to the 1970s and earlier. The problem arises because modern magistrates are ignorant of their own history. I tried to explain what the true position is in a 2002 essay.

While they are correct to point out that stipendiaries (DJMCs) have increased in numbers since 1950, so have lay justices. Lay justices also sit far more often than they did previously. In 1948, over 65 per cent of justices sat less than 26 times and 10 per cent did not sit at all. Nowadays, lay justices are required to sit on 26 occasions per year but they sit, on average, over 41 times a year (Morgan and Russell, below). Most importantly, as I was at pains to point out in 1997, "Neglect", magistrates' jurisdiction has increased out of all recognition in over the last few centuries, as more and more criminal business has shifted down from the assizes, now Crown Court, onto the shoulders of the magistracy. Offences are regularly reclassified downwards, from indictable to either-way, or from either-way to summary only. When new offences are created they are usually summary only or either-way, thus guaranteeing that they will all or mostly be tried by magistrates. The doubling of magistrates' sentencing powers in the Criminal Justice Act 2003 is merely a continuation of this trend.

The Curious Position of London

15–021   In Inner London, for the best part of three centuries, most cases in the magistrates' courts have been heard by stipendiaries, now DJMCs, whereas in outer London and the provinces, most cases were and are heard by lay justices. The position is rendered odder by the fact that Inner London was the first to professionalise its clerks so by the 1970s we had the anomalous position where cases in Inner London were routinely tried by a professional magistrate, advised by a lawyer, whereas elsewhere most cases were decided by lay justices, advised by court clerks who were not lawyers. There is no logic to this difference. It arises from history. Professional magistrates were appointed from the eighteenth century in London in response to concern about corruption among local justices.

When stipendiary numbers increased in the provinces, they were installed at the request of the local benches, usually to help out with a large workload. Since 1999, when the stipendiary bench was organised on a national basis, the Lord Chancellor can appoint a district judge anywhere and shift her around, as the need arises. This means that there are many DJMCs who move round from court to court, sitting in different courts on a rota basis or brought in to handle long and/or complex trials.

The Lack of Logic in our Current Distribution of Criminal Cases

As I pointed out in "Neglect" (1997), there is no logic in the way   15–022
in which we currently allocate criminal cases. This is still the case. While DJMCs may do more of the serious work of the magistrates' courts, they are not confined to that. In the courts where they sit alongside lay justices, parties may not be able to predict in advance if they will be heard by a lay bench or a DJMC, because if one court finishes early, the clerk is sent to fetch work to relieve the list of a busier bench. In the magistrates' court, a defendant may find himself tried by a judge alone but he has no choice. If he is tried in the Crown Court, having pleaded not guilty, again he has no choice. He must be tried by judge and jury. Yet in most other common law jurisdictions he could choose a non-jury trial, or "bench trial".

The Value of Lay Justices

The last Royal Commission to consider this was the 1948 Royal   15–023
Commission on Justices of the Peace. Their reasoning illustrates comprehensively the principled reasons for keeping lay justices.

> "(L)ike that of trial by jury, it gives the citizen a part to play in the administration of the law. It emphasizes the fact that the principles of the common law, and even the language of statutes, ought to be . . . comprehensible by any intelligent person without specialized training. Its continuance prevents the growth of a suspicion in the ordinary man's mind that the law is a mystery which must be left to a professional caste and has little in common with justice as the layman understands it. Further, the cases in which decisions on questions of fact in criminal cases are left to one man ought to be, as they now are, exceptional." (p.7).

Doran and Glenn, commissioned to examine *Lay Involvement in Adjudication* for the review of the criminal justice system in Northern Ireland, provided a very useful survey of issues raised in debate between supporters and detractors of the principle of lay participation.

1. *The right of participation in the adjudicative process*
   Every person has an equal right to participate in matters of
   general concern. Lay participants are more representative of
   the local community and establish a link between the courts
   and local affairs. On the other hand, in reality, some members
   of the community are excluded from participation and lay
   adjudicators are a social elite.

2. *The personality of the participants*
   Lay participants possess an informal and experiential body of
   knowledge gleaned from the local environs, whereas professionals possess formal technical knowledge. The problems
   with this are whether participants are truly local, whether
   'local knowledge' sits happily with the concept of acting as a
   neutral arbiter and whether participants will encounter
   defendants outside the courtroom in an embarrassing or dangerous context. The argument that the professionals' training
   makes them superior can be countered by training lay participants but that might destroy the "layness" for which they are
   valued.

3. *The process of participation*
   It is said to be safe to entrust minor matters to lay participants
   because they are legally advised and because the guilty plea
   rate is high. The problem with this argument, however, is that
   it trivialises the work of the lower courts and, as I have
   pointed out above, English and Welsh magistrates are not
   confined to trivia, as are lay magistrates in other jurisdictions.
   It is also argued that lay involvement injects realism and
   popular values into decision-making so that law and legal
   procedure become less mysterious. Further, lay people are
   said to be cheaper, more flexible and less case-hardened and
   their reasoning based on reasonableness, equity and fairness.
   There are problems with these arguments. There is no evidence that the law is kept less complex by the presence of lay
   persons on the bench. Those who sit regularly may become
   just as case-hardened as professionals. The vague form of reasoning of laypeople produces inconsistent decisions and
   regional disparities that are less susceptible to review, create
   uncertainty and diminish public confidence. Professionals
   are said to be more consistent and procedurally correct. On
   the other hand, some say that professionals can be inflexible,
   legalistic, detached from the community and less sympathetic with arguments raised before them.

Several fairly recent reports mean that we can now reach a better informed opinion on the practical differences between lay and professional magistrates, to test the assumptions underlying the arguments of principle above.

In 1990, Shari Diamond's research affirmed lawyers' long held anecdotal assumption that professional magistrates are harsher in sentencing than lay justices.   **15–024**

In research reported in *The Role and Appointment of Stipendiary Magistrates* (Seago, Walker and Wall, 1995) aimed to examine the function of stipendiaries. They found:

- Very few courts had rules for allocating work to stipendiaries.

- There was a striking difference between the work of stipendiaries and acting (deputy) stipendiaries, who were kept away from more legally and evidentially complex cases.

- Metropolitan stipendiaries appeared to be almost twice as quick to hear contested cases as provincial stipendiaries.

- Most of their judicial work was general list cases but they also heard long trials (especially those lasting more than a day) or complex or highly publicised trials and they had a heavier caseload than lay justices.

- Stipendiaries dealt with all types of work more speedily than lay justices. One provincial stipendiary could replace 32 justices and one metropolitan stipendiary could replace 24 justices.

In discussing the future role of stipendiaries, the authors suggested that pressure could be relieved on the Crown Court. "Consideration could be given to an enhanced jurisdiction (up to two to three years' imprisonment) for a trial tribunal consisting of a stipendiary and two lay magistrates".

In 2000, a major research project was undertaken for the Home Office and Lord Chancellor's Department. It is reported in *The Judiciary in Magistrates' Courts* by Morgan and Russell. Its aims were to investigate the balance of lay and professional magistrates and the arguments in favour of that balance. Apart from the findings on composition, above, they were:

- Lay justices sat on 41.4 occasions per year on average. Additionally, they spent a full working week on training and other duties. They sat in threes, except in 16 per cent of cases, when in pairs.
- All professionals sat in court around four days a week. They rarely sat with lay justices.

- Their finding on stipendiaries' work allocation was the same as Seago, Walker and Wall. Stipendiaries' time was concentrated on either-way rather than summary cases.
- Stipendiaries heard 22 per cent more appearances than lay justices. If their caseloads were identical, they could deal with 30 per cent more appearances.
- Stipendiary hearings generally involved more questioning and challenging.
- Stipendiaries showed more command over proceedings and would challenge parties responsible for delay. People applied for fewer adjournments and were less likely to be granted them.
- Lay justices were less likely to refuse bail or use immediate custody as a sentence.
- Court users had more confidence in stipendiaries. They were seen as more efficient, consistent in decisions, questioning appropriately and as giving clear reasons. Lawyers admitted to preparing better for stipendiaries.
- Court users considered lay justices better at showing courtesy, using simple language and showing concern to distressed victims.
- Few members of the public had heard there were different types of magistrate. Most thought lay justices would be better at representing the views of the community and sympathising with the defendants' circumstances but that stipendiaries were better at making decisions on guilt and innocence.
- One stipendiary could replace 30 lay justices. Doubling stipendiary numbers would cut down court appearances but increase the prison population. The net cost would be about £23 million per year.

15–025   In 2000–2001 the Institute for Public Policy Research commissioned a MORI public opinion poll on the magistracy and then asked Andrew Sanders to compare the skills and experience which lay and professional magistrates brought to the bench. His 2001 paper, *Community Justice—Modernising the Magistracy in England and Wales* reports the following. The MORI poll found a third of the public polled did not know that the majority of magistrates were laypeople and hugely underestimated the proportion of cases heard by magistrates. Only 29 per cent thought magistrates did a good job and 61 per cent thought they were out of touch. Forty-nine per cent were unhappy that magistrates were legally untrained. Forty-two per cent would be more confident in a mixed panel.

Mixed Benches

In 1948, the Bar recommended that peripatetic stipendiaries be   **15–026**
created, to travel around and sit with local lay justices and that was
done in some areas. I briefly discussed mixed benches in 1997, as
did Seago, Walker and Wall in 1995. I mentioned that this pattern as
common in Eastern Europe. As I pointed out in 1997, the obvious
danger here is that the professional will dominate the lay participants and some of the research on the Eastern European models ver-
ifies this, as Vogler was swift to point out in 2001.

Sanders, above, concluded that the skills of both professional and
lay magistrates, sitting as a mixed bench are needed in deciding
complex cases: legal skills to apply the relevant law to the facts;
social skills to assess character and judge honesty and managerial
and administrative skills. Panel decision-making was preferable to
sole decision-making. Justice should be transparent and accountable. This is promoted by lay participation. Public confidence
needed to be safeguarded and increased.

The Civil Liberties Trust, in its 2002 report, "Magistrates' Courts
and Public Confidence   a proposal for fair and effective reform of
the magistracy", called for reform of the magistracy to inspire
public confidence. They recommended mixed tribunals, with the
lay justices and professionals separately responsible for the fact-
finding and the law. Magistrates should be drawn randomly from
the population and required to sit for a specified period of time.
Alternatively, the current lay magistracy should be expanded.

My response to Vogler was to argue, in 2002, that he was not com-   **15–027**
paring like with like. In all the European examples he gave, the lay
participants were and are more like jurors. Our lay justices are
appointed to sit frequently for many decades and are trained and
experienced in fact finding and sentencing. Further, as I had already
pointed out in 1997, this danger could be averted by training the professionals not to dominate the lay justices and training the lay justices not to defer to the professional. Besides, as I have also pointed
out before, we have over 100 examples of mixed tribunals in England
and Wales, dealing with civil cases, as I have described in Chapter
12, on alternatives to the civil courts, above. The mixing of lay and
professionals there does not seem to have caused problems.

Lord Justice Auld, in his 2001 *Review of the Criminal Courts* considered all these arguments of principle and the research above and
made some controversial recommendations, which I will not deal
with in great depth, because they were rejected by the government.
In brief, he recommended the creation of a middle tier of his proposed unified criminal court, called the "district court", with lay
justices sitting together with one DJMC. The lay justices would participate in fact finding but the DJMC would do the sentencing.

Many commentators were opposed to this suggestion. The Law Society thought the cost of running a middle tier would outweigh the benefits and the government must have agreed, because they rejected the proposal in their 2002 response. The problem I had with the mechanism of his proposed mixed bench would be that the lay justices would be relegated to the position of jurors; the DJMC would do the sentencing alone. I can see no logic to this suggestion, given that justices are experienced sentencers and given that the justices are there to represent the community including, presumably local attitudes to the relative gravity of local crimes. Morgan and Sanders, in 2002 criticised Auld's suggestions in relation to magistrates. Both felt he had disregarded their findings and conclusions. Other responses to the Auld *Review*, in relation to magistrates and all other recommendations are to be found on the Criminal Courts Review website *(www.criminal-courts-review.org.uk)*.

Having rejected Lord Justice Auld's proposal for a middle tier criminal court with a mixed bench, the government opted instead to double magistrates' sentencing powers. They announced in the 2002 white paper, *Justice for All* that magistrates would be given the power to pass a sentence of 12 months for a single offence. This has been done in the Criminal Justice Act 2003, s.154. When this comes into force, the potential effect will be to significantly increase the criminal case load of the magistrates' courts, which simply continues the trend of the last two centuries of shifting work down onto the shoulders of the magistracy. Magistrates who were the subject of doctoral research by Andrew Herbert were opposed to this change. Many felt they were already being asked to handle cases at the extreme of their ability.

BIBLIOGRAPHY

15–028   Lord Justice Auld, *Review of the Criminal Courts of England and Wales* (2001): *www.criminal-courts-review.org.uk*

The Civil Liberties Trust is part of the pressure group, Liberty: *www.liberty-human-rights.org.uk*

P. Darbyshire, *The Magistrates' Clerk* (1984).

P. Darbyshire, "The Lamp That Shows That Freedom Lives—is it worth the candle?" [1991] Crim. L.R. 740.

P. Darbyshire, "An Essay on the Importance and Neglect of the Magistracy" [1997] Crim. L.R. 627.

P. Darbyshire, "For the New Lord Chancellor—Some Causes of Concern About Magistrates" [1997] Crim. L.R. 861.

P. Darbyshire, "A Comment on the Powers of Magistrates' Clerks" [1999] Crim. L.R. 377.

P. Darbyshire, "Magistrates", in *The Handbook of the Criminal Justice Process* (McConville and Wilson ed., 2002).

S. Doran and R. Glenn, *Lay Involvement in Adjudication*, Criminal Justice Review Group (HMSO: London, 2000).

DCA, *National Strategy for the Recruitment of Magistrates*, October 2003: *www.dca.gov.uk*

S. Diamond, "Revising Images of Public Punitiveness: Sentencing by Lay and Professional English Magistrates" (1990) *Law and Social Inquiry* 191.

A. Herbert, "Mode of Trial and Magistrates' Sentencing Powers" [2003] Crim. L.R. 314. Synopsis by M. Zander at (2003) 153 N.L.J. 689.

The Home Office, *Review of Delay in the Criminal Justice System*, 1997 (The Narey Report).

House of Commons Home Affairs Committee, Third Report, Session 1995–1996, *Judicial Appointments Procedures, Vol.II* (HMSO, 1996).

Judicial Appointments Annual Report 2003–4: *www.dca.gov.uk*

Justice for All, white paper, 2002, accessible from several websites, such as the DCA and on *www.cjsonline.gov.uk*

H. McLaughlin, "Court Clerks: Advisers or Decision-Makers?" (1990) 30 *British Journal of Criminology* 358.

R. Morgan and N. Russell, *The Judiciary in the Magistrates' Courts* (2000).

R. Morgan, "Magistrates: The Future According to Auld" (2002) 29 *Journal of Law and Society* 308.

G. Robson, "The Lay Magistracy: No Time for Complacency" (2002) 166 *Justice of the Peace* 624.

A. Sanders, *Community Justice* (2000) IPPR.

A. Sanders, "CoPre Values, the Magistracy and the Auld Report" (2002) 29 *Journal of Law and Society* 324.

P. Seago, C. Walker and D. Wall, *The Role and Appointment of Stipendiary Magistrates* (1995).

Seago *et al.*, "The Development of the Professional Magistracy in England and Wales" [2000] Crim. L.R. 631.

Secretary of State and Lord Chancellor's Directions for Advisory Committees on Justices of the Peace, revised 2005, DCA website: *www.dca.gov.uk*

J. Vennard, G. Davies, J. Baldwin and J. Pearce, "Ethnic minority magistrates' experience of the role and of the court environment", DCA Research Report 3/2004: *www.dca.gov.uk/research*

G. Williams, *The Proof of Guilt* (1955).

R. Vogler, "Mixed Messages on the Mixed Bench", *Legal Action*, May 2001, p.8.

FURTHER READING AND SOURCES FOR UPDATING THIS CHAPTER

Updates to this book: *http://www.sweetandmaxwell.co.uk/academic/* **15–029** *updates/darbyshire/index.html*

Judicial Appointments Annual Reports, Department of Constitutional Affairs: *www.dca.gov.uk* (and generally, the DCA website, sections on magistrates, press releases, speeches and research).
The Justices' Clerks' Society: *www.jc-society.co.uk*
The Justice of the Peace journal.
The Magistrates' Association: *www.magistrates-association.org.uk*
Judicial Studies Board: *www.jsboard.co.uk*
Law Journals, such as the *New Law Journal*.

16. The Jury

"Each jury is a little parliament . . . The first object of any tyrant in Whitehall would be to make Parliament utterly subservient to his will; and the next to overthrow or diminish trial by jury, for no tyrant could afford to leave a subject's freedom in the hands of twelve of his countrymen. So that trial by jury is more than an instrument of justice and more than one wheel of the constitution: it is the lamp that shows that freedom lives." (Sir Patrick Devlin, later Lord Devlin, Law Lord, *Trial by Jury*, 1956.)

"(T)he liberties of England cannot but subsist so long as this palladium remains sacred and inviolate; not only from all open attacks (which none will be so hardy as to make), but also from all secret machinations, which may sap and undermine it; by introducing new and arbitrary methods of trial." (Sir William Blackstone, *Commentaries on the Laws of England Vol.IV*, 1769.)

"Out of all the citizens (possibly some three million) who, in the course of any year, find themselves in difficulty with the law, only a small portion (32,000 in 1984) will be tried by a jury. The underlying logic of this situation we find puzzling in the extreme. If society believes that trial by jury is the fairest form of trial, is it too costly and troublesome to be universally applied? . . . But if jury trial is not inherently more fair, given its extra cost and trouble, what are the merits which justify its retention? Society appears to have an attachment to jury trial which is emotional or sentimental rather than logical." (The Roskill Committee on Fraud Trials, 1986, para.8.21.)

"The symbolic function of the jury far outweighs its practical significance . . . this sentimental attachment to the symbol of the jury is dangerous. Adulation of the jury is based on no justification or spurious justification. It has fed public complacency

> with the English legal system and distracted attention from its evils ... The truth is that for most people who pass through the criminal justice system this palladium is simply not available and for those who can and do submit themselves to its verdict, it will not necessarily safeguard their civil liberties."
> (Darbyshire, 1991.)

1. "The Lamp that Shows that Freedom Lives"

16–001   As illustrated by the adulation of Blackstone and Lord Devlin, quoted above, this ancient institution arouses strong emotions in the hearts of the English and Welsh, as it does with the Americans and many others living in common law systems which are daughters of the English legal system. This is because, for centuries, jury trial was central to our legal systems. The use of ordinary people as fact finders in civil and criminal cases was and is perceived by some as the only democratic way of organising a legal system. What most people do not realise, as the opinion surveys cited in the previous chapter show, is that over 95 per cent of defendants to criminal charges are dealt with by magistrates. Of the remainder who appear before the Crown Court, most plead guilty, so, only around one per cent of defendants receive a jury trial (for detail, see discussion below and Darbyshire, 1997). As for civil cases, the jury had almost died out by the beginning of the twentieth century. By 2005, there are very few civil jury trials per year.

2. Selection of Jurors

Widening Jury Participation from 2004

16–002   Jurors are drawn from the electoral roll at random. This is not prescribed by the Juries Act but is a matter of practice. As I pointed out in 1991, statutory excusals and avoidance of jury service destroyed randomness, prior to 2004.

Selection from the electoral roll

16–003   The Juries Act 1974, as amended, specifies that every adult, aged 18–70, who is on the annual electoral register and who has lived in this country for at least five years is qualified to serve as a juror.

In our research for Lord Justice Auld, for his *Review of the Criminal Courts* (2001), we (Darbyshire, Maughan and Stewart, 2001) examined jury research worldwide. We argued that selection from the electoral roll is a flawed system. Research as long ago as the 1960s, in the US, demonstrated that electoral lists are not representative of communities and this has been confirmed in Australia and New Zealand. This is caused by such factors as population mobility and residential status, which are linked to class and income levels. We pointed out that census data in England and Wales show non-registration to be high among ethnic minorities, the 20–24 age group and renters, and it is well known that some people do not register to vote in order to avoid council tax. As long ago as 1968, Federal US legislation required the voters' list to be supplemented with other source lists, such as drivers' licence lists and utility lists and we recommended that the Juries Act should be amended to copy this method. Auld L.J. accepted our recommendation and repeated it in Chapter 5 of his *Review*. He considered that jury eligibility should be based on eligibility to vote not on inclusion on the roll. The Government rejected this in their response to his *Review*. In their 2002 white paper, *Justice for All*, they said that instead, they would continue the work of the Electoral Commission to improve the quality of the electoral roll and ensure in particular that minority ethnic communities register themselves. My objections to this refusal are threefold: it does not respond to our findings on population mobility or wilful refusal to register; no good reason was given for not adopting our recommendation; and thirdly, if the census is to be used as a test of the representativeness of the roll, then that too is defective, as gaps in the 2001 census are already well known. The same groups who do not register to vote also failed to complete the 2001 census, such as young men.

Problems caused by statutory excusals, ineligibility and disqualification

Until 2003, the Juries Act disqualified some people from service 16–004 and contained long lists of people who were ineligible or excusable as of right, according to their occupation or status. For example, members of the legal profession, judges, magistrates, members of the prison and probation services and the clergy were ineligible. The 1965 Morris Report on jury service considered that those with special knowledge or prestige attached to their occupations would be unduly influential over their fellow jurors. The Royal Commission on Criminal Justice 1993 upheld this view but Auld L.J. did not agree.

Members of the armed forces, medical practitioners, chemists, vets, peers and MPs and those aged 65–70 had a right to be excused from jury service as did members of religious organisations, whose tenets or beliefs were incompatible with jury service. Those who had done jury service in the previous two years were also excusable.

In 1991, I complained that exempting long lists of people from jury service was the "very antithesis" of randomness. The problems caused by the Act and the excusal rate were affirmed in 1999 by Home Office research conducted by Airs and Shaw. This was cited by Auld L.J. They found that about a quarter of a million people were summoned for jury service every year. In a sample of 50,000 people summoned in June and July 1999, only one-third were available for service, about half of whom were allowed to defer their service to a later date. Of the remaining two-thirds, 13 per cent were ineligible under the Juries Act, or disqualified or excusable as of right. 15 per cent failed to attend on the day or their summonses were returned as "undelivered" and 38 per cent were excused. As a result of their findings, a Central Jury Summoning Bureau (CJSB) was created, in Blackfriars, taking over the summoning of jurors from individual Crown Court centres. The excusal rate was high and inconsistent between Crown Court Centres so this was an attempt to regularise the position and tighten up on excusals.

16–005   I discovered from the CJSB in the course of our work for Auld L.J., however that, because of the rate of non-attendance and excusals, it was still necessary to summon four times as many jurors as were needed, around England and Wales and six times as many as were needed in London. I found that if people simply did not respond to a jury summons, then they might not be pursued. It was left to each individual Crown Court to chase those who did not attend and in London there was no budget allocated for this. I quoted a circuit judge who told me he was well aware of this and if a friend of his were reluctantly summoned for jury service he would advise them to throw the summons "in the bin". Our research was funded by the Government but because we disclosed how easy it still was to evade jury service, I was told that the Government considered our findings sensitive so they would not be publishing our work. The Auld team, however, considered that our work should be publicised so it exists electronically and can be accessed from the Criminal Courts Review website. Incidentally, it is not uncommon for government to refuse to publish research which they funded if they do not like the findings. Academics are familiar with this. For instance, this has happened to Professor John Baldwin of the Institute of Judicial Administration, University of Birmingham and professors in the Criminal Justice Unit at Leeds University.

In our 2001 paper for Auld L.J. we recommended repeal of the categories of excusable as of right and ineligible in the Juries Act. He received a number of arguments to the same effect. He examined the regime in New York, where the law and procedure had been tightened up to prevent people avoiding and evading jury service. The presumption in NY was that everyone should do jury service, with very limited grounds for excusal.

> People have been trying to get out of jury service for centuries:
>
> "I am summon'd to appear *upon a Jury*, and was just going to try if I could get off". (Hawles' *The Englishman's Right: A Dialogue between a Barrister and a Jury-Man*, (1680)).

The solution—banning ineligibility

Lord Justice Auld considered the reasons for making groups such as lawyers ineligible for jury service but did not agree, "People no longer defer to professionals or those holding particular office in the way they used to do" (see Chapter 5 of his *Review*). He also considered the objection that if people connected with the criminal justice system did jury service, they would lack openness of mind. He could not see why they were expected to be any more prejudiced than shopkeepers or house owners who had been burglary victims, or people who held strong views over such issues as euthanasia or drugs. Nor did he accept the objection that professionals would infer and transmit to fellow jurors the fact that if the accused did not mention his previous good character that was because he had previous convictions. Like the Morris Committee before him (*The Report on The Departmental Committee on Jury Service* (1965)), he considered that such a possibility was widely known among the public and would be known by anyone who had already done jury service. He considered the objections to having judges on the jury but "I consider that it would be good for them and the system of jury trial if they could experience at first hand what jurors have to put up with." He was also heartened by the fact that a number of American judges had had to do jury service and spoke warmly of it. He considered the objection that judge-jurors might know the judge or lawyers in the trial and, depending on seniority or personality, this might inhibit the judge or advocates in their conduct of the case. This problem, he responded, could be dealt with by discretionary excusal on a case by case basis. There was no need for the current blanket ban. 16–006

He noted that the Morris Committee had decided to preserve the ineligibility of the clergy on the grounds of possible embarrassment caused by their pastoral role and compassionate instincts but observed that there were many others in the community with similar roles and instincts. Lord Justice Auld accordingly recommended that everyone should be eligible for jury service, save for the mentally ill.

The solution—abolishing the right to excusals

Turning to scrutinise the long lists of people enjoying the right to excusal, he noted that the Morris Committee had reasoned that this was in the public interest because such groups owed special and 16–007 personal duties to the state or were responsible for the relief of pain and suffering. Again, his Lordship felt any problems could be dealt with by way of discretionary excusal rather than a blanket right of excusal. As for the 65–70 age group, he could see no reason for automatically excusing them unless they could show they were mentally or physically unfit. In relation to those who had recently done jury service, he observed that if all these statutory exclusions were done away with, being summoned twice would occur less frequently. He thought the CJSB could consider, on the basis of their statistical observations, excusing people for longer periods.

The disqualified

16–008   Auld L.J. recommended that the category of the disqualified should not change and this was accepted by the Government. Consequently, the Criminal Justice Act 2003 preserves the disqualification of those who have ever been sentenced to custody or alternatives for five years or more or who, in the last ten years have been sentenced to custody or an alternative for three month. Those on bail are also disqualified. The 2003 Act, Sch.33, continues the ban on mentally disordered persons.

In 2004, the Social Exclusion Unit published a report, "Mental Health and Social Exclusion" suggesting that the categories of mental disorder excluding a person from jury service were too many. The ban failed to distinguish between someone being treated by a doctor for mild depression and someone who had been sectioned under the Mental Health Act 1983. In 2005, the DCA and Home Office issued a joint consultation paper on the subject. Those who cannot participate effectively as a juror because of physical incapacity may have their summons discharged by the judge. This is discussed below.

Discretionary excusal

16–009   In our research for Lord Justice Auld, we found that people try to get out of jury service all over the world and the commonest excuses, worldwide, are childcare, family commitments, problems with employment and loss of wages. Excusals in England and Wales were examined in much more detail by Airs and Shaw. Auld L.J. observed the high excusal rate, 38 per cent, in England and Wales and recommended that, where an excuse appears to be well-founded, CJSB officers should aim to deal with it by way of deferral instead of outright excusal.

The Government's response—Justice for All *and the Criminal Justice Act 2003*

16–010   The Government agreed with Auld's recommendations. In their 2002 white paper, *Justice for All* they set out their plans for reforming criminal justice by changes in law and procedure. In a chapter entitled "Enhancing the Public's Engagement", they expressed the principle that "We believe that members of the community have the responsibility and a duty to carry out jury service if they possibly can".

The principles expressed in the white paper were enacted in the Criminal Justice Act 2003. It amends the Juries Act, s.1 to provide that everyone should be qualified for jury service provided they are not mentally disordered or disqualified. Summoning officers are obliged to excuse serving members of the armed forces if their commanding officer certifies that their absence would be prejudicial to the efficiency of the armed service. The 2003 Act amended s.9 of the Juries Act to place a duty on the Lord Chancellor to issue guidance to the CJSB on how its discretion should be exercised in granting deferrals and excusals.

In *Justice for All*, the Government promised to improve jury service. Jurors, they said, had a right to be treated with respect and to expect minimal disruption to their personal lives. They agreed with our finding that too many jurors were kept hanging around. Jurors should be supported, they said, with more information and advice. They claimed that the CJSB had shifted the balance from excusal to deferral and that this had increased the pool of potential jurors.

The 2003 Act came into force in April 2004 and the Government **16–011** claimed that this would significantly increase the pool of potential jurors. They promised that only those who proved they could not defer service to another period within 12 months would be excused, and then only in exceptional circumstances. Their press release said that compelling reasons for deferral included death or illness of a close relative; health reasons; pre-booked holiday; being a serving member of the armed forces where absence would be detrimental and religious festivals. Compelling reasons why eligible people could be excused included insufficient understanding of English, certain care responsibilities and being a member of a religious order or society whose beliefs are incompatible with jury service. This summarises the Jury Summoning Guidance issued in December 2003, discussed below. In response to concern that some of those summoned for jury service feared for their employment, the Employment Relations Act 2004 protects employees from protection or discrimination resulting from a being summoned or serving as a juror.

Public reaction to widening jury participation

When Lord Justice Auld published his proposals and then again **16–012** during the passage of the Criminal Justice Act as a Bill, through

Parliament, individuals in certain groups predictably objected. Newspapers came out in a a rash of letters from doctors and nurses claiming that the National Health Service would collapse in their absence. My response to this is to repeat a calculation I made in 1997 that we cited in our paper for Auld L.J. I calculated that of all adults aged 18–70 in England and Wales, we each only had a one in six chance of being summoned for jury service during our eligible lifetime. The Government relied on this calculation in its press releases and added that, thanks to the changes made in the 2003 Act, a person's chances of ever doing jury service are now reduced to one in 12. If doctors and nurses, like the rest of us, have a one in 12 chance of doing a fortnight's jury service once in their lifetimes, this is hardly going to cause the collapse of the NHS as we know it. I might add that many members of the medical profession are not UK citizens and so will not be called for jury service.

Another battery of objections in the press came from judges and lawyers, claiming that they might have undue influence over other jurors. My response to this is to express the expectation that lawyers and judges will have the integrity not to try to influence other jurors. After all, the old law did not exclude legal academics like me, or non-practising solicitors. I sat on two juries in 1990 and did not disclose that I taught law; nor did I try to sway my fellow jurors (see Darbyshire, 1990).

Well aware of objections from lawyers, doctors and others, the Government swiftly issued a consultation paper on their new "Jury Summoning Guidance" on deferral and excusals, in December 2003. They reiterated Auld L.J.'s reasoning in his *Review*:

"Concerns have been raised about the possible effect on the fairness of the trial of allowing lawyers and others involved in the administration of justice to sit on juries. The fear is that they might exercise undue influence over their fellow jurors by virtue of their specialist knowledge of the justice system. However, the Government is satisfied that these concerns are unfounded. The American experience, where, in a number of states, judges, lawyers and others holding positions in the criminal justice system have sat as jurors for some time, is that their fellow jurors have not allowed them to dominate their deliberations. In England and Wales, a large number of people with extensive knowledge of the criminal justice system—legal academics, law students and civil servants working in criminal justice—currently do jury service. There is no evidence to suggest that the involvement of any of these groups in jury service has been a problem. More generally, the diluting effect of the process of random selection, and the group dynamic of the jury, serve to protect the integrity of the deliberative process".

Lord Justice Dyson, a Court of Appeal judge was the first judge to be called for jury service. He told me that he was disturbed that one circuit judge had rejected him from a jury on the grounds that he knew him. Considering this to be an unacceptable reason, Lord Justice Dyson wrote to the Lord Chief Justice to object. In the meantime, he did serve on another jury. At the same time, a number of lawyers were attempting to avoid jury service, especially in the Old Bailey, by asking judges to be excused in trials where they knew the advocates. Some excusals were granted until the Recorder of London, the resident judge at the Old Bailey, issued a local Practice Direction that this was unacceptable. Both Auld L.J. and the Government in its consultation paper had recognised that lawyers and judges might need to be excused if they knew trial participants. This problem has now been resolved by requiring judges or recorders to do jury service in an area in which they do not sit as a judge. Of course famous judges, such as Dyson L.J. are known to all judges and lawyers—but then so was Elizabeth Hurley when she did jury service in the Old Bailey.

16–013

The Bar Council issued guidance, in 2004, to barristers summoned for jury service. It warned barristers that it was neither necessary nor appropriate to conceal their profession, nor was it necessary to volunteer such information. They should remember they were sitting as one equal member of a tribunal of fact and not in their capacity as barristers. They should not offer advice or an opinion as to the law and they should not contradict the judge's direction on law.

The Jury Summoning Guidance, now on the website of Her Majesty's Courts Service, reflects the criteria listed in the section above. Additionally, it says that if people find it difficult to get to court they can be offered another court. MPs can be allowed to sit outside their constituencies. Shift workers can ask for deferral. Those with physical disabilities should be treated sympathetically and so on. There were only 29 responses to the consultation. In its conclusions the government clarified the position of those working for the Crown Prosecution Service (CPS). They should not sit on any case where the CPS is prosecutor, that is, most criminal cases. It was accepted that it would be appropriate to extend excusal on the grounds of previous jury service to five years but that would require legislation. They agreed that "extreme circumstance" needed defining.

Randomness

The legal and philosophical sources of the notions of randomness and representativeness are difficult to discover. They do not appear in the Juries Act 1974, which significantly qualified randomness until 2004, but there are statements elsewhere. *The Report of the*

16–014

Departmental Committee on Jury Service (The Morris Committee, 1965) said "a jury should represent a cross-section drawn at random from the community" and a 1973 Practice Note by the Lord Chief Justice stated "a jury consists of twelve individuals chosen at random from the appropriate panel". The *obiter* statement of Lord Denning in the *Brownlow* case (1980, CA (cited at para.16–018 below)) reviewed the two "rival philosophies" as he called them, of our random jury and the highly selected American jury. He stated:

> "Our philosophy is that the jury should be selected at random from a panel of persons who are nominated at random. We believe that twelve persons selected at random are likely to be a cross-section of the people and thus represent the views of the common man. Some may be moral. Others not. Some may be honest. Others not . . . The parties must take them as they come."

Lord Denning's reference to the philosophy behind American jury construction acknowledges that while we believe in random selection, they believe that impartiality can only be guaranteed by a very elaborate selection system, by means of a *voir dire*. This means the completion of questionnaires by and examination of potential jurors in open court and a generous allocation of peremptory challenges exercisable by each party, to exclude those considered undesirable. In high profile trials, such as the Rodney King Beatings trials, the O. J. Simpson trial and the 2005 Michael Jackson trial, jury construction may take weeks or months and wealthy defendants like Simpson and Jackson spend thousands on the hiring of expensive jury consultants to help them select a jury.

Selection from the electoral register is now done randomly by computer, by the CJSB, since late 2000. Before the 1980s, Crown Court jury summoning officers were given the freedom to select jurors from the electoral register, as they chose, and this led to some selecting alphabetically whilst others selected street by street.

Race

16–015   In the 1980s, there were complaints from black defendants that jurors were summoned from white areas. In one trial the judge ordered an adjournment and, in another, ordered a jury to be summoned from a different district, in the hope of producing a mixed jury. The CA has ruled, however, that a jury may not be racially constructed. In *R. v Smith (Lance Percival)* [2003] EWCA Crim 283, they affirmed this rule, as laid down in *R. v Ford* (1989). The US Supreme Court has set down the same rule.

The Royal Commission on Criminal Justice 1993 recommended that the prosecution or defence should be able to apply to the judge, pre-trial, for the selection of a jury containing up to three people from minority communities, in cases with a racial dimension where the defendant or alleged victim is non-white. We reiterated this recommendation in our paper for Auld L.J.'s *Review* and he adopted this recommendation, relying on our research. We concluded, on examining worldwide research on juries that, while the findings on gender and verdict and age and verdict are equivocal, there appears to be a clear relationship between racial composition of juries and verdicts. Research demonstrates that three is the crucial number to have any impact on the verdict. We also pointed out that specially constructed juries are not unprecedented in English law. For over five centuries until 1870, foreigners had the right to be tried by a jury half composed of foreigners, *de medietate linguae*. The Law Society, Race Relations Committee of the Bar Council and the Commission for Racial Equality and others also supported this recommendation.

Auld L.J. pointed out, as we had done, that minorities are under-represented on juries because many do not register to vote, as disclosed by Airs and Shaw's 1999 research. 24 per cent of black citizens, 15 per cent Asian and 24 per cent other ethnic minority citizens did not register to vote. He commented that a limited sample for the *Review* in three centres in 2000 "showed a noticeable lack of ethnic mix in jury trials at all three centres". Other solutions to the problem, contemplated by the RCCJ 1993 and by Auld L.J. would be to allow the judge to transfer a trial to an area with a better ethnic mix or amalgamate the jury panel with another jury panel from a mixed race area. He rejected these suggestions because it smacked of forum shopping and could cause upset where a defendant and an alleged victim disagreed. At the time of writing (2005) research on ethnic diversity and the jury system is in progress. It is being conducted by Sally Lloyd-Bostock and others at the Institute of Judicial Administration, University of Birmingham.

The first obvious objection to our recommendation, which we **16–016** acknowledged, is that racial construction destroys randomness. Auld L.J. considered this and weighed it against the problem that an estimated 400,000 crimes a year are racially motivated and this has recently been recognised by statute and the philosophy of Art.6 of the Convention which requires objective impartiality. He concluded that randomness was not an end in itself.

We had recognised another objection to our suggestion for racial construction—a "thin end of the wedge" argument. If racial construction were permitted in a racially charged case, why not allow parties to demand a jury of mixed sexuality in a "queer-bashing" case? Auld L.J.'s response to this was that, while all jurors may bring their own prejudices, that is invisible compared with colour and will be overcome by the differing views of other jury members. Our research had indicated that white juries were or were perceived to be less fair to black than to white people. He thought the problems of racially constructing a jury were not insurmountable. The Summoning Bureau could ask people to disclose their ethnicity on receiving a summons.

Initially attracted to Auld L.J.'s recommendation to construct mixed race juries, the Government eventually rejected it, in *Justice for All* (2002), para.7.29 because it would:

- undermine the fundamental principle of randomness;
- assume bias on the part of the excluded jurors;
- place the minority jurors in a difficult position;
- generate tensions in the jury room;
- place undue weight on the views of the minority jurors and
- place a new burden on the court to determine which cases should receive special treatment and provide a ground for unmeritorious appeals.

Welsh language

16–017 Some Welsh judges argued to Auld L.J. that, in a case where a witness gives evidence in Welsh (as is her right), and it has to be translated into English, that witness is at a disadvantage. They suggested that it should be possible to select a bilingual jury in such cases. The lack of facility to do so infringed the principle that English and Welsh were to be treated as equal by the courts and caused potential for injustice. Auld L.J. examined other judges' arguments that selecting a bilingual jury would exclude 90 per cent of the defendant's peers, who spoke only English. He declined to resolve the issue but suggested it was worthy of further consideration by someone else.

Vetting

16–018 The group summoned to attend at a particular Crown Court location is called "the panel", from which juries are selected for trials over a certain period (usually two weeks) and the prosecution at this stage may exercise a problematic form of scrutiny known as "vetting" and then the prosecution and defence may exercise rights to challenge. It must be understood, however, that vetting and all types of challenge are *extremely rare*, since the late 1980s. Controversy arose during the highly publicised Official Secrets Act trial in 1978, known as the "ABC Trial" (because of the three defendants' surnames: Aubrey, Berry and Campbell). *The Times* exposed the fact that successive Attorney-Generals, using prerogative power, had been secretly vetting the backgrounds of potential jurors in this and other politically sensitive trials and trials involving professional gangs. The Attorney-General revealed his guidelines on vetting. In 1980 the two divisions of the CA gave rather conflicting rulings on the legality of jury vetting. In *R. v Sheffield Crown Court Ex p. Brownlow*, the Civil Division, led by Lord Denning, unanimously ruled jury vetting by the police to be illegal but the case was closely followed, in the Criminal Division, by *R. v Mason*, in which police vetting had taken place, as part of the routine in Northamptonshire. The Court held that police vetting was supportable as common sense.

In response, the Attorney amended his guidelines, enhancing controls over vetting and distinguishing between: (a) vetting carried out by the police; and (b) "authorised checks", requiring his personal consent:

1. Police may make checks against criminal records, to establish that jurors are not disqualified.
2. "Authorised checks" are now to be carried out only with the Attorney's permission, following a recommendation by the DPP. The DPP decides what part of the information disclosed should be forwarded to the prosecution (note: not the defence). Except in terrorism cases, such checks will not now be carried out in politically motivated cases. In, for example, official secrets trials, vetting will only be permitted where national security is involved and the hearing is likely to be *in camera*.
3. The Attorney will consider and, in other cases, the Chief Constable may consider, defence requests for information revealed on jurors.

The Royal Commission on Criminal Justice 1993 recommended the routine screening of jurors for criminal convictions. In 1997, I asked the Conservative Attorney-General, Sir Nicholas Lyell, how often he authorised vetting. He had never heard of vetting and asked me to explain it, suggesting that the practice is very rare.

Challenges to the Array

All parties have a common law right, preserved by s.12(6) of the Juries Act 1974, to challenge the whole panel, on the grounds that the summoning officer is biased or has acted improperly. For example this was attempted in *Danvers* (Crown Court, 1982) by a black defendant, on the grounds that the all-white jury did not reflect the ethnic composition of the community.

16–019

Challenges by the Prosecution

The prosecution may exclude any panel member from a particular jury by asking them to "stand by for the Crown" without

16–020

reasons, until the whole panel, except for the last 12, is exhausted. Reasons, "cause", must be given for any further challenges but, with panels often consisting of 100 or more, the prosecution rarely needs to explain its challenges. The Roskill Committee recommended the abolition of this right but the Government declined to include it in the Criminal Justice Bill 1986.

The Attorney-General announced, in 1988, that the prosecution's right to stand a juror by without giving reasons would now be limited to two instances: to remove a "manifestly unsuitable" juror or to remove a juror after authorised vetting. This goes some way towards responding to complaints over the imbalance between prosecution and defence rights of challenge.

Challenges by the Defence

16–021   Once the jury are assembled in court, the judge invites the juror to step down if she knows anyone involved in the case. The defence may then challenge any number of potential jurors for cause, (*i.e.* good reason acceptable to the judge) but what is an acceptable "cause" was qualified by a 1973 Practice Note issued by the Lord Chief Justice, who stated that it was contrary to established practice for jurors to be excused on grounds such as race, religion, political beliefs or occupation. This followed a trial of alleged anarchists called "The Angry Brigade", where the defence had requested the judge to ask people to exclude themselves if, for example, they were members of the Conservative Party or if they had relatives in the police force or serving in the forces in Northern Ireland.

It is also clear that the reasons must be those known to the defence and should not normally be ascertained by examining the potential juror in court. In other words, no practice exists such as the *"voir dire"* system in the US, where potential jurors are examined by psychologists and other professionals to discover any prejudices. There have been occasional, well-publicised exceptions, however, in the 1980s, where the judge has permitted examination of jurors on their affiliations or beliefs, notably in cases involving black defendants. In the 1995–1996 Maxwell brothers' fraud trial, potential jurors were questioned on their views of the evidence because of prejudicial pre-trial publicity.

Until 1989, the defence could make a certain number of peremptory challenges, that is, challenges without reasons. This number was reduced from seven to three in the Criminal Law Act 1977 and was abolished by the Criminal Justice Act 1988. This resulted from the Conservative Government's belief that the right to peremptory challenge was being abused by defence lawyers, deliberately trying to skew the jury and from the recommendation of the Roskill Committee on fraud trials (1986) that it be abolished. This leaves a gross imbalance between prosecution and defence rights of challenge. The abolition of peremptory challenge is in sharp contrast to the US where, dependent on state law, each party usually has a generous number of "peremptories", as explained above, to help them exclude from the jury those who they consider may not be sympathetic to their case.

Lord Justice Auld received very few suggestions that challenges be reintroduced in English law and made no recommendations to alter the right to challenge.

Excusal by the Judge

Under the Juries Act, s.10, the judge may discharge from service **16–022** any juror about whom there is doubt as to "his capacity to act effectively as a juror" because of physical disability or insufficient understanding of English. Additionally, judges have a common law discretion to discharge jurors and they occasionally interpret this quite broadly. For example, the whole panel was discharged in a controversial 1979 anarchists trial and the eventual jury were discharged for life, after acquitting most of the defendants.

Following the widening of jury participation aspired to by the by the Criminal Justice Act 2003, a sub-group of judges considered how judges should now exercise their right of excusal but at the time of writing, 2005, the Consolidated Practice Direction, Part IV, para.42 has still not been amended.

Deaf jurors

Under s.9 of the Juries Act 1974, where there is doubt as to a **16–023** person's ability to act effectively as a juror, the summoning officer is obliged to bring that person before a judge. The judge must discharge the summons where she is of the opinion that the person will not be capable of acting effectively as a juror, on account of his disability. The exclusion of deaf jurors is considered by Majid. In 1999, Mr McWhinney had his jury summons discharged by a judge at Woolwich Crown Court because he would need a sign interpreter in the jury room with him and, on consideration of the case law, with the legal assistance of a friend to the court, the judge found that a 13th person could not be allowed into the jury room. She heard evidence that sign interpreters were permitted into the jury room in the US but concluded she was bound by English common law until Parliament decided to admit sign interpreters into the jury room. Sign interpreters are routinely used in open court to assist deaf witnesses, claimants and defendants.

3. Function of the Jury

16–024 The purpose of having the jury is to enable the decision on fact to be taken by a small group from the community, rather than for it to be left entirely in the hands of the lawyers. Thus, in criminal cases tried at the Crown Court, the guilt of the person accused has to be established to the satisfaction of ten of the 12 jurors beyond all reasonable doubt. (Remember that this applies to around one per cent of defendants to criminal charges, because fewer than five per cent are tried in the Crown Court and, of these, most plead guilty and merely appear before the judge for sentence).

After hearing the judge's "summing up" of the evidence and directions on the law, the jury retire and consider their verdict in private. On the pronouncement of that verdict by the foreman of the jury, the accused is found either "guilty" or "not guilty". If "not guilty" the defendant is acquitted and is free to leave the court; if "guilty" he is convicted, and the judge sentences him. The judge will first hear the criminal record of the prisoner and then a plea in mitigation of sentence, which is made by defence counsel. The judge may adjourn for a pre-sentence report to be made before sentencing. The jury has no part to play in the decision as to sentence. Equally the jury has no part in decisions which are concerned with law or legal procedure. A judge will often have to ask the jury to retire, so that she can hear arguments on and decide on a point of law and routinely, legal arguments, such as those on the admissibility of evidence take place before the trial or during the trial but in the absence of the jury. The judge must determine admissibility. Such rulings on law and evidence are discussed in Chapter 10, above.

The Decline of the Civil Jury

16–025 The civil jury declined massively in the twentieth century. Although a jury of eight may be called in the county court at the discretion of the judge, in practice this is rare, except in the one growth area for jury trials since 1990, tort actions against the police. Jury trial is also available in certain cases in the Queen's Bench Division but jury trials here and in the county court only amount to a few hundred per year. In the following tort actions there is, by s.69 of the Supreme Court Act 1981, a right to jury trial: libel, slander, malicious prosecution, false imprisonment and fraud. Even here jury trial can be refused if a prolonged examination of documents, or accounts, or a scientific or local investigation, or other complex material is involved. In all other cases, the judge has a discretion to allow a jury trial. The trend away from jury trial in civil cases has been comparatively rapid since, as recently as 1933, 50 per cent of cases involved a jury. In *Ward v James* (1966) a five-judge CA decided that trial by judge alone should be the usual mode of trial.

The most important reasons for the disuse of the civil jury are the inconsistency in damages awards and exorbitant figures for damages which sometimes result. Examples of this include the award of £600,000 libel damages to Sonia Sutcliffe, ex-wife of the "Yorkshire Ripper", against the publishers of *Private Eye*, which led Ian Hislop to comment: "If this is justice, I'm a banana". This was later reduced to £60,000. The Courts and Legal Services Act 1990, s.8 provided for rules to empower the CA to substitute its own award of damages. It has obviously been easier to achieve consistency in the scale of damages for personal injuries because they are now left to the judges. Throughout the 1990s, however, juries continued to make outlandishly high damages awards in the defamation actions of the rich and famous, much to the exasperation of the judiciary. Notice the disgust of the Master of the Rolls, in December 1995, in *John v Mirror Group Newspapers*, an appeal in which the Mirror group succeeded in getting the CA to reduce to £75,000 the jury's award of £350,000 to Elton John, for alleging that he displayed symptoms of an eating disorder at a Hollywood party:

> "It is in our view offensive to public opinion, and rightly so, that a defamation plaintiff should recover damages for injury to repu- tation greater, perhaps by a significant factor, than if that same plaintiff had been rendered a helpless cripple or an insensate veg- etable. The time has in our view come when judges, and counsel, should be free to draw the attention of juries to these compar- isons."

Also in 1995, a jury award of £750,000 damages made to Graeme Souness, against his ex-wife for calling him a "dirty rat" in *The People*, was settled, pending appeal, for £100,000. In 1996, four large awards of damages against the Metropolitan Police in jury trials for actions such as false imprisonment provoked the Metropolitan Police Commissioner to call for judicial guidelines to be set down for juries in these cases, similar to those in defamation cases.

The Faulks Committee (1974) recommended that juries should no longer be available as of right in defamation actions for these reasons, which give us some insight into why the civil jury declined generally.

1. Judges were not as remote from real life as popularly supposed.
2. Judges gave reasons, whereas juries did not.
3. Juries found complex cases difficult.

4. Juries were unpredictable.
5. Juries were expensive (jury trial is more time-consuming, as explanations have to be geared for them, not a judge).

Coroners' Juries

16–026   The coroner, whose task it is to inquire into sudden death can and in some circumstances must, call a jury for the inquest. The coroner's jury, after hearing the evidence, return a verdict as to the cause of death and the coroner must record this verdict. The issue of coroners' juries giving reasons in certain cases is discussed in Chapter 4 on human rights, above.

4. Majority Verdicts

16–027   For centuries, the English legal system required that the verdict of the jury in both civil and criminal trials should be unanimous. If unanimity could not be achieved then a retrial was necessary. In the 1960s there was increasing criticism of this requirement, particularly on the part of the police who pointed out that one member of the jury if "nobbled" by the defendant or his supporters could cause a retrial by simply refusing to agree with the other 11 jurors in a criminal case. The Criminal Justice Act 1967 permitted a majority verdict of 10–2 to be accepted by the judge in a criminal case, or 10–1, or 9–1 if one or two jury members had been discharged. The jury must spend at least two hours seeking to achieve unanimity. If the verdict is "guilty" the fact that it is a majority verdict must be disclosed. Majority verdicts were permitted in civil cases from 1972 and all the provisions concerning majority verdicts have now been consolidated in the Juries Act 1974, as amended. Lord Justice Auld received few comments that the system should be changed and made no proposal for change.

5. Jury Secrecy

16–028   The secrecy of jury deliberations is protected in English law. They deliberate alone in the jury room and disclosure of those deliberations is a contempt under the Contempt of Court Act 1981, s.8. The application of that section is so broad as to preclude bona fide research into jury decision-making, frustrating would-be socio-legal researchers and reform bodies. The Royal Commission on Criminal Justice, 1993, recommended its amendment, as did the Law Commission, in their 1995 annual report but Auld L.J. disagreed, in his 2001 *Review*. He considered the view of Lord Hewart C.J., expressed in 1922, that the value of the jury's verdict lies only in its anonymity and the view of Glanville Williams, in *The Proof of Guilt*, 1950, that "the real reason for keeping the jury's deliberations secret is to preserve confidence in a system which more intimate knowledge might destroy." (p.205). Auld L.J. asked:

"Should section 8 of the 1981 Act be amended to permit legitimate research (and, while we are about it, to enable the Court of Appeal, Criminal Division, to examine conduct in the jury room the subject of appeal)? Or is public confidence in juries' oracular verdicts so precious to our legal system that we should not put it at risk? Many fear that the very undertaking of intrusive research—that is, into how individual juries reach their decisions—could damage public confidence by sewing doubts as to the integrity of verdicts ... On the other hand, such research might show that all is not well and that changes are needed." (p.166).

He considered the point made in our paper for him, that there is a wealth of jury research, worldwide, from which lessons could be learned and most of it is of a non-intrusive nature. He cited the 1994 New York Jury Project and the 2001 New Zealand criminal trial jury study and thought ample lessons could be learned from non-intrusive research of this kind. He recommended no amendment to s.8. There should, instead be careful consideration of all available existing research material throughout the common law world (summarised in out paper for him) with a view to identifying and responding appropriately to all available information about how juries arrived at their verdicts. If and to the extent to which such information was insufficient, jury research should be considered that does not violate the 1981 Act.

In 2005, the DCA published a consultation paper "Jury Research and Impropriety", again raising the question of whether the s.8 protection of jury secrecy should be amended. The paper states that jury secrecy "has long been regarded as a cornerstone of the legal system" but in recent years, after the incorporation of the European Convention on Human Rights into English law

"there has been increasing debate on whether the current law has got it right. Is there a risk that the necessary confidentiality of the jury process could lead to potential miscarriages of justice and, if so, is there a way of reducing this risk without fundamentally undermining the jury process?" (p.5).

The paper canvassed views on whether:

- any or all aspects of the way in which juries deliberate should be subject to research;

- there are circumstances in which a jury's deliberations should be subject to external investigation; and
- any aspect of the common law rule rendering inadmissible any evidence from jury deliberations should be clarified or amended.

The paper set out the Government's provisional views, proposing that any research into deliberations should only be allowed if permitted by the minister and undertaking in accordance with conditions agreed by him and the Lord Chief Justice. A code of conduct should guarantee confidentiality.

As for impropriety, the paper set out the current law as stated in recent appeals where there had been allegations of impropriety, notably *R. v Mirza* [2004] UKHL 4 and recommended that the law should be left as it is. Such allegations should be dealt with on a case by case basis.

16–029 The paper explained the background to s.8, reminding us that it had not been the intention of the government in 1981 to prohibit bona fide research but, after lengthy deliberation on the dangers of research, the House of Lords made last minute amendments which precluded research. They examined previous debates on this issue and the arguments for and against change. The potential benefits of permitting such research were said to include:

1. An understanding of the factors jurors consider important when determining guilt/innocence.
2. Improving information, guidance and direction to jurors.
3. Discovering what jurors think of the trial process.
4. Examining whether all jurors are able to participate.
5. Determining whether there is any evidence of gender/racial or other bias.
6. Suggesting any other factors which would allow jurors to do their job better.

The risks included:

1. Inhibiting the frankness of jury discussions.
2. Undermining the finality of verdicts.
3. Damaging public confidence in the jury system.
4. Where the research is not bona fide or is slanted, exposing jurors to harassment.

Any change in the law must be designed to improve support for jurors, they concluded.

Examining Allegations of Impropriety

Occasionally, a defendant or a court hears allegations from a juror **16–030** that there was something unsatisfactory about the deliberations or the way in which the jury arrived at their verdict and the trial court or the CA has to decide how far they can breach jury room secrecy to investigate. The consultation paper sets out the common law rule, as articulated in *R. v Mirza* (see above), by Lord Hope

"The general rule is that the court will not investigate, or receive evidence about, anything said in the course of the jury's deliberations while they are considering their verdict in the retiring room."

The consultation paper examined cases in which the court had departed from this rule:

1. *Ellis v Deheer* (1922) Some of the jurors could not hear the verdict announced and disagreed with it. The CA would not hear evidence of jury deliberations.
2. *Hood* (1968) A juror was a relative of the defendant's wife and he may have known of the defendant's record. The CA admitted an affidavit from the juror that he did recognize the accused because this did not deal with what took place in the jury room.
3. *Brandon* (1969) The jury bailiff made remarks to the jury which might have indicated that the accused had a record. The court admitted evidence of what the bailiff said.
4. *Young* (1995) While staying overnight in a hotel, four jury members tried to contact the deceased via a ouija board. He allegedly told them the defendant had murdered him. The CA held that it could inquire into what took place in the hotel but not in the jury room.
5. *McCluskey* (1994) One of the jurors used a mobile phone to make a business call, during deliberations. The CA admitted evidence from him that he did have his phone.

The Impact of Article 6 of the European Convention on Human Rights

Article 6, as described in Chapter 10 of this book, requires fair **16–031** trial. In *Remli v France* (1996) the ECtHR made it clear that the Convention imposes an obligation on the national court to check whether a tribunal was impartial. In *R. v Mirza* (above), the House of Lords held that the s.8 prohibition on the admission of jury deliberations did not breach Art.6. The case law of the ECtHR has not undermined the principle of secrecy of jury deliberations.

In *Gregory v UK* (1998) the ECtHR stressed that the tribunal, including the jury must be impartial from a subjective as well as an objective point of view. in that case, one juror had passed a note to the judge during deliberations which read "Jury showing racial overtones. One member to be excused". The judge had warned the jury to decide according to the evidence and they returned a majority guilty verdict. The ECtHR acknowledged that jury room secrecy was fundamental and made no attempt to overturn the principle.

Sander v UK (2001) was another case in which a juror alleged racial bias. They complained to the trial judge that jurors had been making racist jokes. The judge read out the complaint and adjourned the case overnight, asking the jurors to consider whether they could try this case solely on the evidence. The next morning the jury refuted the allegations and said they could decide according to the evidence. One letter from a juror apologised and said the juror thought he could be the cause of it. He apologised, claimed he was unbiased and outlined his connections with minority people. The ECtHR found a breach of Art.6, because one juror had admitted racist jokes and that could not be reconciled with refutation of racism by the majority.

16–032   In *R. v Mirza* (above) the House of Lords affirmed a line of case law on the common law prohibition against receiving evidence of deliberations. The common law rule only protected the secrecy of jury deliberations, not extraneous evidence of jury bias so was not disproportionate and therefore not in breach of Art.6. The House recognised that there could be cases where evidence should be admitted that the jury had completely failed to discharge its duty, such as by using a ouija board.

Lord Hope said it was the collective decision-making, free from outside interference that gave the jury trial process its strength. The tribunal was presumed to be impartial until the contrary was proven. Attempts to soften the rule in the public interest should be resisted if jurors were to continue to perform their vital function of safeguarding individual liberty. The jury's introductory video, he said, should be amended to warn jurors to raise concerns before the verdict, when they could be investigated and dealt with by the trial judge. (Here, a juror had written *after* the trial, alleging prejudice by other jurors and in the case joined to *Mirza, Connor and Rollock* [2004] UKHL 2 a juror alleged that her jury were prepared to find the accused both guilty just for the sake of reaching a quick verdict). The House dismissed suggestions in previous case law and in by Auld L.J. in his *Review*, indicating that for the court to examine jurors it would be in breach of s.8 of the Contempt Act 1981. This was not correct because the court could not be in contempt of itself.

Better information could be given to appeal courts so they could scrutinise allegations to the high degree required by Art.6. The CA could call for a report from the trial judge. A Practice Direction was swiftly issued by Lord Woolf in February 2004. Jurors should be notified of the importance of bringing to the attention of the judge any concerns about fellow jurors while there was still time to put things right but it was undesirable to encourage inappropriate criticism.

R. v Mirza was applied in another House of Lords Decision, *R. v Smith and R. v Mercieca* [2005] UKHL 12. Here, a juror had written to the judge alleging coercion by some jurors of others and that deals were being done in order to reach a swift decision. The House upheld the trial judge's decision not to question the jurors about their deliberations. The judge had been correct to give the jury further directions and warn them not to be bullied but he was insufficiently comprehensive and emphatic. He should have given them a stern warning to follow his directions on law and to decide on their verdicts without pressure or bargaining.

In *Karakaya* [2005] EWCA Crim 346, a juror downloaded information from the internet, for use in jury deliberations. The CA quashed the defendant's convictions on the ground that this offended against the principle of open justice. The public and the defendant should know the material considered by the decision making body. The prosecution and defence were entitled to a fair opportunity to address all the material considered by the jury. The Court applied *Gearing* (1968), where it was held that no evidence must be introduced after the jury retired. Jurors should not conduct their own private research. Judge L.J., giving the judgment of the court, suggested that this should be explained to jurors in their standard guidance. In *Attorney General v Scotcher* [2005] UKHL 36 the House of Lords upheld the contempt conviction of a juror who had written to the defendant's more expressing concern are th jury's deliberations. His desire to expose a miscarriage of justice was no defence.

6. *"Jury Equity" and the Unreasoned Verdict*

Jurors do not give reasons for their decisions. An interesting historical survival is the rule that jurors cannot be punished if they bring in a perverse acquittal contrary to the direction of the judge. This was laid down in *Bushell's Case* in 1670 where two Quakers were charged with tumultuous assembly. The jury were ordered to convict, but instead returned a verdict of "not guilty". The judge sent the jury to prison until they should pay a fine by way of punishment. On appeal, it was held that the fine and imprisonment could not be allowed to stand. The Ponting trial of 1985 saw a jury bring in a verdict of "not guilty" in an Official Secrets Act case where a conviction had been expected. This freedom to ignore the law and resort to their

16–033

16–034

consciences, we call "jury equity" and Americans call "nullification". There are many more modern day examples. For instance, there have been several acquittals of defendants in the 1990s who have used cannabis to relieve the pain of such illnesses as multiple sclerosis.

In *R. v Wang* [2005] UKHL 9, the House of Lords, applying *Stonehouse* (1978) affirmed that there were no circumstances in which a judge could direct a jury to convict, even in cases where the burden of raising a defence rested on the defendant and he had failed to discharge it. The jury were free to deliver an acquittal that the trial judge considered to be perverse.

In our 2001 work for Auld L.J., we concluded

"We agree with the suggestion being made by many that the Convention may require jurors to give reasoned decisions. They could be given a series of questions, agreed between counsel and judge, as they are in civil trials. Lord Justice Auld might find it helpful to study Thaman's account of how the procedure works in Spain. (The New Zealand Law Commission recommended a series of sequential questions or a flow chart in complex trials, para.318). If jurors are to be asked for reasons, then they must surely be told of their power to acquit in the face of condemnatory evidence, as an exercise of jury equity."

16–035   Since 2001, there has been no case before the ECtHR challenging the unreasoned verdict. Lord Justice Auld disagreed with us on Art.6. He pointed to a decision of the ECtHR expressly ruling that the unreasoned verdict of a Danish jury was not a breach of the Convention. He also made the point that the ECtHR examines the fairness of the trial and appeal taken together.

The problem with an unreasoned verdict is that it can make appeal difficult and it is an anomaly compared with other criminal tribunals. The magistrates and the district judge (magistrates' court) are both required by Art.6 of the Convention to give reasoned decisions. Lord Justice Auld said

"A reasoned judgment tells the parties why they have won or lost; it is more likely to be soundly based on the evidence than an unreasoned one; and, by its openness is more likely to engender public confidence in the decision-making system." (p.169).

He agreed with our suggestion of giving the jury a series of questions but went much further, reaching the opposite conclusion on jury equity. He said he regarded the jury's ability to acquit or convict in the face of the law as "a blatant affront to the legal process and the main purpose of the criminal justice system—the control of crime".

He surprised commentators by recommending that the law should be changed to declare that juries had no right to acquit in defiance of the law or disregard of the evidence (p. 176). This recommendation outraged critics of the *Review* and, unfortunately, destroyed much of its credibility. In 1991, I had attacked the unfairness and irrationality of jury equity, using the same reasoning as Auld L.J. did ten years later but it seems to me that suggesting it should be banned is pointless. The very reason why the English and the Americans heap praise on their jury system is its ability to defy the law. It is argued that the jury acts as a check on officialdom, on the judge's power, and a protector against unjust or oppressive prosecution, injecting jury "equity" by deciding guilt or innocence according to a feeling of justice rather than by applying known law to facts proven beyond reasonable doubt: for example Kalven and Zeisel said, in *The American Jury* (1966),

> "It represents also an impressive way of building discretion, equity and flexibility into a legal system. Not least of the advantages is that the jury, relieved of the burdens of creating precedent, can bend the law without breaking it."

Unsurprisingly, in the furore on this point that followed publication of the *Review*, the Government did not follow this recommendation.

7. History

During its long history, the jury has completely changed its role. Nowadays, every effort is made to ensure that the jury have no prior knowledge of the case, and will be able to reach their verdict entirely on the evidence presented at the trial. Originally, however, the jury's role was a combination of local police and prosecutor. Centuries before a paid police force was created, the responsibility for law and order lay with the community. This meant the local "jury" arresting suspected offenders, and then bringing them before the visiting judge and swearing, like prosecution witnesses, to the guilt of the accused. There was nothing unusual in this use of local representatives in the early community. It can be seen also in the local inquiries which led to the creation of the Domesday Book, and the system of inquisitions post mortem, the inquiry held on a death as to the ownership of the lands and goods of the deceased. Throughout the Middle Ages juries were used in the settlement of civil disputes concerning the ownership and tenancy of land and the right to an advowson (the right to present to the living of a church). It was only very gradually and with the passage of centuries that the use of the jury as uninvolved judges of fact developed. Even then

16–036

the original concept continued to exist and this led to the existence of a grand jury and a petty jury. The grand jury of 24 members met only at the start of assizes or quarter sessions in order to find a true bill of indictment against the accused. Since the accused had previously undergone the preliminary inquiry by magistrates, who had heard the prosecution case and had decided to commit the accused for trial, the decision of the grand jury became a complete formality. It was fully abolished by the Criminal Justice Act 1948. US jurisdictions retain the grand jury to indict the accused in certain cases. The petty jury, trial jury, of 12 members emerged in the thirteenth century to take the place of trial by ordeal, which the ecclesiastical authorities then saw fit to condemn. It became increasingly distinct in its functions from the grand jury, although it long maintained its composition from local witnesses of fact deciding matters from their local knowledge. It was the fifteenth century before the petty jury assumed its modern role in criminal trials as judges of fact.

In civil cases the jury appears to have had its origin in the Assizes of Clarendon in 1166, and the Assizes of Northampton in 1176, establishing the grand and petty assizes. Here again the jury was at first called to decide a case from its local knowledge, and only with the passage of time did it become an impartial judge of the facts. The system allowed for trial to be in two parts. The local jury would hear and deal with the case, then send their findings to the judges at Westminster where the judgment would be given.

8. Current Plans to Reduce Jury Trial

Withdrawing the Right to Elect Jury Trial

16–037   As explained in the Chapter 10 on criminal procedure, above, in cases of medium seriousness, "triable either way", where the magistrates express no preference as to mode of trial, the defendant has the right to elect trial by magistrates in their court or judge and jury in the Crown Court. Governments have been thinking of removing this right to elect jury trial since the Royal Commission on Criminal Justice recommended they do so in 1993. Drawing conclusions from Home Office and other research on mode of trial decisions by magistrates and defendants, they concluded that the system was not being used as intended.

They found that, while defendants often opted for Crown Court trial in the belief that their chances of acquittal were greater, they nevertheless changed their plea to guilty at the Crown Court; that defendants often opted for Crown Court trial in the mistaken belief that, if convicted, the Crown Court judge would impose a lighter sentence than magistrates and that magistrates sent a number of cases to the Crown Court where the defendant ultimately received a sentence within the magistrates' own sentencing powers.

They recommended that the defendant should no longer have the right to insist on jury trial. Where prosecution and defence could not agree on mode of trial, the decision should be referred to the magistrates. The Commission was subject to academic criticism, especially by Warwick Professors McConville and Bridges, alleging that it had misinterpreted the Home Office research. Nevertheless, the (Conservative) Home Office published a consultation document, *Mode of Trial*, in 1995. In it, they outlined three options designed to shift more cases from the Crown Court to the magistrates' courts:

1. The reclassification of more offences as triable only summarily.
2. The withdrawal of the defendant's option to insist on jury trial in the Crown Court.
3. A requirement that the defendant enter the plea before the trial/hearing venue is chosen.

The Government chose to enact the third and least draconian of these options. Given the sentimental attachment of the English to jury trial in criminal cases, it would be politically inexpedient to remove the defendant's right to opt for jury trial in all triable either way cases. Instead, s.49 of the Criminal Procedure and Investigations Act 1996 was passed. This requires magistrates, before determining mode of trial, to ascertain the accused's plea, in the hope of persuading the magistrates to keep more cases in the magistrates' court. This and successive legislation is explained in Chapter 10 on criminal procedure, above.

Before this plan could take effect, however, The Narey Report **16–038** (M. Narey, *Review of Delay in the Criminal Justice System*, Home Office) was published in 1997 and reiterated the recommendation that the defendant's right to elect jury trial be removed. New Labour replaced the Conservatives three months later. In 1998, the Labour Home Secretary, Jack Straw, published *Determining Mode of Trial in Either Way Cases—A Consultation Paper*. In it, he set out the familiar arguments on abolishing the defendant's right to elect jury trial, as follows:

For abolition

- The right is not ancient. It only dates from 1855 and has **16–039** nothing to do with Magna Carta.
- 22,000 defendants elected for Crown Court trial in 1997 but most changed their plea to guilty, after significant inconvenience and worry to victims and witnesses and considerable extra cost.

- By definition, elected cases are those which magistrates have determined are suitable for themselves. The mode of trial decision should be based on objective assessment by the court of the gravity of the case, not the defendant's perception of what is advantageous to him, such as a greater prospect of acquittal.
- It is questionable whether defendants opt for jury trial to defend their reputation, as nine tenths of those electing already have previous convictions.
- Most defendants elect because they want to delay proceedings, to apply pressure to the Crown to accept a guilty plea to a lesser offence, or to deter witnesses or to put off the evil day.
- Few other jurisdictions allow the defendant such an element of choice (*e.g.* Scotland).

Arguments in favour of the status quo

16–040
- The right helps to promote confidence in the criminal justice system.
- Whereas magistrates are broadly concerned with the seriousness of the offence, it is the defendant's reputation which the public sees as a justification for continuing to allow the right to elect.
- When people who have never been accused of a crime defend the right, it is usually on the basis that they would want such a right if they were charged with something of which they were innocent.
- It is assumed that Crown Court trial is fairer. Defendants who choose it rightly believe they have a higher chance of acquittal.
- Some arguments go to the merits of trial by jury, for example, the jury's capacity to acquit contrary to legal proof of guilt.

One proposal in the paper was to take away the right of those defendants who had previous convictions and who had, therefore, already lost their reputations. Consequently, Jack Straw introduced the Criminal Justice (Mode of Trial) Bill in 1999. This would have abolished the defendant's right to elect, placing the mode of trial decision in the magistrates' hands. The prosecutor and accused would have had a right to make representations. The Bench would have to take into account the nature of the case, whether the circumstances make the offence serious, whether magistrates' sentencing powers would be adequate, whether the accused's livelihood or reputation would be damaged and any other relevant circumstances. The magistrates could take account of the defendant's previous convictions. In small cases of theft, where the sum involved was under £5,000, the magistrates would be obliged to treat it as an offence triable only summarily.

The Bill attracted much criticism, notably from the Bar, the Law Society, the Society of Black Lawyers and from lawyers' groups such as the Legal Action Group (LAG). LAG argued the following (*Legal Action*, September 1998):

- The main reason defendants opt for jury trial is that they rightly see their chances of obtaining justice in the Crown Court as significantly higher. In 1997, 62 per cent of defendants who pleaded not guilty to some or all counts were acquitted. Having a professional judge oversee the case was as important as having a jury. Thirty-eight per cent were acquitted because the judge discharged the case and a further 16 per cent on the judge's direction.
- Electing jury trial brings into play a range of other safe-guards, such as greater disclosure of the prosecution case. (This point was also made by many other commentators.)
- Removing the right to elect would significantly disadvantage black defendants. They more frequently elect for the Crown Court. Research indicates that this results in more of them being acquitted or having the charges against them dropped.
- The suggestion that defendants elect jury trial to put off the evil day is not borne out by research.
- Delays would increase, caused by mini-trials on venue.
- In opposition, Jack Straw had called the proposal "short-sighted".

Wolchover and Heaton-Armstong added:

- A defendant who delays a guilty plea to obtain some advan-tage cannot expect the same sentence discount as one who pleads earlier and, since 1986, advocates have had a duty to warn defendants of this.
- Tactical elections will continue to decline because of the intro-duction of the "plea before venue" procedure and because of s.48 of the Criminal Justice and Public Order Act 1994, which allowed the sentencing court to take account of the timing of the guilty plea.
- As experienced defence counsel, they denied that defendants caused delay to "put off the evil day". On the contrary, the most frequent and obvious cause of a last minute plea was the defendant's loss of courage.
- The argument is about the loss of a traditional common law right.

- Loss of liberty is no less serious for an habitual thief than loss of good name for someone with no previous convictions.

Courtney Griffiths QC (*Counsel*, April 1999) added:

- Research by the Runnymede Trust, 1990, showed that, whereas under one third of white defendants, given the option, elected for jury trial, 45 per cent of black defendants elected.
- This is an intelligent choice. Only two per cent of magistrates are non-white. Home Office research at Leicester magistrates' court showed white defendants had a substantially better chance of being granted bail and were less likely to receive immediate custodial sentences than blacks. (Incidentally, when the research was completed in 1999, it showed the reverse. Magistrates acquitted more Asians and blacks than whites. McConville and Bridges however, completed another unpublished study which indicated the opposite and the Attorney General conceded in a House of Lords debate, in 2000, that there is evidence of overcharging of ethnic minority defendants.)

Both the Bar and Law Society opposed the plan to abolish the right to elect. A number of other commentators emphasised that jury trial is inherently superior to summary trial, especially as listing for a Crown Court trial triggered a much more careful review of the case by the CPS, which would often result in dropping the case or reducing the charges. This also implied that, if magistrates were to decide on mode of trial, they would be doing so on inadequate information.

16–041 Further, at the Crown Court, a professional judge reviews the strength and admissibility of the evidence, whereas magistrates are both fact-finders and arbiters of the law. Nigel Ley pointed out that magistrates did not take notes of evidence, that defendants in theft cases were often refused legal aid, and that criminal defence solicitors in magistrates' courts were often ignorant of the law, as were magistrates' clerks. Some critics pointed out that magistrates' courts are seen as police courts; magistrates are seen as part of the Establishment and magistrates are not as socially and ethnically diverse as the jury.

A *New Law Journal* editorial ((1999) 149 N.L.J. 549) argued that there were other ways of cutting down the cost and length of jury trials, such as reducing jurors to six, or having them sit in the magistrates' court with lay justices doing the sentencing, or to cutting out the opening statement and permitting the judge to sum up only on law.

This first Bill was heavily defeated in the House of Lords, in January 2000. The Home Secretary replaced it with the Criminal Justice (Mode of Trial) No.2 Bill, which was again defeated in the Lords in autumn 2000. Prior to the 2001 election, Home Secretary Straw insisted that he would use the Parliament Acts to push though a third Bill.

He did not do this because Auld L.J. was part way through his   16–042
comprehensive *Review*. In it, he reiterated the recommendation that the right to elect jury trial should be removed. After consulting on this, the Government received predictable responses from all the groups cited above, raising the same objections that they had already argued many times before. The Government therefore dropped plans to remove the right to elect. Instead, they passed the Criminal Justice Act 2003, doubling magistrates' sentencing powers. This has the potential to shift a mass of the Crown Court case load down into the magistrates' court, thus achieving most of the Government's aims by a different means.

The Right to Elect Trial by Judge Alone

Lord Justice Auld added, however, that the defendant should, in   16–043
serious cases, be entitled to opt out of jury trial by choosing trial by judge alone. We discussed this in our 2001 paper for him.

I have long argued (1991 and 1997) that it is inappropriate to speak of the "right" to jury trial in indictable cases which must go to the Crown Court, because the defendant has no choice. If he pleads not guilty, then he will be tried by judge and jury. He cannot opt for trial by judge alone, or a "bench trial" as it is called in the US. The English legal system is odd among common law systems because the accused does have this choice in the US, Canada, New Zealand and a number of Australian states. Doran and Jackson have examined judge-alone trials not only in Northern Ireland, in the Diplock Courts but in bench trials in other jurisdictions. Lord Justice Auld was persuaded to investigate this procedure in some depth. He found that in some Canadian provinces, up to 90 per cent of defendants opt for a bench trial. In the US it tends to be used where prosecution and defence cannot agree to a plea bargain but Auld L.J. found there are other reasons why some defendants chose trial by judge alone.

- Those who believed themselves innocent in a factually or legally complex case who were anxious for the tribunal to understand their case.
- Defendants with technical defences who wanted fully reasoned decisions which would ease an appeal.
- Defendants charged with offences which attracted public opprobrium, such as sex or violent offences.

- Minorities who considered a judge to be more objective than a jury.
- Where there has been adverse publicity.
- Defendants in cases turning on alleged confessions or identification.
- Where local lower tier judges are well known to and trusted by the legal profession to conduct fair trials.

He recommended that defendants should, with the consent of the court, be able to opt for judge-alone trial in cases tried on indictment. The Government accepted his recommendation, in *Justice for All* (2002), para.4.2. The Criminal Justice Bill 2003 aimed to introduce a procedure for trial by judge alone, where the accused requested it. This clause met opposition from the Conservatives and Liberal Democrats and did not survive into the Act.

The Judge's Right to Order Trial by Judge Alone

16–044   There has long been a concern by some that jury trial is inappropriate in long and complex frauds. Jurors' difficulty in understanding evidence is most acute in fraud trials and was considered by the Roskill Committee on Fraud Trials in 1986. Fraud trials are notoriously long (sometimes over 100 days), expensive and highly complicated. The Committee said:

> "The background against which the frauds are alleged to have been committed—the sophisticated world of high finance and international trading—is probably a mystery to most or all of the jurors, its customs and practices a closed book. Even the language in which the allegedly fraudulent transactions have been conducted will be unfamiliar. A knowledge of accountancy or bookkeeping may be essential to an understanding of the case. If any juror has such knowledge, it is by chance". (para.8.27).

The Committee recommended the jury be abolished in complex criminal fraud cases and be replaced by a Fraud Trials Tribunal of a judge and two lay members.

This debate was revived in 1992, following the Guinness trial and the Blue Arrow fraud trial, lasting over a year and again in 1996, following the acquittals after the Maxwell trial. The suggestion was revived by Labour Home Secretary, Jack Straw, in 1998, in "Juries in Serious Fraud Trials", a Home Office consultation paper. In his *Review*, Auld L.J. considered fraud and other complex cases at length. He said the problem was compounded by the unrepresentative nature of juries, particularly in fraud and other complex cases. Even the Bar Council had acknowledged that it was difficult to find representative juries for long trials. The Serious Fraud Office had commented to him that these trials are often too much for jurors and ill health or claimed ill health is a cause of delay or severance. Auld L.J. listed the arguments for and against juries in cases of serious and complex fraud:

- the jury is a hallowed democratic institution and the defendant's right in serious cases;
- random selection ensures fairness and independence;
- the question is usually one of dishonesty, essentially a matter for the jury, who because of their number and mix are better equipped than a smaller tribunal of professionals;
- there is no research evidence that they cannot cope with long and complex cases or that their decisions are contrary to the evidence;
- there is openness and impartiality in the parties having to explain the case to the jury in simple and digestible form and there is scope for improvement there.

On the other hand

- if juries are the defendant's peers, they should be experienced in the professional or commercial context of the alleged offence;
- the volume and complexity of evidence may make dishonesty difficult to determine;
- the length of such trials is an unreasonable intrusion into jurors' personal and working lives;
- juries in these trials are unrepresentative;
- such long trials are a strain on the defendant, victim and witnesses;
- judges, with legal and forensic expertise, and/or specialist assessors would be better equipped to deal with such cases fairly and expeditiously;
- there would be the benefit of openness, since there would be a publicly reasoned and appealable decision;
- the length of these trials is very costly to the public and unduly delays the efficient disposal of other cases.

He contemplated the alternatives: special juries; judge alone; a panel of judges or a judge and lay members. He recommended that, as an alternative to jury trial in long and complex frauds, the nominated trial judge should be able to direct trial by himself, sitting with lay members or, where the defendant has opted for trial by judge alone, by himself. The Government responded to his recommendation in *Justice for All*. They rejected the idea of recruiting people experienced in complex financial issues because of the difficulty of recruitment so proposed that such cases be tried by judge alone. They estimated this would not affect more than 15–20 trials a year.

Accordingly, the Criminal Justice Act 2003, s.43 allows the prosecution to apply for a judge-only trial in a long and complex fraud case but the Government promised the Opposition that it would not activate this section without further research and consideration. In *Justice for All*, the Government welcomed views on whether the court should have the power to order judge-alone trials in long and complex cases other than fraud.

16–045   Similarly, s.44 of the Criminal Justice Act 2003 allows an application for a judge-only trial where there is a danger of jury tampering. The inclusion of this clause in the Bill resulted from lobbying by the police.

In March 2005 the Jubilee Line Extension corruption trial collapsed in the Old Bailey, after taking almost two years and wasting £60 million of public money. The trial had suffered massive delays and interruptions. One juror had already been removed from the 12, as he was suspected of benefit fraud. The trial finally collapsed when another juror said he could not afford to go on and a third said he was going on a six week holiday. The Attorney-General ordered an immediate inquiry and the Lord Chief Justice said trials should be organised so they took no longer than three months or, exceptionally, six months. The Bar, who oppose removal of jury trial in such cases, supported his remarks. Naturally the case fuelled the revival of arguments in favour of ordering judge-only trials in such cases.

9. Helping the Jury to do their Job—What the Research Tells Us

16–046   In our research for Auld L.J., we made a number of recommendations to help the jury perform their function of finding the facts and applying them to the law as directed by the judge, based on our analysis of all the relevant jury research, including the following (Auld L.J.'s response is bracketed.):

1. If English judges are to continue to sum up the evidence, they should be told not to recite their notes but to draw attention to the main points, to areas of conflict and to how the law applies to the issues of evidence. (Discussed by Auld, with similar recommendations in Chapter 1, p.537).

2. Juries in criminal trials should be given a series of questions to answer as they are in civil trials. (Adopted by Auld L.J.).
3. Juries have a great deal of difficulty in understanding and applying judicial instructions. They should be rewritten by psycholinguists, taking account of the large body of research from the US. (Auld L.J. went further than this, recommending that the judge should not direct the jury on law save by implication in the series of factual questions he puts to them).
4. Jurors should be given written instructions on the law and pre-trial instructions, where possible, as it is illogical and difficult for jurors to receive instructions on what evidence is important *after* they have heard it, as they now are. (Accepted and discussed by Auld, with recommendations accordingly, at p.522–3. Auld L.J. also recommended that judges should use visual aids where possible and be provided with Powerpoint and presentational software accordingly).
5. Certain basic instructions, such as those on the burden and quantum of proof, could be pinned on the jury room wall. (Not discussed).
6. Juries have immense difficulty in understanding the quantum of proof "beyond reasonable doubt". When judges explain it to mean "sure", many jurors look for absolute proof of guilt, which is impossible. The word "sure" should be eliminated from the judges' explanation of BRD. (Not discussed).
7. Juries should be instructed to discuss the evidence before voting as this makes them deliberate more thoroughly. (Not discussed).
8. Real jurors in England and Wales experience a great inhibition against asking questions, often to the detriment of their deliberation. Encouraging jurors to ask questions, take notes occasionally and discuss the evidence at an interim stage may all help to keep them awake and alert and to make sense of the trial, to help them remember the evidence more accurately, to understand the case and make their deliberation more focussed. (Not discussed).

We also made some recommendations to make life more comfortable for jurors, again resulting from our examination of jury research and personal accounts of jurors:

1. Many people resent giving up time for jury service and the abiding memory of most jurors is boredom, waiting for a trial or for legal argument to take place in their absence. In long

trials, the jury trial should proceed in the mornings, while jurors are more alert and legal argument in the afternoons.

2. Heat, cold, boredom and their passive role may reduce jurors' arousal levels. Court managers should check courtroom temperatures and jurors should have breaks.
3. Small discomforts all irritate jurors. Court personnel should be more responsive and polite to them.
4. Jury service can be emotionally and physically stressful.
5. In long trials, we should copy the US system of sitting two or more "alternates" alongside the real jury, in case of illness or indisposition.

Auld L.J. adopted this last recommendation but the Government rejected it. He summarised our findings and made a number of suggestions for keeping the jury better informed and for providing them with better facilities, including working facilities, so they could carry on their business while waiting around. In *Justice for All* the Government responded very briefly. They promised to continue their reforms of jury service to keep jurors better informed and ensure their time was not wasted.

In 2004, the Home Office published findings on "Jurors' perceptions, understanding, confidence and satisfaction in the jury system: a study in six courts", by Matthews, Hancock and Briggs. The key findings were:

- Most respondents gained a more positive view of jury trial.
- Confidence in the jury system was closely associated with perceived fairness of the process and ability to consider evidence from different perspectives.
- A jury's representation of a broad spectrum of views was a key factor in jurors' confidence in the Crown Court trial.
- Jurors were very impressed with the professionalism and helpfulness of court personnel, especially the performance, commitment and competence of judges.
- The main impediment to understanding was legal terminology. Jurors felt evidence could sometimes be presented more clearly.
- Over half said they would be happy to do service again, reporting a greater understanding of Crown Court trial and a feeling of having performed an important civic duty.

10. Research into Jury Decision Making

16–047   Most research into jury deliberation and decision making is conducted by constructing shadow juries or mock juries. They may be

534

asked to sit in on a real trial, or, more usually, to watch an edited audio or videotape of a real trial. The drawbacks of this type of research are well known. The mock jurors often do not reflect composition of a real jury, as they are paid students. They are volunteers not conscripts, like real jurors. They usually sit through a three hour video rather than a two day trial. Most importantly, they are not under the same pressure as real jurors, since their verdict will not affect a real victim and the liberty and reputation of a real defendant.

Nevertheless, this is all that researchers can hope for, since researchers are banned from sitting in on jury deliberations in virtually all jurisdictions. Apart from this, a researcher's presence is bound to affect deliberations. In some jurisdictions in the US, researchers have been allowed to audio-tape jurors' deliberations.

The 2005 DCA consultation paper, "Jury Research and Impropriety", discussed above, asked whether researchers should be allowed into the jury room. This question is rather pointless, I suggest, as virtually no respondent is likely to favour that and Parliament is highly unlikely to permit it. The paper also asks whether research should be permitted into jury deliberations. This could be conducted by asking jurors questions after they have served. Again, questioning jurors is not permitted in most jurisdictions, although many academics have for years advocated the amendment of s.8 of the Contempt Act to permit this, as explained above. In our paper, we examined all English language jury research, worldwide, up to 2001; we also examined juror's personal accounts of jury service to test the cross-cultural applicability of foreign research, most of which is American. Among our findings, summarising this vast body of research were:

1. The most popular theory on how jurors individually consider the trial and verdict is the cognitive story model. The juror reorganises information into a narrative story by using the trial evidence, prior knowledge (which, as real jurors' accounts show, may be wrong) and what makes a complete story. Accounts of real English and Welsh jurors strongly support the story model and the research finding that the adversarial trial process presents evidence in a way which hampers the juror's construction of a story.
2. It is questionable how effective the average juror is at judging the truthfulness of a witness based on demeanour but real jurors' accounts show that many of them are influenced by whether they approve or disapprove of witnesses.
3. Although *Turnbull* allows a warning that even truthful and impressive witnesses can be in error, some American jurisdictions allow a much greater input from experts on the

reliability of eyewitness evidence and other expert evaluation of different types of evidence.
4. The accounts of real jurors show they are frustrated by the
fact that pieces of evidence have been excluded from the story
and they speculate on what this evidence might be. They
sometimes refer to jury trial as a game.
5. Jurors may be disproportionately influenced by evidence
they are told to ignore and are influenced by previous convictions.
6. Joining defendants and multiple charges can confuse juries.
7. Juries are much better at remembering evidence than individual jurors but real juries sometimes argue in the jury room
over the contents of the evidence.
8. Since juries consider the evidence more thoroughly when
they are not "verdict driven", it may be thought desirable to
encourage them to discuss the evidence thoroughly before
taking a vote on verdict. (The same point made by New
Zealand Law Commission.)

In the meantime, a great deal could have been learned from our
survey of the existing mass of research and from such projects as
the New Zealand Law Commission's research which questioned
real jurors. There is much that could be done without the need
even to question real jurors. For example, I was quite alarmed to
find, in the course of our research for Auld L.J., that judges' specimen directions to jurors are simply drafted by a pair of judges.
They have never been tested on real people. I would have thought
that doing so was an obvious and sensible suggestion but this and
the other practical suggestions by Auld L.J. and ourselves seem to
have disappeared down some black hole, by 2005. Other suggestions, like using alternate jurors, have been flatly rejected.

BIBLIOGRAPHY
16–048 J. Airs and A. Shaw, "Jury Excusal and Deferral", Home Office
Research and Statistics Directorate Research Study No.102, 1999,
available from the Home Office Research and Statistics
Directorate, archived publications: *www.homeoffice.gov.uk/rds*
Lord Justice Auld, *Review of the Criminal Courts of England and Wales*
(2001): *www.criminal-courts-review.org.uk*, Chapter 5.
The Criminal Justice Act 2003: *www.opsi.gov.uk/acts*
P. Darbyshire, "Notes of a Lawyer Juror" (1990) 140 N.L.J. 1264.
P. Darbyshire, "The Lamp That Shows That Freedom Lives—is it
worth the candle?" [1991] Crim. L.R. 740.
P. Darbyshire, A. Maughan and A. Stewart, "What Can the English
Legal System Learn from Jury Research Published up to 2001?

Criminal Courts Review website: *www.criminal-courts-review.org.uk* (click on "research into juries"). It is summarised in "What Can We Learn from Published Jury Research? Findings for the Criminal Courts Review 2001" [2001] Crim. L.R. 970.

Department for Constitutional Affairs, "Jury Research and Impropriety", Consultation Paper CP/04/05, archived on the DCA website: *www.dca.gov.uk*

P. Devlin, *Trial by Jury* (1956).

S. Doran and J. Jackson, "The Case for Jury Waiver" [1997] Crim. L.R. 155 (on judge-only trials).

J. Jackson and S. Doran, *Judge Without Jury: Diplock Trials in the Adversary System* (1995).

"Jury Summoning Guidance", December 2003, an archived consultation paper on the DCA website: *www.dca.gov.uk*. The Guidance for Summoning Officers is also on the website of Her Majesty's Court Service (The Court Service).

Justice for All (2002), white paper. This set out the Government's responses to Auld L.J.'s *Review of the Criminal Courts of England and Wales* and explained Government plans to enact the Criminal Justice Act 2003 and to develop criminal justice policy: *www.dca.gov.uk*. (click on publications, then white papers).

N. Ley, on the superiority of Crown Court trial: (1999) 149 N.L.J. 1316.

A. Majid, "Jury Still Out on Deaf Jurors" (2004) 154 N.L.J. 278.

R. Matthews, L. Hancock and D. Briggs, "Jurors' perceptions, understanding, confidence and satisfaction in the jury system: a study in six courts", Home Office website, Research, Development and Statistics Directorate: *www.homeoffice.gov.uk/rds*

New Zealand Law Commission Report 69, *Juries in Criminal Trials*, 2001: *www.lawcom.govt.nz*

Report of the Departmental Committee on Jury Service (The Morris Report) CMND 2627 (HMSO 1965).

"The Roskill Report", *Fraud Trials Committee Report* (1986) HMSO.

Wolchover and Heaton-Armstrong's arguments are at (1998) 148 N.L.J. 1614, and see 150 N.L.J. 158.

The attempts to suppress Professor Baldwin's findings on the Crown Prosecution Service are discussed by Professor Andrew Ashworth in the editorial of the *Criminal Law Review* for August 1997 (Baldwin's findings are discussed in Chapter 10 of this book, above).

There are thousands of reports of jury research in the English language. Those relevant to the ELS are reviewed in our 2001 paper but there are too many references to list here.

SOURCES FOR UPDATING THIS CHAPTER

16–049   Online updates to this book: *http://www.sweetandmaxwell.co.uk/ academic/updates/darbyshire/index.html*

The Department for Constitutional Affairs: *www.dca.gov.uk* (see press releases and publications).

The Home Office Research and Statistics Directorate: *www.homeoffice. gov.uk/rds*

Newspapers from databases and archived articles on individual newspaper websites.

Part VI: Access to Justice

17. Legal Services from 2000

"The effective replacement in civil litigation of public funding by the conditional fee agreement is in direct contradiction of the message we received when the Human Rights Act was introduced, namely that rights were coming home. If Human Rights have come home, they are largely unemployed. There is all too often no wherewithal to protect or enforce them. The conditional fee provides at best a fig leaf to cover the nakedness of the legal system in protecting those in need of protection." (The Hon. Mr Justice Lightman, of the High Court, Chancery Division in the Edward Bramley Memorial Lecture University of Sheffield, April 4, 2003.)

"Call this access to justice?" (Title of a public meeting called by the Access to Justice Alliance, April 2005.)

If the Rule of Law states that everyone should be equal before the law then, I would argue, this implies that everyone should have equal access to the law, the courts and legal services. Further, the law presumes that we all know the law so I would suggest that one of the requirements of a civilised modern democracy must be the promotion of and access to information on our legal rights and duties. The first principle was broadly accepted in the English legal system from the middle of the twentieth century. It is supported by the European Convention on Human Rights, which was imported into English law in 2000. Article 6 requires fair trials and sets out the principles for the requirement of legal services in civil and criminal cases. It is set out fully in Chapter 10 on criminal procedure, above. The section relevant to legal representation is as follows:

17–001

"In the determination of his civil rights and obligations or of any criminal charge against him, everyone is entitled to a fair and public hearing . . . Everyone charged with a criminal offence has the following minimum rights . . .

b. to have adequate time and facilities for the preparation of his defence;

c. to defend himself in person or through legal assistance of his own choosing or, if he has not sufficient means to pay for legal assistance, to be given it free when the interests of justice so require . . ."

As can be seen, Art.6 requires representation in criminal cases where the interests of justice require it. It also requires legal help or representation in civil cases, according to what the litigant needs to ensure them "equality of arms" with the opposition. This must be determined on a case by case basis, as is illustrated by the cases discussed under Art.6, in Chapter 4, above.

The Department for Constitutional Affairs (DCA) (formerly Lord Chancellor's Department) is responsible for legal services, with the Lord Chancellor and his junior ministers answerable in Parliament.

17–002 As we shall see, there has been much use of the phrase "access to justice" in the 1990s. This means, broadly: being able to make full use of legal rights, through adequate legal services, *i.e.* advice, assistance and representation, regardless of means; also, the ability to make full use of the court structure and rights of appeal. Legal services are dealt with in this chapter and access to justice via the civil courts is dealt with in Chapter 9 on civil procedure, above.

The Royal Commission on Legal Services 1979 defined legal services as "services which should be available to any person or organisation requiring advice or assistance of a legal character, whether payment for the service is made from public or private funds".

Before the twentieth century, although there were various schemes for providing representation to the poor, these were not put on a systematic, state funded basis until civil legal aid was introduced during World War II, for the armed forces and later for the civilian population. In 1945, the Rushcliffe Committee considered how best to provide legal services for those who could not afford them. The legal aid scheme established after this was to provide for services through the private practice lawyer claiming a fee from the State. This model of delivery of publicly funded legal services is sometimes referred to as the judicare model. Their second recommendation, for a network of legal advice centres staffed by fulltime state salaried lawyers was never implemented. At no time did Rushcliffe contemplate developing a National Legal Service, along the lines of the National Health Service.

17–003 They considered whether a state department or local authorities should administer the system but, concerned that both of these had an interest in so many cases, chose to leave administration in the hands of the lawyers. Indeed, when civil legal aid was created, by the Legal Aid and Advice Act 1949, the Law Society administered it. Criminal Legal Aid arrived later, also delivered through private practice lawyers but dispensed via the court. Legal advice was provided under a different scheme. By 1988 the various schemes for these different types of legal aid were put on a systematic basis in one statute, the Legal Aid Act 1988. At the same time, lawyer's fingers were taken off the purse strings. The Legal Aid Board was created to fund and manage the civil legal aid scheme and legal advice. Criminal legal aid, as before, was dispensed by the criminal courts, normally the court clerks in magistrates' courts. All types of aid were available only to those who passed a means test, those who could afford to contribute being required to do so. The means tests were different for each of the three and civil legal aid and criminal legal aid were subject to merits tests.

Despite all of this provision, it proved to be inadequate. Sociologists and lawyers in the 1960s and 1970s exposed the phenomenon of "unmet legal need", which occurs when someone has a legal problem which goes unsolved. The causes were identified (see below) and alternative legal services developed in the voluntary sector, outside the legal aid scheme, in an attempt to fulfil some of those needs. By the 1980s and 1990s, the legal aid budget was increasing out of control but a decreasing percentage of the population was eligible for it. It was clear that, whichever political party was elected, in 1997, it would have to curb the legal aid budget and target it better to provide the right type of help to the right people. When New Labour were elected, in 1997, they devised this radical new scheme, explained here. I come back to the background of the new scheme after describing it.

1. The Access to Justice Act 1999—The Statutory Framework Replacing Legal Aid from 2000

Civil legal aid was largely replaced, in April 2000, by the new **17–004** scheme of publicly funded legal services, provided for in the Access to Justice Act 1999. Criminal legal aid was replaced by criminal defence services, also provided for in the Act, in April 2001. This replaces the whole framework for legal aid established by the Legal Aid Act 1988. The Lord Chancellor, who is responsible for legal services, explained his plans for these schemes in a white paper, *Modernising Justice*, which was published alongside the Access to

Justice Bill, in December 1998 and in numerous consultation papers and speeches. In this section, I explain the Act and its mischief; I then explain the new scheme in practice; I then examine its background in detail and finally examine evaluations of the new system. Notice that, although legal aid was dismantled and replaced with this new scheme of legal services, everyone still refers to it as "legal aid".

The Legal Services Commission

17–005   This was established by s.1 of the Access to Justice Act 1999. It replaced the Legal Aid Board as the body administering legal services. It consists of seven to twelve members, appointed by the Lord Chancellor, according to their knowledge of social conditions, work of the courts, consumer affairs and management. Section 3 empowers the Legal Services Commission (LSC) to make contracts, undertake inquiries and advise the Lord Chancellor.

The Community Legal Service

17–006   Section 4 requires the Commission to establish and fund a Community Legal Service (CLS) "for the purpose of promoting the availability to individuals of services of the descriptions specified . . . and, in particular, for securing (within the resources made available) . . . that individuals have access to services that effectively meet their needs". Section 4(2) describes these services as: providing information about the law and the legal system and the availability of legal services, advice and help in preventing, settling or resolving disputes and enforcing decisions. Section 4(4) provides that everyone involved in the CLS should have regard to the desirability of promoting improvements in the range and quality of services provided by the CLS and in making them accessible and appropriate to their nature and importance and of achieving the swift and fair resolution of disputes. This means lawyers and other "service providers" are bound by this duty too.

The LSC has a duty, under s.4(6), to find out about the need for and provision of services, plan what needs to be done and help other bodies to plan how to use resources to meet those needs. It is empowered to set and monitor standards and provide accreditation schemes for service providers (this means lawyers and others providing legal services) (s.4(6)–(8)). Under s.5, the Lord Chancellor provides the budget for the LSC to maintain a Community Legal Service Fund. The LSC must aim to secure value for money. They may fund services by entering into contracts, making grants and loans, establishing bodies to provide services, or themselves provide services, etc. (s.6). They may provide different services for different areas of England and Wales and the Lord Chancellor may direct them to provide particular services.

The Funding Code

Under s.8, the LSC must prepare a Funding Code, subject to the 17–007
Lord Chancellor's approval, setting out the criteria under which it is
prepared to provide services and providing the form and content of
applications for funding. The Code was established some years ago.
Section 10 provides for regulations as to when recipients should pay
fixed fees or contributions for the legal services they receive and s.11
provides that costs ordered against a funded individual should be
kept to a reasonable amount, taking into account his resources and
making allowances for his clothes, furniture and tools of trade.

The Criminal Defence Service

Under s.12, the LSC must and did establish a Criminal Defence 17–008
Service (CDS) for the purpose of securing that individuals involved
in criminal investigations or criminal proceedings have access to
"such advice, assistance and representation as the interests of justice
require". It can set up an accreditation and monitoring scheme and
fund such advice and assistance as it considers appropriate, by
making contracts, grants, loans or establishing and maintaining
advice and assistance bodies, or employing people to provide advice
and assistance. It can fund advice and assistance by different means
in different areas of England and Wales (s.13). Section 15 provides
that the represented individual may select any representative to act
for him and it may be from a prescribed group *but* the applicant may
not be restricted to a person employed by the LSC (notice this is a
requirement of Art.6 of the Convention). This means a client cannot
be confined to accepting a state employed public defender. Under
s.16, the LSC must prepare a code of conduct for its employees and
funded providers (meaning lawyers and other advisers and representatives), which includes a duty of non-discrimination and duties
to the court, etc. Under s.17, where anyone is represented in a criminal court, the court may ask them to pay for some or all of their representation. Under Sch.3, the criminal courts are empowered to
grant representation.

Conditional Fee Agreements (No Win No Fee Contracts)

Under Part II of the Act, Conditional Fee Agreements (CFAs) are 17–009
defined, in s.58(2) as "an agreement with a person providing advocacy or litigation services which provides for his fee and expenses,
or any part of them, to be payable only in specified circumstances".
This generally means an agreement that a fee will be paid only if the
lawyer wins the client's case. Such contracts are prohibited in relation to criminal proceedings and virtually all family proceedings.
Section 29 provides that insurance premiums for policies insuring
against the risk of losing the case may be recovered in costs awarded

by the court. CFAs are described and then discussed at length below and also discussed in Chapter 9 on civil procedure, above.

Legal Services Consultative Panel

17–010   This small panel is appointed by the Lord Chancellor, with "the duty of assisting in the maintenance and development of standards in the education, training and conduct of persons offering legal services . . . and making recommendations to (the Lord Chancellor)". They are obliged to advise the Lord Chancellor when he calls on them.

Modernising Justice—The "Mischief" of the Act

17–011   The Access to Justice Act 1999, like most modern statutes, really just explains the framework of legal services. We need to turn to the white paper, *Modernising Justice* (1998) published alongside the Bill, for an explanation of the reasoning behind it and the detail of the scheme now in place. The full document is archived on the DCA website (*www.dca.gov.uk*).

The Government identified these problems in the old legal aid scheme:

- inadequate access to quality information—poor co-ordination in services;
- inability to control and target legal aid;

The legal advice sector had grown randomly. The Community Legal Service would:

- develop a system for assessing needs and priorities and monitoring standards;
- co-ordinate plans of various funders;
- treat the advice sector and advice by lawyers under one budget.

A new Legal Services Commission would:

- develop local, regional and national plans to match provision to needs;
- report annually to the Lord Chancellor;
- manage the CLS fund;
- make contracts, fund traditional or other types of provider;
- take account of local views;
- develop partnerships with local authorities, *etc.*

The immediate project in implementing the new scheme in 1999 was to:

- develop systems for assessing need;
- develop core quality criteria;
- build a CLS website on legal advice.

The LSC would develop a quality system by

- developing the scheme of contracting with providers;
- kitemarking non-lawyers.

As for the legal profession, the Government would:

- cut lawyers' restrictive practices (see Chapter 13, above);
- improve standards;
- make legal services more affordable through:
    - — legal insurance;
    - — regulating cost;
    - — expanding provision for conditional fees.

Chapter 6 of the white paper, on criminal defence, said the Government's objectives were to:

- ensure a fair hearing, by putting the defendant on an equal footing with the prosecution;
- protect the interest of the defendant;
- maintain the defendant's confidence and effective participation.

The CDS must reflect domestic law (Police and Criminal Evidence Act) and international law (Art.6 of the ECHR). Weaknesses of the old criminal legal aid system were identified in the white paper as:

- cost;
- the lawyers' pay framework was outdated because of:
    - — inappropriate financial incentives;
    - — a few disproportionately expensive cases;
- the criminal legal aid means test was flawed;
- the legal aid scheme was highly fragmented.

Fundamental reform was necessary. The Government would replace criminal legal aid with a Criminal Defence Service. It would:

- be separate from CLS, with a separate budget but both would be run by the Legal Services Commission;
- cover all services provided under criminal legal aid;

- develop more efficient ways of procuring services, through:
  - — contracts with accredited private practice lawyers;
  - — salaried defenders on the model piloted in Scotland;
  - — restricting client choice to a duty solicitor or accredited solicitor;
- abolish means testing but target rich defendants; and
- establish pilot contracts for representation in youth courts.

The LSC replaced the Legal Aid Board in April 2000 and the Criminal Defence Service was established by April 2001.

2. Developing the New Legal Services Model in Practice

17–012   Thirteen Regional Legal Service Committees were established in 1997–1998 and published their *Assessment of Need for Legal Services* by July 1999. They had organised their priorities. They identified particular groups suffering from an unmet need for legal services: those living in rural areas, the elderly, people with mental health problems, people whose first language was not English and those appearing before employment tribunals.

The Present System for Civil Cases

The community legal service
17–013   In May 1999, the Government published a consultation paper on how they would develop this institution (DCA website). It made the following points.

- People needed basic information and advice on rights and responsibilities, not necessarily to go to court.
- 6,000 professionals (lawyers) and 30,000 volunteers at Law Centres and other advice centres, such as Citizens' Advice Bureaux, etc. provided this for £250 million pounds per year.
- This was enough but service was fragmented and uncoordinated.

The paper gave case studies demonstrating how difficult it was for people with certain problems to obtain satisfactory advice. The lack of an effective referral network meant people got initial advice and were sent away so the new legal services network should include:

- lawyers;
- professionals outside private practice;

- advice workers;
- para-legals with specialist knowledge, *e.g.* Trading Standards Officers;
- volunteers in Citizens' Advice Bureaux, etc.

The CLS should provide information, advice and assistance. The need for legal services varied geographically. Research disclosed no area where strategy had been developed jointly by different funders. Time was wasted by advice agencies demonstrating the quality of their services to their different funders. For instance, one Asian women's group had ten funders. Forty per cent of its manager's time was spent on reporting to them. Quantifying need was difficult. Statistics indicated that unmet need for legal services resulted not from inadequate provision but from "lack of access to appropriate adequate help of adequate quality".

The LSC is the new co-ordinating body. It took over from the Legal Aid Board in 2000. It works with "Community Legal Service Partnerships", targeting funds to local needs. They bring together different funders (*e.g.* local authorities, charities) and providers of legal and advice services (*e.g.* solicitors, paralegals) to organise funding and delivery with the aim of meeting the needs they have identified. By 2002, there were CLS Partnerships for every area of the country.

Core criteria were developed for the legal service providers' quality mark from 1999. A legal services website was developed from 1999 but the Government acknowledged, in the consultation paper, that only two per cent of social classes D/E were online. Historically, this group has been identified as suffering from unmet legal need. The CLS was officially launched in April 2000.

Contracting

The introduction of general civil contracting brought a massive shift in funding of legal services. Whereas, under the old legal aid scheme, any solicitor could give legally aided services, providers of legal help (solicitors and advice agencies) are now limited to those who have a contract with the LSC to deal with a specified number of cases. To get this, an advice agency or firm of solicitors must demonstrate they satisfy the quality criteria, based on an audit. For instance, they need to show that they have a satisfactory management system, that staff work is closely supervised and their systems are computerised. The LSC is required to spend around a tenth of its budget on contracts with providers in the not-for-profit sector, such as charities providing advice.

The predecessor to contracting was the franchising system, introduced by the Conservative Government by about 1994, whereby

17–014

providers could get a franchise to provide services from the Legal Aid Board but did not have to do so. Franchised solicitors' firms and agencies were already subject to rigorous quality criteria and auditing so they became the first contracted providers under the new scheme. A provider may have a general civil contract, a family contract, if on the family panel, or a controlled work contract, in areas such as immigration, mental health, community care, public law and actions against the police. The LSC is thinking of adding new categories, in 2005. Every contracted supplier gets regular payments based on monthly reports to the LSC. Their work is audited by inspection of sample files. Contracted suppliers such as solicitors can call specialist telephone lines for free help in advising clients. For instance, *Shelter* provides training courses and advice on homelessness, possession proceedings, security of tenure and disrepair; the Public Law Project provides help on human rights; the Joint Council for the Welfare of Immigrants provides training and advice to contracted advisers on immigration and nationality law and asylum. The first barristers' chambers to be awarded a contract for advice and representation in employment, immigration and housing law was 2 Garden Court, Temple. Contractors should not take on more cases than are authorised under their contract but if an expensive case takes them beyond their prescribed limit, the CLS will pay for work actually and reasonably done.

Contracts can only be granted to fulfil a perceived need so in 2001, there was an excess of applicants for contracts in immigration work and the LSC announced that applicants would have to demonstrate that they would fulfil a particular need.

Funding certificates can be granted to firms without the relevant contract in special cases. For instance, if a non-contracted solicitor has been working privately for a client and then that person becomes eligible for CLS funding, the solicitor may apply.

The Funding Code—setting out types of legal service the Government is prepared to fund

17–015   This was launched at the same time. Obviously, the Lord Chancellor has the flexibility, under the 1999 Act, to alter the list of what services can be funded, from time to time. This is the scheme in 2005. It provides seven levels of service, which may be provided in different ways and may attract different eligibility and remuneration:

- legal help;
- help at court (these replace the old legal advice and assistance, under the legal aid scheme);
- approved family help (general help or mediation);

- legal representation (investigative help or full representation);
- support funding (either investigative or litigation support);
- family mediation;
- such other services as are authorised by the Lord Chancellor.

As you can see, these statutory categories are quite a mouthful, which is why everybody still calls them "legal aid". Legal help, help at court and certain types of representation are classified as controlled work and can only be carried out by lawyers or legal advisers with a general civil contract. These providers are fully responsible for granting and withdrawing help in these cases. Funding for most cases requiring representation, approved family help and support funding is granted by a certificate awarded by the Commission. The General Funding Code applies to any application for funding. In addition, there are category specific criteria which apply to very expensive cases, judicial review, claims against public authorities, clinical negligence, housing, family, mental health and immigration cases. Following the Court of Appeal's warning that mediation should be tried before judicial review was applied for, as explained in Chapter 12, above, ADR must be considered before funding can be granted for a judicial review.

An exception to the Funding Code criteria may be made in certain deserving cases. For example, as a result of cases arising from deaths in custody, described in Chapter 4 on human rights, above, and *R. (Khan) v SS for Health* [2003] EWCA Civ 1129, the Legal Services Commission extended exceptional funding to representation to bereaved relatives at inquests where an agent of the state (*e.g.* hospital, police station) was involved and Art.2 of the ECHR was engaged.

Eight categories of service are excluded, under Sch.2 to the Access to Justice Act so people will have to pay for them privately, for instance, by persuading a lawyer to act under a conditional fee agreement, or get help from a charity, or a Citizens Advice Bureau (CAB), or from a lawyer acting *pro bono*, or will be left to represent themselves:

- personal injury, apart from clinical negligence, death or damage to property;
- conveyancing;
- boundary disputes;
- wills;
- trust law;
- defamation;
- company or partnership law;
- other business matters.

17–016   Applying the Code criteria means considering the prospects of success of the case and the cost-benefit. The *prospects of success* are evaluated for those clients applying for funding for representation. This means the likelihood of a successful outcome in the proceedings. Generally, at least a 50 per cent prospect of success is required but funding may be granted to borderline cases if, for example, the case has overwhelming importance to the client, has a wider public interest, is a human rights judicial review, involves housing possession, domestic violence or children. The Code provides various cost benefit tests, which usually mean comparing likely cost with likely damages obtainable. This replaces the merits test, under the old civil legal aid scheme.

Investigative help and representation will be refused if the case is suitable for a Conditional Fee Agreement (CFA). Support funding is provided for under the Code. It tops up privately funded personal injury claims, for instance to fund an initial investigation into the claim to establish whether it is worth proceeding under a CFA.

17–017   The Lord Chancellor announced the *priorities* of the new CLS, such as special Children Act proceedings, civil proceedings where the client is at real and immediate risk of loss of life or liberty, social welfare issues which enable people to climb out of social exclusion, domestic violence, child welfare and serious proceedings against public authorities. Cases with a wider public interest have preferential treatment under the Code so even if a case falls into an excluded category it may qualify, even if it has only borderline prospects of success. Significant human rights cases are prioritised.

The Lord Chancellor set up a specific budget for very high cost cases, where costs are likely to exceed £25,000. These are considered by the Special Cases Unit of the Commission. Each of these cases has a special contract and there must be a case plan and fully costed stages. For example a public law Children Act case involving several children and requiring expert reports, or a multi-party action or an action against the police might fall into this category.

Personal injuries, for which legal aid had been available, were removed from the scheme, because the Government considered that most of these cases can be funded through CFAs. This was highly controversial, as I explain below. Clinical negligence cases and actions against the police for tort remain within scope of the fund.

Funding for tribunal cases and ADR

17–018   Note that funding is now extended to representation before some tribunals, such as the Immigration Adjudicators and the Asylum and Immigration Tribunal and the General and Special Commissioners of Income Tax, whereas legal aid had not been available under the old pre-1999 Scheme. The only ADR specifically provided for is mediation but this is likely to be extended and will generally now be funded under legal help or representation. For instance, Early Neutral Evaluation can be funded in this way. Arbitration can be funded, whereas it could not have been provided under the old legal aid scheme. The Commission actively encourages the wider use of ADR, especially in the field of clinical negligence. If a funded client refuses an offer by the other side to enter ADR without good reason, the Commission may limit funding on the case.

Financial eligibility limits

These are updated by regulations, every April, as were the old legal aid means tests. Only clients with very low incomes and capital are entitled to fully funded legal services. Those whose income or capital fall above certain limits will have to pay a contribution towards certain (but not all) legal services, assessed according to means. This is the same as the old legal aid scheme. The Access to Justice Act preserves the statutory charge. This means that the CLS may place a first "charge" on any real property, such as a house, recovered or preserved in funded proceedings. The logic behind this is to ensure people pay towards the cost of their cases if they are able; it encourages people to act reasonably and not to incur excessive legal costs and it puts them in a similar position to a privately paying client.   **17–019**

Conditional fee agreements

Legal representation or investigative help will not be granted in cases suitable for a CFA. Distinguish a CFA from a Contingency Fee Agreement, which is illegal in England and Wales but well known in the US, whereby the lawyer takes a percentage of any damages won. Conditional fees were introduced by the Conservatives in the Courts and Legal Services Act 1990 but widened in scope by the 1999 Act. All civil proceedings may be funded by CFAs, except specified family proceedings.   **17–020**

The Quality Mark

This was launched in April 2000. It is a symbol which the accredited quality providers are allowed to display. This includes over 6,000 solicitors' offices, CABx and other advice centres, websites and the Bar. A Specialist Quality Mark was introduced in 2002.   **17–021**

CLS Direct

The CLS website was launched in 2000, providing a directory of legal services. In 2004, it was relaunched as *www.clsdirect.org.uk*. Citizens Advice provide some advice online. In 2004, the Government launched a self-help website, on debt and tax credits.   **17–022**

CLS information points

17–023   These are available in libraries and law school advice clinics, providing information leaflets.

Telephone advice lines

17–024   These were piloted from 2000. Advisors give a full casework service, as they would with face to face contact. Contracts were granted to a variety of advisers and they initially covered debt, welfare benefits, education and housing. In 2004, Community Legal Service Direct was launched, on a national telephone helpline and a website. Anyone could get information about legal problems and sources of help. Those eligible for legal aid could also get telephone advice on benefits, debt and education.

A variety of methods of delivery

17–025   The CLS keeps announcing novel methods of delivering legal services, some funded by its Partnership Innovation Project, such as a virtual law centre, a work related death advice service, community outreach projects funded by Age Concern, projects for young people, the disabled, ethnic minority communities, women in rural areas and so on.

The New System in Criminal Cases

17–026   In 2000–2001, the Government published several consultation papers on the CDS, which was launched in April 2001. They announced proposals to develop a system of *public defenders* directly employed by the Legal Services Commission but clients are generally able to choose between them and any private practice lawyer, (choice is required by Convention, Art.6, see above) except in cases like serious fraud, where they would be limited to specially qualified lawyers. The first four Public Defenders' Offices were introduced as pilots in March 2001 and there were eight by 2004. For four years, the pilots were the subject of a full review headed by Professors Lee Bridges and Avrom Scherr, two of the most eminent experts in the field of legal services.

A professional Code of Conduct was approved by Parliament in March 2001. It seeks to guarantee minimum standards of behaviour: It imposes duties to:

- protect the interests of the client;
- act with integrity and independence;
- act with impartiality and avoid discrimination;
- respect confidentiality;

- the court;
- avoid conflicts of interest;
- not to offer or accept certain payments.

It also contains rules in relation to:

- their relationship with the legal profession;
- change of legal representative;
- withdrawal of legal representative;
- public interest disclosure;
- excessive caseload;
- standards of conduct.

From 2001, all solicitors' firms undertaking publicly funded criminal defence had to have a contract with the CDS. Only solicitors working to quality standards are eligible for a contract. They are paid agreed monthly amounts, with claims set off against payments. A serious fraud panel was established in 2000. From 2000, the Commission introduced individual case contracts in "Very High Cost Criminal Cases", which are controlled in the same way as very high cost civil cases.

Defendants are allowed to make a reasonable change at any time. The decision will remain in the hands of the court because the judge or magistrates are free from any accusation of economic interest. At a Crown Court, each resident judge usually has a pile of such applications to deal with, every week.

Means and merits test

As announced in *Modernising Justice,* although there is an "interests of justice" merit test (*i.e.* that the case is more than trivial), Labour's original intention was to scrap the means test for representation in magistrates' courts. This has had to be reinstated, because the plan turned out to be too expensive (see below). The Crown Court has power to make a Recovery of Defence Costs Order of up to the full amount of defence costs at the conclusion of the case. Investigations into the defendant's means are undertaken by the LSC The aim is to identify defendants who may have the means to contribute, including criminal assets. The defendant's assets may be frozen pending the outcome of trial. A spouse's assets are taken into account if it appears assets have been deliberately moved. This criminal tactic was the norm under the old legal aid scheme, which explains why many very wealthy fraudsters used to be granted legal aid.

17–027

3. Background to the Reforms—Why was Legal Aid scrapped?

17–028   Throughout the 1990s, both the Conservative Government then their Labour successors were seriously concerned that something radical had to be done to reform the provision of legal services. Why?

- The cost was "spiralling out of control", according to the Conservative Lord Chancellor, Lord Mackay, legal aid was the only demand-led draw on the Treasury. Some years in the 1990s, the cost rose by around 20 per cent, despite the fact that fewer people were being legally aided. Separate representation for children, provided by the Children Act 1989 and the development of duty solicitor schemes in police stations and the magistrates' courts were just two items which accelerated the cost increase. The media were swift to point out that some people who were apparently very wealthy got legal aid. One example was the Maxwells, whose legal aid bill for defence in their fraud trial was over £14.5 million.
- Unmet legal need was identified by social research and social welfare lawyers in the 1970s and never satisfied by 2000. It was caused by:
  - the high cost of legal fees;
  - fear of lawyers, fear of cost;
  - lawyers' lack of training and unwillingness to serve poor clients' needs for advice in welfare law;
  - the inaccessibility of lawyers' offices to poor or rural clients;
  - the creation of new legal rights without the funding to enforce them;
  - people's ignorance that the law could solve their problem;
  - the fact that the legal aid scheme omitted certain services, such as representation at tribunals.
- Funders were unco-ordinated. Legal aid was designed to deliver legal services through the medium of private practice barristers and solicitors so alternative legal services, listed below, received very little of the huge legal aid budget and they were dependent on a precarious mix of sources, such as charities, local authorities and other government departments.
- Criminal legal aid was administered unevenly. Research showed that the "Widgery criteria", merits test was applied inconsistently by different magistrates' courts. The Audit

Commission criticised them eight years running for failure to apply the means test properly. Kenneth Noye was convicted of murder at the Old Bailey in 2000. An inquiry was held into why he was granted legal aid when he was so apparently wealthy, largely as a result of a life of crime. A Court Service inquiry led to the resignation of one official and the disciplining of another.

- Fat cat lawyers, as Lord Chancellor Irvine called them, were charging the Legal Aid Board exorbitant fees (see below).

In 1999, Hazel Genn published a survey of how people solve their legal problems: *Paths to Justice*. She found that people were generally extraordinarily ignorant about their legal rights and obligations.

The Access to Justice scheme was quite visionary and radical. It was first announced in the Labour party policy paper, *Access to Justice*, in 1995. They had the simple idea of finding out how much money was spent on legal aid (by the State) plus the great variety of alternative legal services in England and Wales (by charities, local authorities and other government departments) and working out what people's legal needs were and how they could best be fulfilled, within this overall budget, whether through private practice lawyers or alternatives. Thus they disposed of the assumption underlying the old legal aid scheme that legal services should be delivered through the medium of the private practice lawyer. Lawyers and "alternative" providers were to be funded from the same legal services budget.

4. "Alternative" Legal Services

Because the shortcomings of the legal aid scheme and the causes **17–029** of unmet legal need were identified since the 1970s, alternatives to private practice lawyers had been developed by radical lawyers, charities and others to try and fulfil these needs. Many of these can no longer be seen as alternatives because they have now been absorbed into mainstream, if they have succeeded in getting a contract with the CLS.

- From 1970 law centres were very gradually established in poor areas, with a shop front image, where employed lawyers and paralegals provide advice and representation on such matters as welfare law and immigration. They have always suffered from vulnerable funding. Those financed by local authorities found they were biting the hand that fed them, when they acted for groups suffering bad public housing. Law centre funding was sporadic and sometimes they would have to close temporarily. By 2005 there are 60 law centres.

- Citizens' Advice Bureaux. The Rushcliffe Committee recommended that they should be preserved beyond World War II. Expanding these was a policy of the Thatcher government and they have continued to expand since then. In 2005, their website says they provide advice at 3,200 locations, with the aid of 20,000 volunteers.
- 100s of independent advice centres grew up, some providing general legal advice, some more specialised. They sometimes provide legal services themselves and sometimes make referrals. Examples are the Child Poverty Action Group, Shelter, Youth Access, the Money Advice Association, Dial UK (disability advice), Mind, the Refugee Legal Centre, etc. Lawyers often provide advice free at evening advice centres but will need to make a referral if substantive legal help is needed, beyond advice.
- During the 1990s, both the Law Society and the Bar Council have established *Pro Bono* groups to try to persuade professionals to give some of their services free. The *Free Representation Unit*, a group of Bar students prepared to represent claimants in tribunals, etc. was established in the 1970s. Another example is the CAB in the Royal Courts of Justice providing help for litigants in person. As explained in Chapter 9, above, in addition to its fulltime employed solicitors, another 250 solicitors help out *pro bono.*

In addition, the Conservative administrations of the 1990s devised various other ways of enhancing access to justice, which have been expanded under the new scheme:

- Conditional fees, as described above.
- Simplifying the law (plain English) and making court procedures simpler and cheaper and providing good advice leaflets to help people help themselves. The Conservative Lord Chancellor Mackay was given the crystal award by the Plain English Campaign for simplifying court leaflets. (Incidentally, judges are keen on this too. Lord Chief Justice Woolf seems to have made it his personal mission to eliminate legal Latin. It was he who was asked to simplify civil procedure. The "Woolf reforms" are described in Chapter 9, above).
- Encouraging ADR, discussed in Chapter 12, above.

- Encouraging private legal expenses insurance.
- Duty solicitors, funded under the legal aid scheme, to provide emergency help and representation in police stations and the magistrates' courts.

5. Evaluation of the Legal Services Scheme in 2005—Does it Provide Access to Justice?

When reading evaluations of the new scheme, especially in news- **17–030** papers and the weekly law journals, I would invite the reader to bear in mind the following, which I have observed from studying the legal professions' behaviour for thirty years:

1. The Law Society and Bar Council are not just regulatory bodies, they are trade unions.
2. They are very efficient at promoting their members' financial interests.
3. Their publicity machinery is very powerful. The press is always flooded with comments from the profession when any change is proposed which affects them.
4. They oppose most changes.
5. They argue that what they want is in the public interest.
6. Their professional monopolies have maintained a stranglehold over legal services throughout the twentieth century and their professional bodies mainly defend the interests of private practice lawyers.
7. All of this is illustrated graphically in Chapter 13 on the legal profession, above, exemplified by what Lord Chancellor Irvine has called the "sorry saga" of their behaviour over rights of audience since the ineffective Courts and Legal Services Act 1990.

Conditional Fees to Replace Much of Civil Legal Aid

Development up to 1998

Speculative litigation was illegal under the common law offences **17–031** of champerty and maintenance, abolished in 1967 and unenforceable in English law from the Statute of Westminster 1275 until the Courts and Legal Services Act 1990 permitted conditional fee agreements. In Scotland it has long been permissible for a lawyer and client to conduct litigation on a speculative basis, by entering a straight "no win, no fee" agreement. In the US, a variety of contingency fees is permissible, the most common being that the lawyer takes a percentage of the sum recovered in litigation. No other jurisdiction operates an extensive contingency fee system and the English distaste for it was expressed by Blackstone in his *Commentaries on the Law of England* (1765):

> "This is an offence against public justice, as it keeps alive strife and contention, and perverts the remedial process of law into an engine of oppression" (quoted in Lord Mackay's green paper, below).

The Royal Commission on Legal Services, 1979, decided that any contract between lawyer and client which gave the former an interest in the case was against the public interest but the Civil Justice Review 1988 and the Marre Report 1988 thought the issue should be re-examined. In 1989, Lord Chancellor Mackay published a green paper, *Contingency Fees*, setting out the options. As with his other 1989 green papers on legal services reform, it provoked a very hostile reaction from the judiciary, which I discuss in Chapter 14, above. Note that the subsequent Courts and Legal Services Act 1990 did not permit contingency fees but "no win, no fee" contracts, with the lawyer permitted to take a percentage uplift of 100 per cent above her normal fee if she won the case. Conditional Fee Agreements (CFAs) were permitted in personal injury, insolvency and human rights cases.

In their 1995 policy paper, *'Access to Justice'*, the Labour Opposition condemned CFAs as "little more than a gimmick designed to mask the chaotic state of the legal aid scheme." Lord Chancellor Irvine was reminded of this when he adopted CFAs as one of the main elements of his legal services policy, two years later, at the Law Society conference. He proposed abolishing legal aid for many civil cases and said litigants would instead be able to enter into CFA contracts. His speech was not interpreted as he intended. Commentators concentrated not on the expansion of CFAs but the threatened cutbacks to legal aid, many hysterically warning of "the death of legal aid". The media reaction was hostile. The Lord Chancellor was taken aback by these "savage and grave allegations" (see *Gazette*, December 1997):

> "Under our current arrangements, access to the civil courts is open only to the very poor and the very rich. . ... By extending no-win, no-fee arrangements justice becomes available to all. Legal help will become affordable . . . Civil legal aid has tripled in cost in six years . . . The income received by lawyers has risen on average by 20 per cent a year over the same period . . . The number of cases supported has fallen . . . There is no extra money for legal aid. So we need to extract the maximum value from the money we have. If good alternatives to legal aid exist . . . those alternatives should be used. For too long, legal aid has been abused. Too many weak cases supported by legal aid have been taken on . . . Conditional

fees will make lawyers look harder at the cases which are brought to them."

The speech and articles by Lord Irvine and his junior minister Geoff Hoon provoked an explosion of attacks from lawyers. The Lord Chancellor was forced to make concessions before he detailed the Labour Government's plans in *Access to Justice with Conditional Fees* (1998).

- The risk of litigation should be shared by lawyer and client.
- The Government would be able to redirect funds to securing basic rights in housing, social security and judicial review.
- Legal aid would be delivered through contracts.
- Weak cases would be removed from the legal aid system by toughening the merits test.
- The use of legal expenses insurance would be widened.
- The introduction of conditional fees would be monitored.
- The high success rate of legally aided cases resulted from oppression. Legal aid should not be used to blackmail defendants. Medical negligence should be limited to experienced lawyers because those cases had a very low success rate. Legal aid would be removed once conditional fees developed.
- Defendants would still be eligible for legal aid.
- All personal injury actions would be removed from legal aid.

This consultation prompted 200 formal responses, mainly representing organisations, and much media coverage. Most people supported extending CFAs but not the cutbacks on legal aid. Solicitors were worried that they would not be able to fund the cost of investigating the strength of cases or the CFA insurance premiums for clients. The Bar and the Law Society advocated a Contingency Legal Aid Fund, to which successful litigants would contribute, which would pay the costs of unsuccessful litigants. Other noteworthy comments were:

- The paper contained no proposals for reducing the cost of family or criminal legal aid, yet these took two thirds of the budget.
- CFAs would not cover defendants yet there were about as many aided defendants in contract disputes as plaintiffs.
- Research by the Policy Studies Institute on 197 CFA cases concluded they were not working well.
- If litigants were allowed to recover their success fees from the defendants they defeated, this would significantly reduce the

risk to plaintiff and lawyer so legal aid blackmail could be replaced by CFA blackmail. Insurance companies warned of extra expense to them (as defendants) causing the cost of premiums of all insurance to inflate. The Forum of Insurance Lawyers complained that a windfall of extra fees would be paid to successful solicitors in uplifted fees for no good reason. These warnings turned out to be prophetic, as can be seen below and from the allegations of a "compensation culture", in Chapter 9, above.

- Others described what they considered to be a better system for legal services in Germany, with extensive private legal insurance and fixed fees for legal services.

Despite objections, the Government extended CFAs to all civil cases except family, in 1999. The Access to Justice Act 1999, ss.27–31 amended the Courts and Legal Services Act 1990 to define CFAs much more carefully and permitted the recovery of the success fee and the insurance premium in costs against the losing party.

17–032   The Law Society launched an expensive and graphic press campaign portraying the death of legal aid, in spring 1999. They used full page newspaper advertisements depicting a crying child suffering from bad housing, a beaten woman and a black man who had been falsely imprisoned and discriminated against. Lord Irvine retaliated with a furious press release, pointing out that all such people would still get publicly funded legal services under his new scheme.

Living with CFAs

17–033   In *Nothing to Lose?* researchers Yarrow and Abrams (1999) reported that clients found CFAs confusing. They did not understand success fees. Sometimes they did not understand that the solicitor would get nothing if the case was lost. Clients found the solicitor would not let them drop the case, because the insurance policy would not pay out the solicitor's fees if they did. Nevertheless, clients did not mind paying the success fee.

Research by the Legal Aid Board (1999) indicated that solicitors were good at estimating the chances of success of a case.

In 2001, academic researchers Moorhead and Scherr raised ethical questions in relation to the lack of understanding of the client over the risk they were taking, especially of paying costs if they pull out. Both the Master of the Rolls, Lord Phillips, who chairs the Civil Justice Council, and the Law Society were worried that costs under the new civil justice scheme were not working well because of disputes about who should fund CFAs. Research by Yarrow, *Just Rewards?* revealed that solicitors were using CFAs to overcharge.

In a very important interpretive case in the CA, *Callery v Gray*   **17–034**
[2001] EWCA Civ 1117, Lord Woolf C.J., who designed the Civil
Procedure Rules, Lord Phillips M.R. and Brooke L.J. tried to make
some sense of the mess of litigation over who pays for success fees
and insurance premiums in small claims resulting from traffic accidents. They heard argument from no fewer than seven QCs and five
other barristers. They gave a highly purposive interpretation to the
new regime. The purpose was to achieve access to justice for people
who could not afford it so it was an inevitable consequence of government policy that defendants should be subjected to additional
costs. Defendants, with the help of the court, should be able to limit
success fees and insurance premiums to a reasonable amount. Their
Lordships thought that a reasonable success fee in cases like this
which had a 98 per cent rate was 20 per cent.

Research in 2001 by accountants Stoy Hayward suggested law
firms "cherry picked" cases for CFAs, as was feared by critics. In
December 2004, Citizens' Advice published a damning report on
CFAs, *No Win, No Fee, No Chance* based on 385 evidence reports from
224 Bureaux between January 2002 and September 2004. As predicted, lawyers had cherry picked the most high-value, winnable
cases, leaving people with many meritorious but low value cases
without a remedy. There was no system for regulating the quality or
cost of advice. Consumers, such as accident victims in hospital,
were often subjected to high-pressure sales tactics. Consumers were
not clear of the risks and liabilities involved. People often thought
the contracts were genuinely no win, no fee and failed to appreciate
that they might have to pay the premium to insure against losing.
One woman was left with £15 from a £2,150 compensation payout.

On the other hand there are those who argue that CFAs have
opened up access to justice to people whose problems would otherwise go unremedied. For instance, solicitor Adam Tudor wrote to
The Times (February 8, 2005) to point out that since 1998, his firm
alone had successfully represented over 100 libel claimants from all
walks of life. Under the old legal aid scheme no-one was eligible for
legal aid for defamation and under the new scheme, the grant of
funding in such cases would be very rare.

For further discussion of the "costs war" provoked by the introduction of CFAs and allegations that they have facilitated a "compensation culture", see Chapter 9 on civil procedure, above.

The Need for Legal Services—Unmet Need Persists

Advice deserts

The Law Society and others such as the Legal Action Group   **17–035**
expressed serious concern that, by 2003, so many solicitors' firms had

withdrawn from the legal services scheme that there were "advice deserts", such as Kent, where there were no solicitors doing publicly funded housing law. The CABx chief executive warned, in September 2003, that Bureaux "will find it impossible to continue". In *Geography of Advice* (2004) Citizens' Advice reported a "postcode lottery". 40 per cent of Bureaux considered they operated in an "advice desert". 68 per cent had difficulties finding a publicly funded immigration lawyer. Around 60 per cent had the same problem with family law or housing. Clients had to travel over 50 miles to get help.

Survey of civil problems

17–036   A 2003–4 study for the Legal Services Research Centre of the Legal Services Commission, *Causes of Action: Civil Law & Social Justice,* by Pleasance *et al.*, surveyed over 5000 adults from over 3000 house-holds. Its findings were as follows:

1. One third of adults had experienced at least one civil law problem over 3.5 years.
2. One fifth took no action.
3. About a million problems per year were left unsolved as people did not understand basic rights.
4. Of those who took action, 37 per cent chose to handle their problems alone. Of the 63 per cent who successfully sought advice, almost as many approached an advice centre as a solicitor.
5. Socially excluded groups were especially vulnerable to civil justice problems. Legal problems were experienced by 80 per cent of people in temporary accommodation, two thirds of lone parents and over half of the unemployed.
6. Half the adults surveyed reported multiple problems. Civil justice problems frequently occurred in clusters, such as personal injury leading to loss of home or income. Relationship or marital breakdown could cause multiple problems. This confirmed Genn's finding in *Paths to Justice* (1999).
7. 15 per cent who sought advice did not obtain any, especially with problems of homelessness, rented housing, anti-social neighbours or benefits.
8. People were least likely to take action on mental illness, clinical negligence, unfair police treatment, personal injury or domestic violence.
9. People would often first discuss a problem with a doctor or social worker.
10. The report identified referral fatigue. The more advisers a person was referred onto, the less likely they were to follow up all those referrals.

Commenting on the research findings, an editorial in *Legal Action*, June 2003, added that there was evidence from youth work agencies that young people were reluctant to engage in the legal system. Innovative youth projects had demonstrated that advice services which were integrated into trusted venues achieved a high level of success, such as the Streetwise Community Law Centre, attached to a multi-functional youth project. Another editorial, in April 2004 remarked on the disturbing level of public ignorance revealed by surveys and called for a strategic approach to public legal education.

Responses by the Legal Services Commission

The LSC responded to this research, which it had commissioned.   17–037

1. They launched "Jobcentre Plus, training staff to "signpost" the unemployed and others to advice and information, because they often suffered clusters of problems such as debt and housing.
2. They launched a telephone helpline in 2004, to offer advice on debt, welfare benefits and education (see above).
3. From 2004, they put information on their website in 10 languages.
4. They funded video-conferencing facilities in isolated regions.
5. They established telephone advice lines in magistrates' courts. By 2004, these were being introduced into county courts.
6. They established outreach clinics in town halls, community centres and GP's surgeries.
7. They created a one-stop shop for domestic violence victims.
8. They piloted a duty solicitor scheme at county courts, to give emergency advice to those facing eviction.
9. They acknowledged that a "troubling lack of awareness in basic civil rights". They were considering how they could work with government, the legal profession and not for profit organisations to improve awareness of rights. They were increasing the availability of LSC information leaflets.

Contracting

Under the old legal aid scheme, any barrister or solicitor could   17–038
do legally aided work, with little accountability and no check on the quality of their work. The idea of limiting legal aid provision to lawyers who held exclusive contracts with government was first mooted in the Conservative Government's *Legal Aid Efficiency Scrutiny*, in 1986 and met fierce opposition. It gave the Legal Aid Board the power to make contracts in the 1988 Legal Aid Act and

adopted the less provocative notion of "franchising". The Board offered fixed term contracts to solicitors to deliver certain categories of legal service. Franchisees had to satisfy certain requirements, such as an effective management infrastructure, non-discrimination, capacity to offer advice in welfare benefits, an adequate library and efficiency in keeping clients informed.

The Law Society remained hostile. They warned that clients would be confused. Approaching a solicitor for advice on two topics, they might be sent away on one. By 1996, only 1,300 firms were franchised. To enhance incentives, the Lord Chancellor rewarded franchisees with higher fees and swifter legal aid payments. This was seen as divisive. Eventually, franchises were granted to providers other than solicitors, such as CABx. The present contracting scheme goes much further than this, however. By *requiring* all providers to have contracts, it reverted to the Conservative 1986 model. Firms were given just a few months to apply for a contract to deliver legal advice, in 1998.

This provoked more condemnation from lawyers who said that limiting providers to those who won contracts would exclude many firms of solicitors, such as small ethnic minority practices. This would deprive the public of access to justice. In November 1998, a few weeks before the application deadline, 220 minority practitioners met at the Law Society. Only two were franchised and 20 had applied. The Legal Aid Board (now LSC) had to put back the application deadline. The same performance was repeated over criminal contracts. By March 2001, with an April deadline, under 100 of the 3,400 firms who did criminal legal aid work had signed a contract. Eventually, the Law Society withdrew its opposition and encouraged solicitors to enter contracts.

17–039   There were widespread complaints of excessive bureaucracy, with solicitors being penalised by losing money because of tiny errors in form-filling, and spending many hours preparing for audits (inspections).

Richard Collins, head of the Criminal Defence Service at the Legal Services Commission, defended criminal contracting, in 2000, mainly on the basis of the aim to ensure quality provision: for instance, the requirement for experienced supervisors to check the work of members of staff. Acknowledging that though solicitors considered contracting an affront to their professional judgment, he reminded readers why legal advice at police stations had been limited to accredited representatives:

> "(R)esearch has shown the scheme to have made real improvements in the quality of service to the public . . . However, research has shown that the performance of solicitors themselves in giving

police station advice can fall short of that provided by those who are accredited: it is not sufficient to merely rely on the basic qualification of being a solicitor to assure quality of advice.

It should be recalled that it was often criminal defence solicitors who believed themselves to have an excellent reputation, and considered supervision to be unnecessary, who were deploying unqualified representatives in the police station whose poor standards led to the need for the accreditation scheme."

This quotation understates the mischief that had to be remedied. As Bridges and many others pointed out, the uncontrolled growth of legal aid since 1960 was linked to the massive increase in lawyers, who were not accountable for the quality of services they provided. The rest of us who are paid out of the public purse expect some quality control and accountability for our remuneration. Think about the tight state control over school teachers and universities.

Research such as that reported in *Standing Accused* (1994), exposed **17–040** the appalling state of criminal defence, under the old legal aid scheme, by some solicitors and barristers. Barristers would appear in court having done no case preparation and not knowing the client from Adam. Some solicitors would send the office cleaner to sit behind counsel in court. Mostly, when someone asked to see a duty solicitor in a police station they would not get a solicitor but just anyone the duty solicitor chose to send. This book, and many police investigations uncovered widespread fraud by some firms of solicitors who thought nothing of sending a secretary to sit behind counsel in court and charging the Legal Aid Board for a trainee solicitor. The Royal Commission on Criminal Justice 1993 found most defence counsel did not meet their client until the morning of trial. The National Audit Office complained in *Handling Crown Court Cases* (1997) that 75 per cent of a sample of prosecution briefs were returned and counsel of inappropriate quality took on a third of those cases. In 1998, the CPS reported that only one in ten barristers saw child abuse cases right through their process. Half of briefs were returned by the original barrister. In 2000 Judge John Crocker, at Isleworth Crown Court, publicly complained about inefficient and ill-prepared barristers.

The quality of service under the new contracts showed deficiencies, however. Research on legal advice under the contracting scheme was published after a two-year study by the Institute of Advanced Legal Studies in 2001. It examined 80,000 cases in 100 solicitors' offices and 43 not-for-profit agencies and found:

- quality of advice depended on the time spent and experience of the adviser;
- there needed to be further improvements in quality;

- organisations in the not-for-profit sector took longer to carry out their work than solicitors but gave higher quality advice;
- referral levels were poor and referrals were consistently late;
- contractors needed to address problems experienced by clients in gaining access to their advice.

By 2003, concerns were being voiced that many solicitors' firms were abandoning their contracted legal aid work. The Law Society published a consultation paper in 2003, seeking new ways to provide public legal services. The paper included proposals for a compulsory legal insurance, a state paid service of defenders and, again, a contingency legal aid fund. A Society survey in 2003 found that 90 per cent of respondent practitioners were dissatisfied with the system, citing poor pay, excessive bureaucracy and audits. 78 per cent threatened to drop or reduce publicly funded work (*Gazette*, January 2003). In 2004, the Society President warned at their annual conference that the legal aid system would collapse and large sections of the population would be left without access to justice, unless there were to be a large cash injection. Demoralised solicitors were leaving legal aid work. The Birmingham Law Society President said underfunding had led to the "cancer" of solicitors poaching one another's clients. At the same time, in 2002–3, both the Legal Aid Practitioners Group and the Law Society published consultation papers complaining of a recruitment crisis. Trainee solicitors were not attracted to a career in legal aid work, because of poor pay and bureaucracy.

17–041 In response to the recruitment crisis, the LSC decided to fund trainee solicitors in legal aid firms. To address some of the complaints of overwhelming bureaucracy, they announced, in 2003, that they were establishing a "preferred supplier" pilot. Civil and criminal solicitors would bid for a place in the pilot. Strong performers would be rewarded with new contracting and payment arrangements, guaranteed work and other incentives.

The first batch of criminal defence contracts came to an end and were thus renewable in 2004. The LSC clearly did not feel threatened by the loss of criminal defence solicitors. On the contrary, they planned a significant cut in the number of contracted criminal defence providers. Clare Dodson, Chief Executive of the LSC said that they planned to award criminal defence contracts by a system of competitive tendering. Contracts in London could be cut from 488 to 150, where there was an oversupply of providers. The LSC hoped those who "dabbled" in criminal defence would drop out. Winners would be rewarded with "light touch auditing".

The legal profession was not prepared to cooperate, however. They were concerned at the number of small solicitors firms that would collapse or be forced to merge. The LSC conceded that it would not be able to achieve its aims as planned, by 2005 and, instead, published a 2005 consultation paper on tendering in London. It sought opinions on its stated aims of introducing greater quality assurance for clients while securing better value for money. Competitive tendering would initially be aimed at lower court work, with firms bidding for a share of police station and court duty work. In 2005, the *New Law Journal* reported a "furious" reaction from solicitors. Solicitor Andrew Keogh made an interesting comment on it in February 2005. He started with a realistic warning, cynically opposing the rhetoric of his profession's leaders, above. Contrasting the context of the old legal aid system with the present, he said:

> "Solicitors controlled the market; the state wrote the cheque. Many lament the passing of this state of affairs and long for the days of unquestioning respect for solicitors and a deep pocket . . . Only a fool could seriously believe the government will raise general remuneration rates given a total legal aid spend of £1.1 bn on criminal defence services . . . Those who speak of a collapse in provision do so in the face of evidence to the contrary and a healthy supplier base in crime . . . some are beginning to believe their own rhetoric. There was no collapse in 1994 when franchising arrived, none in 2001, at the start of contracting, and none in 2004, when the second round of contracts were offered. Supply deserts are few."

Nevertheless, he could see nothing in the consultation paper which would increase quality and considered the suggestion that firms could recruit and expand to meet a bid to be "fanciful".

The Cost is still Rising

The cost of legal aid was still rising at 20 per cent a year and by 2004, it was costing £2 billion per year, having risen from £1.5 billion in 1997. The average cost of civil and criminal cases was still rising, despite a drop in the number of civil cases. By 2005, we had the largest legal aid budget in the developed world. Nevertheless, the Legal Action Group argued that this only represented 0.4 per cent of public spending and contrasted it with £135 billion spent on welfare benefits and £73 billion on the NHS.

By 2004, family cases absorbed 80 per cent of the civil budget but most of this cost increase was caused by the rising cost of criminal defence. The causes of this were the abolition of the means test in magistrates' courts, increasing the number of recipients; the number of increasingly complex prosecutions brought by bodies such as the

17–042

Serious Fraud Office and the creation of 360 new offences, in 1997–2004. In the Legal Action Group (LAG)'s view, it was a "scandal" that the Treasury failed to compensate the legal aid budget to cover the increased cost of all its new crime initiatives (*Legal Action* editorial, December 2004). The Criminal Defence Service overspent by £60m in 2002. Critics were concerned that this was reducing the budget available for the Community Legal Service and argued that it should be ring fenced. In December 2004, the DCA published the Criminal Defence Bill, having consulted on a draft version. Minister David Lammy claimed it would cut CDS costs by £35 million per year (it was republished in May 2005, following the general election). The Bill will reintroduce means testing for criminal defence in magistrates' courts, which had been abolished in the Access to Justice Act. The Bill was scrutinised by the parliamentary Select Committee on Constitutional Affairs. The Government accepted their suggestion that defendants should be eligible for non-means tested advice and assistance for the first hearing. The Government was so concerned with the rising cost of legal services that they ordered a fundamental review, co-opting officials from the Prime Minister's Strategy Unit.

Fixed Fees

17–043   Apart from grumbling about contracting, lawyers have complained bitterly over the curb on their fees in publicly funded cases. In 1993, Lord Chancellor Mackay introduced fixed fees in magistrates' courts, after opposition from solicitors and a judicial review by the High Court. Solicitors maintained, and still do, that the amount they are paid does not allow them to provide an adequate service. They predicted a decline in the number of solicitors prepared to do defence work. In an excellent statistical analysis, Bridges showed their argument lacked evidence and historical context. The growth in legal aid, especially in magistrates' courts was linked to the rapid growth of the profession, in the 1970s and 1980s. On lack of quality, Bridges thought this had more to do with solicitors' inability to keep abreast with legal developments through having small case loads.

Even in the late 1990s legal aid was an important source of income. According to the Law Society *Annual Statistical Report, 1999*, it accounted for 14.8 per cent of gross fees in 1997–1998 and 78 per cent of solicitors' offices received at least one payment for legally aided work.

In 2004, solicitors were holding "quiet days of action" and barristers went "on strike" about threats to cut fees in very high cost cases. Junior barristers complained that, once they had paid overheads, they could spend all day waiting around for an appearance in the Crown Court for a fee of about £40. When the LSC announced, in

2004, a plan to introduce fixed fees in civil legal help, the LAG argued there would be incentives for solicitors to cherry-pick articulate, organised clients and they would not be prepared to afford the time for vulnerable clients with mental health problems or multiple problems.

"Fat Cats" and High Cost Cases

As stated above, one of the criticisms of the old legal aid scheme was that much of the budget was eaten up by very high cost cases. By the mid 1990s many newspapers were making a scandal out of the high earnings of some barristers in legally aided cases. At the Bar Conference in 1995, Lord Woolf, then Master of the Rolls, criticised the high level of fees charged in civil cases. He called for a move to fixed fees, alleging wasteful practices, including separate unnecessary representation, unnecessary use of two counsel, unnecessary use of solicitors to sit behind counsel and undue prolixity. The Lord Chancellor's Department LCD (now DCA) warned the Bar of the intention to fix fees for civil legal aid work. The bar response was hostile and unco-operative.

Lord Irvine, then shadow Lord Chancellor, expressed concern, at the Bar Conference, 1996 in over the cost of a few very expensive criminal cases. He repeated this at the Bar conference in 1999:

> "I have and will bear down on excessive fees in the high cost cases which swallow up so much of our budget. It cannot be right that 40 per cent of our criminal legal aid budget is swallowed up by a mere one per cent of cases."

In 1997 the LCD issued league tables of the top 20 barrister recipients of legal aid fees. A number earned over £400,000 for Crown Court work in 1995–1996. In 1997, Lord Irvine defended court fee increases and attacked the price of lawyers as the deterrent to going to law. He told the House of Lords

> "there are a significant number of QCs who earn a million pounds per annum and many who would describe half a million pounds in one year as representing a very bad year for them. . . . Fat cat lawyers railing at the inequity of court fees do not attract the sympathy of the public." (*The Times*, July 15, 1997).

Home Secretary Jack Straw reiterated the attack at the 1997 Bar Conference. In 1999, the Law Society joined in. The Bar objected that there was a big gap in earnings between QCs and other barristers. In the meantime, the Legal Action Group pointed out that, if the Lord Chancellor was concerned about fat cat fees it was up to him

17–044

to do something about it, since he controlled the market in publicly funded cases. In 1997, solicitor Arnold Rosen put forward a powerful argument on this area of "exquisite privilege":

"As if by magic potion, the day after a barrister places the letters QC after his or her name, the fees rise. Can such higher fees be justified when paid for by the tax-payer—not the client? . . . The Criminal Bar and the silks, in particular, have managed to cultivate an assumption which, when analysed, I believe to be false. The assumption is that silks earning £400,000 a year from the Legal Aid Fund could, unless retained by legally assisted parties go and earn it elsewhere. Where else? The entire Criminal Bar is a completely artificial market."

17–045   In November 1999, the Lord Chancellor announced regulations to tighten the criteria regulating the assignment of QCs in publicly funded cases. Orders may now only be made for two counsel or a QC if the defence case involves substantial novel or complex issues of law or fact which could not be adequately presented without a QC and either the prosecution has senior counsel or the defence case is exceptional.

In July 2000, a 10 per cent cut in fees for publicly defended criminal work was announced, to reduce disparity between prosecution and defence fees, again amid protests by the Bar. In 2001 the graduated fees scheme was introduced, including an integrated payment scheme for prosecution and defence lawyers.

As I write, in 2005, the problem of fat cats and high cost cases persist. By 2005, around one per cent of cases were absorbing 49 per cent of the criminal defence budget. The two silks who received the highest payments from the CLS and CDS in 2002–3, earned £606,000 and £620,000. There were similar earnings the following year. A March 2004 editorial in *Legal Action* commented:

"We suggest that keeping silks in the manner to which they are accustomed should not be given a higher priority than, for example, preserving the commendable fairness and simplicity of the police station duty solicitor scheme".

The Criminal Defence Service

Public defenders
17–046   UK lawyers are well aware of the image of the American public defender providing a second class service to criminal clients and this coloured many of the responses to the LCD consultation paper on public defenders in 2000. They proposed salaried defenders alongside

private practice defence lawyers. Their offices would be block funded and would have to build up their own clientele. They listed the benefits, drawing support from evaluations of schemes abroad: quality, better value for money, lack of profit motive, availability of information on the supply of CDS, positive pressure on private practice cost and quality and flexibility. They also considered the drawbacks.

The Justices' Clerks' Society expressed concern over too close a relationship building up between employed prosecutors and defenders. This, coupled with targets could lead to an increase in plea bargaining. The Bar Council naturally opposed salaried defenders. The Legal Services Consultative Panel responded to the draft code of conduct for public defenders in some detail. On the general principles and structure, it emphasised the need to assure quality and independence. "The Crown Prosecution Service provides an example of the systemic problems that can occur if this is not built into the service from the beginning." The service would need to build in mechanisms to prevent overload, ensure proper training and support and "instil a culture that is robust enough to prevent it simply becoming part of the funding or case management strategy of the Legal Services Commission or Court Service".

By 2004, public defenders had been piloted for over three years in Scotland. Goriely *et al.* reported the following findings, comparing case outcomes and client satisfaction between public and private solicitors: The public defender (PD) was more likely to resolve the case at a pleading or intermediate stage. Cases were more likely to end in a conviction. PD cases were more likely to plead guilty. There were similar levels of satisfaction but clients tended to complain the PD was too "businesslike". A 2002 Legal Services Commission report on the public defender system pilot schemes in six places in England and Wales found them to be a "considerable success" after the first year. Most cases handled involved police station and magistrates' court work but the scheme would expand and take on more Crown Court work. The 2004 annual report of the PDS claimed high levels of client satisfaction. It drew attention to their innovative work such as outreach sessions at local CABx and the development of more holistic services for criminal clients. The Liverpool office is part of the team developing defence services for the pilot Community Justice Centre, which opened in 2004, described in Chapter 7, above. The Legal Aid Practitioners' Group nevertheless criticised the PDS as a white elephant, representing poor value for money for taxpayers.

Changing and expanding the CDS

In 2005 telephone advice from police stations was piloted, for matters restricted to telephone advice only and for more serious matters at certain police stations. The Criminal Defence Bill 2005,   **17–047** when enacted, promises to save £35 million per year, by requiring recipients to contribute (see above).

Law Centres—Still Vulnerable

17–048   Since the Access to Justice Act 1999, the number of law centres has increased to 60, including some mobile services for rural areas, but they remain vulnerable to withdrawal of funding. In 2003, Four London law centres were threatened with closure, after the Association of London Government announced that it would not renew funding grants. In 2004, the local council cut Lewisham Law Centre's funding by £41,000. In Leicester, the Council merged the law centre with the CAB and then announced a £100,000 reduction in funding, which, observed the Law Centres Federation Director, exemplified an emerging trend to "advice only" services (Annual Report 2003–4). He advocated copying the Ontario system of law clinics. This would mean 60 clinics in the north west alone, currently served by just 12 law centres (*Legal Action*, November 2003). On the more positive side the same annual report describes LawWorks, a partnership between the Law Centres Federation and solicitors acting *pro bono*. From 2003–2004 23 new clinics had been established and they forecast being able to help and advise 45,000 people by 2007.

6. "The Legal Aid Crisis"—Calls for a fundamental restructuring

17–049   All of the above concerns prompted a battery of reviews in 2004. Here I paraphrase the main findings.

Protecting rights and tackling social exclusion (Law Society)

17–050   1. The civil legal aid budget should be separated, as a matter of urgency, from the rest. (LAG supported this, as did the select committee, below, and Matrix Research).
   2. The government should develop a programme of public legal education.
   3. Other government departments should recognise their role in creating demands on the legal aid budget.
   4. ADR and consumer redress schemes should be promoted.
   5. There should be a greater role for technology and telephone based services.
   6. Salaried services might tackle unmet need.
   7. Peripatetic advisers should be used.

8. There could be more use of legal expenses insurance and CFAs.

Civil Legal Aid—Adequacy of Provision (4th Report of the Constitutional Affairs Select Committee, for the session 2003–2004)

Note that this parliamentary committee, like all select commit- **17–051** tees, is an all-party group of backbenchers, not a government committee. In their fifth report, they examined the Government's proposals on the Criminal Defence Service. After listing all of the defects identified above, they recommended, in these two reports:

1. Peer review of contractors, instead of wasteful, inaccurate and bureaucratic auditing.
2. All government departments should be obliged to cost out the impact of new policy initiatives on the legal aid budget. (The same recommendation was made by Matrix, below.)
3. Spending on criminal legal aid should be curbed. Means testing should be reintroduced but should be done by the LSC, not the courts.
4. Despite denials in evidence from the LSC, unmet need persists. There are deserts.
5. If the LSC keeps reducing suppliers this will reduce provision in rural areas.
6. Over-specialisation could prevent a holistic approach by solicitors.
7. Legal aid is restricted to those who have nothing. It excludes people of modest means and thus denies them access to justice.
8. More research on the viability of salaried schemes should be undertaken.

The Independent Review of the Community Legal Service (for the DCA, by Matrix Research and Sheffield University)

The aims and functions of the CLS should be more transparent, **17–052** clarifying its role in tackling social exclusion, establishing performance management systems.

1. The CLS lacked an evidence base to demonstrate how it meets social exclusion and met other policy objectives. Different forms of provision should be evaluated.
2. Contracting and quality assurance was unduly burdensome and bureaucratic.
3. The LSC should pilot consortia to provide a one stop shop for early advice and prevention.

4. On Community Legal Service Partnerships (CLSPs), there was a dislocation between needs analysis and translation into funding. They had not been able to access new funding for unmet need. Enthusiasm had waned and members had left CLSPs.
5. This government review made a number of specific recommendations, especially in relation to CLSPs.

A market analysis of legal aided services provided by solicitors (by Frontier Economics, commissioned by the LSC and DCA (the results of this smaller scale report are not reviewed here))

Specific Criticisms

17–053   In addition to these reports, there are a number of more specific criticisms. For example, the Advice Services Alliance had misgivings about the new telephone advice line, launched in 2004. The pilot showed that only 23 per cent of users were from target groups and there was a similar problem with the Money Advice Debtline. Also, they were concerned that in an attempt to save money, the Government would see these advice lines as a substitute for face to face advice. See discussion by A. Griffith.

In response to some of these concerns, the LSC published its own consultation paper, *A New Focus for Civil Legal Aid*, in 2004, proposing to re-focus the legal aid scheme away from litigation and into early effective dispute resolution. In family cases they proposed a major restructuring of the Funding Code towards the early diagnostic work of family solicitors. In non-family cases, they would consider whether complaints schemes or ADR should be used before considering funding for litigation. This partly resulted from pressure from the CA, as well as a desire to save money. Lord Woolf in *Anufrijeva v London Borough of Southwark* [2003] EWCA Civ 1406 had criticised the disproportionate and "truly horrendous" cost of appeals under the Human Rights Act in maladministration cases. He said the Administrative Court would only grant permission to apply for judicial review where it could be explained that complaining to the Ombudsman or another complaints procedure was not more appropriate.

Under pressure from the DCA, they considered altering eligibility levels. They also proposed fixed fees for civil help. Benefits were promised for those suppliers who volunteered for this. In 2004, they launched a "Preferred Supplier Pilot". They selected 25 "high performing" suppliers whose participation was rewarded with grants for training contracts, guaranteed payments, more autonomy and guaranteed payments for settling civil cases.

By 2005, they had given £10 million in grants to suppliers to hire   **17–054**
new solicitors under training contracts.

From 2003, the LSC started shifting its much-criticised audit
system over to peer review and refocused audits according to risk.
They introduced salaried solicitors and case workers for legal
advice on asylum and immigration. They limited the suppliers in
this field and the amount of advice and tribunal work they were
prepared to fund. This was in response to criticism that there were
too many suppliers, some of whom were caught touting for business amongst asylum seekers and some of whom provided poor
quality advice. The High Court had criticised one firm for "milking"
the legal aid fund with "grossly incompetent" applications for judicial review in hopeless asylum cases.

Reforms Announced in 2005

In March 2005, the DCA announced the following cuts: **17–055**

1. Eligibility for representation would be cut by 10 per cent, in an
   attempt to encourage early and effective dispute resolution.
2. Financial eligibility for legal help (advice and so on), on the
   other hand, would be increased.
3. In family cases, the structure of legal services would be
   redesigned to emphasise early resolution out of court.
4. Cost protection would be abolished in family cases to deter
   unreasonable conduct by publicly funded clients and stricter
   controls would be exercised over multiple and repeat applications in private law family cases.
5. In clinical disputes and actions against the police, the LSC
   would be expected to take into consideration whether the
   applicant has exhausted all available complaints mechanisms.
6. Restrictions may be introduced to the Very High Cost Cases
   Civil Cases budget.

JUSTICE complained that this would encourage early but ineffective dispute resolution. Poor people would give up even if they had
a good case. In April 2005, the Legal Action Group, legal aid practitioners and advice networks held a public meeting entitled "Call
this access to justice?" calling for the Government to stop the proposed cuts and provide adequate funding for both civil and criminal cases.

BIBLIOGRAPHY

The Access to Justice Act 1999: *www.opsi.gov.uk*   **17–056**
F. Bawdon, on Yarrow and Abrams' research, "Nothing to lose?"
   (1999) 149 N.L.J. 1890.

L. Bridges, "The Professionalisation of Criminal Justice", *Legal Action*, August 1992, at p.7.

L. Bridges, "The Fixed Fees Battle", *Legal Action*, November 1992, at p.7.

R. Collins, defending Criminal Defence Service contracting, "Reports of death greatly exaggrerated" (2000) 150 N.L.J. 1520.

H. Genn, *Paths to Justice—What People Do and Think About Going to Law* (1999), summarised at *www.nuffieldfoundation.org*

"Geography of Advice": *www.citizensadvice.org.uk*

T. Goriely *et al.*, "Does Mode of Delivery Make a Difference to Criminal Case Outcomes and Clients' Satisfaction? The Public Defence Solicitor Experiment" [2004] Crim. L.R. 120.

A. Griffith, "Telephone advice; complement or alternative?", July 2004, *Legal Action*, p.6.

A. Keogh, "Value for money or a leap into the unknown" (2005) 155 N.L.J. 157.

LCD, "Access to justice with conditional fees—a consultation paper" 1998, archived on the DCA website: *www.dca.gov.uk*

The Hon. Mr Justice Lightman, "The Civil Justice System and Legal Profession—The Challenges Ahead" (2003) C.J.Q. 235.

M. McConville, L. Bridges, J. Hodgson and A. Pavlovic, *Standing Accused* (1994).

Modernising Justice (1998), white paper: *www.dca.gov.uk*

"Rights of Audience and Rights to Conduct Litigation", LCD consultation paper, 1998, see DCA website: *www.dca.gov.uk*

R. Moorhead and A. Scherr on CFAs, "Midnight in the garden of the CFA people" (2001) 151 N.L.J. 274.

P. Pleasence *et al.*, *Causes of Action: civil law and social justice*, 2004. *www.lsrc.org.uk* as summarized in *Legal Action*, March 2004, at p.9. LSC's reply is set out in *Legal Action*, April 2004, at p.10.

A. Rosen, "An artificial market?" (1997) 147 N.L.J. 630.

Stoy Hayward's research on conditional fees (2001) 151 N.L.J. 1078.

Yarrow, *Just Rewards?* summarized at (2001) 151 N.L.J. 750.

FURTHER READING AND SOURCES FOR UPDATING THIS CHAPTER

17–057 Online updates to this book: *http://www.sweetandmaxwell.co.uk/academic/updates/darbyshire/index.html*

I used the following additional sources, which the reader can use to update the information in this chapter. The journals listed here are available in all law libraries so if you are a law student working away from your campus, you may be able to access them in the law journals section of a nearby university library:

The Department for Constitutional Affairs: *www.dca.gov.uk* (search publications, especially consultation papers and press releases).

Citizens' Advice: *www.citizensadvice.org.uk*

Law Centres Federation: *www.lawcentres.org.uk*

The Law Society: *www.lawsociety.org.uk* (Research and Trends).

The Law Society's *Gazette*, distributed to all Law Society members and fully available online: *www.lawgazette.co.uk*

Legal Action, published by the Legal Action Group. Its editorials are usefully catalogued and available on their website, as are some articles: *www.lag.org.uk*

The Legal Services Commission: *www.legalservices.gov.uk* (see, especially, their *Focus* news magazine).

The Legal Services Research Centre, the research branch of the LSC: *http://www.lsrc.org.uk*

The New Law Journal, obtainable in hard copy or on *LexisNexis*, a database to which many university law schools subscribe, for their own students' use.

Index

Acquittal
judge, by, 10–063, 10–064
prosecution applications for retrial
following, 10–070
Adversarial procedure, 1–010,
11–001—11–008
criticism of system, 11–006
erosion of, 11–007
judge as unbiased umpire,
11–002—11–005
best case wins, 11–004
orality, principle of, 11–005
parties control evidence, 11–003
Alternative dispute resolution,
12–036—12–052
ACAS (Advisory, Conciliation and
Arbitration Service), 12–037
adjudication, 12–037
avoidance of litigation, and, 12–047
Civil Justice Centres, 12–048
Commercial Court, 12–043
conciliation, 12–037
early neutral evaluation, 12–038
enforcement by courts, 12–047, 12–048
examples, 12–042—12–045
expert determination, 12–038
family mediation, 12–042
formalised settlement conference,
12–038
promotion by courts, 12–050
government contractual disputes,
12–045
med-arb, 12–039
mediation, 12–039
mini trial, 12–039
neutral fact finding, 12–040
NHS (National Health Service),
12–044

Alternative dispute resolution—*cont.*
online dispute resolution, 12–040
public funding for, 12–046
slow growth of, 12–049—12–052
lawyers, and, 12–049
social welfare lawyers, and, 12–052
statistics, 12–051
suitability, 12–041
unreasonable refusal, 12–047
Alternatives to civil courts,
12–001—12–056
Anglo-Saxon laws, 8–002
Appeals, 9–038—9–047. *See also* **Court
of Appeal**
civil, 9–038—9–047
grounds, 9–043
jurisdiction, 9–039
procedure, 9–041
second appeals, 9–046
small claims hearings, from,
9–047
county court, from 9–038—9–047
High Court, from, 9–038—9–047
magistrates' court, from. *See*
Magistrates' court
trial on indictment, from, 10–069
tribunals, 12–008
Arbitration, 12–032—12–035
Arbitration Act 1996, 12–033
challenges to award, 12–033
moving out of London, whether,
12–035
nature of, 12–032
specialist schemes, 12–034
types of disputes, 12–033
when arising, 12–032
Attorney-General, 10–018
References, 10–079

581